# Here's How to Write Well

Elizabeth McMahan
*Illinois State University*

Robert Funk
*Eastern Illinois University*

**Allyn and Bacon**

BOSTON ■ LONDON ■ TORONTO ■ SYDNEY ■ TOKYO ■ SINGAPORE

*To our friend and colleague Susie Day, in gratitude for her invaluable contributions to this book—her inspired advice, her sensible editing, her witty and stimulating company at lunch.*

Vice President: Eben W. Ludlow
Series Editorial Assistant: Linda M. D'Angelo
Senior Marketing Manager: Lisa Kimball
Editorial–Production Administrator: Donna Simons
Editorial–Production Service: Omegatype Typography, Inc.
Composition and Prepress Buyer: Linda Cox
Manufacturing Buyer: Suzanne Lareau
Cover Administrator: Linda Knowles
Cover Designer: Susan Paradise
Electronic Composition: Omegatype Typography, Inc.

Copyright © 1999 by Allyn & Bacon
A Viacom Company
160 Gould Street
Needham Heights, MA 02494

Internet: www.abacon.com

Between the time Website information is gathered and then published, it is not unusual for some sites to have closed. Also, the transcription of URLs can result in unintended typographical errors. The publisher would appreciate notification where these occur so that they may be corrected in subsequent editions.

*Library of Congress Cataloging-in-Publication Data*
McMahan, Elizabeth
    Here's how to write well / Elizabeth McMahan, Robert Funk.
      p.    cm.
    Includes index.
    ISBN 0-205-27382-3
    1. English language—Rhetoric.  2. English language—Grammar.
3. Report writing.  I. Funk, Robert.  II. Title.
PE1408.M39475   1999
808'.042–dc21                      98-24823
                                        CIP

Printed in the United States of America
10  9  8  7  6  5  4  3  2  1    03  02  01  00  99  98

# Brief Contents

# Contents

Chapter **2**

*Addressing Your Readers*                              16

*Chapter* **3**

## Useful Strategies for Developing Ideas 27

*Chapter* **4**

## Reading Critically and Writing Logically

*Chapter* **7**

## The Revising and Editing Process          98

**P A R T   I I     *How to Write a Research Paper*     107**

*Chapter* **8**

## Conducting Your Research          109

**Chapter 9**

*Chapter* **10**

## Documenting Your Sources 150

---

**P A R T   I I I**      *How to Make Your Writing Clear
and Correct*                                    **167**

---

*Chapter* **11**

## Punctuating for Clarity
## and Effectiveness                            *169*

# Preface

This book demonstrates in plain, straightforward language how to become a capable writer. The conversational tone in no way compromises the integrity of the instruction, but it does make the material more accessible—pleasant to read and easy to understand.

*Here's How to Write Well* is organized into three parts. Part I, How to Put a Paper Together, provides a guided tour of the writing process—from gathering, sorting, and organizing ideas to drafting, revising, and editing the final version. Chapter 3 presents strategies for handling writing assignments in six commonly used rhetorical modes. Each section includes ideas for developing the content, sample outlines illustrating how to organize the material, warnings about possible pitfalls, and appealing paper topics to inspire good writing. Next comes advice on thinking logically, on crafting sentences, on composing paragraphs, and then on revising and editing, complete with handy checklists.

Part II, How to Write a Research Paper, constitutes a concise but thorough guide for completing a research paper. Three chapters provide detailed instruction for finding and writing from sources —including electronic sources—and for using two systems of documentation—MLA and APA.

Part III, How to Make Your Writing Clear and Correct, is a handbook explaining the rules of punctuation, grammatical correctness, and usage—all the information writers need to complete the revising and editing stages. These explanations depend only lightly on grammar to make them as easy as possible to understand. The exercises allow anyone in need of extra help to practice the tricky parts. The final chapter, a glossary of usage, provides advice about a number of words and phrases that writers typically find confusing.

Throughout the text, boldfaced **TIP!**s emphasize important concepts and reinforce learning. A number of collaborative activities enable students to work together and learn from each other. Chapter 4, which focuses on reading critically and thinking logically, explains how to detect slanted writing and encourages students to develop inquiring minds.

This slender book—presented in clear, concise, informal language—contains few frills but all of the essentials. Anyone who wants to become a good writer will find ample help within its covers.

## cknowledgments

Our sincere thanks to those who have helped with the polishing and production of this text: our astute reviewers—Kathleen Shine Cain, Merrimack College; Roy Colquitt, Central Piedmont Community College; and Shirley F. Nelson, Chattanooga State Technical Community College; our life-saving computer consultants, Dan LeSeure and Bill Weber; our esteemed editor, Eben Ludlow; his peerless assistant, Linda D'Angelo; and our fine production editor, Bonny Graham. We are especially grateful to our consulting editor, Susie Day, for her always excellent advice.

E. M.
R. F.

# I

# How to Put a Paper Together

# 1

# *The Planning Process*

Don't let anybody kid you: writing well is hard work. But as our friend Charlie Harris says, "I hate to write, but I love to have written." That's it, exactly. Writing is difficult but rewarding—if you do a good job.

## The Need for Good Writing Skills

The rewards are more than psychological. Writing well is one of the most useful skills you can develop—essential even—and extremely valuable to prospective employers. You will improve your chances of landing and keeping a good job if you can write clearly, correctly, and convincingly.

Let's face it: you need to be able to write. This book can help you learn. We'll make the process as painless as possible, but as Monty Python's Graham Chapman notes, "Basically the writing process is a matter of sitting down and thinking—appallingly hard work, really." We struggle and sigh and squint and swear; we chew our nails, furrow our brows, and gnash our teeth—but eventually we write. And you can, too, if you're willing to work at it.

### Allow Plenty of Time

Because of all the thinking that goes into good writing, the process always takes longer than you imagine it possibly could. So plan ahead. Get started early, and you'll have a chance to get your paper done in time to let it cool a day—well, at least a few hours—before revising and proofreading. Otherwise, you'll be pulling an all-nighter for sure, and your work will probably show it.

---

**TIP!** Remember Mark Twain's Rule: writing always takes twice as long as you think it's going to.

---

# W *riting Seldom Goes Step by Step*

Be advised that although we're going to describe writing as a step-by-step process, it's really a lot messier than that. And everybody's process is a little different. Experienced writers, for instance, often revise as they go. But other writers—especially those who have to struggle just to get their ideas down on paper—save the revising until they've completed a first draft. Some people plunge straight into a first draft with no planning whatsoever and then keep generating drafts until they come up with something suitable. Others devise a plan of some sort before they begin. Whatever works for you is what you should do.

So, bear in mind that we're simplifying the writing process as we explain it. We're going to straighten it out, tidy it up, and take it in steps to make it easy to understand.

# T *hink Before You Write*

Before beginning a first draft, you need to consider three things:

- *Your purpose:* Why am I writing?
- *Your readers:* Who am I writing for?
- *Your main point:* What am I writing about?

All of these questions are important, and your answer to one will often affect your response to the others.

---

**TIP!** Try to keep your purpose, your readers, and your main point in mind as you write.

---

## Ponder Your Purpose

Ask yourself, "Why am I exerting all this energy and straining my brain to write this paper?" Although an honest reply might be that someone told you to, that's not a useful answer.

Think beyond that immediate response to find a better reason. What do you hope to accomplish? Are you writing to provide information? Do you hope to persuade your readers to take some course of action or to change their minds on some issue? (You may, of course, be writing in a journal as an aid to learning or just to keep track of your life, but you don't need our help there.)

Your purpose affects your whole approach to writing: how you begin, whether you state or imply your main idea, how you organize the material, which details you choose, how you end, even which words you select. If your purpose is, say, to explain how to follow a process, you'll want to state your thesis clearly up front, arrange your ideas step by step, include easily visualized details, warn about any possible pitfalls at the end, and write the whole thing in easy-to-understand language.

If, on the other hand, your purpose is to entertain with an account of your disastrous visit to Alaska in midwinter, you'll leave your thesis unstated, arrange the details to build up to the worst fiasco, conclude with a vow never to travel again, and use humorous slang and metaphorical language.

---

**TIP!** Determine your purpose early and stay focused on it as you continue planning and writing.

---

## Consider Your Audience

You can't hope to accomplish your purpose without also thinking about who's going to read this piece of writing. Your audience may be a single person—your instructor, a coworker, your boss, your senator, perhaps. Or you may want to reach a more diverse audience—your city council, the urban planning commission, the readers of your local newspaper, or maybe the readership of *Time* magazine, the *Chicago Tribune*, or an interest group on the Internet. If, for instance, you're writing to explain the hazards of mixing household cleaning products, it makes a huge difference whether you're doing it for a college home economics instructor or a fifth-grade health class. Say you're writing to persuade your readers that physician-assisted suicide should be legalized. Consider how different your tactics would need to be depending on whether you were addressing the Knights of Columbus or the American Civil Liberties Union.

---

**TIP!** Think about your readers as you decide what material to present—and exactly how you'll present it.

---

# C ome Up with a Working Thesis

Keep both your purpose and your audience in mind as you search for a *thesis*—that is, *the main idea you intend to focus on.* Because your thesis should clearly relate to every idea in a piece of writing, we think it helps to have it clearly thought out—and down on paper—early in the process. As you proceed with the planning and the actual drafting, you can narrow it, expand it, or change the focus as new ideas occur to you.

## Start with a Topic

First you'll choose (or be assigned) a topic or subject to write about. In composition class you may be allowed to choose your topic. In history class you are more likely to be told the topic. On the job, unless you're the boss, you'll probably be told what to write about. But whether assigned or chosen, a topic is not a thesis—until you turn it into one.

## Narrow the Topic

Let's assume that in your horticulture class, you've been assigned a three- to four-page paper on the topic of home gardening. Because you aren't interested in growing flowers, you narrow the topic to home vegetable gardening. That's still a subject more suited to a book than to a short essay. How about organic vegetable gardening? Better, but four pages isn't much—only six or seven paragraphs, plus a brief introduction and conclusion. You need to narrow the topic still more. What about the problem of insects eating the tender plants? Should the gardener try to control them with insecticides or find other methods? How about focusing on methods of fighting bugs organically? Now, that sounds promising.

## Try *Freewriting* to Reel Out Ideas

If this narrowing down doesn't come naturally, you can try this technique for your horticulture paper. Just scrawl your topic at the top of a piece of paper (or the top of your computer screen) and then start writing down all the ideas that come to mind as you think about this topic. Pay no attention to spelling, punctuation, or organization—not for nothing is this technique called *free*writing. After you've written for ten minutes or so, read over the pages looking for one idea that sounds suitable as a possible thesis. If all the ideas seem too broad, choose the most promising one and do another round of freewriting. Keep writing and choosing until you discover a thesis that pleases you.

---

| **W***riting Exercise 1.1* |
| :--- |

Select one of the following broad topics and freewrite until you find a suitable thesis idea for a paper of about 700 words. Then write this idea in a single sentence that makes a point about your topic.

| | |
| :--- | :--- |
| Parenting | Soap operas |
| Science | Movies |
| Teen pregnancy | Politics |
| Violence | Fashion |
| Sports | TV shows |

---

## Make a Point in Your Thesis

Once you have narrowed your idea, you need to find an approach that will allow you to make a point about the topic. Ask yourself, what *about* fighting bugs organically? Clearly, the point here is to get rid of the voracious bugs without using hazardous chemicals. So, your working thesis might read something like this:

> Fighting bugs organically allows home gardeners to avoid the dangers of pesticides.

---

**TIP!** Before beginning a first draft, write out your thesis in a single clear sentence.

---

## Include a Verb in Your Thesis

A topic is the subject of an essay. It takes a verb to make a point about topic and turn it into a thesis. Notice below the difference between a topic and a thesis (we've italicized the verbs for you):

TOPIC: Drug abuse

THESIS: Drug abuse *can occur* with legal prescriptions.

TOPIC: Air pollution

THESIS: The popularity of gas-guzzling sports utility vehicles *contributes* to air pollution.

TOPIC:   High school sports

THESIS:   High schools *should require* all football players to maintain a C average to be on the team.

---

**TIP!**   **Be sure your thesis sentence makes a statement of some sort about your topic.**

---

## Say Something Solid

A verb won't save your thesis if the point isn't worth making. You want your essay to be interesting, informative, persuasive, and insightful. You do not want it to be obvious, predictable, shallow, or boring. If you can't tell whether your idea is worth writing about, ask somebody—better yet, ask several people. Be especially wary of a thesis that has the ring of a greeting card message: "Happiness is a warm puppy." Think twice about ideas you've heard all your life that may or may not be true: "Playing sports builds character." And try not to bore your readers by telling them something they already know: "Illegal drugs cause a huge problem in our society."

## Changing Your Thesis in Mid-Writing

Keep in mind that the main idea of your paper can change during the writing process. As British author E. M. Forster once observed, "How do I know what I think until I see what I say?" If you come up with a better idea or a different approach as you write, be prepared to shift gears and go with the new insight. Word processors allow you to make changes—even major changes—easily with a few keystrokes. So, don't become locked into the main idea you began with. Let your thesis evolve when it makes sense to do so.

### Starting Without a Thesis

Some writers, in fact, plunge right into writing in order to discover what they have to say. They simply crank out ideas about the topic until they have completed a first draft, a discovery draft. Then they begin revising and keep on revising—adding ideas, taking out ideas, rearranging ideas—until they have a finished product. This method strikes us as less efficient than planning ahead, but if you suffer from writer's block, you might want to give it a try.

## Discussion Exercise 1.2

With a small group of classmates, discuss the following sentences one by one. Some are workable thesis sentences for an essay of two to three typed pages, double-spaced with one-inch margins. But some need to be made more specific. Identify the successful ones, and figure out what's wrong with the losers.

Then, writing individually, turn each unsatisfactory sentence into a reasonably good thesis. When finished, compare results as a group.

1. Many Americans spend so much time in front of the TV set that they never really experience their own lives.
2. Personal freedom and independence carry with them responsibilities and consequences.
3. Making a lemon pie is easy.
4. I think that college students and teachers would be happier with education if people didn't enroll in college before the age of twenty-five.
5. My dog and my boyfriend are much alike.
6. Thousands of Americans go through the vicious cycle of eating until they are overweight and then dieting until they reduce, only to gain the pounds back again.
7. I learned not to worry when I was sixteen.
8. The perfect omelet is fluffy, light, delicately browned, and even attainable if the cook follows five practical guidelines.
9. The purpose of this paper is to compare and contrast Catholic schools and public schools.
10. The prevailing views on capital punishment are quite controversial.

---

# D redging Up Details: Invention Techniques

Once you have established your thesis, your purpose, and your audience, you need to get your mind in gear and come up with plenty of ideas to use in developing your essay. Here are some strategies that will get you started.

## Brainstorming a List

Because you want to come up with as many details as possible, start thinking about your topic, and jot down every idea that comes to mind. Don't be selective at this point. You can eliminate useless or irrelevant material during the arranging stage that follows. You'll probably end up with a jumbled list, something like the one generating ideas for gardening without pesticides shown in Figure 1.1.

### Clustering to Find Ideas

If you aren't a linear thinker, you may want to work out your brainstorming in clusters rather than jotting your ideas down in a

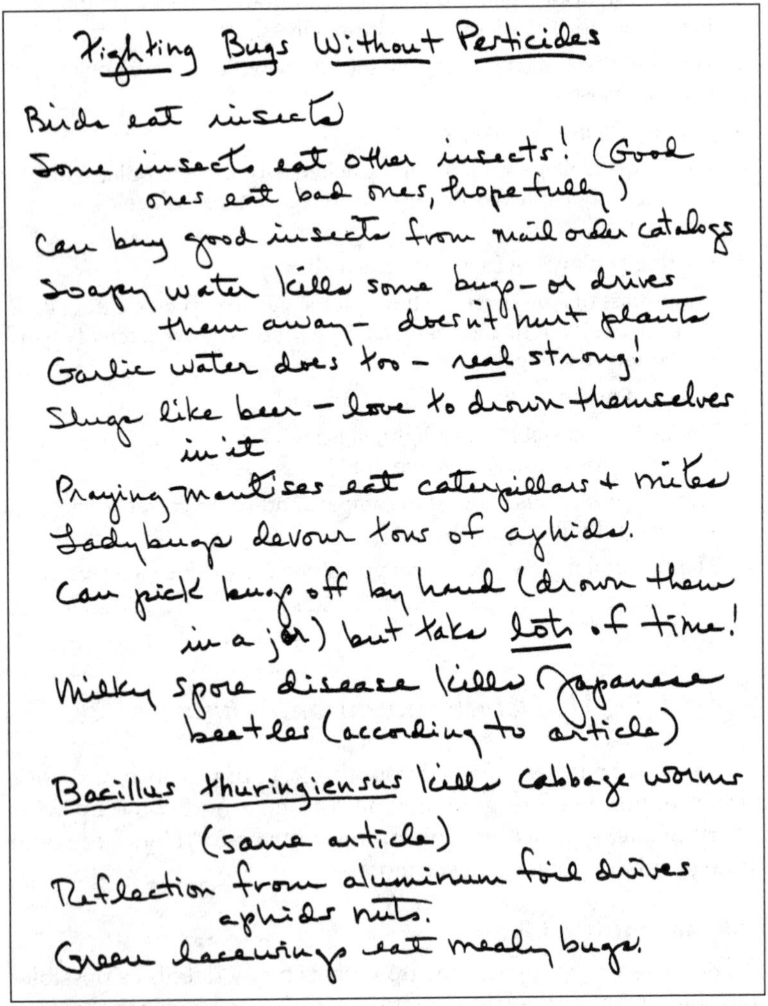

Fighting Bugs Without Pesticides

Birds eat insects

Some insects eat other insects! (Good ones eat bad ones, hopefully)

Can buy good insects from mail order catalogs

Soapy water kills some bugs—or drives them away—doesn't hurt plants

Garlic water does too—real strong!

Slugs like beer—love to drown themselves in it

Praying mantises eat caterpillars + mites

Ladybugs devour tons of aphids.

Can pick bugs off by hand (drown them in a jar) but takes lots of time!

Milky spore disease kills Japanese beetles (according to article)

Bacillus thuringiensus kills cabbage worms (same article)

Reflection from aluminum foil drives aphids nuts.

Green lacewings eat mealy bugs.

**FIGURE 1.1** *Brainstorming List*

list. The process is similar. Write your main idea in the middle of a blank page, draw a circle around it, start thinking, and let your ideas radiate out from there, as illustrated in Figure 1.2, which uses the same gardening material.

### Freewriting to Find Ideas

If freewriting helped you narrow your subject, you can use it again to generate material. This time, write your thesis at the top of the page and continue writing as you think about that idea.

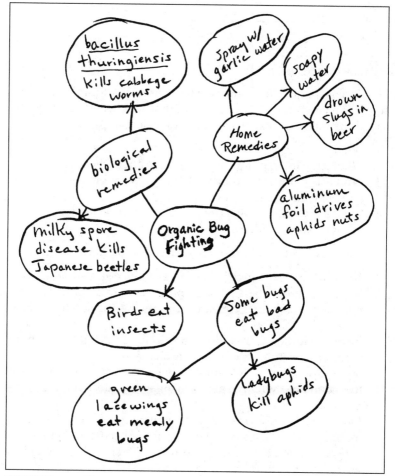

**FIGURE 1.2** *Clustering Ideas*

Continue for at least ten minutes. Then, using a highlighter, mark the lines containing information that you might want to incorporate into your paper. Finally, on a separate sheet, record everything that's useful, and you'll have a list of ideas to choose from when you organize.

## Invention Exercise 1.3

Using the thesis that you devised in Exercise 1.1, develop details for that thesis by brainstorming, clustering, or freewriting. Consider using all three techniques if you have trouble coming up with enough material to support the thesis.

## Prewriting Checklist

Here's a list of questions that will help direct your thinking as you transform your brainstorming, freewriting, or clustering into an essay. Write out your response to each question.

1. What's my topic?
2. What's the main point I want to make about the topic?
3. Who is my primary audience? That is, what group(s) of readers do I want to reach?
4. What's my specific purpose in regard to those readers?
5. What kinds of evidence am I going to use?

Your responses will probably turn out something like these:

1. Topic: needle exchange programs to reduce spread of AIDS.
2. Main point: Needle exchange programs are an effective and relatively inexpensive means of reducing the spread of HIV among drug users.
3. Primary audience: readers who doubt or are unsure about value and usefulness of needle exchanges.
4. Specific purpose: to get doubters to reconsider their opinions— to understand why needle exchanges are effective, not detrimental.
5. Evidence: mainly reasons and explanations, but also summaries of several studies I've read about needle exchanges—a couple of quotations from columnist Clarence Page, who has written on this issue recently.

# B *ringing Order Out of Chaos: Outlining*

Finally, it's time to work out a plan—to arrange all this material into a sequence your readers can follow easily. You'll need at least three or four main ideas to serve as the major points in your outline. In your paper about organic gardening, for example, those major points will be methods of controlling insect pests.

## Sorting Out Main Ideas and Supporting Details

Examine the ideas you have generated, looking for patterns of similarity. First, try to determine which are the major ideas. These are the ones for which you can find *supporting details*—that is, the ideas that explain, identify, illustrate, or qualify a major point.

In the brainstorming list in Figure 1.1, for instance, "Some insects eat garden pests" is clearly a major idea. Several examples support this idea—praying mantises, ladybugs, and green lacewings; you can also mention the specific insects they control and the fact that all of these useful insects can be purchased by mail. That's plenty for one paragraph.

You may detect several supporting details that are similar but that need to have a major heading added. Notice in the list that these items all share a common trait:

Putting out beer for slugs

Laying down aluminum foil to kill aphids

Squirting soapy water or garlic water on plants

These methods all use products usually found in the kitchen. By adding a heading, you can group these three under, "Try safe and easy household remedies."

Two other items on the list clearly belong together: milky spore disease and *bacillus thuringiensis.* (You discover such unusual remedies by reading articles or inquiring at your favorite garden store.) Because these biological techniques work by introducing diseases fatal to insects but harmless to plants and people, you might head this section, "Introduce insect diseases to destroy pests."

Only two items in the brainstorming list remain unused: picking insects off by hand and encouraging birds to come to the garden. Picking bugs off by hand is probably too tiresome to be a practical suggestion. And enticing birds may hurt more than help. Birds eat bugs indiscriminately—the ladybugs along with the aphids—and are exceptionally fond of many succulent garden vegetables as well. You decide to let go of the idea of attracting birds and mention in your conclusion that if all else fails, the fanatical gardener can always pick off the beastly bugs one by one.

## Arranging Your Major Points

After you finish choosing your main ideas and supporting details, the last step before the actual drafting involves deciding how to arrange your ideas. Because there is no chronology (time order) involved in presenting the material, you want to begin with an interesting point to grab your readers' attention. Most importantly, you need to end with your strongest point to leave your audience feeling that they have read something worthwhile.

With this pest control outline, you could almost flip a coin to decide how to organize your material. But because the household remedies are the most practical and the most entertaining to describe, you might want to begin with them. Save the section on importing natural enemies for the end because it sounds like a dramatic and sure-fire solution. A sample scratch outline using this material appears in Figure 1.3.

NOTE: In Chapter 3 you'll find a lot more help with organizing material.

---

### Collaborative Exercise 1.4

The following outline illustrates a number of weaknesses—supporting points that don't really support, minor points that pose as major points, major points that lack supporting points, and so on. With two or three classmates, discuss this sorry example until the group has revealed all its shortcomings; then, still working together, revise the material by adding, omitting, and rearranging ideas as necessary to produce what everyone agrees is a good outline.

**Thesis:** Studying in a dorm is impossible for anyone who lacks unswerving discipline.

1. Phones ringing and stereos playing
2. Friends drop by and keep me from studying
   a. Card playing and bull sessions
   b. Watching TV more fun than studying
3. Neighbors are forever partying
   a. Loud music, talking, and laughing distract me

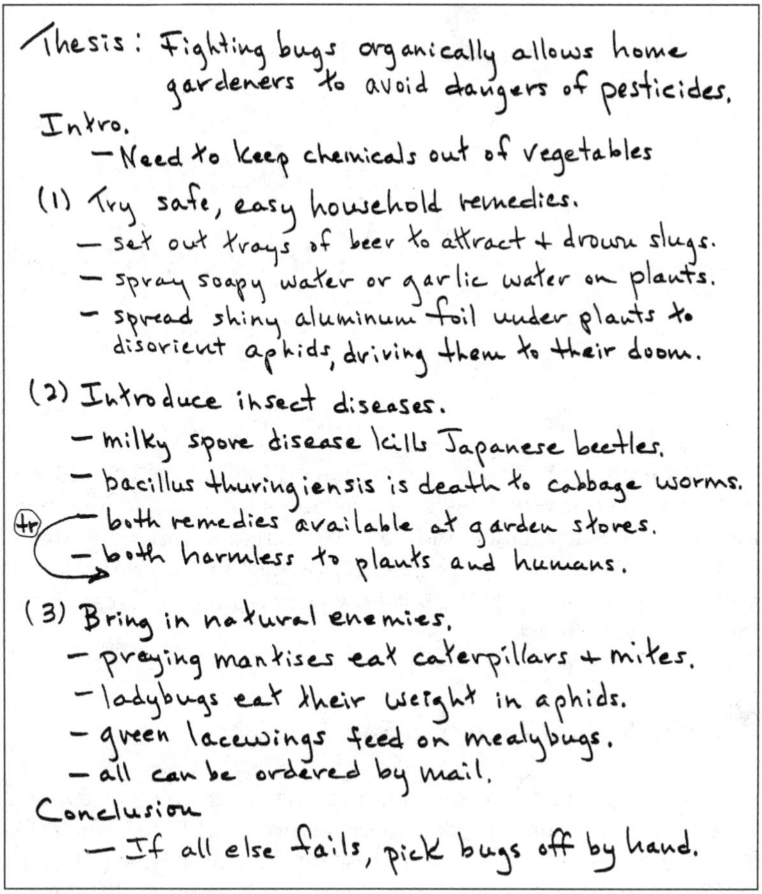

Thesis: Fighting bugs organically allows home
        gardeners to avoid ~~dangers~~ of pesticides.
Intro.
    — Need to keep chemicals out of vegetables
(1) Try safe, easy household remedies.
    — set out trays of beer to attract + drown slugs.
    — spray soapy water or garlic water on plants.
    — spread shiny aluminum foil under plants to
      disorient aphids, driving ~~them to their doom.~~
(2) Introduce insect diseases.
    — milky spore disease kills Japanese beetles.
    — bacillus thuringiensis is death to cabbage worms.
    — both remedies available at garden stores.
    — both harmless to plants and humans.
(3) Bring in natural enemies.
    — praying mantises eat caterpillars + mites.
    — ladybugs eat their weight in aphids.
    — green lacewings feed on mealybugs.
    — all can be ordered by mail.
Conclusion
    — If all else fails, pick bugs off by hand.

**FIGURE 1.3**  *Scratch Outline*

4. Studying is really hard for me
   a. I fall asleep.
   b. Chemistry 101 is beyond me.

**O**utlining *Exercise 1.5*

Look over the material you generated in Exercise 1.3, and construct an outline for a short paper on that topic.

# 2

# *Addressing Your Readers*

In the previous chapter we explained that all the choices you make about your writing—from selecting a topic to deciding how much material to include and how to arrange it—are determined by your purpose and your audience. As part of considering your audience, you need to anticipate how your readers will respond to the words you choose.

## **W** *rite Naturally as You Speak*

As a writer, how do you want to come across to your readers? Do you want to sound like an expert, lecturing the uninformed? Or like an old friend, informally discussing your thoughts and opinions? Do you want to seem serious or playful, warm or distant, excited or detached? The approach you choose determines the *voice* that your readers will hear when they read your writing.

Lewis Lapham, editor of *Harper's* magazine, complains: "I have found that few writers learn to speak in the human voice, that most of them make use of alien codes (academic, political, literary, bureaucratic, technical)." Many people think they're supposed to sound grand and impressive when they write, so they try to produce a form of language they would never use in speaking.

### Use First Person

You should strive for a human voice when you write—preferably your own. Those "alien codes" that Lapham speaks of are usually stuffy and pretentious and often sound like this:

One can appreciate the health benefits of high school athletics for the ones who participate as well as the entertainment value for the ones who observe.

Put that sentence into plain English and you get:

I think high school athletics can be healthful for the players and enjoyable for the fans.

Good writers usually prefer *I* or *we* rather than *one*, and many address their readers as *you*. On rare occasions the use of *one* is still required—in scientific writing, for instance, and in some theses and dissertations. We'll explain later how to handle *one* gracefully, just in case you're backed into a corner and have to write on a very formal level. You should also know that the first person will make your writing sound too familiar and chummy for some readers; college professors and business publications may prefer that you use the first person sparingly. The key is to know your audience and their expectations.

---

**TIP!**   **Avoid the indefinite *you*.**
The words *you* and *your* should always refer to the readers. You may draw an unexpected laugh if you're explaining how to prune a tree and write, "Grasp your diseased limb firmly and saw it off above the joint."

---

### Revising Exercise 2.1

Translate these sentences into clear, straightforward English. You may have to guess at the meaning sometimes, but do your best. We'll rewrite the first one to help you start.

1. One could conclude that the primary cause of her poverty was the number of offspring she possesses.
   *Translation:* I think that she's poor because she has too many children.

2. This writer's report enjoyed a not unfavorable reception by the management.

3. The unacceptability of one's lifestyle can result in the termination of one's employment in some companies.

4. In colonial times, you had to depend on wood for fuel.

5. It was with no little enthusiasm that one's peers inflicted various contusions and lacerations on members of the opposing affinity group.

6. It is the feeling of this committee that the established priorities in management–employee relations are in need of realignment.

---

# A *djust Your Tone*

Sometimes you may want to make your audience angry—about injustice, poverty, bigotry—but you always want to avoid making them angry at you. You need to adopt a tone that will appeal to your readers. *Tone* means the attitude a writer conveys toward the subject matter and the audience. The language you use will tell your readers if you're serious, humorous, interested, bored, cynical, confident, defensive, irritated, enthusiastic, and so on. You have to understand that your writing will have a tone, whether you consciously think about it or not. So you might as well think about it.

The English language offers you a number of ways of conveying the same message, depending on tone. You can word the simplest request to express subtle variations in your meaning:

Lend me ten dollars.

Please send me ten dollars.

Can you spare ten dollars?

I need ten dollars. I'll pay you back tomorrow.

I'd like you to give me ten dollars.

The tone you use should reflect your understanding of the needs and feelings of your readers. It's difficult to make generalizations about tone, but you should avoid talking down to your readers by stating the obvious or talking over their heads by using words and phrases they won't understand. You also don't want to be falsely enthusiastic: readers can usually tell when you're not sincere. Also resist the temptation to be dogmatic, abusive, or overly sarcastic. Mark Twain never published a line or even mailed a letter until his gentle wife Olivia had approved it. His famous letter to the gas company shows you why:

> Hartford
> February 12, 1891

Dear Sirs:

Some day you will move me almost to the verge of irritation by your chuckled-headed goddam fashion of shutting your goddam gas off without giving notice to your goddam parishioners. Several times you have come within an ace of smothering half of this household in their beds and blowing up the other half by this idiotic, not to say criminal, custom of yours. And it has happened again today. Haven't you a telephone?

Ys<br>S L Clemens

Needless to say, Livy didn't let this one pass. Twain revised his correspondence daily as his rage subsided, until he finally produced a temperate version that wouldn't invite a libel suit. Try to do the same with your own writing.

---

**TIP!**   **Imagine your readers reacting to what you've written.**
If you think your readers might get the wrong impression or have the wrong reaction, edit your tone accordingly.

---

# **C** *hoose an Appropriate Level of Language*

The tone of your writing will reflect just how formal you want to be. As always, audience and purpose will dictate the level of language you decide to use. Although these levels overlap, you have three main forms to choose from: *formal, informal,* and *familiar.* You need different levels of language for different writing occasions, just as you sometimes need formal attire for banquets and weddings, informal clothes for dates and shopping, and grubbies for around the house.

The level of language that you choose will depend on your relationship with the topic and the audience. If you're writing to a close friend or family member about something personal, you'll probably use familiar language. For less intimate writing, you'll use informal or formal language. Figure 2.1 illustrates these language levels.

### Formal Writing

Use formal language when your purpose is serious and you want to keep some distance between yourself and your audience. Many textbooks (although not this one) are written in formal English, as are most scholarly articles and books and some magazines. Business writing still observes many of the conventions of formal usage, but nowadays the use of *I* or *we* has replaced the strictly

| Formal: | One should not admit defeat too quickly. |
| | I shall not admit defeat too quickly. |
| Informal: | We should not give up too quickly. |
| | I won't give up too quickly. |
| Familiar: | I'm not throwing in the towel too quick. |

| Formal | Informal | Familiar (slang) |
|---|---|---|
| automobile | car | ride |
| comprehend | understand | get it |
| depart | leave | take off |
| residence | home | crib |
| odious | offensive | gross |
| debilitated | exhausted | wasted |
| morose | sad | bummed out |

**FIGURE 2.1** *Levels of Language for All Occasions*

formal third-person approach. Here are the main features of formal writing:

1. No contractions or slang
2. Third-person approach *(one, he, she, it, they)*; do not address the readers directly as *you*.
4. No sentence fragments
5. A serious or neutral tone

**TIP!** Use formal language when you want to downplay your personal involvement and emphasize the factual content of your writing.

**E**xercise on Tone 2.2

Rewrite each sentence to make the tone consistent and more appropriate for the subject. We'll show you how with the first sentence.

1. Many students who matriculate in a curriculum leading toward medical school really dig biology.
   *Revised:* Many premed students like to major in biology.
2. People who want to improve physically can undertake several schemes to shed poundage and acquire robustness.
3. I think Desdemona is such a wimp; she just lies down and dies.
4. When running for office, a candidate can always try to make the other guy look like a dufus.
5. The very people who bug one the most are often those who most want to please one.

6. We must suppose, then, that the figures cited are OK.
7. You can't help expressing yourself, unless one resides in a vacuum.
8. If you want to hold the attention of your reader, you should cultivate a bitchin' style.
9. Scientists have recommended that one strategy for alleviating the threat of global warming is to cut way back on car fumes.
10. The governor explained his reform proposal at length, but the audience was clearly tuned out and just didn't get it.

## Informal Writing

The formality or informality of language is a matter of degree. Few pieces of writing are exclusively formal or informal. Most of the writing you'll be called on to do will be informal, although some teachers and bosses may insist on a more formal approach. Here are the guidelines for informal language:

1. Use contractions, if you want to.
2. Use slang *only* if it's appropriate for your audience.
3. Write in the first person; address your readers as *you,* if you wish.
4. Use an occasional sentence fragment for stylistic effect.
5. Adopt any tone that's appropriate for the purpose and audience.

**TIP!** Use an informal tone when you want your readers to know something about your personal feelings or attitudes.

## Familiar Writing

The language found in personal letters, journals, and diaries is called familiar writing. You use it when you feel close to your readers and can assume they will understand the context of your writing. It also comes in handy for reproducing the feel of an actual person's speech in an essay that is otherwise more formal. In this kind of writing contractions are expected, slang is fine, the first person *(I)* and second person *(you)* are typical, sentence fragments are acceptable, and the tone is often light or even humorous.

**TIP!** Use a familiar tone only when you are completely sure that your readers will enjoy and approve of this style of writing.

## Colloquialisms and Slang

Colloquialisms are expressions used in everyday conversation and are found primarily in familiar writing. You might talk about "hanging out" with your friends or "getting even" with someone who "ripped you off," but you would probably *write* that you "spent time" with your friends and "retaliated" against someone who "cheated" you. Colloquialisms also include shortened versions of words, such as *prof* for *professor, lab* for *laboratory, grads* for *graduates*. Called clipped forms by language experts, these give a conversational tone to informal prose but are not appropriate for more formal writing.

Slang is extremely informal language; it is often imprecise and understandable only to a certain age group or social set. Terms like *geek, wimp, dis,* and *phat* and phrases like *schizzed out* and *book it* can be lively and colorful, but they go out of style quickly.

---

**TIP!**   You run the risk of not being understood or of not being taken seriously if you use slang and colloquialisms in your writing. Some readers will object to its use on any level.

---

### Writing Exercise 2.3

Compose a brief paragraph in which you try to persuade the members of your household that they should conserve electricity or gasoline or natural gas. Then rewrite the paragraph twice more, choosing a suitable level of language to address each of the groups below. You will end up with three paragraphs. Be prepared to explain the differences in your three versions.

- The Lost Souls Motorcycle Mates
- The local chapter of the American Association of University Women (AAUW)

---

## U se Jargon Carefully

The term *jargon* has several meanings. In his famous essay "On Jargon," Sir Arthur Quiller-Couch defined the term as vague and "woolly" speech or writing that consists of abstract words, elegant variations, and "circumlocution rather than short straight speech." This kind of language, which is used to make thoughts and ideas sound more important than they are, is almost always ineffective because it sets up a barrier to communication with the reader.

Jargon can also refer to the technical vocabulary used within a trade, profession, or field of interest. This language is understood perfectly well by members of that specialized group but not by outsiders. Computer users, for example, mean something entirely different by *bit, mouse, crash, drive, disk, boot,* and *virus* than nonusers do.

Again, consider your audience and your purpose. If you know your readers will be familiar with the jargon, go ahead and use it. But the kind of jargon you should always try to avoid includes those pretentious phrases that creep into the language from all sides—phrases like "increased propensity to actualize" (meaning "apt to happen"), "employee repositioning" (meaning "demoting and firing workers"), and "sociologically compatible behavioral parameters" (meaning who knows what).

## **W***riting Exercise 2.4*

Think of some group you belong to or an activity you engage in; make a list of its specialized words and phrases. Then write a paragraph to a general audience in which you define several of these terms. For instance, you might explain the basic shots in tennis—serve, ground stroke, volley, approach shot, lob, passing shot—for people who don't know what these terms mean.

---

## **U** *se Gender-Free Language*

In considering your audience, keep in mind that many of your readers may be displeased by gender-biased language—that is, words and phrases that unfairly ignore one sex or inappropriately call attention to gender. Fortunately, it's fairly easy to avoid sexist language. Here are some pointers to follow as you write and revise:

- Don't use the words *man* and *mankind* to refer to both men and women. Use the words *person, individual, human being, humankind, humanity,* or *the human race* instead. This advice also applies to words containing *man* or *men:*

| INSTEAD OF | USE |
| --- | --- |
| chairman | chairperson, moderator, chair |
| clergyman | minister, pastor |
| congressman | representative, legislator, member of Congress |

| | |
|---|---|
| fireman | firefighter |
| foreman | supervisor |
| mailman | mail carrier, postal worker |
| manpower | personnel, workers, staff |
| policeman | police officer |
| salesman | salesperson, sales representative |
| weatherman | weather forecaster, meteorologist |
| workman | worker, laborer |

- Use parallel terms when referring to members of both sexes. If the males are *men,* then the females should be *women,* not *girls.* If you write about *ladies,* then also write about *gentlemen.*

- Don't mention gender when it's not necessary. Avoid such phrases as *male nurse, woman engineer, lady doctor, female architect.*

- Don't use the pronouns *he, him,* or *his* to refer to a singular noun that includes both genders. Instead of writing

> Every writer should be careful with the pronouns *he* chooses.

use the plural:

> All writers should be aware of the pronouns *they* choose.

or use *he or she,* if you can do it sparingly:

> Every writer should be careful with the pronouns *he or she* chooses.

or eliminate the pronouns:

> Every writer should be careful when choosing pronouns.

---

## G*endered Language Exercise 2.5*

See if you can eliminate all the gendered language from the following sentences without changing the meaning or creating awkward phrasing. We'll rewrite the first one for you.

1. Man must work in order to eat.

   (revised)   People must work in order to eat.
   Humans must work in order to eat.

2. Anyone with a brain in his head can see the dangers of using atomic reactors.

3. A homeowner can pay his taxes by mail or at the county courthouse.

4. The gregarious dog is man's best friend, but the aloof cat keeps his distance.

5. Girls outnumber the men on campus by almost two to one.

6. Gertie's mother is a computer repairman for the university.

7. The lady surgeon who performed Clyde's bypass operation got her medical degree from the University of Illinois.

8. The hippopotamus is happiest when he is half submerged in mud.

9. American pioneers loaded up their wagons and moved their wives and children westward.

10. "As long as man is on earth, he's likely to cause problems. But the man at General Electric will keep trying to find answers." (advertisement for GE)

---

# A void Biased Language

You should avoid any derogatory language directed at a group, race, religion, or nationality. Identify all groups of people by their accepted proper names, and take care to avoid assigning stereotypical physical or behavioral characteristics to members of a particular group. Also, be aware that usage changes and that certain descriptive terms for groups of people may acquire unfavorable connotations. As a matter of respect to your readers, be sensitive to these details, and always use the terms that groups choose for themselves.

# T o Say It Or Not to Say It: Euphemisms

There may be times when you want to soften your language if you're writing about an unpleasant or emotionally loaded subject. In such cases you can employ linguistic smokescreens called *euphemisms*, most of which are quite innocent. Rather than bluntly saying that "He died of cancer," you can say "He passed away following a lingering illness." It takes the shudder out and cloaks the whole grim business of dying in a soothing phrase. Undertakers (or "funeral directors," as they prefer to be called) sometimes carry euphemism to grotesque extremes, like calling the room where the body lies the "slumber chamber." And in Victorian times, people would refer to the "white meat" of the chicken (instead of the "breast") and to the "second joint" (instead of the "thigh").

Such delicacy is quaint and amusing, but some people use euphemisms to evade the truth and conceal their meaning. In political discourse, this kind of language is called *doublespeak*. The CIA, for example, substitutes the meaningless phrase "terminate with extreme prejudice" for the blunt word "murder." The Pentagon refers to lethal weapons as "antipersonnel implements," and civilian deaths are glossed over as "unintended military consequences." Such transparent attempts to make human slaughter sound inoffensive are far from innocent.

This deceptive misuse of language has become widespread. Killing masses of people is called "ethnic cleansing." Police officers don't shoot to kill; they aim "to neutralize the adversary." The Air Force didn't lie to Congress about the B-1B bomber; they just "inadvertently disclosed incorrect information." An accident at a nuclear power plant is an "abnormal evolution" and an explosion is an "energetic disassembly." When the patient dies on the operating table, it's a "therapeutic misadventure" or "a negative patient-care outcome"; a death in the emergency room is "an adverse occurrence." Such euphemisms are deliberately misleading and border on being unethical.

You have to decide if innocent euphemisms are appropriate for your readers. Certainly you should never use deceptive ones. In most cases, your readers will probably want you to be honest and direct.

---

### Euphemism Exercise 2.6

Translate these euphemisms into more direct language.

1. employee downsizing
2. preowned automobile
3. chemical dependency
4. adult entertainment
5. intelligence gathering
6. correctional facility
7. misspoke
8. at-risk students
9. information specialists
10. revenue enhancement
11. substandard housing
12. encore telecast

# 3

# Useful Strategies for Developing Ideas

Experienced writers employ a number of strategies for developing their ideas, usually without ever consciously thinking about how they're doing it. You may find your own planning and drafting easier if you become familiar with some of these techniques. Usually you'll combine several strategies within one paper. For instance, you may include a narrative or a description or both while writing the explanation of a process.

We're going to present the basic strategies one by one because that's the only way to explain them clearly. After each explanation, we'll ask you to write an essay focusing primarily on that strategy to give you practice in using it.

## S trategies for Narrative

A *narrative* is simply a story, and *narration* involves telling a story. People use narrative a lot, both in everyday speech and in writing, because stories, especially those about personal experiences, provide convincing examples. Stories also can be quite engaging, if skillfully told.

---

**TIP!**  Use a narrative when you want to illustrate a point or in your introduction to catch your readers' attention.

---

## Organizing a Narrative

Because a narrative recounts an event or an experience, you can simply arrange the details in the order in which they happened—that is, in *chronological order*. Sometimes, though, a *flashback* is effective. A jump into the past can reinforce a mood, explain someone's motivation, or give background to help readers understand the event. How do you decide whether such out-of-sequence material is a useful flashback or a tiresome digression? Keep your purpose firmly in mind. Ask yourself how much the proposed addition contributes to that goal, and give it space in proportion to its contribution.

Get your story straight by outlining before you begin—or else straighten it out when you revise. Eliminate any dull, unnecessary, or repetitious material, and then work hard to make it interesting by coming up with just the right examples and illustrations. All good writing is full of specific details, but a narrative will fall flat as a floodplain without them.

## Developing a Narrative

The process of deciding which details to include or exclude is critical to successful narrative writing. Give a lot of thought to these choices. No one wants to hear about the syllabus of your college philosophy course when the main point of the story has to do with the unusual way you disposed of the textbook when the class was over.

As in all good writing you'll want to make a point of some sort in your narrative, but avoid just tacking on a moral at the end. Neither does your point have to involve weighty revelations about the Meaning of Life or the Human Experience. Your purpose can be to tell an amusing, entertaining, exciting, unusual, or puzzling story. This kind of narrative can have a worthwhile point too. Just keep in mind that when you're describing a peaceful stroll on a perfect fall day, you may want to ignore the squashed squirrel in the gutter.

---

**TIP!** In writing a narrative essay, do not state your thesis in the introduction.

Put your thesis or purpose on your outline but leave the main point implied in the paper itself. You don't want to take the edge off.

---

## Pitfalls of Narrative Writing

Narratives are the easiest kind of writing to organize but probably the most difficult to write well. Ask someone reliable, preferably a classmate, to read your draft and help you figure out what needs improvement. It's hard to be objective about your own writing—hard to see what needs adding and what needs taking out.

With your helper, go over the following questions, and take notes recording any changes that should be made.

1. Is the point of the narrative clear? Can the reader understand why I'm telling this story?
2. Are the events in order? Are there any gaps? any flashbacks?
3. Are there enough details? Are these details specific and interesting? If not, which ones need improving?
4. Are there any boring or unnecessary details that should come out?

---

## Topics for Narrative Writing

Before you begin, think about who your audience is and what point you want to make in this narrative, but refrain from including that point in the introduction. After completing your first draft, find someone to help you evaluate what you've written and plan your strategies for revision.

1. I learned _____ the hard way.
2. Think of a conflict between two people: teacher–student, parent–child, employer–employee, man–woman. Narrate the conflict first as though you were one person and then as though you were the other.
3. Write an account of your initiation into some element of the adult world that you were unaware of as a child: violence, hypocrisy, prejudice, sexuality, and so forth.
4. Write the story that your older relatives most often tell about something you did as a child.
5. Tell about the first time you remember being punished at school (or at home).
6. Describe a misunderstanding of the world or of language that you had as a child, and tell how the misunderstanding was corrected.
7. Recount a situation in which you fortunately or mistakenly followed someone else's judgment rather than your own.

8. Narrate an experience that led you to a new realization about yourself (or someone else).
9. Tell the story of a tough ethical decision you once had to make and of what happened afterward.
10. Write a narrative to support or disprove some familiar proverb, such as "Honesty is the best policy," "Nice guys finish last," or "Home is where the heart is."

# S *trategies for Descriptions*

Seldom will a description form the basis of an entire essay, unless you're writing for practice or pleasure. But you will probably use description in virtually everything you write—especially if you write creatively and interestingly.

## Organizing a Description

Writing specialists point out that most descriptions are organized spatially—top to bottom, left to right, near to far, back to front, and so on. True. You can describe your cat from nose to tail. But where do you include the texture of the fur, the stripes or spots, the color of the paws? And what about the meow? And the way the cat moves?

Good description involves working a number of carefully chosen details into some sort of spatial arrangement. There's no convenient way (such as presenting details in chronological order) that will work with description. You have to tailor the arrangement of details to suit your subject.

## Developing a Description

First, consider your purpose. Do you want to arouse an emotional response in your readers? Or are you trying to convey a word picture, without emotion but sharp and clear as a photograph? Your choice of words and details will differ according to the effect you want.

Before you begin to write, look—really *look*—at what you plan to describe. Maybe you'll want to smell and taste and touch it as well. Then try to record your sense impressions—the exact shapes, the lights and shades, the textures, the tastes, the sounds, the smells. Don't include everything, of course, or you may overwhelm your readers. Carefully select the details that suit your purpose in order to give your readers an image of what you're describing. Then, as you revise what you've written, you can search for the precise words that will let them see what you see.

---

**TIP!**   Try to put a picture in the reader's mind.

---

Notice in the following passage how Annie Dillard, through her selection of details and choice of words, allows us to both see and hear the ocean:

> The white beach was a havoc of lava boulders black as clinkers, sleek with spray, and lambent as brass in the sinking sun. To our left a dozen sea lions were bodysurfing in the long green combers that rose, translucent, half a mile offshore. When the combers broke, the shoreline boulders rolled. I could feel the roar in the rough rock on which I sat; I could hear the grate inside each long backsweeping sea, the rumble of a rolled million rocks muffled in splashes and the seethe before the next wave's heave.
>
> —"Innocence in the Galapagos"

## Pitfalls of Descriptive Writing

Remember that good descriptive details can clarify and enliven almost any kind of writing, but they are the very essence of descriptive writing. Including too few is fatal. Using tired, colorless words will also kill a description. Search your mind for lively verbs and choice descriptive words.

---

## Topics for Descriptive Writing

This assignment is designed to exercise your descriptive skills. You are not expected to produce a fully-developed essay with a point, unless you happen to be so inspired.

1. Describe as thoroughly as possible two of the following: how soft rain feels, how hard wind feels, how modeling clay feels, how whipped cream tastes, how a snake moves, how a cat leaps, how your dog greets you—or how a vampire looks, or a werewolf, or a visitor from outer space.
2. With as much sensory detail as possible, describe a food you hate or love.
3. Describe something you know more about than most people.

4. Describe a place (such as a classroom, a coffee shop, the local pool hall, a jail cell, a hospital room, your grandmother's kitchen, a professor's office), and try to convey how you feel about it through your use of specific details. Avoid making an explicit statement of your feelings.
5. Describe a place in which you feel at peace—or one in which you feel ill at ease.

---

# S *trategies for Explaining a Process*

One of the most practical kinds of writing tells readers how to do something. Being able to provide an accurate, step-by-step explanation of how something is done or will be done or how something works is an essential skill.

## Organizing Process Writing

Chronological structure, step by step, is usually the best way to explain a process. No flashbacks here. If you suddenly remember a detail that you should have included earlier, go back and insert that point where it belongs. You know how frustrating it is when someone giving you directions says, "Oh, wait a minute! I forgot to tell you to hang a left at the courthouse." A scratch outline will help you avoid such discouraging mishaps in writing.

Be careful to start at the actual beginning. Mention any necessary preparation, any gathering of supplies, any tips on how to get started. If, for instance, you're going to explain how to bathe a large reluctant dog, you'll first want to suggest putting on old clothes or a bathing suit and proceed from there. Your outline might look something like this:

### Sample Process Outline

**Thesis:** How to wash a dog without losing your temper or frightening the washee.
1. What to wear
   a. In summer—old clothes or bathing suit
   b. In winter—next to nothing in the shower
2. Gathering the implements
   a. Mild soap or dog shampoo
   b. Lots of old towels
   c. Handheld hairdryer, if winter

3. Where to do it
    a. In summer—on driveway or patio to avoid killing grass with soap
    b. In winter—in bathtub with shower curtain drawn
    c. If no shower curtain, wait till summer
4. Reassuring the animal
    a. Be gentle (dog thinks you plot a drowning)
    b. Talk continually in soothing tones
5. The actual washing
    a. Wet entire dog, apply soap or shampoo, work up lather
    b. Keep soap out of eyes and ears
    c. Don't forget the underside and tail
    d. Rinse thoroughly—then stand back
6. Drying the dog
    a. Dog will shake, like it or not
    b. Rub until damp-dry with towels
    c. If winter, finish with hairdryer

You might conclude that having a shiny, fragrant, flealess dog makes all this tribulation worthwhile. Or you might instead conclude that dog owners in their right minds who can afford the fee should pack the beast off to the groomer and let the experts do it.

There are, of course, other sorts of process papers that do not lend themselves to this easy chronological organization—topics like "How to choose a personal computer" or "How to care for an aquarium." For such subjects, you must fall back on classification, which is covered later in this chapter.

## Developing Process Writing

The process paper, although easy to organize, is difficult to make interesting. You might begin with a brief narrative introduction recounting your first failed attempt to wash your Labrador retriever. Best to leave out the swearing, but include as many descriptive words and lively verbs as you can without making the whole process sound grotesque.

You may assume that if you're describing a technical process, such as how to clean a carburetor or how to replace a hard drive, your readers will follow out of a desire for enlightenment. There's no obligation to entertain. But instead, you must be doubly sure to identify all parts and to explain each and every step clearly in language your reader will be able to understand. Define any terms that you suspect your readers may not know.

Make your word choice precise and concrete. If you're explaining how to change a light switch, don't say, "Strip a *short* piece of wire"; say, "Strip *one inch* of wire." If you're describing how to repair a toaster, label the parts (*A, B, C, D*) to help your reader visualize what fits where.

Include reasons whenever possible, especially if knowing the reason helps to understand the process. After you tell your reader to mix the dry yeast with lukewarm water, mention that cold water won't activate the yeast and hot water will kill it—either way, the bread won't rise.

If your process has any foreseeable mishaps, like a wet, shaggy dog shaking in the bathtub, you should warn your readers in advance—pull the shower curtain. If a dangerous mistake is possible, use italics or capital letters: "Before sticking your fingers in the fuse box, TURN OFF THE ELECTRICITY BY PULLING OUT THE MAIN FUSE."

---

**TIPS!**   Don't forget the getting ready part.
Include all the necessary steps—in order.
Warn about any possible mishaps.

---

## Pitfalls of Process Writing

The problems you encounter in process writing often have their roots in not completely understanding your audience. Give careful consideration to how much—or how little—your readers know before deciding where to start your explanations. You need to back up far enough that you don't lose them at the outset.

Your best bet is to enlist the help of someone whose knowledge of the process is about the same as that of your intended audience. Ask this person to read your draft and respond to these questions:

1. Have I chosen the right starting point? Did I give too much background information? Too little?
2. Have I defined enough terms? If not, which ones need clarifying?
3. Have my details been specific enough? Was the explanation unclear at any point? If so, where? How can I make it easier to follow?

---

## Topics for Process Writing

Before you begin, think about who your audience is and how much (or how little) they already know about your topic.

1. How to train an animal (dog, parrot, turtle, cat).
2. How to get rid of a bad habit—nail biting, smoking, interrupting others, procrastination, habitual lateness.
3. Find out and explain how some simple, familiar thing works (soap, can opener, ball-point pen, automatic pencil sharpener).
4. Think of an established process that could use improvement (registration, income tax preparation, courtship). Describe how a preferable substitute system would work.
5. Think of an everyday operation that you'd like to have automated. Describe in detail how a fantasy machine would perform this function.

---

# S *trategies for Classifying and Analyzing*

We classify and analyze things all the time with no struggle at all. We classify political candidates into Republican, Democrat, Socialist, or Independent. We classify doughnuts into plain-glazed, chocolate-covered, and jelly-filled. We analyze whenever we try to figure out a friend's behavior or decide the best way to store the potatoes. If you're an English major, you might classify people into those who like Tolstoy, those who like murder mysteries, those who like spy novels, and those who like Harlequin romances. If you then try to figure out why some readers choose Tolstoy while others favor romance novels, you're analyzing.

For much of the writing you'll be doing in your life, classification provides an effective means of organizing your ideas. Also, breaking a subject down into categories facilitates critical thinking by enabling you to examine and analyze the relationship of the parts.

## Organizing Classification and Analysis Writing

To make an outline using classification, devise a way to separate the material into categories, preferably into orderly, meaningful categories. For instance, in a paper for your child psychology class, you might classify various methods of disciplining five-year-olds this way: (1) scolding, (2) calling time-outs, (3) withdrawing privileges, and (4) spanking.

In deciding how to arrange your points, you have lots of choices: easiest to hardest, least effective to most useful, earliest to most recent, top to bottom, least complicated to most complex, smallest to largest, or even least annoying to most annoying. The trick is to find a reasonable, logical division that suits your material.

The following outline shows how journalist Florence King organized her analysis of a stereotype, the "Good Ole Boy."

### Sample Classification Outline

**Thesis:** The Good Ole Boy is a Southern WASP type easy to recognize but difficult to pin down.

Introduction
1. Physical characteristics
   a. Middle-aged, jowlish, beer belly
   b. Big buckle, white socks, ten-gallon hat
2. Dominant types
   a. Pearl, the playful masher
   b. Calhoun, the kindly fascist
3. Typical attitudes
   a. A lover of little dinky females
   b. Always searching for the oversexed Melanie
   c. A worshiper at Johnny's Cash 'n' Carry Tavern
Conclusion

## Developing Classification and Analysis Writing

Usually you will announce what you are classifying or analyzing in your introduction: four methods of disciplining five-year-olds, three unfair government subsidy programs, six signs of a troubled marriage, three types of stress, and so on. Each section could be a single paragraph or several, but the major sections should be fairly equal in length. If you write about 150 words concerning one type of stress, you should use approximately the same number of words for each of the other two types.

If the material is complex, you can do your readers a favor by using headings. Under each heading, include similar information and present it in the same order. For instance, in writing about three kinds of stress, you might give the first type a heading, like *Stress on the Job*, followed by a description, followed by examples. Then you would present the material about the other two kinds of stress in the same way. This parallel development helps readers to process the information more easily and clarifies the distinctions between categories.

## Pitfalls of Classification Writing

Here are a couple of things to watch out for when you work with classification.

1. *Be careful not to shift the basis of your division.*
   If that sounds confusing, look at the following skimpy outline, and you'll understand what we mean.

### Types of Aardvarks

   A. The fuzzy aardvark
   B. The hairless aardvark
   C. The friendly aardvark

   The first two categories of aardvarks are based on physical characteristics, while the last type shifts to personality. You see the worry this causes: Can a hairless aardvark be friendly? Are fuzzy aardvarks ill-tempered? How much hair does a friendly aardvark have?

2. *Be careful not to shift the rank of your division.*
   This simple outline will show you what can go wrong.

### Types of Recorded Music

   A. Classical
   B. Easy Listening
   C. Marilyn Manson

   Although Marilyn Manson represents a type of music quite distinct from classical or easy listening, the third category is not parallel, not equal in rank, to the first two. It's too narrow. It should be heavy metal, with Marilyn Manson used as an example.

---

**TIP!**   Check your outline for shifts in categories.

---

## Topics for Classification and Analysis Writing

Before you begin, think about who your audience is and what point you want to make. Analyze your material thoughtfully.

1. If you've ever been a salesperson, receptionist, or food server, analyze and classify your clientele.
2. Interview ten people to discover their attitudes toward the death penalty. Classify and then analyze their responses.

3. What types of TV shows are the most popular this season? Analyze the appeal of each type.
4. Study a magazine advertisement or an ad campaign (a series of related ads, such as the Taster's Choice coffee commercials or the Joe Camel cigarette ads). What emotions or beliefs is this advertising designed to appeal to?
5. Divide into types and analyze any of these subjects: neighborhoods, marriages, laughter, prisoners, automobiles, intelligence, dreams, teachers, students, tennis players, drinkers, pet owners, jokes, novels, bicycles.

---

## S *trategies for Comparing and Contrasting*

One of the most common methods of development involves focusing on similarities and differences—or perhaps on one or the other—in order to make a point. Sometimes writers use a comparison to clarify. An effective way, for instance, to explain impressionism in literature is to compare it with impressionism in painting, which is visual and thus easier to grasp. Writers frequently employ a comparison to persuade, as many have done by paralleling the failure of Prohibition in the 1920s with the ineffectiveness of the current war on drugs.

When focusing on differences, writers often seek to show that one category is somehow better than the other. You could, for example, establish a useful contrast between two products, focusing on their differences, in order to recommend one as a better buy. You could contrast the campaign promises of two candidates to establish which would be the better choice for mayor. Or you could humorously contrast the differences between toads and snakes in order to contend that toads make better pets than snakes.

### Organizing a Comparison or Contrast

Whether focusing on differences or similarities, you have two ways of organizing a piece of comparison or contrast writing.

### Using *Block* Organization

Especially handy for responding to essay examinations, this simple method of organization is also perfect for showing how something has changed or developed: your earliest views about AIDS compared with your views now; Americans' attitudes toward Communism in the fifties compared with attitudes today; Henry James's early novels compared with his later ones. In general, here's how to organize using the block plan:

1. State your purpose.
2. Present your points for the first part of the comparison.
3. Provide a transition.
   (for contrasts: *on the other hand, but, however, yet, in contrast, contrary to, nevertheless, nonetheless*).
   (for similarities: *similarly, also, likewise, in the same way, in a similar manner*).
4. Present similar points for the second part of the comparison.
5. Draw your conclusions.

If, for example, you were going to write a paper comparing the relative merits of airbeds versus waterbeds for people contemplating a purchase, your block outline might look like the one below.

### Sample Block Comparison or Contrast Outline

**Thesis:** Airbeds have several major advantages over waterbeds but cost a great deal more.

Introduction
A. Features of a waterbed
   1. Fills with a hose
   2. Adjusting for comfort tricky
   3. Needs an electric heater
   4. Extremely heavy when full of water
   5. Reasonable cost
B. Transition
C. Features of an airbed
   1. Inflates with a button
   2. Adjusting for comfort easy
   3. No need for a heater
   4. Light because full of air
   5. Expensive
Conclusion

## Using *Point-by-Point* Organization

A more precise way of showing a contrast involves setting it up point by point. This arrangement sharpens the contrast, but it also requires more planning because you have to thoroughly classify your material. You choose as your major points of comparison those ideas that best illustrate the similarities or differences.

For instance, say you decide to write an essay contrasting married life without children and married life with children. After thinking of several important ways that parenthood alters lifestyle, you might come up with an outline like this one.

### Sample Point-by-Point Comparison or Contrast Outline

**Thesis:** Having children causes life changes that bring major increases in responsibilities.

1. Sleep—and lack of
   a. Before kids
   b. After kids
2. Household chores
   a. Before kids
   b. After kids
3. Expenses—present and future
   a. Before kids
   b. After kids
4. Leisure time activities
   a. Before kids
   b. After kids
5. Romance in the marriage
   a. Before kids
   b. After kids

Conclusion: Parenthood involves sacrifices as well as joys.

You could, of course, use exactly this same material to write an essay in block organization. The choice depends on which arrangement best suits your purpose.

## Developing a Comparison or Contrast

The introduction of your essay should disclose the subject and set it in context. Here's a summary of the purposes mentioned earlier for using comparison and contrast:

1. to clarify (explaining the unfamiliar by comparing with the familiar);

2. to persuade (showing that one element is better than another);

3. to inform (comparing past and present or showing differences between similar elements).

You may want to mention one of these purposes in your opening paragraph. For example, here's an introduction written by a student in a paper focusing on differences between similar events—in this case, two Elton John concerts:

> Time changes everything, or so we are told. Over a period of time our looks, opinions, and viewpoints change. When I was a kid, I was a rabid fan of Elton John. I idolized Captain Fantastic when I saw him perform at McCormick Place in June of 1976. Still a devoted admirer, I recently attended another concert and was surprised by the differences in the two performances.
>
> —Debbie Brown

Using the block pattern, Debbie then went on in the body of her paper to describe her response to the first concert; then, after making a transition, she described her response to the second concert, concluding with the following paragraph, which summarizes her changed impressions:

> As his third encore, he gave us "Your Song." I stood on that hillside, tears streaming down my face, once again listening to my favorite singer performing my favorite song. By now my initial disappointment at discovering that Captain Fantastic had turned into Reg Dwight was totally gone. Idolizing had changed to respect. Yes, time changes many things—but not everything.

Notice that the first sentence of her introduction is, "Time changes everything, or so we are told." She neatly echoes that line in her final sentence, giving her essay a satisfying closure.

## Pitfalls of Comparison and Contrast Writing

You can avoid one major pitfall by presenting the material in each category in the same order. Here are a couple of other mistakes to avoid.

1. *Don't use too many transitional words.*
   Point-by-point comparison and contrast writing naturally involves a lot of shifting back and forth between ideas. But you won't need to signal each shift with a transitional word because your reader will become familiar with the pattern and will be expecting the shifts. If you use too many transitional words, your reader will become annoyed at being forcibly led rather than guided.
2. *Don't apologize in your conclusion.*
   After presenting a strong case for the superiority of one item over another, you may get to the conclusion and panic. You're

tempted to write, "Of course, this is just my opinion; others might disagree." Don't do it. This modesty undercuts the effectiveness of your paper.

## Topics for Comparison and Contrast Writing

Before you begin, think about your purpose, who your audience is, and what point you want to make.

1. Discuss one or more illusions that are presented as reality on television, and compare the illusion with the reality as you know it.
2. Compare and/or contrast: two lifestyles you have experienced, two novels, two films, a film and the book it was based on, two television characters, two cars you have driven, two sports you have played.
3. A group of extraterrestrial beings visits Earth. On their planet people are neither male nor female: each person is both. Using one of these beings as a first-person narrator, explain how their society is different from ours.
4. Write about a situation in which you expected one thing and got another—in other words, the expectation and the reality were different. Consider: your first day of school, your college roommate, your first date, your high school prom, your wedding day, dining in an expensive restaurant.
5. Find a typical magazine for men and one for women. Discuss three or four major differences that set these publications apart.

## S trategies for Explaining Causes and Effects

Human beings are naturally curious. We want to know why. Why won't the lawnmower start? Why does the computer keep giving me that error message when I've done nothing wrong? Why are some people better at math than others? What happened with Princess Diana and the Mercedes in the tunnel in Paris? This common human impulse to understand why things happen provides a powerful motive for reading and writing.

A lot of the writing done in college courses requires cause and effect thinking. Students are frequently asked to explain: the causes of the Civil War, the origins of prejudice, the consequences of divorce on children, the effects of sleep deprivation on learning. As a bonus, once you learn to analyze causes and effects, you'll become good at problem solving—a useful skill both on the job and in everyday life.

## Organizing Cause and Effect Writing

When you develop a piece of writing by analyzing causes, you are explaining to your readers *why* something happened. If you go on to explore the effects, you are analyzing *what* happened—the consequences. For example, if your topic is divorce and you write "Why Teenage Marriages Fail," you are planning a cause paper. But if you write "What Divorce Does to Young Children," you're planning an effect paper. You'll probably stick to one purpose in a single essay, but you might take up both causes and effects if you have the time and the assignment allows you to.

## Focusing on Causes

Begin by describing a condition or result or problem (such as having claustrophobia, failing your philosophy course, having your car's engine overheat), and then explain as fully as possible the causes or reasons.

Sometimes you may be able to use chronological organization. If, for instance, the problem is your claustrophobia, you could trace its development from the earliest cause at age five (getting locked in a broom closet), through another incident at age eleven (getting locked in a restroom), to the latest trauma at age twenty (getting locked in a stairwell).

More likely, though, your organization will fall into some logical pattern based on the relative importance of the causes—from least significant to most vital, from the most subtle to the most obvious, from local to nationwide. The following sample outline is arranged from the most understandable causes (poor reading and writing skills) to the least defensible one (missing class).

### Sample Outline Focusing on Causes

**Thesis:** I failed Philosophy 101 for several reasons, mostly due to my own shortcomings.
A. I couldn't do the reading.
   1. Abstract material is especially hard for me.
   2. I couldn't follow the textbook.

B. I wasn't good at writing either.
  1. I couldn't express the complicated ideas asked for on exams.
  2. I put off writing the papers for so long that every one was turned in late.
C. I was intimidated by the class discussion.
  1. Usually I could not answer when called on because I did not understand the ideas.
  2. Because I felt so stupid, I never asked questions that might have helped me.
D. The class met at 8 A.M., so I often slept through it.
Conclusion: Because this class is required, I resolve to work harder next time.

## Focusing on Effects

You can start with some condition or event and explain the consequences. For example, you might begin by describing the breakup with your girlfriend and then go on to show how it affected you. Again, you can present the effects as they happened. At first you were depressed; then you began to spend more time with your friends. You also had more time to study, so your grades improved. Finally, you began to date again and found a much better girlfriend.

More likely, though, you'll want to sort your ideas into some logical arrangement that has more to do with the importance of the effects than simply with chronology, as we suggested above. In the following outline, the effects are classified into negative and positive. Because the writer wants to emphasize the positive effects, she puts them last.

### Sample Outline Focusing on Effects

**Thesis:** My family has adjusted well to having Mom become a college student.
Introduction: After ten years as a housewife, I have gone back to college, amid a chorus of whining.
A. Negative effects
  1. My husband feels a bit intimidated.
  2. The children's clothes don't always get ironed.
  3. The house is not as clean as it used to be.
  4. I no longer have time to read for pleasure.
B. Positive effects
  1. My husband is learning to know our children better by sharing their care.

2. The kids are learning to accept personal and family responsibilities.
3. I enjoy a rewarding sense of accomplishment and have been freed from some boring housework.

Conclusion: The family has risen to the challenge, has accepted the changes, and now takes pride in my good grades.

## Developing Cause and Effect Writing

Since people are naturally curious about causes and effects, a good introduction will stimulate your readers to ask "Why?" For instance, if you're writing about what causes a hangover, you could begin by saying, "When you take two aspirin with a glass of water to cure a hangover, the water probably does you more good than the aspirin." Then you go on to explain in detail how alcohol dehydrates the cells, causing headache, dry mouth, and general malaise.

Another good way to begin is by making a prediction. Then in the body of the paper, you discuss the reasons that allow you to make such a statement. For example, you might begin an essay by declaring, "If you put radial tires on your car, you will probably save thirty-five dollars on gas next winter." Your readers will want to know how radial tires save gas, so you tell them.

In your conclusion, you can use any of the standard strategies—advise the reader, predict the future, or issue a call for action. Another strategy that works well in some cause and effect papers involves suggesting larger areas that your subject might branch into, leaving your reader with something additional to think about. If you're explaining how agricultural chemicals get into the grain fed to animals, for instance, you could close with an observation on the probable contamination of drinking water and soil by herbicides and pesticides.

## Pitfalls of Cause and Effect Writing

An explanation of causes and effects won't be successful if your readers find your thinking fuzzy or flawed.

1. *Avoid oversimplifying.*
   Most conditions and events are complex, involving multiple causes and numerous effects. In a short essay, you may have to focus on only the primary reasons, so be sure to let your readers know that's what you're doing.

2. *Be sure your causes are valid.*

   Just because you catch a cold after forgetting your sweater on a cold day doesn't mean that getting chilled caused the cold. More likely, someone sneezed on you. Before writing on causes, study the *post hoc fallacy* in the section on logic in the next chapter (page 54).

3. *Don't confuse the words* effect *and* affect.

   Check these terms in Chapter 14 if you have a problem keeping these words straight.

---

## Topics for Cause and Effect Writing

Before you begin, think about who your audience is and what point you want to make. After completing your outline, examine the logic of your causal analysis.

1. Discuss the probable causes of any situation, practice, law, or custom that strikes you as unfair.
2. Imagine that a close friend tells you that she/he is homosexual. The friend is the same sex as you. What are your reactions? Why would you have these reactions?
3. All school attendance has just been declared voluntary. How will this change the schools?
4. Explain the causes (or effects) of any drastic change of opinion, attitude, or behavior you've undergone in your life.
5. Write a paper in which you explain what causes some natural phenomenon (for example, rain, dew, blue sky, twinkling stars, sweat, hiccups, the phases of the moon).

---

# 4

# *Reading Critically and Writing Logically*

The most important element in the writing process is the thinking that produces what you write. Most of the knowledge and many of the insights you use in writing are acquired through reading. As you read, you'll be exposed to ideas, theories, and opinions as well as facts. Reading, discussing, and synthesizing all this new information constitutes a large part of becoming educated.

## **C***ultivate a Questioning Attitude*

The educational process bogs down if you don't keep an open mind. You shouldn't reject a new idea just because it conflicts with an opinion you presently treasure. Because you've heard and accepted a statement all your life doesn't make that statement true. As Mark Twain observed in his *Notebook*, "One of the proofs of immortality is that myriads have believed it. They also believed that the world was flat."

You should be willing to consider new ideas, examine them, think about them, and decide on the basis of the available evidence what is and is not valid. You'll be bombarded by facts and opinions from all sides. Much of what we read and observe is designed to sway our opinions or sell us something—or both. Just consider the barrage of messages we are subjected to daily from advertising alone—in magazines and newspapers, on television, at the movies, on billboards and matchbooks, even on clothing. Not to mention all the misinformation that flows from Washington, DC. In order to avoid being manipulated or deceived, you must try to distinguish the truth from the tripe. Truth may be mighty, but it doesn't always prevail.

---

**TIP!**   **Adopt a questioning mindset.**
Look for the unstated assumption that often underlies apparently objective statements.

---

## Be Suspicious of Slogans

As you form the habit of questioning statements, examine first those that come in the form of *epigrams* or *slogans*. These prepackaged ideas are neat and tidy, easy to remember, pleasant to the ear. We've been brought up on them and have Ben Franklin to thank for a sizable number, like "A stitch in time saves nine" and "Early to bed, early to rise, makes a man healthy, wealthy, and wise." Epigrams usually state a simple truth, but often they cleverly disguise opinion as fact. For instance, you've heard that "Home is where the heart is," but George Bernard Shaw rewrote that one as, "Home is the girl's prison and the woman's workhouse." Clearly, the truth of either statement is debatable and may lie somewhere in between.

A slogan is a catchphrase or motto designed to rally people to vote for a certain party, buy a certain product, or agree with a certain group. During the Spanish–American war a popular slogan was "My country, right or wrong!" Those same sentiments were voiced again during the Vietnam conflict as "America—love it or leave it!" Both are ringing, patriotic-sounding phrases, for sure, but not the least bit logical. Good citizens do not encourage their country to do wrong. They want their country to do right. Slogans may sound inspiring, but don't mistake them for reasoned ideas. Your job as reader is to question such statements. Demand evidence and decide rationally, not emotionally, which opinions are valid, which are propaganda, and which are a mixture of both.

## D etecting Slanted Writing

More difficult to detect than the bias of slogans is the subtle persuasion of *slanted writing*. Once you become aware of the emotional quality of many words, you'll not likely be taken in by slanted writing.

## Be Cautious About Connotations

Words are symbols that can have both a *denotative* meaning (the actual meaning) and a *connotative* meaning (the emotional response to the word). The term *mother,* for instance, denotes a female who gives birth, but the word typically connotes warmth, love, comfort, and apple pie. Most words have connotations in varying degrees— some so strong as to be considered *loaded* or *slanted.* Whether you call the President a *statesman* or a *politician* may well reveal your political affiliation. Consider the connotations of these pairs of words with similar denotative meanings:

| | |
|---|---|
| egghead | intellectual |
| pornographic | erotic |
| jock | athlete |
| penny-pinching | thrifty |
| mob | crowd |
| cur | doggie |

Whether you choose from the negative words on the left or the favorable words on the right will reveal your attitude to an alert reader.

Don't get the impression that connotative language is necessarily bad. It isn't. In fact, without the use of emotional words, writing would be fairly lifeless. But you need to become alert to connotations.

The tone of righteous conviction achieved in the following passage is admirable. The argument is eloquent, emphatic, and persuasive. But it also is pure hogwash—blatant propaganda. See if you can pick out the emotionally charged words on which the appeal rests:

> If we stand idly by, if we seek merely swollen, slothful ease and ignoble peace, then bolder and stronger peoples will pass us by, and will win for themselves the domination of the world.

Note that the writer says not just "stand by" but "stand *idly* by." He fears we may seek "ease"—but not a good rest earned by hard work. No, it's a *"swollen, slothful* ease." Certainly the word "peace" alone would not serve his purpose: he calls it an *"ignoble* peace." Notice, too, that those who will "pass us by" are *"bolder* and *stronger*

peoples," implying that only wimps would let them go unchal-
lenged, for they are clearly standing in the way of our rightful, glorious conquest of the world.

That sentence, written by Theodore Roosevelt, deserves high
marks as effective propaganda. But you as reader must be able to
detect that the chinks in his logic are effectively plugged with stirring words. It's this kind of misuse of the language that gives
rhetoric a bad name.

You'll hear similar appeals every day, not just from politicians
but from advertisers and special interest groups as well. Your best
protection from slanted writing is your ability to think—to examine the language and the logic, to sort out the sound ideas from the
sound effects.

## Consider the Source

Anyone familiar with U.S. history would know not to hope for
an unbiased comment from Theodore Roosevelt concerning the
causes of the Spanish-American War, which he helped start. This
doesn't mean, however, that you should ignore Roosevelt's statements if you're writing an appraisal of the reasons the United States
began that war. Neither should you ignore the opinions of the opposing attorneys, William Jennings Bryan and Clarence Darrow, if
you're analyzing the fairness of the Scopes trial concerning evolution in the 1920s. But you should be aware that the sources you're
reading are not objective and let your readers know about these biases when you quote. Don't just report them at face value.

Some sources you would recognize as biased without even
reading them. You would know to be suspicious of information on
gun control published by the National Rifle Association, data about
smoking from the Tobacco Institute, or views on racism from the
Web page of the Ku Klux Klan. You would also know not to trust
the *National Inquirer* if you're doing a paper on conspiracy theories
surrounding the Kennedy assassination. But the bias in many other
magazines is far more subtle. In a discussion of affirmative action,
you would want to balance the viewpoint of an article in *Ms.* magazine with that of a less liberal publication, like *U.S. News and World
Report.*

You could probably scare up most of the facts from reading one
unbiased source, but the problem is discovering which source that
is. The only way to make sure is to read widely. After you've read
opinions on both sides of an issue, you should be able to recognize
the middle ground—if and when you find it.

## Keep an Open Mind

Don't make the mistake of embracing what you consider a reliable source and then placing your trust in it till death do you part. Too many of us do just this: we plight our troth to the Bible, to *The Nation*, to *The Wall Street Journal*, or to *Newsweek* and assume we never have to think again. You will discover writers and publications whose viewpoint is similar to yours. These will naturally strike you as the most astute, cogent, perceptive, well-informed, reliable sources to consult. But be careful that you don't fall into the comfortable habit of reading these publications exclusively.

## A *Quick Look at Logic*

Developing a logical mind is important for you, both as a reader and as a writer. Whenever you write—especially when you write to persuade—your aim is to convey your thoughts and ideas into the minds of your readers. To be convincing, these thoughts and ideas must be logical. You should know the important principles of logic so that you can apply them to your own thinking and writing—as well as detect slippery logic in the writing and arguments of others.

## Cite Authorities with Care

You're probably going to quote authorities whenever you write on any controversial subject. But you need to be sure your authority is convincing to your audience. Some people think that once they've clinched a point with "The Bible says . . . ," they've precluded any rebuttal. If your reader happens to be one of the faithful, you'll be on solid ground. But not everyone would agree with the upright citizen who wrote a letter to the editor of our local paper offering this solution for helping the poor:

> The only remedy against poverty is to worship God as God, honor His word and obey His doctrines, call upon Him and humble ourselves. Then He will hear and heal the land.

Your more practical-minded readers are not likely to accept an argument requiring divine intervention to solve social problems.

Cite authorities, by all means, but try for impartial authorities—noted scholars and researchers who have published on your subject and are accepted as experts by most educated people.

---

**TIP!**    Be especially questioning about sources from the Internet. You'll find more extensive warnings about using electronic sources in Chapter 8.

---

## Avoid Oversimplifying

Most of us have a tendency to like things reduced to orderly, easily grasped, *either/or* answers. The only problem is that things are seldom that simple. Be wary of arguments that offer no middle way—the "either we do away with affirmative action or else deserving white males are going to go jobless" sort of reasoning.

## Avoid Stereotyping

Stereotypes involve set notions about the way different types of people behave. Homosexuals, according to the stereotype, are neurotic, promiscuous, immoral people bent on sex and the seduction of innocents. Such stereotypes seldom give a truthful picture of anyone in the group and could never accurately describe all members.

## Avoid Sweeping or Hasty Generalizations

You will do well to question easy solutions to complex problems. A *faulty generalization* (a general statement that is far too broad) can result from stating opinion as fact:

> Heavy metal music causes serious social problems by creating an attitude of irresponsibility in listeners.

That statement needs evidence to prove its claim, and such proof would be nearly impossible to come by.

Since you can't avoid making generalizations, be careful to avoid making them without sufficient evidence. At least, qualify your statements:

(faulty)    All Siamese cats are noisy and nervous.

(better)    Many Siamese cats are noisy and nervous.

Statements involving *all, none, everything, nobody,* and *always* are tough to prove. Instead, try *some, many, sometimes,* or *often.*

## Watch for Hidden Premises

Another sort of generalization that may prove deceptive involves a *hidden premise* (the basic idea underlying the main statement). To those who accept information without questioning, the following observation may sound plausible:

> If those animal rights demonstrators had left when the police told them to, there would have been no trouble and no one would have been injured.

The hidden premise here assumes that all laws are just and fairly administered; that all actions of the government are honorable and in the best interest of all citizens. The statement presumes, in short, that the demonstrators had no right or reason to be there and hence were wrong not to leave when told to do so. Such a presumption overlooks the possibility that in a free country, the demonstrators might legitimately protest the right of the police to make them move.

## Use Analogy with Care

An *analogy* involves taking two similar situations and claiming that what holds true for one holds true for the other. For instance, psychologist Naomi Weisstein, in her article "Woman as Nigger," contends that women are conditioned into a slave mentality and exploited for the economic benefit of society just as African Americans were for centuries. As this example suggests, analogies can add interest and clarity to a persuasive paper, and they often illustrate points effectively. But conclusions derived from an analogy are not logical proof. Make certain your analogy is indeed convincing before giving it too much weight in your essay.

A *false analogy* occurs when the two situations are not comparable. For example, you often hear people say something like this:

> If we can put people on the moon, we should be able to find a cure for AIDS.

Although both of these situations involve solving a problem with scientific knowledge, the difficulties facing medical researchers are quite different from those solved by space engineers.

## Do Not Dodge the Issue

People employ a number of sneaky logical fallacies in order to sidestep a problem while appearing to pursue the point.

1. *Appealing to Emotion*
   Perhaps the most common—and the most underhanded—involves playing on the emotional reactions, prejudices, fears, and ignorance of the audience instead of directly addressing the issue, like this:

   > If we allow condom distribution in the public schools, the moral fiber of the nation will be endangered.

That sentence, which contains no evidence to prove that condom distribution is either good or bad, merely attempts to make it sound scary.

2. *Attacking the Person* (the *ad hominem* fallacy)
   Illogical thinkers and unprincipled people frequently attack the person they are arguing against, rather than addressing the issue being argued. They call their opponents "effete, effeminate snobs" and hope nobody notices that they haven't actually said anything convincing.

3. *Employing Circular Reasoning*
   People who use this dodge offer as evidence arguments which assume as true the very thing they are trying to prove, as a devout person might do by quoting the Bible to prove the divinity of Christ. Here's an example of circular reasoning:

   > If we want a society of people who devote their time to base and sensuous things, then pornography may be harmless. But if we want a society in which the noble side of humans is encouraged and mankind itself is elevated, then I submit that pornography is surely harmful.

   That writer says, in effect, that pornography is evil because pornography is evil. The statement might be true, but that doesn't make it logical.

4. *Jumping to Conclusions*
   A common problem in reasoning is called the *post hoc* fallacy (from the Latin *post hoc, ergo propter hoc,* meaning "after this, therefore because of this"). This fallacy assumes—without any concrete evidence—that because one event follows another, the first is the cause of the second. Because we humans often employ cause-and-effect reasoning in attempting to make sense of our lives, *post hoc* reasoning is common.

   For example, suppose you've just read that the early symptoms of mercury poisoning are restlessness, instability, and irritability. Because ecologists have warned that our waters are polluted with mercury in dangerous amounts, and because everyone you know is restless, unstable, and irritable these days, you conclude that the population is succumbing to mercury poisoning. And we may well be, for that matter, but if you expect to convince anyone who wasn't already eager to make the same leap in logic, you'll need to gather more evidence, such as medical reports showing that human beings (as well as fish and cattle) are actually ingesting dangerous amounts of the poison.

# T *hink for Yourself*

All of these techniques used to sway readers are frighteningly successful with untrained, unanalytical minds. Your best defense is critical thinking. Think while you're reading or listening, and think some more before you write. Be prepared to change your mind. Instead of hunting for facts to shore up your present opinions, let the facts you gather lead you to a conclusion.

And do not insist on a nice, tidy, clear-cut conclusion. Sometimes there isn't one. Your conclusion may well be that for various reasons both sides have a point. Simply work to discover what you honestly believe to be the truth of the matter, and set that down— as clearly and convincingly as you can.

## D *iscussion Exercise 4.1*

Find, photocopy, and bring to class four copies of an example of the use of faulty logic. Good places to look: TV or radio commercials (write a brief description and make copies), magazine ads, political speeches, letters to the editor, editorials, or opinion-page columnists. In a group with two or three fellow students, distribute and discuss everyone's examples. Identify the fallacies, and explain what makes the underlying thinking illogical.

## R *evising Exercise 4.2*

Dig out the last paper you wrote that involved argument or persuasion. Jot down your main points and decide whether your logic was good or flawed. If you find flaws, figure out what went wrong and how to fix the problem.

## W *riting Exercise 4.3*

Think of a stereotype that you once believed in—for instance, the absent-minded professor, the dumb jock, the flighty blonde, the overbearing mother-in-law, the short-tempered redhead, the boring accountant, the greedy boss, the snobbish intellectual. Why did you believe this stereotype? How did you learn the stereotype was wrong? Write a paper in which you answer these questions.

# 5

# Composing Effective Paragraphs

Your writing will be made up of paragraphs: first, an effective introduction; then several interesting, unified, well-developed body paragraphs; and finally, a forceful, emphatic conclusion. Because the body paragraphs are the heart of any piece of writing, let's begin with them.

## U nderstanding the Basic Paragraph

If you are doing academic, business, or technical writing, the paragraphs that constitute the body of your paper should each have a topic sentence supported by plenty of concrete details. The average paragraph runs from about 100 to 150 words—somewhat longer for formal writing, considerably shorter for newspaper and magazines stories where the small type in narrow columns requires frequent breaks to avoid eye strain and to make reading easier.

### Use a Topic Sentence

Every paragraph is going to be about something: it will describe something, question something, demand something, reject something, define something, explain something. That "something" can be identified in a topic sentence. Although narratives and descriptions may not include an explicit topic sentence, most informative writing does.

When writing reports, position papers, academic essays, summaries, and examinations, you will almost always place the topic sentence first. Like the thesis sentence for an essay, a topic sentence states the controlling idea for the paragraph. The ideas and details within the paragraph will support, elaborate, interpret, illustrate, or justify that idea. As you develop your thoughts in a paragraph, be sure that all the points and details pertain to the idea stated in the topic sentence. If, for instance, you decide to write a paragraph about the undeserved good reputation of dogs, you might begin with this topic sentence: "Far from being our best friends, dogs are slow-witted, servile, useless beasts that seldom deserve their board and keep." Then you trot out examples of slavish spaniels and doltish Great Danes you have known in order to convince your readers that dogs are more trouble than they're worth. But if you observe, "Cats are pretty contemptible, too," you need a new paragraph or a new topic sentence. Otherwise, toss that comment out as being beside the point, the point being the idea you committed yourself to in the topic sentence—the uselessness of dogs.

## Build on the Topic Sentence

The topic sentence states the main idea in each paragraph. You build on that idea by supplying facts, figures, examples, reasons, explanations, and specific details that relate to the topic sentence. A building strategy that works for some writers is based on the theory that each sentence in a paragraph stems directly from the sentence before it and in some way responds to it. Thus, adding material in a paragraph becomes a matter of expectation and response: each sentence responds to the one before it and also provides the expectation (or idea) that the next sentence will relate to.

Let's look at a paragraph that begins with the following topic sentence:

> The new McDonald's system was predicated on careful attention to detail.

As a reader, what do you expect from that sentence? You probably want to know about that "attention to detail," right? So if the next sentence were something like

> The McDonald brothers began their business in Chicago.

you might feel a slight confusion or a momentary letdown because you were expecting something else. As a matter of fact, the next sentence in the original paragraph does pick up on the expectation about attention to detail:

> The McDonald brothers shortened the spindles on their Multi-Mixers so that shakes and malts could be made directly in paper cups.

Now, what do you expect from that sentence? You may want to know why that detail is important. So the writer explains with this next sentence:

> There would be no metal mixing containers to wash, no wasted ingredients, no wasted motion.

The writer then adds a series of similar details, as you might expect:

> They developed dispensers that put the same amount of catsup or mustard on every bun. They installed a bank of infrared lamps to keep French fries hot. They used disposable paper goods instead of glassware and china. They installed a microphone to amplify the customer's voice and reduce misunderstandings about what was being ordered.

After this series of examples, what do you expect next? You probably want to know what all this attention to detail adds up to, so the writer concludes with these statements that sum up the significance of the paragraph and bring it to a close:

> By 1952 the McDonald brothers' employees, all men dressed neatly in white, were said to be capable of serving the customer a hamburger, a beverage, French fries, and ice cream in twenty seconds. Word of their proficiency began to spread through the restaurant industry.
>
> —Philip Langdon

---

**TIP!** Stay focused on the main idea expressed in your topic sentence.

Make sure that whatever you put in a paragraph helps your readers to understand that main idea.

---

## **W**riting Exercise 5.1

Choose one of the topic sentences below and write a paragraph of about 150 words using the "expectation and response" strategy for paragraph development explained in the preceding section. Feel free to alter and adapt the topic sentence to fit your interests and experience.

1. My "bargain" used car caused me no end of trouble in my first week of ownership.

2. When I offered to build a fire at our campsite, I thought I could have it roaring in about five minutes.

3. I know that claustrophobia is all in the mind, but I still feel panic coming on when I'm in a closed space. [Substitute your own favorite phobia.]

4. If I'm having trouble getting started writing, I go through a few familiar rituals.

5. Because I am by nature a night person, having to get up at six in the morning brings out the worst in me.

---

# D *eveloping the Ideas Fully*

Adequate and interesting development of material is crucial to writing effective paragraphs. Most experienced writers make their ideas clear and convincing by providing support for every observation or generalization. This supporting material may appear as descriptive details, factual items, illustrations and examples, or a combination of these varied modes of development.

## Use Descriptive Details

Descriptive details are usually intended to convey an impression—how something looked, smelled, tasted. They are especially effective in recounting personal experiences or eyewitness accounts, as in the following vivid picture of the plight of Chicago's poor during the Great Depression of the 1930s.

> There is not a garbage dump in Chicago which is not deliberately haunted by the hungry. Last summer in the hot weather when the smell was sickening and the flies were thick, there were a hundred people a day coming to the dumps, falling on the heap of refuse as soon as the truck had pulled out and digging in it with sticks and hands. They would devour all the pulp that was left on the old slices of watermelon and cantaloupe till the rinds were as thin as paper; and they would take away and wash and cook discarded onions, turnips, and potatoes. Meat is a more difficult matter, but they salvage a good deal of that, too. The best is the butcher's meat which has been frozen and hasn't spoiled. In the case of the other meat, there are usually bad parts that have to be cut out or they scald it and sprinkle it with soda to kill the taste and the smell.
>
> —Edmund Wilson

## Supply Factual Information

If you have them, you can use facts and figures to develop your ideas. Note how the author of the following paragraph uses factual details to support the topic sentence at the beginning:

> No one change led to the virtual demise of the train robbery. A combination of stronger steel cars, modern law-enforcement techniques, and improved methods of transferring wealth made robbing trains too risky and unrewarding. Other forms of illegal activity in the 20th century occupied men (and a few women) who might have preyed on passenger trains 50 years ago. Bootlegging liquor, for example, seemed to be the 1930s equivalent of blowing up express cars.
>
> —John P. Hankey

This next paragraph is developed primarily by citing statistics:

> Although the Health Ministry projects that by the year 2002 Japan will have a cumulative total of eighteen thousand people who have AIDS or are HIV-positive, two Japanese epidemiologists who recently published a paper on the subject have reached a very different conclusion. They say that if the number of customers for prostitutes and the rate of condom use stay the same, "the estimated number of HIV-infected persons will reach a million three hundred thousand in 1996, which will result in two hundred and thirty thousand AIDS cases in 2000."
>
> —Stan Sesser

## Provide Illustrations and Examples

Most of the time, writers use illustrations and examples to flesh out paragraphs. Here is a paragraph that develops the claim in its topic sentence with one main example:

> The history of medicine is replete with accounts of drugs or modes of treatment that were in use for many years before it was recognized that they did more harm than good. For centuries, for example, doctors believed that drawing blood from patients was essential for rapid recovery from virtually every illness. Then, midway through the nineteenth century, it was discovered that bleeding served to weaken the patient. King Charles II's death is believed to have been caused in part by administered bleedings. George Washington's death was also hastened by the severe loss of blood resulting from this treatment.
>
> —Norman Cousins

In this next paragraph the writer illustrates her main point by quoting lines and titles from several country-western songs:

It is taken for granted in country music that "men will be men" and "women will be women." In "I Can't Be Myself," Merle Haggard implies he'll be leaving a woman who wants him to change. George Jones demands, "Take Me as I Am," and Billy Edd Wheeler says straight out, "If you're expecting me to change my old ways for the new / Baby, don't hold your breath until I do." Dottie West, however, is pictured on one of her album covers as a paper doll about to be cut out by a huge pair of scissors held by a big male hand ("Take your scissors and take your time / And cut along the dotted line"). She begs her man to keep his scissors in hand and trim her edges now and then, and "Fit me in with all your plans / For I want to be what I'm cut out to be."

—Ann Nietzke

## Be Specific and Concrete

Abstract words such as *democracy, truth, justice,* and *liberty* mean different things to different people. And sometimes they convey little meaning at all. Consider the following paragraph, which purports to explain what a "democratic" education can do for a child:

A democratic plan of education includes more than the mere transmission of the social heritage and an attempt to reproduce existing institutions in a static form. The purpose of democratic education is the development of well-integrated individuals who can live successfully in an ever-changing dynamic culture. The democratic school is also required to indoctrinate individuals with the democratic tradition which, in turn, is based on the agitative liberties of the individual and the needs of society.

If you can divine meaning from this paragraph, it's a vague, shadowy sort of understanding that can't be pinned down precisely because of the numerous abstract words: *democratic, social heritage, well-integrated, dynamic culture.* And what *agitative liberties* are, only the writer knows; he doesn't provide a hint. The entire passage contains not a single concrete example to help us grasp the ideas.

You can't avoid abstractions entirely, of course, but try to follow abstract words with concrete illustrations. For example, if you say that motorcycle riding can be *dangerous* (an abstract concept), mention the crushed noses, the dislocated limbs, the splintered teeth, the broken bones. Or provide some statistics about the high cost of insurance for motorcyclists and the frequency and severity of their accidents.

## **R***evising Exercise 5.2*

Rewrite the following paragraph about first dates, adding specific details and concrete examples that will bring the material to life. Be as creative as you wish. Feel free to alter wording. Use first person (*I, me, my*) if that approach works best.

> A first date is always a risky occasion, with endless possibilities for disaster and disappointment. Sometimes both people realize at the very beginning of the date that it is a mistake. At other times they get to know each other a little before they see that their interests and personalities don't fit well at all. And frequently, only at the end of the date does the mismatch become clear.

## **W***riting Exercise 5.3*

Think of a concept or an idea that is hard to explain to someone else. It might be a scientific principle, a belief about love or friendship, a political term, a formula for success. Write a paragraph about this concept, using examples and concrete details to help you clarify your thinking. Show your paragraph to several classmates; ask them if they understand what you mean. If they have trouble understanding, ask them to help you decide what changes or additions are needed to make your explanation clear.

## **K** *eeping Your Readers with You:*
## *Unity and Coherence*

As you are constructing paragraphs and putting them together to make a paper, remember that you want your readers to understand what you've written and to understand it easily on the first reading. You don't want them to get lost when you move from one idea to the next or when you change the direction of your ideas. The things you do to make your writing *unified* and *coherent,* to make it hang together, are fairly simple, yet they can often mean the difference between a first-rate paper and a merely passable one.

### Maintain Coherence Within Paragraphs

The first principle of writing a coherent paragraph is to make sure the sentences follow one another in a clear, logical sequence. Using the "expectation and response" strategy described earlier in this chapter will help to insure that your thoughts flow smoothly.

But there still may be places where you need to provide signposts to guide your readers through your prose.

*Repeat Key Words.*   One way to achieve coherence in a paragraph is to repeat key terms. Most of this repetition occurs naturally as you write, but being aware of the process will help you revise. In the following paragraph, observe how the sentences are held together through the repetition of the key term *addict* and the pronouns that refer to it (all italicized for easy identification):

> What to do about drug *addiction?* I give you two statistics. England with a population of over fifty-five million has eighteen hundred *addicts.* The United States with over two hundred million has nearly five hundred thousand *addicts.* What are the English doing right that we are doing wrong? They have turned the problem over to the doctors. An *addict* is required to register with a physician who gives *him* at controlled intervals a prescription so that *he* can buy *his* drug. The *addict* is content. Best of all, society is safe. The Mafia is out of the game. The police are unbribed, and the *addict* will not mug an old lady in order to get the money for *his* next fix.
>
> —Gore Vidal

*Supply Connectors and Transitions.*   You can also use certain words and phrases to indicate the connections between details and ideas. These include coordinating conjunctions—*and, but, or, for, nor, yet, so*—to link words, phrases, and clauses; subordinating conjunctions, such as *if, although, when, because, since, unless,* which mark different levels of importance among ideas. And you can use conjunctive adverbs, such as *however, thus, therefore, indeed, furthermore,* and *consequently*—as well as transitional phrases like *for example, in addition, on the other hand,* and *in fact.*

Figure 5.1 (p. 64–65) lists the most common shifts in thought that writers make (such as moving to a new point, adding an example, providing a contrast) and then offers a wide selection of words and phrases to fit each shift. Take note of the different types of transition illustrated; then tuck in a bookmark in case you get stuck and need a transition to help you over a rough spot.

In the following paragraph, biologist Stephen Jay Gould achieves coherence by skillfully blending transitional words and phrases, which we've italicized, with a series of repeated key terms (**brain, body, animal, large, small**), which we've set in boldface type:

> I don't wish to deny that the flattened, minuscule head of the **large bodied** "Stegosaurus" houses **little brain** from our subjective,

top-heavy perspective, *but* I do wish to assert that we should not expect more of the beast. *First of all,* **large animals** have relatively **smaller brains** than related, **small animals.** The correlation on **brain** size among kindred **animals** (all reptiles, all mammals, *for example*) is remarkably regular. *As* we move from **small** to **large animals,** from mice to elephants *or* small lizards to Komodo dragons, **brain** size increases, *but* not so fast as **body** size. *In other words,* **bodies** grow faster than **brains,** *and* **large animals** have low ratios of **brain** weight to **body** weight. *In fact,* **brains** grow only about two-thirds as fast as **bodies.** *Since* we have no reason to believe that **large animals** are consistently stupider than their **smaller** relatives, we must conclude that **large**

---

**To move to the next major point:**

| | | |
|---|---|---|
| *too* | *moreover* | *next* |
| *in the first place* | *second* | *third* |
| *again* | *besides* | *in addition* |
| *further* | *likewise* | *also* |
| *furthermore* | *beyond this* | *admittedly* |
| *like* | | |

Examples: We *also* can see that the quality of most television programs is abysmal.

*Furthermore,* the commercials constantly assault our taste and insult our intelligence.

**To add an example:**

| | | |
|---|---|---|
| *for example* | *for instance* | *such as* |
| *that is* | *in the following manner* | *namely* |
| *in this case* | *in the same manner* | *as an illustration* |
| *at the same time* | *in addition* | |

Examples: The daytime game shows, *for instance,* openly appeal to human greed.

Soap operas, *in the same manner,* pander to many of our baser instincts.

**To emphasize a point:**

| | | |
|---|---|---|
| *especially* | *without doubt* | *primarily* |
| *chiefly* | *actually* | *otherwise* |
| *after all* | *as a matter of fact* | *in fact* |
| *without question* | *even more* | *more important* |

Examples: The constant violence depicted on television, *in fact,* poses a danger to society.

*Even more* offensive are deodorant commercials, *without question* the most tasteless on TV.

**FIGURE 5.1** *Useful Transitional Terms*

**animals** require relatively less **brain** to do as well as **smaller animals.** *If* we do not recognize this relationship, we are likely to underestimate the mental power of very **large animals,** dinosaurs in particular.

—"Were Dinosaurs Dumb?"
*The Panda's Thumb*

## Try Rhetorical Questions and Short Sentences

In the paragraph about drug addiction quoted earlier, Gore Vidal uses two rhetorical questions: one to get the paragraph started ("What to do about drug addiction?") and one to move the

---

**To contrast a point:**

| | | |
|---|---|---|
| *but* | *still* | *on the other hand* |
| *on the contrary* | *nevertheless* | *contrary to* |
| *however* | *nonetheless* | *conversely* |
| *yet* | *although* | *in contrast* |
| *neither* | | |

Examples: We abhor violence, *yet* we cannot approve of censorship.

*Although* commercials may enrage or sicken us, they do, *after all,* pay the bills.

**To qualify a point:**

| | | |
|---|---|---|
| *in some cases* | *admittedly* | *of course* |
| *granted that* | *no doubt* | *certainly* |

Examples: There are, *of course,* fine educational programs on public television and some cable networks.

*Admittedly,* these shows enrich our culture; *in some cases,* they are inspiring and enlightening.

**To conclude or sum up a point:**

| | | |
|---|---|---|
| *consequently* | *therefore* | *so* |
| *accordingly* | *then* | *as a result* |
| *hence* | *in sum* | *in conclusion* |
| *in other words* | *thus* | *before* |
| *in short* | *finally* | *at last* |

Examples: Soap operas *thus* contribute to the subtle erosion of moral values.

Commercials, *therefore,* are not worth the sacrifice of our integrity.

Television, *in short,* costs more than society should be willing to pay.

---

**FIGURE 5.1** *Useful Transitional Terms (continued)*

discussion along ("What are the English doing right that we are doing wrong?"). This technique of posing a question that you intend to answer can be effective for leading your readers into the next point, but you probably can't get away with it too often in a short paper. You must have other devices in stock.

Like the rhetorical question, the short-sentence transition must not be used often, but it comes in handy when you need it. You simply state briefly and clearly what you intend to discuss next, like this:

> Europeans think more highly of Americans now than they ever did. *Let me try to explain why.* [Italics added.]
>
> —Anthony Burgess

Molly Ivins uses both a question and a short sentence (along with several transitional expressions) to move her readers along in this paragraph:

> While we're meditating on Christmas gifts, let us consider who got coal and switches this year. According to the Center on Budget and Policy Priorities, 93 percent of all the entitlement reductions passed by Congress in the last two years were in cuts for programs for poor people. *This is an appropriately Dickensian plot for the season, don't you think?* Ninety-three percent of everything that's been done to balance the budget in this way is being taken out of the pittance of low-income people. *Of course, not all the news is bad.* CEO Michael Ovitz, for example, will receive at least $95 million in compensation for leaving the Disney Company after 16 months of what is widely regarded as an unsatisfactory performance. [Italics added.]
>
> —"Early Christmas for Aerospace Giants"

## Exercise on Transitions 5.4

In the paragraph below, we have removed the transitional terms and have inserted blanks in their place. Read each sentence carefully to determine which word or phrase from Figure 5.1 best conveys the meaning of the transition needed. Write your choice in the blank. Notice the punctuation so that you know when to use a capital letter.

> The federal government deregulated the Savings and Loan business; _____, greedy money managers defrauded the taxpayers out of billions of dollars. The fleeced taxpayers were outraged, _____ they were helpless. The news media revealed the scandal; _____ Congress reacted with shock. Some people

suggested, _____, that Congress had known about the thievery for some time. Several members of Congress were clearly implicated; _____, two or three were known to have accepted huge campaign contributions from failed Savings and Loans. First, Congress promised a thorough investigation. _____, they set up committees to gather evidence. The taxpayers waited to see the rich managers brought to justice. _____ they hoped that some of the money would be recovered. _____ few of the guilty were even brought to trial, _____ getting the lost money back proved nearly impossible. _____, the American people are now saddled with this huge new debt, _____ the already staggering national debt. We taxpayers will have to shoulder this financial burden for years to come. _____, we might as well face up to it.

---

## Provide Transitions Between Paragraphs

You may sometimes need signposts for your readers when you change paragraphs. The indention for a new paragraph provides a visual clue that you are moving on to another main idea, but indention alone isn't always sufficient. Often you can use the same devices you use when your thought changes direction or you want to add another example within the same paragraph: transitional expressions, rhetorical questions, and short transitional sentences. For instance, here are the opening sentences from several paragraphs of an essay entitled "Fighting Back" by Stanton Wormley Jr. (the transitional words and phrases have been italicized).

*In the spring of 1970,* I was an 18-year-old private at Fort Jackson, South Carolina.

*Afterward,* I was angrily confronted by a young black streetwise soldier named Morris.

*Nevertheless,* that question—Why didn't I fight back?—haunted me long after the incident had been forgotten by everyone else.

*And* we American men buy that attitude—*especially* those of us who are members of minority groups.

I suppose there are *still* situations in which immediate, violent retaliation is necessary.

*Once in a great while,* past events are repeated, granting people a chance either to redeem themselves or to relive their mistakes.

*As I walked away,* I was filled with a feeling of exultation.

### Writing Exercise 5.5

Stanton Wormley's organization and transitions are so effective that you can probably follow the development of his argument even though you don't have the complete text of the article. Write a paragraph in which you summarize Wormley's main ideas.

---

**Use Echo Transitions** An *echo transition* gives you a subtle way to move smoothly from one paragraph to the next. You manage this artful transition by "echoing" the last idea in one paragraph at the beginning of the next. You create the echo by repeating the same word or by using a word meaning the same thing, thus echoing the idea. It's a neat technique and not difficult to perform once you understand how it works. Here's an example from Stanton Wormley's essay:

> Fighting back, on the other hand, is active and defiant. It involves the adoption of *an attitude* that one's retribution is morally justified—or even, at times, morally obligatory.
> And we American men buy *that attitude*—especially those of us who are members of minority groups. [Italics added.]

You can see how the repetition of the word *attitude* in the opening sentence of the new paragraph forms a link to the previous paragraph and at the same time leads into Wormley's next idea: explaining how and why *that attitude* appeals to minority males.

You don't have to repeat the very same word. You can use a synonym or a related phrase, as in this next example, which gives you the final sentence from a paragraph by Frederick Lewis Allen about the big Red scare in the 1920s, followed by the opening sentence of the next paragraph, which explains the reasons for the scare. The transitional words are italicized in our examples.

> It was an era of lawless and disorderly defense of law and order, of unconstitutional defense of the Constitution, of suspicion and civil conflict—in a very literal sense, *a reign of terror.*
> For this *national panic* there was a degree of justification.

Finally, notice the easy transition from a paragraph describing the deafening noises of a large city to the next paragraph suggesting possible relief:

> Reveille is celebrated in New York these frantic days by the commencement of *pneumatic drills.*

The only way to escape *the din of the asphalt bashers* is to move out or up.

—Horace Sutton

*Pneumatic drills* are, of course, one kind of *asphalt basher.*

---

**E***xercise on Coherence 5.6*

Locate an essay, article, or chapter of a book that uses a variety of strategies for achieving unity and coherence. Identify each of the strategies—transitional expressions, repeated words, rhetorical questions, short sentences, echo transitions—and comment on their effectiveness.

---

# C*omposing Special Paragraphs*

Not all of your paragraphs are going to conform to the advice we've been giving you about the content and organization of typical paragraphs. Most notably, introductions and conclusions have special requirements that you need to consider.

## Advice About Introductions

You can draft the introduction to a paper at any point during the writing process. Some people like to write it first as a way of getting started; others wait till last so they can tailor it to fit the rest of the essay. Regardless of when you write the introduction, remember that because your audience reads it first, it should make a favorable impression.

***State Your Thesis.*** Although getting your readers' attention is an important element of most introductions, the chief function is to let readers know what you're writing about. You will not always need a straightforward announcement of your central idea, but the more formal the writing, the more likely you are to need a clear thesis statement. In the following introduction the writer comes straight to the point:

> Today in the United States there is one profession in which conflict of interest is not merely ignored but loudly defended as a necessary concomitant of the free-enterprise system. That is in medicine, particularly surgery.
>
> —George Crile, Jr.

This is point-blank as introductions go. Normally, you take several sentences to work up to your main idea, giving a little background information or making some fairly broad remarks about your subject, then narrowing the focus to the specific idea in your thesis. This more typical method is used in the following introduction (thesis statements are italicized throughout this section):

> To her, tight jeans and no bra mean she's in style. To him, they mean she wants to have sex. So it goes among adolescents in Los Angeles, according to a survey by four researchers at UCLA. Despite unisex hair salons, the women's movement, and other signs of equality between the sexes, *boys still read more sexual come-ons into girls' behavior than girls intend.*
>
> —*Psychology Today*

The article then presents other examples of dress and behavior that are often misinterpreted, just as the introduction promises.

*Catch Your Readers' Attention.*   Unless you are writing for readers that already have a professional interest in the topic of your paper, you need an introduction that will catch their attention and encourage them to continue reading. One good way involves putting a picture in their minds, as the writer does in this introduction:

> You know the couch potato: the flabby muscles and a generous waistline, one hand on the remote control and the other in a bag of chips. Medical research now has confirmed the aptness of this depiction. *Long hours in front of the tube and obesity, it turns out, go together like Monday Night Football and beer nuts.*
>
> —Elizabeth Stark

*Find Fascinating Facts.*   Another way to hook your readers is to begin with some eye-opening facts and figures, as in this introduction:

> Every two-and-a-half minutes someone in the United States is robbed at gunpoint, and every forty minutes someone else is murdered with a gun. The weapons find their way into the hands of the criminals in a manner that almost nobody understands. Made in factories owned and operated by the most secretive industry in the country, the guns move through various markets and delivery systems, all of them obscure. Each year police seize about 250,000 handguns and long guns (rifles and shotguns) from the people they arrest. *Given the number of guns that the manufacturers produce each year (2.5 million long guns and 4 million handguns) the supply-and-demand equation works against the hope of an orderly society.*
>
> —Steven Brill

*Select a Quotation.* Sometimes a relevant and interesting quotation provides an effective way to introduce your main idea. In the following introduction from an essay on free speech, the author uses quotations from two famous Supreme Court justices to set up the thesis:

> There are two free speech traditions in America, not merely one. The first finds its pre-eminent expression in the great dissenting opinions of Justice Oliver Wendell Holmes. Holmes spoke of "free trade in ideas," and thought that "the best test of truth is the power of the thought to get itself accepted in the market." The second tradition can be found in the great dissenting opinions of Justice Louis Brandeis, who said that "the greatest menace to freedom is an inert people" and that "public discussion is a political duty."

After piquing the readers' interest with these two views, the author then brings them together to establish her main line of argument:

> No one believes that the free speech principle protects everything that might come out of a human mouth, a pen or word processor: perjury, conspiracy, attempted bribery, fraud, threats, unlicensed medical and legal advice, child pornography. *The real issue, as Holmes and Brandeis agreed, is not whether all speech is protected but how to draw sensible lines.*
>
> —Cass R. Sunstein

*Try a Definition.* Another useful way to get started is by defining your subject:

> The Indian and Hispanic people of Arizona and New Mexico eat blue tortillas, tissue-thin blue bread, and a blue milk-drink. *What gives these foods their color and much of their nutritional value is blue corn, a versatile corn that has been raised in the Southwest for centuries.* The farmers who have cultivated it so long have developed it into an extremely drought-tolerant, disease-resistant corn that can be steamed, boiled, or roasted in the milk stage, and ground into a delicious meal when mature.
>
> —Richard Flint

---

**TIP!** **Avoid Mindless Generalizations.**

In your effort to begin with a general observation and narrow that down to a thesis statement, you want to avoid obvious generalizations like these:

> Life can be very interesting.
>
> People are funny sometimes.

If you begin with such clichéd comments, your readers may never get beyond the opening sentence.

---

---

| **R**evising Exercise 5.7 |
| :--- |

Find a paper you have written recently, and look at the introduction. How can you improve it? Write two more versions of the introduction, using the strategies described in this chapter.

---

## Advice About Conclusions

Like introductions, conclusions ought to be forceful and to the point. Work especially hard on your last paragraph. Its effectiveness will influence the way your readers react to the whole paper. If you trail off at the end, they will sigh and feel let down. Avoid any sort of apology or hedging: you need an impressive ending.

*Echo Your Thesis Statement.*   What you want in a conclusion is a tidy ending that reinforces the point you set out to make in the beginning. An echo of your thesis statement can be perfect. Consider the conclusion of the article on misinterpreting sexual signals (the introduction appeared on page 70):

> The young people's ethnic backgrounds, ages, and previous dating and sexual experiences had almost no effect on their reactions. The girls' "relatively less-sexualized view of social relationships," the psychologists suggest, "may reflect some discomfort with the demands of the dating scene"; women do, after all, have more to lose from sexual activity, facing risks of pregnancy and/or a bad reputation. The girls in the study were more likely than the boys to agree with the statement, "Sometimes I wish that guys and girls could just be friends without worrying about sexual relationships."
>
> —*Psychology Today*

The quotation at the end echoes the thesis ("boys still read more sexual come-ons into girls' behavior than the girls intend"), restating it in different terms and giving the article a neat unity.

*Summarize Your Main Points.*   If your essay is long and complex, your readers may appreciate a summary of the major ideas. You want to be careful, however, not to write an ending that sounds forced and simply repeats your introduction. It's a good idea to combine your summary with another strategy. For example, the professional author of an essay on the problems of young black males in the inner cities concludes by combining a review of her main points with a general call for action:

If black youths are given real opportunities for education, if they are provided with meaningful jobs, if they have adequate income to care for their families, if they have hope for future mobility, then they will contribute their fair share to the larger community. We have the knowledge, the technology, and the resources to improve life chances for young black males. What we need is the compassion, commitment, and consensus to create a human environment for all youth in this country.

—Jewelle Taylor Gibbs

*Suggest Solutions.* If you're writing an analysis or a persuasive piece, a useful closing strategy involves offering suggestions—possible solutions to problems discussed in the paper. This approach is valid only if you can come up with some sound ideas for solving the problems. Here is the conclusion of the article about containing the proliferation of guns in the United States (the introduction is on page 70):

All these small steps toward sanity are possible if we force the people who profit from America's free-wheeling gun traffic to be open, accountable, and fully responsible to law-enforcement needs. If we're going to continue to allow the RGs or the Smith and Wessons to make guns at all for civilian use, we ought to at least demand that they become partners in the effort to curb the carnage their weapons cause. When we think of people murdered or robbed at gunpoint, we have to start thinking of brand names.

—Steven Brill

*Offer Encouragement.* Especially in process writing, which explains how to do something, it's constructive to close with a few words of encouragement. Tell your readers how delicious they will find the cheesecake if they follow your instructions carefully. Or tell them how rewarding they will find growing their own tomatoes, as the writer does in this conclusion:

When you shop for tomato seeds or plants this season, consider trying at least one new variety. There are hundreds to choose from and if you keep looking, one of them may find a home in your garden. Even if you find nothing to match your favorite, you'll have fun, and the pleasure of gardening is not just in the eating.

—Mark Kane

*Speculate on the Future.* Think about the long-term implications of what you have said in your paper. You might want to conclude by warning of hazards or by suggesting possible benefits. In the next example, the writer does both, concluding his argument that Americans need to become bilingual:

> The benefits, not only in economic terms but also in terms of enhancing our understanding of other cultures and of ourselves, would be beyond measure. The costs, should we fail to act decisively, could eventually prove to be catastrophic.
>
> —Daniel Shanahan

Conclusions aren't really all that difficult. Often they turn out weak because we write them last, when our energy and inspiration are lagging.

---

**TIP!** Treat your conclusion like your introduction: Think about it off and on while you are writing—during coffee breaks or whenever you pause to let your mind rest.

---

### Revising Exercise 5.8

The following conclusion is flat and doesn't leave much of an impression on the reader. Use one of the strategies just discussed to put more punch in this ending. Even though you didn't write the essay, you should be able to improve the concluding paragraph. Work especially hard in crafting the final sentence.

> College is a big change for thousands of students every year. As I have indicated, these students are expected to be fairly mature; they must develop independence and self-discipline; and they have to take more difficult tests and compete for grades. Almost everyone finds college more difficult than high school.

---

### Writing Exercise 5.9

Using any of the strategies just described, write two additional conclusions for a paper that you have written recently. Show these alternate endings to several friends or classmates, and ask them which one seems the most effective for your paper and if they have any suggestions for improvement.

# 6

# *Polishing Your Sentences*

In order to perfect your paragraphs, you need to revise your sentences—to make them more clear perhaps, more vivid, more concise, more interesting, more forceful. Before any paragraph can be effective, the sentences within that paragraph must be both coherent and readable.

## S *entence Combining: Coordination and Subordination*

One way to improve coherence is through skillful sentence combining, which involves placing ideas within each sentence according to their importance so that the readers' attention stays focused on your major points.

Perhaps you've noticed that when little children talk, they tend to string simple sentences together, like this:

> We got hats and balloons and Buffy got presents and Angie was late and we had cake with candles and ice cream and I blew my balloon up big and . . .

So it goes, on and on and on, with little variety, few modifiers, and no distinction between important events and passing details. That's *coordination*—linking ideas together—in its most primitive form. We learn to read and write with a similar simplicity. But by the time we progress to the third grade, we become sophisticated enough to start putting sentences together in patterns that depend on subordination.

## Clauses Versus Phrases

Subordination involves tucking less important ideas into dependent (or subordinate) clauses and small details into phrases. Then, major ideas are elevated into independent (or main) clauses, where they receive proper emphasis. If you're hazy about the difference between phrases and clauses, remember that a clause has both a subject and a verb, whereas a phrase has only one or the other. Notice the difference:

PHRASES:   having lost my head

to lose my head

after losing my head

CLAUSES:   after I lost my head   (dependent)

I lost my head         (independent)

that I lost my head    (dependent)

An independent clause can be a complete sentence all by itself. Because a dependent clause begins with a subordinating word (see list on page 187), it must be attached to an independent clause in order to form a complete sentence.

## H *ow Sentence Combining Works*

Most of this subordinating—this stashing of details into phrases and clauses—we do automatically as we speak and write. But it helps to understand the process when you revise and want to combine ideas to improve your sentence structure. Here's how it's done.

### Subordinating in a Phrase

Say you want to incorporate the following ideas into a single sentence:

Garfield is a cat.

Garfield is orange.

Garfield is striped.

Garfield weighs fifteen pounds.

Garfield is incorrigible.

Garfield is a glutton.

Garfield is a cartoon character.

You could combine several of these details into a phrase this way:

Garfield, an orange-striped, fifteen-pound cartoon cat, is an incorrigible glutton.

You have subordinated the color, stripes, weight, and cartoon status of the cat in one fell swoop. But suppose you wanted to stress Garfield's being a cartoon cat rather than his gluttony. The sentence might come out this way:

Garfield, an incorrigibly gluttonous, fifteen-pound, orange-striped cat, is a cartoon character.

Same details, but see the difference in emphasis? Because the English language depends on word order for meaning, the way you put a sentence together affects the sense as well as the style. In the first example, the key positions in the sentence are these:

| subject | verb | complement |
|---------|------|------------|
| Garfield | is | incorrigible glutton |

In the second one,

| subject | verb | complement |
|---------|------|------------|
| Garfield | is | cartoon character |

---

**TIP!** When combining ideas, be sure to get your important ideas into the main clauses, not the subordinate clauses.

---

### Subordinating in a Clause

Of course, a clause can also become far less important in a sentence if you make it a subordinate clause, like this:

Garfield, who weighs fifteen pounds, is an orange-striped, incorrigibly gluttonous cartoon cat.

Or you could do it this way:

Because he is an incorrigible glutton, Garfield, the orange-striped cartoon cat, weighs fifteen pounds.

But you would not want to arrange the ideas this way:

Because he is an incorrigible glutton, Garfield, who weighs fifteen pounds, is an orange-striped cartoon cat.

That's called upside-down subordination, and you can see why. It makes no sense to say that because the cat eats too much, he has orange stripes and appears in a cartoon.

# **W**hen to Use Sentence Combining

1. *If you are writing a lot of short, choppy sentences, consider combining some of them.*

   For example:

   > Maria became a doctor. She didn't become a regular doctor. She became a medical missionary.

   Combined:

   > Rather than becoming a regular doctor, Maria became a medical missionary.

2. *If you notice needless repetition of a word or phrase, consider combining.*

   For example:

   > LaDonna judges all her friends severely. LaDonna always judges according to her own rigid standards.

   Combined:

   > LaDonna always judges all her friends severely according to her own rigid standards.

3. *When a sentence begins with "This is" or "It is," you may want to combine that sentence with the previous one.*

   For example:

   > To Michael, his car establishes his place in society. It is a sleek, shiny, luxurious Jaguar.

   Combined:

   > To Michael, his car—a sleek, shiny, luxurious Jaguar—establishes his place in society.

---

**S**entence Combining Exercise 6.1

Look at the last paper you wrote. Did you find a fair number of short, choppy sentences? If so, this exercise may help you write more fluently.

If you need this practice, combine each group below into one easily understood sentence by subordinating the less important ideas. We'll do the first one to show you the idea.

1. Fido is a dog.

   Fido belongs to me.

Fido needs a bath.

Fido has muddy paws.

Fido has fleas.

(Combined) My dog Fido, who has muddy paws and fleas, needs a bath.

(Combined) Because he has fleas and muddy paws, my dog Fido needs a bath.

2. Uncle Zou is coming to visit.

   He lives in Dallas.

   He drives a city bus there.

   He is coming on the early train.

   He will stay with us a week.

3. My garden is in the backyard

   Rabbits ate the lettuce.

   Worms got the tomatoes.

   The cucumbers got trampled.

   Somebody stepped on them.

4. I get off work at 4:30.

   I pick up the kids.

   The kids are at day care.

   I fix dinner.

   I wash the dishes.

   I fall asleep in front of the TV.

5. All the characters in this bestseller are stereotypes. Some of these stereotypes are the Idealistic Young Man, the Disillusioned Older Man, the Scheming Siren, and the Neglected Wife.

---

### Sentence Combining Exercise 6.2

If you are a fairly fluent writer who wants to practice sentence combining to avoid wordiness and improve your sentence structure, try the following exercise. Combine the following pairs of sentences, all of which were written by students in one of our classes on writing about literature.

1. Flowers serve an important role in Cather's "Paul's Case." Therefore, they are worthy of closer examination.

2. The boy's illusion is conveyed even more clearly through Joyce's description of the girl. Joyce describes her as turning a silver bracelet on her wrist.

3. Edna was so happy that she shouted for joy. Learning to swim was a big achievement for Edna.

4. The similarities between Dr. Sloper and Morris Townsend are numerous. They can be seen throughout the book.

5. Dr. Sloper warns his daughter about the dangers of marrying Morris. He does this because he sees so many of his own weak points in his daughter's suitor.

---

### $S$*entence Combining Exercise 6.3*

Find the last paper you wrote and read through it slowly, paragraph by paragraph. Look for short sentences, needlessly repeated words or phrases, and sentences beginning with "This is" or "It is." If you find any of these signals, combine sentences to improve your style.

---

# $C$ *ut Out Unnecessary Words*

Try to make your writing clean, clear, and concise. We don't mean to deprive you of effective stylistic flourishes, but ineffective stylistic flourishes have to go. So does just plain lazy wordiness. It's far easier to be verbose than to be concise. As Pascal wrote, "I have made this letter longer than usual because I lack the time to make it shorter." And as Hugh Henry Brackenridge tellingly observed, "In order to speak short on any subject, think long." Nothing will annoy your readers more than having to plow through a cluttered paragraph because you neglected to spend time cleaning it up.

You must diligently prune your prose. Sentences like the following may cause even a gentle reader to contemplate justifiable homicide:

> It is believed by a number of persons in this country that the young people of today do not assume as much responsibility for their actions as it might be hoped that they would. (34 words)

You can say the same thing more clearly with fewer words:

> Many people believe that young people today assume too little responsibility for their actions. (14 words)

---

**TIP!** No need to be telegraphic. Just don't get too flowery.

---

**E*xercise on Conciseness 6.4***

If you have trouble saying things succinctly, practice by tidying the following wordy sentences. Keep the same meaning but eliminate the extra words. We'll revise the first one.

1. The male-gendered style used online in listserver communications is characterized by adversariality.

   (revised)   The male style used in communications on a listserver is adversarial.

2. It is my desire to be called Ishmael.

3. In my opinion there are many diverse elements about this problem that one probably ought to at least think about before arriving at an opinion on the matter.

4. The obnoxious child was seldom corrected or reprimanded because its baffled and adoring parents thought its objectionable behavior was normal and acceptable.

5. There came a time when, based on what I had been reading, I arrived at the feeling that the food we buy at the supermarkets to eat is sometimes, perhaps often, bad for us.

# U *se Mostly Active Voice*

If your writing is somewhat lifeless, the passive voice may be part of the problem. In the passive (which always involves some form of the verb *to be* plus a past participle), the subject is acted upon instead of doing the acting. Notice the difference between active and passive:

(active)   The guard fed the prisoner.

(passive)   The prisoner was fed by the guard.

As you can see, it takes more words to express an idea with a passive verb—unless you leave out the performer of the action. Thus a passive sentence like this one,

   A decision on the matter has been made by the court.

takes longer to read and process than the active version,

   The court decided the matter.

## The Devious Passive

Notice that the passive allows us to leave out information. You don't have to mention who fed the prisoner, you can just say,

"The prisoner was fed." That's not a misleading sentence, because probably nobody was perishing to know who fed the prisoner anyway. But consider the same sentence with the verb changed:

(passive)   The prisoner was beaten.

Now we want to know *by whom?* By the sheriff? By one of the deputies? By a guard? By a fellow prisoner? There's no way to tell from the passive construction. As Richard Gambino, an authority on doublespeak observes, "The effect of the habitual use of the passive is to create a world where events have lives, wills, motives, and actions of their own without any human being responsible for them."

## The Appropriate Passive

Notice, it's the *habitual* use of the passive that is questionable. We don't mean that you should never employ the passive voice. Sometimes it can be the best way to convey information. You would likely choose the passive to announce that "The President was elected by a comfortable majority," rather than using the active voice: "A comfortable majority elected the President."

The passive is also a good choice when you want to stress the action or the receiver of the action:

(passive)   The city hall was damaged by an earthquake.

(passive)   My bicycle was demolished by a truck.

(passive)   The candidate's credibility has been questioned by the media.

## $\mathbf{R}$*evising Exercise 6.5*

If you have trouble distinguishing active from passive—or if you suspect that you use the passive too much—rewrite the following passive sentences in the active voice. We'll do the first one to get you going.

1. Let our daily bread be given to us on this day.

   (revised)   Give us this day our daily bread.

2. The whistle was blown by the referee.

3. It was believed by the police that the child was kidnapped.

4. The day that he discovered sex was never forgotten by Cosmo.

5. Some basic human rights were violated by the officers.

6. Bribes were accepted frequently by the city engineer.

# Practice the Passive

Despite all these warnings against habitual use of the passive, we are aware that writers in a number of jobs and in some academic disciplines are expected—even required—to use the passive voice. If you are taking courses in education, corrections, or any of the hard sciences (chemistry, biology, physics, and the like), you must learn to write gracefully in the passive voice. It can be done, but you may need to practice to get the hang of it.

Proceeding from the pen of an accomplished writer, the passive voice is not in the least objectionable. Jessica Mitford, for one, employs the passive so skillfully that you never notice its presence:

> Today, family members who might wish to be in attendance would certainly be dissuaded by the funeral director.

That sentence is not noticeably improved by making it active voice:

> Today, the funeral director would certainly dissuade family members who might wish to be in attendance.

In order to help you perfect your use of the passive, we have collected some useful and fairly simple sentences as models. If you'd like to learn to use the passive skillfully, try working out the following exercise.

## Sentence Modeling Exercise 6.6

Copy each sentence carefully. Then, choosing subject matter from your academic major, write five sentences imitating the passive structure of each of the originals. Pretending to be agriculture majors, we'll do the first one to show you how it's done.

1. Certain things were not mentioned.    (Jane O'Reilly)

    (imitations)

    Synthetic fertilizers were not invented.

    Pesticides were not advised.

    Crop rotation was not used.

    Early harvesting was not recommended.

    Organic methods were not tried.

2. The SKIP option can be used in input and output statements.
    (J. S. Roper)

3. The poor are slated to take the brunt of the federal budget cuts.
   (Barbara Ehrenreich)
4. The emphasis is generally put on the right to speak.
   (Walter Lippmann)
5. All others are excluded by law from the preparation room.
   (Jessica Mitford)

# B e Specific and Vivid

Paul Roberts once wrote that most subjects—except sex—are basically boring, so it's up to the writer to make the topic interesting. Because you can't write about sex all the time, you need to incorporate some of the following suggestions aimed at keeping your readers awake.

## Choose Action Verbs

One way to liven up your writing is to use vivid, specific words whenever possible. Although you often can't avoid the lifeless *to be* verb (*am, is, are, was, were, been, being*), when given a chance, toss in an action verb. James Thurber writes of a "world made up of gadgets that *whir* and *whine* and *whiz* and *shriek* and sometimes *explode*." (Our italics.) The force of the verbs conveys the feeling of anxiety produced by machine-age living.

George Orwell describes a dog that "came *bounding* among us with a loud volley of barks, and *leapt* round us *wagging* its whole body with glee." (Our italics.) The italicized words and the descriptive detail about the barking allow us to visualize the excitement of the dog.

Thomas Heggen, in *Mister Roberts*, writes, "Surely an artillery shell fired at Hanover *ripples* the air here. Surely a bomb dropped on Okinawa *trembles* these bulkheads." (Our italics.) These verbs and the specific place names produce precisely the effect he wants: the suggestion of being touched, but only barely touched, by events far away.

Of course, other stylistic elements combine to make the above examples effective. But if your writing is colorless and vague, consider adding specific details and substituting more descriptive verbs for these limp ones: *is, are, was, were, has, have, had, get, go, come, make.* If you've written, "We all got into the truck," try "All four of us piled into Billy Bob's rusty pickup." You can, of course, overdo the use of forceful verbs and specific details, but most writers err in the other direction.

---

**TIP!**   Avoid these overworked words *terrible, wonderful, very.* Find more precise terms, like *inept, skillful, excellent.*

---

### Find the Exact Word

Mark Twain once observed that the difference between the right word and almost the right word is the difference between the lightning and the lightning bug. Our language is full of synonyms; but synonyms have different shades of meaning. Don't write *ambiguous* if you really mean *ambivalent.* Don't write *healthy* if you really mean *healthful.* Don't write *deduce* if you really mean *infer.* Especially, be careful not to confuse words that sound alike but mean something entirely different. Don't write *apprise* if you really mean *appraise.* Don't write *disinterested* if you really mean *uninterested.*

### Dust Off Your Dictionary

Any good desk-size dictionary can enlighten you on distinctions of meaning. But in order to get reliable help from your dictionary, you should first learn how to use it. Nobody has ever standardized the format for dictionaries, so each publisher arranges the material in slightly different ways.

Many people believe that the first meaning listed for a word will be the one they want. Not necessarily true. The first meaning will often be the oldest meaning and thus the least used. The same is true of alternative spellings. Lots of people think the first spelling is preferred. But unless some usage label is inserted (such as "also" or "variation of"), all spellings listed are equally acceptable.

The only way to find out how your dictionary handles these matters is to force yourself to read the "Explanatory Notes" at the beginning. It's not lively reading, for sure, but it can be rewarding. You'll discover, for instance, that in most dictionaries the principal parts of verbs, degrees of adjectives, and plurals of nouns are not listed unless irregular. You'll find, if you persevere, explanations of various usage labels, which warn you about words that may not be acceptable in standard English (archaic, slang, substandard, etc.).

You may also, if you have an inquiring mind, discover interesting material in the back (or sometimes in the front) that you never suspected was there. Many dictionaries include lists of abbreviations, proofreader's marks, signs and symbols; rules for spelling, punctuation, and capitalization; and occasionally a list of all the colleges (with locations) in the United States and Canada. One dictionary even offers lists of common first names and of words that rhyme.

---

**TIP!** Good writers keep a dictionary handy and consult it often.
If the only thing you ever do with your dictionary is use it to prop up books, that may be part of your problem.

---

## Trot Out Your Thesaurus

A thesaurus, which is a dictionary of synonyms, comes in handy for locating just the right word. Your word processing program probably has one that's quick to consult. It may not be as good as those in book form, but it's better than none and considerably easier to use.

If you need a synonym, either because you think the word you've used is not precise enough or because you've used it three times already, call up that word on your word processor's thesaurus or look it up in the book version you keep on your desk. Sometimes we use both if the electronic thesaurus fails to offer enough choices. Did you notice that we've used a form of the word *use* four times already in this paragraph? That's a signal to consult a thesaurus.

We just called up *use* on our popular word-processing program and found five words—*employ, utilize, exercise, manipulate, operate*—and only the first two fit our meaning. The word *consult*, which we thought up ourselves, wasn't even listed. So, we checked our pocketbook-size thesaurus and found almost a full page of synonyms arranged according to meaning and part of speech (verb, adjective, adverb, etc.), with a *See* at the end citing four other words we could look up to find additional meanings. Clearly, you need a backup for your electronic thesaurus if you want to discover all your verbal options.

---

**TIP!** Synonyms are not always interchangeable.
Never choose an unfamiliar word from your thesaurus. Look it up in your dictionary first.

---

## E *xercise Your Imagination: Figures of Speech*

Try to come up with a few lively figures of speech—analogies and other imaginative comparisons—to add interest and clarity to your writing. Ralph Waldo Emerson once remarked that "New York is a sucked orange." Now there's an observation full of meaning, phrased with great economy. Maya Angelou writes that some social changes "have been as violent as electrical storms, while others creep slowly like sorghum syrup."

Such comparisons are a form of analogy, a useful method of comparing something *abstract* (like the quality of life in a city) to something *concrete* and visual (like a sucked orange). Here's an apt analogy from Sharon Begley: "The immune system is notorious for falling apart like a dishwasher past its warranty."

When Dorothy Parker declares, "His voice was as intimate as the rustle of sheets," her *simile* (a comparison stated with *like* or *as*) is more interesting than just telling us that the man was speaking seductively. Notice how forcefully Barbara Ehrenreich conveys the hazards of smoking when she asserts that the "medical case against smoking is as airtight as a steel casket."

Brigid Brophy uses a *metaphor* (an implied comparison) to assert her belief that monogamy is too confining: "At present, monogamy is the corset into which we try to fit every married couple—a process which has on so many occasions split the seams that we have had to modify the corset."

### Make Your Metaphors Meaningful

In writing expository prose (the kind we're focusing on in this text), your figures of speech should clarify your meaning—unlike metaphoric language in poetry, which often conceals meaning. Part of the pleasure of poetry involves puzzling out the meaning. Not so in expository prose. The cardinal rule here is Thou Shalt Not Puzzle Thy Readers. Better no metaphors at all than one that is confusing or mixed up. A *mixed metaphor* presents an inaccurate comparison, like this gem from the *Nashville Tennessean*, "I may be just a little grain of salt crying in the woods, but I deplore this kind of thing." Just try to visualize that image and you'll see why it's a mistake. Lapses like this may bring, not admiration for your fine turn of phrase, but an unwanted chuckle from your bemused readers.

## Avoid Clichés

Be sure your figures of speech really *are* lively. Don't settle for the first phrase that comes to mind, as it will likely be a *cliché*—an expression that people pick up because it sounds good and then tend to use again and again until it loses its force, like these chestnuts:

| | |
|---|---|
| bottom line | ballpark figure |
| burning questions | high and mighty |
| crystal clear | last but not least |
| few and far between | pretty as a picture |
| first and foremost | untimely death |
| at this point in time | have a nice day |

---

**TIP!** The simple word "fine" is preferable to the tarnished phrase "worth its weight in gold."

---

### Revising Exercise 6.7

To limber up your imagination, rewrite the following grammatically correct but lackluster sentences. Add details and substitute action verbs and descriptive words wherever appropriate. Here's how we would revise the first one.

1. She was up late last night trying to finish typing her term paper.
(revised)  Selina sat hunched over her typewriter, pecking away doggedly until three o'clock in the morning, trying to finish her term paper.
2. Lou left his office, walked to a store, and made a purchase.
3. The person I went out with last night was a character.
4. She came into the room, took off her shoes, and sat down.
5. Some person had removed the article I needed from the magazine in the library.

---

### Revising Exercise 6.8

Drag out your last paper, and revise your word choices as you go through it, sentence by sentence, replacing or eliminating overworked, tired words with more precise, colorful language.

---

# C onstructing Impressive Sentences

Another way to make your prose effective involves writing an occasional forceful or unusual sentence. If every sentence built to a climax, the technique would lose its effectiveness, so don't work at it too hard. But in a key position—such as at the beginning or end of a paragraph or as the last line in your essay—a carefully constructed sentence is worth the time it takes to compose it.

## Save the Clincher for the End: Periodic Structure

Most of the time we don't deliberate about our sentence structure. We string ideas together, automatically subordinating the less important ones, until we come to the end of the thought, where we put a period and start in on the next idea. These everyday sentences—like the one we just wrote—are called *cumulative* and constitute the bulk of our writing. If, however, you need a Sunday-best sentence, you either consciously plan it or rearrange it when you revise. You want to order the details to build to a big finish, so you don't disclose your main idea until just before the period, where it gains emphasis. These sentences are called *periodic*. Notice the difference in these examples:

cumulative:     Sylvester made the honor roll while holding down a part-time job and playing the lead in *Hamlet*.

periodic:     While holding down a part-time job and playing the lead in *Hamlet*, Sylvester made the honor roll.

cumulative:     Our first consideration is the preservation of our environment, even though preventing pollution costs money.

periodic:     Even though preventing pollution costs money, our first consideration is the preservation of our environment.

If you have a feel for prose, you probably already write periodic sentences when you need them without being aware that you're doing it. If, on the other hand, you're not long on style, you can develop some by cinching up a few of your sentences. Here are a few more useful strategies.

## Try a Short One for Variety, Emphasis, or Transition

The short-short sentence is easier to handle than the periodic sentence and is remarkably effective—as long as you don't overdo it. Often short-short sentences appear at the beginning or at the end of a paragraph, because these are the most emphatic positions. But you can lob one in anytime if you want to vary your sentence structure. Remember, though, not to overdo it. You can't use short-short sentences often or you'll lose the effect; your writing will merely seem choppy.

Notice the emphasis achieved in the following examples by the brief sentence preceding or following one of normal length:

> This is our hope. This is the faith with which I return to the South to hew out of the mountain of despair a stone of hope.
>
> —Dr. Martin Luther King

> Webster's dictionaries and the endless multiplication of handbooks and courses in English composition represent a desperate effort to prevent class distinction from revealing itself in language. And, of course, it has failed.
>
> —John Hurt Fisher

> What, therefore, is the prognosis of our terminally ill planet? It is gloomy.
>
> —Helen Caldicott

The short sentence also functions effectively as a transitional device between paragraphs (our italics):

> Economics, foreign policy, the split in the party as it relates to racial equality, and some resulting questions of political style all require a special word. *To these matters I now turn.*
>
> —John Kenneth Galbraith

## Experiment with the Dash

Because the end of a sentence is an emphatic position, you can use a dash there to good advantage, as Woodrow Wilson did in this warning:

> I have seen their destruction, as will come upon these again—utter destruction and contempt.

The dash can be used to tack on an afterthought, but you'll find it more impressive for reinforcing a point or for elaboration, like this:

> Hollywood offered the public yet another marvel—talking films.

> This was the year of the big spectaculars—Biblical extravaganzas spiced with sex and filmed in glorious Technicolor.

The dash, like the short sentence, can't retain its effect if overused. In fact, a flurry of dashes produces an unfortunate, adolescent style.

---

**TIP!** For emphasis, use dashes and short sentences sparingly.

---

# **U** *se Parallel Structure*

Another way to keep your ideas clear and make your sentences impressive is to use parallel structure. This technique depends on deliberate repetition—sometimes of the same words, always of the same grammatical structures (phrases, clauses). Virginia Woolf repeats the same adverb (*well*), changing the verb each time to achieve this elegant sentence:

> One cannot think well, love well, sleep well, if one has not dined well.

Mark Twain, in a less elevated tone, repeats independent clauses:

> It was marvelous, it was dizzying, it was dazzling.

## For Everyday Writing

While parallel structure lends itself particularly well to emphatic sentences, the technique is fundamental to all good writing. If by chance you put together a sentence involving two similar elements or a series of them, your readers expect these similar parts to be balanced using parallel structure. Whenever you join parts of a sentence with a coordinating conjunction (*and, but, or, for, nor, yet, so*), you need to make those parts parallel.

Consider the problem caused by lack of parallelism in this first simple example:

> Clyde likes *to smoke* and *drinking*.

Your readers expect those italicized parts to sound and look alike— to be parallel in construction, like this:

> Clyde likes to *smoke* and *drink*.

Or you could revise it this way:

> Clyde likes *smoking* and *drinking*.

Let's look at a more typical example, the kind of sentence you might write in a first draft and should make parallel in structure when you revise:

> Politicians today face the difficult tasks of *solving urban problems* and *how to find the money* without raising taxes.

You need to match the two parts connected by *and*. The easiest way is to make *how to find* sound and look like *solving*—that is, use *finding:*

> Politicians face the difficult task of *solving urban problems* and *finding the money* without raising taxes.

## For Sunday-Best Sentences

Once you become adept at constructing parallel sentences, you'll find the technique perfect for composing splendid climactic sentences—the kind you need to summarize key points, to conclude paragraphs, and to bring your essays to a resounding finish. Martin Luther King learned from the Bible how to repeat parallel phrases with ringing effect:

> With this faith we will be able to work together, to pray together, to struggle together, to go to jail together, to stand up for freedom together, knowing that we will be free one day.

Here is Thomas Jefferson expressing righteous outrage in the Declaration of Independence:

> He [King George III] has plundered our seas, ravaged our coasts, burnt our towns, and destroyed the lives of our people.

Parallel structure also provides the most effective way to compress a number of ideas into a single sentence with perfect clarity and easy readability. Notice how many ideas T. E. Kalem packs into this nicely balanced comment on one of George Bernard Shaw's plays:

> Shaw steadily sounds his pet themes: the chicanery of politics, the corruptive power of money, the degrading stench of poverty, the servile dependencies of marriage and family, the charlatanism of medicine, the fossilization of learning, the tyranny of the state, the stupidity of the military, and the bigoted, sanctimonious zeal of the church.

**TIP!**   There's no better strategy than parallel structure to deliver so many ideas so clearly in so readable a way.

You can also use parallel structure to good effect in separate sentences by repeating key words in the same grammatical structure. Because the technique involves building to a climax, you can't use it often, but the effect is impressive when well done. Notice how Pastor Martin Niemöeller, a Lutheran minister, achieves eloquence by using simple, parallel sentences to explain how he ended up in a Nazi concentration camp during World War II:

> In Germany, the Nazis first came for the Communists, and I didn't speak up because I wasn't a Communist. Then they came for the Jews, and I didn't speak up because I wasn't a Jew. Then they came for the trade unionists, and I didn't speak up because I wasn't a trade unionist. Then they came for the Catholics, and I didn't speak up because I was a Protestant. Then they came for me, and by that time there was no one left to speak for me.

## Revising Exercise 6.9

The following sentences were written by students whose grasp of parallel structure was less than perfect. We want you to restore the parallelism. Don't aim for impressive or emphatic sentences in this exercise. Just try to produce good, clear, everyday sentences.

First, read each sentence and decide which parts need to be made parallel. Look for elements in series or connected by coordinating conjunctions (*and, but, or, for, nor, yet, so*). Then change the part that's irregular so that it matches the other part or parts.

Often you can find several equally good ways to revise such sentences. Here's how we would do the first one:

1. The plan is not workable: it delegates too much power to the states and because it is unconstitutional.

That sentence consists of three clauses. All three should be parallel. The first two are independent:

> The plan is not workable
>
> it delegates too much power to the states

Fine so far. The clauses don't have to be precisely parallel as long as the basic structure is the same. The trouble comes with the third clause, which is not independent but dependent (beginning with the subordinating word *because*):

> because it is unconstitutional.

Probably the easiest way to revise the sentence is to make all three clauses independent by dropping the subordinating word *because:*

> The plan is not workable: it delegates too much power to the states, and it is unconstitutional.

Or you could make the last two clauses both dependent, like this:

> The plan is not workable because it delegates too much power to the states and because it is unconstitutional.

Now have a go at revising these sentences:

2. The final step involves making a ninety-degree kick turn and then start the pattern over from the beginning.

3. European trains are frequent, punctual, having easy connections, and travel at high speeds.

4. In the movies, college men are portrayed as single, driving a nice car, well-off financially, good looks, and wearing cool clothes.

5. Progressive education aims to teach children to be open-minded, thinking with logic, know how to make wise choices, having self-discipline, and self-control.

6. This proposal would alert society to the fact that rape is a prevalent crime and also only a few convictions are made each year.

---

## Revising Exercise 6.10

Look at that last paper again. Do you find any sentences that are out of kilter—that need parallel structure? If so, whip them into shape.

Have you written an emphatic closing sentence? If not, write an impressive sentence using parallel structure.

---

## Use Repetition Wisely

Deliberate repetition, such as you observed in many of those impressive parallel sentences, can be one of your most effective rhetorical devices. But needless repetition will probably offend your readers because they can tell it stems from lack of thought and inadequate revision, as in this student's sentence:

> Walking up to the door, I came upon the skeleton head of a cow placed next to the door.

That's too many *to the door* phrases. Just changing the first one solves the problem:

> Walking up to the house, I came upon the skeleton head of a cow placed next to the door.

You need to eliminate any word or phrase that's been needlessly used twice:

Clarence found the challenge of trying to make the honor roll a great challenge.

When you revise, just eliminate the first challenge:

Clarence found trying to make the honor roll a great challenge.

*Deliberate repetition* can be powerful, as you saw in many of the examples of parallel sentences. Another way to achieve the same clarity and emphasis is to repeat a key term deliberately, as Katherine Anne Porter does in this sentence describing the execution of Sacco and Vanzetti (our italics):

They were put to death in the electric chair at Charleston Prison at *midnight*, a desolate dark *midnight*, a *night* for perpetual mourning.

You see the difference between well-executed deliberate repetition and careless repetition of the same word. Porter's *midnight* tolls like a bell reinforcing the darkness of the deed.

---

**TIP!**  A deliberately repeated word or phrase can reinforce a key idea.

---

## S *traightening Out Screwed-Up Sentences*

Some sentence problems are impossible to categorize as other than messed up. And these are the worst kind because the sentences make no sense and are likely to drive readers to drink—or induce them to quit reading.

### The Confusion of Mixed Constructions

The sorry sentences known, for want of a better term, as *mixed constructions* apparently result when a writer begins to say something one way, loses track in the middle, and finishes another way because the brain is faster than the fingers. That's our guess, anyway. The people who write them are more surprised than anyone when confronted with these prodigies.

These are the kinds of sentences that make readers do a double take. We shake our heads, rub our eyes, and read them again, hoping for a better connection next time. But we never get it from mix-ups like these:

When students have no time for study or moral training also breeds a decadent society.

> The first planned crime will tell how well a boy has learned whether or not he is caught to become a juvenile delinquent.

Now, these are pretty hopeless cases. They need to be scrapped. You'll lose more time trying to revise sentences like these than you will by backing off and starting a different way. Take that last example. It needs a totally new beginning, perhaps like this:

> Whether or not he is caught in his first planned crime may determine whether a boy will become a juvenile delinquent.

Occasionally, a screwed-up sentence can be easily revised, like this one:

> When frequently opening and closing the oven door, it can cause a soufflé to fall.

All you need to do to correct that one is scratch out the *when*, the *it*, and the comma:

> Frequently opening and closing the oven door can cause a soufflé to fall.

Nobody will hold you accountable if you accidentally write a mixed up sentence in a first draft, but it's your job to catch and correct the problem when you revise.

## The Problem of Faulty Predication

We can describe what goes wrong in a sentence to produce faulty predication: the subject doesn't match the predicate—the part that includes and follows the verb. Apparently, the writer loses track of the subject when supplying the predicate, so that the sentence ends up not quite making sense, like this:

> The excuse for earning money offers Paul the job of ushering at Carnegie Hall.

Everybody knows that *excuses* don't *offer jobs,* so the statement contains a lapse in logic.

Some faulty predication problems are easy to fix, like this one:

> Your first big city is an event that changes your whole outlook if you grew up in a small town.

Clearly, a *big city* is not an *event,* but we can set this one to rights just by adding a new subject:

> Your first trip to a big city is an event that changes your whole outlook if you grew up in a small town.

---

**TIP!**  Pay close attention to meaning as you proofread to be sure every sentence makes perfect sense.

---

### Revising Exercise 6.11

Straighten out the following sentences, written by students. Some are mixed constructions; some suffer from faulty predication. If a sentence can't be easily revised, consider backing off and beginning a different way.

1. The Rites of Spring Festival has been postponed because of too many students are sick with the flu.
2. Illegal parking is towed away at the owner's expense.
3. In time of crisis must be handled with cool judgment.
4. The second qualification for my ideal roommate would have to be easygoing.
5. Whether a person makes the choice to go to college or not has both its problems and rewards.
6. Miss Brill tries to convince herself that she really is a significant contribution to society.
7. By no means is the novel to glorifying war.
8. No matter if she is loved or not, did not matter any more.
9. Mrs. Pontellier carried herself in a way that people thought she would only be the mother of strong, gallant sons.
10. The importance of remaining married is essential in Edna's society.

---

# 7

# The Revising and Editing Process

A common myth about writing is that good writers get it right the first time. The truth is that good writers almost never say what they want to on the first try; they nearly always plan on revising. Teacher and writer Anne Lamott says that every piece of writing should go through at least three drafts. The first draft she calls "the down draft—you just get it down"; the second draft is "the up draft—you fix it up"; and the last draft is "the dental draft, where you check every tooth, to see if it's loose or cramped or decayed, or even, God help us, healthy."

We agree that these drafts are essential, but we call them the rough draft, the revision draft, and the editing draft. If you don't work through those last two, you won't achieve the best results, no matter how good you think your first draft is.

## R evising Your First Draft

Revision involves more than just tidying up your prose. The process of correcting your spelling, punctuation, and mechanics is called *editing*, but after finishing your rough draft, your paper is not ready for editing yet. First you need *re-vision*—seeing again—to discover ways of making your writing more effective.

**TIP!** Schedule your time so that you can put the rough draft aside at least overnight before revising.

While a draft is still warm from the writing, you cannot look at it objectively. And looking at it objectively is the basis of productive revision. Your fondness for a well-turned sentence should not prevent you from cutting it when, in the cold light of morning, you realize that it doesn't relate to your thesis.

## R *evising from the Top Down*

Not all revising is the same. One kind of revision involves large-scale changes, changes that significantly affect the content and structure of your paper. Such changes might include enlarging or narrowing your thesis, adding more examples or cutting irrelevant ones, and reorganizing points to improve logic or gain emphasis. A second kind of revision focuses on improving style: checking paragraph unity, strengthening transitions, combining and refining sentences, finding more effective words, adjusting tone. We recommend that you take a top-down approach to revising by starting with the large-scale issues and working down to the smaller elements. If you try to do the fine-tuning and polishing first, you will burn up valuable time and energy and may never get around to the main problems.

---

**TIP!** **Distinguish between larger problems (like content and organization) and smaller ones (like sentence structure and word choice). Work on large problems first.**
Tackling the simple problems first may seem reasonable, but you will find that dealing with a major difficulty may eliminate some minor problems at the same time—or change the way you approach them.

---

### Outlining the Draft

To be sure that your discussion is unified and complete, you should briefly outline your rough draft. This kind of after-the-fact outlining is not a waste of time, as it allows you to detect flaws in your organization and to review the development of your main ideas at the same time. First, write down your thesis statement; then add the topic sentence of each paragraph along with your important supporting ideas. Don't bother with complete sentences; short phrases are easier to check and evaluate.

After completing this scratch outline, you should use it to check your paper for unity and completeness by considering these points:

1. Make sure that the topic sentence in every paragraph relates directly to your thesis.
2. Consider whether your support is adequate. Sometimes a paragraph can be developed with a single extensive example, but more often you will need at lease three or four examples, details, or reasons. If you fail to find adequate support for a topic sentence, perhaps you need to rethink it, omit it, or combine it with another main idea.
3. Examine your supporting details to see if any are irrelevant or overlapping and need to be cut.
4. Look at the order of your paragraphs and the order of the supporting details in each paragraph. Your sentences and paragraphs should follow one after the other with no breaks and no confusion.
5. Make sure you have tied your sentences and paragraphs together with transitional hooks and signposts. For a handy list of transitional terms, see Chapter 5, Figure 5.1.

## Adding Headings to Highlight Your Points

Writers are using headings in all kinds of publications these days to highlight main ideas and to indicate shifts in topics, making the text easier to follow. Headings have always been appropriate in technical writing and business reports. Textbook authors also use them to focus attention on key concepts, provide greater clarity, and make the material easy to review. You'll notice headings in newspaper and magazine articles. Whenever you present complex material that your readers might have difficulty following, consider inserting meaningful headings to signal your major points.

Word processing programs make using headings a snap. With a single command, you can center them, set them flush left, or make them boldface. You can also indent material to set it off and thus call attention to it. If you glance at the formatting of this book, you'll see a number of options for breaking up blocks of type, adding emphasis, and thus achieving greater readability. You can perform every one of them with your word processor.

Remember, though, that the essential factor in making a text easy to follow is having it clearly and logically organized. All the formatting in the world is not going to save a paper that is not unified or lacks continuity.

## Revising for Style

Once you are satisfied that your ideas are developed fully and proceed smoothly and logically, you need to consider the shape of each sentence. Is any phrasing wordy or repetitious? Does the writing sound natural and interesting? Are the sentences forceful and varied? Rewrite those sentences that carry key ideas to make them elegant and emphatic. Work particularly hard on the opening and closing sentences—especially that last one. Don't let your otherwise fine essay trail off limply at the end because you ran out of steam.

Now is also the time to look up word meanings and use your thesaurus, if necessary, to find just the right words. Also make sure that the tone and language level are suitable for your purpose and audience. (See Chapter 2 for guidance about tone and language levels, Chapter 4 for a brief review of logic, and Chapter 6 for specific direction about words and sentences.)

## Getting Feedback: Peer Review

Writers routinely seek the help of potential readers to find out what is working and what is not working in their drafts. Even professional writers ask for suggestions from editors, reviewers, teachers, and friends. In college your composition instructor may divide your class into small groups to review one another's papers and provide suggestions for improvement. In the workplace, much of the writing you do will be passed around, with various writers adding their sections and making suggestions about yours.

Someone else can often see places where you *thought* you were being clear but were actually filling in details only in your head, not on the page. You can help people who are reviewing your paper by assuring them that you want honest critical responses. Here are some guidelines to follow when asking for help with your revision:

1. *Specify the kind of help you want.*
   If you already know that the spelling needs to be checked, ask your readers to ignore those errors and focus on other elements in the draft. If you want suggestions about the thesis or the introduction or the tone or the organization or the examples or the style, then ask questions about those features.
2. *Ask productive questions.*
   Be sure to pose questions that require more than a yes or no answer. Ask readers to tell you in detail what *they* see. You can use the questions in the Revising Checklist (Figure 7.1, p. 103) to help you solicit feedback.

3. *Don't get defensive.*

Listen carefully to what your reviewers have to say, and interrupt only when you don't understand their comments. Above all, don't argue with your readers. If something confused them, it confused them. You want to see the writing through *their* eyes, not browbeat them into seeing it the way you do.

4. *Make your own decisions.*

Remember that this is your paper; you're responsible for accepting or rejecting the feedback you get. If you don't agree with the suggestions that are offered, then don't follow them. But also keep in mind that your peer reviewers are likely to be more objective about your writing than you are.

## **R** *evising on a Word Processor*

Revision is much easier if you are using a word processor. Probably the biggest advantage of word processing is that it helps you to see that writing is *changeable.* You can consider every word, sentence, or paragraph as just one possible choice among many. Because you can delete, move, and save the text in different files, the word processor invites you to explore alternatives. You can try a change and see how it reads; if the revision flops, you can easily restore the original draft.

Computer software can also help with sentence-level revisions. Many word-processing programs have spell checkers that identify questionable spellings and suggest possible correctly spelled alternatives. Of course, a spell checker does not understand your text and can't determine if its suggestions are appropriate or even plausible, but it can focus your attention on words that you may need to change. Other programs, called *text analyzers* or *style checkers,* will give you information about word choice, sentence length, and other features of style. These programs can only point out *possible* problems, such as a long sentence or a weak verb; you have to decide whether the verb is effective or the sentence really is too long.

### Avoiding Computer Pitfalls

There are some disadvantages to revising on a computer. Early versions of your essay are lost as your revise. In most cases, this loss is no problem, but if you make big changes, you need to stop and print out old drafts as you go. They may contain work that can be retrieved later and used elsewhere. We encourage you to print your rough draft even when you know it's due for a major rewrite.

In addition, certain problems are easier to see on a printed copy than on the computer screen. For example, you see more paragraphs at a time on the page. On the screen, you may not notice that you've used the same transitional phrase at the beginning of several paragraphs, or that the paragraph lengths are wildly unbalanced. And when you revise sentences on the screen, you are much more likely to neglect to delete the old version or perhaps a word or two of it, leaving you with a garbled sentence.

A final caution about revising on computers: instructors expect clean, neat, correct final copy when papers are done on word processors. Some allow for tidy corrections done in ink, but others insist on a new printout when you find an error. Your instructor may be righteously indignant over a misspelling that should have been flagged by the spell checker, attributing the error to your laziness or haste.

## **S** *etting a Revision Agenda*

Your revision will be easier and more efficient if you establish some priorities to guide your rethinking, rearranging, and rewriting. Not all revisions require the same amount of time and energy. You need to consider how much time you have and how effective your first draft is. If you have left enough time for your writing to evolve, you may not need a wholesale revision. On the other hand, a hurried first draft will need more thorough reworking.

The list of questions in Figure 7.1 will help you set up your own revising agenda. This checklist focuses on general questions first and takes up smaller matters later.

---

1. Does the paper meet the assignment and make the point I set out to make?
2. Is the thesis clear and intelligent?
3. Is the main idea of each paragraph directly related to the thesis?
4. Are the paragraphs fully developed with examples and details?
5. Do the ideas flow coherently? Are the transitions easy to follow?
6. Are the sentences clear and effectively structured?
7. Does the introduction capture the reader's attention and make the main point of the paper clear?
8. Does the conclusion provide intelligent closure for the paper?

---

**FIGURE 7.1** *Revising Checklist*

# E *diting the Final Draft*

After you've finished your revisions, you must force yourself—
or someone completely trustworthy—to read the paper yet one
more time to pick up any careless mistakes or typos. Jessica Mitford
rightly says that "failure to proofread is like preparing a magnificent dinner and forgetting to set the table." So, be polite—
proofread and then correct any errors. This correcting is called the
editing process.

Careless errors can be unintentionally funny, like these from
the real-life job applications of people who apparently didn't edit
their copy:

> I am a rabid typist and have a proven ability to track down and cor-
> rect erors.

> I was instrumental in ruining the entire operation of a Midwest chain
> store.

> Thank you for your consideration. I hope to hear from you shorty.

Do you suppose any of those applicants got the job?

Many careless errors are just plain witless and annoying—like
repeating a word needlessly ("and and") or leaving off an -s and
producing an illiteracy:

> The protester were arrested and herded off to jail.

Such errors do nothing to encourage your readers to admire the
brilliance of your ideas—no matter how keen they are. So watch the
little things. Don't write "probable" for "probably," or "use to" for
"used to" or "you're" for "your" or "then" for "than." Check possessives to be sure the apostrophes are there—or not there, in the
case of "its." Figure 7.2 gives you some other points to keep in mind
as you edit your draft.

## Proofreading Advice

Most of us have difficulty proofreading our own writing because we know what we wanted to say and thus don't notice that
we haven't said it flawlessly. We become caught up in the content
and fail to see the errors. If you have this trouble, try reading the
sentences from the bottom of the page to the top, out of order; you
can't become interested in what you're saying because it won't
make sense. Try to read slowly, word by word. Figure 7.3 gives you
a list of points to check for when you proofread.

1. Make sure that each sentence really is a sentence, not a fragment—especially those beginning with *because, since, which, that, although, as, when,* or *what* and those beginning with words ending in *-ing*.
2. Make sure that independent clauses joined by *indeed, moreover, however, nevertheless, thus,* and *hence* have a semicolon before those words, not just a comma.
3. Make sure that every modifying phrase or clause is close to the word it modifies.
4. Check your manuscript form to be sure it's acceptable: Have you skipped three lines between the title and the first line of the essay? Did you double-space throughout? Did you leave at least one-inch margins on all sides, including top and bottom? Did you prepare a title sheet, if requested to do so? Did you clip the pages together?

**FIGURE 7.2** *Editing Checklist*

Pay no attention to content. Read only for errors to make certain that you have

1. No words left out or carelessly repeated;
2. No words misspelled—or carelessly spelled (*use to* for *used to*);
3. No plurals left off;
4. No apostrophes omitted in possessives or in contractions;
5. No periods, dashes, commas, colons, or quotation marks left out;
6. No confusion of *to/too, their/they're/there, its/it's, then/than, your/you're*.

**FIGURE 7.3** *Proofreading Checklist*

## A Word of Encouragement About Spelling

In the past people were considerably more relaxed about correct spelling than we are today. William Shakespeare, demonstrating his boundless creativity, spelled his own last name at least thirteen different ways. John Donne wrote "sun," "sonne," or "sunne," just as it struck his fancy. But along about the eighteenth century, Dr. Samuel Johnson decided orthography was out of hand. He took it upon himself to establish a standard for the less learned and brought out his famous dictionary. Of course, the language refused to hold still even for the stern-minded Dr. Johnson, and his followers have been trying to make it do so ever since.

Today educated people are expected to be able to spell according to the accepted standard. Nobody encourages creativity in this area. So, if you didn't learn to spell back in grade school, you may need help.

*Use Your Spell Checker, If You Have One.* Help with spelling is easy to come by if you write on a word processor. You just need to run your handy spell checker after you finish revising and make the necessary corrections.

---

**TIP!** **Your spell checker won't flag those troublesome words that are easy to confuse.**

Your checker won't flag *its/it's, to/too/two, then/than, there/they're/their, altogether/all together, choose/chose, effect/affect* and all those other pesky sound-alike words because you're not misspelling them. You're just using the wrong one. So, you still need to proofread carefully in case you've accidentally typed the wrong word.

---

*Keep a List and Study It.* If you have serious trouble with spelling, you need to keep a list of the words you get wrong and learn how to spell them. Start now. Add to the list whenever you discover you've misspelled a word. If you keep adding the same word—especially an easy, often-used word, like "writing" or "coming"—make a point of *remembering* that you can't spell it so you can look it up or choose a synonym that you *can* spell.

*Find a Friend to Help.* If you're fortunate enough to have a friend or relative who can spell, you are in luck. Beg or bribe this gifted individual to check your papers for misspelled words.

---

**TIP!** **Remember to add those misspelled words to your list.**

This proofreading help won't be available to you in the business world where almost everyone has to write and hardly anyone has a secretary anymore. You must improve your spelling to avoid embarrassing errors on the job.

---

# II

# *How to Write a Research Paper*

# 8

# Conducting
# Your Research

At some time, you may be asked to write a paper that doesn't draw entirely on your own knowledge and experience. In fact, many kinds of writing involve the use of source materials. You may be required to do research: that is, to read fairly widely on a certain subject, to combine and organize this accumulated information, and then to present it in clear and coherent prose.

Traditionally, research papers involve *argument*. You may be expected to choose a topic that is somewhat controversial, investigate the issues on both sides, and take a stand. But you can, of course, engage in valuable and interesting research that simply involves finding and synthesizing information on any subject to increase your and your readers' knowledge.

In many ways, the writing process for a research paper is the same as for any other. You still need to narrow the subject to a topic that you can handle in the number of assigned pages, and you still have to come up with a thesis statement and outline or plan before you begin writing. But first you have to locate the material you're going to read; then you'll need to take notes as you read so that you can give credit to your sources as you write the paper.

## S cheduling *Your Research Paper*

Writing a research paper is a time-consuming job. This is one paper that you simply cannot put off until the last minute. As usual, the writing will be better if you do it in stages. Dividing the project into units will allow you to keep the work under control.

## Setting Deadlines for Yourself

If your completed paper is due in, say, six weeks, you could put yourself on a schedule something like this:

*1st week:*    Locate your possible sources, and record all the necessary bibliographical information about them.

Try to narrow the topic to a workable thesis question to investigate.

*2nd week:*    Read and take notes.

Settle on a preliminary thesis question.

Try to come up with a preliminary outline.

*3rd week:*    Continue reading and taking notes.

*4th week:*    Complete your reading and note-taking.

Turn your thesis question into a statement.

Arrange your notes and organize your ideas.

Develop a complete, detailed outline.

*5th week:*    Write the first draft and let it cool.

Begin revising and editing.

Get someone reliable to read your second draft and tell you whether the paragraphs are coherent, the sentences are clear, and the quotations are effectively integrated.

*6th week:*    Polish the second draft or write a third one.

Type the final draft and let it rest at least overnight.

Proofread and edit the final draft carefully.

This is a fairly leisurely schedule. You can, of course, do the work in a shorter time if required to. You will just have to be more industrious about finding sources and taking notes. Some instructors deliberately ask students to complete the project within a month in order to prevent procrastination. Whatever your time limit, devise a schedule for yourself and stick to it.

## Narrowing Your Topic

If you have an area of interest but no ideas about any way to limit that topic, your first step might be to consult a good encyclopedia. Perhaps you have just taken up tennis, and you would like to know more about the sport. An encyclopedia article on tennis will give you information about the origin and history of the game, the court and the equipment, strategy and techniques, outstanding players, professional tournaments, and the state of the sport today.

As you read, you will learn that improved equipment and increased physical training have changed the nature of the game in the last twenty years. Precisely how has the game changed? In what ways has the equipment been improved and how have the improvements affected play? Have these changes been positive or negative? All it takes is a sentence, a subtopic, or an example in a general encyclopedia article on your subject to provide a focus for your research.

## T *opics for Researched Writing*

If your mind remains a blank and your instructor will allow you to take one of our suggestions, here are some ideas that we think might be interesting to research.

### For Informative Writing

1. Research the history of a familiar product or object, such as Coca-Cola, Mickey Mouse, the dictionary, disposable diapers, the nectarine, the title *Ms.*, frozen yogurt, the typewriter.
2. Research and analyze a fad, craze, custom, or holiday: fraternity hazing, body piercing, tattoos, quick weight-loss diets, Beanie Babies, St. Patrick's Day, Mother's Day, Kwanzaa, Cinco de Mayo, Hanukkah.
3. Research how a troubled group of people can be helped: autistic children, alcoholics, rape victims, anorexics, agoraphobics, battered women, people with HIV, nicotine addicts, steroid users.
4. Research the history of some feature of your hometown: a landmark, street names, architecture, an industry.
5. Research some hobby or job in order to inform someone unfamiliar with the activity.

### For Persuasion or Argumentation

After doing the appropriate research, defend either side of one of the following issues.

1. The use of animals in research should (should not) be allowed.
2. It should (should not) be harder than it is now for married people to get a divorce.
3. Today's toys often contribute (do not contribute) to violent behavior in children.

4. Having a working mother does (does not) harm a child's welfare and development.
5. The fashion industry does (does not) exploit consumers. Or substitute another area of business: the cosmetics industry, the funeral business, car manufacturers, the oil industry.
6. Genetic screening of fetuses should (should not) be prohibited.
7. Sexual harassment is (is not) a serious problem in the workplace.
8. The government should (should not) cut welfare benefits for single parents.
9. News reporters should (should not) be required to reveal their sources in criminal cases.
10. English should (should not) be the only official language of the United States.
11. Affirmative action should (should not) be discontinued.
12. Homosexuals should (should not) be allowed to serve openly in the military.
13. It is (is not) better for children if their incompatible parents get a divorce.
14. Teaching phonics would (would not) solve the literacy crisis in this country.
15. Laws restricting the use of pesticides should (should not) be repealed.
16. Free speech should (should not) be restricted on the Internet.

## O *rganizing Your Search*

Once you have narrowed your topic, you need a plan for efficiently tracking down your source materials. Consider how much time you have and what kinds of sources you will probably be using. A good strategy is to begin with sources that give a broad overview of the subject and then move to ones that provide more detailed information. If you were to write about changes in tennis equipment, you might first look at a specialized reference work on the sport—something like *Bud Collins' Modern Encyclopedia of Tennis,* a book listed at the end of that encyclopedia article on tennis. Then you might search for articles of general interest and end with more technical articles in trade publications.

In order to locate all the relevant information in the library, you may need to think of headings under which your subject might be indexed. The encyclopedia and general reference works will supply you with some clues. The *Library of Congress Subject Headings (LCSH)* can be very useful in providing terms or key words to search with as well as additional terms you might not have considered. Most of the entries in the *LCSH* give alternative terms listed as BT (broader topic), RT (related topic), and NT (narrower topic). For example, when we looked up "tennis," we found "racket games" and "ball games" as broader topics and "rackets (game)" and "rackets (sporting goods)" as narrower topics. We can use these alternative terms as we search for sources about the effects of improved equipment in tennis.

## S ome Suggestions for Using the Library

One of the first things you need to do before writing a research paper is get acquainted with your library. Most college libraries offer orientation courses to show students how to find materials. If the course is not required, take it anyway. An orientation course is the surest way of learning your way around the library. Libraries also have tours and guidebooks telling you where to find various materials. Taking one of these tours or studying the guidebook may save you hours of aimless wandering.

---

**TIP!**   **If you fail to find what you need, ask for help.**
Librarians are usually willing to answer questions and will often lead you to the material you want and give you valuable advice.

---

### Searching for Sources

In the old days, the first things you were likely to see upon entering a library were imposing rows of polished wood cabinets with small drawers: the card catalog. In most libraries those cabinets have been replaced with row upon row of computers. It is almost certain that you will conduct your search for sources on a computer. Computer searches, online databases, and Internet search engines vary in the way you can use them; they are being expanded and improved all the time. We can offer here some general instructions to help you find your way around the modern library.

*The Online Catalog.*   The computer version of the card catalog is called a *public access catalog* (PAC) or an *online catalog* (OC). The PAC or OC terminal itself will tell you how to use it. The opening screen of the OC at the library we use shows that we can search by subject, title, and author, as well as by call number, shelf position, and international standard book number (ISBN). We can search for books, titles of journals, and other items owned by our library or by other libraries in the state.

After choosing the subject option (#1 on the menu), we are directed to enter the key words in the topic we want to search for. We're also reminded at this time that "You will achieve better results if you use a valid Library of Congress subject heading." Entering the topic "tennis" gets a message that there are 176 items in the library on that topic. We can look at a list of all 176 items if we want to, but we're encouraged to limit our search by choosing one or more of the 34 subcategories on tennis. We choose "Tennis—equipment and supplies" and find that there is only one book in our library on that topic. So we decide to search for articles in magazines and other periodicals.

*Indexes and Databases.* Most libraries now subscribe to large online database networks. One of the largest of these is DIALOG, which provides access to more than 300 million items in over 400 separate databases in the humanities, business, and the social and natural sciences. There are a number of specialized databases, such as NEXIS, which catalogs news sources, and LEXIS, which can be used to locate legal and government publication. If your library subscribes to one or more of these services, you will find them either on the OC terminal or on computers in the library's reference area. You may also be able to access many of these databases from your computer at home or in your dorm room, if it has the necessary software and a modem (a device that connects your computer through the phone lines to other computer networks, like the ones in your school library).

The library terminals in our library allow us to switch from the Online Catalog to search four data systems: WILSONLINE, ERIC, PsychINFO, and InfoTrac SearchBank. Each of these targets a different set of sources. WILSONLINE, for instance, provides electronic access to the printed indexes published by H. W. Wilson Co., including *Readers' Guide to Periodical Literature, Education Index,* and *Social Science Index.* ERIC focuses on educational materials; PsychINFO covers journals and reports from psychology and the behavioral sciences.

In our search for tennis equipment, we choose the *Readers' Guide Abstracts,* one of the Wilson indexes, because we don't want articles that are too scholarly or specialized, and the *Readers' Guide* catalogues popular periodicals. After typing in the search term "tennis equipment," we discover that there are eighty-two references. We can view these entries one at a time if we want, or we can print out the entire list. Each citation includes the article title, name of the magazine, volume, date, and page number; it also supplies the call number of the magazine if our library owns it. Some of the entries contain a brief description or a summary of the article's contents. We can even send the data to our home computers by way of e-mail.

***CD-ROMs and Commercial Vendors.*** Our library also owns a number of specialized databases on CD-ROM (compact disk, read-only memory), which are often easier to use than those online. Many reference works, such as *The Oxford English Dictionary* and various encyclopedias, are now available on CD-ROM, as are numerous indexes, like the *General Science Index*, the *Music Index*, and the *Philosopher's Index*. One important CD service is InfoTrac, which provides access to *The New York Times* and *The Wall Street Journal*, as well as to articles in more than a thousand business, technological, and general-interest periodicals. Figure 8.1 shows the abstract and first page of an article on new tennis rackets, which we found and printed out using InfoTrac SearchBank.

In addition, our library subscribes to several computerized bibliographic utilities, which are provided by commercial vendors. For example, we can connect to *FirstSearch*, which accesses databases for academic journals, corporations, congressional publications, and medical journals, and to *Newsbank CD News*, which indexes articles from a variety of newspapers. Sometimes these services are not free; we have to get special permission to log on to some of them. It costs the library considerable money per minute to subscribe to national vendors, and the library may pass the charges along to its users. When you ask the librarian to help hook you up, be sure to find out whether you will be charged.

As you can see, the library's computers provide an overwhelming number of sources and service options. With so many possibilities, you can see why it's important, if not crucial, to take that orientation course we mentioned earlier. You will also have to spend some time with these data systems to find out how they work and how useful they are for your work. But it's time well spent. Once you get the hang of it, you will be able to research this or any other topic with astonishing ease and thoroughness.

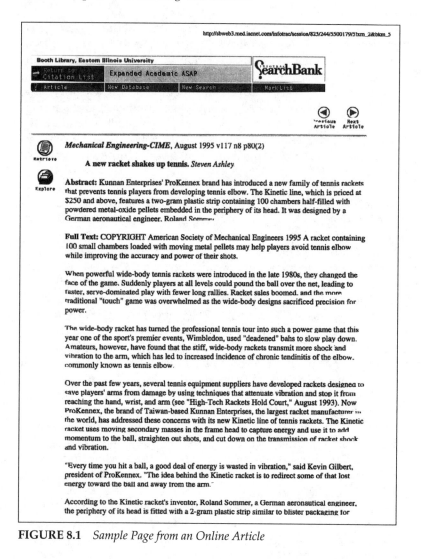

**FIGURE 8.1**    *Sample Page from an Online Article*

---

**TIP!**    Remember that most libraries still hold almost all of this material in old-fashioned print.

The *Readers' Guide,* for instance, still comes out in book form. If the computer terminals are crowded or not working—or if you simply want some peace and quiet while researching—your librarian can tell you where on the shelves the references you seek are kept.

# U *sing the Internet*

The Internet links computers around the world; it's a vast storehouse of information that can be accessed in a number of ways. It's relatively easy to get on the Internet. All you need is a computer, a modem, and a browser (software that helps you find places on the Internet). If you don't have a computer at home, your college library probably has computers that are hooked up to the Net (as it's called).

On the Net you can find government documents and archives, newsgroups, online publications, texts of published materials, and databases provided by commercial servers such as America Online, Prodigy, and Campus Networks. You can browse the noncommercial contents of the Internet through the World Wide Web.

It would take up too much space to give you detailed instructions for using the Internet, but we can briefly describe three of the basic tools that are available there: electronic mail, newsgroups, and the World Wide Web. If you are interested in finding out more, consult a book like *Online!: A Reference Guide to Using Internet Sources* by Andrew Harnack and Eugene Kleppinger (St. Martin's, 1997) or *Casting Your Net: A Student's Guide to Research on the Internet* (Allyn and Bacon, 1998) by H. Eric Branscomb.

## Electronic Mail

If you've used the Internet at all, it's probably been with electronic mail (e-mail), communicating with friends and family. But e-mail can be a valuable research tool as well. Many people participate in special-interest discussion groups via e-mail; these groups are called *mailing lists,* and they use a *listserver* to send mail automatically to all the people on the list. Once you join a mailing list, the listserver will send you all messages on standard e-mail.

Because there are thousands of mailing lists, it will be difficult to find ones on your topic. The easiest way to find a listserv is to check one of the directories on the World Wide Web (see page 118). One of the most popular directories is *Liszt,* which claims to list over 70,000 e-mail discussion groups. It's available at <http://www.liszt.com> and gives you simple instructions for searching and subscribing to any list you might find useful.

---

**TIP!** **Evaluate the reliability of an e-mail source in the same way you would judge any person you have interviewed.** When referring to this source in your paper, provide background on the source and indicate why he or she is qualified to give information on your topic.

---

## Newsgroups

A newsgroup is a kind of public bulletin board containing comments, questions, and responses on a particular topic. It's more extensive and better organized than an e-mail listserv. Asking a question of a mailing list or a newsgroup is a great way to get information about sources and to find people who can help you with your research. The newsgroup message board keeps track of several discussions at once, organizing the messages and replying in groups called *threads*. A thread begins with the original message, or *posting*, and includes all of the replies made by every participant in the discussion.

A program called a *newsreader* is used to read newsgroups and follow the threads. If your school subscribes to a news feed (a central computer that stores all messages and feeds them to other providers), you will have access to a newsreader and will be able to locate a newsgroup to follow.

---

**TIP!** **Use material gathered from a newsgroup with caution.** Try to confirm from other sources the reliability of any information from a newsgroup that you want to use in a research paper.

---

## World Wide Web

The most popular tool for searching the Internet is the World Wide Web (also called the Web and WWW). The WWW is not the same thing as the Internet; the Web is a complex system for organizing and viewing information on the Internet. The primary attraction of this system is that its documents, called *Web pages,* are linked to other pages by a technique called *hypertext.* Hypertext links are usually in blue type and underlined. By pointing and clicking at these links on a Web page, you can find paths to additional material, such as cross-references and explanations, on other pages and at other Web sites on the WWW. (A *Web site* is a collection of related Web pages.)

To navigate the Web, you need a *browser* program such as Netscape, Mosaic, or Microsoft Internet Explorer. Figure 8.2 shows the *home page* (the first page that appears when you access a Web site) for the Library of Congress, viewed through Microsoft Internet Explorer. The WWW is also searchable. You can use one of several different *search engines*—such as Webcrawler, AltaVista, Yahoo!, Lycos, and Infoseek—to search for key words in the Web addresses,

**FIGURE 8.2** *Sample Web Page*

headings, or text. Figure 8.3 gives the first page of results from a key word search that was conducted using Yahoo! powered by Alta-Vista (key word: *Kwanzaa*).

## Some Advice About Using the Web

The Internet and the Web give you access to a great deal of information that is often more current than anything available in

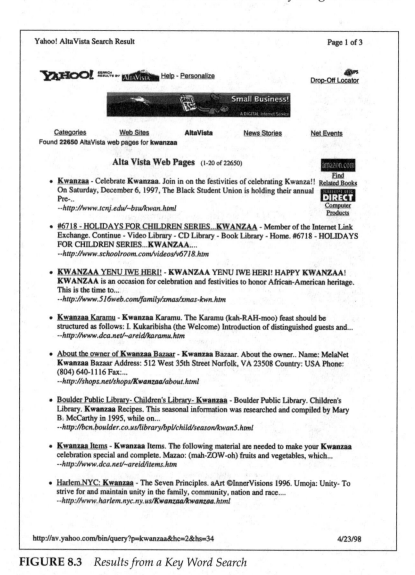

**FIGURE 8.3**    *Results from a Key Word Search*

printed sources, and the Web's hyptertext feature allows you to explore a topic quickly and thoroughly. Nonetheless, there are a couple of serious pitfalls in using the Web that you need to consider.

First, it's difficult to know how to judge the vast array of information that's available. You will find research reports, online journals, and government publications, but you will also find unsupported opinion, propaganda, inaccurate information, and tasteless junk. Anyone can publish on the Web; there is no editorial board to screen the material. Therefore, you must apply sound judgment in evaluating each of your electronic sources, just as you would the print sources that you find in the library. Check the information against other sources, and consider carefully the credentials, and the biases, of the person or organization supplying the data.

Second, searching on the Internet, especially on the WWW, can eat up a lot of valuable time. Because it's so easy to move from site to site through numerous interlinked sources, you can spend hours browsing the Web. Your time might be better spent reading your source materials, taking notes, and writing your paper. To avoid wasting time, always go to the Web for specific purposes, skim the sites first, and note the size and downloading time of a document before printing it out. (The slow downloading time on some equipment can consume a lot of time.)

---

**TIP!**   **Always record or store the address and references from an Internet source.**
You'll need these details for return access and later for documentation in your paper.

---

## S *weating Through the Research*

Once you've located the sources—the books and articles you'll need to read and assimilate—you can begin the actual reading, taking notes, and synthesizing of the material.

### Get It All Down

Every time you consult a new source, copy all the information necessary for indicating your source to the reader. If you fail to record all the pertinent data, you may find yourself tracking down a book or article weeks later in order to look up an essential publication date or volume number that you neglected to record initially.

By this time, the book may checked out, lost, or stolen, so get it all down the first time.

We recommend that you use 3" x 5" note cards to keep track of this information. They are easy to carry with you to the library, and you can easily insert new entries in alphabetical order. Figures 8.4 through 8.7 give examples of what these cards should look like.

If you work on a computer, you can create a separate file for your list of sources and use a printout when you are not near your computer. Remember to keep the file up to date, and don't delete a citation until you're sure you will not be using that source.

Library
call
number

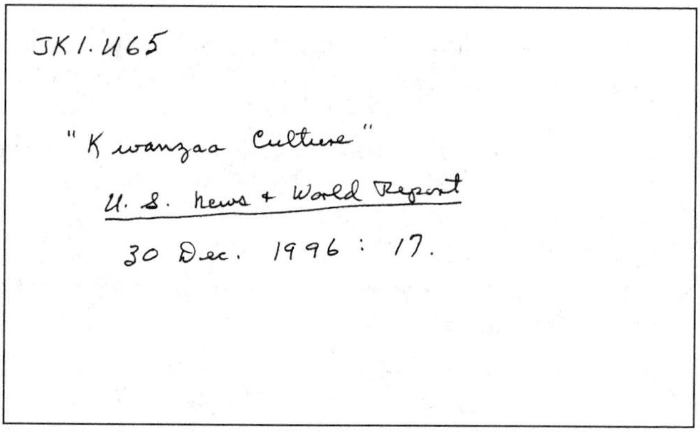

JK 1. U65

"Kwanzaa Culture"
U. S. news + World Report
30 Dec. 1996 : 17.

**FIGURE 8.4** *Article from a Magazine Without a Volume Number*

Library
call
number

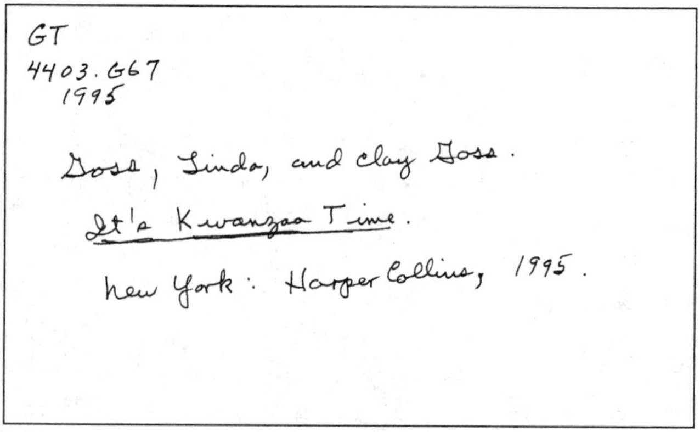

GT
4403. G67
1995

Goss, Linda, and Clay Goss.
It's Kwanzaa Time.
New York : Harper Collins, 1995.

**FIGURE 8.5** *Book*

Database name

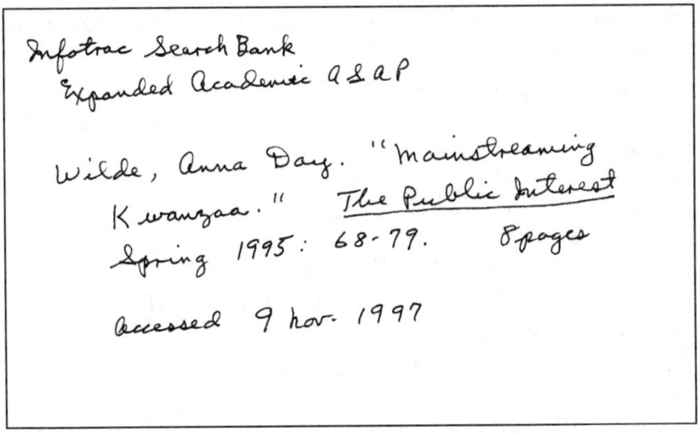

Infotrac Search Bank
Expanded Academic ASAP

Wilde, Anna Day. "Mainstreaming Kwanzaa." The Public Interest Spring 1995: 68-79. 8 pages

Accessed 9 Nov. 1997

**FIGURE 8.6** *Full-Text Article Available Through a Library Database*

WEB site name and protocol

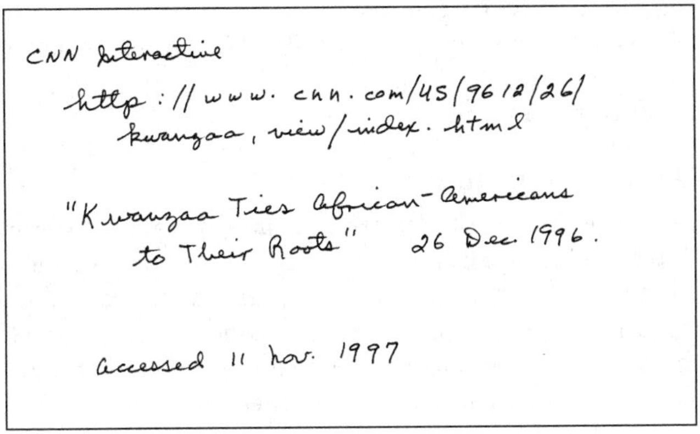

CNN Interactive
http://www.cnn.com/US/9612/26/kwanzaa,view/index.html

"Kwanzaa Ties African-Americans to Their Roots" 26 Dec. 1996.

Accessed 11 Nov. 1997

**FIGURE 8.7** *Web Site Source*

---

**TIP! Always remember to get *all* the pertinent data about your sources!**

---

For whatever documentation system you are using, you will need to record the following information.

*FOR BOOKS:*

1. Author or editor
2. Title
3. Place of publication
4. Publisher

5. Date of publication (plus date of edition, if the book has more than one)
6. Library call number

*FOR ARTICLES:*
1. Author (or "no author")
2. Title
3. Name of magazine, newspaper, or journal
4. Volume number (if the journal uses them)
5. Date of the issue
6. Complete pages the article covers

*FOR THE ELECTRONIC FORM OF EITHER BOOKS OR ARTICLES, YOU WILL ALSO NEED:*
7. Title of database (if relevant)
8. Medium (like CD-ROM)
9. Name of the vendor or utility (*FirstSearch* or *InfoTrac*—if relevant)
10. Electronic publication date.

## On to the Reading

Using the list of sources you have developed so far, your next step is to locate all the materials that look promising and decide which ones will be genuinely useful. As you consider which articles and books to study thoroughly and which ones to eliminate at this stage, you need to give some thought to their reliability as well as their relevance to your thesis question.

---

**TIP!**   Just because a statement appears in print, it is not necessarily honest or accurate. Be wary as you read.

---

## Evaluate Your Sources

You might expect an unbiased analysis of an event from journalists who were there, but again you must stay alert because not all publications present—or even try to present—objective reporting. The conservative *National Review* will give a substantially different assessment of an event than the ultraliberal *Mother Jones*. And the *Congressional Record*, which sounds like an impeccable source, is actually one of the least reliable, as any member of Congress can read any foolishness whatsoever into the *Record*. You must consult several sources and sample a variety of authorities to weigh the issues and discount the prejudices.

The date of publication often makes a difference in its value or reliability. If you are writing a paper about the treatment of AIDS, an article from 1980 will be of little use. If, on the other hand, you are writing a paper on the *history* of treating AIDS, then a 1980 article could be quite important. In general, we place the highest value on recent sources simply because the latest scholar or scientist has the advantage of building on all that has gone before.

---

**TIP!** Look for sources that address the topic from different perspectives. Avoid relying too heavily on a single source.

---

## Tips on Note-Taking

Many researchers use note cards for keeping track of the information they find. If you decide to use note cards, work out some system for recording information. Here are some suggestions to guide you:

1. First record the essential information about the source on each and every card: the author's last name, an abbreviated title, and the page number or numbers. If you get in the habit of writing down these essentials before you start taking notes, there is less chance of forgetting an item.
2. Write only one idea or point of information on each card. This allows you to shuffle the cards as you figure out the precise organization of your paper. Taking notes on consecutive sheets of paper makes this handy sorting of ideas impossible.
3. Put subject headings on the cards: one or two words in the upper right-hand corner to tell you what each note is about. If all works well, these subject headings will probably correspond to sections of your outline.
4. Summarize the ideas in your own words. If you think you might want to quote directly from the source, copy the author's exact words and enclose them in quotation marks. If you forget the quotation marks and use these words in your paper, you will be guilty of *plagiarism* (claiming another person's work as your own), which is a serious academic offense.

## The Photocopying Option

If the time you can spend in the library is limited and your finances aren't, you might want to photocopy an article or pertinent portions of books in order to have these materials available to study at your convenience. You can underline or highlight key ideas, even color coding these highlighted passages to fit different subtopics in your paper. You can also write comments or cross-references to other sources in the margins.

---

**TIP!** **It's a good idea to put the photocopied information on note cards.**

This procedure forces you to summarize the material in your own words—thus avoiding plagiarism—and makes it much easier to sort the separate items into categories.

---

## Constructing a Working Outline

At the time you're reading and taking notes, you should also be working on your outline. Chances are that the best arrangement of points and ideas won't emerge until you're fairly well along in your research—possibly not until you've finished it. As you collect more and more cards, leaf through them occasionally to see if they can be arranged into three or four main categories that will become the major headings of an outline. The sooner you can get an outline worked out, the more efficient your research becomes. You can see exactly what you're looking for and avoid taking notes that would prove irrelevant and have to be discarded.

If an idea sounds potentially useful, copy it down whether it fits exactly or not. If the idea recurs in your reading and gathers significance, you may decide to add a section to your outline or to expand one of the present sections. Then later, at the organizing stage, if you have cards with points and ideas that just don't seem to fit in anywhere, let them go. Let them go cheerfully. Don't ruin the focus and unity of your paper by trying to wedge in every single note you've taken. Unless you're an uncommonly careful note-taker, you'll have a number of cards that you just can't use.

In the next chapter you will find advice on synthesizing all this diverse material into a unified, informative, well-documented research paper.

# 9

# *Using Your Sources*

After you've read and taken notes on all the material you feel is necessary to cover your topic thoroughly, gather together your notes, your bibliography cards, your photocopied pages, your working outline, and anything else you need for writing your first draft. The actual drafting of the paper is a lot like writing any other paper, except that you'll incorporate the material from note cards into your text (either in your own words or through direct quotations) and give credit to the original authors for information, ideas, and quotations that you gathered from them. The following sections will give you advice on how to take all of this raw material and craft it into a smooth, readable research paper.

## F *ocusing the Thesis*

You first need to refine the thesis question or idea that you devised before you started reading about the subject. The refined thesis should convey the point you want to make after studying your sources. If, for instance, you began by investigating the question "Do breakfast cereal ads manipulate and exploit children?" you might, after doing your research, end up with a thesis statement something like this one written by our student Barb Taylor:

> Advertisers use jingles, slogans, cartoon characters, incentives, and promises of athletic prowess to lure and mislead young consumers into getting their parents to buy sugary, low-nutrient cereals.

---

**TIP!**  Your thesis may change as you work with your source
material, but get a fairly clear idea of where you're going
before you start your draft.

---

## Imagine Your Readers

If your teacher doesn't specify an audience for you, you'll find
it helpful to think of your readers as people who want to learn
about your topic but don't know much about it. Your focus will be
clearer if you have in mind a specific group of readers and perhaps
a specific publication your writing could appear in. For example,
Barb Taylor's research essay could be directed at parents of small
children and might appear in *Parents, Good Housekeeping,* or *Mother
Jones,* magazines that often criticize shoddy television fare and fal-
sity in advertising.

## O rganizing Your Notes

Once you have a clearly focused thesis and a strong sense of
your target audience, go back and read through your note cards.
Use the headings that you put on the cards while taking notes, and
group the cards with similar ideas together in stacks. (If you photocopied most or all of your sources, write headings on the first
page of the photocopy and sort the articles that way.) Then consult
your working outline, and arrange the stacks in the order that the
headings appear there. As you write, following this plan, you will
have the information you need in front of you, ready to be incor-
porated into the first draft of your paper.

If your stacks of cards don't match the outline but lie there in
a confused, overlapping, mind-boggling mess, all is not lost. You
can still bring order out of chaos. Here are a few methods:

1. *Tinker with your outline.* It may seem like a step backward, but
   now that you have new information from your research, the
   whole topic may look different. Look at the main headings and
   change any that don't seem to fit; add others that you have
   good material for but overlooked when you created the working outline.
2. *Cluster your note cards again.* This process may suggest an organizing strategy that you wouldn't think of any other way.

3. *Put your notes aside and begin writing*—even if you begin in the middle of a thought. Force yourself, as in freewriting, to keep going, even if your paper seems repetitive, disorganized, and sketchy. Eventually, the writing will begin to take shape, giving you an idea about where to start your first draft.
4. *Find a key article on the topic, and examine its structure.* You may be able to find an organizational scheme that will work for your paper.

## I ntegrating Sources

One important difference between writing a paper using your own ideas and writing a paper incorporating research involves acknowledging your sources. Whether you are quoting directly or simply paraphrasing someone else's ideas and observations, you should always give credit in the text of your paper to the person from whom you are borrowing. Both the MLA and APA documentation styles require you to cite all sources *within* the paper. Many people who do researched writing make no attempt to work in direct quotations or provide complete citations in the first draft because pausing to do so interrupts the flow of their ideas. They just jot down the name of the person who has provided the information or idea; they go back later to fill in page numbers and integrate exact quotations.

### Use the "Hamburger" Model

Think of each use of a source as a hamburger, with its two buns and a burger. The top bun is your introduction of the source, telling your reader that material from some authority is coming up, who or what the source is, and what the person's credentials are, if you know them. The burger is the information from the source, quoted or paraphrased. The bottom bun is the *parenthetical documentation,* which tells your reader that you've finished using the source and gives the page number for that particular material.

Following the hamburger model is crucial because your reader needs to know where your own ideas stop and others' begin—and end. The following example from student Bob Harmon illustrates the hamburger approach to documentation:

Behavior research has clearly shown that different types of music have different effects on different people. Music can increase or decrease anxiety, but its use in business to improve morale is questionable. In the *Journal of Marketing*, researcher John Milliman points out that past decisions to use music in the marketplace have been based on folklore or intuition rather than on empirical results (88). His study focused primarily on the experimental manipulations of no music, slow music, and fast music. The results indicate music does control the speed with which subjects move through a store. Slow music results in subjects spending more time, and fast music means less time spent (Milliman 86–91). If music does affect the speed with which people move through a store, does it affect their perceptions of time? If fast music is used for music-on-hold, it may decrease people's sense of how long they are on hold; and slow music may expand the perceived length of time. Here again, proper selection is critical.

In this example, you can trace Harmon's transition from a preceding paragraph, his use of a paraphrase of the thesis of Milliman's article, his summary of Milliman's research, and then his own application of the research. And you never confuse which is which, because the hamburger system of source citation makes clear where all the ideas come from.

---

**TIP!**   Attribute sources ("According to Professor White, ... ") in the text of your paper, besides giving parenthetical citations.

---

## T o Cite Or Not to Cite

The main purpose of documentation—of citing sources used in a research paper—is to give credit for ideas, information, and actual phrasing that you borrow from other writers. You cite sources in order to be honest and to lend authority to your own writing. You also include citations to enable your readers to find more extensive information than your paper furnishes, in case they become engrossed in your subject and want to read some of your sources in full.

Although we are all occasionally unsure about when a citation is necessary, we can say with authority that you must include a citation for:

1. All direct quotations,
2. All indirect quotations,
3. All major ideas that are not your own, and
4. All essential facts, information, and statistics that are not general knowledge—especially anything controversial.

The last category is the one that causes confusion. In general, the sort of information available in an encyclopedia does not need a citation. But statements interpreting, analyzing, or speculating on such information should be documented. If you write that President Warren G. Harding died in office, you do not need a citation because that is a widely known and undisputed fact. If you write that Harding's administration was one of the most corrupt in our history, most people would not feel the need for a citation because authorities agree that the Harding scandals were flagrant and abundant. But if you write that Harding was sexually intimate with a young woman in the White House cloakroom, you should cite your source. Because such information is not widely known and is also debatable, you need to identify your source so that your readers can judge the reliability of the claim. Then, too, they might want further enlightenment on the matter, and your citation will lead them to a more complete discussion.

---

**TIP!** It's better to bother your readers with too many citations than to have them question your integrity because you have too few.

---

### Accuracy Is the Aim

Get the form of your citations correct every time, right down to the last comma, colon, and parenthesis. After years of being told to be original and to think for yourself, you are now being told— on this one matter, at least—to fall into line and slavishly follow the prescribed format. What you might consider a blessed bit of variety in citing your source information will not be appreciated by your readers. The crucial information (date, publisher, place of publication) is located on the title page and on the copyright page (the back of the title page) of each book. For magazines you can usually find it all on the cover.

### When in Doubt, Use Common Sense

Keep in mind that the purpose of documentation is twofold:

1. To give credit to your sources;
2. To allow your readers to find your sources in case they want further information on the subject.

If you are ever in doubt about documentation form (if you are citing something so unusual that you can't find a similar entry in the samples here), use your common sense and give credit the way you think it logically should be done. Be as consistent as possible with other citations.

# To Quote Or Not to Quote

Never quote directly unless (1) the material is authoritative and convincing evidence in support of your thesis, (2) the statement is extremely well phrased, or (3) the idea is controversial and you want to assure your readers that you are not slanting or misinterpreting the source. You would probably quote an observation as well-put as this one:

> Charles Darwin concluded that language ability is "an instinctive tendency to acquire an art."

There is no need, however, for the direct quotation in the following sentence:

> The ICC, in an effort to aid the rail industry, has asked for a "federal study of the need and means for preserving a national passenger service."

You could phrase that just as well yourself. But remember, even after you put the statement into your own words, you still have to indicate (in a parenthetical citation) where you got the idea.

## Quoting Quotations

Sometimes in your reading you will come across a quotation that says precisely what you've been looking for and says it well. If the quotation is complete enough to serve your purpose, and if you honestly don't think you would benefit from tracking down the original source, then don't bother. Instead, include that quotation in the usual way. But notice that your parenthetical citation will include "qtd. in" before the source and page number:

> Oscar Wilde once said about education, "It is well to remember from time to time that nothing that is worth knowing can be taught" (qtd. in Pinker 19).

---

**TIP!** Too much quotation can suggest that you have too few ideas of your own.

Use quotations to support your points, not to make them for you.

---

# **W** *orking Quotations in Smoothly*

If you want your research paper to read smoothly, you must take care when incorporating quotations into your writing. You'll need to have a ready supply of introductory phrases to slide the quotations in gracefully—phrases like "As LeSeure discovered," "Professor Weber notes," and "According to Dr. Lee." These attributions help your readers to evaluate the source material as they read it and distinguish source material from your remarks about it. If you run through the examples in this section on quoting, you will find a generous assortment of these phrases. Borrow them with our blessing.

Notice, please, that the more famous the person, the less likely we are to use Mr., Miss, Mrs., or Ms. in front of the name. "Mr. Shakespeare" sounds quite droll. If the person has a title, you can use it or not, as you think appropriate: Dr. Pauling or Pauling, Senator Feinstein or Feinstein, President Wilson or Wilson.

## **Lead into Your Quotations**

Don't drop quotations in without preparing your readers. Provide clear lead-ins, usually including the author's name, to connect the quotation to your text:

> Many fluent native speakers of English will claim they don't understand grammar. As Professor David Crystal points out, "Millions of people believe they are failures at grammar, say that they have forgotten it, or deny they know any grammar at all—in each case using their grammar convincingly to make their point" (191).

For variety, you may want to place the connecting phrase in the middle every so often, this way:

> The fundamental purpose of language is to communicate intelligibly. "But if thought corrupts language," warns George Orwell, "language can also corrupt thought" (38).

You don't always have to quote full sentences from your sources. You can quote only the telling phrases or key ideas of your authority, like this:

> Barbara Strang remarks that worrying about split infinitives is "one of the most tiresome pastimes" invented by nineteenth-century grammarians (95).

Or like this:

> The play's effectiveness lies, as E. M. W. Tillyard points out, in "the utter artlessness of the language" (34).

> The self-portraits of Frida Kahlo are bold and personal. Art critic Hayden Herrera describes them as "autobiography in paint" (xii).

But do introduce your quotations, please. Identifying the source before presenting the borrowed material helps your readers to know which ideas are yours and which come from sources.

---

**TIP!** If you have difficulty finding new ways to introduce your authorities in the text of your paper, perhaps you are using too many direct quotations.

---

## Make the Grammar Match

When you integrate a quotation into your own sentence, you are responsible for making sure that the entire sentence makes sense. You must adjust the way your sentence is worded so that the grammar comes out right. Read your quotations over carefully to be sure they don't end up like this one:

> When children are born, their first reactions are "those stimuli which constitute their environment."

"Reactions" are not "stimuli." The sentence should read this way:

> When children are born, their first reactions are to "those stimuli which constitute their environment."

What a difference a word makes—the difference here between sense and nonsense. Take particular care when you are adding someone else's words to your own; you get the blame if the words in the quotation do not make sense, because they *did* make sense before you lifted them out of context.

## Use Special Punctuation: Ellipsis Dots and Brackets

When you write a documented paper, you may need to use ellipsis dots and brackets to condense quotations and blend them in smoothly with your text.

To shorten a quoted passage, use *ellipsis dots* (three periods with spaces between) to show your readers that you've omitted some words:

> "The time has come . . . for us to examine ourselves," declares James Baldwin, "but we can only do this if we are willing to free ourselves

from the myth of America and try to find out what is really happening here" (18).

Ellipsis dots are not needed if the omission occurs at the beginning or end of the sentence you are quoting. But if *your* sentence ends with quoted words that are not the end of the original quoted sentence, then use ellipsis dots:

> Thoreau insisted that he received only one or two letters in his life "that were worth the postage" and commented summarily that "to a philosopher all news, as it is called, is gossip. . . ."

That fourth dot is the period. If you include documentation, such as a page number, add the period after the parentheses:

> "is gossip . . ." (27).

Use *brackets* (square parenthetical marks) to add words of your own to clarify the meaning or make the grammar match:

> In her memoir, Jessica Mitford confirms that "In those days [the early 1940s] until postwar repression set in, the [Communist] Party was a strange mixture of openness and secrecy" (67).

## Handling Long Quotations

If you quote more than four typed lines of prose or more than three lines of poetry, set the quotation off by indenting it one inch or ten spaces. Introduce the quotation, usually with a complete sentence followed by a colon; begin the indented quotation on the next line; double-space the quotation and do not use quotation marks (because the indention signals that the material is quoted).

> In 1892 George Bernard Shaw wrote to the editor of the London *Chronicle*, denouncing a columnist who had complained about split infinitives:
>
> > If you do not immediately suppress the person who takes it upon himself to lay down the law almost every day in your columns on the subject of literary composition, I will give up the *Chronicle*. . . . I ask you, Sir, to put this man out . . . without interfering with his perfect freedom of choice between "to suddenly go," "to go suddenly" and "suddenly to go." Set him adrift and try an intelligent Newfoundland dog in his place. (qtd. in Crystal, 195)

Notice that in an indented quotation, the page number is cited in parentheses *after* the period. The quotation marks within the indented material indicate that Shaw punctuated those phrases in that way.

# A voiding Plagiarism

Plagiarism means using somebody else's writing without giving proper credit. You can avoid this dishonesty by using a moderate amount of care in taking notes. Put quotation marks around any material—however brief—that you copy verbatim. As you're leafing through your note cards trying to group them into categories, circle the quotation marks in red so you can't miss them, or else highlight the quoted material as a reminder.

You must also avoid the author's phrasing if you decide not to quote directly but to paraphrase. We all naturally tend to write down an idea using the same language as the source, perhaps changing or omitting a few words. *This close paraphrasing is still plagiarism.* To avoid it, read the passage first, then look away from the original as you put the idea down in your own words. You will be much less likely to fall into the original phrasing that way.

---

**TIP!** When you summarize, try to condense several pages of reading on a single notecard.

---

## Writing an Acceptable Paraphrase

Sometimes, of course, you must do fairly close paraphrasing of important ideas. Because plagiarism can often be accidental, we will give you a couple of examples to show you exactly what unintentional plagiarism looks like. Here is a passage from *The Language Instinct* by Steven Pinker. Assume that you want to use this idea to make a point in your paper.

> Language is not a cultural artifact that we learn the way we learn to tell time or how the federal government works. Instead, it is a distinct piece of the biological makeup of our brains. Language is a complex, specialized skill, which develops in the child spontaneously, without conscious effort or formal instruction.

If you incorporate this material into your paper in the following way, you have plagiarized:

(wrong)    Humans do not learn language the way we learn to tell time or how the federal government works. Language is a part of the biological makeup of our brains, a complex skill that a child develops spontaneously, without conscious effort or formal instruction (Pinker 18).

The fact that the source is cited suggests that this plagiarism resulted from ignorance rather than deception, but it is plagiarism nonetheless. Changing a few words or rearranging the phrases is not enough. Here is another version, somewhat less blatant but still plagiarism:

(wrong)    Humans do not learn language in the way we learn to count or understand how a steam engine works. Language is part of our physical makeup, a complex, specialized skill that develops automatically, without conscious effort or formal instruction (Pinker 18).

There are still two phrases that are distinctly Pinker's: "a complex, specialized skill" and "without conscious effort or formal instruction." It is quite all right to use those phrases but *only if you put them in quotation marks*. You should also acknowledge your source in the text of your paper whenever possible, like this:

(right)    According to linguist Steven Pinker, humans do not learn language in the way we learn to count or understand how a steam engine works. Language is part of our physical makeup, "a complex, specialized skill" that develops automatically, "without conscious effort or formal instruction" (18).

Notice, by the way, that the phrase "in the way we learn" and the words "makeup" and "develops" do not have quotation marks around them, even though they appear in the original. These words are so common, so frequently used that quotation marks are unnecessary. Here is another acceptable paraphrase in which none of the original phrasing is used:

(right)    Linguist Steven Pinker claims that human beings do not learn language in the way that we learn to count or understand how a steam engine works. Language is a part of our physical makeup; it's a sophisticated skill that children acquire automatically and effortlessly without explicit training (18).

## Writing Exercise 9.1

Write paraphrases of two of these paragraphs from Chapter 5: Ann Nietzke's paragraph on country-western songs (p. 61), Stephen Jay Gould's paragraph on dinosaurs (p. 63), Steven Brill's paragraph on handguns (p. 70), and Cass Sunstein's paragraphs on free speech (p. 71). If you have the chance, compare your paraphrases with your classmates' to see how well you did at capturing the original meaning while avoiding plagiarism.

# R *evising the Draft*

Because a research paper requires the incorporation of other people's ideas and the acknowledgment of these sources, you need to take special care in revising. Consult the Revising Checklist for Researched Writing in Figure 9.1.

## Preparing the Final Copy

Before you work on your final draft, give your entire attention to the following instructions on format.

1. Provide margins of at least one inch at the top, bottom, and sides.
2. Double-space throughout.
3. Do not put the title of your own paper in quotation marks.

---

**Check the Usual Things**
1. Be sure the introduction states your thesis.
2. Be sure each paragraph is unified, coherent, and directly related to your thesis.
3. Be sure that the transitions between paragraphs are clear and effective.
4. Be sure your conclusion evaluates the results of your research. If the paper is argumentative, be sure the last sentence is emphatic.

**Check the Special Things**
1. Be sure that you have introduced direct quotations gracefully, using the name and, if appropriate, the title or occupation of the person quoted.
2. Be sure each citation is accurate.
3. Be sure that paraphrases are in your own words and that sources are clearly acknowledged.
4. Be sure that you have not relied too heavily on a single source.
5. Be sure that you have written most of the paper yourself; you need to examine, analyze, or explain the material, not just splice together a bunch of quotations and paraphrases.
6. Be sure always to separate quotations with some comment of your own.
7. Be sure to use ellipsis dots if you omit any words from a quotation; never leave out anything that alters the meaning of a sentence.
8. Be sure to use square brackets, not parentheses, if you add words in a quotation.
9. Be sure to underline or italicize the titles of books and magazines; put quotation marks around titles of articles and chapters in books.
10. Be sure to indent long quotations ten spaces—without quotation marks.

---

**FIGURE 9.1** *Revising Checklist for Researched Writing*

4. Put page numbers in the upper right-hand corner, starting on the first page (but do not number the title page or the outline, if you include these). Note correct page numbering on the sample student paper, which follows.
5. Proofread. You may well be close to exhaustion by the time you finish typing the final copy, and the last thing you will feel like doing is rereading the blasted thing. But force yourself. Or entice somebody else to do it. But do not skip the proofreading.
6. Edit. If you find mistakes, insert the corrections neatly in ink *above the line* (if allowed by your instructor) or retype the page (which is easy to do on a word processor).

---

**D***iscussion Exercise 9.2*

Interview someone who has written a successful research paper to find out what the person did to make the process work. Report back to your class on this interview, and discuss what advice and warnings you picked up.

---

## S*ample Student Research Paper*

The following documented essay was written by Amelia Doggett, a student at Eastern Illinois University. Amelia chose to follow the MLA (Modern Language Association) style commonly used in the humanities. We have annotated Amelia's paper to call attention to certain features of this style. Complete instructions for the MLA style of documentation appear in Chapter 10.

If you want to follow the APA (American Psychological Association) style of documentation, which is used in the social sciences, you will find directions on pages 160–165. You should, of course, follow the documentation style that your instructor requests.

Doggett 1

Amelia Doggett

English 1091C.095

Professor Funk

5 December 1997

Kwanzaa: An American Creation

Many people have heard of the African American celebration called Kwanzaa, but few outside the African American community know exactly what it is about. In fact, many African Americans do not know all the details about the origins and purposes of this festival. Although an estimated 18 million people celebrate Kwanzaa worldwide ("Kwanzaa Culture" 17), there are those who question the holiday's legitimacy and others who claim its goals and values are already being compromised and commercialized.

Origins

Kwanzaa is a recent invention. In 1966 Ron Karenga, a leader of a black nationalist group called US ("United Slaves"), traveled to Africa to learn more about the history of his people ("Only" 1). According to author Janet Riehecky, Karenga wanted to educate African Americans, especially young people, about their rich heritage (3). While in Africa he observed the celebrations of

---

Sidebar notes (left margin):

Be sure to date your paper. In a few years, you'll be glad you did.

Give your paper a title that suggests not only the topic but also your point of view or main idea.

This article had no author byline. Use the article title, in its entirety or shortened, within quotation marks. Alphabetize in the Works Cited by the first main word of the title.

Here the title of the article is shortened from "Only in Afro-America."

The 3 is the exact page number that the information in the sentence came from.

Doggett 2

many tribes when the first crops of year were harvested. In Swahili these celebrations were called <u>matunda ya kwanza,</u> meaning first fruits; according to Karenga the Africans offered the first fruits of their harvest to their ancestors. Karenga decided to combine these commemorative celebrations with other African traditions and with customs borrowed from other holidays to create a festival in which African Americans could rejoice and remember their culture and their ancestors. He took the word <u>kwanza</u> from the Swahili phrase, added an extra <u>a</u>, and called the new holiday <u>Kwanzaa</u> (Riehecky 4-5).

This citation shows that the information in the last 3 sentences came from pages 4–5 of the Riehecky book. Provide just the pages you use, not the whole page span of the article.

The Seven-Day Festival

The extra <u>a</u> was added to give the word seven letters. Karenga wanted the seven-letter name to go along with the seven days of the celebration, the seven candles lit for each day, the seven symbols, and the seven principles he created for the holiday. The basic doctrines of Kwanzaa, the <u>Nguzo Saba</u> (seven principles), come from the values that Karenga saw in the harvest festivals. These are <u>umoja</u> (unity), <u>kujichagulia</u> (self-determination), <u>ujima</u> (collective work and responsibility), <u>ujamaa</u> (cooperative

Doggett 3

economics), <u>nia</u> (purpose), <u>kuumba</u> (creativity), and <u>imani</u> (faith). These values are celebrated over seven days and nights, from December 26 through January 1, with each day focused on one of the seven principles (Goldsmith 8-10). Most families light a candle each night in honor of the principle of the day. The candles (called <u>mishumaa saba</u>) are black (representing the African people), red (symbolizing their struggles), and green (denoting both Africa itself and the hope of deliverance from the struggles) and are placed in a simple seven-candle holder called a <u>kindra,</u> reminiscent of a Hanukkah menorah (Goss 2).

The rituals, as described by Karenga, also involve fruits and vegetables, each identified by its Swahili name and symbolizing "the rewards of collective productive labor" (<u>mazao</u>); a straw mat symbolizing tradition or history (<u>mkeka</u>); ears of corn for each child in the family (<u>vibunzi</u>); and simple, homemade gifts that emphasize education and African culture (<u>zawadi</u>) (Wilde 3). The <u>kindra</u> is placed on the straw mat among the fruits and vegetables. The gifts are distributed each night or just on the final night, December 31, when family members gather for the communal feast (<u>karamu</u>). This

Notice that there is no punctuation between the author's name and the page number—just a space. The same goes for an article title in your parenthetical citations: only a space before the page number.

Doggett 4

closing feast often includes some kind of
tribute or salute to ancestors or famous
African Americans, usually in the form of
a song or poem or even a speech by a
guest (Goss 2-3).

Controversy and Divisiveness ———————— Use subhead-
ings to help
   Kwanzaa is the product of the Ameri-    your reader
                                           grasp your
can civil rights and black power move-     organization.
ments of the 1960s. Its creator, Ron
Karenga, is now a professor of black
studies at California State University in
Long Beach, and he has changed his first
name to Maulana ("master teacher"). In
the '60s, however, Karenga was the leader
of a Los Angeles-based organization
called US (as opposed to "them") and became an important figure in the rebuild-
ing of Watts after the riots there (Early
2). Kwanzaa was born in the aftermath of
Watts and was an attempt "to reaffirm
African culture," says Karenga; "it was
at the same time a political act of self-
determination. . . . We were talking
                                           —— The *qtd. in* means
about re-Africanization" (qtd. in "Kwan-   that the person's
                                           words were
zaa Culture" 1). And, indeed, one of the   quoted in the
                                           cited article.
common features in some larger Kwanzaa
ceremonies has been a name-changing ceremony, in which the participants convert
their "slave names" into African ones
(Wilde 3).

Doggett 5

In the beginning, Karenga's Afrocentric and anti-white rhetoric was often polemical and confrontational:

If you use more than four typed lines of direct quotation from a source, indent all the lines 10 spaces (or 1 inch) from the left margin. Don't use quotation marks around the indented material.

> The more you learn, the more resentful you are of this white man. Then you see how he's tricking your people, emasculating your men, raping your women and using his power to keep you down. (qtd. in Wilde 3)

But since that time, Karenga has mellowed, and Kwanzaa has lost much of its polemical style and content. The inventor of the holiday now describes its goals in more general and tranquil terms, saying that it promotes "The good life. The good of existence. The good of family, community and culture. The good of the awesome and the ordinary. The good of the divine, the natural and the social" (qtd. in "Kwanzaa Ties" 1).

While Kwanzaa has been transformed in the thirty years since its original conception, it still retains some traces of divisiveness and anti-white sentiment.

When you give the name of the person or author you're using and you place a parenthetical citation at the end of the same sentence as the name, put only the page number in the parentheses.

Professor Gerald Early, director of the African and Afro-American Studies Program at Washington University in St. Louis, points out that "Kwanzaa's success depends on exacerbating, consciously or un-

Doggett 6

consciously, black people's sense of alienation from Christmas" (4). In this respect, then, Kwanzaa becomes, as the Afrocentrist writer Haki Madhubuti claims, an "Afro-American celebration [that] is truly progressive and revolutionary" (qtd. in Early 4).

The divided opinion about Kwanzaa extends into the black community. Although many African Americans embrace the holiday, others think that it presents a false history (Wilde 4). They question the need to celebrate an idealized African past, especially when there is so much to celebrate in the real history of blacks in America. "It's not an authentic black American holiday, not a part of our tradition," says Clarence Walker, a black professor at the University of California at Davis (qtd. in "Only" 2).

Professor Early feels that the seven principles of Kwanzaa are "less ideas than a set of slogans." He describes the philosophical foundation of the holiday as a "pastiche" drawn from a range of political and cultural sources:

> There's a good deal of the African political philosopher Julius Nyerere, some of the former Senegalese president Leopold Senghor's "Negritude,"——

Because it's in an indented quotation without quotation marks, the word "Negritude" has double quotations marks around it, just as it appeared in the source.

a bit of Mao, a dash of Marx,
a serving of Garveyite Pan-
Africanism, and a pinch of
nature religion. (2)
But this concoction of ideas is entirely
fitting for an American creation: Americans have been inventing their culture
from scratch since the country began.
Early concedes that the principles
of Kwanzaa "combine the beatitude of
willpower, an old American preoccupation,
with the righteousness of racial uplift,
an old African-American preoccupation"
(2-3).

Entering the Mainstream

Kwanzaa was originally intended as a
way to unite African Americans against
those (whites) who are trying to hold
their race back, but its positive goal of
increasing community cohesiveness has diminished the racial resentment. Yes,
there is still some anti-white feeling,
but as Anna Day Wilde observes, "Most
African Americans view Kwanzaa not as an
opportunity to bash whites but as a force
for oneness among blacks" (7). This constructive concern has made it a holiday
that many people feel comfortable
embracing.

Doggett 8

And there are many signs that African Americans have enthusiastically embraced Kwanzaa. Bookshops carry Kwanzaa cookbooks and audiotapes; schools and museums include Kwanzaa in their holiday celebrations; communities hold parades and public celebrations; Kwanzaa expositions draw thousands of merchants and customers; and Hallmark since 1992 has been selling Kwanzaa cards, featuring designs by African American artists, as part of its Mahogany line (Wilde 3-4). As journalists Kenneth Woodward and Patrice Johnson point out, "All this activity means that Kwanzaa has made it into the mainstream. If it's featured in shop windows and McDonald's ads, then it has arrived" (2).

Notice that the quotation marks close the sentence. Then the parenthetical citation appears, followed by the period to close the whole thing.

Some people do not approve of the increased popularity of the holiday. They fear that commercial exploitation will take away from the positive communal goals of Kwanzaa (Horne 2) and contribute to its decline. After all, many people say the main reason they started celebrating this new holiday was to escape the over-commercialism of Christmas (Wilde 4). "I'm wondering when they're going to announce a big Kwanzaa clearance sale," says Dawad Phillip, an editor at the <u>Daily Challenge,</u> a black newspaper in

Whenever possible, give the credentials and titles of the people you quote.

Doggett 9

Brooklyn (qtd. in Woodward and Johnson
2). But others feel that the holiday is
safe because most people who really celebrate Kwanzaa realize what it stands for
(Horne 3). Gerald Early thinks that the
commercialization of Kwanzaa is not a
sign of the corruption of the holiday but
an indication of the increasing economic
power of blacks (6).

Conclusion

There are those who feel that no matter how commercialized the holiday becomes it will not endure. These cynics
scoff at this relatively new holiday and
dismiss it as "a marginal, slightly ludi-
crous idea that is unlikely to last long,
let alone 2,000 years"--like Hanukkah and
Christmas ("Only" 2). But behind all the
commercialism and controversy, there is a
holiday moving steadily toward its potential. Kwanzaa is no longer a tool for
racial separatism, as it was when it
started. It has become, instead, a strong
force for cooperation and unification in
the African American community and in
American society in general.

Doggett 10

Works Cited

Early, Gerald. "Dreaming of a Black ◄─────── The Early article
   Christmas." <u>Harper's</u> Jan. 1997:                 appeared in print
                                                           in *Harper's* maga-
   55-61. Online. <u>InfoTrac SearchBank.</u>             zine and then
                                                           was distributed
   8 pp. 9 Nov. 1997.                                      electronically
                                                           through InfoTrac.
Goldsmith, Diane Hoyt. <u>Celebrating Kwan-</u>

   <u>zaa.</u> New York: Holiday House, 1993.             With multiple
Goss, Linda, and Clay Goss. <u>It's Kwanzaa</u> ◄─── authors, reverse
                                                           the order of only
   <u>Time.</u> New York: HarperCollins, 1995.            the first author's
                                                           name.
Horne, Malaika. "The Seeds of Kwanzaa

   Have Spawned a Cultural Revival."

   <u>Crisis</u> Nov. 1994: 2-3. ◄─────────── In the Works
                                                           Cited listing for a
"Kwanzaa Culture." <u>U.S. News & World Re-</u>          printed article,
                                                           give the number
   <u>port</u> 30 Dec. 1996: 17.                           for the whole
                                                           span of the arti-
"Kwanzaa Ties African-Americans to Their                  cle, even if you
                                                           used material
   Roots." CNN Interactive. 26 Dec.                        from only one or
                                                           a few pages. This
   1996. <http://www.cnn.com/US/9612/26/                  article spanned
                                                           pages 2 and 3.
   kwanzaa,view/index.html.> (11 Nov. 1997).

"Only in Afro-America." <u>The Economist</u> 17

   Dec. 1994: A32. Online. <u>InfoTrac</u>

   <u>SearchBank.</u> 2 pp. 11 Nov. 1997.

Riehecky, Janet. <u>Kwanzaa.</u> Chicago: ◄─── The Works Cited
                                                           form for a book
   Children's Press, 1993.                                 gives the city of
                                                           publication, the
Wilde, Anna Day. "Mainstreaming Kwanzaa."                 publisher's
                                                           name, and the
   <u>The Public Interest</u> Spring 1995:                copyright date—
                                                           but no page
   68-79. Online. <u>InfoTrac SearchBank.</u>             numbers.

   8 pp. 9 Nov. 1997.

Woodward, Kenneth L., and Patrice John-

   son. "The Advent of Kwanzaa." <u>Newsweek</u>

   11 Dec. 1995: 88. Online. <u>InfoTrac</u>

   <u>SearchBank.</u> 2 pp. 9 Nov. 1997.

# Documenting
# Your Sources

This chapter provides complete instruction for documenting papers according to the two most widely used academic styles:

1. MLA (Modern Language Association) for the humanities,
2. APA (American Psychological Association) for the social sciences.

If you are writing a paper incorporating library sources for any of the remaining academic disciplines, you should identify a leading journal in that field and follow the style employed there.

## T *he MLA Documentation Style for the Humanities*

The Modern Language Association (MLA) recommends that source citations be given in the text of the paper, not in footnotes or endnotes. This in-text style of documentation involves parenthetical references. It works like this:

A. Normally you will introduce the cited material by mentioning the name of the author in your lead-in and giving the page number (or numbers) at the end in parentheses:

```
Edmund Wilson tells us that the author of Uncle Tom's
Cabin felt "the book had been written by God" (5).
```

B. Your readers can identify this source by consulting your Works Cited at the end of your paper (see items H through K). The entry for the source cited above would appear like this:

```
Wilson, Edmund. Patriotic Gore: Studies in the Litera-
    ture of the American Civil War. New York: Oxford
    UP, 1966.
```

C. If you do not mention the author in your lead-in, then include his/her last name in parentheses along with the page number:

```
One of the great all-time best-sellers, Uncle Tom's
Cabin sold over 300,000 copies in America and more
than 2 million copies world wide (Wilson 3).
```

D. If you have to quote indirectly—something from another source not available to you—use "qtd. in" (for "quoted in") in your parenthetical reference. The following example refers to a book written by Donald Johanson and Maitland Edey.

```
Richard Leakey's wife, Maeve, told the paleoanthropolo-
gist David Johanson, "We heard all about your bones on
the radio last night" (qtd. in Johanson and Edey 162).
```

E. If you are using a source written or edited by more than three people, use only the name of the first person listed, followed by "et al." (meaning "and others") in your lead-in:

```
Blair et al. observe that the fine arts were almost
ignored by colonial writers (21).
```

F. If you refer to more than one work by the same author, include a shortened title in the parenthetical reference:

```
(Gould, Mismeasure 138).
```

G. If the author's name is not given, then use a shortened title instead. Be sure to use at least the first word of the full title to send the reader to the proper alphabetized entry on your Works Cited page. The following is a reference to a newspaper article entitled "Environmental Group Calls DuPont's Ads Deceptive":

```
The Friends of the Earth claimed that, despite DuPont's
television ads about caring for the environment, the
company is the "single largest corporate polluter in
the United States" ("Environmental Group" F3).
```

H. On a separate page at the end of the paper, alphabetize your Works Cited list for all sources mentioned in your paper. Use *hanging indention;* that is, after the first line of each entry, indent the other lines five spaces.

I. Omit any mention of *page* or *pages* or *line* or *lines.* Do not even include abbreviations for these terms. Use numbers alone:

```
Kinsley, Michael. "Continental Divide" Time 7
    Jul. 1997: 89-91.
```

J. Shorten publishers' names. For example, use Allyn instead of Allyn & Bacon, Inc.; Norton instead of W. W. Norton and Co.; Oxford UP instead of Oxford University Press; and U of Illinois P instead of University of Illinois Press. See sample entries 1 through 13.

K. Use regular (not roman) numerals throughout, even to indicate act and scene in plays: "In <u>Othello</u> 2.1, the scene shifts to Cyprus." Exceptions: Use *lowercase* roman numerals (ii, xiv) for citing page numbers from a preface, introduction, or table of contents; use roman numerals in names of monarchs (Elizabeth II).

L. Use raised note numbers for *informational notes* only (i.e., notes containing material pertinent to your discussion but not precisely to the point). Include these content notes at the end of your paper just before your Works Cited page, and use the heading Notes.

M. Abbreviate months and titles of magazines as shown in the sample entries.

## S *ample Entries for a Works Cited List*

The following models will help you write Works Cited entries for most of the sources you will use. If you use a source not illustrated in these examples, consult the more extensive list of sample entries found in the *MLA Handbook for Writers of Research Papers,* 4th ed., or ask your instructor for guidance.

### Books

1. Book by one author

```
Chused, Richard H. Private Acts in Public Places: A
    Social History of Divorce. Philadelphia: U of
    Pennsylvania P, 1994.
```

2. Two or more books by the same author

> Gould, Stephen Jay. <u>The Mismeasure of Man</u>. New York:
> Norton, 1981.
>
> ---. <u>The Panda's Thumb: More Reflections in Natural
> History</u>. New York: Norton, 1980.

3. Book by two or three authors

> Anderson, Terry, and Donald Leal. <u>Free Market Environ-
> mentalism</u>. Boulder: Westview, 1991.
>
> McCrum, William, William Cran, and Robert MacNeil. <u>The
> Story of English</u>. New York: Viking, 1986.

4. Book by more than three authors

> Medhurst, Martin J., et al. <u>Cold War Rhetoric: Strat-
> egy, Metaphor, and Ideology</u>. New York: Greenwood,
> 1990.

[The phrase *et al.* is an abbreviation for *et alii,* meaning "and others."]

5. Book by an unknown author

> <u>Literacy of Older Adults in America: Results from the
> National Adult Literacy Survey</u>. Washington: Cen-
> ter for Educ. Statistics, 1987.

6. Book with an editor.

> Gallegos, Bee, ed. <u>English: Our Official Language?</u> New
> York: Wilson, 1994.

[For a book with two or more editors, use "eds."]

7. Book with both editor and author.

> Whorf, Benjamin. <u>Language, Thought, and Reality: Se-
> lected Writings of Benjamin Lee Whorf</u>. Ed. J. B.
> Carroll. Cambridge: MIT P, 1956.

8. Book by a group or corporate author

```
National Research Council. The Social Impact of AIDS
    in the United States. New York: National Academy
    P, 1993.
```

[When a corporation, organization, or group is listed as the author on the title page, cite it as you would a person.]

9. Work in a collection or anthology.

```
Gordon, Mary. "The Parable of the Cave." The Writer on
    Her Work. Ed. Janet Sternburg. New York: Norton,
    1980. 27-32.
```

10. Work reprinted in a collection or anthology

```
Sage, George H. "Sport in American Society: Its Perva-
    siveness and Its Study." Sport and American Soci-
    ety. 3rd ed. Reading: Addison-Wesley, 1980. 4-15.
    Rpt. in Physical Activity and the Social
    Sciences. Ed. W. N. Widmeyer. 5th ed. Ithaca:
    Movement, 1983. 42-52.
```

[First give complete data for the earlier publication; then add "Rpt. in" and give the reprinted source.]

11. Multivolume work

```
Blom, Eric, ed. Grove's Dictionary of Music and Musi-
    cians. 5th ed. 10 vols. New York: St. Martin's,
    1961.
```

12. Reprinted (republished) book

```
Jespersen, Otto. Growth and Structure of the English
    Language. 1938. Chicago: U of Chicago P, 1980.
```

13. Later (second or subsequent) edition

```
Gibaldi, Joseph. MLA Handbook for Writers of Research
    Papers. 4th ed. New York: MLA, 1995.
```

14. Book in translation

> Grmek, Mirko D. <u>History of AIDS: Emergence and Origin</u>
> <u>of a Modern Pandemic</u>. Trans. Russell C. Maulitz
> and Jacalyn Duffin. Princeton: Princeton UP, 1990.

## Newspapers

15. Signed newspaper article

> Krebs, Emilie. "Sewer Backups Called No Problem." <u>Pan-</u>
> <u>tagraph</u> [Bloomington] 20 Nov. 1995: A3.

[If the city is not part of the name of a local newspaper, give the city in brackets, not underlined, after the newspaper's name.]

> Weiner, Jon. "Vendetta: The Government's Secret War
> Against John Lennon." <u>Chicago Tribune</u> 5
> Aug. 1984, sec. 3: 1.

[Note the difference between "A3" in the first example and "sec. 3: 1" in the second. Both refer to section and page, but each newspaper indicates the section in a different way. Give the section designation and page number exactly as they appear in the publication.]

16. Unsigned newspaper article

> "No Power Line-Cancer Link Found." <u>Chicago Tribune</u> 3
> July 1997, final ed., sec. 1: 5.

[If an edition is specified on the paper's masthead, name the edition (late ed., natl ed., final ed.) after the date and before the page reference. Different editions of the same issue of a newspaper contain different material.]

17. Letter to the editor

> Kessler, Ralph. "Orwell Defended." Letter. <u>New York</u>
> <u>Times Book Review</u> 15 Dec. 1985: 26.

18. Editorial

> "From Good News to Bad." Editorial. <u>Washington Post</u> 16
> July 1984: 10.

## Magazines and Journals

19. Article from a monthly or bimonthly magazine

    Lawren, Bill. "1990's Designer Beasts." <u>Omni</u> Nov.-Dec.
        1985: 56-61.

    Rosenbaum, Dan, and David Sparrow. "Speed Demons:
        Widebody Rackets." <u>World Tennis</u> Aug. 1989: 48-49.

20. Article from a weekly or biweekly magazine (signed and unsigned)

    Coghlan, Andy. "Warring Parents Harm Children as Much
        as Divorce." <u>New Scientist</u> 15 Jun. 1991: 24.

    "Warning: 'Love' for Sale." <u>Newsweek</u> 11 Nov. 1985: 39.

21. Article from a journal with continuous pagination throughout the entire volume

    Potvin, Raymond, and Che-Fu Lee. "Multistage Path Mod-
        els of Adolescent Alcohol and Drug Use." <u>Journal
        of Studies on Alcohol</u> 41 (1980): 531-42.

22. Article from a journal that paginates each issue separately or that uses only issue numbers

    Holtug, Nils. "Altering Humans: The Case For and
        Against Human Gene Therapy." <u>Cambridge Quarterly
        of Healthcare Ethics</u> 6.2 (Spring 1997): 157-60.

    [That means volume 6, issue 2.]

## Other Sources

23. Book review

    Emery, Robert. Rev. of <u>The Divorce Revolution: The Un-
        expected Social and Economic Consequences for
        Women and Children in America</u> by Lenore Weitzman.
        <u>American Scientist</u> 74 (1986): 662-63.

24. Personal interview or letter.

Ehrenreich, Barbara. Personal interview. 12 Feb. 1995.

Vidal, Gore. Letter to the author. 2 June 1984.

[Treat published interviews and letters like articles, with the person being interviewed as the author.]

25. Anonymous pamphlet

How to Help a Friend with a Drinking Problem. American
    College Health Assn., 1984.

26. Article from a reference work (signed and unsigned)

"Psychopharmacology." The Columbia Encyclopedia. 5th
    ed. 1993.

Van Doren, Carl. "Samuel Langhorne Clemens." The Dic-
    tionary of American Biography. 1958 ed.

[Treat a dictionary entry or an encyclopedia article like an entry from an anthology, but do not cite the editor of the reference work.]

27. Government publication

United States Dept. of Labor, Bureau of Statistics.
    Dictionary of Occupational Titles. 4th ed. Wash-
    ington: GPO, 1977.

[GPO stands for Government Printing Office.]

28. Film or videotape

Citizen Kane. Dir. Orson Welles. Perf. Orson Welles,
    Joseph Cotton, Dorothy Comingore, and Agnes Moore-
    head. RKO, 1941. 50th Anniversary Special Edition
    videorecording: Turner Home Entertainment, 1991.

29. Lecture

Albee, Edward. "A Dream or a Nightmare?" Illinois
    State University Fine Arts Lecture. Normal, IL.
    18 Mar. 1979.

For any other sources (such as televised shows, performances, advertisements, recordings, works of art), include enough information to permit an interested reader to locate your original source. Be sure to arrange this information in a logical fashion, duplicating so far as possible the order and punctuation of the entries above. To be on safe ground, consult your instructor for suggestions about documenting unusual material.

## Electronic Sources

If you use material from a computer database or online source, you need to indicate that you read it in electronic form. In your research, most of the electronic items suitable for use have also appeared in print. Give the print information, followed by the computer source.

30. Article from an online full-text database
    [Cite the following information: Author. "Article Title." <u>Magazine Title</u>. Date: paging. <u>Database Name</u>. Online. Access date.]

    Viviano, Frank. "The New Mafia Order." <u>Mother Jones</u>
      May-June 1995: 44-56. <u>InfoTrac SearchBank</u>. On-
      line. 17 July 1995.

31. Article from a commercial online service
    [Cite the following information: Author. "Article Title." <u>Newspaper Title</u>. Date, Edition (if given): paging. <u>Database Name</u>. Computer service. Access date.]

    Howell, Vicki, and Bob Carlton. "Growing up Tough: New
      Generation Fights for Its Life: Inner-City Youths
      Live by Rule of Vengeance." <u>Birmingham News</u>. 29
      Aug. 1993: 1A+. <u>Nexis</u>. 26 Apr. 1997.

    [Nexis is both the database and the name of the online service.]

32. Article from an online encyclopedia
    [Cite the following information: Author or editor. "Part Title." <u>Title of Print Version of Work</u>. Edition statement (if given). Publication information (Place of publication: publisher, date), if given. <u>Title of Electronic Work</u>. Medium. Information supplier. Date of access. Uniform Resource Locator (URL) enclosed in angle brackets.]

```
Daniel, Ralph Thomas. "The History of Western Music."
     Britannica Online: Macropaedia. 1995. Online En-
     cyclopedia Britannica. 14 June 1995. <http//
     www.eb.com:180/cgi-bin/g:DocF=macro/5004/
     45/O.html>.
```

[It is not necessary to give place of publication and publisher when citing well-known reference works.]

33. Sources from a database published on CD-ROM

```
Shakespeare. Editions and Adaptations of Shakespeare.
     Interactive multimedia. Cambridge, UK: Chadwick-
     Healey, 1995. CD-ROM. Alexandria: Electronic Book
     Technologies, 1995.

"Silly." The Oxford English Dictionary. 2nd ed. CD-
     ROM. Oxford: Oxford UP, 1992.
```

34. Web site

```
Cummings, Shelly. "Genetic Testing and the Insurance
     Industry." Electronic Genetics Newsletter 18 Mar
     1996 17:442. 23 Dec. 1997. <http://
     www.westpub.com/Educate/mathsci/insure.htm>.
```

For more detailed information about citing electronic sources, consult *The MLA Style Manual,* 2nd ed. (1998) or the MLA's World Wide Web site <http://www.mla.org>.

### Citation Exercise 10.1

To practice composing entries for a Works Cited list, complete an entry for each of the works described below. You need to supply underlining or quotation marks as appropriate around titles. The first example will you show you how.

1. The author of the book is Charles K. Smith
   The title of the book is Styles and Structures: Alternative Approaches to Student Writing.
   It was published in 1974 by W. W. Norton and Co., Inc.

```
Smith, Charles K. Styles and Structures: Alternative
     Approaches to Student Writing. New York: Norton,
     1974.
```

2. Author: Robin Lakoff
   Title of the book: Language and Woman's Place
   Published by Harper and Row in New York in 1975.

3. Author: Max Spalter
   Title of the article: Five Examples of How to Write a Brechtian Play
       That Is Not Really Brechtian
   Periodical: Educational Theatre
   Published in the 2nd volume in 1974 on pages 220 to 235. The periodical has continuous pagination throughout the volume.

4. Author: Daniel S. Greenberg
   Title of the article: Ridding American Politics of Polls
   Newspaper: The Washington Post
   Published on September 16, 1980, in section A, on page 17.

5. Authors: Clyde E. Blocker, Robert H. Plummer, and Richard C.
       Richardson
   Title of the book: The Two-Year College: A Social Synthesis
   Published in Englewood Cliffs, New Jersey, by Prentice-Hall in 1965.

6. How would this textbook, Here's How to Write Well, appear in the Works Cited list? Include the exact data.

7. In which order would the publications from 1 to 6 above appear in your list?

   a) 5 4 2 6 1 3     b) 1 2 3 4 5 6     c) 4 3 6 1 5 2
   d) 6 4 3 5 1 2

---

# T he APA Documentation Style for the Social Sciences

The APA style focuses more on the date of the source than the MLA style does. The year appears in the parenthetical documentation in the text, instead of only in the References list. APA documentation works this way:

A. Always mention your source and its date within the text of your paper in parentheses:

```
The study reveals that children pass through identifi-
able cognitive stages (Piaget, 1954).
```

B. Your readers can identify this source by consulting your References list at the end of your paper. The entry for the information above would appear like this:

```
Piaget, J. (1954). The construction of reality in
the child. New York: Basic Books.
```

[Note the use of sentence capitalization for titles in the References section. Note, too, that APA style requires you to underline the punctuation that follows underlined titles.]

C. If you are quoting directly or if you want to stress the authority of the source you are paraphrasing, you may mention the name of the source in your sentence. Then include just the date in parentheses:

```
In Words and Women, Miller and Swift (1976) remind us
that using the plural is a good way to avoid "the
built-in male-as-norm quality English has
acquired . . ." (p. 163).
```

D. If the author's name is not given, then use a shortened title instead. Be sure to use at least the first word of the full title to send the reader to the proper alphabetized entry on your References page. The following example is a reference to the newspaper article entitled "Environmental Group Calls DuPont's Ads Deceptive":

```
The Friends of the Earth claimed that, despite DuPont's
television ads about caring for the environment, the
company is the "single largest corporate polluter in
the United States" ("Environmental Group," 1991).
```

E. If you are using a source written or edited by more than two people and fewer than six, cite all authors the first time you refer to the source. For all subsequent references, use only the surname of the first person listed, followed by *et al.* (meaning "and others") in your lead-in:

```
Blair et al. (1980) observe that the fine arts were
almost ignored by colonial writers.
```

When there are only two authors, join their names with the word *and* in the text:

```
Hale and Sponjer (1972) originated the Do-Look-Learn
theory.
```

In parenthetical materials, tables, and reference lists, join the names with an ampersand (&):

```
The Do-Look-Learn theory (Hale & Sponjer, 1972) was
taken seriously by educators across the country.
```

F. If you are quoting more than *forty* words, begin the quotation on a new line and indent the entire quotation five spaces, but run each line to the usual right margin. Omit the quotation marks. Do not single-space the quotation.

```
In Language and Woman's Place (1975) Lakoff has con-
cluded that
        men tend to relegate to women things that are not
        of concern to them, or do not involve their
        egos. . . . We might rephrase this point by say-
        ing that since women are not expected to make de-
        cisions on important matters, such as what kind
        of job to hold, they are relegated the noncrucial
        decisions as a sop. (p. 9)
```

G. If there are two or more works by the same author in your References list, put the earliest one first. When more than one work has been published by the same author during the same year, list them alphabetically, according to the name of the book or article, and identify them with "a," "b," "c," and so forth, following the date. (Include the "a," "b," "c," in your in-text citations, too.)

```
    Graves, D. (1975). An examination of the writing
processes of seven-year-old children. Research in the
Teaching of English, 9, 227-241.

    Graves, D. (1981a). Writers: Teachers and chil-
dren at work. Exeter, NH: Heinemann Educational
Books.
```

> Graves, D. (1981b). Writing research for the
> eighties: What is needed. <u>Language Arts, 58,</u> 197–206.

# S *ample Entries for a References List*

The following models will help you write entries for most of the sources you will include in your References list. If you use a source not illustrated in these samples, consult the more extensive *Publications Manual of the American Psychological Association,* 4th ed. (Washington: APA, 1994), or ask your instructor.

Alphabetize your list by the author's last name. If no author is given, alphabetize the entry by the title. Use regular paragraph indention; use author's initials for given names; put the dates after the authors' names; and use sentence capitalization for article and book titles, but capitalize the first word in the subtitle after a colon.

## Books

1. Book by one author

> Abernathy, C. F. (1980). <u>Civil rights: Cases and</u>
> <u>materials</u>. St. Paul: West Publishing.

2. Book by two or more authors

> Cook, M., & McHenry, R. (1978). <u>Sexual</u>
> <u>attraction</u>. New York: Pergamon Press.

> Brusaw, C., Alfred, G., & Oliu, W. (1976). <u>The</u>
> <u>business writer's handbook</u>. New York: St. Martin's.

[In the list of references, use the ampersand sign instead of writing the word *and*.]

3. Book by a group or corporate author

> National Research Council. (1993). <u>The social</u>
> <u>impact of AIDS in the United States</u>. New York: National Academy Press.

4. Book with an editor

> Gallegos, Bee (Ed.). (1994). <u>English: Our offi-</u>
> <u>cial language?</u> New York: Wilson.

5. Article in a collection or anthology

> Emig, J. (1978). Hand, eye, brain: Some basics in
> the writing process. In C. Cooper & L. Odell (Eds.),
> Research in composing: Points of departure
> (pp. 59-72). Urbana, IL: National Council of Teachers
> of English.

6. Multivolume work

> Asimov, I. (1960). The intelligent man's guide to
> science. (Vols. 1-2). New York: Basic Books.

7. Later (second or subsequent) edition

> Gibaldi, J. (1995). MLA handbook for writers of
> research papers (4th ed.). New York: MLA.

## Periodicals

8. Article from a journal paginated by volume

> Messner, M. (1990). When bodies are weapons: Mas-
> culinity and violence in sport. International Review
> for the Sociology of Sport, 25, 203-220.

[Do not put quotation marks around article titles. Capitalize all important words in journal or magazine titles.]

9. Article from a journal paginated by issue

> Holtug, Nils. (1997). Altering humans: The case
> for and against human gene therapy. Cambridge Quar-
> terly of Healthcare Ethics, 6(2), 157-160.

10. Article from a magazine

> Neimark, J. (1991, May). Out of bounds: The truth
> about athletes and rape. Mademoiselle, 196-199.

11. Article from a newspaper

Eskenazi, G. (1990, June 3). The male athlete and
sexual assault. The New York Times, Section 8, 1.

## Other Sources

12. Personal or telephone interview
    Not cited in References list, only within your paper.

13. Article from a specialized dictionary or encyclopedia
    Treat as an article in a collection (item 5 above).

## Electronic Sources

14. Article from a full-text database
    [Cite the following information: Author. (Year, month, day).
    Article Title. Magazine Title [Online], volume (if given), pag-
    ing. Available: name of database. [Access date].]

    Viviano, F. (1995, May/June). The new mafia or-
    der. Mother Jones [Online], 44–56. Available: InfoTrac
    SearchBank. [1995, July 17].

15. Article from a CD-ROM
    [Cite the following information: Author. (Year, month, day).
    Article Title. Newspaper Title [Type of medium], paging or in-
    dicator of length. Available: Supplier/Database name (Data-
    base identifier or number, if available)/Item or accession
    number. [Access date].]

    Howell, V., & Carlton, B. (1993, August 29).
    Growing up Tough: New Generation Fights for Its Life:
    Inner-City Youths Live by Rule of Vengeance. Birming-
    ham News [CD-ROM], p. 1A (10 pp.). Available: 1994
    SIRS/SIRS 1993 Youth/Volume 4/Article 56A. [1995,
    July 16].

16. Article from an online encyclopedia
    [Cite the following information: Author or editor. (Year). Title.
    In Source (edition), [Type of medium]. Producer (optional).
    Available Protocol (e.g., HTTP): Site/Path/File [Access date].]

```
    Daniel, R. T. (1995). The history of western mu-
sic. In Britannica online: Macropaedia [Online].
Available HTTP: http//www.eb.com:180/cgi-bin/
g:DocF=macro/5004/45/O.html [1995 June 14].
```

For more details about citing electronic sources, see Xia Li and Nancy Crane's *Electronic Style: A Guide to Citing Electronic Information* (Westport: Meckler, 1993), which is based on the APA style; or Janice R. Walker and Todd Taylor's *Columbia Guide to Online Style* (New York: Columbia UP, 1998).

# How to Make Your Writing Clear and Correct

# 11

# Punctuating for Clarity and Effectiveness

When we speak, we nod, gesture, change facial expression, and raise and lower the tone and volume of our voice to help communicate the meaning of our words. When we write, the only aids we have are word choice, word order, and punctuation. The conventions for punctuating our written sentences are not numerous, but they are complicated and flexible enough to give inexperienced writers more trouble than help.

## S eparating and Connecting

Punctuation marks have one main function: to signal the separation between ideas. For example, if you want to show that two ideas are completely separate, you put a period or question mark after one and start a new sentence. On the other hand, if you want to show that two parts of a sentence (like the subject and verb) are closely connected, you don't put in any punctuation at all. The following list of punctuation marks describes the amount of separation (from most to least) that you can signal within and between sentences:

- period, question mark, exclamation mark: maximum
  separation

- semicolon: medium separation

- colon: medium separation (anticipatory)

- dash: medium separation (emphatic)
- comma: minimum separation
- no mark: no separation

As the list suggests, the colon and the dash signal more than just the amount of separation. Their precise uses will be explained later in this chapter.

Another way of understanding the differences among these punctuation marks is to look at the grammatical units they separate. These units can be divided into two kinds: independent clauses and non-independent elements. You may remember that an independent clause is a group of words that contains a subject and a verb and can stand alone as a sentence. Non-independent elements include words, phrases, and dependent clauses that do not stand alone as sentences. Figure 11.1 presents the list of punctuation marks arranged according to the grammatical units they separate.

---

*To separate independent clauses*  ——  Use **periods, question marks, or semicolons.**

American novelist Willa Cather was born in Virginia. When she was ten her family moved to Nebraska.

Have you read any of Cather's novels? Many of them deal with the immigrant settlers of the western prairies.

The Cather family settled near the Kansas border; they later moved from the prairie to Red Cloud.

*To separate independent clauses or to separate non-independent elements from independent clauses*  ——  Use **dashes or colons.**

Cather came to know various immigrant groups who settled on the Divide—a high area of grassy, windblown plains.

The plains area was often affected by harsh conditions: blizzards, droughts, and invasions of insects.

*To separate non-independent elements from independent clauses*  ——  Use **commas.**

Six years after her family moved to Red Cloud, Cather enrolled in the University of Nebraska.

Planning to study science, Cather, however, turned to writing.

Several of Cather's early novels, such as *My Ántonia* and *O Pioneers!*, deal with the people of the prairies.

In 1912 Cather visited the Southwest, an area that influenced her later novels.

---

**FIGURE 11.1** *Using Punctuation to Separate Sentence Elements*

With these differences in mind, we can now look at the specific conventions for using punctuation marks both within and between independent clauses. And we'll begin with the most frequently used mark of punctuation, the comma.

## P *unctuating Within Sentences: Using Commas*

*Commas* are used to set off non-independent elements within sentences. Learn to look at a basic English sentence—with a subject, verb, and completer—as a single structure (an independent clause):

| subject | verb | completer |
|---------|------|-----------|
| Liz | loves | cleaning the house. |

You don't want to separate the three parts of an independent clause with commas. But when you attach non-independent elements (words, phrases, dependent clauses) to this structure, you need to put in commas.

You can add non-independent attachments in three places: before the independent clause, after the independent clause, and in the middle of the independent clause.

(before)   Though it seems odd to most of us, Liz loves cleaning the house.

(after)   Liz loves cleaning the house, a preference we find hard to believe.

(middle)   Liz, who hates to do laundry, loves cleaning the house.

These non-independent additions are usually separated from the independent clause by commas. If you leave the commas out, the reader may be confused or disconcerted, because your punctuation has not marked off where the main (independent) clause begins and ends.

### Using Commas to Set Off Beginning Elements

Put a comma after an introductory word or phrase, a dependent clause, or a long phrase that precedes an independent clause. Dependent clauses, you will remember, contain a subject and a verb but do not make complete sense by themselves. (See page 186 for more information about dependent clauses.)

After a heavy downpour with lightning and high winds, the yard was littered with branches.

Surprisingly, the roof was still intact.

Before going outside, my roommate checked the basement.

Indeed, he found an inch and a half of water down there.

Because the electricity had gone out, the sump pump quit working.

Sighing heavily, we got out the wet-vac and went to work.

## Using Commas to Set Off Ending Elements

Put a comma before a word, phrase, or dependent clause tacked onto the end of an independent clause.

The counselor intended to help you, obviously.

Her advice wasn't all that bad, considering the hopelessness of the situation.

Do not be angry with her, whatever you decide to do.

She was completely honest, which suggests she had your best interests at heart.

Dependent clauses that begin with *after, as soon as, before, because, if, since, unless, until,* and *when* are not set off with a comma when they follow an independent clause:

You will feel better after you get a good night's sleep.

But dependent clauses that begin with *although, even though, though,* and *whereas* convey a contrast and are usually set off when they come after an independent clause:

The play seemed to go on for hours, although my watch said it lasted only forty minutes.

## Using Commas to Set Off Elements in the Middle

Put commas before and after a word, phrase, or dependent clause that interrupts the flow of thought in an independent clause.

Honesty, in my opinion, should always be tempered with kindness.

Being totally honest is, after all, sometimes an excuse for being cruel.

Mr. O'Malley, my friend from school, has taught me a lot about etiquette.

A noncommittal remark may be, it seems, the proper response to questions about personal appearance.

George, taking into account my frame of mind, told me that my swimsuit had beautiful colors.

My swimsuit, which is bright red and flaming orange, does fit a bit tightly.

In these last two sentences, the interrupters (the parts between commas) could be dropped out of the sentence without changing the overall meaning:

George told me that my swimsuit had beautiful colors.

My swimsuit does fit a bit tightly.

---

**TIP!** You can also use this dropout rule to decide whether to enclose an interrupter in commas.

---

## Using Dashes and Parentheses to Set Off Elements

You can also use dashes or parentheses instead of commas to set off non-independent elements.

A *dash* is a comma with clout. Dashes are used for emphasis or variety—to highlight whatever they set off.

In the twentieth century it has become almost impossible to moralize about epidemics—except those which are transmitted sexually.

—Susan Sontag

The real interest rate—the difference between the nominal rate and the rate of inflation—has averaged about three to four percent over long periods.

—Milton Friedman

If the interrupting material contains commas, dashes will help to make the sentence easier to read:

Although we are by all odds the most social of all social animals—more interdependent, more attached to each other, more inseparable in our behavior than bees—we do not often feel our conjoined intelligence.

—Lewis Thomas

---

**TIP!** Remember the difference between a hyphen and a dash: Hyphens connect, dashes separate.

On your keyboard, strike two hyphens to make a dash.

---

*Parentheses* function just the opposite of dashes. (Parentheses downplay whatever they enclose.) Use parentheses to separate material that is indirectly related or less crucial to the main idea in a sentence.

John Stuart Mill (1806–1873) promoted the idea of women's equality.

Although Ernest has lapses of memory (often forgetting what he went to the store to buy), he is the best auditor in the company.

## Using Commas to Separate Items in a Series

Put commas between elements in a series—words, phrases, or short parallel clauses. The comma before the final item (usually before the *and*) is now optional, but we recommend using it.

The restaurant in the elegant shopping mall specialized in fresh fish, lobster, shrimp, clams, and crabs.

We strolled through the mall, looked at expensive clothes, and admired the fountains.

Jeanne lusted for a diamond pin, she panted for a crystal vase, she pined for a chiffon gown, but she bought a pair of pretorn blue jeans.

---

**TIP!** **For variety you can sometimes omit the *and*:**
Some values never go out of style: love, pity, compassion, honesty.

**For emphasis, you can replace the commas with *ands*:**
We could all be more loving and compassionate and honest and caring.

---

When writing descriptive modifiers in series, put in a comma only if you could insert the word *and* between the modifiers:

Jeanne loves fresh, creamy lobster thermidor.

You could easily say "fresh *and* creamy." You could not sensibly say "creamy *and* lobster," though. Neither would you say "lobster *and* thermidor." Consider this one:

Jeanne bought pretorn, stonewashed blue jeans.

You could say "pretorn *and* stonewashed," so the comma is all right. But you can't reasonably say "stonewashed *and* blue jeans," nor would you say "blue *and* jeans."

## Using Semicolons with Items in a Series

If one or more of the items in a series already includes commas or if the individual items are lengthy, *semicolons* will increase the amount of separation and help the reader to sort out the boundaries between items:

> Thom asked me to bring wine, preferably a chablis; baby Swiss cheese; and freshly baked whole wheat rolls.

## Using Commas with Dates, Addresses, and Titles

In dates, the year is set off from the rest of the sentence with a pair of commas:

> On May 5, 1993, I'll be moving to Colorado.

If you give only the month and year, you don't need to separate them with a comma:

> July 1997 was an extremely hot month.

The elements in an address or place name are separated by commas, although a zip code is not preceded by a comma:

> My new address will be 4378 Oak Street, Englewood, Colorado 81118.
>
> Our aunt in Pine Bluff, Arkansas, sent us some gold-plated candlesticks.

If a title follows a name, separate it from the rest of the sentence with a pair of commas:

> The committee chose Delores Sanchez, attorney-at-law, to represent them.

## Using Commas to Prevent Confusion

Occasionally you may need to put in a comma simply to make the sentence easier to read:

> The main thing to remember is, do not light a match.
>
> Everything that we thought could happen, happened.
>
> Before kicking, a player may want to visualize her target.

---

**TIP!** Don't write an unclear sentence and depend on a comma to make it intelligible. If in doubt, rewrite the sentence.

---

### Exercise 11.1

Try your hand at putting commas in the following sentences to separate non-independent elements from the independent clause and to separate elements in series.

1. My father who leads a sheltered life took a dim view of my being arrested.
2. My mother however saw the injustice involved.

3. All students who can't swim must wear life jackets on the canoeing trip.

4. Melvin's cousin who can't swim has decided to stay home.

5. Date rape after all occurs in a culture that still expects men to be assertive and women to be resistant.

6. Before you complete your plans for vacationing in the Bahamas you should make plane reservations.

7. Reservations which may be submitted either by mail or by phone will be promptly acknowledged.

8. Reservations that are not secured by credit card or check will be returned.

9. If you go out please get me some cheese crackers pickles and a case of cola.

10. Anyone who wants the most from a college education must study hard.

11. Eudora who was born November 15 1950 in Santa Fe New Mexico moved to Dallas Texas before she was old enough to ski.

12. Before getting all excited let's find out if the money is real.

13. Irving can't seem to pass math although he studies for hours and hours.

14. My cousin Clarice is the tall willowy red-haired girl with the short bow-legged long-haired dog.

15. Robert Frost tells of a minister who turned his daughter his poetry-writing daughter out on the street to earn a living saying there should be no more books written.

---

# **W** hen Not to Use Commas

Remember that commas separate or set off non-independent elements from the rest of the sentence. If you toss in commas whenever you feel the need, you may confuse or mislead your readers. Here are some situations that seem particularly tempting to comma abusers.

1. *When main sentence parts are long.*
   Some writers mistakenly separate the subject from the verb or the verb from the complement. These are required parts of the independent clause and should not be separated from each other.

| (misleading) | A lively lecture followed by a good discussion, is entertaining, and instructive. |
| (clear) | A lively lecture followed by a good discussion is entertaining and instructive. |
| (misleading) | I was told by several people, that this speaker would be boring. |
| (clear) | I was told by several people that this speaker would be boring. |

In the second example, the dependent clause serves as the completer of the verb *told* and thus should not be set off with a comma.

2. *When a restrictive clause occurs in the sentence.*
   The term *restrictive* means that the modifier is necessary to the meaning of the sentence or is needed to identify the word it modifies.

| (restrictive) | People who compose on word processors can use spell checkers to catch their misspellings. |

In this example, the modifier "who compose on word processors" identifies the subject of the sentence, "people"; it tells us which people are being talked about.

| (nonrestrictive) | Sid, who composes on a word processor, is too lazy to use the spell checker. |

In this example with the subject identified as *Sid*, the modifier adds a bit of information but does so without changing the basic meaning of the sentence. Because you could drop the modifier, you set it off with commas—one before and one after.

3. *When the word* and *appears in the sentence.*
   Some people always put a comma before the word *and,* and they are probably right more than half the time. It's correct to put a comma before *and* when it joins the last item in a series or when it joins independent clauses. But when *and* does not do either of these things, a comma before it is usually inappropriate.

| (nonstandard) | His problems with spelling, and his reluctance to proofread make Ned's writing seem illiterate. |
| (standard) | His problems with spelling and his reluctance to proofread make Ned's writing seem illiterate. |

# **P** *unctuating Between Sentences*

Most of your writing will consist of multiple independent clauses. To guide your readers through your sentences and paragraphs, you need to mark the places where the independent clauses begin and end. If you don't, your writing will be confusing and difficult to follow.

There are two devices for marking the boundaries of independent clauses: conjunctions and punctuation marks. The rules for using these devices effectively are not complicated, but they offer you several choices that require thought and understanding.

## Using Periods and Other End Marks

A period, question mark, or exclamation mark provides the greatest amount of separation between independent clauses. Each of these marks tells the reader to come to a full stop.

Use a *period* to end sentences that make statements or give mild commands:

> Professional tennis players keep their eye on the ball until the point of impact with the racket.
>
> Keep you head down, and swing through the ball.

Also use a period to close an indirect question, one which reports a question instead of asking it directly:

> The players wondered whether the tournament will start on time.
>
> Many parents ask if their children need individual tutoring.

Use a *question mark* to end a direct question. Direct questions often begin with an interrogative word (such as *who, when, what, how, why,* and so forth) and usually have an inverted word order, with the verb in front of the subject.

> When will the tournament start?
>
> Does my child need individual tutoring?

Use *exclamations points* to end sentences that express strong feelings or deserve special emphasis.

> O kind missionary, O compassionate missionary, leave China! Come home and convert these Christians!
>
> —Mark Twain, "The United States of Lyncherdom"
>
> I'm mad as hell, and I'm not going to take it anymore!
>
> —Paddy Chayefsky, *Network*

---

**TIP!** Don't use an exclamation point to give punch to an ordinary sentence; instead, write a good emphatic sentence.

(ineffective)    LeRoy was in a terrible accident!

(improved)    LeRoy, whose motorcycle collided with a pickup on US 51, lies in a hospital near death.

---

## Using Coordinating Conjunctions and Commas

To mark the boundary between two independent clauses, you can use a coordinating conjunction (*and, but, or, nor, for, yet,* and *so*) with a comma before it.

> Children's reactions to grief vary, *yet* educators have found a well-defined set of common responses.
>
> Children intuitively know something is wrong, *and* they fill in the gaps with their fantasy thinking.
>
> Educators must pay attention to the warning signs, *for* the key to successful grief counseling is early intervention.
>
> Children at this age are interested in tangible things and want to know the facts about death, *but* they are also interested in causality and want to know why someone has died.

Notice, there are three coordinating conjunctions in that last example, but a comma precedes only one of them. The *ands* connect compound verb phrases (are interested in *and* want to know), not independent clauses the way the *but* does. Thus, a comma before a coordinating conjunction signals readers that another complete sentence is coming up.

If the independent clauses are short and parallel, you can use the coordinating conjunction without the comma:

> Adults seek emotional help but children do not.

---

**TIP!** If independent clauses are short and parallel in structure, separate with commas for stylistic effect.

> We shall fight on the beaches, we shall fight on the landing grounds, we shall fight in the fields and in the streets, we shall fight in the hills; we shall never surrender.
>
> —Winston Churchill

---

## Using Semicolons

A *semicolon* functions very much like a period but doesn't provide as much separation. Thus, you can use a semicolon between two independent clauses that are closely related in thought.

Gustavo Kuerten must rethink his strategy; he is losing more games than he's winning.

Perhaps he needs better equipment; a wider racquet and some lightweight tennis shoes might help him.

You should also use a semicolon to separate two independent clauses, even though they appear to be connected with a conjunctive adverb (*therefore, nevertheless, consequently, then, thus, however, indeed, furthermore, besides, otherwise, moreover, hence, meanwhile, instead*).

Practicing more might help Gustavo; however, he already practices four hours a day.

He should skip the next tournament; then he and his coach can decide how to improve his game.

For more on conjunctive adverbs, see page 182.

Notice that when independent clauses are connected with a coordinating conjunction (*and, but, or, for, nor, yet, so*), you do not need a semicolon. A comma is enough.

Practicing more might help Gustavo, but he already practices four hours a day.

He should skip the next tournament, and he and his coach can then decide how to improve his game.

---

**TIP!** Memorize the seven coordinating conjunctions—*and, but, or, for, nor, yet, so*—so you won't be fooled into mistaking a conjunctive adverb for a coordinating conjunction.

---

---

**TIP!** Both clauses connected by a semicolon should be independent clauses.

(nonstandard)  I thought surely Kuerten would win the tournament; although I didn't bet any money on him.

(standard)  I thought surely Kuerten would win the tournament, although I didn't bet any money on him.

(standard)          I thought surely Kuerten would win the tournament; I
                    didn't bet any money on him, though.

## Using Colons

You can use a *colon* to separate independent clauses, but the colon
marks more than a separation: it also signals that an explanation or
summary is coming. So use a colon between independent clauses
only when the second clause summarizes or explains the first, as
these examples demonstrate:

> John Merrick, the Elephant Man, was not a pretty sight: his forehead
> and the right side of his face were so hideously deformed that he al-
> ways wore a large bag over his head.

> The students had an inspired idea: they would publish a course guide
> for next year's class.

If the second clause poses a question, begin with a capital letter:

> Our policy makers should ask themselves this question: Are we do-
> ing everything we can to reduce poverty?

You can also use a colon after a single independent clause to
call attention to a list or a quotation.

> You will need the following supplies for this course: three camel's hair
> brushes, one 15-by-30-inch watercolor pad, and 10 tubes of paints.

> Oscar Wilde's epigrams are often thought-provoking: "The truth is
> rarely pure," he says, "and never simple."

---

**TIP!**   **In formal writing, make sure that a complete independent
clause precedes the colon. Do not use a colon after part
of a sentence, even if it contains words like *including* or
*such as*.**

(informal)          This chapter discusses punctuation marks such as: com-
                    mas, semicolons, colons, dashes, and apostrophes.

(formal)            This chapter discusses such punctuation marks as com-
                    mas, semicolons, colons, dashes, and apostrophes.

---

# M *arking Sentence Boundaries Clearly*

If you run independent clauses together without any punctuation
or with only a comma, you may confuse some readers and annoy

others. Sentences that are run together with no conjunction or no punctuation are called *fused* or *run-on sentences.*

(run-on)          Oubykh is a highly complex language it has eighty-two consonants but only three vowels.

Sentences that are separated by just a comma are called *comma splices.* A comma alone is not enough to divide independent clauses.

(comma splice)    Almost all languages change in one way or another, the written form of Icelandic is a rare exception.

## Using Conjunctive Adverbs and Semicolons

Only coordinating conjunctions—*and, but, or, nor, for, yet, so*—can link two independent clauses with just a comma. If you use another connective word with a comma, you will create a comma splice:

(comma splice)    We read our papers aloud first, then we discussed them.

Other connective words—also known as *conjunctive adverbs*—may seem like coordinating conjunctions, but they are not. Figure 11.2 provides a list of the most commonly used conjunctive adverbs.

One way to tell a conjunctive adverb from a coordinating conjunction is to see whether you can reasonably move the word around in the sentence. If you can move it, it's a conjunctive adverb:

We read the poem first; *then* we analyzed it.

We read the poem first; we *then* analyzed it.

We read the poem first; we analyzed it *then.*

If you use a conjunctive adverb between independent clauses, you must put a semicolon in front of it:

Learning a language is a challenging experience; therefore, a learner must be persistent and hardworking.

Children pick up languages easily; however, the older we get, the harder it becomes to learn a new language.

| also | however | nevertheless | still |
|------|---------|--------------|-------|
| besides | indeed | next | then |
| consequently | instead | nonetheless | therefore |
| finally | likewise | otherwise | thus |
| furthermore | meanwhile | similarly | hence |

**FIGURE 11.2** *Commonly Used Conjunctive Adverbs*

Many common transitional expressions also function as conjunctive adverbs:

| | | |
|---|---|---|
| as a result | in addition | of course |
| for example | in fact | on the other hand |

You should put a semicolon in front of these expressions when you use them between two independent clauses:

> Language acquisition is natural; in fact, every normal human child learns to speak at least one native language.

## Revising Run-Ons and Comma Splices

You can revise these two sentence boundary problems in a number of ways. You have to decide which method fits your writing situation.

1. Use a semicolon:
   Oubykh is a highly complex language; it has eighty-two consonants but only three vowels.
2. Use a period and a capital:
   Almost all languages change in one way or another. The written form of Icelandic is a rare exception.
3. Use subordination to eliminate one independent clause:
   Although almost all languages change in one way or another, the written form of Icelandic is a rare exception.
4. Use a comma plus a coordinating conjunction:
   Oubykh is a highly complex language, for it has eighty-two consonants but only three vowels.
5. Use a semicolon plus a conjunctive adverb:
   Almost all languages change in one way or another; however, the written form of Icelandic is a rare exception.

---

## Exercise 11.2

Revise any run-ons or commas splices in the following sentences. You may be able to revise them in more than one way.

1. Many people are left-handed, some of them belong to an organization called Lefthanders International.
2. Lefthanders International fights discrimination against the left-handed, it informs the public about the special problems of left-handed people.
3. More men than women are left-handed hand preference doesn't become established until about the age of six.

4. The right side of the brain controls the sense of space, in addition it governs the left side of the body.

5. Left-handed people can drive or sew or paint as well as any right-hander, still it is not easy for them to use many ordinary tools and mechanical gadgets.

6. Stores now sell objects designed especially for left-handed people these include watches, scissors, cameras, and pencil sharpeners.

7. Creativity is not the same thing as intellect, in fact there is no relation between intelligence and originality.

8. Intelligence tests measure knowledge and skill, however they do not accommodate inventiveness.

9. Creative people ask questions intelligent people want to know the answers.

10. Creative scientists have a lot in common with creative artists, they both prefer things to be complex instead of simple.

---

## Revising Exercise 11.3

Rewrite the following paragraph; revise the six run-on sentences and comma splices by using the methods described in this chapter.

### WATER SUPPLY

Years ago river water and rain water provided all the water people needed. The farmer working in the fields used river water, the people in the towns used rain water. There was no shortage in the water supply, however, population growth and town development have changed the situation. Nowadays geologists are looking for new underground reserves, engineers are trying to find cheap ways to get drinking water from the salty sea. Newspaper advertisements ask people to save water towns have passed ordinances against watering lawns in the summer, farmers who have no irrigation system fear a dry winter. Townsfolk once disliked the winter rains, they now wait for the clouds that will bring the needed water.

---

## Recognizing and Revising Sentence Fragments

A *sentence fragment*, as the term suggests, is only part of a sentence but is punctuated as if it were a complete sentence. Many accomplished writers use fragments for emphasis, or simply for convenience, as in the portions we have italicized in the following examples:

Man is the only animal that blushes. *Or needs to.*

—Mark Twain

I did not whisper excitedly about my Boyfriends. *For the best of reasons.* I did not have any.

—Gwendolyn Brooks

If there is to be a new etiquette, it ought to be based on honesty, mutual respect and responsiveness to each other's real needs. *Regardless of sex.*

—Lois Gould

Although professional writers sometimes use grammatically incomplete sentences for emphasis and variety, the writing that you do in school and in business should be in complete sentences. To make sure that you are not writing sentence fragments, you first need to be able to recognize a complete sentence. Then you need to know how to revise the fragments.

## Recognizing a Complete Sentence

A group of words must meet three grammatical tests to be a complete sentence:

1. It must contain a subject.
2. It must contain a verb.
3. It must contain at least one clause that does not begin with a subordinating word.

Groups of words that do not pass all three tests are fragments and need to be revised.

---

**TIP!** A clause is a group of words that has a subject and a verb. Subordinating words—such as *if, when, although, who, which, that*—turn independent clauses into dependent fragments.

---

### Subjects and Verbs

Look at the following examples, and notice the difference between the ones that contain a subject and a verb (the sentences) and the ones that don't (the fragments). Subjects are underlined and verbs are double underlined.

(sentence)    My <u>uncle</u> in New Jersey <u>has worked</u> in a zinc mine most of his life.

(fragment)    My uncle in New Jersey.

(sentence)    This <u>mine</u> in New Jersey <u>produces</u> the richest zinc ore in the world.

(fragment)    Produces the richest zinc ore in the world.

### Dependent Clauses

Some groups of words may contain a subject and a verb but do not pass the third test for grammatical completeness: they need at least one clause that does not begin with a subordinating word. Look at the following examples to see the difference:

(fragment)    When I was twelve years old.

(sentence)    I started mining when I was twelve years old.

(fragment)    Who worked here forty years ago or more.

(sentence)    On the walls I can read the names of miners who worked here forty years ago or more.

(fragment)    Although mining may not be the easiest job in the world.

(sentence)    Although mining may not be the easiest job in the world, I don't think it's dangerous.

(fragment)    Because the mine is never too hot or too cold.

(sentence)    I like working underground because the mine is never too hot or too cold.

Word groups that begin with a subordinating word are fragments because they *depend* on another statement to complete the thought. *When I was twelve years old* leaves the reader hanging, expecting to find out what happened when the writer was twelve years old. These word groups are called *dependent clauses.* Unlike independent clauses, which can stand alone as sentences, dependent clauses don't make complete sense by themselves. Figure 11.3 lists words that begin dependent clauses. Whenever you begin a sentence with one of these words, be sure to attach it to another clause so that the whole thought sounds complete.

### Verbal Phrase Fragments

Some groups of words that appear to be grammatically complete may be verbal phrases. These fragments usually begin with a word that looks and sounds like a verb but isn't. Some words ending in

| after | in order that | when, whenever |
|---|---|---|
| although | once | where, wherever |
| as | since | whereas |
| as if | so that | whether |
| because | than | whether |
| before | that | which |
| even though | though | while |
| ever since | unless | who, whom, whose |
| how | until | whoever |
| if, even if | what, whatever | why |

**FIGURE 11.3**  *Subordinating Words*

*-ing* (working, repairing, using) or with *to* in front of them (to love, to produce) name actions but are not complete verbs. Notice the differences in the following examples (subjects are underlined and verbs are double underlined):

| (verbal phrase) | Working underground for eighteen months. |
|---|---|
| (sentence) | <u>Daniel Flores</u> from Argentina <u><u>has been working</u></u> underground for eighteen months. |
| (verbal phrase) | To love his job in the mine. |
| (sentence) | <u>He</u> <u><u>seems</u></u> to love his job in the mine. |
| (verbal phrase) | Repairing machinery in the mine. |
| (sentence) | <u>Richard Vreeland</u> <u><u>has worked</u></u> for five years repairing machinery in the mine. |
| (verbal phrase) | Using modern machinery. |
| (verbal phrase) | To produce the richest zinc ore in the world. |
| (sentence) | The <u>miners</u> <u><u>work</u></u> nearly two thousand feet under the ground, using modern machinery to produce the richest zinc ore in the world. |

## Revising Sentence Fragments

In general, you can revise a fragment by combining it with an independent clause or by turning it into an independent clause. The following examples show you how to eliminate sentence fragments from your writing. (Fragments are italicized.)

1. A group of words that lacks a subject or verb can often be joined to the independent clause that comes before or after it:

(fragment)  A steeplejack paints and fixes church roofs, clocks, and steeples. *The highest parts of tall church buildings.*

(revised)  A steeplejack paints and fixes church roofs, clocks, and steeples—the highest parts of tall church buildings.

(fragment)  *The entire O'Neil family, Jerry O'Neil, his wife Beverly and their two sons and the sons' wives.* They all work as steeplejacks.

(revised)  The entire O'Neil family, Jerry O'Neil and his wife Beverly and their two sons and the sons' wives, all work as steeplejacks.

2. Dependent clauses can be added to a nearby independent clause or rewritten as complete sentences:

(fragment)  *Because many old church buildings became damaged by wind and water.* Their roofs began to leak, the paint peeled, and the decorations wore off.

(revised)  Because many old church buildings became damaged by wind and water, their roofs began to leak, the paint peeled, and the decorations wore off.

(fragment)  The church members then decided to hire someone to make repairs. *Which can be very expensive.*

(revised)  The church members then decided to hire someone to make repairs, which can be very expensive.

(revised)  The church members then decided to hire someone to make repairs. Such work can be very expensive.

3. Verbal phrases can be combined with an independent clause or turned into separate sentences:

(fragment)  The O'Neils enjoy working together. *Traveling around the country. Finding jobs as they go.*

(revised)  The O'Neils enjoy working together, traveling around the country and finding jobs as they go.

(revised)  The O'Neils enjoy working together. They travel around the country, finding jobs as they go.

---

**TIP!** It's O.K. to use fragments in asking and answering questions, even in formal writing.

When should the reform begin? At once.

How? By removing self-serving politicians from office.

---

---

**R***evising Exercise 11.4*

Rewrite the following paragraphs, correcting any fragments that you find. The first one has three fragments in it.

1.     Next year I am going to cooking school. I got the idea from a friend of my brother's. A business manager for a cruise line. He said that cruise ships build their reputations on the meals they serve. Which must be superbly prepared and elegantly presented. Consequently, cruise lines are always looking for chefs. Trying to find people who are well trained as expert cooks.

2.     There are many ways to exercise and have fun at the same time. Such as, swimming, hiking, or playing tennis. But some people are exercise puritans. Insisting that exercise must be serious and painful. My next door neighbor, for example, makes fun of me because I prefer walking to jogging. But I walk several miles every day. While he jogs only once or twice a week. I figure that exercise isn't going to help if a person doesn't do it regularly. So why not find something enjoyable to do?

3.     To do their work, steeplejacks have to sit on seats that hang down from ropes. Attached to the very tops of the church steeples. If you watch them at work, you can see them. Swinging gently in midair. While they repair a roof. Or replace the old numbers on a church clock. With newly painted ones. Would you have the nerve to do that kind of work? Probably not. Most people wouldn't.

---

# **C***oping with Apostrophes*

*Apostrophes* probably cause more problems than any other mark of punctuation. Many experienced writers feel shaky about using them. If you study carefully the various uses of the apostrophe, you should be able to straighten them out.

1. Use an apostrophe plus *s* with singular nouns to show possession.

| | |
|---|---|
| the length of the rope | the rope's length |
| the star of the show | the show's star |
| a lease of one year | a year's lease |

As you can see from the above examples, the *'s* ending is a substitute for a phrase beginning with *of* that shows possession.

2. Do not use an apostrophe to form the plural of a noun.
   You may have problems with the apostrophe plus *s* ending because the letter *s* gets pressed into service in a number of ways. Its most common use is to show that a noun is plural (more than one of whatever the noun names). No apostrophe is needed:

   > three professors
   > two encyclopedias
   > two athletes

3. Use an apostrophe with plurals that are possessive.

   > three professors' letters of recommendation
   > two encyclopedias' different interpretations
   > two athletes' difficulties with drugs

   You do not need another *s* after the apostrophe in the above examples because it can't be pronounced aloud.
   In deciding where to place an apostrophe to show possession with plural nouns, first write down the plural form. Then add just an apostrophe to those plurals ending in *s*.

   | Singular | Plural | Plural Possessive |
   |---|---|---|
   | lady | ladies | ladies' lunch |
   | society | societies | societies' problems |
   | bartender | bartenders | bartenders' tips |

   But if the plural does *not* end in *s*, then you have to add an apostrophe plus *s*:

   | child | children | children's clothes |
   |---|---|---|
   | man | men | men's fashions |

4. Use an apostrophe plus *s* with singular nouns ending in *s*.

   > the boss's daughter        Janis's singing
   > Keats's poetry             the albatross's curse

   If pronouncing the added '*s* would be awkward, some writers use only the apostrophe. Either use is acceptable.

   > Jesus' teachings          Jesus's teachings
   > Socrates' death           Socrates's death

5. Do not use an apostrophe with any of the possessive pronouns.
   You won't even be tempted to use an apostrophe with most of the possessive pronouns—*his, hers, theirs, ours, yours.* But one

of these pronouns—*its*—causes considerable grief because it gets confused with the contraction *it's*. Notice the difference:

That dog just bit *its* kindly owner.

*It's* an ungrateful beast.

---

**TIP!** If you simply can't keep track of the difference between *it's* and *its*, the only safe thing to do is to quit using the contraction entirely. Then all you have to remember is that *its* never takes an apostrophe.

---

6. Use an apostrophe to show omissions in contractions and numbers. The apostrophe goes where letters are left out, not where the two words are joined.

does not = doesn't (not *does'nt*)

will not = won't (not *wo'nt*)

would not = wouldn't (not *would'nt*)

class of '95 = class of 1995

---

**TIP!** Use contractions with care. Many people consider them inappropriate in academic and business writing.

---

7. If you wish, use an apostrophe in forming the plural of numerals, letters, words used as words, and abbreviations.

Your 5's look like 8's to me.

This paragraph has three *very*'s in it.

Her last name contains three m's.

The 1960's were years of great social change.

He claims to have three Ph.D.'s.

You may also correctly add the *s* with no apostrophe.

Your 5s look like 8s to me.

The 1960s were years of great social change.

---

## Exercise 11.5

Copy the following sentences, inserting an apostrophe or an apostrophe plus *s* as needed.

1. Many adults distrust of computers stems from lack of understanding the way that the machines function.

2. Childrens love of computers may indicate that they are not concerned with the machines internal workings.

3. Grade school teachers are often surprised by their students achievements on computers.

4. One students accomplishments were the main topic of talk in the teachers lounge.

5. Students attendance improves when they are allowed to do assignments in class on computers.

6. When he was given a computer, James attitude changed completely, greatly to his mothers surprise.

7. "For goodness sake," his mother exclaimed. "I used to question James intelligence."

8. Many of societys problems have been eased by computer use.

9. But the computers usefulness is offset by problems caused by programmers mistakes.

10. A computers mistake can ruin a persons credit, for instance.

---

### Exercise 11.6

Using *its* or *it's*, fill in the blanks in the following sentences with the correct form.

1. The army forces _____ recruits to do aerobic exercise.

2. Undoubtedly _____ a good idea to keep the soldiers fit.

3. The military needs _____ forces in fighting shape.

4. To gain _____ full benefits, exercise must be strenuous.

5. In order to exercise regularly, _____ helpful to have a drill sergeant to force you.

---

## P unctuating Quotations

If you want to report the actual words that someone has spoken or written, you need to enclose those words in *quotation marks*. It is customary to use a *reporting tag* to identify the person being quoted: "she said" or "he replied" or "Darwin observed" or some such phrase. For variety, these reporting tags can appear at the beginning, in the middle, or at the end of the quoted material.

## Identifying Quotations at the Beginning

Put a comma after the reporting tag and before the opening quotation marks:

> Samuel Johnson observed, "Marriage has many pains, but celibacy has no pleasures."

If you quote a full sentence, capitalize the first word in that sentence, unless it blends into the sentence that introduces it:

> In his essay on punctuation, Lewis Thomas writes, "The commas are the most useful and usable of all the stops."

> It is Thomas's opinion that "exclamation points are the most irritating of all."

## Punctuating the Ends of Quotations

If the quotation ends the sentence, put a period, a question mark, an exclamation mark, or a dash before the final quotation marks:

> The mayor announced, "Our landfills are completely full."

> The city manager asked, "What are we going to do?"

> A concerned citizen shouted, "We *must* begin recycling!"

> One board member smugly observed, "I'm recycling already, but you folks—"

The dash in this last example indicates that the speaker stopped in midsentence—or was interrupted.

If a question mark or an exclamation mark belongs to the whole sentence, not just to the quoted material, put this mark after the closing quotation marks:

> Did the mayor actually say, "Let's postpone this issue"?

> I could not believe that the mayor said to the council, "Let's table this recycling business tonight"!

If you are not reporting the exact words that were spoken, you don't need quotation marks:

> Did the mayor actually want to postpone recycling?

> He told the city council he wanted to table the recycling proposal.

## Identifying Quotations in the Middle

If your reporting tag interrupts a sentence, set it off with commas:

> "I hope," sniffed the mayor, "that we can remain civil about this matter."

If a complete sentence comes before the reporting tag, put a period after the reporting tag and capitalize the first word of the rest of the quoted material:

> "You cretin!" shouted the concerned citizen. "Can't you see that this is a pressing issue?"

> "What do you mean?" asked the mayor. "I don't feel any great need for haste."

If the reporting tag is placed between two independent clauses that are separated by a semicolon, the semicolon follows the tag:

> "Everyone needs to calm down," pleaded the city manager; "we must try to discuss this issue rationally."

## Identifying Quotations at the End

If the quoted sentence would ordinarily end in a period, put a comma before the quotation marks:

> "We must come to some decision tonight," said the city manager.

But use a question mark or an exclamation mark when it is appropriate:

> "Why do we have to decide tonight?" the mayor asked.
> "Because time is running out!" yelled the manager.

In these cases, do not add a comma as well.

## Punctuating Dialogue

When you are writing dialogue or reporting a conversation, start a new paragraph when there is a change in speaker, no matter how brief the quoted remarks may be:

> "I saw you listening to those two little creeps," she hissed.
> "Were they talking about me?"
> "I don't know," I said.
> "You don't know! Why not?"
> "They were speaking Spanish."

## Quoting Within Quotations

When you need to put quotation marks around material that is *already* inside quotation marks, use single quotation marks around the material inside.

Jim whispered, "I think I heard one of them say, 'We launch the attack as soon as it gets dark.' "

Notice that both single and double quotation marks go outside the period.

## Using Quotation Marks to Punctuate Titles

Put quotation marks around the titles of short works—such as the titles of short stories and poems that are usually part of a longer work like a book or magazine:

"Spunk"—a short story by Zora Neal Hurston

"We Real Cool"—a poem by Gwendolyn Brooks

"Not Poor, Just Broke"—an essay by Dick Gregory

"Your Reflex Systems"—a chapter in a book by Jonathan Miller

## Exercise 11.7

Copy the following paragraphs, inserting quotation marks in the appropriate places.

Motherhood is not for every woman, moaned Michelle, as she wiped up the milk. Why doesn't anyone ever tell you that having children can be hazardous to your health?

Do you mean your mental health? inquired her friend Laverne, who was holding the dripping Billy at arm's length.

That too! snapped Michelle, stripping off the milk-soaked T-shirt. This makes the third time today I've changed Billy's clothes. And it's not even afternoon yet!

But he's so cute, observed Laverne, glancing at the grinning Billy who was already planning more mischief. Isn't he your pride and joy?

Maybe, if I live through his childhood, sighed Billy's mother, I may be able to see some profit in this venture. But right now I agree with Roseanne, who says, When my husband comes home at night, if those kids are still alive—I've done my job.

# U *sing Italics (Underlining)*

Italic type slants upward to the right. We use *italics* to set off words and phrases for emphasis or special consideration. Some word processors and printers can produce italic type. In handwritten or typed papers, you underline material that would be italicized if set in type.

## Italicizing Titles and Names

We generally italicize (or underline) the titles of long or complete works. Figure 11.4 lists examples of titles to italicize.

The titles of sacred books, such as the Bible or the Koran, and of notable public documents, such as the Bill of Rights or the Constitution, are not italicized or underlined. The titles of shorter works—such as poems, short stories, songs, and essays—are enclosed in quotation marks: "My Last Duchess," "Good Country People," "Dancing in the Dark," "On Keeping a Notebook." The same is true for sections of works, such as chapter titles ("The Rise of the Middle Class") or titles of magazine articles ("An Interview with Jessica Lange").

## Italicizing Words and Phrases

We underline (italicize) foreign words and phrases that have not yet been adopted into English:

> Standing *en pointe* is useful only if the candy bars are on the top shelf.

Words and phrases used so frequently that they have become part of the English language—for example, "pasta," "bon voyage," "habeas corpus" and "karate"—do not need to be underlined or italicized. Most dictionaries will tell you whether the words you want to use should be underlined or marked for italics.

| | |
|---|---|
| **Books** | **Long Poems** |
| *The Grapes of Wrath* | *The Odyssey* |
| *The Internet for Dummies* | *In Memoriam* |
| | |
| **Plays** | **Films** |
| *The Glass Menagerie* | *Courage Under Fire* |
| *A Midsummer Night's Dream* | *Citizen Kane* |
| | |
| **Long Musical Works** | **Paintings and Sculptures** |
| Gershwin's *Rhapsody in Blue* | Rodin's *The Thinker* |
| the Beatles' *Abbey Road* | the *Mona Lisa* |
| | |
| **Television and Radio Programs** | **Magazines and Newspapers** |
| *Chicago Hope* | the *St. Louis Post Dispatch* |
| *All Things Considered* | *Entertainment Weekly* |

**FIGURE 11.4** *Titles to Italicize*

We also underline or italicize words, letters, or numbers referred to as words:

> In current usage, the pronouns *he, him,* and *his* outnumber *she, her,* and *hers* by a ratio of almost 4 to 1.

> Some people have trouble pronouncing the letter *r,* especially when it follows an *i* or an *a.*

### Using Italics for Emphasis

Underlining or italics can add emphasis to written language:

> We want our freedom *today,* not tomorrow.

But this means of adding emphasis is obvious and easy to overdo. It is usually more effective to create emphasis through sentence structure and word choice.

## U *sing Hyphens*

1. Use a *hyphen* to connect two or more words that go together to modify a noun.

> hard-hearted lover          up-to-date sources
> lighter-than-air balloon    world-renowned pianist

Do not hyphenate the modifiers when they come after the noun.

> lover with a hard heart     sources that are up to date
> balloon lighter than air    pianist who is world renowned

Do not use a hyphen between an *-ly* adverb and the word it modifies:

> a hopelessly dull person     a happily divorced couple

2. Use a hyphen to connect *all-, self-, ex-* and *-elect* to other words.

> self-esteem     ex-wife     all-important     governor-elect

Never use a hyphen with the following words:

> yourself     himself     itself
> themselves   herself     oneself
> ourselves    myself      selfless

3. Use a hyphen when spelling out fractions and compound numbers from twenty-one to ninety-nine.

   People over fifty-five make up almost two-fifths of the population.

4. Use a hyphen to avoid ambiguous or awkward combinations of letters. For instance, *re-creation* means "create anew"; the hyphen distinguishes it from *recreation,* which means "a refreshing or diverting activity." Words like *anti-inflammatory, cross-stitch,* and *bell-like* are easier to read with the hyphens.

5. Consult a dictionary about compound words: some are two words, some are hyphenated, some are written as a single word. Usage changes rapidly and is unpredictable. Even compounds that begin with the same word are treated differently: blue cheese, blue-collar, blueprint.

6. Use a hyphen to divide a word at the end of a line of type. Words can be divided only between syllables. Consult your dictionary when in doubt. The tendency today is to *avoid* dividing words if at all possible.

# 12

# *Working with Verbs*

You probably remember from somewhere back in junior high school that in English subjects have to agree with their verbs in *number*, meaning a singular subject takes a singular verb and a plural subject takes a plural verb. And then there are irregular verbs, which lots of people have trouble with. Most of the time getting your verbs right is easy, but complications can occur.

## G *etting Subjects and Verbs to Agree*

When the Bible declares that "the wages of sin is death," we're not supposed to question—either grammatically or theologically. But if you write, "The wages at McDonald's is lousy," you'll likely get corrected by someone saying your subject–verb agreement is off. There's no point in protesting the inequity of this double standard. Just grant poetic license to the Bible and concentrate on making your own subjects and verbs agree.

### Singular Verb Forms

In English the only singular verb form occurs in the present tense. We add an -s or -es ending to a present-tense verb when its subject is a singular noun or the pronoun *he, she,* or *it.* (In the examples throughout this chapter, subjects are underlined and verbs are double underlined.)

> Our biology instructor wants us to write three lab reports a week. She expects them to be handed in on Friday.

My <u>roommate</u> <u>washes</u> his hair twice a day. He <u>flosses</u> his teeth after every meal.

That <u>color</u> <u>looks</u> good on you; it <u>matches</u> your eyes.

Two verbs—*have* and *be*—are exceptions to this rule. *Have* changes to *has*, and *be* changes to *is*.

My <u>uncle</u> <u>has</u> false teeth.

He <u>is</u> only thirty-five years old.

*Be* is the only verb that has a singular form in the past tense. Use *was* with *I*, with singular nouns, or with *he, she*, or *it*.

I <u>was</u> late for class yesterday.

My <u>teacher</u> <u>was</u> not happy with me.

Otherwise, use *were*.

The other <u>students</u> <u>were</u> all on time.

Most of the time, subject–verb agreement poses no problem. With a plural subject (*wages*), supply a plural verb (*are*), and everybody's happy:

The <u>wages</u> at McDonald's <u>are</u> lousy.

Only it's not always that simple, because people don't always use the normal subject-followed-by-verb sentence pattern. In this chapter, we'll explain a few of the less-than-simple situations. For variety, writers shuffle the order around so that sometimes the verb gets ahead of the subject—or sometimes modifiers crop up between the subject and verb, causing confusion. Another construction you need to watch out for involves *expletives*, words that often pose alluringly as subjects, even though they're not. You also have to be alert for collective nouns and indefinite pronouns, which can sometimes lead to agreement problems.

## Subject–Verb Reversals in Questions

You naturally expect one of the first words in a sentence to be the *subject*—what the sentence is about. Usually the *verb* follows, explaining what's going on with the subject or what the situation is:

These <u>papayas</u> <u>taste</u> delicious.

But questions often reverse this normal order:

Where <u>are</u> the <u>papayas</u>?

---

**TIP!** **To find the subject, turn the question into a statement.**
If you make a statement out of a question, the subject usually ends up at the beginning of the sentence:

> The papayas are where.

---

As you can see, the reversal won't necessarily make sense. But the real subject becomes clear—*papayas* (plural), so the verb should be *are* (plural). No problem.

The going sometimes gets tricky when the questions get longer:

(wrong)    Which version of the ending has the show's producers decided to use?

If you turn that into a statement, you can see that the agreement is off:

(wrong)    The show's producers has decided to use which version of the ending.

Because the subject—*producers*—clearly is plural, you need a plural verb:

> The show's producers have decided to use which version of the ending.

(right)    Which version of the ending have the show's producers decided to use?

If you have difficulty with agreement in questions, get into the habit of quickly changing them into statements as part of your editing process. Once you get the subject and verb in the normal order, you're not likely to go wrong.

### Subject–Verb Reversals for Style

Sometimes you may deliberately put a verb ahead of its subject as a stylistic device. If not overdone, this technique is a dandy. The variation from the expected sentence pattern automatically produces emphasis:

(wrong)    In poverty, injustice, and discrimination lie the cause of many social problems.

But just glance at that sentence again. What is the subject? Not *poverty, injustice, and discrimination:* those words are the object of the preposition *in.* Because a noun can't serve as the subject *and* as an object in the same sentence, you need to look elsewhere. The subject actually is *cause*—and *the cause lie* doesn't sound right. It should be *the cause lies* or *the causes lie.* You could change either word, but both words have to be singular or both plural to make subjects and verbs agree.

(right)    In poverty, injustice, and discrimination lies the cause of many social problems.

(right)    In poverty, injustice, and discrimination lie the causes of many social problems.

Of course, we know that most people who aren't composition teachers probably wouldn't be much bothered by the lack of agreement in that sentence. But see if you pick up the problem in this less complex construction:

(wrong)    Here comes the defending champions.

The sentence should read,

(right)    Here <u>come</u> the defending <u>champions</u>.

---

**TIP!**  *Here* and *There* can never be subjects.
If a sentence begins with *here* or *there,* turn the sentence around, find the true subject, and make the verb agree.

(right)    There <u>are</u> a few *flaws* in your plan.

(right)    Here <u>is</u> a small *case* of larceny.

---

## Agreement with Intervening Modifiers

Sometimes even when the subject–verb order is normal, a modifier gets sandwiched between them and confuses things:

(wrong)    The seriousness of these injustices have been revealed to the public.

*Injustices have been revealed* sounds fine, but the subject of that sentence happens to be *seriousness,* with *injustices* serving as object of the preposition *of* (which means that it can't also be the subject). So, how does *The seriousness have been revealed* sound? Not good, since *seriousness* is clearly singular. The sentence should read,

(right)    The <u>seriousness</u> of these injustices <u>has been revealed</u> to the public.

Because this problem won't be revealed by simply turning the sentence around, let's look at a few more examples. You have to recognize the intervening modifiers and take them out in order to get the subject and verb next to each other. Try this sentence:

(wrong) The boredom of dusting furniture, folding laundry, cleaning floors, cooking meals, and washing dishes have driven many women to drink.

Doesn't sound bad, does it? But actually, all of these plural-sounding tasks are objects of the preposition *of.* The true subject is singular—*boredom.* The sentence should read,

(right) The <u>boredom</u> of dusting furniture, folding laundry, cleaning floors, cooking meals, and washing dishes <u>has driven</u> many women to drink.

Here's one more example:

(wrong) Ling's reasons for developing his gymnastics style was essentially the same as Jahn's—to promote nationalism.

*Style was* sounds fine. But *style* is not the subject. It's the object of the gerund *developing;* the subject is *reasons.* So, *reasons was* can't be right. The verb needs to be plural:

(right) Ling's <u>reasons</u> for developing his gymnastics style <u>were</u> essentially the same as Jahn's—to promote nationalism.

## Agreement with Compound Subjects

Sentences having *compound subjects* (meaning more than one subject) usually cause no bother. With singular compound subjects connected by *and,* you can apply simple arithmetic:

The <u>pitcher</u> and the <u>catcher</u> <u>are</u> both fine players.

*Pitcher + catcher* = 2 people = plural subject requiring plural verb. But matters can get a tad more complicated:

1. *When you have more than one singular subject connected with "but," "or," or "nor."*
   These subjects take singular verbs, even though the idea expressed may be plural:

   Not only the pitcher <u>but</u> the catcher also <u>is</u> tired.

   Both are tired, but the verb arbitrarily should be singular. Go figure. If you use *nor,* the agreement is at least a bit more logical:

   Neither the pitcher <u>nor</u> the catcher <u>is playing</u> well.

   Both are still tired but neither one is playing well.

2. *When you have one singular and one plural subject.*
The verb agrees with the one that is closest:

> Champagne or sad <u>movies</u> <u>remind</u> me of you
> Sad movies or <u>champagne</u> <u>reminds</u> me of you.

3. *When you have subjects that sound plural but really are not.*
Singular subjects followed by any of these terms remain singular:

| | | |
|---|---|---|
| with | like | along with |
| besides | including | together with |
| as well as | namely | no less than |

The meaning of the sentence may be distinctly plural but the subject is still grammatically singular:

> The Attorney General, as well as the President, is responsible for the decision.

Obviously, two people are responsible, but the verb remains faithful to the singular subject. This next example is more logical:

> Seymour, together with his St. Bernard, his pet alligator, and his seventeen goldfish, is planning to move in with us.

Although the group moving in is incontestably plural, only Seymour is doing the planning.

---

**TIP!**   Commas often set off these troublesome constructions, giving you a good clue that the subject remains separate.

---

## The Expletive *There*

Although an indispensable little word, the expletive *there* causes more than its share of bother. An *expletive* is a filler word that stands enticingly at the beginning of a sentence, looking for all the world like the subject, when actually it's nothing of the kind. It's just taking up space until the real subject comes along.

---

**TIP!**   *There* can never be a subject.

---

The word *there* is either an expletive or an adverb. You need to find out what the subject really is before sliding in a verb.

(wrong)   There is among all the weeds in my garden several exquisite begonias.

The actual subject is *begonias:*

(right)    There <u>are</u> among all the weeds in my garden several exquisite <u>begonias.</u>

***Expletives in Questions*** Don't forget that *there* can complicate
questions as well as statements (and *there* won't necessarily be the
very first word, either):

(wrong)    Is there in this line of work many opportunities for advancement?

Ask yourself, *what* is? Answer: *opportunities is.* But *opportunities* always *are*, so the verb needs changing. Or you can make those *opportunities* singular and write the sentence that way.

(right)    <u>Are</u> there in this line of work many <u>opportunities</u> for advancement?

(right)    <u>Is</u> there in this line of work any <u>opportunity</u> for advancement?

## Collective Nouns and Indefinite Pronouns

*Collective nouns*, which name a group or a collection of people,
are usually considered singular:

Theodore's <u>family is</u> quite small.

Our school <u>orchestra plays</u> extremely well.

The <u>audience was clapping</u> wildly.

Sometimes, if the members of the group are acting as individuals,
a plural verb is used to indicate that the group is not considered a
single unit:

The curriculum <u>committee disagree</u> on every issue.

Our old <u>gang have gone</u> their separate ways.

---

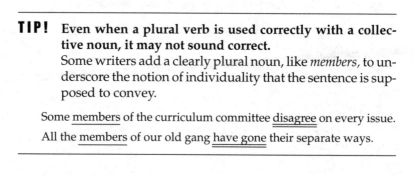

**TIP!**  **Even when a plural verb is used correctly with a collective noun, it may not sound correct.**
Some writers add a clearly plural noun, like *members*, to un-
derscore the notion of individuality that the sentence is supposed to convey.

Some <u>members</u> of the curriculum committee <u>disagree</u> on every issue.

All the <u>members</u> of our old gang <u>have gone</u> their separate ways.

---

Several collective nouns (such as *rest, remainder,* and *number*) and some *indefinite pronouns* (*some, all, enough, neither,* and *none*) can be either singular or plural, depending on how they are used:

(singular)     The <u>rest</u> of the movie <u>is</u> sloppy and sentimental.

(plural)     The <u>rest</u> of us <u>are</u> leaving.

(singular)     <u>Some</u> of the players <u>are</u> already on the bus.

(plural)     <u>Some</u> of the pizza <u>has</u> anchovies on it.

(singular)     <u>All</u> of the seats <u>are</u> taken.

(plural)     <u>All</u> of the pizza <u>is</u> stone cold by now.

---

**TIP!**  When referring to *a number,* use a plural verb; when referring to *the number,* use a singular verb.

<u>A number</u> of students <u>are</u> ill; <u>the number</u> <u>is</u> getting larger every day.

---

When the indefinite pronouns *none* and *neither* are used alone, they take a singular verb:

(singular)     <u>None</u> <u>is</u> immune to this disease.

(singular)     <u>Neither</u> <u>has</u> arrived.

But when followed by phrases with a plural meaning, usage varies:

(plural)     <u>None</u> of us <u>are</u> ever going to eat there again.

(singular)     <u>None</u> of us <u>is</u> sick today, at least.

---

**TIP!**  Be warned that some writers and editors insist that *none* and *neither* should always be singular.

---

The rest of the indefinite pronouns are singular and cause little trouble with verbs: *anyone, something, any, anybody, each, either, everybody, everyone, everything, nobody, no one, somebody, someone.*

<u>Anyone</u> <u>is allowed</u> to attend.

<u>Everything</u> <u>seems</u> in order.

<u>Somebody</u> <u>is pounding</u> on the door.

## Exercise 12.1

Revise any of these sentences whose subjects and verbs do not agree. Some may be correct.

1. A child's personality and behavior is influenced to a great extent by environment.
2. In this new stage of our relationship comes new adjustments.
3. There has never been any concerted attempts to solve the mystery.
4. Financial support, like volunteer workers and effective speakers, are hard to get.
5. Movies packed with violence is still a favorite with the public.
6. There by the bank of that stream is a mass of lovely flowers.
7. Melba Starstruck, along with her agent, her latest husband, and her Bengal tiger, are staying at the Plaza.
8. In the center of the superstore lies various departments ranging from electronics to kitchenware.
9. Where has my toothbrush and the toothpaste gone?
10. The prime audience for advertising, mainly young people, are an easy target.

---

## Exercise 12.2

If you still feel shaky about subject–verb agreement, see how you do choosing the correct word in the following sentences.

1. There (is/are) Yolanda and Chris, talking furiously.
2. Bananas and peanut butter (make/makes) a tasty snack.
3. Peanut butter or bananas (make/makes) a tasty snack.
4. The major impact of these statistics (has/have) not yet been analyzed.
5. Ingesting tar, as well as nicotine, (cause/causes) cigarette smoking to be hazardous to your health.

---

# W atching Out for Irregular Verbs

Although sometimes the language seems irritatingly irregular, English is actually a well-patterned language. Only because we are accustomed to its regularity do we get thrown off track by its quirks—like irregular verbs.

Verbs in English regularly form their past tense and their past participle by adding *-d* or *-ed* or *-t*. The past participle is the form used with the helping verbs *has, have,* or *had* and with forms of *be* in passive verbs (*are used, was seen, will be changed*).

I <u>hope</u> today,    I <u>hoped</u> yesterday,    I <u>have hoped</u> always.

I <u>laugh</u> today,    I <u>laughed</u> yesterday,    I <u>had laughed</u> before.

I <u>spend</u> today,    I <u>spent</u> yesterday,    I <u>have spent</u> too much.

As you can see, the past tense and past participle are the same for regular verbs.

But with irregular verbs, you just have to memorize the principal parts. Here are the most common irregular verbs:

| PRESENT | PAST | PAST PARTICIPLE |
|---|---|---|
| bring | brought | brought |
| begin | began | begun |
| break | broke | broken |
| burst | burst | burst |
| choose | chose | chosen |
| come | came | come |
| do | did | done |
| drag | dragged | dragged (not drug) |
| drink | drank | drunk |
| forget | forgot | forgotten (or forgot) |
| get | got | gotten |
| go | went | gone |
| lay | laid | laid (meaning placed) |
| lead | led | led |
| lie | lay | lain (meaning reclined) |
| ride | rode | ridden |
| rise | rose | risen |
| run | ran | run |
| see | saw | seen |
| swim | swam | swum |
| take | took | taken |
| wake | waked (or woke) | waked (or woke) |

You can also look up the principal parts of verbs in your dictionary. If you don't find any listed, that means the verb is regular, adding -*d*, -*ed*, or -*t*.

## Dictionary *Exercise 12.3*

Look up in a dictionary the principal parts of these verbs:

climb                          dive

freeze                         awake

| | |
|---|---|
| say | go |
| drown | shine |
| eat | drag |

Were any alternate forms presented? Did any of the answers surprise you? If so, why?

---

## Exercise 12.4

In the following sentences, insert the form of the verb given in parentheses beforehand. Check the verbs against the list on p. 208. The first one is done for you as an example.

1. (*break:* past participle) You have _broken_ your promise.
2. (*lay:* past) Yesterday I _____ my watch on the sink.
3. (*lie:* past) She was so tired that she _____ down.
4. (*set:* past) I _____ my watch ten minutes fast.
5. (*lie:* past participle) We had just _____ down when the telephone rang.
6. (*lay:* past participle) The goalie _____ down his face mask and chin protector.
7. (*drown:* past) His son almost _____ in the pool.
8. (*cost:* past participle) It has _____ me a lot to move.
9. (*go:* past participle) She has _____ to Arkansas.
10. (*begin:* past participle) I have just _____ to fight.
11. (*see:* past) The director _____ to it that I knew my part.
12. (*bring:* past participle) What have you _____ to the picnic?
13. (*be:* past participle) They had _____ soundly defeated.
14. (*do:* past participle) You have _____ it again.
15. (*swim:* past) We _____ to the other side of the lake.

---

## S *taying in the Same Tense*

Sometimes your prose gets rolling along and you shift into the wrong gear while moving, which causes an unpleasant grinding noise in your readers' heads. You should choose either present or past tense and stay with it. *Tense* in verbs has nothing to do with being uptight; it just indicates time. Here's an example of present tense:

Carlos <u>is swimming</u> in his running shorts.

Past tense would be

Carlos <u>was swimming</u> yesterday too.

Carlos <u>has been swimming</u> every day this week.

Tenses exhibit a good bit of variety. There's no need to go into all of the varieties here, but the thing to remember is to choose one tense and stay in it—unless you have some reason, like this, to change:

Carlos <u>is swimming</u> today, but yesterday <u>he played</u> tennis.

Here's an example of a faulty tense shift, the kind that happens by accident and needs to be changed when you revise:

(inconsistent)    Carlos <u>was swimming</u> across the pool, when suddenly he <u>sinks</u> under the water and <u>failed</u> to come up. I <u>yell</u> and <u>jumped</u> in to rescue him, when he <u>shoots</u> to the surface and <u>laughed</u> at me.

The passage sounds much better this way:

(consistent)    Carlos <u>was swimming</u> across the pool, when suddenly he <u>sank</u> under the water and <u>failed</u> to come up. I <u>yelled</u> and <u>jumped</u> in to rescue him, when he <u>shot</u> to the surface and <u>laughed</u> at me.

---

**TIP!**   Be consistent: choose present tense or past tense and stick with it.

---

## The Literary Present Tense

If you are writing about literature, you will probably want to use the present tense even though you may be referring to works written decades ago, authors long dead, and characters never alive. The use of the present tense makes sense if you consider that the works, the authors, and the characters still live in our imaginations.

*Adventures of Huckleberry Finn* by Mark Twain <u>is</u> one of our greatest American novels.

Despite his deep and abiding cynicism, Mark Twain <u>remains</u> our most famous American humorist.

Huck Finn <u>tells</u> fibs to get himself and Jim out of scrapes, yet honesty <u>is</u> one of his great virtues.

## Writing Exercise 12.5

Think about some person, some friend or relative, whom you have known for years. How has this person changed? How does he or she act toward you now that you are older? Write a paragraph describing how your friend or relative has changed. Use present tense verbs to describe how the person is now and past tense verbs to describe how the person used to be.

## Revising Exercise 12.6

The following paragraph contains uncalled-for tense shifts. First, revise it to make all the verbs present tense; then go through it again to make all the verbs past tense.

(1) Bowser, the huge sheepdog who lives next door, had a shaggy coat and a loud, resounding bark. (2) He was friendly and loves to be petted, but his size frightened children. (3) He got so excited when kids came around that he knocks them down like bowling pins. (4) So he spent his time barking at squirrels, or else he gallops along the fence and terrorized our tiny fox terrier. (5) Bowser really needed to live on a farm and have animals his own size to play with.

# 13

# Managing Pronouns and Modifiers

Pronouns, for the most part, don't cause any more bother than do nouns, the words they replace. But you remember that pronouns must agree with their antecedents in number (singular or plural) and gender (male or female). Gender never causes agreement problems, but agreement in number can get tricky.

And although modifiers usually know their place, an occasional one will stray off and nudge up next to the wrong word, leaving your readers either puzzled or amused. But more on that later. We'll take up pronouns first.

## S orting Out Agreement with Indefinite Pronouns

The indefinite pronouns that have been decreed singular (such as *everyone, everybody, anyone, anybody, everything*) can cause confusion with the pronouns referring to them. Consider these grammatically correct sentences:

*Everyone* applauded, and I was glad *he* did.

After *everybody* finished writing, the instructor passed among *him* and collected the papers.

The lack of logic in such constructions has always made the agreement rule difficult to follow. So standard usage is changing to allow these once singular indefinites to be followed by plural pronouns:

*Everyone* should wear *their* seat belts.

*None* of those arrested would admit *they* were involved.

This change takes care of what used to be a truly troublesome problem with pronoun agreement.

---

**TIP!**  Be warned: some people out there will not like this usage. Some may declare you in error if you write *everyone* followed by *their*. To avoid ruffling such readers, you can use both singular pronouns:

*Everyone* should wear *his or her* seatbelt.

*None* of those arrested would admit *he or she* was involved.

Or rewrite to avoid the issue:

Everyone should wear a seatbelt.

None of those arrested would admit to being involved.

---

## S trategies for Avoiding Sexist Pronouns

If your indefinite pronoun is singular in meaning, standard English once required you to write,

*Each* student must show *his* permit to register.

Writers now take care to avoid sexist language that makes all people appear to be male. You can totally eliminate the difficulty by writing in the plural:

*Students* must show *their* permits to register.

Or you can revise this way:

*Each* student must show *a* permit to register.

Occasionally, you may need to write a sentence in which you emphasize the singular, like this one:

*Each* individual must speak *his* own mind.

But the sentence will be just as emphatic this way:

*Each one of us* must speak *our* own mind.

---

**TIP!**   **If you write in the plural, the problem disappears.**

---

> **E**xercise 13.1

In the following sentences, select one or more pronouns to fill in the blanks. If you can't think of suitable words, rewrite the sentences in the plural.

1.  Anyone living outside of town should leave _____ job early to avoid getting _____ car stuck in a snow drift.

2.  A good student does _____ own homework.

3.  Someone has left _____ car lights on.

4.  Anyone wishing to improve _____ tennis game should work on _____ backhand.

5.  Each must cast _____ own vote.

---

# **C** onfusion with the Pronouns **This** and **Which**

Most of the time when you use the pronoun *this,* your meaning is clear. You say, "This is my new tennis racquet," and because you're standing there holding it, your meaning is understood. But at other times, we use *this* to refer to ideas or events, and if the pronoun gets too far from its antecedent (the idea or event it refers to), your meaning becomes hazy.

---

**TIP!**   **Whenever you use the word "this," try to follow it with a noun telling what "this" refers to.**

---

If you're going to write,

> The importance of this becomes clear when we understand the alternatives.

at least give your readers a clue: this *plan,* this *principle,* this *problem,* this *stipulation,* this *qualification,* this *dichotomy,* this *stalemate,* this whatever. And if you have trouble supplying a noun to follow *this,* that's nature's way of telling you that the whole idea is vague, and you need to go back and clarify what *this* means in your own mind before you totally befuddle your readers.

The word *which* causes similar problems. Often this handy pronoun refers to an entire clause preceding it. Sometimes the meaning is clear, sometimes not. Suppose you write,

(wrong)   Jolyne has received only one job offer, which depresses her.

That sentence can be interpreted two ways:

Jolyne is depressed about receiving only one job offer, even though it's a fairly good one.

or

Jolyne has received only one job offer—a depressing one, at that.

Whenever you use the word *which*, make sure that your readers will be able to tell exactly what it means.

### Exercise 13.2

Revise the following sentences to eliminate any unclear pronoun reference.

1. Al asked if Carlos allowed a speck of egg yolk or a particle of grease to get into the egg whites. This might keep the whites from fluffing up the way they should.
2. Jamal ate Chinese food and went out jogging, which caused him to feel unwell.
3. Eating a simple meal in an outdoor setting, which I prefer, relaxes me after a hard day.
4. This makes all my symptoms of stress disappear.
5. I was late and skipped dinner, which got me in trouble.

## Choosing Pronoun Case: I or Me? He or Him?

Nouns do not change form when they move from being subjects to objects in a sentence. For instance, you can write,

Kesha resembles my sister.

My sister resembles Kesha.

But alas, as a holdover from Old English, pronouns still show *case* (subjective, objective, or possessive). So, with pronouns, we write,

*She* resembles my sister.

My sister resembles *her*.

The case forms are easy.

| SUBJECT | OBJECT | POSSESSIVE |
|---------|--------|------------|
| I | me | my, mine |
| he | him | his |
| she | her | her, hers |
| you | you | your, yours |
| it | it | its |
| we | us | our, ours |
| they | them | their, theirs |
| who | whom | whose |
| whoever | whomever | whosever |

Except for the confusion of *its* with the contraction *it's* and *whose* with *who's*, the possessives are easy to use correctly. But writers must make choices among the other forms in constructions like these:

1. *When you have more than one subject or object.*

(wrong)    Seymour and *me* went to a lecture.

(right)    Seymour and *I* went to a lecture.

(wrong)    LaWanda sat with Seymour and *I*.

(right)    LaWanda sat with Seymour and *me*.

---

**TIP!** **Drop the word before (or after) the "and" to see how the pronoun sounds alone.**

> *Me* went to a lecture or *I* went to a lecture?

> LaWanda sat with *I* or LaWanda sat with *me*?

Your choice is now a no-brainer.

---

**TIP!** **Although prepositions are usually short words (*in, on, at, by, for* and the like), a few are deceptively long—*through, beside, among, underneath, between*.**
Long or short, prepositions always take object pronouns:

> between Clyde and *me*

> among Clyde, Clarence, and *him*

> beside Clyde and *me*

---

2. *When pronouns are used as appositives.*
   You remember what appositives are. They go like this:

   | | |
   |---|---|
   | we football fans | us football fans |
   | we pizza lovers | us pizza lovers |
   | we students | us students |
   | we teachers | us teachers |

   Whether you choose *we* or *us* depends on whether the construction is the subject or the object.

   | | |
   |---|---|
   | (wrong) | *Us* fitness freaks are slaves to exercise. |
   | (right) | *We* fitness freaks are slaves to exercise. |
   | (wrong) | Weather can be bad news for *we* joggers. |
   | (right) | Weather can be bad news for *us* joggers. |

---

**TIP!** **If you're in doubt, just drop the appositive.**
Would you say *"Us* are slaves" or *"We* are slaves"? Your ear should tell you that *we* is the correct choice. And would it be "bad weather for *we*" or "bad weather for *us*?" Of course, it's "bad weather for *us*."

---

3. *When pronouns are used in comparisons.*

   | | |
   |---|---|
   | (wrong) | My sister is smarter than *me.* |
   | (right) | My sister is smarter than *I.* |

---

**TIP!** **Just finish the incomplete comparison in your mind.**
Would you say, "My sister is smarter than *me* am"? If so, you're right about your sister but wrong about the pronoun. Most of us would say, "smarter than *I* am."

---

4. *When choosing between "who" and "whom."*
   In speaking, you don't have to worry about this choice any more; you can just use *who* in any construction. But if you're writing, you're expected to figure out whether to use the subject *who* or the object *whom.*

   Kate Chopin was a superb writer (who/whom) literary critics have neglected until recently.

**TIP!**   **Substitute the subject pronoun "he" (or "she") or the object pronoun "him" (or "her").**
Ask yourself, "Critics have neglected *she*"? or
            "Critics have neglected *her*"?
We would all choose *her*, of course. Because *her* is an object, the sentence needs the object *whom*:

> Kate Chopin was a superb writer *whom* literary critics have neglected until recently.

**TIP!**   **You can avoid the choice by using "that":**

> Kate Chopin was a superb writer *that* literary critics have neglected until recently.

Although some people still find this usage distasteful, it is now standard English.

**TIP!**   **Do not substitute "which" for "who" or "whom."**
Standard usage still does not allow *which* to refer to people.

(wrong)     the woman *which* I adore

(right)     the woman *whom* I adore

(right)     the woman *that* I adore

### Exercise 13.3

Choose the correct pronoun in each sentence.

1. You can't win if you run against Orville and (she/her).
2. At the prom next Saturday, Ashley and (I/me) are going to wear blue jeans.
3. For too long, (we/us) taxpayers have been at the mercy of Congress.
4. (Who/Whom) is going to deliver the keynote address?
5. Jose went to visit his mother (who/whom) he called "Muma."
6. Stanley and (I/me) are planning to become vegetarians as soon as we finish our Big Macs.
7. Did both (she/her) and Cecil promise to come early to help?
8. The Senator is the person on (who/whom) I base all hope of the future.

9. We should be spared commercials (who/whom/that/which) are an insult to our intelligence.

10. We arranged to study for the big exam with Selina and (she/her).

# R *evising Dangling and Misplaced Modifiers*

The word *modify* means to change. Thus a modifier in a sentence changes in some way the meaning of whatever it modifies. Here's a sentence with no modifiers:

Maria graduated.

We'll add a couple of modifiers in italics:

*Yesterday* Maria graduated *with honors.*

Positioning modifiers is usually easy, but sometimes they get stranded with nothing to modify—or else they stray off and modify the wrong thing, as in the following examples. The first is from the *Daily Bulletin,* the campus newspaper of the University of Tennessee:

In 1978, Tennessee became the first state to adopt a child passenger protection law requiring the parents of children under four years of age to be restrained in a child safety seat.

From the *San Bernadino Sun:*

A mountain lion suspected of killing at least two suburban dogs was shot to death after a state warden spotted it taking a report near the scene of the latest attack.

## Repairing Dangling Modifiers

Modifiers that dangle aren't always funny. They can be annoying because they indicate that the writer isn't paying attention:

Driving through the lush, pine-scented forest, the air was suddenly fouled by the sulphurous belchings of a paper mill.

Clearly, the *air* isn't driving though the forest. The opening modifier dangles with nothing in the sentence to modify. You can revise in a couple of ways:

As we drove through the lush, pine-scented forest, the air was suddenly fouled. . . .

Driving through the forest, we gasped as the air was suddenly fouled. . . .

To catch wayward modifiers, read your last draft carefully, paying attention to each sentence individually.

**TIP!**   **Modifiers often dangle in passive constructions, so take special care with the passive voice.**
The passive voice allows you to omit the person or entity doing the acting, thus positively inviting dangling modifiers:

(faulty)   Knowing that the airliner was off course, only two conclusions can be drawn.

Clearly, it wasn't the "conclusions" that knew the plane was off course. Whoever did the knowing got left out of the sentence entirely. When you revise in active voice, you'll need to supply a subject for the modifier:

(revised)   Knowing that the airliner was off course, *the investigators* could draw only two conclusions.

## Moving Misplaced Modifiers

Misplaced modifiers may not be quite as annoying as dangling ones, but they can still mess up the meaning of your sentence:

(faulty)   Once married, the Church considers that a couple has signed a lifelong contract.

The Church isn't getting married, so you need to move the modifier:

(revised)   The Church considers that a couple, once married, has signed a lifelong contract.

Sometimes a misplaced modifier can badly skew the meaning of a sentence, as in this example taken from a college newspaper:

(faulty)   DARE is sponsoring a series of presentations on drugs for college students.

That sentence wrongly gives the impression that DARE is in the business of acquainting college students with drugs to use. The meaning is less ambiguous this way:

(revised)   DARE is sponsoring a series of presentations for local college students on the dangers of drug use.

As you revise, check your sentences for lapses in logic caused by misplaced modifiers.

### $E$*xercise 13.4*

Revise the following sentences to eliminate all misplaced or dangling modifiers. You may need to add information to help some of these make sense.

1. After deciding which section will be sewn first, the material must then be cut.
2. I had been driving for forty years when I fell asleep and had an accident.
3. Otis was robbed at gun point in the elevator where he lives.
4. At college I hope to start singing with a scholarship.
5. A crutch is a device used to take weight off an injured leg by sticking it under the arm and leaning on it.
6. I do not see my Aunt Frieda much in Colorado.
7. With this total lack of responsibility, more and more items were purchased.
8. Consider this letter to the editor of an urban newspaper a few years ago.
9. The poem exemplifies the patriarchal success of the socialization of women.
10. After reading the essays, papers were written discussing the ideas.

---

## Exercise 13.5

Explain how the following sentences might be misread. Then rewrite them to make the meaning clear and unambiguous.

1. The company packages natural meals for children that can be shipped anywhere.
2. North Dakota citizens' groups are sending volunteers to help flood relief workers in Manitoba.
3. The Senate plans to resume consideration of legislation to restrict campaign contributions next week.
4. Phil Jackson signed a $5.7 million contract to coach the Bulls yesterday.
5. A municipal task force announced its plan to increase parking at a city hall press conference.
6. The plan will increase parking in congested areas.
7. The representative called for a meeting to talk about increasing teenage drug use with members of Congress.
8. They wanted their ordeal to end desperately.
9. The Grishams decided their daughter would be a lawyer before she was ten years old.
10. The restaurant had many autographs of celebrities on the walls that had eaten there.

# 14

# A User's Guide to Troublesome Words and Phrases

*Usage* means the way the language is used. But different people use the language in different ways. And even the same people use the language differently on different occasions. You probably speak one way in the classroom or on the job and another way at a party or a ball game. Good usage, then, is a matter of using language *appropriate* to the occasion.

In this chapter, we describe the current usage of terms that are often confused and misunderstood; we also point out when words and expressions are unacceptable or questionable for formal or even informal writing. (To refresh your memory about the characteristics of the various levels of language, see pages 19–22.) In making decisions on usage, we have been guided by *Webster's Dictionary of English Usage; Fowler's Modern English Usage,* 3rd ed.; *The American Heritage Dictionary of the English Language,* 4th ed.; and several popular composition handbooks.

If you are still in doubt about some terms or have questions about words that don't appear in this chapter, consult your trusty collegiate dictionary. But be sure it's a recent one: even the best dictionaries will be out of date on usage within ten years.

# H *azardous Usage*

*Standard usage* means the language used by educated people; *nonstandard usage* means any language that fails to conform to this accepted standard. Unfortunately, dialectical expressions are considered nonstandard. Some dictionaries label such usage as *illiterate*, which seems harsh, but be advised that many people are unalterably opposed to the use of nonstandard English in business and academic writing. Avoid the following words and phrases, or use them only with extreme caution for stylistic effect.

**ain't**   People have been using this word in speech for at least two hundred years, but it's still considered nonstandard. Don't use it unless you're writing dialogue or trying to get a laugh. Use *am not, are not (aren't)*, or *is not (isn't)*.

**alot**   It's still two words: *a* + *lot* (a noun meaning a large extent or amount).

> Your complaints have caused *a lot* of trouble.

> We are feeling *a lot* better.

**analyzation**   The standard term is *analysis;* tacking on extra syllables doesn't make it any grander—only incorrect.

**anyways/anywheres**   These terms are nonstandard. Use *anyway* and *anywhere*.

**could of/should of/would of**   These phrases are nonstandard for *could have, should have, would have.*

**enthused**   Many people prefer that you use *enthusiastic.*

> (familiar)      The critics were *enthused* about our performance.

> (preferred)     The critics were *enthusiastic* about our performance.

**etc.**   This abbreviation means "and so forth." Do not use it just to avoid thinking of good examples, and avoid ending a list with *etc.* unless the other examples are obvious (such as large cities: Paris, Rome, London, etc.). Even then, it's usually more effective to end with an example or to use the more graceful phrase *and so on.* Never write *and etc.;* it's redundant.

**hardly** This adverb carries a negative meaning, so don't combine it with a negative verb.

| (nonstandard) | She *can't hardly* see without her glasses. |
| (standard) | She *can hardly* see without her glasses. |
| (standard) | She *can't* see without her glasses. |

**hisself** This word is nonstandard. Use *himself.*

**irregardless** Most people still steadfastly refuse to accept *irregardless* as standard English. Use *regardless* or *nonetheless.*

**myself** This word is a reflexive or intensive pronoun: *I cut myself shaving* (reflexive); *I will fix the faucet myself* (intensive). Do not use *myself* in place of *I* or *me.*

| (familiar) | Jocasta and *myself* are going to be partners. |
| (preferred) | Jocasta and *I* are going to be partners. |
| (familiar) | Will you play tennis with Jocasta and *myself?* |
| (preferred) | Will you play tennis with Jocasta and *me?* |

**quote** *Quote* is a verb:

Leroy *quotes* Shakespeare in his sleep.

In writing, avoid using *quote* or *quotes* as a shortened form of *quotation* or *quotation marks.*

**suppose to/use to** These are nonstandard; the correct forms are *supposed to* and *used to.* Be careful to add the *-d* in writing, even though you don't hear it in speech.

**theirself/theirselves/themself** These are all nonstandard forms of *themselves.*

## D ouble Trouble: Words That Are Easily Confused

The English language is filled with words that look alike or sound alike or are alike in meaning, and they cause problems for many writers. The only way to handle these similar terms is to stay alert for them and double-check every use when you proofread. It's not just a matter of learning how to spell the words correctly; you also have to match the spelling with the meaning. Keeping a list of the ones that give you trouble will increase your awareness and save you time when you edit. And remember: the spell checker on your computer won't help you with the words that sound and look alike.

**a/an**  Use *a* before words that begin with consonant sounds; use *an* before words that begin with vowel sounds (*a, e, i, o, u*).

| | |
|---|---|
| a martini | an Irish coffee |
| a tree toad | an armadillo |
| a hopeful sign (the *h* is sounded) | an honest decision (the *h* is silent) |
| a hostile crowd (sounded *h*) | an hour exam (silent *h*) |
| a one-car accident (*o* sounds like *w*) | an only child |
| a university (*u* sounds like *y*) | an unusual request |

*An* once was used before unaccented syllables beginning with *h*: *an historian*, *an hotel*. But that usage has changed; it's now acceptable to write *a historian* or *a hotel*.

**accept/except**  *Accept*, a verb, means "to receive or to agree with."

We *accept* your gracious apology.

*Except*, a preposition, means "other than" or "leaving out."

He didn't utter a word *except* to complain.

Everyone will attend the banquet, *except* Dinsdale.

*Except* isn't used often as a verb, but it means "to exclude."

Senior citizens are *excepted* from paying full price.

**advice/advise**  *Advice* is a noun; *advise* is a verb. When you *advise* someone, you are giving *advice*.

vb.
We *advise* you to stop smoking.

n.
Sun-Lee refuses to follow our good *advice*.

**affect/effect**  The verb *affect* means "to influence." The noun *effect* means "the result of some influence."

n.                                        vb.
The *effect* on my lungs from smoking should *affect* my decision to quit.

vb.
Smoking adversely *affects* our health.

n.
Carleton smokes expensive cigars for *effect*.

Just to confuse things further, *effect* can also be a verb meaning "to bring about." And *affect* can be a verb meaning "to put on or simulate" or a noun meaning "emotional response."

vb.
We need to *effect* [bring about] some changes in the system.

vb.
He *affects* [puts on] the petulance of a rock star.

n.
Psychologists say that inappropriate *affect* [emotional response] is a feature of schizophrenia.

These last three meanings are seldom confused with the more widely used words above. Concentrate on getting those first common meanings straight.

**all right/alright**  Although *alright* is gaining acceptance in the world of advertising, you should stick with *all right* to be safe. *Alright* is definitely not yet *all right* with everybody.

**almost/most**  See *most/almost*.

**already/all ready**  *Already* means "before," "previously," or "so soon."

Julia has *already* eaten two cheeseburgers.

*All ready* means "prepared."

Juan is *all ready* to deliver his anti-junk food lecture.

**altogether/all together**  *Altogether* means "entirely, thoroughly."

Reba's analysis is *altogether* absurd.

*All together* means "as a group."

Let's sing the last chorus *all together*.

**among/between**  Use *among* when referring to more than two items.

Ashley found it difficult to choose from *among* so many delectable desserts.

Use *between* when referring to only two.

> She couldn't decide *between* the raspberry tort and the butterscotch mousse.

**anymore/any more**    Use *any more* if you mean "any additional."

> Ashley won't be eating *any more* desserts.

Use *anymore* with negative verbs if you mean "any longer."

> She doesn't live here *anymore*.

Don't use *anymore* with positive verbs; use *now* or *nowadays*.

> (familiar)        All we do *anymore* is watch television.
>
> (preferred)     All we do *nowadays* is watch television.

**apprise/appraise**    To *apprise* means to "inform or serve notice."

> The judge *apprised* the defendant of her right to counsel.

To *appraise* means to "evaluate or judge."

> The fugitive *appraised* the situation and caught the next flight to South America.

**bad/badly**    *Bad* is an adjective; use it after linking verbs (*be, feel, seem, appear, look, become, smell, sound, taste*).

> We feel *bad* about missing your birthday.
>
> I feel *bad* because I'm coming down with a cold.

*Badly* is an adverb; use it to modify verbs.

> The car is vibrating *badly*.
>
> The car was *badly* damaged.

---

**TIP!**    If you just can't remember these distinctions, choose another word.

---

> We feel sorry about missing your birthday.
>
> I feel awful because I'm coming down with a cold.
>
> The car is vibrating alarmingly.
>
> The car was seriously damaged.

**between/among**    See *among/between*.

**choose/chose**   *Choose* (rhymes with *ooze*) means a decision is being made now.

> Please *choose* a new lab partner for me.

*Chose* (rhymes with *toes*) means a choice has already been made.

> The one you *chose* for me last semester was incompetent.

**cite/site/sight**   *Cite,* a verb, means "to quote as an authority or example."

> In her speech, Molly Ivins *cited* three passages from the Bill of Rights.

*Site,* a noun, means "a particular place."

> We found a perfect *site* to hold our rally.

As a verb, *sight* means "to observe or notice."

> Astronomers recently *sighted* a new comet.

As a noun, *sight* means something that is seen or foreseeable or worth seeing.

> There is no end in *sight* to this heat wave.

> One of Brussel's most famous *sights* is the Manneken-Pis.

**compare/contrast**   These words overlap in meaning. While *compare* generally means to focus on similarities and *contrast* means to focus on differences, you are comparing when you make a contrast.

**complement/compliment**   *Complement* is a verb meaning "to go together with or complete" and a noun meaning "something that completes."

> Sherry's lilac scarf *complements* her lavender sweater.

> The scarf is also a good *complement* to her eyes.

*Compliment* is a verb meaning "to praise or flatter" and a noun meaning "an expression of praise or flattery."

> Many people *complimented* Sherry on her outfit.

> She received many *compliments* on her sense of style.

**continual/continuous**   There is a slight difference between these two words, although many people treat them as meaning the same. *Continual* describes an action that is repeated at intervals; its synonyms are *recurrent* or *intermittent. Continuous* means something that is extended or prolonged without interruption; its synonyms are *uninterrupted* or *incessant*.

> The *continual* banging of the shutters kept me awake.

> They kept a *continuous* watch for approaching storms.

**desert/dessert** People who get their just *deserts* are getting what they deserve. People who get *desserts* are eating something like cheese cake or pie with ice cream at the end of a meal.

**disinterested/uninterested** Although the distinction between these words is important, many people carelessly confuse them. *Disinterested* means "impartial or objective."

> You need a totally *disinterested* counselor to help you with your marriage problems.

*Uninterested* means "not interested."

> Andre is totally *uninterested* in environmental causes.

**dominant/dominate** *Dominant* is an adjective.

> Bud has a *dominant* personality.

> Brown eyes are genetically *dominant*.

*Dominate* is a verb.

> Cecil's brothers *dominate* him.

**effect/affect** See *affect/effect*.

**everyday/every day** Use *everyday* as an adjective to modify a noun.

> Jamal is wearing his *everyday* clothes.

Use *every day* to mean "daily."

> It rains here almost *every day*.

**hung/hanged** These are the alternate past and past participle forms of the verb "to hang." If you are talking about hanging inanimate objects, then *hung* is the correct form:

> The people at the art museum *hung* the pictures upside down.

But if you are referring to executing people by suspending them by the neck, then *hanged* is the one you want.

> They *hanged* the prisoner at dawn.

**imply/infer**   *Imply* means to state indirectly or throw out a suggestion.

>   Theo *implied* that he was a computer expert.

*Infer* means to draw a conclusion or take in a suggestion.

>   The boss *inferred* that Theo had exaggerated his credentials.

**its/it's**   Do not confuse these two terms. Memorize the two definitions if you have trouble with them, and when you proofread, check to be sure you have not confused them accidentally. *Its* is a possessive pronoun.

>   That dog wags *its* tail whenever *its* owner walks into the room.

*It's* is a contraction of "it is" or "it has."

>   *It's* a great day for taking the dog for a walk.

>   *It's* been a long time since you walked the dog.

---

**TIP!**   **If you never can keep the two straight, quit using the contraction. If you always write *it is* or *it has*, then all you have to remember is this: no apostrophe in *its*.**

---

**lay/lie**   *To lay* means to put or place; *to lie* means to recline. Be sure you know the principal forms of each verb; then decide which verb you need:

>   (to place)     lay, laid, laid, laying

>   (to recline)   lie, lay, lain, lying

Remember that *lay* requires a direct object: you always *lay* something. But you never *lie* anything: you just *lie down*, or *lie quietly*, or *lie under a tree*, or *lie on a couch*.

>   (no direct object)     Selma *lies* in the hammock.

>   (direct object)        Selma usually *lays* the mail on the hall table.

---

**TIP!**   **If you absolutely can't keep these verbs straight in your mind, choose another word.**

>   Selma *lounges* in the hammock.

>   Selma usually *puts* the mail on the hall table.

---

**lead/led**   Pronunciation causes the confusion here.

*Lead* (rhymes with *bed*), a noun, means "a heavy, grayish metal."

> Our airy hopes sank like *lead*.

*Lead* (rhymes with *seed*) is present tense of the verb meaning "to guide."

> He *leads* me beside the still waters.

*Led* (rhymes with *bed*) is the past tense of the verb *lead*.

> Marcelo *led* the march last year, but he vows he will not *lead* it again.

**lose/loose**   This is another problem in pronunciation and spelling. *Lose* (rhymes with *ooze*) is a verb meaning "to fail to keep something."

> If we *lose* our right to protest, we will ultimately *lose* our freedom.

*Loose* (rhymes with *goose*) is an adjective meaning "not tight."

> The noose is too *loose* on your lasso.

**most/almost**   *Most* is colloquial when used to mean "almost."

> (familiar)      *Most* everyone in the office took Friday off.
>
> (preferred)    *Almost* everyone in the office took Friday off.

**prejudice/prejudiced**   *Prejudice* (without the *-d*) is a noun.

> *Prejudice* remains engrained in our society.

*Prejudiced* (with the *-d*) is the past participle of the verb *to prejudice;* it means "affected by prejudice." Do not leave off the *-d* when using this word as an adjective.

> adj.                                  n.
> A *prejudiced* person is someone who harbors *prejudice.*

> pred. adj.
> Our society remains *prejudiced* against minorities.

**principal/principle**   *Principle* means a rule: a person of high moral *principle*, a primary *principle* of physics, the *principle* of equal justice. You can remember the *-le* spelling by association with the *-le* ending of *rule*. All other uses end with *-al*: a high school *principal*, the *principal* of a loan, a *principal* cause or effect, the *principal* (main character) in a film or play.

**probable/probably**   Both of these words mean "likely." *Probable* (sounds at the end like *capable*) is an adjective, and *probably* (ends with a long *e* sound, like *capably*) is an adverb.

> adj.                                                                              adv.
> The *probable* involvement of the CIA in the uprising *probably* caused the rebels to lose.

**quite/quiet**   *Quite* means "entirely" or "truly"; use it to qualify adjectives and adverbs: *quite* suddenly, *quite* often, *quite* right. *Quiet* means the opposite of "loud."

> Carlos was *quite* ready to yell, "Be *quiet*, please!"

**raise/rise**   You never *rise* anything, but you always *raise* something. Prices *rise,* spirits *rise,* curtains *rise,* temperatures *rise;* but you *raise* children, *raise* corn, *raise* prices, or *raise* the window.

> Taxes are *rising* because Congress has *raised* the defense budget again.

---

**TIP!**   **If you cannot keep these verbs straight, avoid them.**

> Taxes are going up because Congress has increased the defense budget again.

---

**real/really**   Do not use *real* as an adverb or qualifier in writing.

> (familiar)        Maya saw a *real* interesting movie.
>
> (standard)       Maya saw a *really* interesting movie.

**rise/raise**   See *raise/rise.*

**sit/set**   You seldom *sit* anything. You *sit* down or *sit* for a while or *sit* in a chair. One notable exception: *sit* can mean "to cause to be seated." Thus, it's quite correct to write: "The parole officer *sat* Buffy down and gave her a lecture."

But you always *set* something. You *set* a glass down or *set* a time or *set* the table. Exceptions: in some common phrases *set* does not have an object—the sun *sets,* jello and concrete *set,* and hens *set*—but people seldom have a problem with these uses.

**than/then**   See *then/than.*

**their/there/they're**   These words are easy to confuse because they sound exactly alike. But their meanings and uses are quite different.

*Their* is a possessive modifier or pronoun.

> *Their* dog is friendly. That dog is *theirs.*

*There* is an adverb or an expletive (a filler word that delays the subject).

(adverb)          Sylvia is over *there*.

(expletive)       *There* is no one with her.

*They're* is a contraction of *they are.*

(contraction)     *They're* gone now.

---

**TIP!** If you have trouble spelling *their,* remember that all three—*they're, there,* and *their*—start with *the-*.

---

**then/than** These words have quite different meanings. *Then* means "at that time in the past" or "next in time, space, or order."

We were all much younger *then.*

We watched the late movie and *then* went to bed.

*Than* is used in comparisons.

No one talks more *than* Michael does.

Claudia would rather talk *than* eat.

**to/too/two** *To* is usually a preposition and sometimes an adverb; it also introduces an infinitive.

*to* the depths, push the door *to, to* swing

*Too* is a qualifier or an adverb meaning "also."

Don't make *too* much noise. (qualifier of "much")

Selina is going, *too.* (means "also")

*Two* is the number.

*two* paychecks, *two* miles

**weather/whether** *Weather* is what goes on outside; *whether* introduces an alternative. Using the wrong one causes serious misunderstandings.

We cannot decide *whether* the *weather* will be suitable for a picnic.

**who/which/that** Use *who* to refer to people (or to animals you are personifying).

The person *who* lost the car keys. . . .

Lenin, *who* is Susie's cat, . . .

Use *which* to refer to animals and nonliving things.

> The earth, *which* blossoms in the spring, . . .
>
> The cat, *which* is sitting in the window, . . .

Use *that* to refer to either people or things.

> The person *that* lost the car keys . . . (*who* is preferable in formal usage)
>
> The earth *that* blossoms in spring . . .
>
> The cat *that* is sitting in the window . . .

**your/you're** *Your* is a possessive modifier or pronoun.

> Here is *your* book; this book is *yours.*

*You're* is a contraction of *you are.*

> Let me know when *you're* leaving.

---

## Exercise 14.1: Assorted Matters of Usage

Most of the sentences below contain examples of questionable usage. Revise those sentences that need changing in order to be acceptable as standard English. Some contain more than one dubious usage.

1. My roommate and myself moved into a new apartment.
2. Did the budget committee write this report all by theirselves?
3. You could of broken your toe on that rock.
4. Lou is disinterested in urban entertainment.
5. For once, try to do what you're suppose to.
6. I am going to put quotes around this slang expression, irregardless of what the book says.
7. Most everyone which is likely to come has all ready arrived.
8. A banquet is where you eat alot of food and listen to alot of long speeches.
9. If we go altogether, we should be alright.
10. I am not coming because I'm not interested anyways.
11. Amanda can't hardly describe her feelings about her new job.
12. Kim use to be enthused about the virtues of step aerobics.
13. If I had known you were coming, I would of left.
14. His powers of analyzation use to be sharper.
15. Boris hurt hisself in a hunting accident.

## Exercise 14.2: Frequently Confused Words

The following sentences contain words that sound alike but have different meanings. In each sentence, select the appropriate word from the choices in parentheses.

1. I have been (lead, led) astray again.
2. Tristan is plumper (then, than) a teddy bear.
3. (Its, It's) not the money; (its, it's) the (principal, principle) of the thing that bothers me.
4. Those most in need of (advice, advise) seldom welcome it.
5. Tony cannot study if his room is (to, too) (quiet, quite).
6. The automobile is a (principal, principle) contributor to air pollution.
7. Our spirits (rose, raised) with the sun.
8. They had a frisky time when (there, their) mongoose got (lose, loose).
9. Let's (lie, lay) down and talk this over.
10. That (continual, continuous) drip from the faucet is driving me to drink.
11. You ought to (appraise, apprise) the situation carefully before you decide (weather, whether) to file a complaint.
12. (You're, Your) decision could (affect, effect) your career.
13. If you (choose, chose) to file, you should not harbor the illusion that all (your, you're) problems will be solved.
14. Why don't we (sit, set) this one out?
15. (Your, You're) going to be sent to the boondocks if you (accept, except) this job.
16. The IRS is really (uninterested, disinterested) in Virgil's (continual, continuous) complaints.
17. I could (infer, imply) from his complaints that he owes back taxes.
18. If the (weather, whether) improves, (then, than) we will plant the garden.
19. Any news program will usually (appraise, apprise) you of a late frost.
20. Snow peas will not be (affected, effected) by a light frost.
21. I (advice, advise) you to pick them young.
22. The dean has (lain, laid) down firm rules concerning class attendance.
23. I (chose, choose) strawberry last time, and it was (alright, all right), (accept, except) there weren't any strawberries in it.

24. How did that dog (lose, loose) (its, it's) tail?

25. Please (set, sit) that plant over (their, there) near the window.

26. Whenever I (lie, lay) down for a nap, the children outside (rise, raise) a ruckus.

27. Miguel is a person of firm moral (principle, principal) who should (rise, raise) to national prominence.

28. This recipe (implies, infers) that using artificial chocolate sometimes (affects, effects) the taste of the cookies.

# Index

# Credits

from demanding payment or lodging complaints: "My son is in the hands of the law since December 8 and I know nothing concerning your bills," he wrote, for instance, to *L'Ecran français* when they demanded to be paid for the ads François had placed. "I'm taking the liberty of warning you against this fly-by-night Cercle Cinémane founded without my knowledge, and I would be grateful if you would cancel any orders or requests for service under that name which you might receive. I feel I should also warn you that since my son's arrest, some of his friends might have used the name to place orders." Though Roland's colleague Monsieur Guillard had refrained from lodging a complaint, there was still another problem in François's file, concerning the typewriter theft. A lawyer, Maurice Bertrand, had been assigned, and François had confessed. The court judge for the ninth arrondissement had to rule on all these points—acknowledged debts paid by the father and thefts confessed to by the son. He proved to be rather lenient, sentencing Roland Truffaut to pay a 12,000-franc fine on behalf of his son, and ordering that François be placed in a home after his release from Villejuif, until he reached his majority or age of legal independence, with the possibility of part-time outside employment if he found an employer.

Still, Truffaut did find some small consolations during his detention. Because he was cultivated and engaging when he opened up, several adults in the correctional institution and the judiciary took an interest in his case. Raymond Clarys, director of the Villejuif Observation Center, grew fond of him in spite of his misdemeanors, and brought François a regular supply of newspapers and movie magazines. There was the all-important Mademoiselle Rikkers, the "spychogist," as Antoine Doinel would call her in *The 400 Blows*. She met with him for several long conversations and played a decisive role in improving his legal situation; soon the initial diagnosis—"psychomotor instability with perverse tendencies"—was dropped and replaced by a detailed portrait of a youth "using repeated lies to escape" a family environment and an emotional situation that the psychologist saw as "traumatizing."[35] Her fondness for him was such that she met with his parents and his close friends, such as Lachenay, to help speed up his release. Then, in March 1949, she contacted André Bazin and requested his intercession on her young patient's behalf. Though Bazin hardly knew François at the time, he went to see Mademoiselle Rikkers at her home on rue du Pot-de-Fer. Not only did he agree to vouch for François; he promised to find him a job at Travail et Culture. Mademoiselle Rikkers agreed to continue monitoring François's progress after his release. Thanks to all these guarantees, the judge decided to place François Truffaut in a religious home in Versailles three months before his scheduled release. On March 18, 1949, the seventeen-year-old youth was granted semifreedom.

# I DON'T GAZE AT THE SKY FOR LONG

On the morning of March 18, 1949, François Truffaut was taken to the Guynemer home, on rue Sainte-Sophie, in Versailles. A religious boarding school under the authority of the Seine-et-Oise Association familiale et sociale, its regulations were strict, though less restrictive than those of the Villejuif Observation Center. The nuns of the Notre-Dame parish were an improvement over the Villejuif educators, though Truffaut would not have fond memories of the dormitory, the attendance checks, the strict schedules, and the prayers preceding meals.

François still bore the psychological marks of his recent ordeals. This is clear from the essay he wrote for his literature teacher at the boys' day school he attended on boulevard de la Reine in Versailles. The assignment was to "describe the most beautiful or saddest adventure in your life." Truffaut approached the theme existentially, describing his whole life as a "sad adventure." His despair is expressed in simple, logical language, devoid of ornament and as naked as a prison wall: "My life, or rather my slice of life to this day, has been banal to the utmost. I was born on February 6, 1932; today is March 21, 1949, therefore I'm 17 years 1 month and 15 days old. I've eaten almost every day and slept almost every night; I think I've worked too much and haven't had very many satisfactions or joys. My Christmases and birthdays have all been ordinary and disappointing. I had no particular feelings about the war or the morons who took part in it. I like the Arts and particularly the movies; I consider that work is a necessary evil like excreting, and that any person who likes his work doesn't know how to live. I don't like adventures and have avoided them. Three films a day, three books a week and records of great music would be enough to make me happy to the day I die, which will surely occur one day soon and which I egoistically dread. My parents are no more than human beings to me; it is mere chance that they happen to be my father and mother, which is why they mean no more to me than strangers. I don't believe in friendship, and I don't believe in peace either. I try to stay out of trouble, far from anything that causes too much of a stir. For me, politics is merely a flourishing industry and politicians intelligent crooks. This sums up my adventure; it is neither gay nor sad; it is life. I don't gaze at the sky for long, for when I look back down again the world seems horrid to me."[36]

Yet François Truffaut had decided to struggle and pull through. He tried to adapt to the supervised schooling, though eventually his rebellious streak would reassert itself. In the beginning of August he would be punished for "leading a big disorderly outbreak into which he had dragged three of his younger classmates," resulting in broken windowpanes and insulted teachers. On September 13, 1949, the director of the home would write Roland Truffaut that "unfortunately" his son was "a bad influence" and he was obliged to expel him.[37] On September 17, Roland Truffaut would have to sign a check in the amount of 19,860 francs to pay for damages, room and board, and accumulated debts. His expedition to the Kilimanjaro was once again postponed.

François's extremely tense return home hastened his falling-out with his mother. He took everything out on her and blamed her directly, while appealing to Roland for understanding and trust. Yet, though Janine Truffaut had gone to see François infrequently in Villejuif and Versailles, and had stayed only very briefly each time, making him feel she visited him out of pure obligation, Roland had never gone to see him at all. But therein was the family paradox—in the inversion of symbolic roles. The revelation of his adoption, instead of estranging Truffaut from his substitute father, brought him closer to a man whom he considered basically kind, although weak— weak in being too much in love with his wife. It was his mother whom he now hated and resented. He confided his intimate feelings to Roland, on April 2, 1949: "Dear Daddy, the reason I'm divulging my sorrows to you is that, contrary to what you think, you're the one I trust. I did not, as you believe, feel estranged from you by discovering my filiation. Though it estranged me from Mom, it brought me closer to you. Indeed, before knowing the truth, I suspected there was something abnormal in my family situation and I even thought that though you were my real father, Mom wasn't my real mother. I believed this for a long time for your behavior and mother's confirmed this idea. This is why I was shattered to learn that the opposite was true. But psychologically you're still my real daddy and Mom a stepmother. She may not be an evil stepmother but she's not a mother either. . . . In my new life, I want to make you my confidant and tell you all my little problems."[38]

Roland Truffaut felt obliged to show this letter to his wife. François felt betrayed. His divisive strategy further exacerbated Janine's hostility. The April 2 letter had been a result of growing animosity. Janine, aiming for his most sensitive spot, had blamed all his troubles on Robert Lachenay, "the evil genie" who had led his younger friend down the path of truancy, financial irresponsibility, and even debauchery. According to her, not only had Robert taken François to prostitutes but the two boys had had a homosexual relationship at the elder's initiative, "which could be clearly proved through medical analyses and tests on the syphilis strain,"[39] she had written him in stinging terms. Deeply hurt by this accusation, François had defended himself as best he could, pleading complete awareness and maturity, and argued for a second medical assessment: "I will forestall any medical inquiry," he had written his parents on March 27, 1949, "by expressly requesting from Mademoiselle Rikkers a medical exam for Robert Lachenay to dispel all suspicions in that area. By the way, speaking of him, I should tell you that your ideas about him are completely wrong. He is a much more scrupulous boy than I and he never would have done half of what I did. Furthermore, he was an excellent friend since, to help with the film club and my debts, he didn't hesitate to sell a bound set of Buffon's complete works and lots of other books."[40]

These exchanges, filled with suspected betrayals, hatred, and libelous accusations, provoked a quasi-definitive rift between François and his parents. He yearned for his complete independence, which he would obtain a year later, on March 10, 1950, a month after his eighteenth birthday, when Roland Truffaut signed a declaration granting him legal emancipation.[41] François then became free, released from parental guardianship, but his freedom was founded on a family trauma that would forever leave its mark and occasionally show its deep effects in the coming years.

In reform school, in Versailles, his freedom was relative; he was penniless, had no clothes, and wore shoes with holes. But on Thursdays and Sundays, he could borrow the gardener's bicycle and get to Paris in an hour: "It was beautiful weather and I raced like a madman," he wrote to Lachenay in April 1949. "I went to see Madame Duminy and Claude Thibaudat, on rue des Martyrs. As I approached the house, which I had not seen for four months, I pictured a cold welcome and reproaches, which is why, on Place Pigalle, I continued along the same road down the boulevards and decided to go see an assistant director friend who lives at La Chapelle. At his mother's insistence, I ate at their house, and in the afternoon I left the bicycle there and we went to see Bazin at Travail et Culture, on rue des Beaux-Arts. We wrote to Jacques Becker. I've started to look for work. Mademoiselle Rikkers, the psychologist whom I go to every Sunday, is also looking into it."[42] Paris belonged to him once again.

## UPSETTING THE APPLECART

François Truffaut again devoted his free moments to cinema. In Versailles, he helped Abbé Yves Renaud—French teacher, film enthusiast, and friend of André Bazin—in programming the day school's film club. As for Bazin, he did not forget his promise to find work for his young protégé. He appointed François as his personal secretary at Travail et Culture, a job that did not pay very much, only about 3,000 francs a month, but which helped convince the judge to allow François to live on his own in Paris. To fully enjoy "his new life," he had to find a room to live in. He had suffered too

much in Villejuif and Versailles to want to return to those places; he preferred "to live on 200 francs a day and tighten my belt,"[43] as he wrote to his
father. Roland, who had given him a stern warning that if he got the least bit
into debt or if Roland heard the least complaint, he would "strike back,
without any compunction,"[44] agreed to make a last effort. Starting in September 16, 1949, he rented a room for him on the fifth floor of a building on
rue des Martyrs, at 1,500 francs a month.

Thanks to André Bazin, François attended the meetings of the film society Objectif 49, a gathering place of artists, writers, students, and Parisian
critics. Founded by the advocates of the new criticism—Bazin, Astruc, Kast,
Doniol-Valcroze, Bourgeois, Tacchella, and Claude Mauriac—and benefiting from the sponsorship of such filmmakers and writers as Jean Cocteau,
Robert Bresson, René Clément, Jean Grémillon, Raymond Queneau, and
Roger Leenhardt, Objectif 49 showed its members only new, unreleased
films. An exclusive but highly influential club (those "snobs,"[45] as the Communist filmmaker Louis Daquin called them in L'Ecran français), Objectif
49 was launched by the big premiere of Jean Cocteau's Les Parents terribles
(The Storm Within) at the Studio des Champs-Elysées. Cocteau brought his
prestigious literary backing to the club and played a crucial role in coordinating plans and initiatives. Truffaut met him for the first time in the offices
of Objectif 49.

It was the beginning of the Cold War, with tensions running high in intellectual circles, and film criticism was divided along political lines. The Communists had taken over L'Ecran français and thrown out Bazin, who was
probably considered a "Catholic leftist." In addition, Jean George Auriol's
La Revue du cinéma, whose contributors included Bazin, Doniol-Valcroze,
Astruc, and Kast, filed for bankruptcy after being dropped by its publisher,
Gaston Gallimard. Objectif 49 became the forum of the new criticism. Its
screenings were jam-packed, and important filmmakers came to present
their work—among them, Roberto Rossellini, Orson Welles, William Wyler,
Preston Sturges, Roger Leenhardt, Jean Grémillon, and René Clément.
Encouraged by their success, the organizers of Objectif 49 decided to create
a festival, which they hoped could rival Cannes: the Festival indépendant du
Film Maudit (Independent Festival of the Accursed Film) in Biarritz.

The first festival took place in late July 1949. Naturally, Bazin, a key figure in the movement, insisted that his young personal secretary join him; so
Truffaut boarded the night train at the Gare d'Austerlitz on the evening of
July 29. Penniless, he could not afford a berth and traveled in discomfort
amid the noise and heat. The morning of July 30, he wrote Robert Lachenay
a postcard: "Dear old pal, trip dreadful, weather so-so. The festival opens
tonight with Marcello Pagliero's La Nuit porte conseil. Cocteau has arrived.
Photos and more photos, the beach is straight out of Jean Vigo, with fram-

ings straight out of Hathaway, a depth of field out of Welles, and perspectives out of Fritz Lang. Will write long letter on Tuesday. I'm almost broke. François Toréador."[46] Put up, like a great number of young festivalgoers, at the dormitory of the Biarritz Lycée, Truffaut was caught up in the slightly mad, eccentric ambiance and the all-night festivities—such as the costume ball on August 2, an "Accursed night" organized by Alexandre Astruc and Marc Doelnitz, near a place called the Lac de la Négresse (Lake of the Negress). To get in, Truffaut had even bought himself a bow tie, but he found the atmosphere too social and fashionable: "The festival is unfolding quietly with no great surprises," he confided to his friend Lachenay. "To my great amazement, Cocteau recognized me because of bow tie and Bazin, but he gains nothing from being approached, in fact no more so than Grémillon or Claude Mauriac. The town is horrible and so are the inhabitants and the tourists, but Bazin is very well liked for his film presentations and discussions."[47]

Fortunately, the four films he saw every day took up most of his time. A group of young film enthusiasts was formed during some of the special screenings (the long version of Vigo's *L'Atalante,* shown for the first time; the preview of Welles's *The Lady from Shanghai;* or the European premiere of Renoir's American film *The Southerner*) and during the nocturnal discussions in the Lycée dormitory—a group that would soon be talked about: Truffaut, of course, as well as Jacques Rivette, Claude Chabrol, Charles Bitsch, Jean Douchet, and several others. Eric Rohmer, who was also in Biarritz and was the eldest in the group, vividly remembers meeting François Truffaut there for the first time, and how he was introduced to him, with a big wink, as Bazin's secretary. These radical and insolent young people made it a point of honor to dissociate themselves from Objectif 49; they spent their time denigrating the way the festival was organized, though those in charge were critic friends who were better established than they were, like Bazin and Doniol-Valcroze. This polemical spirit was what bound the group of film enthusiasts together, as did their common passion for actresses and filmmakers like Gloria Grahame and Ingrid Bergman, Alfred Hitchcock and Fritz Lang.

When he returned to Paris in the late summer of 1949, Truffaut lived through his most intense period as a film enthusiast. His loneliness and troubles were over; he was now part of a group. Others joined the clique from the Biarritz dormitory—Jean-Luc Godard, Suzanne Klochendler (soon Schiffman), Jean Gruault, Paul Gégauff, Alain Jeannel, Louis Marcorelles, Jean-José Richer, and Jean-Marie Straub. They assembled at the weekly screenings of the main Paris film societies. On Tuesdays, they met at the Studio Parnasse, where Jean-Louis Chéray led the discussions with energy and passion, ending with a film quiz that entitled the winner to a free

1. François Truffaut. *I had to read in silence . . .*

2. ABOVE: Roland and Janine Truffaut.
*The great injustice has been redressed*
*by a man with a noble heart* . . . (Bernard
de Monferrand).
3. LEFT: François on vacation with his father,
Roland Truffaut.
4. BELOW: François Truffaut and his grandmother, Geneviève de Monferrand, in 1939.

5. RIGHT: François Truffaut with his paternal grandmother in Juvisy. *Vacations were usually spent at the edge of the road watching the cars leave for the weekend.*
6. BELOW: Class portrait at the school on rue Milton in 1944. François Truffaut is seated in the first row, third from left. In the same row, at far right, is his friend Claude Thibaudat (who later made a career as Claude Vega). *Good little student, though occasionally a bit talkative . . .* (report card).

7. TOP: Weekend in Fontainebleau. *From left:*
François, Roland, and Janine Truffaut. *My son*
*François will never understand anything about*
*mountaineering . . .* (Roland Truffaut).
8. CENTER: François's film society membership
card.
9. RIGHT: I.O.U., December 8, 1948.
10. OPPOSITE: François Truffaut and Robert
Lachenay on Boulevard Saint-Michel, in 1948.
*We had joined forces to resist . . .* (Robert
Lachenay).

11. ABOVE: Jean-Pierre Léaud in *The 400 Blows:*
Antoine Doinel as a juvenile delinquent.
12. RIGHT: Notebook containing the first draft of
the screenplay for *The 400 Blows*.

13. ABOVE: Self-portrait by Truffaut, showing him handcuffed between two soldiers.
14. LEFT: François Truffaut in 1951. *A self-hating autodidact.*

15. LEFT: Paris, 1952: François Truffaut, free at last . . .

16. ABOVE: André Bazin, Truffaut's spiritual father. *A man of conscience* . . .

17. ABOVE: François Truffaut and Jacques Doniol-Valcroze at *Cahiers du cinéma*.
18. LEFT: *Cahiers du cinéma*, April 1951, number 1.
19. BELOW: First polemical essay: *A Certain Tendency of the French Cinema* . . .

UNE CERTAINE TENDANCE
DU CINEMA FRANÇAIS

par François Truffaut

Jean Aurenche

« On peut aimer que le sens du mot art soit
tenté de donner conscience à des hommes
de la grandeur qu'ils ignorent en eux. »
André Malraux
(Le Temps du Mépris, préface).

Ces notes n'ont pas d'autre objet qu'essayer de définir une certaine tendance
du cinéma français — tendance dite du réalisme psychologique — et d'en
esquisser les limites.

DIX OU DOUZE FILMS...

Si le cinéma français existe par une centaine de films chaque année, il est
bien entendu que dix ou douze seulement méritent de retenir l'attention des
critiques et des cinéphiles, l'attention donc de ces CAHIERS.

Ces dix ou douze films constituent ce que l'on a joliment appelé la *Tradition
de la Qualité*, ils forcent par leur ambition l'admiration de la presse étrangère,
défendent deux fois l'an les couleurs de la France à Cannes et à Venise où, depuis
1946, ils râflent assez régulièrement médailles, lions d'or et grands prix.

★

Au début du parlant, le cinéma français fut l'honnête démarquage du cinéma
américain. Sous l'influence de *Scarface* nous faisions l'amusant *Pépé le Moko*.
Puis le scénario français dut à Prévert le plus clair de son évolution, *Quai des
Brumes* reste le chef-d'œuvre de l'école dite du *réalisme poétique*.

La guerre et l'après-guerre ont renouvelé notre cinéma. Il a évolué sous
l'effet d'une pression interne et au réalisme poétique — dont on peut dire
qu'il mourut en refermant derrière lui *Les Portes de la Nuit* — s'est substitué
le *réalisme psychologique*, illustré par Claude Autant-Lara, Jean Delannoy,
René Clément, Yves Allégret et Marcel Pagliero.

15

20. LEFT, ABOVE: The critic at work, 1959.
21. RIGHT, ABOVE: François Truffaut and M*
Ophuls. *I have the feeling, though I can*
*explain why, that you will become some*
*important.* (Max Ophuls).
22. LEFT: Truffaut and Jean Cocteau on th
set of *Testament of Orpheus* in 1960.
23. BELOW: François Truffaut and Jean
Renoir.

TOP: Madeleine and François Truffaut's wedding,
ber 29, 1957, in Paris.
ENTER, LEFT: Truffaut with his mother, Janine, on the
f his wedding.
ENTER, RIGHT: Madeleine and François Truffaut, with
llini, a witness at their marriage.
GHT: The family at La Colombe d'or: François,
leine, Éva, and Laura.

28. LEFT: Truffaut with Bernadette Lafont and Géra[
Blain, the lead actors in *The Mischief Makers*.
29. BELOW: Summer 1957, shooting *The Mischief
Makers* in Nîmes: Truffaut, Claude de Givray,
Bernadette Lafont.
30. BOTTOM: The last day of the shoot of *The 400
Blows* on the beach.

31. LEFT: Jean-Pierre Léaud and Madeleine and François Truffaut, May 4, 1959, in Cannes, just before the screening of *The 400 Blows*.
32. BELOW: The front page of *Arts:* Jacques Audiberti's article on *The 400 Blows*.
33. BOTTOM: *Clockwise, from left:* The actress Claire Maurier (Antoine Doinel's mother), Cocteau, Truffaut, Albert Rémy (Doinel's father), the American actor Edward G. Robinson, and Jean-Pierre Léaud.

34. ABOVE: Truffaut, Charles Aznavour, and Marie Dubois on the set of *Shoot the Piano Player*.
35. RIGHT: A Cocteau drawing with an inscription in praise of Truffaut.
36. BELOW: Hitchcock's telegram to Truffaut.

Samedi 3 sept 1960

mon François ton film est un chef d'oeuvre, une manière de prodige et j'éclate Jean

F602/WLA252

WEST LOS ANGELES CALIF 107 1/52 11 308P PDT

LT
MR FRANCOIS TRUFFAUT 25 RUE QUENTIN BAUCHART PARIS

CHER MONSIEUR TRUFFAUT VOTRE LETTRE MA FAIT VENIR LES LARMES AUX YEUX
ET COMBIEN JE SUIS RECONNAISSANT DE RECEVOIR UN TEL TRIBUT DE VOTRE
PART STOP JE SUIS TOUJOUR EN TRAIN DE TOURNER THE BIRDS ET CELA CONTINUERA
JUSQUAU 15 JUILLET STOP APRES

F602/WLA252 2/55
CELA JE DEVRAI COMMENCER LE MONTAGE CMA CE QUI PRENDPA QUELQUES
SEMAINES STOP JE PENSE QUE JATTENDRAI QUE LE TOURNAGE SUR THE
BIRDS SOIT TERMINE ET JE ME METTRAI ALORSEN CONTACT AVEC VOUS
AVEC LIDEE DE NOUS RENCONTRER VERS LA FIN AOUT STOP MERCI ENCORE
POUR VOTRE CHARMANTE LETTRE SINCERES AMITIES CORDIALEMENT VOTRE
    ALFRED HITCHCOCK

37. François Truffaut, Alfred Hitchcock, and Helen Scott, in August 1962, during their interview sessions.
38. Truffaut and Helen Scott.

39. Hitchcock and Truffaut, 1962.

entrance ticket. Thursdays were reserved for the Ciné-Club du Quartier Latin, where the key figure was Maurice Schérer. Thirty years old in 1950, with a stern appearance, schoolboyish and deadpan, Schérer taught French at the Lycée Lakanal in Sceaux and signed his articles on cinema with the pseudonym Eric Rohmer. He used his Thursday afternoon screenings to teach film aesthetics. He was also editor in chief of the monthly *Bulletin du C.C.Q.L.* (Ciné-Club du Quartier Latin), first issued in January 1950. The young film enthusiasts regarded Rohmer as a kind of older brother and addressed him with the polite *vous* form to show their respect. "He was honest, upright, very professorial. He always lent us a bit of money when we were broke, but in exchange you had to give him a receipt, anything from a used métro ticket to a train ticket, or a grocery-store bill,"[48] his friend Paul Gégauff later wrote.

The other evenings of the week were spent at the Artistic, at the Cinéac-Ternes, at Langlois's Cinémathèque, at the Reflets, or at the Broadway. The screenings were followed by endless discussions and wanderings in the streets of Paris with Jacques Rivette and Charles Bitsch. "As soon as we had walked one of us to his door," Bitsch recalled, "we would start walking the second one to his door, and then we'd resolve to walk the third to his door. And so on and so forth, until fatigue and thirst would drive us into one of the cafés that were still open at that ungodly hour, which inevitably made us go back to our favorite neighborhood, between the Place Clichy and the Place Pigalle. Rested, refreshed, and even giddier from talk, we would resume our rounds until morning."[49]

Jacques Rivette had come to Paris at the beginning of 1949 from Rouen, his native city, to take courses at the Sorbonne. He was barely twenty-one, and he had a distinct preference for film screenings over university lecture halls. Thin, with an emaciated face, lively and passionate, he already lived ascetically and with minimal resources. "He looked like the Cheshire cat in *Alice in Wonderland*," Claude Chabrol recalled. "He was tiny. Hardly visible. He seemed not to eat. When he smiled, he disappeared completely behind his magnificent teeth, which made him no less ferocious."[50] Rivette was the group's conscience and spokesman, and as such, he would leave a deep mark on Truffaut, incarnating an opinion and film judgment for which he would have the highest respect. "Rivette was the great talker," Jean Douchet later remarked. "He was the group's secret soul, the occult thinker, a bit of a censor. In fact we called him 'Father Joseph.' His judgment was always very abrupt, very contradictory, he never hesitated to burn what he had adored."[51] Nicknamed "Carolus" by his young companions, Charles Bitsch had an entirely different personality. He was the faithful follower, someone to confide in, always ready to give a helping hand. His father ran a bistro on Place du Palais-Royal, directly opposite the Comédie-Française, where the group often gathered around a table with some drinks and discussed films.

François Truffaut's entry into this crowded, hectic scene of Paris film enthusiasts[52] upset the applecart. The youngest of the group, he was considered a troublemaker. "In the beginning, for about six months, we couldn't take him seriously, he was too bruised,"[53] Chabrol said, a remark confirmed by Gruault: "Let's admit it, François's aggressiveness, his state of perpetual agitation, like a crazed mosquito, got on our nerves."[54] The first thing that struck everyone was Truffaut's physical appearance. Short, five feet four, he had a lively, thin, almost skinny body. He was excitable and had quick, jerky gestures and a dark, piercing gaze. He exuded intensity and elation, in contrast to the photos of him from that period; in these, he is often striking a pose, so that one sees a presentable young man, sometimes smoking a pipe and smiling behind a pair of obtrusive, heavy glasses—for Truffaut was nearsighted, having only 4/10 vision in each eye.

Younger, more rebellious, and more impecunious than the others, Truffaut had to prove himself before being adopted by the small, closed, demanding circle of film enthusiasts. This required time—time to see more films, subdue his impulsiveness, and gain self-confidence in discussions, as well as time to work and write. One of his outstanding qualities was his great capacity for work. He was surely one of the most faithful members of the audience at the Cinémathèque screenings—along with Rivette, Douchet, Godard, and Suzanne Klochendler—and also one of the most diligent: He had a mania for making files and clipping articles, for devouring the specialized press and taking abundant notes. Though he lacked Rivette's ease in speech and writing, or Godard's intuition, his most important asset at the beginning of his career was this scholarly labor, which was evident in his very first essays. Truffaut began as a typical Eric Rohmer disciple, since his first two film reviews were accepted by the *Bulletin du C.C.Q.L.* and published in the spring of 1950. The first describes René Clair's visit to the film club and is a straightforward account by a habitué. The second, a month later, discusses *The Rules of the Game* at great length. Since he had seen the film twelve times by then, when he saw the uncut version, he was able to spot thirteen new scenes and four new shots—precious pearls that he listed learnedly in a column of the *Bulletin*. "Thanks to these thirteen scenes, thanks to Renoir, it was a wonderful evening,"[55] he wrote in conclusion. Far from making a sensational entrance into the world of criticism, Truffaut entered discreetly, combining precision and modesty, as though he wanted to erase the memory of his first months as an embarrassing troublemaker. An eighteen-year-old autodidact under the friendly patronage of Rohmer— whom he soon felt he could nickname *"le grand Momo,"* taking inspiration from Rohmer's real first name (Maurice)—Truffaut learned to train his eyes and write. Working relentlessly, he would not be long in finding his own personal style.

## LOVE AT THE CINÉMATHÈQUE

On his own at last, François Truffaut was living in a room on rue des Martyrs, in the heart of his childhood neighborhood. But he had difficulty adjusting and making ends meet, for his salary from Travail et Culture grew more and more irregular. Bazin was no longer in good graces. The Cold War was raging and the Communists, who controlled the association, looked disapprovingly upon this left-winger who had had the pluck to denounce the "Stalin myth" in the journal *Esprit*. In January 1950, Bazin suffered an acute attack of tuberculosis and had to leave Paris for over a year to take a cure in a sanitarium in the Alps. Truffaut, who hadn't been paid since Christmas 1949, had to resign.

That same January, Robert Lachenay found him a job as an acetylene welder in a factory in Pontault-Combault, in the Seine-et-Marne, a half hour from Paris by bus, "a place which was miles from anywhere, with a church, two hotels, a few farms and a population of around 2,000."[56] There was very little here to delight a young Parisian film enthusiast, except for the prospect of a regular salary. Indeed, the work was exhausting, but well paid—almost twelve thousand francs a month. But then came some bad news—Lachenay was being sent to Germany for his military service. Deprived of his childhood friend and Bazin, Truffaut would once again be alone. On New Year's Day, 1950, they threw a going-away party for the future soldier at the home of a girl Robert was madly in love with. François, too, was in love with his date that night, Mireille G., an ardent film lover, clever and pretty, slightly older than he. The two had been living together for three weeks, in the room on rue de Martyrs, the first lasting relationship in Truffaut's love life.

Work at the Pontault-Combault factory was strenuous—ten hours of welding a day. But then came the first paycheck, on January 18, 1950: 5,748 francs. The very next day, his day off, Truffaut attended the 4:00 p.m. screening at the Cinémathèque. It was on that day, after having watched her and hesitated for a long time, that he first spoke to Liliane Litvin, a young aficionada of the Cinémathèque. As an excuse to speak to her, he used the book by Hervé Bazin that was tucked under her arm; this led to a lively conversation and the promise to meet again at a forthcoming screening on avenue de Messine. This meeting turned François's life upside down. He decided not to return to the factory. His constant wish was to see Liliane, not realizing that he wasn't the only young man courting her. Jean Gruault and Jean-Luc Godard were also captivated by the young girl, whom Gruault later described as "a gang leader with a very lively personality, petite, slightly plump, with a round face, and light brown, very curly hair."[57] Charting her love life with virtuoso skill, the fickle Liliane set up separate dates with each one of her suitors at the Cinémathèque. They also took turns calling at the Litvins' home, which was in the seventeenth arrondissement. Liliane's step-father was a garage owner, her mother cooked excellent kosher meals, and both parents were sociable and talkative. Jean-Luc, Jean, and François were warmly welcomed for lunch or dinner. Each one paid discreet court to the girl and her parents, and caught the occasional television broadcast at their house—a rare treat in Paris in 1950. They discussed literature to impress both mother and daughter, the latter a great admirer of André Gide. Truffaut knew Gide's work almost as thoroughly as he knew Balzac's, but to no avail: Liliane would give herself to none of them.

Of the three suitors, Truffaut was the one who took this platonic romantic relationship most to heart, alternating between joy and despair, with fits of jealousy and rage, while Liliane considered him only a friend. "Normally I shouldn't be in love with her. Each time we have a serious discussion, she laughs. All the same, I wait for hours in front of her door, freezing my balls off,"[58] he wrote in his journal. Later that June, after four months of ups and downs, Truffaut would take a daring step; he would move into a hotel directly across the street from the Litvins, on rue Dulong, so he could spy on Liliane. Delighted, Liliane would visit his room, even taking her parents there, but she still would resist throwing herself into this love quadrille with Gruault, Godard, and Truffaut. In the meantime, during the spring and summer of 1950, Truffaut had countless liaisons—with Mireille, Madeleine, Janine, Gisèle, Geneviève, Monique, and Charlotte. But Liliane Litvin "still remained as elusive as Proust's Albertine."[59] Truffaut would retain a taste for concurrent relationships, happy and unhappy, for a long time to come. Each woman was not only lovable but essential because different. *The Man Who Loved Women* was probably born in that spring of 1950; Truffaut had just turned eighteen.

Without his salary as an apprentice welder, Truffaut found himself penni-less at the end of January 1950. Lachenay, though no longer present, had left him his room, which François had rented to a friend for 1,880 francs a month. And he earned a bit of money helping Rohmer contact film distribu-tors, carry reels, and edit the *Bulletin du C.C.Q.L.*, but not enough to live on. So he borrowed small sums here and there, three hundred francs or so. Then, in the beginning of March, he sold off half of Robert's library to a bookseller for three thousand francs. This infuriated his "dear old soldier," causing the first real quarrel between the two friends.

## THE CLUB DU FAUBOURG

Probably to impress Liliane Litvin, Truffaut started going to the prestigious Club du Faubourg. Founded in 1917, this old institution welcomed inquisitive minds, enthusiasts, journalists, and the Paris smart set three times a week (in the late afternoon, Tuesday, Thursday, and Saturday) to meet and discuss recent shows, books, and social issues or to attend debates between writers. Every year, at the end of June, the Faubourg organized an eloquence competition; the qualifying contests held throughout the season were very popular events. Liliane's parents attended on Tuesdays, for the meetings were at the Villiers-Cinéma, not far from their house. During the week of February 27 to March 3, 1950, Truffaut participated in a discussion on gangster films and another on the Festival du Film Maudit. Though at first confining himself to cinema, he soon ventured easily into literature, or subjects he knew from personal experience, such as the competence of juvenile judges. François Truffaut felt at ease, for his talent was recognized. His ardor and competence impressed the club's habitués, among them Aly Khan, the fabulously wealthy playboy; Armand Piéral, a writer and the literary editor at Laffont; and the actor Jean Servais. Léo Poldès, the club's director, was also impressed, as was Marc Rucart, a senator and former minister, one of the many politicians who attended the gatherings there. On December 26, 1950, he wrote to Truffaut:

> Be assured of my esteem since the day I first saw you speak at the Club du Faubourg. This esteem stems from the courage you seemed to have, the clarity of your talks and "objections"; and from the fact that you spoke as if you were twenty years older than you are. Of course, you almost always shocked me, as you shocked nearly the whole audience. . . . Rightly or wrongly, you took pleasure in rising up against those who seemed stronger, more experienced, or older than you; and in the fear that people would think you incapable of further "plunging into the fray," you used the words most likely to offend and to provoke indignation. This was the mark of an inferiority complex that had to be overcome at all costs, a need for preventive attacks, an expression of your youthful rebellion against the less youthful, a manifestation of your ruthless opposition to all forms of conformism and traditionalism. Not being one to judge by results, I suspected the causes for your atti-

tude. I never learned what these were, but my suppositions strengthened my esteem, and gave rise to my sympathy, and even to a tender
curiosity.[60]

During the spring of 1950, Truffaut thereby became the Club du
Faubourg's mascot, and he attracted a growing list of admirers, many of
whom were writers or aristocrats. Hence, Louise de Vilmorin, Aimée
Alexandre, and the Countess du Pasthy would be his three benefactresses
for a long time to come. The first, a well-known writer, the author of
*Madame de . . .* , was a friend of Cocteau and André Malraux, and her salon
at Château de Verrières-le-Buisson was renowned. Aimée Alexandre was
Russian, a writer and a disciple of Bachelard. Following a brilliant presentation by Truffaut, she sent him the following note, echoing Rucart's impression: "My dear, delightful friend, you've suffered and struggled so much that
your mental age is at least double your physical age. And I'm convinced that
one day you'll become a marshal without having been a corporal."[61] Aimée
Alexandre would remain one of François Truffaut's confidantes until her
death, in the early seventies. As for Countess du Pasthy, a great collector of
valuable objects, she wrote Léo Poldès a letter filled with affection for "our
youngest member, François Truffaut": "This person has unquestionable
genius. This genius has not yet manifested itself, for up to now the struggle
for daily bread has fully absorbed him, but he knows what he wants, and has
willpower. He'll become an artist. He'll produce a life's work. He'll succeed.
Furthermore, he's a kind soul and has a treasure trove of tenderness."[62]

The ease and culture of this aristocratic milieu fascinated Truffaut and he
felt encouraged to display his brilliance. Later, he would recall Louise de
Vilmorin, Aimée Alexandre, and Countess du Pasthy in conceiving Fabienne Tabard, the incarnation of the seductive and refined woman played by
Delphine Seyrig in *Stolen Kisses.*

## SOCIETY REPORTER

In April 1950, Pierre-Jean Launay, *Elle* magazine's literary editor and a
friend of Louise de Vilmorin, Aimée Alexandre, and Léo Poldès, attended
an eloquence competition François Truffaut had signed up for. On that day,
Truffaut won his set, and Launay immediately made him an offer to work at
the well-known women's weekly.

This first experience as a journalist allowed Truffaut a new lifestyle for
several months. He "treated his pals," dressed up, took Liliane to the theater, spending everything he earned. He was now thrown into Parisian liter-

ary and journalistic life as a society reporter. In addition to *Elle,* he contributed to other publications, *Ciné-Digest, Lettres du monde,* and *France-Dimanche,* sometimes as a photographer: "I took my first 'photo-flash' steps at Le Méphisto cabaret and one of my pictures is going to appear in *France-Dimanche*—the actress Annette Poivre and her daughter at the bar."[63] For six months, from May to October 1950, Truffaut took on a large number of assignments to maintain his new lifestyle, and his metamorphosis. He had never been so prosperous and now he could even support his friend Lachenay in the army, sending him money, clothes, books, and food.

But he soon found himself overworked because of his double career as journalist and photographer. His articles included a report on the fashion shows, the elegant shops near the Opéra, and several portraits of popular actresses—Michèle Morgan, whom he met at the Gare de l'Est on the set of René Clément's *Le Château de verre;* Martine Carol, with whom he lunched at the Billancourt studios, where she was being filmed in *Caroline chérie.* "She's a very decent girl, the victim of stupid publicity, she has a lot of talent,"[64] he wrote to Lachenay at the beginning of August.

The event Truffaut followed most attentively for *Elle* had nothing to do with film; it was the trial of Michel Mourre, a twenty-two-year-old man famous throughout France. A former novice, who had been expelled from a Dominican monastery for atheism, he had managed, a year before, to ascend the pulpit at Notre-Dame on Easter Sunday and proclaim in a loud, clearly audible voice, "God is dead." This scandalous blasphemy almost got him sent to Sainte-Anne psychiatric hospital. The Church of France's trial against him was followed intently at the end of May 1950. Truffaut saw Mourre as a figure he could identify with, the kind of outlaw who was inevitably attacked by the establishment—whether political, academic, institutional, or—as in this case—religious. It was like the compassion that he had felt for Marshal Pétain, not a political sympathy, but one for lost causes generally, whatever they might be, and "a shared emotion with all the maligned of the earth,"[65] he wrote. Mourre was acquitted on June 14, and Truffaut got on well with him when the two men had lunch together the following day. Three days later, Truffaut had written four articles on the affair, which he intended to offer to the various magazines he was writing for.

He went to Hesdin, in the Pas-de-Calais, from June 8 to 13, 1950, to watch Robert Bresson shoot the final scenes of *Diary of a Country Priest,* adapted from the novel by Georges Bernanos. Meeting Bresson "is fantastic," he wrote Lachenay, but five days on the sad and rainy set "is too long and boring."[66] Truffaut extracted five articles from this experience, but he was beginning to tire of his new profession. Though journalism had its good sides—meeting people, living well, the enjoyable frenzy of deadline writing—it also had its shortcomings, particularly its superficiality. "I'm bored . . . and I'd like to give it all up," he confided to Lachenay as early as July 21, 1950.

## TWENTY-FIVE RAZOR SLASHES

François Truffaut was weary of journalism, but also drained by his relationship with Liliane Litvin, which was turning into a farce. On the evening of June 13, 1950, just after returning from the set of *Diary of a Country Priest,* he moved into the furnished room on rue Dulong that he had rented a week before, across the street from the Litvins; he wrote a long letter to Lachenay, describing the room in detail, and he even included a sketch of the layout.[67] His dream was for Liliane to move in with him, but she seemed unwilling to do so, for she was very busy preparing for her baccalaureate examination.

Truffaut was preparing for a kind of exam himself, that of the eloquence competition at the Club du Faubourg, to be held on Tuesday, June 27, at the Villiers-Cinéma. He was among the eleven finalists and the great favorite of the habitués. The competition included an assigned topic—"Paris in 1950"—and an improvisation on a theme to be divulged only at the last minute. Truffaut hoped against hope that Liliane would come, but in vain. On the night of the competition, deprived of his desired listener, he sulked: "I disappointed everyone because I had an infinitely bored, tired, monotonous air, implying 'what a stupid subject.' I came out third out of eleven."[68] He was given consolation prizes—a bottle of Ricard, some beauty products, and several lottery tickets, which he gave to Liliane's parents.

The beautiful Liliane flunked her exam as well, and did not get her baccalaureate degree. But this hardly deterred her from celebrating her birthday, on July 4, and inviting all her friends and acquaintances to an empty ground-floor apartment across the street from her parents' house. "There were over 40 people, including Claude Mauriac, Schérer, Alexandre Astruc, Jacques Bourgeois, Ariane Pathé, Michel Mourre, the cream of 16mm and journalistic Paris," Truffaut reported to Private Lachenay, languishing in his German barracks. Godard, Rivette, Chabrol, Gruault, Suzanne Klochendler, and her sisters also attended the party. "The rest of the evening was straight out of *The Rules of the Game.* Intrigues, rows in the street, doors slamming, Liliane played Nora Grégor, she switched 'Saint-Aubains' 4 or 5 times, I was Jurieu, there was bound to be a victim."[69] Who the victim would be was obvious. In the early morning, Truffaut went home, lay down in bed, and administered twenty-five razor slashes to his right arm, drenching the sheets in blood. Then he fainted. At 11:00 a.m., Liliane walked in and found him unconscious. She revived him, nursed him, and bandaged his arm. "Now, with my arm in a sling,

I'm like Frédéric Lemaître in *Children of Paradise* and I tell everyone I suffered a sprain,"[70] wrote Truffaut, ironically transposing the events of his life into fiction. As for Liliane, she disappeared for two days, whereabouts unknown, leaving her young neighbor weak and depressed.

By way of recovery, Truffaut stepped up his activities in the summer of 1950, attending the second Festival du Film Maudit in Biarritz from September first to twelfth. Over the course of a year, he had gained status; and as the special correspondent for *Elle,* he was put up at the Casino-Bellevue Hotel instead of in the lycée dormitory. But the ambiance on the Basque coast was morose; indeed, the festival would turn out to be the last project of a dying Objectif 49. Truffaut then went to spend about ten days in Antibes, Cannes, Nice, Saint-Tropez, and Cap-Ferrat, seeking scoops and hanging around the entrances of the villas and luxury hotels of the Riviera, in the hope of intercepting a film star or a leading Paris personality.

When he returned to Paris at the end of September, Truffaut was joyfully reunited with his friend Lachenay, who was on leave. They went to the movies and had long conversations, as in the past. Truffaut was slowly recovering from a bad patch, and once again André Bazin would try to help him. At the end of August, Truffaut had gone to a sanatorium in the Alps to visit him. During their meeting, the critic suggested they collaborate on a biography of Jean Renoir, his favorite director. Truffaut would have the task of establishing a complete filmography. The project had been commissioned by the English journal *Sight and Sound* and Bazin offered to split the payment of 26,000 francs. Truffaut had started his research when the deal fell through.

Truffaut then focused on a film project. He hoped that in writing his first screenplay, *La ceinture de peau d'ange* (The Angel Skin Belt), he would regain a zest for living. In August, he had written to his friend Lachenay, "I have 25 reels of film stock, in other words, 1 hour and 40 minutes of screen time. My film will be about 45 minutes long, so I have some leeway. I have the 16-mm camera and the cameraman, I have all the actors. I'm only missing some costumes and a large room as the set of a dining room with a 40-amp meter for the lighting."[71] *La ceinture de peau d'ange* is about a communicant, and he had obviously conceived and written the story with the idea of casting Liliane Litvin in the female lead. On the day of her First Communion, a young girl is raped by her cousin in the family attic. Six years later, she gets married, and during the wedding dinner she goes up to the attic to look for her childhood toys, which are locked away in an old trunk. Her husband's boss, a guest at the wedding, joins her in the attic; under the pretense of consoling her for her melancholy, he throws her down on an old couch.

In this fantastical screenplay, with its sexual and blasphemous overtones, there were parts for Jacques Rivette (the cousin) and Alexandre Astruc, as well as a part for Truffaut himself, as the communicant's brother. Truffaut hoped to win support from the Church of Paris, presenting the film, therefore, as a documentary on First Communions. To win over the religious authorities, he relied on the help of Abbé Gritti, Abbé Ayfre, and Father Yves Renaud of the Versailles film club, all close friends of André Bazin. But the Paris bishopric decided not to support this unorthodox documentary, and in later years, when Truffaut became a filmmaker, he wisely never reconsidered this first youthful screenplay.

## ENLISTMENT

In October 1950, Robert Lachenay returned to Germany to finish his military service. Liliane was still as elusive as ever, and André Bazin's tuberculosis kept him far from Paris. Truffaut was alone and still bored with journalism. On an impulse he decided to enlist for military service instead of waiting to be drafted. On October 29, he went around to the Reuilly-Diderot barracks, the Ministry of the Armed Forces on rue Saint-Dominique, and the Palais de Justice to get a certificate of his police record. Then the countdown began: In two weeks he would leave. "Of course, I've requested the occupation troops in Germany,"[72] he wrote Lachenay, who was enthusiastic at first: They would be closer to each other and could spend their leaves together in Coblenz. But two months later, when he heard what Truffaut had really signed up for, Lachenay changed his mind. Instead of leaving for Germany at the beginning of November as planned, Truffaut enlisted for a three-year term in the artillery—motivated by unrequited love, bravado, disgust with his Paris life, and, no doubt, the sizable bonus awarded to enlisted men. He was now due to leave for Indochina six months later. Robert Lachenay could not comprehend his friend's decision: "François, why did you do this? François, now we'll be separated for three years; I can't believe it, it's hard for me to accept the idea that you won't be in Paris when I return. I wonder what I'll do, how I'll live, how I'll get used to not seeing you, you and your briefcase, your papers, your eyeglasses, your humble pants and socks. . . ."[73]

On December 30, 1950, François Truffaut crossed the German frontier to go to Wittlich and join the Eighth Artillery battalion. He would do basic training for six months before leaving for Saigon. He started his military experience enthusiastically: "I have deliberately made a gift to the French army of three years of my life, three years with no films, no books, no running around, no friends, no initiatives," he wrote his father on January 3, 1951. "I consider this noble. The army is very often misunderstood. To say that military life is devoid of meaning or logic is as childish as kicking Arabs in police stations or laughing at Russian films."[74] But three days later, Truffaut had already recovered from his illusions and was begging for help from Bazin, Rohmer, and Launay—*Elle*'s literary editor—urging them to pull strings so he could be posted to Baden-Baden as a journalist for the *Revue d'information des Troupes d'Occupation en Allemagne* (Journal of Information of the Occupation Troops in Germany). In a letter to Rohmer on January 7, he described the Wittlich camp as a hellhole—the exercises, the discipline, the snow and mud, the compulsory marches with a pack of sixty-six pounds. He pleaded, "Don't forget that on the other side of the Rhine a friend is counting on you. If I die in Indochina, it will be your fault! Hurry."[75] Rohmer, Bazin, and Launay all intervened with the military authorities, but to no avail; the enlisted man remained a "prisoner" in Wittlich. He described to Lachenay his inadequacies as a soldier: "When I say, 'Platoon, at my command, forward . . . march!' no one moves, since only the officer cadet can hear me. . . ." He is incapable of holding a gun: "Of the entire barracks (2,000 guys), I'm the one who least knows how to set the weapon on my shoulder. It's staggeringly awkward and earns me a slew of punishments."[76] It is hardly surprising that Truffaut became the whipping boy of the regiment's noncommissioned officers and that they made his life hell.

The end of basic training felt like a relative liberation. On March 10, 1951, he was finally given a somewhat cushy secretarial job taking phone messages, which left him time to read and write. Truffaut made frequent visits to the infirmary during the harsh German winter, owing to recurrent sinus and hearing problems. He would suffer from these ailments contracted in Wittlich for a long time to come; it was only in the early sixties that he would undergo a nasal septum operation, and the hearing deficit in his right ear, caused by the cold and the noise of cannon fire, turned out to be permanent. "Several times a day I feel like my right ear is being torn off with an enormous pair of tongs, so great is the pulling sensation when a detonation rocks the camp,"[77] he had written to Lachenay in February. Later, Truffaut would use this characteristic for Ferrand, the director he plays in *Day for Night*, who wears a hearing aid.

From his cushy job, Truffaut corresponded with all "his women." First with Liliane Litvin, for whom he still carried a torch. She looked after him, forwarded his mail, and sent him packages of books and magazines. Truffaut hoped for much more—a declaration of love, which never came. But, as he told his friend Robert, my "love life is rather complicated," and "the objects of my love are either 16 years old or 40, with a few ambiguous relationships between these two ages—young women from good families, widows, and my Pigalle 'ladies.' "[78] Truffaut corresponded with Louise de Vilmorin, Aimée Alexandre, and the Countess du Pasthy, his Faubourg benefactresses. "I write them worn-out lies. They respond favorably to these letters which are all feverish declarations of love (success no doubt stems from the fact that I'm not sincere)."[79] The young serviceman vacillated between the melancholy of frustrated passion for Liliane and the cynicism of a ladies' man who was already a blasé manipulator. And in between there were the loose women—the prostitutes he visited regularly, and Geneviève, his first mistress from the autumn of 1946, with whom he corresponded from Germany. "She lives alone and her letters are very tempting. My 1946 dream is beginning to materialize, Geneviève, a Balzacian heroine, my lily in the valley whom I'll once again defile!"[80] he wrote to Lachenay on February twelfth. These real women would later serve as models for the women in his films. Liliane Litvin would be the Colette of *Love at Twenty,* played by Marie-France Pisier; the proper young girls would recognize themselves in the Christine Darbon of *Stolen Kisses* and *Bed and Board,* played by Claude Jade; the mature, elegant women would be perfectly incarnated by Fabienne Tabard (unforgettably played by Delphine Seyrig); while prostitutes would appear in all his works.

## THE DIARY OF A THIEF

Deprived of films during basic training, François Truffaut read intensively in the Wittlich barracks. He discovered Marcel Proust, whose *Remembrance of Things Past* he read and reread in January 1951: "It's wonderful and decisive for the fate of the novel: Balzac and Proust are the two greatest novelists in the French language,"[81] he wrote Lachenay on January 26. Another revelation was Jean Genet. Truffaut read *The Thief's Journal* just before he enlisted and recopied one specific passage in a datebook on December 19, 1950. "I was born in Paris on 19 December 1910. It was impossible for me, as a ward of Public Welfare, to know anything else about my civil status. When I was twenty-one, I obtained a birth certificate. My mother was named Gabrielle Genet. My father remains unknown. I came into the world at 22, rue d'Assas."[82] Truffaut, the former inmate of the Villejuif Observation Center, was bound to identify with Genet—the child of an unknown father, the delinquent sent from juvenile centers to prisons, the victim of punishments, humiliations, and unbridled animal sexuality, who finally found salvation in writing.

François Truffaut recopied this excerpt because the date was particularly important to him, as well; on December 19, 1950, he wrote to Jean Genet on the occasion of his fortieth birthday. At the time, Genet was living in a small room at the Hotel Terrass in the eighteenth arrondissement, right near the Montmartre cemetery, and was undergoing a deep moral and intellectual crisis, as well as a physical one—he was suffering from gallstones and would require several hospitalizations in 1950 and 1951. He was destitute as well, and survived by relying on friends who were better off. He also seemed dried up in terms of work, after the intense excitement of the "glory years," from 1942 to 1947. "For six years I remained in that miserable state," he later said, "in that imbecility which is the dregs of all life: opening a door, lighting a cigarette. . . . There are only certain bright spots in the life of a man. Everything else is grayness." Genet would also write in 1954: "The thought—not the appeal, but the thought of suicide, appeared clearly in me toward my fortieth year, brought there, it seems, by my weariness with living, after an inner void opened up in me that nothing except the final sliding away, would seem to be able to abolish."[83] One sees here a meeting of two suicidal souls, and this kindred outlook, in spite of differences in background and age, was surely what brought Truffaut and Genet together. However, despite his state of mind, Genet was also becoming one of the most famous French writers of the period. Each of his books and each of his plays—such as *Haute Surveillance,* which had been performed the previous year at the Théâtre des Mathurins—caused a furor. In 1951, Gallimard started publishing his complete works. And in *Saint Genet: Actor and Martyr,* Jean-Paul Sartre saw him as the poet and protagonist of the century.

In his letter, Truffaut enclosed the essay he had written on *The Thief's Journal* and "The Criminal Child," entitled "Jean Genet, mon prochain" ("Jean Genet, My Fellowman"), originally intended for the journal *Lettres du monde* but, unfortunately, now lost. On March 24, 1951, Truffaut mentioned to Robert Lachenay that he had been "surprised to receive an answer": "He wrote me a really nice letter expressing thanks and kind feelings: he tells me to come and see him when I'm in Paris. It's a fine autograph to have."[84] Genet had indeed written a warm letter: "Dear Monsieur, I am very touched by your note. I am also very surprised that anyone should think of writing to me and writing about my work. You might be disappointed, for I have not fallen out with Sartre, whom I like enormously and very sincerely. Besides, his critical work on me hardly concerns me—it's mostly about himself. Of what you write, I don't know what to say, except that it seems to me much too glowing. If you get a few days off from the army to come to Paris, come by and say hello to me. It would be a pleasure to shake your hand. Kind regards."[85]

The meeting took place in Genet's little hotel room in mid-April of 1951, as soon as Truffaut had his first leave. We can measure the full effect it had on Genet by his inscription on the first page of *The Thief's Journal,* which he gave to François a short time later: "My dear François, don't be hurt, but when I saw you come into my room, it was like seeing myself—in an almost uncanny way—when I was 19 years old. I hope you'll retain your grave expression for a long time and your simple, slightly unhappy way of expressing yourself. You can count on me." With his military haircut, frail appearance, short stature, slightly crooked nose, lively, worried gaze, and melancholy air, Truffaut certainly looked like the self-portrait Genet described in April 1951. But this apparition, in the door frame of a hotel room, also illustrates something Sartre wrote about *The Thief's Journal* at that same time: "Genet sees himself everywhere; the dullest surfaces reflect his image; even in others he perceives himself, thereby bringing to light their deepest secrets."[86] Truffaut's secret, of course, was his unknown father, whom he sought to replace with the artists he most admired. Jean Genet and André Bazin were the first to fit into this surrogate role. Truffaut wrote as much to Lachenay on August 15, 1951: "In three weeks Bazin and Genet did for me what my parents never did for me in fifteen years."[87]

Genet responded to all of Truffaut's letters and requests in the spring and summer of 1951. He wrote him in Wittlich "a very brief word to let you know I haven't forgotten you. Send me news of yourself, ask me for anything you desire, and stop by to see me if you come to Paris. Consider me always your very faithful friend." Above all, Genet sent him dozens of books through Gallimard and it was he who first introduced Truffaut to the publisher's *Série Noire* crime thrillers in August 1951. "I arranged to have some detective novels (hospital reading) sent to you and two packs of Gitanes. Did you receive these?" This would turn out to be essential reading for Truffaut, who would later adapt for the screen works by William Irish, David Goodis, Henry Farrell, and Charles Williams, all authors who had been translated and published in the prestigious *Série Noire*.

This important friendship was documented by a total of eleven letters[88] and two book inscriptions on the part of Genet: "I'm amused by your letter," Genet wrote at the beginning of June 1951. "Do what you want, but don't ask me for such inane explanations. It's true, I don't like letters very much. Forgive me if mine are short. The important thing is that they express my friendship." Truffaut's answers, of which there are about fifteen in all, were longer. Though this friendship had very little concrete effect on the physical conditions of Truffaut's military life, it helped him greatly during that difficult time. So he wrote to Lachenay on November 22, 1951, from his prison cell, when he had thoughts of suicide, "I get only short, infrequent letters from Genet, but it's thanks to them I can hold out."[89]

Their relationship would last after Truffaut's return to civilian life; he and Genet would often take long walks together down the boulevard de Clichy. But it would come to an abrupt end in November 1964, when Truffaut arrived very late to an appointment Genet had set up for him to meet his friend Abdallah, who was looking for work. Truffaut received his last note from Genet on the following day: "Yesterday I asked you to do a young Moroccan a favor, a lost soul, and you kept him waiting for an hour and a half. For his mental health, it was good for him to see how people in film behave and the kind of treatment they deserve. I'm deeply sorry, François, that you've learned to play the part, because I liked you. You can let your laughable misplaced pride go to your head but drop the bad manners, François, and keep up the habit of roaming around the Boulevard de Clichy, because sometimes I need dough. . . ."[90]

## THE DESERTER

On May 12, 1951, François Truffaut was pronounced fit for duty by the military physician in Wittlich; he could therefore be posted to Saigon. His departure was set for July 14. He was given several leaves during his final two months, and, naturally, he spent those in Paris, where he fell back into his old life—seeing friends again, going constantly to the Cinémathèque, meeting Genet. He saw a great deal of Liliane Litvin; they went to the movies together and she invited him to her country house. She even became jealous and demanded he break up immediately with Geneviève S., who housed and supported Truffaut while he was in Paris.

Truffaut now began to regret he had enlisted for service in Indochina. On June 8, he wrote to Robert Lachenay for advice, weighing things for and against, only to conclude, "I feel like deserting."[91] On June 21, his letter is replete with cinematic references: "I'll soon find myself in the same situation as Jean Gabin at the beginning of the film set in Le Havre [*Port of Shadows*], except I'll have clothes, work, housing, dependable friends. I'll then be in Gabin's shoes at the end of the film that takes place in Algiers [*Pépé le Moko*], when the ship leaves without him! I don't know if you'll approve of my decision, but I'm convinced it's the best. Don't let anything surprise you when we see each other in Paris, and trust me."[92]

Truffaut had made up his mind: It was utter madness to go to Saigon. He turned in his kit in Wittlich on July 13, said farewell, and boarded the 4:00 p.m. train for Strasbourg. "Incredibly depressed," he wrote in his date book during the train trip. The following day, he was supposed to be in Marseilles to start a month of intensive combat training prior to his departure for Indochina on August 20. On the overnight trip from Strasbourg to Paris, he met a "delightful" young German girl named Charlotte who shared his compartment and helped him regain a taste for civilian life. And in Paris, in the early morning, he ran into Genet—miraculously—on the boulevard de Clichy, and spent the rest of his departure allowance with him. By the early afternoon, he had joined Liliane, Robert, Chris Marker, Alexandre Astruc, and Jacques Rivette, who were waiting for him so they could throw a bash in Rivette's apartment on rue de Clignancourt. Truffaut was therefore not in Marseilles on the night of July 14 to 15, which made him a deserter—or at least put him in what was officially called "a state of illegal absence." He didn't hide at first, and his friends saw him proudly resume his Parisian lifestyle. But soon it became dangerous for him to roam the streets at night because of the possibility the police might ask for his papers. So Truffaut looked for a place to hide. He spent one or two nights at Jean Douchet's, then was back on the street. Once again, André Bazin, who had just returned from a long convalescence in Vernet-les-Bains, in the Pyrénées, proved to be the providential friend, offering to put Truffaut up. Bazin, his wife, Janine, and Chris Marker spent a whole day looking for Truffaut, waiting outside his favorite movie houses for the shows to let out. They finally found him on July 21 and took him back to Bry-sur-Marne, where the Bazin couple lived with their two-year-old son, Florent, and their many pets. They had a small, modest apartment, but it was pleasant—three rooms and a kitchen on the second floor of a house, surrounded by a quiet park, in a peaceful Paris suburb. Though it wasn't fixed up, the maid's room in the attic was habitable—and this was where Janine and André put François up. Bazin felt that, first and foremost, Truffaut should legalize his situation, and he convinced him to go and plead his case before the officers in the Paris area, saying this was the only chance he had of really regaining his freedom. On July 28, Liliane was invited for lunch at Bry-sur-Marne; then they all went to see Robert Flaherty's *Elephant Boy* at the Cinémathèque; afterward, Bazin and his protégé, accompanied by Janine and Liliane, went together to the Prévauté at the Invalides. The plea for conciliation failed; charged with illegal absenteeism, Truffaut was sent forthwith to the prison of the Dupleix barracks and incarcerated. He was detained for seven days. The Bazins came to see him, and so did Liliane, who even sent him a parcel of books. He was then told that he would have to join the Thirty-second Artillery battalion in Coblenz. This seemed like relatively good news, since his departure for Indochina appeared to have been called off.

On the afternoon of August 3, Truffaut was discovered to have a new bout of syphilis and was rushed to the military medical unit at Villemin hospital, near the Gare de l'Est. Under surveillance and knocked out by the treatment, he was in a state of dreadful boredom and depression; he was cheered only by the visits of the Bazins and Abbé Gritti and by a few letters of friends. Jean Genet tried unsuccessfully to see him after returning from a trip to Stockholm, but he lacked the necessary authorization paper from the examining judge. So he sent François a letter and a big package of books. "Actually, everything is now for the best," he wrote. "Your pox made its appearance at the right time. As a moralist, I would be sorry if you were spared Indochina: the sick are the first who should be sent to slaughter. Jean Domarchi will bring you other books, [Sartre's] *Situations*. What should I wish for you? Recovery? Prison? Psychiatric hospital? Freedom? You don't really seem to me to want it. I'm afraid you have the soul of a desperado. If that's the case, you should come to terms with it, submit to your fate and croak holding a grenade. I like you anyhow, with kind regards and love."[93]

François Truffaut stayed at Villemin hospital from August 3 to September 3, 1951, in a state of physical and mental disrepair, from which he emerged only gradually. The Bazins had left for vacation in the Charente; his Paris friends were out of town. Again, he was alone, ill, and in prison. Genet did his utmost to help him. He remembered René Leibowitz, a psychiatrist friend of Sartre, whom he thought might be able to help Truffaut get out of his predicament. But in order to reach him, they had to wait for Sartre to return from his trip to the North Pole. None of the steps taken by Genet would change the situation, but under his influence, Truffaut started keeping a journal on August 21. The cover of this schoolboy's notebook, a montage of photos and drawings, is itself an homage to Genet and also a kind of self-portrait—sketches of faces, women's bodies, a Pierrot, a picture of Genet's face cut out from a magazine, and the manacled hands of a young man. And under the title *Diary* was this epigraph: "May this notebook be for Truffaut what the *Pierres* [*Stones*] were for Hugo."[94] Inside were notes, drawings, comments on filmmakers and writers, as well as daily impressions, punctuated by letters he'd received and his successive transfers from prison to prison, and barracks to hospital. Locked up and ill, he had plenty of time to read the many books sent to him by Genet, Bazin, Lachenay, and Liliane and to write about them at length. In this journal, Truffaut defined the literary tradition he most admired—Balzac, Proust, and Genet—and rejected "moralizers," such as Eugène Sue and Hervé Bazin, and "writers of contempt," such as Flaubert and Gide. He described his revolts and revelations, and discussed cinema, sharply dismissing postwar French movies as "studio filmmaking based on adaptation." Truffaut also worked on his own image in his journal, molding himself into a provocative figure, worthy of both Balzac and Genet, actor and martyr. "We're handcuffed when we go to the showers. The first time around, I was embarrassed because you have to go through the hospital and people stared at us, but later I was ashamed at being ashamed, because doesn't the 'Genet' position dictate pride in deserving handcuffs? So, now, before going to the showers, I light a cigarette and smirk in a kind of satisfied, slightly aggressive way."[95]

On Monday, September 3, 1951, Truffaut was informed of his impending departure for Germany. He requested a day to put his affairs in order and say his farewells; as soon as this was granted and he was set free, he deserted. For three days, he roamed around Paris, looking for less impecunious friends. Bazin was out of town, and so was Genet. Jean Domarchi and Jean Cau, friends of Genet to whom he had been recommended, were nowhere to be found. And none of the friends he ran into at the Cinémathèque—Rivette, Gruault, or Liliane Litvin—had any money to lend him. On September 7, utterly penniless, Truffaut went to see a doctor who worked at the Cité Universitaire, and a military chaplain, to ask for help. They tried to get him admitted into the Val-de-Grâce hospital with a false certification of ill health. But he was missing a necessary document—permission from the military health unit. On September 8 at 4:00 p.m., as he was going to meet a friend of the doctor's who was prepared to give him the precious document, Truffaut was arrested at the entrance of the building by soldiers who asked to see his identity papers. He was taken to the Dupleix barracks and put in the very same cell where he had been held several weeks before.

## ME, FRANÇOIS TRUFFAUT, A SELF-HATING AUTODIDACT

He remained locked up for three days. At 6:00 a.m. on September 12, he was transferred to a police van and taken to the Gare de l'Est. "People look at me, particularly because of my handcuffs. Hatred or sympathy? Neither, probably, just a morbid, animal curiosity, nothing more. In the reserved compartment, I have two guards all to myself and those dopes won't even remove my handcuffs. More asses than bastards, and close to retirement, so they don't want trouble. If only they knew that behind the contemptuous, haughty airs I put on, there's a little boy who would break out in tears from just an affectionate squeeze on the shoulder,"[96] he wrote in his journal. In Strasbourg, Truffaut and his two guards got into a car, and after driving across the German frontier, they handed him over to the police in Kiel, a small German village. His handcuffs were removed, and he was even allowed to buy cigarettes while he waited for his departure to Coblenz at 5 a.m. on Thursday, September 13. He arrived at the barracks at noon, and his hair was cropped.

On the following day, Truffaut was brought before the camp's judicial officer, who suspected him of being a Communist. Truffaut described his youth, "including Villejuif and syphilis," so that on September 15, he was transferred to the army hospital in Andernach, nineteen miles from Coblenz. A new treatment was started as soon as he arrived—more than fifty injections over a period of ten days. When he was cured, he was returned to Coblenz and locked up in the disciplinary area, which was completely deserted. Books were scarce and Truffaut was bored to death; his only entertainment was to get drunk every day with his guards. On the morning of September 30, the guards found him with many razor slashes on his face, neck, and chest. This second suicide attempt landed him once again at the Andernach hospital, this time in the neuropsychiatric unit. "I'm with a guy who never talks, a rookie who couldn't get used to the army; there's also a case of delirium tremens who gets over 40 shots a day; a mental retard who never stops stroking his feet; and another retard who put on his shoes in the middle of the night and grabbed his haversack to go home. Another guy, very young, went crazy from a bazooka exploding right next to him. His name is Dany, but his nickname is Tino Rossi, because he sings incomprehensible songs all day. There's also Terasse, a swinging daddy's boy, and Brault, a painter I like a lot. But he has very violent tantrums. His fingers are contorted, twisted, he brings a hand to his throat and tries to strangle himself, uttering little shrieks and cries. And then there's me, François Truffaut, a self-hating autodidact."[97]

Truffaut would spend a month and a half in the company of the madmen, watched over by brutal male nurses, though they were conscripts like himself. He kept his journal but lived in solitude and self-hatred. It was not until November 27 that he was released from the Andernach neuropsychiatric unit and sent back to the Coblenz barracks. Working in the canteen, he found a more convivial, warmer atmosphere; he was the only man among five women, with one of whom—Laura, a young German domestic—he had a passionate affair.

Meanwhile, in Paris, André Bazin tried to rescue Truffaut from his plight. His direct appeals to the military authorities were fruitless; sometimes his efforts even turned against him, for he was seen as an "antimilitary, Communist intellectual,"[98] and against Truffaut, the "guy with connections." Helped by Abbé Gritti, Bazin finally succeeded—through Raymond Clarys, the director of the Villejuif Observation Center for Minors, and Senator Marc Rucart, Truffaut's old admirer at the Club du Faubourg—in contacting the military examining judge, Lieutenant Le Masne de Chermont. He was the person conducting the investigation of the Truffaut case in view of the trial set for November 22, 1951, before the Coblenz military tribunal. Raymond Clarys forwarded to him the psychiatric file that had been drawn up two years earlier by Mademoiselle Rikkers, while Senator Rucart, a former minister, contacted General Noiret, stationed at Baden-Baden. These appeals seemed promising, as indicated by the note the examining judge wrote to Bazin on October 22: "Let things settle down now and stop moving heaven and earth. . . . From my investigation into this case, I can encourage you to hope for a favorable outcome for your protégé."[99] Similarly, General Noiret reassured Senator Rucart concerning the young man's future: "You can rest assured that this young soldier's case will be given favorable consideration as a result of the particular circumstances you brought to my attention."[100] On Friday, December 7, Truffaut learned from his commanding officer, Captain Wittmann, that there was a very good chance that he would be given a "second-class temporary discharge" and sent back home.[101]

Good news came with its share of humiliations. The Coblenz officers had trouble accepting the decision and submitted the malingerer to harsh discipline. Truffaut now spent most of his time in jail, including Christmas, but a telegram from Janine and André Bazin brought him a bit of comfort: "Thinking of you, be patient, with love."[102] On January 3, 1952, Truffaut went before the discharging board and stood at attention, hair shaved and in an oversized uniform. After a two-hour discussion, during which three captains and two majors described the soldier's "unstable character" and his "perverse delinquent tendency," he was finally given a temporary discharge. His military enlistment was annulled, but he still had eighteen days of duty as a legal requirement. He would spend them back in prison again—a way of depressing the "guy with connections" just a little while longer.

He received letters from his friends—Bazin, Aimée Alexandre, Louise de Vilmorin, Marc Rucart, Lachenay. On January 16, Cocteau even sent him the proofs of his new anthology, *Bacchus,* with a warm and cheering inscription. Nor did Genet forget him: "You're really unlucky! Still in prison! The army is beginning to realize the blunder it made in accepting you. In any case, it's good that you're returning to France. But it's unfortunate you'll be leaving the army for Saint-Germain-des-Prés. Personally, I'd rather see you a soldier. Return anyhow and stop by to say hello. I'm well. I see very few people. You're very nice and I like you a lot."[103] Truffaut, for his part, wrote many letters, and kept track of his readings in his diary—Balzac, Raymond Radiguet, Julien Gracq, and a new journal with a yellow cover that Bazin had sent him, *Cahiers du cinéma.* Liliane's silence weighed heavily on him and intensified his feelings of isolation and humiliation. On February 6, 1952, his twentieth birthday, Captain Wittmann subjected him to insults in front of five witnesses. Truffaut noted down the juicy dialogue in his journal; he would later use it for inspiration in *Stolen Kisses,* for the scene where Antoine Doinel is discharged.

> —*Ah, Truffaut! I believe you're leaving us. Do you know where you'll go when you return to Paris?*
>
> —*Yes, to Bazin's . . .*
>
> —*Bazin's? Well, tell your Bazin he'd better give you better advice in civilian life than in military life, because if you'd gone before a military tribunal, you wouldn't have gotten off so easy, nor would he in fact; it's expensive to house a deserter, he must be something your Bazin, he and his friends, antimilitarists, Communists, homosexuals, these people, I spit in their faces, you understand, that's French, right, get it, that's French!*

*—It's French, but inaccurate. . . .*
*—Shut your trap, you're just a quitter, a loudmouth, a stinker, that's*
*all; I'd like to come across you at war; while there are guys getting*
*killed over there in Indochina.*[104]

Ten days later, the degradation ritual took place before the disciplinary committee, in the officers' presence. "It is customary to present gunners with a record of good conduct at their release, even when they've committed some minor misdeeds, but those you committed voluntarily are of the type that taint your honor,"[105] the colonel said as Truffaut remained dignified and saluted properly, keeping his thoughts to himself. On the afternoon of Wednesday, February 20, 1952, François Truffaut, finally freed, boarded the train at the Coblenz station. The next day, at 7:00 a.m., he arrived at the Gare de l'Est as a civilian and could inscribe page 184 of his journal in capital letters: "IN PARIS."

# 3.
# LIFE WAS THE SCREEN:
# 1952–1958

wo hours after getting off the train at the Gare de l'Est, François
Truffaut went to boulevard Masséna to see Madame Kirsch, Janine
Bazin's mother, who fed him a good meal and gave him the keys to
the Bazin apartment, since the couple was out of town. He moved back into
his attic room, in Bry-sur-Marne, and tried to forget his year in the military.
He realized how much he owed the Bazins, and soon he acquired a taste for
the kind of family life he had never known before. "You can laugh, but admit
that parents like these are rare. I've had enough of loneliness that gives rise
to squalor, listlessness, low morale, etc. . . ."[1] he wrote to Robert Lachenay,
who was sad that he had not immediately come to join him in Paris after his
return from Germany.

## AT THE BAZINS'

Truffaut found material comfort in Bry-sur-Marne, and, more important, an
atmosphere that was conducive to work. The only thing troubling him was
his relationship with Liliane Litvin, which ended before it had ever really
started. Liliane told him that she was pregnant and planned to marry the
father of her child. This romantic breakup probably marked the final crisis
in Truffaut's youth. In his journal, on May 6 and 7, he wrote, "I've now loved

Liliane for two and a half years and loved only her. It's beginning to last too long. I'm fed up with it. I shouldn't have invited her on Saturday and Sunday. I feel it's putting me through the worst suffering. I won't invite her anymore. This whole thing has to come to an end as soon as possible. I'm waiting impatiently for Janine and André to return."[2]

In the first weeks of his new life at Bry-sur-Marne, Truffaut went to a few screenings at the Ciné-Club du Quartier Latin, with Lachenay, Rivette, Godard, and Rohmer. He also resumed his conversations with Jean Genet, in the latter's little studio behind the Sacré-Coeur. But he devoted most of his time to reading the many books in Bazin's library. Often, he went to Paris with Bazin to see a couple of films. He gradually regained his taste for the cinema, but his moviegoing was far less obsessive than in previous years—as though he were searching for something else, or wanted to extend this period of convalescence. He was perfectly content in this family atmosphere, with André, Janine, and their son, Florent, and there developed a reciprocal relationship between François and André: "They both educated each other,"[3] Janine wrote in 1961, referring to the ties between Bazin and Truffaut. It's easy to see what the critic offered his protégé—experience, an attentive ear, a lively intelligence, and great kindness. The disciple responded with his own qualities—lively conversation, laughter, complicity, vitality. Indeed, Truffaut's arrival enlivened the couple's existence, and it was the most joyous period of their life. "It was the only time I saw André laugh and be happy in spite of his illness,"[4] Janine recalled in a letter to Truffaut in February 1965. Or, as she put in 1984, "a two-year state of grace between a mildly insubordinate young man and a 'man of conscience.' "[5]

But this was only an interlude. In the beginning of April 1952, Truffaut had to find employment. He asked all his friends and connections for help, such as Jean Cau, Jean-Paul Sartre's secretary, whom he'd met through Genet, and Senator Marc Rucart, whom he knew from the Club du Faubourg. Several leads opened up but subsequently fell through. Then he wrote to Louise de Vilmorin, who answered immediately, inviting him to come visit her in Verrières: "I know quite a few people in journalism, including some magazine editors. However, I can't talk to them about you unless I know you better,"[6] she wrote him on April seventeenth. There in Verrières, in her blue living room, Louise de Vilmorin gave him an excellent lead. A new magazine, *L'Express,* was being launched and her friend Françoise Giroud was on the editorial staff. Unfortunately, this lead fell through, as well. Depression threatened again; he was broke and at loose ends.

Many months went by without employment, but Truffaut's tastes and intellect continued to be formed by contact with Bazin, who once again stepped in to help his protégé, getting him some freelance assignments at *Cinémonde* and some work in the film department of the Ministry of Agriculture. The latter involved assisting the directors of ministry-financed doc-umentary films and lasted only a few weeks; the *Cinémonde* work, including a piece on the "new sensual bombshells," allowed Truffaut to write an impassioned homage to one of his favorite actresses: "In the fierce sex derby that makes the whole world focus on Hollywood, Marilyn Monroe is in a class of her own. Among fifty others, Gloria Grahame has had the best start and is a very close contender. You don't need a telescope to follow the progress of this new breed of fillies: they're thoroughbreds, unequivocally. No pair of binoculars or scientific lens could resist the sensual radiations that emanate from their utterly desirable beings."[7] Protected by anonymity, Truffaut wrote at length, in a short, lively, rapid style. If nothing else, *Ciné-monde* gave him his first opportunity to focus his journalistic writing specifi-cally on cinema.

## THE TIME OF CONTEMPT

François Truffaut next set himself a specific objective whose attainment would bring little money but much prestige—to write for *Cahiers du cinéma,* the magazine founded by Jacques Doniol-Valcroze, Joseph-Marie Lo Duca, and André Bazin in April 1951. He worked for several months on a long article which he handed to Bazin at the end of December 1952: "The Time of Contempt: Notes on a Certain Tendency of the French Cinema." It was a harsh indictment, initially conceived in Germany, where, deprived of movies, he had sifted through countless notes, trying to classify and analyze the films he had seen in his youth. These dozens and dozens of films consti-tuted what Jean-Pierre Barrot, in the postwar *L'Écran français,* called, with marked respect, the "tradition of quality."[8] It was this very tradition that Truffaut would take pains to denounce.

In an early version of this essay, Truffaut confessed to his youthful fasci-nation for the dark atmosphere and seamy stories of traditional French films, particularly those written by the most famous screenwriting team of the period, Jean Aurenche and Pierre Bost. Indeed, this fascination was dis-cernible in *Ceinture de peau d'ange,* the story of the First Communion girl which he had wanted to direct in the fall of 1950. "I'm ashamed I was once able to invent a story that is so stupid and nasty, but you could see the influ-ence of the kind of movies I believed in at the time."[9] A taste for blasphemy, a hatred of family, perverse, cynical characters—these were the main themes of the French cinema of the period, and they could be found even in Truffaut's three-page synopsis. No doubt his own "experience of infamy," being locked up in a military prison, marked a decisive and painful stage in his development. He could no longer bear the "infamous stories" of French movies, or the contemptuous superiority directors and screenwriters displayed toward their screen characters. "The director should have the same humility toward his characters that St. Francis of Assisi had toward God. For us to accept infamous characters, the person who creates them must be even more infamous. Anathema, blasphemy, sarcasm are the three passwords of French screenwriters. Griffith, to take a counter-example, is always great because he was even more ingenuous than his screen characters. These 'superior' artists claim to be superior to their creations; this presumption explains, but fails to excuse, the bankruptcy of the arts since the invention of motion pictures."[10]

The other focus of his attack concerned the French tradition of adapting literary works. Truffaut was convinced that French cinema was a screenwriter's cinema which owed its failings to those of the screenwriters. In the military prison in Andernach, Truffaut had reread Radiguet's *Devil in the Flesh*, which was being serialized in *Ici Paris*. And he drew up many instances of "equivalencies-betrayals" between the novel and Claude Autant-Lara's film adaptation from Aurenche and Bost's screenplay. Truffaut decried the mediocrity of a school that liked to think of itself as true-to-life and psychological, formed by the war, and represented by the screenwriters Aurenche and Bost, Charles Spaak, Henri Jeanson, Roland Laudenbach, Robert Scipion, Pierre Laroche, and Jacques Sigurd. "For them, psychological realism inevitably requires that men be base, infamous and vile . . . the films they write are even more base, vile and spineless than anything French art has produced to date."[11] Truffaut also inveighed against films like Jean Delannoy's *La Symphonie pastorale* (*The Pastoral Symphony*) and *Le Garçon sauvage* (*Savage Triangle*), Christian-Jaque's *La Chartreuse de Parme* (*The Charterhouse of Parma*) and *D'homme à hommes* (*Man to Men*), Yves Allégret's *Manèges* (*The Cheat*), *Dédée d'Anvers* (*Dedee*) and *Une si jolie petite plage* (*Riptide*), and *Retour à la vie*, a film made up of sketches by André Cayatte, Henri-Georges Clouzot, Jean Dréville, and Georges Lampin.

Truffaut continued to work on his article after moving in with the Bazins in February 1952. In the course of his research, he even approached Bost and, by flattery, succeeded in borrowing four screenplays including an adaptation of Bernanos's *Diary of a Country Priest*, which the novelist had rejected during his lifetime and which Aurenche hoped to direct himself. Truffaut would use these documents, obtained in such an inelegant and opportunistic fashion, against Bost, as damaging firsthand evidence in the campaign he intended to wage.

Truffaut gave Bazin the first version of his article in December 1952.[12] Thirty-one typed pages, it was often awkward and violently polemical in tone. His attack on the "blue chips" of French cinema was sometimes personal. Aurenche is characterized as "a dropout from directing who made one or two commercial shorts," Jeanson is written off as "base and ignoble," and Françoise Giroud is accused of having "boundless bad taste." He denounces the plots of "quality films" with great violence: Autant-Lara's *Le Blé en herbe* (*The Game of Love*) is "a gross lesbian story," and Yves Allégret's *Les Orgueilleux* (*The Proud and the Beautiful*) elicits an outraged witticism: "If Yves Allégret is really honest with himself, within the next three years he should show us Madame Michèle Morgan in Australia without panties surrounded by kangaroos decimated by typhus, transformed for local reasons into a nasal hemorrhage. If my prediction doesn't come true—which is probable—I will have been right in accusing Monsieur Allégret of being the most conformist of film directors."

The essay appealed to André Bazin, but not for a minute did he imagine it in *Cahiers du cinéma* without changes; he asked his protégé for a revision with fewer examples, fewer quotes, and fewer personal attacks, as well as a positive section to offset his denunciations. Truffaut followed this advice and worked on the article for almost a year. In the meantime, Bazin suggested he write a few brief essays on current films in order to practice his critical writing skills, promising to get them published in *Cahiers du cinéma*. In March 1953, Truffaut's first piece appeared in the magazine—a few pages on a small American film that had gone more or less unnoticed, David Miller's *Sudden Fear*, with Jack Palance, Gloria Grahame, and Joan Crawford. "The craftsmanship of Hollywood motion pictures is perfect even in 'Z movies.' This upsets the hierarchy . . . for the only things that count here are an ambitious screenplay and the director's reputed market value. . . . There, in contrast, a clever, beautiful and sober story, directed with professionalism and precision, Gloria Grahame's face and a steep Frisco street—all contribute to the stature of a cinema that proves to us every week that it is the greatest in the world." From month to month, Truffaut extolled American B movies, praising their modesty and production speed, compared to the sluggishness of French films. His admiration for vitality in cinema would have an effect: Samuel Fuller, Nicholas Ray, Edgar G. Ulmer, Allan Dwan, Ernest Schoedsack, Richard Fleischer, Tay Garnett, André de Toth, to name only a few, owe their critical fate in France partly to Truffaut's informed gaze.[13]

In March 1953, Truffaut was publishing so many articles in *Cahiers* that he soon decided he couldn't sign them all with his own name. A certain "François de Monferrand" broke into print and then, in November 1953, one "Robert Lachenay"—his two favorite pseudonyms. The critic could thereby vary the style of his contributions: François de Monferrand used jokes, puns, and spoonerisms, while Robert Lachenay indulged in suggestiveness and fetishism. The latter, for example, started a cult for Marilyn's underwear in a passionate review (November 1953) of *Niagara* entitled

"*Niagara's* Underpinnings." But on each, the polemical mastery bears the unmistakable mark of their creator.

On November 5, 1953, Truffaut gave Bazin and Doniol-Valcroze the new version of his long article, now entitled "A Certain Tendency of the French Cinema." Two days later, he returned the scripts, which he had borrowed a year earlier, to Pierre Bost with a malicious, rude note: "I didn't expect that reading these screenplays would be so fruitful and revealing. That's my excuse, as well as the desire not to leave anything to chance and to do a comprehensive job. I hope I haven't put these documents to too bad a use. With all my gratitude and respectful good wishes."[14]

Doniol-Valcroze and Bazin hesitated. By attacking the establishment head-on, they felt, the article might puzzle readers with such proclamations as this: "Though the French cinema exists thanks to about a hundred films each year, it is understood that only ten or twelve deserve the attention of critics and film enthusiasts, hence of *Cahiers*. These ten or twelve films constitute what has nicely been called the tradition of quality; because of their literary ambition, these movies compel the admiration of the foreign press, and uphold France's colors twice a year, in Cannes and Venice, garnering medals, gold lions and first prizes quite regularly since 1946."

Fearing "A Certain Tendency . . ." would shock part of the readership, and wishing to mitigate its offense to director friends such as Clément and Clouzot, Doniol-Valcroze felt he had to run a nuanced explanatory editorial in the same January 1954 issue of *Cahiers du cinéma*. He found an elegant way of taking responsibility for publishing the article while declaring that he did not necessarily share all the views expressed: "Clearly, we realize the polemical style of some of the assessments could raise objections, but we hope that beyond the tone—which involves only the author—and regardless of certain specific value judgments—these are always individually questionable and we are far from unanimously agreeing with them—the reader will nevertheless recognize a critical orientation, or better yet, a point of theoretical convergence that is ours." Doniol-Valcroze's preemptive commentary was courageous, but customary precautions were useless and soon the devastating effects of this article written by a twenty-one-year-old unknown became manifest.

On January 28, the main subject of conversation at the professional critics' luncheon was Truffaut's article. The camps were clearly divided. On one side were the indignant defenders of French cinema, led by Denis Marion of *Paris-Cinéma;* on the other were Doniol-Valcroze and Claude Mauriac, who sided with the young critic. A writer and movie reviewer for *Le Figaro*, Claude Mauriac offered staunch support. On February 13, he wrote, "We have long felt there were flaws in the work of those recognized masters of

French motion picture quality, Jean Aurenche and Pierre Bost. . . . We should be thankful to a young critic, Monsieur François Truffaut, for shedding light on this subject for us in a brilliant article just published in *Cahiers du cinéma.*" The following week, Mauriac discussed the article again, and though he reproached the author for "a certain moralizing tone," he added, "We cannot help but agree with Monsieur Truffaut's conclusions."

The counteroffensive was not long in coming. On February 25, a second critics' luncheon was devoted to the "Truffaut affair." This time, the screenwriters came to defend themselves. Doniol-Valcroze gave the following account: "Present are Charles Spaak, Georges Cravenne, Jacqueline Audry, Pierre Laroche, Kast and Astruc . . . and the discussion is far-ranging. Neither Bazin nor I, though we reflected at length before publishing the study, could imagine that it would have such an explosive effect."[15] Feeling singled out by Truffaut, who had denounced "Charlespaak" as "the language that is fluently spoken in French films," the screenwriter Charles Spaak wrote Doniol-Valcroze a bad-tempered note, typifying the indignation, surprise, and also superiority the screenwriters' guild felt toward the "young whippersnapper": "A single thought came to my mind on reading *Les Cahiers du cinéma.* In a note, at the bottom of page 29, your collaborator expresses how impatient he is to see 'Feyder and Spaak fall into permanent oblivion.' On the face of things, I think many of us will find it far more difficult to forget Jacques Feyder's name than to recall François Truffaut's."[16]

Aside from the furor among film professionals, *Cahiers du cinéma* also received quite a few letters from indignant readers. Many of them felt betrayed, and reproached the magazine for abandoning the serene spirit of film studies for the sake of a polemic. Some readers faulted Truffaut's article for its anti-French, pro-American bias; others hated its "reactionary and pious tone."[17] Opinion was split at the magazine itself concerning the article. Pierre Kast, who was close to René Clément and Jean Grémillon, was its fiercest opponent; he denounced the article's imprecatory tone and its moral judgments, which he called "critical dogmatism," or "the colonization of *Cahiers* by the priest party."[18] André Bazin also answered his young protégé. In his critique of Autant-Lara's *Blé en herbe,* published in February 1954, he brought up the subject of fidelity to literary works: "It cannot be doubted that Aurenche and Bost have imposed the notion of fidelity as a positive value. I know that François Truffaut challenges this, but he is wrong, at least to the extent that the liberties taken by the screenwriters of *La Symphonie pastorale* stay within the relatively narrow framework of equivalencies that are seen as necessary. . . . In sum, like hypocrisy to virtue, their very infidelities are yet another homage to fidelity." While he didn't consider them masterpieces, Bazin defended Autant-Lara's films—and he defended them specifically against Truffaut.

"A Certain Tendency . . ." was the subject of much discussion at the time of its publication and the affair turned a large group of French critics against Truffaut. But over time, this essay would determine the new orientation of *Cahiers du cinéma*, because it rallied a great number of film devotees who completely ignored and scorned the French tradition of quality, heaping praise on Hollywood auteurs instead.

## THE YOUNG TURKS

Since *Cahiers* had supported Truffaut's polemical stance, he felt he had to involve himself completely in the fight on its front lines. Bazin and Doniol-Valcroze had shown real tolerance in publishing an article whose ideas they didn't completely share. They also worked for other newspapers; Bazin wrote every day for *Le Parisien libéré;* Doniol-Valcroze was the film critic at *France-Observateur.*

In the winter of 1953–54, they welcomed Truffaut onto the *Cahiers* staff.[19] The magazine had its offices on the Champs-Elysées, at number 146. It was a comfortable space, about sixty feet square, with a view on the avenue, loaned by the magazine's financial backer, Léonid Keigel, a film distributor who directed *Cinévogue* and a Paris movie theater called the Broadway. There was also a small, darker room at the end of a hallway, giving out on an inner courtyard; this was reserved for editorial meetings. There were three worktables: one for Doniol-Valcroze, one for the secretary, and a large one for the editorial staff, where discussions took place and the layout was designed. Each editor kept his own hours. The morning was good for quiet discussions with Doniol; 3:00 p.m. on Tuesdays was the time to listen to Bazin; early afternoon was the time to go over a piece with Truffaut; and somewhere around 6:00 p.m., between film showings, was when articles were assigned. In 1954, *Cahiers's* founders, Bazin and Doniol-Valcroze, had as collaborators former critics from Objectif 49, such as Alexandre Astruc, Pierre Kast, and Jean-José Richer. There was also a group of "Young Turks," followers of Eric Rohmer, who had forced open the door of the prestigious magazine thanks to François Truffaut: Jacques Rivette, Jean-Luc Godard, Claude Chabrol, Charles Bitsch. Being familiar with each person's qualities and faults, his tastes and knowledge, Truffaut decided who got assigned what.

There were occasionally eventful moments, as when Godard was caught "borrowing" from the cash box, or when Michel Dorsday challenged Pierre Kast to a duel. At other times, there was much laughter—when Chabrol stopped by, and starting in 1956 and 1957, when young actor friends like Jean-Claude Brialy and Jean-Paul Belmondo made it a habit to drop in and clown around whenever they were near the Champs-Elysées. The staff members were good listeners, and very soon novice directors Jacques Demy, Pierre Schoendoerffer, and Agnès Varda came by to describe their projects, get advice, and make contacts.

Between March 1953 and November 1959, François Truffaut published 170 articles in *Cahiers,* mostly film reviews of five to six typewritten pages, or interviews with film directors, a genre that he was particularly fond of. Aside from his long January 1954 essay, "A Certain Tendency of the French Cinema," he didn't publish theoretical articles, leaving them to Bazin, Rohmer, Rivette, or Godard. Truffaut didn't claim to be an intellectual; his aim was to meet film directors, attack opponents, and assert his opinion—unconventionally, cunningly, offhandedly, and sometimes with a certain arrogance—on *all* the films showing in Paris. On average, Truffaut saw more than one film a day, thereby living up to his reputation as the critic who "saw four thousand films between 1940 and 1955."

The group of young critics at *Cahiers* whom André Bazin had nicknamed the "hitchcocko-hawksians," in reference to their two favorite film directors, clustered around Truffaut. Each had his role. Jacques Rivette was the best friend and the true movie-loving companion, whose opinions were most authoritative and reliable and whom the younger Truffaut consulted constantly. Eric Rohmer was like an older cousin, somewhat strict and austere, although Truffaut sometimes cajoled him. Truffaut and Rohmer even collaborated on several projects, among them a screenplay written at the end of 1953, *L'Eglise moderne (The Modern Church).*[20]

Some other "cousins," with similar tastes, joined this trio, such as Chabrol and Godard. Chabrol, then a skinny live wire, found time amid studies in pharmacology, literature, and the law to worship Hitchcock. The first to settle down (Chabrol married in 1956 and lived in the middle-class comfort of an apartment, as opposed to a room), he was of great help to the group, thanks to his knowledge of English—an invaluable asset in meetings with Hollywood directors—and his position as press attaché for Fox, which gave him access to previews and reliable information. Jean-Luc Godard was Swiss, from a good family, and had come to Paris to complete his studies, first at the Lycée Buffon, then at the Sorbonne. His love of movies brought him to the Ciné-Club du Quartier Latin, where he met the other Young Turks. Put in contact with Doniol-Valcroze (their mothers were friends), he was first given the opportunity to write for *Cahiers du cinéma* in January 1952 and quickly carved a niche for himself there thanks to his impertinence and taste for paradox. He was the most taciturn of the group, acting most like an artist and dandy, and he fascinated the others, probably because he also kept his private life shrouded in mystery—his trips to Switzerland and throughout the world, his family, and his love life.

Truffaut, a true group leader at *Cahiers du cinéma*, also attracted several very young critics into its fold. Charles Bitsch, a Paris friend; André Martin, the animation specialist; Fereydoun Hoveyda, a young Persian science fiction enthusiast; François Mars, a lover of burlesque; Jacques Siclier from Troyes; André S. Labarthe from Sarlat; and Claude Beylie, Claude de Givray, and Luc Moullet—these were the younger members who would take over the magazine when Truffaut, Godard, Chabrol, Rivette, and Rohmer would go on to direct. Truffaut, for them, was a charismatic figure with whom they could identify. But he was also very demanding, and he didn't hesitate to curb polemical passions when he felt they were unjustified—for example, he refused to publish a piece on the Venice Film Festival by a friend, Jean-Marie Straub, because he found it very violent and radical. Indeed, Truffaut feared overly imitative behavior on the part of his young disciples, as he wrote to Luc Moullet in March 1956: "Your pieces are difficult to publish in their present state. I should have written to you at greater length explaining how things had been for us, how our pieces had been rejected. One article, with which I'm hardly satisfied today, 'A Certain Tendency of the French Cinema,' required several months' work and five or six complete rewrites. Yes, I admit, we were a bit frightened of you. First of all because we once shared your aggressiveness (sincere and fanatical) and it's a shock to see this eternal recurrence at the *Cahiers*, this perennial revival of the same sarcastic attitude. . . ."[21]

Truffaut would often approach writers to solicit articles or excerpts of screenplays. The most decisive meeting was with Jacques Audiberti. Audiberti was known for his plays, but Truffaut was particularly taken with his novels (*Monorail, Le Maître de Milan,* and especially *Marie Dubois*), where he saw a world that reflected some of his own obsessions. "The same question is asked tirelessly in all his books: why don't women desire us the way we desire them, i.e., a priori, systematically, physically and abstractly, and for what they are: the hunchback for her hump, the bourgeoise for her hat, the prostitute for her thighs, the prude for her virtue, the plump girl for her curves and the thin one for her bones?"[22] In the beginning of 1954, Audiberti published a new novel with Gallimard, *Les Jardins et les Fleuves,* which Truffaut read with great eagerness. He was particularly struck by a passage about Charlie Chaplin's Tramp. Truffaut seized the opportunity; on the last Wednesday of May 1954—it became a memorable date for him—he wrote Audiberti: "Would you be willing to write a column which would be entitled 'Le Billet d'Audiberti [Audiberti's Letter]' or a kind of 'Perpetual Column on Woman on Screen,' thoughts on the actresses and heroines in the films you were seeing?"[23] Audiberti accepted immediately, and he wrote a monthly column for *Cahiers* from July 1954 to December 1956. This gave Truffaut the opportunity to meet with him regularly. They were instantly taken with each other, and would always remain so. Later, Audiberti would be the first devotee of Truffaut's films, praising *Les Mistons* (*The Mischief Makers*) and, later, *The 400 Blows* in *Arts*. Truffaut considered him one of his masters, and the only one, except for Cocteau, who knew "how to describe both films and film actresses."[24] In an homage to him, Truffaut wrote, "Jacques Audiberti, with his scarred mug of a vacationing old sea dog, was a colossus of Antibes, as handsome and powerful as his books."[25]

## PRESS CAMPAIGNS

The publication of "A Certain Tendency of the French Cinema" in 1954 changed François Truffaut's life.[26] A short time later, he was contacted by Jean Aurel, a journalist just a bit older than he, who was editor of the movie pages in the cultural weekly *Arts-Lettres-Spectacles*. In the late forties, *Arts* was the home of the intellectual right wing, a group nicknamed the *"hussards"* (hussars, for their unsubtle, rough-and-tumble style), which included Jacques Laurent, Michel Déon, Roger Nimier, Marcel Brion, and Antoine Blondin. The weekly was unabashedly polemical and attracted famous contributors. Aside from the *"hussards,"* these included Cocteau, Audiberti, Louise de Vilmorin, Claude Roy, Maurice Clavel, Maurice Pons, Claude Roger-Max, Pierre Seghers, Pierre Marcabru, Ferdinand Alquié, and Jean Cathelin. Ruthless and provocative, *Arts* instigated big cultural debates; in the fifties, it was the true rival of the left-wing journals and magazines like *Les Temps modernes*, *Les Lettres françaises*, and *L'Express*.

The magazine belonged to a wealthy art dealer, Daniel Wildenstein, who gave the weekly's managing editor, Jacques Laurent, complete editorial freedom. Laurent put Aurel in charge of the movie pages, with the task of developing an incisive and original tone. Seduced by the verve and style Truffaut exhibited in *Cahiers*, Aurel asked him to write for *Arts*. Truffaut was quick to seize the opportunity, for not only was *Arts* an unhoped-for platform; it also offered substantial freelance pay (seven hundred francs per manuscript page, five times more than *Cahiers du cinéma*), and writing for them would solve his financial problems. Truffaut continued his demolition job on the "tradition of quality" in the columns of *Arts*. Rough, polemical, moralizing, and imprecatory, Truffaut attacked left-wing intellectuals and their "cultural political activism."[27] He showed his worth, publishing 528 articles in five years—in other words, an average of two articles a week, filling almost single-handedly the entire movie page, under his own name or a pseudonym.

Truffaut was in great demand during this period. Between January and September 1954, he published twelve articles under the name François de Monferrand in the Catholic weekly *Radio-Cinéma-Télévison,* the forerunner of today's *Telerama.* Between July and September, at Doniol-Valcroze's request, he suggested several articles to the left-wing weekly *France-Observateur.* Between May and August 1956, he contributed to *La Parisienne,* a literary and socialite magazine with right-wing tendencies. Then in April 1956, when Philippe Boegner launched a new liberal daily, *Le Temps de Paris,* with the ambition of rivaling Hubert Beuve-Méry's *Le Monde,* Truffaut was asked to be editor of the film section. The paper was a commercial failure and folded a month later, but Truffaut wrote about twenty articles for it during its brief existence.

A film a day, an article every other day—this was the pace the young man kept up, working every night, imbibing Maxiton, cigarettes, and coffee. Life and work were one. He confided movingly to Jean Mambrino, a Jesuit priest and fellow film critic, "Actually I'm very limited, very uncultured (I'm not proud of the fact); I'm just lucky to have some understanding of cinema, to like it, and work like a dog. That's all. Beyond that, any deeper reflection on content is above my poor head. As I hate the fact that I'm self-taught, I don't 'teach' myself anything, or hardly. I'll be saved by the fact that I 'specialized' in the cinema very early on and used the position as much as possible, working every night if need be."[28]

Truffaut put all his energy into his work, letting his personality show through in his writing. He established a "Truffaut tone" with his very first articles in *Arts;* a style blending vehemence and humor, it was rich in wordplay, jokes, and hoaxes and was clearly intended to draw in the reader. "He rewrote all the screenplays with his criticisms, recreated the films with passion, both the positive and negative elements, as he thought he had seen them,"[29] said the producer Pierre Braunberger, an avid reader of *Arts.* Truffaut also gave free rein to his erotic fetishism in his descriptions of the gestures and bodies of women on the screen, praising the "practiced eye" who "is learning the angles suited to revealing a brassiere's fabric and color, and consequently the very life of the breasts it supports," who sees "the sharp angles that capture the diagonal patterns and hems of underpants outlined by a woman's gait." For "the face can pretend, modesty can be false, and virtue simulated, but the brassiere never lies."[30]

Criticism, for Truffaut, was like an intimate journal, unveiling the secrets of an ever-alert sensibility. He was plainspoken in his judgment of works and put all his energy into convincing his readers by means of what he called his "press campaigns." He proclaimed on the first page of *Arts,* in one of his most famous and violent tracts,[31] "You are all witnesses to this trial. . . ." On several occasions, Truffaut supported particular causes; he defended Henri Langlois's Cinémathèque when it was threatened with closure in early 1955; he also brought attention to certain films that had been unappreciated or neglected by critics, such as Joseph L. Mankiewicz's *The Barefoot Contessa,* Alexandre Astruc's *Les Mauvaises Rencontres,* and especially Max Ophuls's *Lola Montès.*

Reactions to his spirited temperament differed. In an internal memo written on November 2, 1955, André Parinaud, the editor in chief of *Arts,* requested Truffaut to show a little restraint: "Letters of complaint are piling up lately, and I know that your present mood won't help matters. You're responsible for yourself, but when the paper is implicated, I request that you be cautious and stay polite. There are things you should avoid, and from now on, in your articles for *Arts,* I forbid you to use terms like 'plagiarized' or 'copied,' or to make physically and sexually discriminatory remarks. You're entitled to dislike skinny women or homosexuals, but you must refrain from expressing this in your columns." However, Jacques Laurent, at about the same time, decided to encourage Truffaut's open revolt against all academicism, feeling that his polemical tone fit into the magazine's way of thinking. Indeed, on July 6, 1955, at Jacques Laurent's and Jean Aurel's request, Truffaut published "Criticism's Seven Deadly Sins." "On the margins of the movies, there is an unrewarding, painstaking and little-known profession— that of 'film critic.' What is a critic? What does he eat? What are his habits, tastes and obsessions?" he asks in the beginning of the article, which is illustrated by an acerbic Siné drawing entitled "A Critique of Criticism." Truffaut's answers, stated in seven points, suggest that critics are neither free nor intelligent. Rather, he says, they are ignorant of both the history and technique of motion pictures, and lack imagination. They are professorial and full of prejudices. He even accuses them of being chauvinistic and of selling out to the highest bidder, since "it is impossible to have a successful career as a critic in Paris without eventually meeting Delannoy, Decoin, Cayatte or Le Chanois." The list of sinners includes Jean Dutourd, François Nourissier, Georges Sadoul, Georges Charensol, Louis Chauvet, Jean-Jacques Gautier, André Lang, Roger Régent, Jacques Lemarchand, and André Billy. The elite critics of the daily and weekly press are all implicated. As a counterpoint, Truffaut adduces the "noncritic film enthusiast," actually a self-portrait of someone defined by two characteristics: a radical point of view—"Everyone has his system. Mine leads me to praise or pan unreservedly"—and honest judgments. Hence, in reviewing Mervyn LeRoy's *The Bad Seed* in *Arts* (1956), and describing a promotional press luncheon he attended where the director was present, he had no compunctions about writing, "I remember eating very well, but I guess gastronomic gratitude is not my strong point, and anyway, it's better never to have met Mervyn LeRoy lest one lose any desire to see a film made by him."

Jacques Laurent openly supported Truffaut, making him the leader of what he called "criticism from the catacombs."[32] In an editorial published in *Arts* in February 1955, he wrote:

There are two brands of film criticism. The first kind could hang a shingle announcing "good plain fare." It doesn't make waves, agrees eagerly with the tastes of the general public and is practiced by people for whom cinema is not a religion but a pleasant pastime. And then there is an intelligentsia that practices criticism in a state of anger. Truffaut is one of the most gifted representatives of this second kind of criticism, a recent development requiring scrutiny. The intelligentsia I am referring to sees itself as being, or wanting to be, in a state of belligerence. All attacks are worthwhile since the god of cinema will recognize its own. Whether approving or disapproving, these critics are always angry because, judging films according to ethics and esthetics evolved at the Cinémathèque, they are perpetually at war with middle-class criticism and frequently in disagreement with box office receipts, in other words with the public.

Truffaut, then, had sired a new form of film criticism—frank, direct, violent, sectarian, founded on value judgments, always detailed but often provocative and scathing, with no qualms about being peremptory and unfair. This new brand of criticism preached by the Young Turks came to dominate *Cahiers du cinéma* and *Arts*, but throughout critical circles at the time, there was great shock. After the publication of "Criticism's Seven Deadly Sins," Jean Néry, president of the French Association of Film and Television Critics, asked Truffaut to resign from the association. "I assume," Néry wrote him on October 27, 1955, "it is painful for you to belong to a group of film critics whose incompetence, stupidity, cowardice and ineptitude you are constantly stressing, and unbearable for you to remain in their company as a member of an association where we seek to develop mutual respect rather than systematic boorishness."[33] Truffaut replied several days later: "Quite frankly, I regard myself as an excellent—if temporary—critic, and as someone who justifies and honors a group that is not so much an association as a union, needing to protect its members from possible (and permanent) political, police, censorship and publicity pressures. But since it is not for me to judge, I thought it might be useful to include with this letter some testimonials from readers, fellow members and film directors."[34] These testimonials are glowing assessments from such critics as Henri Agel,

Claude Mauriac, André Bazin, and Jacques Doniol-Valcroze, and from prominent directors like Max Ophuls, Abel Gance, Fritz Lang, Nicholas Ray, Roger Leenhardt, and Jean Cocteau. This clearly illustrates Truffaut's tactic of working within, and not outside, the system, and of making it implode under the well-organized, carefully staged blows of his own press campaigns. With Jacques Laurent's protection, the "hussar" could appeal to the readers of *Arts* and call them to witness in the trial he was conducting, while benefiting from the refuge and authority provided by *Cahiers du cinéma* and its group of angry young men who supported him with unfailing loyalty.

## A HUSSAR WITH HIS SWORD DRAWN

François Truffaut's writing style, press campaigns, and taste for provocation were typical of the literary right. It's no coincidence, since the papers he wrote for—*Arts, La Parisienne, Le Temps de Paris,* and even *Cahiers du cinéma*—his personal contacts, and his pamphleteering style all suggest rebellion against academicism and the culturally dominant left-wing intellectual circles of the postwar period. Polemics raged between the two camps in the fifties, even if the Communist, social-Christian, humanist left vastly outnumbered the right. *Les Temps modernes* denounced the danger of a "resurgence of fascist intellectuals,"[35] *L'Express* published its first feature on "the right-wing writers,"[36] and in a December 1952 article in *Les Temps modernes,* Bernard Frank singled out the "hussars" as "crusaders of the pen" who charge their enemies "with swords drawn." Jacques Laurent was the leading "hussar," but he founded *La Parisienne* and accepted the editorship of *Arts* under the banner of "political noncommitment." He expressed his objective in an editorial in the first issue of *La Parisienne,* dated January 1953: "Literature has become a means to an end. It is disapproved of as soon as it is anything other than a means"; he wished to sever the ties between literature and politics—that is, between literary circles and left-wing activism.

This was a cause François Truffaut could identify with. In *Cahiers,* he fought against supporters of "films with a message," praising form and mise-en-scène over the screenplay. But this cause was considered reactionary; lack of political commitment was associated with individualism, egoism, formal innovation, dandyism—so many attitudes denounced as impeding the values of cultural, political, and moral reconstruction inspired by the Liberation. Truffaut's many opponents went even further—they assimilated him into the extreme right; his sworn enemies at the journal *Positif,* for example, regularly referred to him as the "fascist" in their letters and columns.[37] They saw in Truffaut an "intellectual vigilante" whose "political choices go hand in hand with a distinct taste for authority and the police."[38]

Truffaut himself enjoyed being provocatively right-wing. His moralistic intransigence in attacking the leading lights of French cinema sometimes induced him to take extreme, dubious, contrarian positions, as when he went so far as to praise American censorship in the January 1954 issue of *Cahiers:* "We can thank American screen censorship for the fact that Marlowe is no longer a homosexual and that the characters become clearly either likable or hateful. Hence the need for moral censorship. . . ." His determination to be a redresser of wrongs, while identifying with minority intellectual groups that were decried, and sometimes even banned, occasionally led him to pure political provocation.

Truffaut pulled no punches in writing about Maurice Bardèche and Robert Brasillach's *L'Histoire du cinéma,* the latter having been executed at the Liberation for collaborating with the Nazis: "Brasillach's political views were also those of Drieu La Rochelle; views that earn their advocates the death penalty are bound to be worthy of esteem. . . ."[39] Two months later, in a complimentary review of Sacha Guitry's *Si Versailles m'était conté (Royal Affairs in Versailles),* Truffaut paid tribute to the monarchy of the Ancien Régime, "which contributed to the grandeur of France for several centuries: Christian feeling and a sense of honor, respect for the clergy and the nobility, the keystones of a justly hierarchical society."[40] But more important, in the winter of 1955–56, he was pleased to establish contact with Lucien Rebatet, a thirties film critic of undeniable talent and a scathing style, who had written for *L'Action française* under the pen name of François Vinneuil, and later for *Je suis partout.*[41] During the Nazi Occupation, Rebatet had been a powerful anti-Semitic voice supporting the purges in the motion picture sector; and in a 1941 book, *Les Tribus du cinéma et du théâtre (The Tribes of Film and Theater),* part of a series entitled "The Jews in France," he called for the "regeneration" of the entertainment arts: "Whatever is undertaken or decided regarding French cinema, it should first be cleansed of Jews. Sooner or later we will have to drive out of our country several hundred thousand Jews, starting with those who do not have residency papers, the nonnaturalized Jews, the most recent arrivals, those whose evil political and financial effects are most manifest, in other words all the Jews in cinema." Does the writer's talent and polemical verve justify forgetting these odious books? Did these writing qualities bring Truffaut close to Rebatet, or Rebatet close to Truffaut? One might be led to believe so by a comment Henri Langlois made to his friend Lotte Eisner shortly before his death in 1977: "There were only two great film critics in this century, François Vinneuil and François Truffaut."[42] This opinion was shared by Claude Elsen, a far more dubious character, the author of a 1943 work that was pulped at the Liberation, *Destin du cinéma* (*Cinema's Fate*), himself a collaborator who was condemned to death in absentia in 1944. Having taken refuge in Spain, he wrote Truffaut a long letter of congratulations in early 1956 at the suggestion of "our mutual friend François Vinneuil-Rebatet," which concluded with this nostalgic sentence: "You very much remind me of what I tried to be before the deluge. Bravo."[43]

Lucien Rebatet himself wrote to Truffaut on November 25, 1955, after having read and appreciated one of his most vitriolic articles in *Arts,* ridiculing Jean Delannoy's *Chiens perdus sans collier:* "I have been wanting to meet you for a year, because you remind me of the young Vinneuil of the thirties. My old friend Jacques Becker said wonderful things about you. . . ."[44] Far from refusing any contact, Truffaut replied to Rebatet politely, and kept up a correspondence with him as "from critic to critic," recommending some small American films to him, such as Tay Garnett's *The Naked Dawn,* Edgar G. Ulmer's *Cause for Alarm,* and Samuel Fuller's *House of Bamboo.* Released in 1952 after spending eight years in jail, Rebatet had resumed work as a critic at *Rivarol.* He thanked Truffaut for his valuable advice: "Colleagues my own age couldn't possibly give me the kinds of tips you generously give me. . . ."[45] Curious to meet the former collaborator, Truffaut even accepted his invitation and spent a whole day with him in late 1955, lunching on board a Paris *bateau-mouche.*

Not all his friends approved of this relationship; Doniol-Valcroze, for example, a former Resistance fighter and left-winger, categorically refused to meet Rebatet,[46] and Pierre Kast expressed great indignation at this "acute attack of Maurrassism."[47] Truffaut saw it as echoing one of the major nonconformist traditions in French culture, the one that leads from the *Action française* to the "hussars," from Maurras to Rebatet.

As a film critic at *Arts,* beginning in the spring of 1954, François Truffaut enjoyed an improved financial situation. His regular freelance work brought in from fifteen to twenty thousand francs a month, thus allowing him to live in furnished hotels and to eat proper meals. He was also able to repay his debts to Doniol-Valcroze, Astruc, and Lachenay. Work absorbed him completely; he spent all his time in movie theaters, editorial offices, and seeing film directors. He avoided society events and literary cafés. Eric Rohmer described the relative colorlessness of this "life outside movies": "We didn't have 'happy years' or 'happy times,' and if anything could claim to apply to us, it would be the sentence of Nizan, 'I'll never let anyone tell me that being twenty years old is the best moment of one's life.' Those years were not only unhappy but colorless: . . . To anyone who asked us, 'What do you live on?' we liked to answer, 'We don't live.' Life was the screen, it was movies, it was discussing movies, writing about movies."[48] They had in common this devotion to cinema and, oddly enough, an extreme reserve about their private lives, which remained secret. Rohmer, Rivette, Godard, and Truffaut shared a puritanical streak; there were ties of friendship among them, but no familiarity. There existed a barrier, a sense of dignity and moral inflexibility that favored reciprocal respect rather than emotional out-pourings.

Though movies monopolized François Truffaut's life, he nonetheless reserved a place for women—seeing them daily, in large numbers, and obsessively. Once again, he had to be treated for venereal disease. His rela-tionships with women were in tune with the frenzied life he led—liaisons and conquests matched his insatiable appetite for films and his critical over-activity. In the notes exchanged between Truffaut and Lachenay during this period, there are many recommendations about girls, good addresses, and pickup spots between the Porte Saint-Denis and Pigalle. Most of Truffaut's involvements at that time were still anonymous and unconnected to movie circles. But these ephemeral affairs were an undeniable part of his life, and he often informed Lachenay of his schedule. "After leaving you," he wrote, "I picked up a girl near the Studio Parnasse; I only had 400 francs left; the hotel cost 500; she lent me 100 francs. I was joining the Bazins at 11 o'clock at the Champs-Elysées and didn't have a cent left to get there, or for break-fast. So I stopped by and pinched 1,000 francs from your black wallet, under the mattress."[49]

This frenetic rhythm might have been an aftereffect of the trauma caused by his definitive breakup with Liliane Litvin; Truffaut seems to have wanted both passing liaisons and one woman to whom he could become attached. In February 1954, he met Laura Mauri, a friend of Jean-José Richer, a young critic at *Cahiers* who was a close friend of Doniol-Valcroze. Truffaut and she lived together for a while in a two-room apartment on boulevard des Batignolles. In 1955, when Truffaut stayed at Roberto Rossellini's house in Rome, and then went to cover the Venice Film Festival for the first time, Laura accompanied him. A pretty brunette, she was lighthearted, short and curvy, and wore elegant, flowing dresses; she seemed the female type he was most attracted to.

Two years later, on January 29, 1956, at a point where his affair with Laura Mauri was fizzling out but hadn't quite ended, Truffaut met Joëlle Robin. In the beginning of March, he left the Hôtel de Tunis, near Place Clichy, where he was living at the time, and moved in with Joëlle on rue de Lincoln, near the Champs-Elysées. He would stay there for eight months. A budding actress, Joëlle Robin had already had supporting roles in several French films and had appeared in Vincente Minnelli's *Lust for Life* in 1956. Having noticed her in a film, Truffaut wrote a profile of her in the February 22, 1956, issue of *Arts*. "Well directed, Joëlle Robin can bring a new flavor to certain films—that of a modern Alice in a reconsidered 'wonderland.' " His article must certainly have furthered their relationship.

## FIRST FOOTAGE

Though successfully launched on a career in film criticism, Truffaut did not forget his desire to direct films. Indeed, he was always writing short screenplays and jotting down ideas for films, on his own or with his friends from *Cahiers*. But since *La Ceinture de peau d'ange* in 1950, all his filmmaking attempts had failed. Finally, at the end of 1954, he and Jacques Rivette set up a project for a silent ten-minute short entitled *Une Visite*. Truffaut would have the opportunity to "waste his first film stock."[50] Robert Lachenay was both producer and assistant, and Rivette, who could get film stock at a discount and had access to a silent 16-mm camera, was the cameraman. Truffaut had found a set—Jacques and Lydie Doniol-Valcroze's apartment on rue de Douai, in his old neighborhood. He had also chosen three actors—Laura Mauri, and her friends Jean-José Richer and Francis Cognany. Lydie Doniol-Valcroze insisted he cast her two-and-half-year-old daughter, Florence, whom the members of the film crew had to take turns baby-sitting for. Truffaut created a part for the child in his story, structured around amorous play. A young boy is looking in the classified ads for a room to rent; he finds one in an apartment where a young woman is living alone. She welcomes him amicably, gently making fun of his shyness, for he is rather awkward and provincial. The young woman's brother-in-law, played by Jean-José Richer, comes to the apartment to drop off his little girl for the weekend. During his brief visit, he clowns around, blowing puffs of cigarette smoke like a locomotive, and tries in vain to flirt with the young woman, stealing a kiss on her neck. After this episode, the new tenant also tries his luck with her, awkwardly attempting to hold her hand. Rebuffed, he packs up his suitcase and leaves the apartment. Night falls over Paris, near Place Blanche. The young girl puts her niece to bed, draws the curtains, and pensively sits down beside the child.

In spite of the speed of the shoot—five days—this eight-minute film, with its numerous cuts, required many camera movements. But Truffaut wasn't pleased with it and showed it to no one, not even his friends at *Cahiers du cinéma*. The little reel would lie dormant for many years in a closet in the rue de Douai apartment. It was thirty years later, in 1982, that he came across his first cinematic endeavor again. "At the time he wanted to destroy it, since he felt it was of no interest," recalls Lydie Mahias, the former wife of Jacques Doniol-Valcroze. "But he left me a print because it was a souvenir of my daughter at two. In 1982, François and Rivette summoned us to a screening. He had blown up the short to 35 mm. We had a good time, because Rivette was absolutely delighted with his camera work."[51] After this first setback, Truffaut was very depressed, doubting he had the ability to become a director. Disappointed by what he regarded as mere amateur work, he decided to become better acquainted with the secrets of the great masters and return to criticism.

## TRUFFETTE AND RIVAUT

A polemicist with a mischievous spirit, but also a sincere film enthusiast, François Truffaut was very intrigued to meet the film directors he admired. For him, criticism, journalism, and interviews went hand in hand; they were all part of a way of viewing cinema that was based on real involvement, stated preferences, and an intimate knowledge of the secrets of the art. Truffaut and Rivette spent the whole morning of January 20, 1954, taping a long conversation with Jacques Becker. While this method seems obvious today, at the time it was deeply innovative and would radically change the approach to films. The twelve-page spread that appeared the following month would be the first such piece to be published by *Cahiers du cinéma*. The form was not new—Truffaut himself had been very impressed by the publication of Paul Léautaud's radio interviews with Robert Mallet[52]—but to date it had been used only in magazines to report the comments of stars, the moods of producers, or anecdotes about film directors. Truffaut and Rivette had a completely different, very specific goal: to become intimately acquainted with a filmmaker by inviting the auteur to talk freely about himself, his work methods, and his career. They had but one rule—the use of a portable tape recorder to all its advantage. This, too, was new. At the time, the Grundig machine, with its heavy reels of magnetic tape, weighed nearly nine pounds, so that this unheard-of practice did not go unnoticed. On May 14, 1954, *Cinémonde* stressed its "exceptional interest": "These articles are transcribed from tape-recorded interviews, and reproduced intact with all the repetitions and hesitations of spoken language, and all the more precious in that these repetitions and hesitations allow the reader to follow the interviewee's thoughts step by step, down to the smallest details and subtlest twists and turns."

It was "Truffette and Rivaut"—as they called themselves, so inseparable in their work that for a long time Becker thought they were a homosexual couple—who created the rules and chose the first interviewees. They described their method clearly for their meeting with Abel Gance which appeared in the January 1955 issue of *Cahiers du cinéma*: "There are two rules governing our 'interviews with . . .' First, we only choose directors we like. Secondly, we let them express themselves freely and never burden them with embarrassing or insidious questions."

The first interview, with Jacques Becker, the director of *Casque d'or*—one of Truffaut's favorite films—was published in February 1954. "The most authentic and flawless director,"[53] according to Truffaut the critic, was the first of the "masters" to hit it off with the young *Cahiers* rebels. Becker talked with great simplicity and detail for nearly three hours, about his work, his films, and his concept of directing. Between the spring of 1954 and the autumn of 1957, *Cahiers* would publish a series of interviews, conducted mostly by Truffaut and Rivette, with Jean Renoir, Luis Buñuel, Roberto Rossellini, Abel Gance, Alfred Hitchcock, Howard Hawks, Robert Aldrich, Joshua Logan, Anthony Mann, Max Ophuls, Vincente Minnelli, Jacques Tati, Orson Welles, Gene Kelly, Nicholas Ray, Richard Brooks, Luchino Visconti, and, finally, Fritz Lang. This constitutes a corpus that is one of the great innovations of *Cahiers du cinéma*, and it still remains a foundation and pillar of modern criticism. François Truffaut expected a great deal from each of these meetings. They no doubt derived from a deep trait in his personality: the need to find masters and learn from them.

## I ADMIRE YOU . . .

Truffaut had carefully thought through his idea and planned it out. In the beginning of spring 1954, he drafted a letter he would send to several directors. "I admire you; I would like to meet you; I would like to write about you and give you exposure in the press. . . ."[54] The letter went out at about the same time to Preston Sturges, Jean Renoir, Luis Buñuel, Max Ophuls, Abel Gance, Roberto Rossellini, Fritz Lang, and Nicholas Ray. They almost all replied, including the foreigners, though some respondents were somewhat blasé, such as Preston Sturges, who wrote on September 1, 1954, "Come to see me whenever you want but you should know that I'll be happy to welcome you only because you're a pleasant young man who is sincerely interested in an art that I very much like. The fact of being spoken about in movie magazines, or having my face reproduced—I don't give two hoots about all of that. . . ."[55]

During the same period, Truffaut started to spend time on the sets of the directors he admired. In October 1954, for instance, he spent ten days on the set of Jean Renoir's *French Cancan* at the Studio Francoeur, and he recounted the experience in *Arts* in the form of a shooting journal. Renoir must have approved of his article, for several times he invited Truffaut to his house on avenue Frochot, near Pigalle, and subsequently allowed him to visit the set of *Éléna et les Hommes* (*Paris Does Strange Things*). In those years,

Truffaut was also a privileged spectator of all of Renoir's theater experiments. That July, he had assisted Renoir when he was directing Grisha and Mitsou Dabat's translation and adaptation of Shakespeare's *Julius Caesar*. This was when Truffaut first met Jean-Claude Brialy, who was completing his military service in Germany at the time, in the army motion picture unit. There, Brialy had become friends with Pierre Lhomme, the future cinematographer, who suggested that during their leave they go to Arles with some other film enthusiast friends to see Renoir's *Julius Caesar*. These friends were Charles Bitsch, Claude Chabrol, Jacques Rivette, and Jean-Luc Godard. During the entire trip from Paris to the south of France in a beautiful Buick, the only subject of conversation was movies. Jean-Claude Brialy, who had had a strict upbringing and whose father was a military man, couldn't believe his ears. "It was like an underground group preparing a revolution," he recalled. In the morning, the gang arrived at the arena. The ambiance was that of a bullfight, with dust and two hundred extras. "In the midst of all this, Jean Renoir, magnificent, and next to him a young man in black with fiery eyes—François Truffaut." During the return trip, Brialy, who was obsessed with becoming an actor, did everything he could to impress the gang and acted out a whole series of roles—"dancer, old man, young man, Carmen. . . ."[56] The *Cahiers du cinéma* team was certainly smitten, and Brialy would later become their mascot actor. He can be seen in their first films—in short subjects like Eric Rohmer's *La Sonate à Kreutzer* (*The Kreutzer Sonata*) and Jacques Rivette's *Le Coup du berger*, both in 1956; in Jean-Luc Godard's *Tous les garçons s'appellent Patrick* in 1957; and, more importantly, in Claude Chabrol's first two features, *Le Beau Serge* (*Bitter Reunion*) and *Les Cousins* (*The Cousins*), in 1958 and 1959, respectively.

From his contact with directors, Truffaut developed an increasing desire to become a director. Strangely enough, it was Julien Duvivier, an old-timer in French cinema, who suggested that they collaborate on the writing of a screenplay. Truffaut had not always been kind to Duvivier, but he had liked his most recent film, *Voici le temps des assassins* (*Deadlier than the Male*). The two men met in Cannes and discussed a project called *Grand Amour*, about an average man's love life. But Duvivier was monopolized by another project, the adaptation, with René Barjavel, of a murder mystery, *L'Homme à l'imperméable* (*The Man in the Raincoat*).

In mid-August, he wrote Truffaut a wonderful letter: "Last night I had a strange dream. You and I were at Le Havre. We were about to embark for America on a huge ocean liner whose name I saw very clearly: *L'Atlantique*. . . . I was inviting you on the trip!!! But when it was time to board, I noticed that I hadn't booked your passage. . . . You flew into a mad rage, and told me a few plain truths. So I went to see the chief purser, who remembered that I had crossed in 1948 and gave me a cabin. Then all of a sudden we were at sea and I was called to the telephone. . . . I'll never know who was calling me because at that point I woke up." A trip to America, a Freudian slip (one ticket for two!), an angry young man telling an experienced director some plain truths—Duvivier's dream reveals the nature of an ambiguous relationship between an experienced director and a critic who still has some way to go before crossing over to the other side. Yet Duvivier's letter ends on a very amicable note: "I would like to have you as a collaborator, if you still desire it as well. Let me know what you've been up to recently and what your plans are. Please see me as a friend who thinks highly of you and likes you."[57]

## OPHULS

Max Ophuls was one of Truffaut's great "masters." They first met in 1953, when the director was shooting *Madame de . . . ;* for the release of the film, Truffaut and Rivette interviewed Ophuls at length in his home in Neuilly. Ophuls had asked his son Marcel to be present on that day to help him with the two *Cahiers* journalists, who he suspected might be slightly confused intellectuals. "As soon as they walked in, something clicked between my father and François. There was no need to translate; one could just sit in a corner and listen to them talk,"[58] Marcel Ophuls recalls. With his mixture of timidity and self-confident judgment, Truffaut seduced the great director. The two men understood each other and later developed the habit of meeting at the bar of the Plaza Athénée Hotel, on avenue Montaigne, for long conversations. This was the period when Truffaut organized vigorous press campaigns to gain appreciation for the "Ophuls style." He had to convince a public that was extremely skeptical and saw the German director as a gentle and eccentric dreamer specializing in slightly sugary Viennese pastries. Neither *Le Plaisir (House of Pleasure)* nor *Madame de . . .* had met with any critical success in France.

In the course of their many conversations, Ophuls and Truffaut discussed *Lola Montès*, the film that Ophuls was scheduled to start shooting in February 1955. Truffaut offered to work for him as an assistant. Ophuls encouraged him and, at the end of January, Truffaut signed up with Gamma Films and its head of production, Ralph Baum, as an assistant-trainee for five weeks, at a salary of 12,000 francs a month. But the contract was annulled because of union opposition. With his years of experience in movies, Baum was probably wary of the idea of giving an indiscreet critic a hands-on job on the set of an ambitious and difficult film. Ophuls, sorry about the decision but unwilling to clash with Baum, wrote to Truffaut on February 17 to express his regrets: "Next time, we will have to make use of you earlier, in the directors' camp rather than the assistants'. I hope Monsieur Rossellini will employ you thus. . . . I have the feeling, though I can't explain why, that you will become someone important in the creative end of motion pictures and that your conversion—from criticism to filmmaking—will occur smoothly."[59]

It was, therefore, in his capacity as journalist that Truffaut spent a week in Nice on the set of *Lola Montès* at the beginning of March. His reportage came out in *Arts* a short time later. At the time of its release, in the end of December, *Lola Montès* provoked quite a critical uproar. When it was first shown in Paris, on December 20, 1955, at the Marignan theater on the Champs-Elysées, the distributor ran an announcement informing the public that it was about to see a film that was "out of the ordinary" and that they still had time to get their money back. During the first screenings, part of the audience made such heckling noises that on two or three occasions the police had to be called in. François Truffaut was on the front lines of what he called the "battle of the Marignan": "Just like the heroine of the title, this film courts the danger of provoking a scandal and exacerbating passions. We will fight, if fight we must! We will argue, if argue we must! This is certainly the kind of cinema we must support, today, in 1955—auteur cinema, which is also a cinema of ideas, with a burst of invention at every image, a cinema that doesn't revive the prewar period, a cinema that beats down doors that have been boarded up for too long."[60] After a three-week run, the film's theatrical release was already threatened.

Truffaut resorted to a petition in a grand attempt to save the film. On January 6, 1956, a short statement written by Rossellini and Truffaut and signed by Astruc, Becker, Christian-Jaque, Cocteau, Kast, and Tati appeared on the front pages of *Arts* and the *Figaro,* requesting that the film's run be extended: "*Lola Montès* is, above all, an act of respect toward the public, which is so often mistreated by low-level entertainments that alter its taste and sensibility. To support *Lola Montès* is to support cinema in general since any serious attempt at renewal is in the best interest of cinema and the public." This was probably the first time in the history of motion pictures that a united front of influential filmmakers stood up for one of their own and dared to go against public opinion. Deeply moved and grateful, Ophuls wrote Truffaut a letter the next day to thank him for his help: "Now that I know you very well, I can confess a daydream I had a while ago. I had a lot of money. I had so much money that I could finance a big production house, a sort of 'European United Artists' and during the whole morning, so they could make their own films and express themselves, the following personalities were signing contracts: Jean Cocteau, Roberto Rossellini, Jacques Becker—how I love to write these names—Christian-Jaque, Jacques Tati, Pierre Kast, Alexandre Astruc. Please be so kind and be my emissary to them."[61]

Truffaut made his way in fits and starts down the road leading from journalism to directing, helped by decisive encounters. His talent and charm constituted undeniable assets, as did the polemical verve he applied to the causes he supported. Above all, he had a gift for delighting the film directors he met, whether it was Julien Duvivier or Max Ophuls.

## ROSSELLINI

Max Ophuls hoped François Truffaut would be employed by Roberto Rossellini. In 1954, Rossellini was forty-eight and unappreciated by the Italian critics; his latest films, *Stromboli, I Fioretti, Europa '51 (The Greatest Love)*, and *Viaggio in Italia (Strangers)* were all commercial failures and remained misunderstood. He had just returned from Germany, where he had made *La Paura (Fear)*, an adaptation of a Stefan Zweig story; he was discouraged and pondering the idea of giving up filmmaking. He had moved to Paris and taken up residence in a suite at the Hotel Raphaël, on avenue Kléber, with Ingrid Bergman, their oldest son, Robertino, and their three-year-old twins, Isabella and Ingrid. He had been engaged to direct *Jeanne au bûcher (Joan of Arc at the Stake)*, the Paul Claudel oratorio with music by Arthur Honegger, at the Paris Opéra in June, with Bergman in the title role.

This artistic event filled the gossip columns, for Ingrid Bergman and Roberto Rossellini were among the most famous couples at the time. In its April 3, 1954, issue, *Paris-Match* published a front-page color photograph of the actress holding her two little girls in her arms. For the critical establishment, Rossellini was merely a ghost from the Italian neorealist past. But for the young *Cahiers* rebels, he was one of the world's greatest film directors.[62] Neither outdated nor scandalous, he embodied modern cinema, and the cinema of the future. Once again, Truffaut was on the front lines and publicly hailed the arrival in France of Rossellini and Bergman. On April 6, he made the front page of *Arts* for the first time, thanks to his exclusive interview with Ingrid Bergman and the flashy headline I ESCAPED FROM HOLLYWOOD . . . AND FROM SACHA GUITRY. From then on, Truffaut began a press campaign in support of Rossellini, producing about a dozen articles on the great master over a period of sixteen months. On May 12, in *Arts,* a profile entitled "Rossellini's Life in Eleven 'Fioretti' "; on June sixteenth, a first interview: "I am not the father of neorealism," the director declares, "I work in absolute mental solitude. I suffer from being scorned and insulted from all sides. I have to finance my films myself." On July fourth, another profile, this time in *Radio-Cinéma-Télévision:* "A Man Alone, Roberto Rossellini." Again in July, a second interview in *Cahiers,* conducted this time by Eric Rohmer. Finally, on July 19, a kind of preview in *Arts* of the five Rossellini films that were to be shown in Paris that year: *L'Amore* (*Ways of Love*), *Dov'è la Libertà?*, *Jeanne au bûcher*, *Viaggio in Italia*, and *La Paura*.

For the passionate film devotees at *Cahiers*, undeniably, it was exposure to Rossellini that put to the test their desire to make films. With *Viaggio in Italia*, Rossellini proved to them that it was possible to make films with great simplicity by telling a love story between two people in a real location. When the film was released in Paris on April 15, 1955, with the title *L'amour est le plus fort*, it was not just a lesson in filmmaking for Truffaut, Godard, and Rivette but a real revelation.[63] At the same time, the producer Henri Deutschmeister—who had just made Renoir's return to France possible by financing *French Cancan*—gave his friend Rossellini carte blanche. He decided to make a series of full-length 16-mm features, each of which would show an aspect of French life in the mid-fifties. These films would be made under his supervision by Rivette, Rohmer, Godard, Truffaut, Rouch, Reichenbach, Chabrol, Aurel—that is, the future New Wave group four years ahead of its time. "Each of us had to write a screenplay," Claude Chabrol recalls. "This is how I started writing the one for *Le Beau Serge* [*Bitter Reunion*]. Our desire to make films crystallized at the same time. François took the plunge first by directing a short, so I said to myself I would do one, too; it's as simple as that."[64] Significant locations were investigated—the Cité Universitaire, by Rivette and Gruault; the milieu of the press, by Truffaut; the construction site of a large dam in the Alps, by Godard. Several synopses were written, then contracts signed. But the project was too far ahead of its time; it didn't come off—not one foot of film was produced, either by Rossellini or by his disciples.

Of all of them, Truffaut was certainly closest to Rossellini, who made him his assistant—or "factotum," as Truffaut preferred to say, at the whim of projects of the moment and their urgency. For Rossellini could commit himself to a subject one day and ditch it just as quickly, depending on his mood. But as soon as he came up with an idea, Truffaut was enlisted. "And, immediately, one had to buy all the books on the subject, collect research material, contact vast numbers of people, begin writing, and start 'moving.' "[65] Truffaut's first collaboration with Rossellini was in February 1955. From Stockholm, where he was sojourning, the Italian director asked François to find a comedy he could film, with a part for Ingrid Bergman. In response, Truffaut wrote *La Décision d'Isa* (*Isa's Decision*), an eighteen-page treatment for a screenplay. It is the story of a woman screenwriter who discovers, launches, and marries a young Hollywood comedian named Jimmy. But she leaves him when her former husband dies in an accident. The project would be ditched, like many others.

Between 1955 and 1956, Truffaut worked on a dozen film ideas, assembling considerable research material each time, summoning actors, scouting locations, writing synopses. Included among these projects were a filmed biography of Georges and Ludmila Pitoëff and the adaptation of Montherlant's *La Reine morte* (*Queen After Death*). In the spring of 1955, the two men went to Lisbon, where Rossellini planned to shoot the Montherlant, to negotiate a contract. After spending a day in Vevey, where he had gone to visit Chaplin, Rossellini met Truffaut in Lyon. Truffaut described the journey thus: "We tear down the road in his Ferrari, speeding all the way to Lisbon; he drives day and night, and I have to tell him stories to keep him awake; each time he thinks I might be getting drowsy, he hands me a mysterious flask to inhale from."[66] The two men worked in Lisbon for a few days, and tried to meet the director Manuel de Oliveira. But Rossellini, who didn't feel comfortable in Portugal, gave up the project. They returned to France through the south of Spain and Castile. Suddenly, the Ferrari's steering wheel went out of control while they were speeding; miraculously they avoided an accident. Some workers in a small Castilian village managed to make the needed part overnight, and they were able to get back on the road. So, as Truffaut explained, "Moved by the talent, courage and conscientiousness of the garage mechanics, Rossellini decides to return to Castile to film *Carmen*."[67] As soon as he returned to Paris, Rossellini started to approach distributors. Skeptical, they demanded a treatment. Truffaut set to work, equipped with three copies of *Carmen*, a pair of scissors, and a big pot of paste; three days later, he handed Rossellini a script. Rossellini dropped the project almost immediately.

The next idea was to make a "Soviet *Paisan*," an anthology of six or seven stories typical of modern life in the Soviet Union. Over a period of several weeks, Rossellini and Truffaut had *Pravda* translated for them, read books, and started to shape stories, with the confidential advice of a Russian diplomat. The project, which was doomed from the start, fell through because of a story that the diplomat considered too irreverent. A Soviet citizen spots his wife from a distance and suspects she is on her way to a romantic assignation. He follows her jealously, loses sight of her, and then sees her arm in arm with another man. This happens several times in the space of a few hours. But in the end, one discovers that the city's main department store has received about a hundred samples of the same dress, so on that day, a great many Muscovite women are identically attired.

In September 1956, on his return from the Venice Film Festival, Truffaut spent ten days or so at Rossellini's house in Santa Marinella, near Rome. The project this time involved Truffaut directing his first feature, *La Peur de Paris* (Fear of Paris), which Rossellini would produce with the support of Franco-London Films, Deutschmeister's production company. A contract was signed on November 21. Truffaut was paid 100,000 old francs for the forty-page screenplay, and his contract stipulated a total payment of 1 million francs for directing the film and making the final edit. The project was a coming-of-age story[68]: A young man, returning from military service in Germany, learns about life in Paris through his uncle, a wealthy artist who houses him and gives him an introduction into journalism. Soon sickened by this superficial, cynical life, the young man is saved from suicide by his friend Robert who works with him in the editorial offices of the newspaper. He gives up journalism and ekes out a living for a while illicitly selling poetry pamphlets and books on the street. Then he meets two women; with one, he shares a passionate but platonic romance; the other is an older woman who runs a nightclub and supports him in luxury. Finally, a decisive revelation brings the young man back to his true love. In this story the influence of Rossellini's screen characters is blended with Truffaut's own military, journalistic, and romantic experiences. But once again the project came to naught.

His two-year collaboration with Rossellini ended abruptly, after a last project that Truffaut worked on actively—a documentary on India, produced by the RAI (Radio Televisione Italiana) and directed by Rossellini. The filming was supposed to take nearly two years. As on prior occasions, Truffaut assembled considerable research material; he also acted as the intermediary with Jean Renoir, whose Indian experience—from making *The River* near Calcutta in 1950—was invaluable. Finally, since Truffaut couldn't allot more than a year to a trip so far away, Rossellini went off to shoot *India* on his own in 1957, with Jean Herman as his assistant. "I think it is wise for me to stop working with R.R. before he himself tells me that he can't take me to India or something like that,"[69] Truffaut wrote to Lachenay from Venice on September 16, 1956.

His experience with Rossellini, though outwardly fruitless, played a crucial part in Truffaut's life; it taught him resourcefulness, cunning with producers, and, above all, how to go from project to project, as dictated by imagination or financial opportunity. Though Rossellini lost interest in fiction and turned his attention to filmmaking projects with a documentary slant, Truffaut, for his part, was never attracted to the documentary form and even rejected its philosophy. One can understand his distress, between 1954 and 1956, working on stories, narratives, and scripts with a filmmaker who rejected them on principle. Yet from Rossellini, Truffaut learned the most essential thing—the filming of life.

## THE AUTEUR THEORY

Meeting directors such as Max Ophuls and Roberto Rossellini provided François Truffaut with important opportunities to support them. He also developed another, more theoretical but just as radical way of promoting them, which was the *"politique des auteurs* [the auteur theory]," a decisive concept that Truffaut himself formulated.[70] The expression became famous, but even today it is often ambiguous. To trace its genesis and comprehend it requires understanding François Truffaut's critical persona. As early as January 1954, his article on *The Big Heat,* with the explicit title, "Aimer Fritz Lang [Loving Fritz Lang]" sets out the basis of his theory: "Shouldn't all of this lead us to suspect that Fritz Lang might be a true film auteur, and if his themes and stories come to us cloaked in the banal appearances of a thriller, war film, or western, shouldn't we see this as a sign of great probity on the part of a cinema that feels no compulsion to adorn itself with enticing labels? We should love Fritz Lang."[71]

Deliberate love and the desire to follow a body of work in the making—for Truffaut, these are the essential elements of the *"politique des auteurs."* This implies, first of all, closeness and intimacy with the author, all of whose films must be defended, even those that are flawed. Indeed, it is no coincidence that Truffaut's *"politique des auteurs"* developed into a coherent theory with the release of two movies generally scorned by the critics—Jacques Becker's *Ali Baba et les Quarante Voleurs (Ali Baba and the Forty Thieves)* and Abel Gance's *La Tour de Nesle.* These films provided Truffaut with the opportunity to make his manifesto more explicit.

On September 1, 1954, Truffaut published in *Arts,* the laudatory "Sir Abel Gance," wherein he considered the paradox that Gance's silent films were admired while his talkies were disparaged. This was the quasi-unanimous opinion of the critical establishment. Truffaut maintained that Gance's talkies were born of the same visionary genius as his silent films, and that it was inevitably contradictory to praise the latter and denounce the former. "Perhaps I should make the following confession. I believe in the *'politique des Auteurs,'* or, you might say, I refuse to accept the theory, which is so valued in motion picture criticism, of great directors 'aging,' or becoming 'senile.' Nor do I believe in the genius of the émigrés—Fritz Lang, Buñuel, Hitchcock, or Renoir—drying up." In setting down his theory, Truffaut attacks two highly ingrained critical prejudices: aging, and the loss of cultural roots. The directors he loves are "sages," "masters," cosmopolitan spirits, filmmakers who transcend boundaries. "The ten greatest directors in the world are over fifty,"[72] he wrote confidently in January 1958, with the New Wave on the horizon.

Truffaut was in fact disappointed by Abel Gance's *La Tour de Nesle* when it was released in March 1955. But virtuoso strategist that he was, he turned this disappointment into his principal argument in subsequent affirmations of his theory. "There is nothing very interesting to say about *La Tour de Nesle.* Everyone knows it is a commissioned film with a ridiculous budget whose best parts have remained in the distributor's drawers. *La Tour de Nesle,* you might say, is Abel Gance's least good film."[73] Judging Gance essentially on the basis of his potential and the one successful scene he notices in *La Tour,* Truffaut defends its author precisely for having botched his film, but botching it with sublime ease: "Since Abel Gance happens to be a genius, *La Tour de Nesle* is a brilliant film. Abel Gance doesn't possess genius: he is possessed by genius. . . . If you can't see Gance's genius, then you and I don't have the same conception of cinema, mine being the right one, of course. The question now is to see if it is possible to be both brilliant and a failure. I tend to believe that failing is a talent. Succeeding is failing. I would ultimately like to defend the thesis, Abel Gance failed auteur of failed films. I'm convinced that there are no great directors who don't sacrifice something. According to the criticism of our elders, a successful film is one in which all the elements partake equally of a whole which then deserves the adjective perfect. But I decree that perfection and success are abject, inde-cent, immoral and obscene."[74] With his taste for paradox, here at its extreme, Truffaut used the very deficiency in Gance's work to illustrate his auteur theory. Every auteur film becomes the story of a failure, of perfec-tion sacrificed; and only the whole body of his work, retracing a personal, unique journey, can allow us to understand an auteur. The whole theory is based, therefore, on what could be called the "paradox of the minor film."

His defense of *Ali Baba and the Forty Thieves,* a film Jacques Becker was commissioned to make with Fernandel, published in the February 1955 *Cahiers du cinéma,* also seems intended as a manifesto—as suggested by its title, *"Ali Baba et la 'politique des auteurs.'"* The movie was ignored by the critics upon its release and Truffaut himself was embarrassed by its failings. Again, he used the art of paradox to extricate himself from a difficult posi-tion, subscribing to Becker's body of work, "with no exception," in the name of coherence in taste. "Even if *Ali Baba* were a failure, I would still defend it by virtue of the auteur theory to which I and my fellow critics subscribe. This theory, based on Giraudoux's statement, 'There are no works, there are only authors,' consists in denying the axiom dear to our elders, which main-tains that films are like mayonnaise, you either succeed in making them or fail." What Truffaut is plainly suggesting, in a way, is a theory of taste as intransigent as the one he had used to attack "quality French cinema" a year earlier in "A Certain Tendency of the French Cinema." As for André Bazin, *Cahiers's* tutelary figure, he was very skeptical about this critical approach, fearing the perverse effects of the systematic and formalistic praise of minor films.[75] But in spite of Bazin, the auteur theory soon won over a large part of the *Cahiers* editorial staff, for it fit in well with the magazine's personal approach (interviews with the chosen directors) and reinforced its polemi-cal orientation.

Though Truffaut had put forward a critical strategy and a polemical line of defense, the notion of "auteur" still needed to be defined. Like Godard, Rivette, and Rohmer, Truffaut advanced a simple argument: An auteur is primarily and exclusively a director. *Mise-en-scène* is the auteur stripped bare; it is what remains when all the subsidiary aspects of film disappear (screenplay, promotion, etc.). The *only* thing that is beautiful in the movies is the *mise-en-scène;* and this alone defines the auteur. Rohmer expressed it with a quip: "No man shall enter the *Cahiers* Olympus who is not a director."[76] Bazin found it at the core of his study of *Cahiers's* "hitchcock-hawksian" (that is, auteurist) tendency: "They so value *mise-en-scène* because they detect in it a large part of a film's very substance, an organizing of people and things which has a meaning unto itself, both moral and esthetic."[77]

For François Truffaut, the ideal instance of the "auteur-director" was Alfred Hitchcock, about whom Truffaut wrote profusely—twenty-seven articles in the fifties. The "master of suspense" was the object of true worship. "The greatest inventor of forms," the director par excellence, the one who "makes us experience the vertigo felt by his characters, thanks to the fascination which any formal, quasi-geometric figure exercises upon us. And beyond vertigo, [he] makes us discover the depth of a moral idea, a vision of the world."[78]

What the critic sees in the film, thanks to the mise-en-scène, is a (self-) portrait of the director, the auteur himself. An auteur, then, when all is said and done, is a director who allows his intimate self to be seen on the screen, either through a multiplicity of masks, like Hitchcock, or by revealing himself with complete frankness, like Nicholas Ray. So said Truffaut about Ray and *Johnny Guitar,* a film that moved him so deeply that he saw it over ten times in two weeks: "The mark of his talent lies in his absolute sincerity, his hypersensitivity. . . . Unlike André Bazin, I believe it is important for a director to recognize himself in the way we depict him and his films. Otherwise we have failed."[79] Recognizing the man who has revealed himself emotionally on screen is the ultimate consequence of the auteur theory. In this absolute love, there is a quasi-anthropomorphic conception of cinema; he who sees one of Ray's films and recognizes him, also sees and recognizes cinema as a whole. Ergo, Ray is cinema.

The auteur theory, as conceived by Truffaut, entails a strategy of continually harassing the enemy—and the enemy, in the mid-fifties, is again, or still, "quality French cinema." Truffaut relied principally on *Arts* to launch his attacks, for it had a wide circulation and as a weekly was better suited to polemic than the monthly *Cahiers du cinéma.*

On March 30, 1955, Truffaut published in *Arts* a tract entitled "The French Cinema Short on Ambition," wherein he suggested a precise rating of the "89 French directors of the day," whom he divided into five categories: the "auteurs"—he identifies nine—Astruc, Becker, Bresson, Cocteau, Gance, Leenhardt, Ophuls, Renoir, Tati; the representatives of "quality": Yves Allégret, Autant-Lara, Carné, Cayatte, Christian-Jaque, Clair, Clément, Clouzot, Delannoy, Grémillon; fifteen "semiambitious directors"; twenty-five "honest commercial" directors; and twenty-nine "deliberately commercial" directors. Similarly, on June 8, 1955, he berated the screenwriters, extending his attack on Aurenche and Bost to the whole profession, which "apes the worst literature" and aspires only to a "stillborn quality" with adaptations of best-selling books.

Truffaut regularly summoned the readership of *Arts* to "rise up against French cinema" and the audiences to "smash the seats when faced with these revolting films."[80] But he was at his most skillful and effective in direct combat—for example, in his lively, vitriolic attack on Jean Delannoy's *Chiens perdus sans collier,* adapted by Jean Aurenche and Pierre Bost from a novel by Gilbert Cesbron. In his November 9, 1955, article in *Arts,* Truffaut seemed to seek a confrontation with Delannoy—he insulted him in order to draw him out in the open, then called public opinion to witness. "It is custom-tailored writing for the Gaumont-Palace by two disillusioned and cynical screenwriters, Aurenche and Bost, who have written 'moving' dialogue, put into images by a man who is not intelligent enough to be cynical, too cunning to be sincere, and too pretentious and solemn to be straightforward." The hoped-for answer was not long in coming; on November 13, Delannoy sent him a registered letter: "What you wrote . . . is so low that I have never encountered anything like it in my twenty years in the profession. You've just broken a record. This deserves to be pointed out."[81] Naturally, Truffaut took advantage of this godsend by publishing an excerpt from Delannoy's letter in *Arts,* along with some of the letters of support he, Truffaut, had received. He thereby orchestrated a Manichean battle between the "incorruptible righter of wrongs" and one of the most eminent representatives of official academicism. On November 26, Truffaut triumphed: "Monsieur Jean Delannoy is the most commercial French director; what more does he want? Unanimous praise from the critics? Impossible! In reply to Jean Delannoy's *lettre recommandée* [registered letter], let me contrast three other letters whose signatories *recommend* themselves only to the grace of God. I guarantee I received no letter supporting *Chiens perdus sans collier*—nor has the management of *Arts;* if I had, I would have published it, not out of esteem for Jean Delannoy, but to balance this futile polemic."

After a year of combat, François Truffaut began a new stage in his career. In the spring of 1956, his popularity was such that his articles commanded the front page of *Arts*. In May 1956, there were four consecutive pieces on what he called the "progressive degeneration"[82] of the Cannes Film Festival. Cannes was an institution celebrating its ninth year; though more open than ever to the international film scene, it was also a fortress of the most established French cinema. On May 23, Truffaut launched an assault on the festival and the Ministry of Culture, which supported it, headlining his piece, CANNES, AN UNQUESTIONABLE SUCCESS? NO, MR. MINISTER! His critique staged a dialogue between the "little guy" who is the keeper of truth and the "big guy" blinded by power: "Movies are for the people who make them, who love them, who go to see them, and not for those who profit by them. The jury should be discharged and the diplomats sent back to their compromises." By violently and insolently attacking the festival, Truffaut gained yet further authority. From then on, every year in May, reports of the Cannes Film Festival in *Arts* would be colored by his moods.

## VENICE 56

At the beginning of September 1956, François Truffaut attended Venice's Mostra, a prestigious film festival older than Cannes.

During his ten days at the Lido, Truffaut saw two or three films a day, including Robert Bresson's *Un condamné à mort s'est échappé* (*A Man Escaped*), Kenji Mizoguchi's *Street of Shame,* Nicholas Ray's *Bigger than Life,* Joshua Logan's *Bus Stop,* and Robert Aldrich's *Attack!* He very much wanted to meet Aldrich, a director whom he greatly admired. The meeting finally took place, a memorable event for him: "I met the corpulent genius on the beach and we chatted," he wrote in *Arts* on September 19. "I asked him 60 questions. Watch for the results of this delightful, sublime interchange in our next issue."

In Venice, between two screenings and during the lunch hour, French journalists and film professionals congregated on the Lido beach. The crowd included André Bazin, Jean de Baroncelli, Jean Néry, and Claude Mauriac. Here the foremost polemicists in the "paper war" that was raging in French cinema rubbed shoulders. It was a place for countless small humiliations, poses, and displays of contempt. "I sunbathe next to Carlo Rim," Truffaut confided, "but we make believe we don't know each other, which is sometimes comical since people try to introduce us three times a day, and we have to put on a show of not catching the names.... It's insane!"[83] Pierre Braunberger also hung around the Lido beach. He was one of the rare producers in Paris who was interested in young directors and willing to finance their films, mainly shorts. Braunberger admired the young Truffaut's critical talent and wanted François to make a short film for his production house, Les Films de la Pléiade. The two men hit it off, and Truffaut discussed several projects with the producer, whom he nicknamed "Batala," a reference to the fascinating swindler played by Jules Berry in Renoir's *The Crime of Monsieur Lange*.

On the Lido beach, Truffaut also met Madeleine Morgenstern, a pretty brunette with short hair. This perceptive, cheerful young woman was the only daughter of an important distributor, Ignace Morgenstern, the director of Cocinor (Comptoir cinématographique du Nord). While Morgenstern and his wife, Elizabeth, were vacationing in Switzerland, their daughter was representing him in Venice and had the task of finding films that could be distributed in France. Madeleine was twenty-five years old; she had studied English and lived in the United States for several months, and she was now working in Cocinor's publicity department. One evening, Pierre Braunberger introduced her formally to François Truffaut at the Hotel Excelsior, the fashionable festival hangout. The two would meet again on subsequent days, sometimes in the front rows at festival screenings. They enjoyed talking to each other, even though Madeleine didn't feel she impressed the hot-headed critic, whom she knew by his reputation and articles. "When we parted, he promised to write me, which he never did,"[84] she recalls. They would only see each other again six weeks later, thanks to a chance meeting on the Champs-Elysées. "Oh, I wrote you, but I tore up the letter!"[85] he told her, as a way of justifying his silence, shrouding himself in mystery and playing the seducer. They started to see each other regularly and go to the movies together, but it was still only a friendship.

When he left Venice on September 10, 1956, Truffaut went to stay at Roberto Rossellini's in Rome. Exhausted by his strenuous journalistic activity, he yearned for some other occupation, and even considered giving up criticism. Though he remained skeptical about his projects with Rossellini, he found it stimulating to be in close contact with the Italian director. Making a film became his top priority. But the contract signed with Rossellini and Deutschmeister for *La Peur de Paris* would remain in the drawer.

## HENRI-PIERRE ROCHÉ

At this point, Truffaut was deeply moved by Henri-Pierre Roché's novel *Jules and Jim,* which he discovered by rummaging through the stalls of secondhand books at the Librairie Delamain on Place du Palais-Royal. He had been intrigued by the title of the novel, which had been published two years earlier by Gallimard and had gone more or less unnoticed. Henri-Pierre Roché was completely unknown and seventy-six years old; *Jules and Jim* was his first novel. "From the very first lines, I fell in love with Henri-Pierre Roché's prose," Truffaut would later explain. "At that time, my favor-

writer was Cocteau for his brisk sentences, their seemingly dry tone and his precise imagery. Now, with Henri-Pierre Roché, I was discovering a writer whom I thought superior to Cocteau, for he obtained the same kind of poetic prose with a less extensive vocabulary, making very short sentences, and using everyday words. With Roché's writing, emotion is born from the void, from emptiness, from all the rejected words, in short from the ellipsis itself."[86]

Overflowing with enthusiasm, Truffaut mentioned *Jules and Jim* at every opportunity. Thus, in his review of Edgar G. Ulmer's intimist Western, *The Naked Dawn,* he ventured a comparison, clearly far-fetched for anyone but him: "One of the most beautiful modern novels I know is Henri-Pierre Roché's *Jules and Jim,* which shows us the lifelong relationship of two friends and their common female companion, and the tender love they have for each other, with hardly any conflict thanks to a new aesthetic moral code which is constantly reassessed. *The Naked Dawn* is the first film to make me feel that a cinematic *Jules and Jim* is feasible."[87] This declaration of love soon reached its intended beneficiary. Indeed, one month later, Roché wrote Truffaut a card in his tight, shaky handwriting, thanking him warmly: "I was very touched by your comments on *Jules and Jim* in *Arts,* in particular 'thanks to a new aesthetic moral code which is constantly reassessed.' I hope you will find it again, even more clearly, in *Deux anglaises et le continent* [*Two Englishwomen and the Continent*] which you will be receiving shortly."[88] Several days later, Truffaut received the writer's second novel, just published by Gallimard. After reading it, he felt even more strongly convinced of Roché's greatness, and during the summer, Truffaut went to visit him at his pretty little house in Meudon. He found a tall, thin, lively elderly man, who was working on his third novel, *Victor,* which would remain unfinished and whose hero was based on his friend Marcel Duchamp. Roché described his life to Truffaut, a dilettante's life spent among women, similar to Cocteau's, punctuated by trips and many encounters with his painter friends—André Derain, Francis Picabia, Max Ernst, Wols, Georges Braque (whose boxing companion he was), Marie Laurencin (one of his most faithful mistresses), and Picasso (whom he introduced to Gertrude Stein).

The exceptional bond he developed with a man three times older than himself strengthened Truffaut's desire to adapt *Jules and Jim.* In mid-November 1956, he even considered hiring Roché to write the dialogue for Kathe, the woman Jules and Jim both love. Roché responded enthusiastically to the idea and on November 23, he arranged to have five copies of *Jules and Jim* sent to Truffaut. The latter worked uninterruptedly, annotating, cutting, and restructuring, using Roché's sentences to create a simple, linear narrative. Henri-Pierre Roché would not write the dialogue for Kathe—who became Catherine in Truffaut's version—but he did offer much advice. The truth is, Truffaut was not really ready to make his first film on such a literary and sensitive subject, and the project of filming *Jules and Jim* was constantly postponed. But he maintained his correspondence with Roché, whose last letter was dated April 3, 1959. Because of illness, he was unable to accept Truffaut's invitation to one of the first screenings of *The 400 Blows*. "Dear young friend, your kind letter! If I feel better, I'll go see *The 400 Blows* in Paris. You'll let me know where it is showing. I reread *Jules and Jim* as well. I won't try to visualize it on screen until I've discussed it thoroughly with you, and know how you plan to adapt it. Would you like more copies? A heartfelt thanks for the photos of Jeanne Moreau. I like her. I couldn't go out to see *The Lovers*, of course. I'm glad she likes Kathe! I hope to meet her one day. Yes, when you return, come to see me whenever you want, I look forward to it."[89] Henri-Pierre Roché died on April 9, 1959, without having seen *The 400 Blows* or having read the screenplay for *Jules and Jim*. At least he had seen Jeanne Moreau's face.

## MAKING A FILM

Aware that he was not ready or mature enough to handle the subject successfully, François Truffaut put aside his adaptation of *Jules and Jim*. Other projects occupied him in the final months of 1956: ideas for films, some fully worked out, others not. Among these were several lines jotted down after a long conversation with Jean-Luc Godard one December morning on a bench at the Richelieu-Drouot Métro stop. The story was the following: Having missed the last train for Le Havre, Michel steals an American car near the Saint-Lazare station. After shooting a police motorcyclist who was hot on his tail, Michel, now back in Paris, goes to find his fiancée Betty, a young and pretty American journalist. In the streets of Paris on a late summer day, a frenetic chase takes place, from one movie theater to another. When she is arrested by the police, Betty ends up ratting on Michel, who is hiding out in a barge. He then gives himself up, although he claims to have taken a fatal dose of aspirin. No one believes him and he is hauled into the office of the inspector in charge of the case. "But for once Michel was not lying. As soon as he walks into the office, he collapses, arms stretched out on either side Christ-like, backward, in a single heap. They rush to his side, but Michel is already dead."[90] Three years later, in the summer of 1959, Truffaut's four-page synopsis was developed and changed, thus becoming the screenplay for Jean-Luc Godard's first film, *À bout de souffle* (*Breathless*).

Truffaut had suggested his most promising projects to Pierre Braunberger when they saw each other on the Lido beach. On January 10, 1957, they signed their first contract together, for a short film entitled *Autour de la tour Eiffel* (Around the Eiffel Tower). Truffaut received 75,000 francs for his four-page shooting script of the projected twenty-five-minute film scheduled to be shot in ten days, in 35 mm, with an estimated budget of around 2 million old francs. Joëlle Robin, Jean-Claude Brialy, Edith Zedkine, and Raymond Devos were cast in the four parts. Oddly enough, Truffaut wrote two versions of this story about a person obsessed with seeing the Eiffel Tower. In the first version, Juliette, a young provincial girl who is in Paris to settle an inheritance, wants to go up to the top of the Eiffel Tower, which she sees wherever she goes but is never able to get to. She meets people who could help her—a cattle dealer (Devos) on a short Paris trip, who delivers a monologue on the condition of the peasants instead of giving her directions; an attractive, talkative, cheeky young hussy (Joëlle Robin) who is waiting for a client and whose profession the young provincial girl is clearly far from suspecting; and a playboy (Brialy) who easily seduces her and finally drives her to the Eiffel Tower in his sports car. The other version gives Jean-Claude Brialy the leading role. He portrays a "Paris peasant" who first appears "leading an enormous, reluctant cow at the end of a rope" as he heads toward the Vaugirard slaughterhouses. He walks out of the slaughterhouse with a wad of bills in his hand and sets about visiting the capital. The Eiffel Tower is the first monument to attract him. He sees it from afar but seems to get lost every time he tries to approach it. A talkative, absentminded bistro owner (Devos) is of no use to him, nor is a prostitute. However, a young woman, Juliette, notices him sniveling at the edge of the sidewalk. She invites him to get into her convertible and then drives him to the Eiffel Tower. There, she drags him along on a quick tour of the monument. On their elevator ride up the tower, "the peasant changes imperceptibly: his beret, pulled down to his eyebrows, gradually rises until it vanishes in the emptiness." Up at the top, the peasant discovers "a Parisian Paris down to the fingertips." On their ride down, they are clearly in love and make "the most Parisian of couples"—she still smiling and elegant, he unrecognizable, clean-shaven, and witty—"An Adam of 1957 on the arm of an eternal Eve."[91] Truffaut quickly dropped this project, which no longer amused him. But a remnant of it can be seen in the credits of *The 400 Blows,* with the camera scanning the streets in the west of Paris and coming to a standstill at the foot of the Eiffel Tower. Several years later, Truffaut would collect replicas of the Eiffel Tower in all sizes, and they would be displayed on the shelves of his living room on avenue Pierre-Ier-de-Serbie.

He signed a second contract with Braunberger in March 1957 to contribute to a film with children as the theme. Truffaut, Richard Leacock (the British-born documentary filmmaker, disciple of Robert Flaherty), Claude de Givray, the novelist René-Jean Clot, Jacques Doniol-Valcroze, and Pierre Kast were each supposed to direct an episode. Truffaut's contribution was entitled "Le Mensonge de Bernadette [Bernadette's Lie]." It is the story of an adolescent girl accused by her teacher of cheating. The schoolgirl lies to defend herself and the teacher believes her. Several weeks later, before her First Communion, Bernadette stops eating and speaking. Finally, she leaves a letter on the kitchen table confessing her lie to her parents, then drowns herself in the river.[92]

This collective project was also soon abandoned. For a while, Truffaut envisaged making the film on his own, and he continued writing down anecdotes on childhood and classifying them by theme along with "Le Mensonge de Bernadette." Some of these would be reworked much later, in 1975, in *Small Change,* while one heralds a theme of *The 400 Blows:* "François's truancy. Cuts school. Returns. The note. The schoolbag behind the door."[93] In the spring of 1957, Truffaut was absorbed by the thought of making a film on childhood, but the link was still missing that would allow him to make the creative leap simply and naturally.

## BERNADETTE'S SKIRT

In the *Arts* offices on rue du Faubourg-Saint-Honoré, François Truffaut met Maurice Pons, a young fellow contributor to the cultural weekly. Pons was also the author of a book of short stories entitled *Virginales,* which had been published by Julliard two years before. Truffaut very much liked one of the stories, "Les Mistons," and wanted to adapt it for the screen. Pons, who felt an immediate fondness for Truffaut, whom he later described as "a nervous young man, always hurried, with wild hair and beautiful dark eyes, like 'Bonaparte at the bridge of Arcole',"[94] was delighted at the thought. As for Truffaut, he was very impressed by the elegant, concise, almost precious style used by Maurice Pons to tell the story of a group of kids, nicknamed "*les mistons,*" and how they spy on the love affair of a student couple, Yvette and Etienne, intruding on their tennis games and movie dates. And then, how on a beautiful May afternoon, in a clearing where they have followed the couple, one of the boys is caught and given a stern hiding by Etienne. After the vacation, the children learn that Etienne died over the summer in a mountain-climbing accident, and they watch Yvette walk by one last time, in mourning clothes and engrossed in melancholy thoughts. Truffaut was moved by this short story and its evocative sensual power—the physical agitation conveyed, for example, in the description of Yvette's bath. "When she went to the baths at the river, she would leave her bicycle padlocked outside the entrance. Since her skirt always fluttered as she biked, and she certainly wore no petticoat, on hot days the saddle of her bicycle would become very humid. As the weeks went by, the outline of pale rings on the saddle became more visible.

Fascinated, we would walk around this flower of curdled leather, an ace of hearts perched high, whose trips we envied. It was not unusual for one us, unable to endure the strain, to walk away from the group and, with no exhibitionism or false shame, go up and press his face momentarily against this saddle—the confidant of what mystery?"[95]

In April 1957, Truffaut was finally in a position to make his first film. Robert Lachenay, who had just come into a small inheritance, had promised to help him, and Truffaut's confidence was buttressed by having found the actor who could play the part of Etienne—Gérard Blain, whom he had noticed in Julien Duvivier's *Voici le temps des assassins* (*Deadlier than the Male*), a brooding, handsome, and robust young man with a rather touchy personality. In his review of Duvivier's film in *Arts*, on April 18, 1956, Truffaut made a point of praising the new actor to his readers: "Gérard Blain, in his first real appearance, is perfect in the most difficult part." Blain responded immediately on the following day: "When I read you yesterday, it brought tears to my eyes and I didn't dare believe it. I've read almost all your articles and being perfectly aware of the reputation you have among us, I'm even more flattered. You're the only one to have understood me." Several days later, the two young men met and got on well; they began seeing each other in a café near the Champs-Elysées and at the actor's house in Boulogne. At dinner at Blain's house, Truffaut made the acquaintance of his young wife, Bernadette Lafont, whom Blain had met at the Nîmes Festival of Dramatic Art in the summer of 1955, when she was only seventeen years old. Captivated by Bernadette's spontaneity and convinced of Gérard Blain's talent, Truffaut suggested the couple play the lovers in *Les Mistons* (*The Mischief Makers*). He decided to shoot the film in Nîmes, Bernadette's hometown.

Bernadette Lafont had never acted in a film and Blain didn't look favorably upon his wife's embracing an acting career. But Truffaut's offer was an opportunity not to be missed. "I was rather shy; I spoke very little and I was ashamed of my accent," she says today, recalling her debut. "When I asked Truffaut why he had chosen me, he answered, 'I felt you wanted to work in films as much as I did.' And it was true."[96] The young woman began preparing for her part immediately and stopped studying for the baccalaureate exam, which she was supposed to take in June 1957. In May, she took up tennis to prepare for her role, and she followed Truffaut's costume instructions scrupulously: "The dressmaker told me she could make me a complete outfit in two days. I have nothing in white. So I could have two skirts made in that color—a very full skirt for the bike scenes and a narrow one with a slit as you mentioned. Will that be good?"[97] she wrote her Pygmalion on July 8. On two long weekends in April and June 1957, Truffaut scouted the region, accompanied by Rivette, Chabrol, and Brialy, as well as by Bernadette

Lafont and Gérard Blain, who served as guides. He decided on his shooting locations—the Nîmes arena, the Tennis Club, the Place de la Fontaine, and the outskirts of Saint-André-de-Valborgne. Now he only needed to find the money. The budget was far from enormous, particularly since Truffaut could benefit from equipment loaned by Jean Malige, the cameraman who had been approached for the film. Malige owned a ministudio near Montpellier, with a lightweight camera, dolly tracks, an editing table, and sound equipment. The actors were prepared to work on a profit-sharing basis and friends—Robert Lachenay, Claude de Givray, and Alain Jeannel—would be enlisted as assistants. However, there were essential expenses that had to be covered during the shooting and editing, which would take forty-five days.

Madeleine Morgenstern, who had become very intimate with François, asked her father to help finance *The Mischief Makers;* he handed the matter over to Marcel Berbert, his collaborator at Cocinor. The latter still remembers his boss's instructions: "Monsieur Morgenstern said to me, 'This young man wants to make a film. He should go ahead, but I'd rather he set up his own company so he'll be on his own. See what you can do.' "[98] Truffaut was thus able to create his own production company, les Films du Carrosse—an explicit homage to Jean Renoir (his 1952 film *Le Carrosse d'or* [*The Golden Coach*])—with the backing of 2 million old francs, the equivalent of the film's budget, from UFIC, an organization that financed movies. A phone call from Marcel Berbert was enough to convince the official at UFIC to grant this loan to a young unknown, though the volume of work in production at Cocinor was such that the risk involved was really minimal. "For a long time, Truffaut believed that he had been loaned this money because of his pretty face! Similarly, we were held financially liable when he brought his film in to be developed. It was only years later that François realized the truth,"[99] says Marcel Berbert. Helped, without his knowing it, by the man who would become his father-in-law, Truffaut got ready to direct his first film.

## THE FILM OF TOMORROW WILL BE AN ACT OF LOVE

Before shooting *The Mischief Makers,* François Truffaut, still a star journalist, was careful not to miss the opportunity of a last press campaign. Shortly before the opening of the Cannes Film Festival, he published an article in the April 20, 1957, issue of *Arts* predicting the worst academicism. On May 15, when the festival was almost over, Truffaut drove the point home, once again in *Arts:* "You are all witnesses in this trial: French cinema is dying from its false legends." The following week, he delivered his final blow: "Cannes: a failure dominated by compromises, schemes and faux pas." According to Truffaut, the French film industry was producing "too many mediocre films," too much of that "quality cinema" he had been denouncing for nearly four years, restricted to narrow formulas, manufactured artificially in obsolete studios, with polished screenplays and actors, fossilized and flaunting a haughtiness and scorn for novelty and youth. As always, Truffaut counterbalanced his attack with praise for the directors he admired—in this instance, Renoir, Ophuls, and Rossellini, three auteurs whose "films are as personal as a fingerprint."[100] In analyzing the crisis in French cinema, Truffaut mentioned higgledy-piggledy the bankruptcy of producers, screenwriters, and directors, all of whom were passing the buck among themselves. He saw only one possible remedy: trust vested in the auteur, simultaneously director and screenwriter, who would freely choose his crew, actors, set, music, and story and converse with his producer as an equal. "The film of the future will be shot by adventurers," he concluded in an article that resembles both a critical testament and an anticipation of his own evolution:

> The film of tomorrow appears to me as even more personal than an individual and autobiographical novel, like a confession, or a diary. The young filmmakers will express themselves in the first person and will relate what has happened to them: it may be the story of their first love or their most recent; of their political awakening; the story of a trip, a sickness, their military service, their marriage, their last vacation . . . and it will be enjoyable because it will be true and new. . . . The film of tomorrow will not be directed by civil servants of the camera, but by artists for whom shooting a film constitutes a wonderful and thrilling adventure. The film of tomorrow will resemble the person who made it and the number of spectators will be proportional to the number of friends the director has. The film of tomorrow will be an act of love.[101]

Once again, Truffaut provoked an outcry in the film industry. (The following year, the directors of the Cannes Festival sanctioned Truffaut and refused to give him journalistic accreditation. He attended nonetheless.) Then Claude Autant-Lara got on the front lines. The director, whose adaptations—Stendhal's *The Red and the Black,* Radiguet's *The Devil in the Flesh,* and Colette's *Le Blé en herbe* (*The Game of Love,* based on *The Ripening Seed*)—were representative of "French quality" but who had also directed more personal, *noir* films, such as *Douce* (*Love Story*), *Occupe-toi d'Amélie* (*Oh Amelia!*) and *La Traversée de Paris* (*Four Bags Full*), tried to silence the angry young man of movie journalism. A week after Erich von Stroheim's death, on May 19, 1957, Autant-Lara took advantage of a radio homage to the deceased director to settle his score with Truffaut. "While I was attending the funeral of the jinxed director Erich von Stroheim this morning, I thought of that young thug of journalism who shamelessly claims that censorship doesn't exist, and I felt like grabbing him by the ears and dragging him in front of the grave of the director of *Greed* and showing him the grave of a director who was the preeminent victim of censorship." Truffaut responded on June 19 with a virulent article, certainly the most polemical one of his entire career. He accused Autant-Lara, whom he called a "false martyr," of being a "bourgeois director," of abdicating intellectually, of lacking courage and hiding behind screenplays written by other people, and of working within a system "spoiled rotten by money," which allowed him to "earn a salary of 25 million to direct Brigitte Bardot in *En cas de malheur* [*Love Is My Profession*] without ever taking the risk of personal creative work." The journalist concluded by saying, "The word courage keeps recurring in this article which is devoted to the kind Claude Autant-Lara lacks. He has only the courage to grumble and denigrate."[102]

On July 3, 1957, Truffaut savored his victory in *Arts*. In answer to Autant-Lara's incensed reaction, he published letters from readers who supported his views and were indignant at the contemptuous term "young thug of journalism"; these letters paint a dark, defamatory portrait of a defeated, embittered director "sold out to a system that is in complete decay."

Autant-Lara was not the only established director with whom Truffaut dueled publicly at this time. Yves Allégret, for example, was accused of contemptuously and artificially reconstructing the world of prostitution in *Méfiez-vous fillettes* (*Young Girls Beware*). Truffaut criticized Allégret for being completely cut off from life, for having never set foot in Pigalle, for being, in sum, one of those "French directors who are bourgeois and have no problems, and whose knowledge of life is limited to the hackneyed gossip of the Elysée-Club, the escalator of the Rex and the Kermesse aux Etoiles."[103] Truffaut also denounced Michel Audiard for his vulgar dialogues and his contempt for his characters.[104] In writing about Carlo-Rim, a director known for his clichés, Truffaut assumed a moral stand, asserting that a filmmaker must never "show contempt for the audience by underestimating it," but, rather, treat "the spectator as his equal" and respect the rule of never including anything in a film "that is supposed to make people laugh unless it makes you laugh yourself, or to make people cry unless it moves you yourself," he wrote on November 6, 1957. Truffaut's diatribe against the "money that makes the bourgeois directors rotten," the corrupt system, and the "civil servants"[105] of the French cinema was completely in keeping with the protest language of the final months of the French Fourth Republic, which called into question the decaying French political and parliamentary system. In the late fifties, France needed fresh air, and a complete overhaul. The need was felt in all areas—political, social, and cultural. In film circles, Truffaut embodied this need for renewal.

Henri-Georges Clouzot and René Clément were the only important directors of "quality French films" who had so far been spared by Truffaut. In fact, Truffaut nicknamed them "the Untouchables."[106] Though Doniol-Valcroze and André Bazin were close to both directors, neither had the power to prevent Truffaut from doing a real hatchet job on Clouzot in the December 1957 *Cahiers du cinéma,* in an article entitled "Clouzot at Work, or the Reign of Terror," which is still surprising today for its violence. "With *Les Espions,* Clouzot has made Kafka in his pants, a seven-word statement which perfectly conveys the exact level of the enterprise," he wrote, basing his demonstration on an account of the shoot of the film, and denouncing the reign of terror the director had enforced on the set. Clouzot and Clément were both expelled from the "cinema of the future," whose advent Truffaut was yearning for; he was particularly harsh in his review of *Barrage contre le Pacifique (The Sea Wall):* "For Clément the main thing is that he shoot a film which costs more than the preceding one and less than the next."[107] Clouzot, the terrorist; Clément, the thoroughly corrupt: The hatchet job was complete.

## IF GUITRY WERE TOLD TO ME

In the mid-fifties, Sacha Guitry was still regarded primarily as a man of the theater, an author and wit, and was still tainted by the political and moral charges made against him after the Liberation. As a result, he was ignored by film devotees and scorned by left-wing critics. But Truffaut had remained loyal to the director of *The Story of a Cheat,* one of the films that had most influenced him in his youth. Consequently, any film by Sacha Guitry became the occasion for a merciless fight against the "prejudices of French cinema." In March 1956, he led a crusade in defense of *Si Paris nous était conté,* which he regarded as greatly undervalued by the critics. But the rift—or abyss—that had grown between the critics and the director of *Désiré* and *Donne-moi tes yeux* was even more apparent when Guitry's last two films were released, *Assassins et Voleurs (Lovers and Thieves)* and *Les trois font la paire,* made when he was already disabled and gravely ill. Truffaut took up the challenge and embarked on a particularly bellicose rehabilitation campaign, perhaps his most brilliant fight of those years. On February 13, 1957, with provocative humor, Truffaut entitled his article on *Lovers and Thieves* "Sacha in Top Form," maintaining it was one of the best films of the year, an opinion most critics did not share. Truffaut indignantly affirmed that Sacha Guitry's "unbelievably casual shooting style is a wonderful directing idea, for it is perfectly suited to his sense of humor. I love Sacha Guitry because given the choice between suggestiveness and obscenity, he always chooses obscenity, because his sense of humor knows no boundaries and the infirm, the elderly, children and the dead clink their glasses like everyone else." The young critic's only regret was that he never got to meet the man whom he unhesitatingly compared to Renoir. "In 1955, during the filming of *Lovers and Thieves,* I wanted to interview Sacha Guitry; his secretary replied I could do so only if I prepared my questions ahead of time and submitted them to the master first. Foolishly I refused; I was a dope that day,"[108] he admitted in July 1957, in an homage published at the time of the director's death.

## VADIM RIGHT ON TIME

The crusade against "quality cinema" and the desire for renewal focused, in the mid-fifties, around two young directors—Alexandre Astruc and Roger Vadim. For Truffaut, these two names were synonymous with a new, intimate cinema, in touch with life. "Vadim will deal only with the things he knows well—today's girls, quick cars, love in 1957 (and not love copied from prewar films). Alexandre Astruc, on the other hand, has a more abstract temperament and will shoot lyrical films which could be very beautiful and very commercial when the characters are in period costume, and very beautiful and noncommercial when the same characters expressing the same thing are in modern dress," he wrote on May 15, 1957 in *Arts.* His point of view, once again, was hardly shared by most of the critics. Astruc's "precious social whirl" was mocked when *Les Mauvaises Rencontres* was released in 1955, and Vadim was upbraided for his effrontery when he undressed Brigitte Bardot in *Et Dieu créa la femme* (*And God Created Woman*) a year later.

The affair even caused quite a stir when Bardot's picture was splashed all over the front page of *Arts.* FILM CRITICS ARE MISOGYNISTS. B.B. IS THE VICTIM OF A CABAL, was the weekly's headline on December 12, 1950, written by Truffaut. Judged harshly by intellectuals and virtuous censors, French cinema's new star was also the object of constant rumors and malicious gossip in the popular press. Once again, Truffaut outspokenly chose sides: "Bardot, who had the bad luck of appearing in three films in one month, has an army of gossips ganging up against her who, being deficient in mental arithmetic, count on their fingers and are amazed to discover that three times thirty million is far beyond anything they will ever earn with their pathetic freelance assignments as undernourished intellectuals."[109] With the emergence of the Bardot myth, Truffaut finally believed he saw a rift within French cinema—the advent of the liberated female body, and a new eroticism that contrasted completely with the soppiness or bawdiness of most films of the period. "I thank Vadim for directing his young wife by making her repeat everyday gestures in front of the camera, insignificant gestures like playing with her sandal, or less insignificant ones like making love in broad daylight—less insignificant but just as real! Instead of imitating other films, Vadim wanted to forget the movies and 'copy life,' true intimacy, and, with the exception of two or three slightly self-indulgent endings in some scenes, he achieved his goal perfectly."[110] Truffaut's statement certainly didn't displease Brigitte Bardot, who sent the young man a timid and grateful note on December 13: "Dear Monsieur Truffaut, I was immensely touched by the article you published in *Arts,* it encouraged me and I thank you with all my heart."[111]

Truffaut found Brigitte Bardot the equal of Marilyn Monroe and James Dean, a screen presence that rendered most other actors archaic, relegating them to the rank of "quaint mannequins." Vadim was the only one to be filming a woman of his time; other directors were twenty years behind the times. Indeed, *Sait-on jamais?* (*No Sun in Venice*), Vadim's second film, was featured as *Cahiers du cinéma*'s cover story in April 1957. Then, in July, in *Cahiers* once again, Jean-Luc Godard recognized the importance of the phenomenon: "Roger Vadim is 'with it.' No question. His fellow directors, for the most part, are still shooting 'on empty.' No question again. Vadim must be admired for the natural way in which he does what should have long ago been the ABCs of French cinema. For what could be more natural than to *breathe the air of the times?* Therefore we shouldn't be congratulating Vadim for being ahead of time, for actually it's just that while all the others are late, he's right on time."

## THE MISCHIEF MAKERS

Being "right on time"—for François Truffaut, 1957 was a turning point. In Nîmes, everything was ready for the shoot, except one small detail: The mischief makers were missing. Truffaut's first task, therefore, when he moved into the Hotel Imperator on July 30, 1957, was to choose the boys who would play in his film. To do so, he placed an announcement in *Le Midi libre:* "Film director seeks 5 boys, 11 to 14 years old, to play 'mischief makers.' " On July 31, out of about fifty boys who paraded through the newspaper's premises, five were selected. August 2 was the first day of shooting in the city's arena, an event that was closely followed by the local newspaper. "It is this morning," reported one journalist, "that the critic (become director) François Truffaint [*sic*] started shooting the scenes of his first film."[112]

The technical equipment was truly rather rudimentary: eight-meter dolly tracks, a dolly that did not need to roll silently since there would be no sound recording, a lightweight 35-mm camera, three sun reflectors, and a photoelectric cell. These were in the hands of a very small crew, consisting of Jean Malige, Robert Lachenay, Claude de Givray, and Alain Jeannel. Thrift called for this minimal crew and equipment, recalls Bernadette Lafont: "There was no money. I lived at my parents' house, and they agreed to put up Claude de Givray. François wanted to be at the Imperator. 'When Madeleine calls me, I have to be in a good hotel,' he said to justify himself. But just to be provocative, he would walk into the hotel with his bike, wearing blue shorts, the hotel being elegant and strict at the time."[113]

On August 5 and 6, the cast and crew moved to the Nîmes Tennis Club, where the progress made by Bernadette Lafont and Gérard Blain seemed very relative, even though they had taken intensive courses since the spring. The first litmus test came on the morning of August 7—with the rushes of the four preceding days. Truffaut analyzed his work with great lucidity, finding these first results uneven, pinpointing a "certain static aspect" and wary of "overly meticulous camera work."[114] On August 8, Truffaut shot the lovers' separation scene at the Montpellier train station, on the platform of the train for Palavas. Bernadette Lafont recalls it was a difficult moment: "François wanted me to cry and I was having trouble. So, to stimulate me, he said, 'You know, Brigitte Bardot (whom we adored, he and I) is not a very good actress. I don't think she could cry, but you'll be able to!' I cried and cried, but the shot wasn't kept in the editing."[115] On the next day, the big scene was shot, in the country near Saint-André-de-Valborgne, when Gérard Blain catches a boy and tells him off: "You nasty little mischief maker!"

In the middle of the filming, during a weekend of rest, Truffaut made a first assessment and decided to give Bernadette Lafont's role greater importance, and to focus more on the children, whom he very much enjoyed directing: "There's such a difference between what I obtained from them in the final days and at the beginning of the shoot that I've completely regained my self-confidence,"[116] he wrote his friend Charles Bitsch. The truth of the matter was that his relationship with Gérard Blain was strained. The actor proved to be capricious and jealous of the attention Truffaut was paying to his young wife. Blain was deliberately pushed aside, and he left the shoot before the rest of the actors and crew. After his departure, the atmosphere on the set improved, probably because Truffaut had also acquired greater self-confidence. Bernadette Lafont recalls that they nicknamed him *"le petit caporal"* (the little corporal), because in profile "he resembled Napoléon at the bridge of Arcole, very inspired, impassioned, consumed with ambition. There was something feminine about him, this way of stealing from others, with genius."[117]

When he returned to Paris on September 7, 1957, François Truffaut was relieved, though exhausted from his five weeks of intensive work in Provence. The first screening of *The Mischief Makers* was held on November 17, in the BBC screening room on avenue Hoche, and the second one, ten days later, at the U.G.C. movie theater on the Champs-Elysées. Truffaut was literally sick with anxiety: An X ray showed he had aerophagia, something he would often suffer from before and after his shoots.[118] He dreaded the cold, impersonal social ambiance of this type of screening. Consequently, he mobilized numerous friends, from *Cahiers* and *Arts,* as well as directors he felt close to—Alex Joffé, Roberto Rossellini, Pierre Kast, Norbert Carbonnaux—and also Audiberti and Cocteau, who saw the film for the first time on November 27. "The theater is very large," Truffaut complained to Lachenay on the eve of this screening, "and I hope you'll be able to come and bring whomever you want."[119] Truffaut was well aware that, this being his first creative endeavor, some people were waiting to get back at him. Indeed, his many enemies would be ready to jump upon the smallest flaw. He was cheered by the reactions of his friends, Rivette, Rohmer, Godard, Doniol-Valcroze, and Bazin, but he would only really be quieted after the private screenings for journalists and industry professionals on December 18 and 19, at the Centre national de la cinématographie. Such producers as Pierre Braunberger, Henry Deutschmeister, and Paul Graetz responded favorably to the film. And so did Simone Signoret, regardless of her misgivings toward a critic who hadn't always been kind about her films. On November 23, Truffaut presented *The Mischief Makers* before a packed audience at the Tours Festival of Short Films, though he didn't dare enter the film in competition. The response was enthusiastic, which immediately made him regret his not daring. Truffaut had won his gamble: His enemies were silent—some had already come around—and only his friends took sides publicly.

Yet it would take a year for *The Mischief Makers* to get a commercial release. On November 6, 1958, it began a run at La Pagode movie theater. In the meantime, it was presented at the Festival du film mondial in Brussels in February 1958, where it won the prize for best director. Press coverage was extensive and often full of praise. "They were waiting to catch him out. He survived the test with honor. He doesn't know how to tell a full-blown story yet, but his humorous sketch is bursting with talent. He has a feeling for imagery, he knows how to direct actors, and above all he has a 'tone' that is both poetic and cruel," reported *France-Soir.*[120] His writer friends at the weeklies orchestrated unanimous approval for his first venture. Claude Mauriac in *Le Figaro littéraire,* Jacques Siclier at *Radio-Cinéma-Télévision,* Jacques Doniol-Valcroze in *France-Observateur,*

Jacques Audiberti in *Arts,* and Paul-Louis Thirard in *Les Lettres françaises*
were all complimentary, as well as Claude Beylie at *Cahiers du cinéma.*

Jean Delannoy introduced the only jarring note in this chorus of praise.
True, he had been targeted directly, since in one scene in the film, the boys
have fun ripping up a poster for *Chiens perdus sans collier.* In February
1958, *France-Soir* reported Delannoy's comments: "The story of *The Mischief Makers* acquires special pungency when you realize that François
Truffaut only got to direct his first film thanks to the backing of the prominent distributor of whom he has recently become the son-in-law, and who
handled my last two films, *Notre-Dame de Paris* and *Chiens perdus sans collier,* among other things. So, I have the satisfaction of having contributed, to
some extent, to the debut of my fiercest opponent."[121] Ambitious critic marries daughter of wealthy distributor to further his career—this rumor would
fuel the dark side of the François Truffaut legend for a long time to come.

## MADELEINE

Over the last several months, François Truffaut and Madeleine Morgenstern had gotten to know each other well. They saw each other with increasing frequency, shared a common passion for books, and often went to the
movies together. He liked to watch her drive when they were in a car; it
made him think of the women in Hawks or Hitchcock films. The summer
had been devoted to the filming of *The Mischief Makers,* but as soon as it
was over, there was talk of a fall marriage. An only daughter, Madeleine
lived on rue de la Tour, in the prosperous sixteenth arrondissement, with an
intractable mother and a father she adored, and with whom she worked.
Marriage with an "antisocial, heretical young journalist"[122] may not have
been an act of rebellion against her parents, but it was certainly very daring
for the period. A young woman whose upbringing was strict but not religious, Madeleine was captivated by François, by the intense look in his eyes,
and by his shyness, "which he used like a screen so he could spend time only
on the things he liked, and with the people he liked."[123] He also had a loner
quality that made him different from all the young people from good families whom she had met up until then. With François, she had the feeling of
discovering another world, another way of living: "He never said anything
inconsequential or neutral,"[124] she commented. Her tastes in movies
evolved under his influence: "I liked what François liked; even if I was
grudging about certain films, I could understand his choices."[125] For Truffaut, Madeleine embodied intelligence and humor, and a certain seriousness, as well as the strangeness of another culture, which he found very

appealing. She had great gentleness, and a little something about her reminded him of Leslie Caron. Their love was based on an immediate bond, which, nonetheless, concealed a few misunderstandings. They each fulfilled a deep desire in the other: He could settle down and find stability after his long years of adventure; she could finally escape the family stronghold and taste adventure, after years of being extremely sensible.

The wedding took place on October 29, 1957, at the town hall of the sixteenth arrondissement. For family reasons, the two youths wanted a discreet ceremony, as simple as possible. Madeleine was very worried about her father's health, for he was gravely ill. As for François, his relationship with his parents was so strained that he put off introducing his future wife to them until the very last moment. This is clear from a somewhat curt letter he wrote to his mother in the summer of 1957, informing her of the practical details of his wedding: "It is best that you meet Madeleine after the vacation, and her parents only on the day of the wedding so as to simplify interfamily relationships as much as possible. Madeleine and I are going about things so that this marriage won't be a nuisance for anyone. For the time being, let's not talk about it in the family. At the last minute, so no one will be offended, we might have to invoke a bereavement on the 'opposing side' to justify the 'strict intimacy.'[126]

François made a point of explaining that he was getting married "at the town hall only, since the Morgensterns are Hungarian Jews." This sentence could be regarded as simply informative, but he wrote it as a slap at the Monferrands, whose values he was well aware of—straitlaced, basically nationalistic, and attached to a traditional, Catholic France. Truffaut had deliberately done nothing to bring the two families closer. Indeed, Madeleine Morgenstern confirms that "introducing me to the Bazins was more important to François than my meeting his parents";[127] it was as though the future bridegroom was embarrassed, or too aware that any emotional bond between two families of such disparate cultures was impossible. "His parents weren't unfriendly—they were rather enlightened and pleasant, not brutal at all—but there was such hatred and rebellion in François," Madeleine adds.

Madeleine's father, Ignace Morgenstern, born in 1900, had fled Hungary in 1921, in the aftermath of the counterrevolutionary regime's bloody suppression of the Béla Kun movement. On his arrival in Paris after a stay in Germany, he got a job as an unskilled worker at Renault; then he worked as a runner in the accounting department at Paramount-France. He had very good organizational skills, and learned to speak French, though he never lost his Hungarian accent. Gradually, he moved up through the ranks and became head of production for Adolphe Osso when Osso, founder and president of Paramount-France, created his own company, Les Films Osso.

In 1927, Ignace Morgenstern married his cousin Elizabeth, who had come from Hungary to join him in Paris. In July 1931, Madeleine was born. When Osso Films went bankrupt in 1934, Morgenstern found himself without a job. During the period of the Front populaire, he moved to Lille with Elizabeth and Madeleine and set up the local branch of SEDIF, a film distribution company, whose parent company was owned by the producer Joseph Lucachevitch. In 1939, Morgenstern was drafted. The following year, Elizabeth Morgenstern and her daughter joined the exodus and left Lille, squeezing into a taxi headed for Lyon with six other people. Morgenstern had rented a farm in the village of Frontenas, in the Beaujolais area, where he and his family hid during the Occupation, arduously working the land for a living. Here, Madeleine found solace in reading the classics. At the time of the Liberation, Morgenstern reopened the SEDIF. Then, in 1948, he created his own distribution company, Cocinor, buying up SEDIF from Lucachevitch, who had moved to the United States during the war.

In the 1950s, Ignace Morgenstern became one of the major distributors in Paris. "He was a man who didn't regard making money as contemptible," Madeleine says, "but he was not a big-time gambler. He liked playing chess, and for him, doing business was like winning at chess. It so happened that he won more often than he lost."[128] Morgenstern, who distributed mostly popular films, starring actors like Fernandel or Jean Gabin and directed by such commercially successful directors as Henri Verneuil, was extremely respected at the time among French film-industry professionals. He was a man of his word, discreet, shrewd, intelligent, generous.

When he met François Truffaut, Ignace Morgenstern made no comment to his daughter about this young man who bit his nails and had a timid look in his dark eyes. Morgenstern didn't read *Arts,* which he regarded as too right-wing; he preferred *L'Humanité* and *Les Lettres françaises,* out of ideological conviction, and *Le Figaro,* to keep track of the reviews of the films he distributed. An established and respected distributor working within the popular cinema, he found nothing to draw him close to the young "hussar," this "thug of journalism," whom Madeleine was seeing. But out of respect and love for his daughter he accepted him.

Elizabeth Morgenstern, on the other hand, never hid the fact that she would have preferred her daughter to marry a Jewish doctor or lawyer, or, in any case, someone Jewish. Madeleine describes her mother as an engaging person who nevertheless had an explosive temper. "My only act of independence was to marry François. My mother was possessive, while my father respected the other person's freedom."[129] Clearly, this marriage seemed incongruous to Elizabeth Morgenstern, but she wanted her daughter's happiness above all. She could only look on with disquiet, however, as the wedding ceremony took place.

Truffaut had asked André Bazin to be his witness, and he was also glad of Rossellini's friendly presence at the town hall that day. Claude de Givray was the only member of the *Cahiers du cinéma* group to be present. Madeleine wore a white wedding dress—the only traditional note in the quick, simple, somewhat tense civil ceremony. After the wedding ceremony, the young couple went to see Ignace Morgenstern, who had been advised by his physicians not to leave his room. Then Madeleine and François joined their guests at the Pavillon Dauphine near the Bois de Boulogne for their wedding luncheon.

Fortunately, a few congratulatory messages from the friends at *Cahiers* brought a bit of merriment and humor to this melancholic celebration. For instance, Jean-Luc Godard's: "One must be against one's wife. Congratulations." Or Doniol-Valcroze's: "After Schérer married in Paramé, we have Truffaut becoming Mado's hero. *Cahiers* are becoming bourgeois, and it's all to the good, we'll eat better. Bravo."[130] That night, the couple took the train to Monte Carlo for their honeymoon. Boredom and bad weather made it easy for them to shorten their stay in the principality and leave for Nice, where there was at least a greater choice of films playing at the movie theaters!

Star critic, budding director, happy husband—at twenty-five, François Truffaut had settled down; his bohemian existence was over. The couple moved into the apartment that Ignace Morgenstern had bought for his daughter, on rue Saint-Ferdinand in the seventeenth arrondissement, five minutes away from the Place de l'Etoile. The building was unexceptional, modern and impersonal, but the three-room apartment was comfortable, well laid out, and tastefully furnished. Thanks to the large living room and its many bookshelves, Truffaut finally had space for all the books and most of the files he had accumulated since adolescence, for they had followed him from room to room, hotel to hotel, at the mercy of his moods, his finances, and his restless love affairs.

## PUTTING AN END TO CRITICISM

After *The Mischief Makers*, François Truffaut regarded himself as a full-fledged director—young, inexperienced, but a director nonetheless. He wanted to give up movie criticism, since from the outset, he considered the two professions incompatible. "Criticizing a film comes down to criticizing a man, and this I no longer want to do."[131] Refusing to play the role of the "wolf in the sheep barn" and no longer wishing to tell a lazy or unworthy fellow director a few plain truths, Truffaut restricted himself, from that time on, to supporting a few director friends by praising them in writing, especially if they were in need. He let others take over his columns. This posed no problem at *Cahiers du cinéma,* where a new editorial staff formed around Eric Rohmer; it included Jean Douchet, Luc Moullet, André Labarthe, Jacques Siclier, Claude Beylie, and Michel Delahaye. But the situation was more complicated at *Arts,* where Truffaut was nearly as much of a star as Jacques Laurent. Yet, since 1956, Truffaut had brought in his friends—first Rohmer, followed by Rivette and Siclier; then Charles Bitsch, Claude de Givray, Jean-Luc Godard, and Jean Douchet the following year. The Young Turks had developed an efficient infiltration strategy. In 1958, then, Truffaut's name appeared more and more infrequently; he seems to have planned his withdrawal from criticism just as easily as he had previously—thanks to the same friends—stormed onto the movie page of the same cultural weekly.

However, sensing the danger of losing a star journalist, André Parinaud, the editor in chief of *Arts,* became more and more insistent. He was even prepared to give Truffaut a raise rather than see him resign from the movie page. On September 7, 1957, Parinaud tried to clarify matters, requesting in passing that Truffaut attend the Tuesday-afternoon editorial meetings: "I'd like to know whether you're serious about your work. Over the last three years you've achieved a certain success in the profession and I think we've played a part in getting your talent recognized. But it so happens that for the last few weeks your sloppiness has become a serious matter. The movie page has lost its punch. Your little friends, like Eric Rohmer, whatever their competence, lack experience, and as far as that's concerned I think it might be good if Monsieur Eric Rohmer were to school himself elsewhere. I request that you tell him so. . . ."[132]

Simultaneously courted and threatened, Truffaut had to make up his mind. So he chose confrontation through escalation of pressure. The tactic was clear: Either the editorial board would reject his demands and the two parties would break off for good or it would accept that he write for the weekly whenever he wanted and that he could freely assign to his friends the regular articles that he now refused to write. Things came to a head on September 18, 1957, when *Arts* published on its front page his interview with Jean Renoir, who was in Paris for rehearsals of *Le Grand Couteau,* adapted from the Robert Aldrich film *The Big Knife,* which was itself based on a Clifford Odets play. The interview was heavily cut and included an unflattering photo of the director; he looked downcast, his features were drawn, he was gesturing grotesquely with both his hands, and a balloon had him saying, "I don't believe in well-structured theater." Furious, Truffaut complained to Parinaud and reissued his demands for real control of the movie page, including the right to have anyone he chose write for it. At the end of his letter, Truffaut called Parinaud a liar, since he had promised to publish the interview in its entirety. The editor in chief reacted sharply to this demand and justified his cuts on technical grounds: "It saddens me to see how far you're driven by the pretensions of your 'inflated ego,' but your tough-guy airs are too amusing for me to be angered. One of these days, with your bullying attitude I'm sure someone will get a big thrill bringing you back to earth with a couple of slaps. As for me, I have too much work."[133]

At that point, Truffaut tried a more subdued approach, aware that he wouldn't obtain anything through anger: "I don't have an inflated ego, but I feel at this point that merit—yes, merit—entitles me to the complete supervisory capacity that Aurel exercised through terror and intimidation when I first started here. I received enough slaps between the age of ten and fifteen so that new ones wouldn't change my behavior in any way. And that's just it, I knock about in circles (journalism and cinema) where no one knows where to give slaps anymore: they prefer to say yes, and betray me as soon as my back is turned." And he concluded with the following admission: "All I ask for is one thing, control on cinema here."[134] He demanded a letter signed by his editor in chief defining his role. It seems that in this power struggle with Parinaud, Truffaut failed to get his way, though he did get much better payment for his freelance work.

Between the autumn of 1957, when he returned to Paris after shooting *The Mischief Makers* and the following spring, Truffaut underwent a severe crisis in confidence; getting to direct a first feature turned out to be far more difficult than he had realized. Several of his projects—with Pierre Braunberger, for instance—had come to nothing, one after the other. "I have to continue writing articles to make a living, particularly since *Arts* now pays me quite well. But how difficult it is to try to get a bit more film exposed this year!"[135] he wrote on May 6, 1958. This disillusioned, indeed pessimistic, state of mind can be seen in his articles at the beginning of 1958. At a time when renewal and youth could be sensed in a large portion of the press— the first waves of the cinema to come—Truffaut, in *Arts*, systematically went against critical fashion. On January 15 he wrote, "It's too early to clean out the dead wood. The ten greatest directors in the world are over 50." For the first time, Truffaut seemed outstripped by the movement he himself had launched—the coming New Wave—and, indeed, some of his readers reproached him for it.

Though his last articles of spring 1958 constitute an interesting, if rather pessimistic, testament, they are hardly representative of Truffaut's journalism, the medium by which he first achieved fame. It is hard to grasp just how much hatred and admiration he summoned in the mid-fifties. Truffaut wrote that Orson Welles was famous before he had shot a single foot of film; this could also be said about Truffaut. One need only note how often he was alluded to in films at the time. In Christian-Jaque's *Nathalie (The Foxiest*

*Girl in Paris*), the screenwriter Jean Ferry gave the name Truffaut to a crooked cop; in Edouard Molinaro's documentary on the Banque de France, a man picks up the telephone and says, "Get me Truffaut in the risk department"; and in Léo Joannon's *Le Désert de Pigalle,* one can see a shady character in a disreputable café reading a front-page article in *Arts* signed François Truffaut.

For an entire generation, Truffaut played the part of a catalyst for debate and an authority on taste. He became the spokesman for a culture that had been scorned up to then, the culture of film devotees. Witness this emblematic letter, among so many, written to Truffaut on December 12, 1956 by the very young future editor Christian Bourgois:

I know you only as a byline, but it is affixed to such wonderful rages and such just enthusiasms, week after week for months, that you're a friend: I beg you, continue to express all our disgust at the lazy and dull way of writing film criticism or making films. . . . It seems you have bad press and a bad reputation in film circles, but it takes all the impudence and intellectual dishonesty of our so-called critics and directors not to see in your "executions" and your fits of rage an immense love of cinema. . . . Please keep in mind, dear François Truffaut, that there are many of us, all over Paris and in all the cellars of the neighborhood movie houses, that hate this cinema and film criticism, and we will never think you're violent enough in defending our pale and deeply moving Marilyn. We, too, are in love with cinema, we passionate audience members.[136]

# 4.
# NEW WAVE:
# 1958–1962

After *The Mischief Makers,* François Truffaut's goal was to attempt a first feature film. During the spring of 1958, his plans were still rather vague, but as an apprentice director, he was prepared to seize any opportunity.

Paul Graetz, one of the most important postwar French producers, suggested he write and direct a film on childhood in collaboration with Jean Aurenche. There was talk of casting Yves Montand in the lead as the head of a school. The offer appealed to Truffaut, even though he realized he would be forming an unnatural alliance with the advocates of the kind of cinema he had violently fought against. In January 1958, he regularly lunched and dined with Graetz at the Relais-Augustins to discuss the project, and he had a long meeting with Yves Montand on the afternoon of January 14. But since Truffaut and Aurenche had no real desire to work together, the project lagged and was finally abandoned.

## DAYS OF HEAT

On January 24, Truffaut accepted the job of first assistant director on a Belgian feature, *Quelqu'un frappe à la porte.* The shoot was scheduled for March and April of 1958, in Brussels; but in the end, Truffaut would not show up. For in the meantime, he had been invited to a party at the producer Pierre Braunberger's house, on January 25, and had been lured by what he had once called, not without malice, "*l'ami Pierrot's* belly dances."[1] Pierre Braunberger had already talked to him a month before about a novel by Jacques Cousseau, *Temps chaud* (Days of Heat), which depicted the summer romances of several young women in a light and lively tone. Braunberger brought up the book again and convinced Truffaut it would make a good first feature film. On March 14, 1958, the two men signed a contract stipulating that Truffaut was to collaborate on the screenplay, direct and edit the film, and receive 6 percent on box-office receipts, with an advance of 1 million francs—200,000 francs on signing the contract and 800,000 on the first day of shooting.

Truffaut was fully aware of his compromise in accepting an assigned project that Braunberger saw as resembling the films of Vadim, which were all the rage at the time. "As you know," he confided to his friend Charles Bitsch, "I'll be shooting *Temps chaud* in ten weeks in the Midi. . . . For Pierrot it will be a super *And God Created Woman in Black and White*, for me a new *Diary of a Chambermaid*, delirious and baroque. Braunberger thinks it will be pretty to look at and tragic. I hope it will be unnerving and farcical. In short, we understand each other very well, as always. . . ."[2] He worked diligently on the adaptation of the novel and presented Braunberger with a screenplay as early as mid-February. He planned to cast Bernadette Lafont in the lead, rehire the technical crew of *The Mischief Makers,* and cast Jean-Claude Brialy instead of Gérard Blain. By the middle of February, everything was ready for the shoot, but at the last moment, Braunberger decided to wait until the first days of summer: "It's a slightly erotic story, with the heat bringing out unusual behavior in people,"[3] he wrote to Truffaut. To keep Truffaut busy, he suggested he spend a few days directing a short film on the subject of his choice. Truffaut decided to take advantage of the floods just south of Paris to quickly shoot a whimsical story about a young couple in a car trying to drive through blocked roads and flooded fields. Godard helped him with the editing and reworked much of the dialogue. *Histoire d'eau,* shot in two days in the outskirts of Montereau, is an eighteen-minute film dedicated to Mack Sennett, in which Jean-Claude Brialy, dubbed by Godard, displays his comic gifts, while Caroline Dim talks about the rain and the bad weather, literature and love.

Knowing that he would be filming *Temps chaud* in June, Truffaut felt unworried and devoted most of the spring to critical writing and settling into domestic life. He presented *The Mischief Makers* at various festivals,[4] and once again he haunted the offices of *Cahiers du cinéma* and *Arts.* He also took driving lessons so he could get his license. He saw a great many films, one or two a day, spent quite a bit of time with Madeleine, and several evenings at André Bazin's home in Nogent-sur-Marne, where he helped celebrate Bazin's fortieth birthday on April 18, 1958. This quiet waiting period came to a sudden end in the last days of April, when Bernadette Lafont suffered a serious injury. The shooting of *Temps chaud,* scheduled to start on June 15, was once again postponed. Therefore, Truffaut decided to turn to a new project.

## ANTOINE'S TRUANCY

In May 1958, Truffaut went to the Cannes Film Festival as a critic for the last time. In retaliation for his virulent attacks of the previous year, the festival directors had refused to accredit him as a journalist. Truffaut counterattacked by signing his front-page byline in *Arts* as "François Truffaut, the only French critic not invited to the Cannes Festival."[5] One week later, he proclaimed, "Unless radical changes are made, the next festival is doomed."[6] Yet the festival was instrumental in Truffaut's directing his first feature.

That year, Ignace Morgenstern made one of the best deals in his career as a distributor. On April 21, 1958, he attended a preview screening in Paris of the Soviet entry at Cannes, Mikhail Kalatozov's *The Cranes Are Flying.* With its fast pace and lyricism, its young, romantic heroes and bold cinematography, the film perfectly expressed the political thaw of the Khrushchev period. Morgenstern saw the film again in Paris on the morning of May 3, this time with his son-in-law, François Truffaut, who immediately convinced him to acquire the rights. A deal was made "for next to nothing"[7] before the festival even opened. Within weeks, Kalatozov's film began showing a profit, as it was awarded the prestigious Palme d'or by the festival jury and became a big commercial success when it was released in June. Given this success, Morgenstern had fewer misgivings about coproducing his son-in-law's first feature. "My father trusted him," Madeleine recalls, "but François had no money; he had only his screenplay, which in the beginning wasn't substantial. My father respected François and found him intelligent, but he hadn't particularly liked *The Mischief Makers.* So, of course, he produced *The 400 Blows* to help our marriage, to give his daughter's husband the opportunity to prove he could make films."[8] For Ignace Morgenstern the financial risk was slight; the estimated budget for *The 400 Blows* was around 40 million old francs, a sum (the equivalent of about 2 million present-day francs) markedly below the cost of the standard French film of the period. On June 22, 1958, Truffaut could therefore calmly note in his diary: "Everything is ready to go."[9]

Optimistic once again, he now had to write a screenplay. He decided to rework "La Fugue d'Antoine [Antoine's Flight]," originally conceived as one episode in a film on childhood. It depicted a specific incident from his own adolescence when he was still a student at the school on rue Milton. He had cut class because he had forgotten to do the assignment he had been given as a punishment. His excuse ("My mother died") had not gone unnoticed, and the following day, his father had come for him in the middle of class and given him a good smack in the face. In the beginning of June, Truffaut fleshed out this incident with childhood memories—his truancies with Lachenay, their trips to the movies, the rotor at the fair grounds, scenes at home with his parents, and the scene on Place Clichy when the adolescent sees his mother in her lover's arms. These were the first pages, a few ideas strung together, that he showed his father-in-law in order to convince him to finance the film.

To complete the screenplay, Truffaut again drew material from his own adolescence, including his stay at the Villejuif Observation Center for Minors in December 1948. He put Lachenay to work: "Note down your ideas and memories, for La Fugue d'Antoine. Take a look at our letters from Villejuif, etc."[10] Claude de Givray points out how much the character of Antoine owes to Lachenay: "Antoine isn't Truffaut; he's a combination of the two. He stole a bit from his friend Lachenay's youth. Lachenay was more of the driving force at the time. Truffaut was a bit shy; he was pulled along by Lachenay."[11] Though the narrative was autobiographical down to the last detail, Truffaut wanted to present it as a fiction. He therefore compressed five years of his life into a relatively brief period, which he transposed from the Occupation and the immediate postwar years to the present-day fifties. Finally, he avoided some obvious autobiographical giveaways. For example, Truffaut initially gave his runaway adolescent the name of Antoine Loinod, an anagram and pseudonym of Doniol (Valcroze). Robert Lachenay became René Bigey, in memory of his grandmother. And Truffaut changed his father's passion from mountaineering to amateur car racing.

To better define his characters and master his narrative, he contacted Marcel Moussy, a novelist and screenwriter, and the author of a very popular television series, Si c'était vous. "I know you work quickly and structure things with a rigor that I completely lack. On the other hand, I'm thoroughly familiar with this world of twelve-year-old kids that I want to capture on film,"[12] Truffaut wrote Moussy. The two started working together on July 9, 1958, and met about ten times in one month. Moussy worked quickly and was very helpful in constructing the narrative. By the end of the summer of 1958, the screenplay was ninety-four pages long and had acquired its definitive title: Les Quatre Cents Coups (The 400 Blows; in French, this is a double entendre, because faire les quatre cents coups means "to be up to no good").

Now that the film's financing was assured and the screenplay completed, Truffaut devoted his attention to practical matters. He decided to film The

*400 Blows* in black-and-white Cinemascope and to recruit one of the best cinematographers, Henri Decaë, who had worked with Jean-Pierre Melville (*Bob le flambeur* had very much impressed Truffaut), Louis Malle, and Claude Chabrol. With his sharply contrasted black and white, his liking for natural lighting, and his great working speed, Decaë was an ideal collaborator for Truffaut, who probably needed to feel confident on the technical level. But hiring Decaë was the greatest investment of the production—he received the highest salary, 1.5 million old francs, while Moussy and Truffaut were paid 1 million francs each, and all the actors' fees together came to about 3 million.

Permission still had to be obtained from the Centre national de la cinématographie (CNC). In those days, you couldn't just become a director. There were requirements: three professional training courses, three jobs as second assistant director, and three jobs as first assistant director. As the director of two short films, the first of which had never been shown commercially, Truffaut couldn't meet these criteria, and was rather worried when he went before the union committee assembled at the CNC in early September 1958. This was why he chose a first assistant who was more experienced than he, Philippe de Broca. At twenty-six, Truffaut was given a special dispensation entitling him to shoot his first feature.

Truffaut had learned from his experience with *The Mischief Makers* that it was not easy to direct children, but the success of *The 400 Blows* would essentially rest on two adolescents. Given the largely autobiographical screenplay, Truffaut feared the danger of a "whiny, self-indulgent confession,"[13] since his aim was the opposite, to transmit the universal aspect of childhood. He gathered a vast amount of material on adolescent psychology, and especially on difficult, unhappy, delinquent childhoods. During the summer of 1958, he consulted two juvenile-court judges, Mademoiselle Lamotte and Monsieur Chazal, several times. He also worked with Joseph Savigny, the director of the division of supervised education at the Ministry of National Education, and read a great deal, for example *Graine de crapule, Les Vagabonds,* and Fernand Deligny's book *Adrien Lhomme,* which influenced some of the sequences in the film. Bazin put him in touch with Deligny, whom he had met after the war at Travail et Culture and who was carrying out experiments that Truffaut wanted to know more about. Settled in the heart of the countryside with about ten autistic children "snatched from the gates of psychiatric institutions,"[14] Deligny was trying to make them "live differently." Truffaut sent him his screenplay in early August 1958, asking his advice. Deligny had some harsh criticism for the scene that involved the conversation with the psychologist, which he called "embarrassing and artificial";[15] Truffaut cut the scene during the filming and replaced it with the young Antoine's improvised confession before the camera. In September, Truffaut spent two days at Petit-Bois with Deligny. In a letter written to Deligny on October 29, 1958, a few days before shooting began, Truffaut mentioned these meetings, which were decisive "in preventing me from rushing into all the possible errors."[16]

The last phase of preproduction for *The 400 Blows* consisted in choosing the actors. Truffaut cast Guy Decomble—whom he had seen in many supporting roles, in particular Tati's *Jour de fête*—in the part of the French teacher nicknamed "Petite Feuille" (Small Leaf). After seeing the comedian Pierre Repp and Henri Virlojeux in the same variety-show program, Truffaut chose them, respectively, for the parts of the English teacher and the menacing night watchman who presides over Antoine's arrest after the typewriter theft. Georges Flamant, who had acted in Renoir's *La Chienne* and in Gance's *La Vénus aveugle,* portrays Monsieur Bigey, René's father, a compulsive gambler and horse lover. With his humorist's fantasy and his sauciness, typical of a Parisian joker and grumbler, Albert Rémy, an actor much in demand in the forties and fifties, was perfect for the part of Antoine's stepfather. Antoine's mother would be played by Claire Maurier, a pretty thirty-five-year-old brunette (her hair would be dyed blond for the part), whose prior experience had been mostly onstage, not on the screen.

To cast the two adolescents, Truffaut published an announcement in *France-Soir* and auditioned several hundred children in September and October 1958. Jean Domarchi, a critic at *Cahiers du cinéma,* had earlier recommended the son of an assistant scriptwriter, Pierre Léaud, and the actress Jacqueline Pierreux. Truffaut was immediately captivated by the fourteen-year-old adolescent, who had already appeared the previous year with Jean Marais in Georges Lampin's *La Tour prends garde!* He recognized traits they both shared, "for example a certain suffering with regard to the family. . . . With, however, this fundamental difference: though we were both rebels, we hadn't expressed our rebellion in the same way. I preferred to cover up and lie. Jean-Pierre, on the contrary, seeks to hurt, shock and wants it to be known. . . . Why? Because he's unruly, while I was sly. Because his excitability requires that things happen to him, and when they don't occur quickly enough, he provokes them."[17]

Jean-Pierre Léaud, then in the eighth grade at Verrières, a private school in Pontigny, was far from an ideal student. "I regret to inform you that Jean-Pierre is more and more 'unmanageable,' " the director of the school wrote to Truffaut. "Indifference, arrogance, permanent defiance, lack of discipline in all its forms. He has twice been caught leafing through pornographic pictures in the dorm. He is developing more and more into an emotionally disturbed case."[18] But this unstable boy, who often ran away with the older students on their nights out, could also be brilliant, generous, and affection-ate. Extremely cultured for his age, he was already very good at writing, and he even claimed to Truffaut that he had written a "verse tragedy," *Torquatus*.

Jean-Pierre Léaud's screen tests were instantly conclusive, at every stage, his personality and naturalness commanded admiration. This just confirmed Truffaut's intuition and soon became obvious to the rest of the crew. The fig-ure of Antoine was born. "I think in the beginning," the director wrote, "there was a lot of myself in the character of Antoine. But as soon as Jean-Pierre Léaud arrived, his personality, which was very strong, often led me to make changes in the screenplay. So I consider that Antoine is an imaginary character who derives a bit from both of us."[19] In the part of René, Truffaut cast Patrick Auffay, who was slightly older than Jean-Pierre Léaud, taller, with a more bourgeois appearance, less the young Paris hoodlum than the boy from a good family. A few improvisations quickly persuaded Truffaut that he had finally found his duo.

During the night of November 10–11, 1958, André Bazin died of leukemia. That very morning, Truffaut, tense and anxious, had started shooting *The 400 Blows*. In the evening, he went to Nogent-sur-Marne, where the Bazins had been living for three years. He stayed with Janine by the bedside of the man he considered his adoptive father, mentor, and friend. An atmosphere of bereavement would permeate the shoot, most probably heightening the film's bleakness. While a fictional character was being born, the "real" father met death.

Truffaut explained in writing on several occasions what he owed Bazin. Once, he described him as "a sort of saint in a velvet cap living in complete purity in a world that became pure from contact with him."[20] But he proba-bly never said it with as much emotion as in the special issue of *Cahiers du cinéma* published immediately after the critic's death: "Bazin helped me make the leap from film buff to critic, to director. I blushed with pride when, in the midst of a discussion, he agreed with me, but I felt even greater pleasure in being contradicted by him. He was the Just Man by whom one likes to be judged and, for me, a father whose very reprimands were sweet, like the marks of an affectionate interest I had been deprived of in child-hood."[21]

As soon he could, Truffaut left the set of *The 400 Blows* to go to Nogent-sur-Marne and be among Bazin's close relatives and friends. On November 16, 1958, the day of the funeral, he wore a black suit while directing his actors, and he would dedicate his film "to the memory of André Bazin." The most important postwar critic passed away as the New Wave was being born, just as Truffaut was filming the first scenes of *The 400 Blows*. The coincidence was not just symbolic: Becoming a director, for Truffaut, was a way of settling his score with a clandestine childhood and a reckless adolescence. *The 400 Blows* bears the marks of those heartbreaking times and of his painful liberation.

François Truffaut chain-smoked and was racked with anxiety as he started shooting *The 400 Blows*.[22] The first week's shoot took place in a small apartment on rue Marcadet, on the hill of Montmartre, in a three-room apartment that was so tiny it couldn't accommodate the twenty-odd members of the cast and crew. The building was so run-down that sudden voltage changes caused power cuts, interrupting the filming several times. Tense, ill at ease, and feeling judged by his crew, Truffaut limited his appearances on the set to a minimum. As for Albert Rémy, he was almost paralyzed by back pains. In the end, Jean-Pierre Léaud was the most relaxed of the lot, even if he nearly choked on the thick smoke that filled the room during the scene when the Balzac photograph in the little niche above Antoine's bed went up in flames. Truffaut, worried sick about bungling things, paced up and down the set. Hence it was a great relief for the whole crew when, on November 19, they finally went outside on Place Clichy to shoot the scene of the kiss between the mother and her lover—a fleeting figure played by the critic Jean Douchet.

The second part of the shoot, from November 20 to 25, was mainly devoted to the sequences of the two adolescents at René's house. For this, Truffaut returned to the heart of his childhood neighborhood, rue Fontaine, where Claude Vermorel, a film critic close to Bazin and Doniol-Valcroze, had loaned him a large apartment. It is one of the key moments in the film, and the complicitous bond among Jean-Pierre Léaud, Patrick Auffay, and Truffaut worked wonders. Thereafter, the filming was much more broken up, with changes of location every day. Friends stopped by, like Audiberti, Jacques Laurent, and Doniol-Valcroze, and some even performed bit parts, like Jacques Demy and Charles Bitsch, disguised as policemen in the scene at the police station on rue Jouffroy. A very young film enthusiast and avid reader of *Arts* by the name of Bertrand Tavernier asked his teacher for permission to watch the filming for a day. A few days later, to save money, Truffaut's cast and crew moved into the offices of SEDIF, the company directed by Ignace Morgenstern, on rue Hamelin to film the sequence where Jean-Pierre Léaud returns the stolen typewriter and is caught by a night watchman. This is the first time in the film when Antoine gets called by his last name, which Truffaut had suddenly changed the previous evening; Antoine Loinod became Antoine Doinel, a discreet homage to Jean Renoir, who had a close collaborator named Ginette Doynel.

During the sequences in a printing shop, which lasted two days, Jean-Pierre Léaud injured his hand rather seriously and the filming fell slightly behind. On the night of December 10, while the crew was shooting the

Doinel family coming out of the Gaumont-Palace—where they had just seen *Paris nous appartient* (*Paris Belongs to Us*) (Truffaut's wink at his friend Rivette, the director of that film)—and returning home in their Dauphine (specially rented for the occasion), the police interrupted the filming, accusing them of disturbing the peace. On Christmas Eve, the filming was interrupted once again, this time by a police van summoned by the owner of the café Le Rendez-vous du Bâtiment; during the sequence with the gym teacher, which required several takes, Jean-Pierre Léaud repeatedly insulted the café owner, while two of his classmates stole cutlery and ashtrays.

Before this, from December 16 to 22, the shoot had moved to Normandy for the film's final sequences, the ones where Antoine is put under observation in a reformatory and runs away to the sea. A big sign saying (in French) OBSERVATION CENTER FOR MINORS had been hastily placed at the entrance of a property that bore no resemblance whatsoever to a prison—the Moulin d'Andé, a very beautiful estate located near Saint-Pierre-du-Vauvray where Suzanne Lipinska, Maurice Pons's friend, welcomed writers and artists. Antoine's long race toward the sea, which closes the film, was shot in the vicinity of Villers-sur-Mer, with a camera Henri Decaë had placed on a camera truck, allowing him to follow Jean-Pierre Léaud as he ran. This sequence ends with Antoine Doinel looking directly into the lens—What right have you to judge me? Léaud seems to be saying to the audience—a rather rare stylistic device at the time, inspired by a shot in Ingmar Bergman's *Monika*.

The many classroom scenes were shot right after Christmas at the Ecole technique de photographie et de cinéma, on rue de Vaugirard, as the school was closed for the vacation. After forty days of work, Truffaut gained self-confidence. The shoot had been carefully planned out. He could now face with greater equanimity the group scenes of adolescents, which were the hardest to direct.

The filming of *The 400 Blows* ended on January 5, 1959. Marie-Josèphe Yoyotte had already started the editing, so that by early February, Truffaut would be able to view a first version. Jean Constantin composed guitar music, simple but insistent, like a ritornello, which was perfectly suited to the mood of the film. Within two months, Truffaut would deliver the answer print of his first feature film.

On January 22, 1959, Madeleine Truffaut gave birth to a little girl at the American Hospital in Neuilly. They named her Laura Véronique Annie Geneviève, after her grandmothers. Although the first day of filming had been marked by mourning, the postproduction period was heralded by a birth.

Doniol-Valcroze, Rivette, Godard, and Rossellini reacted enthusiastically at the first screenings of the film, and on April 2, the press screening at the Marbeuf was equally encouraging. On the 14th, to everyone's surprise, the Cannes Festival committee, influenced no doubt by the movement that was emerging in support of young cinema, suggested to André Malraux, the Minister of Cultural Affairs, that the film be included as one of the official French entries, along with Marcel Camus's *Orfeu Negro* (*Black Orpheus*) and Alain Resnais's *Hiroshima mon amour.* "When I told Monsieur Morgenstern that I had received a phone call from Jacques Flaud, the director of the Center, informing me that the film had been selected, he didn't believe me,"[23] Marcel Berbert recalls. On April 22, in his violent attack on "quality" French directors in the columns of *Arts,* Jean-Luc Godard could exclaim, "Today, as it happens, we have won a victory. It is our films that make it to Cannes to prove that France has a pretty face, cinematographically speaking. And next year it will be the same. Repress all doubts! Fifteen courageous, sincere, lucid, beautiful new films will again block the road for the conventional productions. For though we have won a battle, the war is not yet over."

## THE FESTIVAL OF CHILD PRODIGIES

On April 27, 1959, François Truffaut and Jean-Pierre Léaud rented tuxedos in Paris, in anticipation of the official screening of *The 400 Blows* in Cannes. The director arrived on the morning of May 2 with Madeleine, Marcel Berbert, Jean-Pierre Léaud—who was accompanied by his parents—Henri Decaë, Claire Maurier, and Albert Rémy. Everyone stayed at the Carlton Hotel. "We didn't even have a poster for the film, just an enlarged photograph of Jean-Pierre Léaud, which we pasted on the wall. And I had someone come and paint the title of the film and Truffaut's name,"[24] Marcel Berbert recalls. He was far less anxious than Truffaut as he had already accomplished a remarkable feat—selling the film to the Americans before the festival, "for $50,000, which was the exact equivalent of the 47 million francs the film had cost."[25] But the real test was the official screening on the evening of Monday, May 4. In the meantime, Truffaut roamed the streets of Cannes looking for friendly faces. Jean Cocteau, the honorary president of the jury, Roberto Rossellini, and Jacques Audiberti, sent by *Arts* to cover the festival, all brought him a bit of comfort; the three men had already seen the film in Paris and were confident of its success. On the night of the screening at the Palais des Festivals, Truffaut was pale and tense. Jean-Pierre Léaud winked at him when the lights were dimmed. The director was soon reassured on hearing the applause that greeted some scenes even before the end of the screening. And when the lights went up, it was a regular triumph; everyone turned toward the young filmmaker to see his face. Coming out of the Palais, Jean-Pierre Léaud was carried by the crowd, amid an indescribable crush, to be presented to the festivalgoers and photographers who were clustered at the bottom of the steps. Introduced by Cocteau, Truffaut greeted people and shook the many anonymous hands that reached up to him; then he led Cocteau to a Provençal restaurant for supper with the actors and the crew of the film.

On the following day, there were big front-page headlines in all the major newspapers. *France-Soir,* for instance, ran the following caption above a photograph of Truffaut coming down the steps: "A 28-year-old director: François Truffaut. A 14-year-old star: Jean-Pierre Léaud. A triumph in Cannes: *The 400 Blows.*" *Paris-Match* described this triumph over four full pages in its May 9 issue: "The Festival of Child Prodigies." *Elle* magazine stressed this newfound youthfulness: "Never has the festival been so youthful, so happy to live for the glory of an art which youth loves. The twelfth film festival has the honor of announcing to you the rebirth of French cinema."[26] Truffaut's film fully embodied this youthfulness, and Léaud, who became the darling of the festival, even more so. Reports on him, his family, his difficult life, his ambitions, and his personality proliferated in the press and on the radio. His Cannes escapades—in restaurants, bars, and nightclubs—his rash statements, his arguments with his parents, fascinated journalists and paparazzi. The serious press followed suit and in a matter of days Truffaut, too, became an emblematic figure. *Le Monde* ran a flattering profile of the young director, as did *France-Observateur.* On May 7, Jean-Pierre Léaud's picture was on the cover of *L'Express. Arts* was not to be outdone, and Jacques Audiberti wrote the following about the "Truffaut epic": "All those who, with no particular animosity toward Truffaut, condemn what they call his careerism and Machiavellianism gave in, reluctantly and instantly, to the breathtaking attraction of the inevitable, the intensely passive pleasure of imagining, ahead of time and in detail, this triumph which was going to occur and which did indeed occur."[27] In *Cahiers du cinéma,* Jacques Doniol-Valcroze wrote, "*The 400 Blows* would really just be a deeply moving film and the confirmation of our friend François's talent, if it were not also a sudden missile exploding right in the enemy camp and that consecrates its defeat from the inside."[28]

Added to these glowing commentaries were congratulatory telegrams from people all over the world, including Georges Braque, Pierre Brasseur, Jacques Flaud, Abel Gance, Jean Renoir, Robert Aldrich, Nicholas Ray, Louise de Vilmorin, and Georges Simenon. The festival jury awarded *The 400 Blows* the prize for best direction. Within two days, foreign distributors scrambled for the film, negotiating with Marcel Berbert for the rights for Japan, Italy, Switzerland, and Belgium. Sales, including in the United States, had already reached 87 million old francs—twice the budget of the film. In the wake of all this attention, *The 400 Blows* opened on June 3, in two movie theaters on the Champs-Elysées. It was an enormous success— almost 450,000 people went to see the film.

The popular as well as the critical press seized on Antoine Doinel's misadventures to illustrate the social issues of child neglect and education of adolescents. PARENTS, WHAT IF THIS WERE YOU? read the headline of the magazine *Nouveaux Jours,* while its competitor, *Bonheur,* warned adults, PARENTS, BEWARE! DON'T LET YOUR KIDS BECOME HOODS! As Truffaut's film came to be used as a pretext for discussions about the abdication of parental responsibilities, its audience widened considerably. But above all, it benefited from and helped propagate the "New Wave" phenomenon. Rapid filming, contemporary characters played by a new generation of actors, shooting in exterior locations with natural lighting rather than in studios, small technical crews and small budgets—thanks to the success of *The 400 Blows* in Cannes, these new ideas gained unexpected popularity. Truffaut's film really seemed to be kicking off the movement, with French film production focusing on the "youthful film" for some time to come. Over the next three years, nearly 170 directors shot their first feature and the trademark New Wave almost became a kind of (uncontrolled) *appellation contrôlée.* Dozens of producers who had previously been wary of youthful cinema suddenly sought to produce small-budget films with unknown actors in the hope of getting a good return on their investments. This marked an important turning point in the history of French cinema.

In fact, the term *Nouvelle Vague* (New Wave) had appeared a year and a half earlier (in *L'Express,* October 3, 1957) in the headline of an article by Françoise Giroud ("Rapport sur la jeunesse [Report on Youth]"). In June 1958, Giroud published a successful book, *La Nouvelle Vague: Portrait de la jeunesse (The New Wave: A Portrait of Youth);* although it did not deal directly with cinema, it expressed a need for change within French society. It was the critic Pierre Billard who first applied the term to the new French cinema in February 1958.[29] In the spring of 1959, the expression was heard around Cannes and was used again in the autumn by the regional press when *Les Cousins* and *Les Quatre Cents Coups* were released. Soon the term was echoed in the international press. From then on, there wasn't a single festival in France or anywhere else in the world that didn't include a roundtable discussion on the New Wave. Even publishing tried to exploit a good thing and analyze the phenomenon—three books on the New Wave were hastily published after the Cannes revelation.[30]

In 1959, though the New Wave was generally well received, a counter-offensive was already being launched by its enemies, mainly the advocates of traditional French cinema and a contingent of left-wing critics. At the Cannes Festival, several recognized directors and screenwriters, such as Jean Delannoy, René Clair, Claude Autant-Lara, Henri Jeanson, Michel Audiard, and Charles Spaak—those whom François Truffaut ironically called the "Old Wave" in *Cahiers*[31] attacked the movement acrimoniously. "Amateurism," "intellectualism," "boredom," "self-promotion," "careerism," were the comments that recurred most often in the interviews and writings of the representatives of the established cinema at the time. Another anti–New Wave center was the magazine *Positif, Cahiers du cinéma*'s rival, which accused the movement of being gratuitous, mannered, Parisian, and, above all, of having right-wing tendencies, and which criticized the films for their lack of political commitment.[32]

Though Truffaut himself mistrusted the idea of being recruited for any cause, he tried to analyze the New Wave phenomenon. Through his many polemical articles in *Arts,* he had been the privileged and active witness to the crisis in traditional French cinema. He had called for a profound renewal in subject matter, actors, production, and shooting methods. Under the influence of Renoir, Rossellini, and Ophuls, he had praised the independent auteur, freed from the pressures of stardom and the dominance of screenwriters. This theoretical position provided a strong link between Truffaut the director and Truffaut the critic. For starting with *The Mischief Makers,* he had implemented a rapid and economical filming method, surrounded by loyal technicians, and had written his own stories and dialogues, opening up opportunities for new actors. But he realized that as it was being described in the large-circulation papers, the New Wave, with its many, very uneven "youth" films, represented a trendy phenomenon, a kind of sociological concept, rather than a definite break in the French cinema's habits and practices. Yet, in spite of his denials, he was definitely considered by both his friends and enemies as the leader of the new cinema, while Resnais and Godard tended to be seen as its theoreticians and experimenters. For better or worse, Truffaut's personal fate was bound up with that of the New Wave. In 1959, the worst was yet to come, and for several years, the young director would invest a good part of his energy in defending the movement.

## AN EASY TARGET

Being on the front line of the cinema revolution, François Truffaut was an easy target. Some criticized him for resembling what he had formerly fought against, for duplicating the values of a cinema that he himself had denounced. CRITICISM'S TERRIBLE MISCHIEF MAKER HAS BECOME THE ACADEMICIAN OF THE NEW WAVE[33] was the headline in the monthly *Lui,* while on May 15, 1959, another paper announced TRUFFAUT'S BETRAYAL on its cover: "I liked the tough, uncompromising Truffaut," the anonymous journalist exclaimed in this virulent opinion piece, "I liked his pecking on the skull of the pompous old-fashioned film farts, I liked when he was excommunicated by the Cannes establishment. Now I'm mad at him for going to Cannes. . . . He let himself be dressed in a tuxedo, he let himself be swallowed by the big buttering-up factory. Tossed in granulated sugar, tamed and sweetened, what will be left of the former Truffaut?"[34] Adding to this betrayal syndrome was the ironical assessment made by the old-timers whom the young director had greatly helped to shove out: Perhaps the heralded revolution had given birth to a mouse and the youth cinema would soon fall into line with the most commercial productions, they postulated. This is what Charles Spaak wrote in *France-Soir* in early June 1959: "Once launched, Truffaut is blithely preparing himself to cross over to the other side, among the 'real' directors who make films costing 250 or 500 million francs. . . ."[35]

There were also rumors in the press of Truffaut as an arriviste consumed with ambition, ready to make any compromise for the sake of success, cynical, cunning, crafty, hypocritical, and underhanded. "He married the daughter of his worst enemy in order to get financing,"[36] wrote Claude Brulé bluntly in *Elle,* during the 1959 Cannes festival. This part of the story was reiterated in a great many profiles of the "Rastignac of the New Wave": "And then Truffaut got married," noted one journalist, "as was his right, after all. But his father-in-law, alas!, is one of the shrewdest, most reliable producer-distributors of the old French cinema. I say 'alas!' for the tough, uncompromising Truffaut that used to be. We are told that *The 400 Blows* did not cost much. Yet, thirty to forty million still needed to be found and normally this is not so easy. There are many young people, let alone those no longer so young, who have aged with their talent and their ideas merely because they never inherited from a parent, like Chabrol, or married Mademoiselle Morgenstern, like Truffaut. Between the art of motion pictures and its expression there lies money, and I'm afraid that François Truffaut gave it too much thought."[37] Philippe Labro reports a story told by Jean-Pierre Melville, who was a kind of mentor for the directors of the New Wave in the very early sixties: "I see myself walking down the Champs-Elysées with François Truffaut, who says to me in an undertone, 'Beware of Louis Malle, he's an arriviste!' And I see myself walking up the opposite side of the Champs-Elysées with Louis Malle, who whispers: 'Beware of Truffaut, he's an arriviste!' They each used pejorative terms to describe the other, but this was simply because Malle and Truffaut were both ambitious directors."[38]

"Among the men I have known," confirms Jeanne Moreau, "François was the most ambitious, while remaining true to his youthfulness. This kind of ambition is always needed. What you receive from others is different from what you receive from yourself. François received nothing compared to Louis Malle, whose ambition was more raw."[39]

Though the success of *The 400 Blows* had given him self-confidence, François Truffaut was nevertheless extremely sensitive to the attacks and the rumors circulating about him. In a certain sense, he had expected to be mistreated, but he was hurt at being so often the butt of personal attacks, though he himself, in former times, had not hesitated to use such tactics. In retaliation, he decided to give himself another image through several carefully prepared interviews. This authorized self-portrait consisted of a mixture of goodwill and reticence. He stressed his difficult childhood, dominated by his failure at school; he spared his parents as much as he could, banalizing the portrayal of himself as an adolescent, and deliberately underplayed his influence as a critic. Above all, he stressed his passion for film, maintaining that it allowed him to subdue his most shameful passions and forget his difficult relationship with his parents, the juvenile delinquent centers, his violence as a critic and in his love affairs, his distress at being illegitimate, and his ideological position as a "hussar." The violence imputed to him vanished in this moving portrait of an autodidact who had been integrated into the system, raised by cinema, and made the symbol of a classical French art form, full of halftones and subtleties.

## FAMILY WOUND

Truffaut was soon faced with hostility on another front. In reading accounts of their son's youth splashed all over the press, Roland and Janine were astounded by what they considered outrageously blackened portraits of themselves. Their reaction was so violent that there was absolutely no question of their going to see *The 400 Blows*. Dishonored, they found themselves being pointed at in their own neighborhood, now recognized as that of Antoine Doinel in the film. Truffaut had failed to foresee the impact his film would have, or the fact that the press would pry into the private life of a filmmaker as it might into that of a famous actor or actress. But though it was too late to correct matters, the director did everything he could to smooth things over, even claiming that his film was not autobiographical. For their part, Roland and Janine took the offensive and encouraged the family to react, before themselves writing indignant letters to their son.

In fact, from the moment he began to shoot *The 400 Blows*, Truffaut had grown aloof. He had no doubt sensed that the autobiographical nature of

the film and the rather negative portrait of his parents were going to provoke his family. He adopted a clumsy, underhanded strategy of avoidance.
He played dead and gave no more news of himself. Roland and Janine
learned of their granddaughter's birth in the press, two months after the
fact: "We hope little Laura is in excellent health," wrote a surprised Roland
Truffaut. "Have we done anything to you? If there is a misunderstanding,
don't hesitate to tell us. . . . It must be possible to clear it up." Roland also
congratulated him about *The 400 Blows* having been selected for Cannes,
confessing "a certain pride at the thought that [he] will represent French
cinema."[40]

Their disillusionment was all the greater when they read the first articles
about the film. Roland made notes on several loose sheets of paper, which
he angrily labeled "The press gone wild: concerning *The 400 Blows*": "You
probably want to make us believe that we're responsible for the way you
are," Roland wrote. "Love of camping maybe, but you, little shit, how much
did you cost me in movies? . . . And what about IDHEC, which I offered to
pay for, little idiot, and which you turned down. . . . Bazin's death is costing
us a pretty penny." Roland's final comments draw the portrait of an arriviste,
an unscrupulous son, a sly and skillful cynic: "Why come to see us on Thursdays for four years running? Sheer hypocrisy. What self-interested sham. . . .
This film, a masterpiece before anyone has seen it. Well-orchestrated publicity. . . . The Morgenstern millions certainly come in handy. . . ."[41]

On May 20, 1959, Roland Truffaut wrote his son a brief, bitter letter:

Maybe you'll now find time to grant me an interview concerning articles that have appeared in the press, obviously very ill-informed, since
I can't imagine you allowed so many inaccuracies to be published. I
leave the day and time of this rendezvous up to you, but I think we'd
better meet at 33, rue de Navarin. In fact, you'll surely be moved to
see these squalid lodgings again where you were so "mistreated" by
ignorant parents that they later allowed you to become a glorious and
disinterested "child martyr." I'm counting on your usual frankness to
accept this little conversation. See you soon . . . ? Your father (merely
legal). P.S. I wish to make it clear that you'll be physically safe when
you come: the garbage will be emptied and I won't inform the police
stations.[42]

He included with his letter a photo of his son on the set of *The 400 Blows*,
where he is wearing a tie, has a cigar in his mouth, and exudes a conquering
air; Roland had inscribed it on the back with this caption: "Portrait of an
authentic shit." For Roland and Janine, it was probably the suddenness of
such public revelations about their son's childhood that provoked such a

strong reaction: A childhood that everyone seemed to have successfully forgotten had reemerged in a devastating manner. The Truffauts ascribed this dark portrayal of his childhood to their son's hypocrisy and careerism, and saw him as corrupted by an unhealthy, dishonest "cosmopolitan milieu."

To justify himself, Truffaut on May 27 wrote his father a long letter, a deeply moving confession in which he revealed his feelings of helplessness:

> I regret, like you, the abuses of this publicity; they questioned people who had known me, they purchased pictures from army chums, they simplified, magnified, deformed things, all of which is common in this type of journalism. However, I'm going to denounce all of this exaggeration in *Arts* and partially deny the "autobiographical" side of the film. I think it might be good for us to have an earnest discussion, but only after you've seen the film. . . . Of what happened to me, I only filmed what happens or could happen in other families. I didn't show a little saint, but an adolescent who plays hooky, forges his parents' handwriting, steals money from them, and constantly lies. . . . Despite the unpleasantness of seeing some silly things published in the papers, I haven't the slightest regret about having made this film. I knew I would hurt you, but I don't care, for since Bazin's death I have no parents. I would have shot a truly horrifying film had I depicted what my life was like on rue de Navarin between 1943 and 1948, and my relationship with Mom and you. During the whole period of rations, I didn't eat a single piece of chocolate; you used to take it to Fontainebleau. You went away on Saturdays and left practically nothing for me. I got by stealing lumps of sugar (whole rows so it wouldn't be too visible). On Sunday nights, I started to live in falsehood and fear. A child who finds he is the only one in school not to have a "snack" can't help wondering. There were also moments of exceptional tension between Mom and me, as when I was on the ground and she kicked me, on a morning when I had stood on line for two hours but had only brought back a box of biscuits. I swear this is true. I became cowardly and underhanded, I "clammed up" and your friends admired my good behavior at the table: I hated Mother in silence and liked you but felt contempt. During medical checkups, what a tragedy when I had to take off my shoes and reveal the state of my socks. . . . There was also a ridiculous little tragedy that influenced my whole life—the test at the Lycée Rollin, a second chance to get into sixth grade. At that time I was still a good student and my flunking had been accidental. I had every chance of doing well on the October test. I was on vacation in Juvisy, and I wrote asking you to come get me on the Sunday before the exam. You didn't come and I couldn't take

the test. So then you registered me at the local elementary school where I started to get into trouble. You told me you never got my letter. An extraordinary coincidence: you had spent that weekend in Fontainebleau—surprise, surprise—as usual. How dreary to give up a weekend in the forest to go to Juvisy and pick up the kid. . . . You sign your letter: 'Your father (merely legal)' and I can imagine your bitterness. It so happens that this revelation was a great shock to me and I think I told you it occurred while I was rummaging in a cupboard and found the 1932 diary and then the family record book. Did I also tell you that the family ambiance was such that I was almost sure of a secret concerning my birth; Mom hated me so much that, for a year, I thought she wasn't my real mother. I could go on for pages and pages. No, I wasn't a "mistreated child," but simply one who wasn't "treated" at all, unloved and feeling completely "unwelcome" from the time you took me in to my emancipation. I'm aware of all the facts involved: I had become a lying, thieving, underhanded, secretive and "difficult" child, but I can assure you that my daughter will not be a difficult child. So she can already have her "own" room, we set up our bed in the dining room and we spoil her as much as possible because I believe it's best to err along those lines than the other. The film, which is infinitely less violent than this letter, will certainly hurt you, and it's not true that I don't care. I thought of you constantly while making it and I improvised a few scenes to avoid being unfair, convince you of my good faith and show you, partially, what I think was the truth. You're ironical in your letter about my returning from Cannes "finally freed of my many complexes." You couldn't have stated it better: for two months I've had the feeling of having dispelled an old nightmare and of having become a man who is fit to bring up a child.[43]

Keeping his promise to his father, the day his film opened, June 3, Truffaut denied in *Arts* that he had made an autobiographical movie: "If the young Antoine Doinel sometimes resembles the turbulent adolescent I was, his parents bear absolutely no resemblance to mine, who were excellent. . . ." Truffaut's rewriting of the family saga began on that day, in a radical break with the interviews granted up to then. He thought he had protected the most important thing, his own parents, whom he had lectured vehemently and sincerely in a private letter but whom he preferred to forget about publicly. As his ultimate gesture, he took on financial responsibility for his Truffaut grandmother and started sending her a monthly money order of 20,000 francs as of the autumn of 1959. He met with his father at the Brasserie du Courcelles in early June, but it was a dialogue of the deaf, concluded several days later with this little note from Roland: "We should be happy and thrilled to read or hear about your success. Alas, it merely reminds us of a son who 'scorns and despises us.' "[44]

These exchanges undermined Truffaut's morale considerably. But if he felt guilty, he also felt liberated. He came to regret having publicly stated that the film was not autobiographical. Faced with what he now saw as artistic success but a great mess in his personal life, he decided to break off permanently with his parents. The estrangement would last three years; the silence would be oppressive. It was Madeleine, his wife, who would decide on her own to get back in touch with her in-laws. In January 1962, she secretly sent them a short conciliatory letter, saying, "Forgive my long delay in writing this letter. I should have done so long ago."[45] The Truffauts appreciated her gesture: "Your courageous letter, dear Madeleine, has softened a great bitterness within us. . . ."[46]

In the meantime, on June 29, 1961, a second daughter, Eva, had been born. Madeleine Morgenstern tells of this family schism: "For a very long time, François didn't want his parents to see our daughters. He did a lot for his grandmother, who had left Juvisy to move into a retirement home. On her ninety-second birthday, in 1976, François took his daughters to see her. She died in February 1979. As for Roland, he only met Laura in 1979, when she was twenty. Roland and Eva only saw each other several years later. But Janine, she never knew her granddaughters."[47]

One event would favor something like a reconciliation—Roland and Janine Truffaut's divorce. François immediately wrote to his father in May 1962:

> Hearing of your separation, my first reaction was one of absolute joy, but this satisfaction wasn't directed against either of you. It was strange, and I later analyzed the feeling in great detail. I think I love you more separately than together, that's the explanation. On the one hand there's the father and the mother, on the other the parents, it's a different notion. I've always loved my father and my mother, but I haven't always loved my parents, that's the thing. I hope I'm not shocking you by dissecting this so bluntly. I often think of Mom and you, not as parents or in relation to me, but as a couple. I think I've inherited many of mother's traits, for example, critical judgment, quick mood changes from cheerfulness to sadness, and as a husband, I resemble you a lot; at mealtime and before leaving the house in the morning, I make Madeleine and the children laugh with jokes that I got from you.[48]

From then on, François Truffaut saw his father regularly. In the autumn of 1963, he started having lunch once again every other Thursday at rue de Navarin with his mother; by then, she had married Robert Vincendon, the former lover who had brought François gifts when he was a boy. The outcome, therefore, was on the happier side, even if it was a bit forced. The fact remains that this family drama undermined Truffaut for many long years. The impact of film on his personal life was a painful shock to him, exposing feelings, hatreds, resentments, and memories that had long been repressed.[49] He enjoyed quick, immediate success, but paradoxically this very success bruised him. Hence, the heyday of the New Wave he had helped to inaugurate was not a happy period in François Truffaut's life. In fact, he confided as much to his mother: "I have the profession I like, unconditionally, the only possible one for me, and yet it doesn't make me happy. I'm sad, Mom, very often so sad."[50]

## A NEW LIFE

The success of *The 400 Blows* changed Truffaut's way of life; he adopted the look of a young man from the Right Bank, conventionally elegant, with all the external signs of success. "François was established in the world; he knew how to discuss contracts; he wasn't at all marginal; and yet at the same time he was still a complete rebel,"[51] says Florence Malraux, who first met him in the early sixties, when he was among a group of directors on the brink of success—Resnais, Chabrol, Rivette, Godard, Varda, and Demy. "I never knew which part of his personality overshadowed the other," she continues, "the two strains coexisted. Especially compared to all of us who weren't set up as yet. François had an office, but he was more of an anarchist than we were. I always saw these two sides of him, which was his distinctive feature and therefore his charm."

On the one hand, there was this attachment to his childhood haunts, the culture of his youth, the songs, the music hall, the insolent Parisian humor and extravagance, and his ingrained gestures, the Gitane cigarette between his fingers, the prostitutes he continued to visit, his odd habits—he couldn't stand certain fabrics, he always followed certain itineraries, he always ate the same quick meals in the same places, and he always thoroughly emptied his pockets when he got home. And on the other hand, he had material comfort and everything it entailed, allowing him to support his family and his own lifestyle, and to help out his friends as well. Simone Jollivet, who was a close friend of Sartre and Simone de Beauvoir, and whom Truffaut had considered casting in the part of Madame Bigey in *The 400 Blows*, described him accurately by comparing him, in a certain way, to Jean Renoir and his "noble, working-class" bearing: "I think, dear Truffaut, that your outstanding qualities are working-class—passions which are sudden, almost instinctive, sentimental and melodramatic, a taste for the burlesque, for melodrama, novels, fantasy—while, on the other hand, your appearance and thought have an aristocratic and subtle orderliness. These two kinds of gifts are more difficult to reconcile than any other (it will happen when you will truly have found the 'form' which is yours) and yet these rare qualities are the ones the good fairy left in your cradle and that you cannot disown without renouncing your own self."[52]

In the mid-fifties, when he was already a star critic, his freelance writing assignments and odd jobs brought in 500,000 francs a year, the equivalent of 45,000 francs today. In 1958, with several film contracts added to his earnings from journalism, Truffaut declared a taxable income of over 3 million francs. In 1959, the year of *The 400 Blows,* he declared earnings of 65 million—that is, twenty times more than the preceding year; his 1960 income was about the same. From that time on, Truffaut was a young man who earned a very good living and whose affluence was visible. He dressed well and, since he hated fittings ("He couldn't stand being touched by a man,"[53] says Madeleine Morgenstern), he would order four or five suits twice a year (and for Jean-Pierre Léaud at the same time), as well as solid-color shirts by the dozen, first from Ted Lapidus in 1959 and 1960, then from Pierre Cardin, whom he met through Jeanne Moreau.

Another external sign of success was the beautiful Facel-Véga Truffaut bought himself in late 1959. "At its wheel I bring James Dean irresistibly to mind, but my wife is none too pleased with the comparison,"[54] Truffaut commented. Indeed, the comparison almost became too real when he had a serious accident on December 17, 1962, while driving the "rolling masterpiece."[55] He escaped unharmed, but the car was completely wrecked. "He was a 'nouveau-riche' for two years," says Claude Chabrol, "up until he wrecked the Facel-Véga. . . . This changed him: afterward, he stopped being nouveau-riche."[56] Cautiously, Truffaut resigned himself to a Jaguar sedan, more comfortable for driving his little family around. Money also allowed him to satisfy his curiosity. While tourism and museums would never interest him, and he confined his travels to those required for the shooting and promotion of his films, he always had a passion for music and especially for reading. He therefore built up a fine collection of records, mostly of French popular music (Trenet, Aznavour, Mistinguett, Béart, Francesca Solleville), but also the work of the Québécois Félix Leclerc and some classical music; he owned very little jazz and no opera at all, since he hated it. He also possessed a wonderful library, which included all the books he had kept from his youth, as well as all the latest novels, especially crime novels, and books on cinema. He was the faithful customer of several bookstores near the Palais-Royal, and of Contacts, on rue du Colisée, reputed to be the best cinema bookstore in Paris. He spent hours there, leafing through new publications, rummaging around the old stock, and conversing with the "beautiful Creole saleswoman," Elaine Micheaux-Vigne. He owned a collection of classical nineteenth- and twentieth-century novels, which he had bought at secondhand bookstores whenever he had come across a bargain or something hard to find. He also bought works on child psychology and history books, particularly on the Occupation, the Belle Epoque, or certain major nineteenth- and twentieth-century law cases; he loved Gordeau's comic-strip versions of these cases in *France-Soir*, which served him well in finding subjects for films. When he wasn't filming, Truffaut allowed himself time to read and write, pleasures he considered essential. He also read the daily press (*France-Soir, Le Monde, Combat*), weeklies (*L'Express, France-Observateur, Le Canard enchaîné, Paris-Match*), and many monthlies—film publications, of course, but also *Critique, Les Temps modernes, Diogène, Le Crapouillot*, and *Détective*, for news items and as inexhaustible sources of ideas and subject matter.

## PARALLEL FAMILIES

When he was preoccupied or melancholic, as he often was, François Truffaut found solace with his two families, the one he had started with Madeleine, and his professional one, centered around Les Films du Carrosse. "I'm tired, demoralized, and have more and more doubts about the point of making films. My only joy is playing with my daughter, who is becoming terrific. So, I stay home—and I'll stay home all year, as much as possible, so I can play with her and read, read, read, because I wasn't reading enough,"[57] he wrote to a friend on March 29, 1960.

At the end of March, Madeleine, Laura, and François moved into a five-room apartment in a beautiful building on rue du Conseiller Collignon, in the heart of the sixteenth arrondissement. Truffaut agreed to this move reluctantly. Though his family was beginning to feel cramped in the sixth-floor rue Saint-Ferdinand apartment, which was flooded with light, Truffaut liked it. Still, the new apartment had character and family life that was harmonious. Madeleine was distressed by her father's illness, but she was happy, devoting most of her time to taking care of Laura and preparing for the birth of her second daughter, Eva, due in early summer 1961. In her free moments, Madeleine, fluent in English, helped her husband by reading and translating manuscripts, screenplays, letters, and books that he received from England or the United States. She was in good health and in good spirits— Truffaut described her as gentle, charming, and wonderfully sincere[58]—and the couple got on well, usually surrounded by laughter, good humor, and amorous whimsy. Madeleine and François often spent time away from Paris—in Brittany (near Concarneau) or, beginning in July 1959, in Saint-

Paul-de-Vence, where they stayed at the well-known Colombe d'Or. When Truffaut was not making films, they sometimes traveled abroad; in 1960, they went to London, and in the spring of 1962 to Argentina, Brazil, New York, and Montreal.

Truffaut was a fully committed father. "My way of reacting to my children is the exact opposite of what I have lived through," he wrote in 1963. "But I'm still too much of a joker; I think mostly about entertaining my daughters and sparing them any worry, and I don't have very many serious occupations with them, perhaps because they're girls. It is really their mother who takes on the greater responsibility."[59] According to Madeleine, "François got married so he could start a family. This was one of the misunderstandings between us. I got married so I could have a man in my life, get away from my parents, and be left alone. When we had Laura, François was deliriously happy and he wanted to have another child quickly, because he thought I was a good mother."[60] His daughters gave him moments of true happiness at times when he was not directing; he took pictures of them, or filmed them with a small 8-mm camera. He showed them movies very early on; the first film Laura remembers seeing was Charlie Chaplin's *Shoulder Arms,* which she saw with her father at the Cinémathèque when she was four.

In a way Jean-Pierre Léaud was also a member of the family. Since the filming of *The 400 Blows,* Truffaut had adopted him, so to speak, and he spent quite a lot of time at rue Saint-Ferdinand. At the beginning of 1960, Truffaut secured a place for him at the Institut de la Muette, on rue Cortambert, very close to the couple's new apartment. But Jean-Pierre was expelled a few weeks later, at the headmaster's request: "We could have extended the trial period," he wrote to Truffaut, "but he himself made it impossible because of the accounts he gave to his classmates of his marvelous life and his daily earnings, so much so that the families protested against this contagion spreading in class and dangerously stimulating the lust for money that holds sway among today's youth."[61] Truffaut then placed Léaud with a retired couple in Colombes, but despite their goodwill, Léaud displayed volatile and insolent behavior and regularly ran away to Paris. Truffaut then took matters directly in hand again and made him the offer of living alone, at seventeen, in a maid's room, much as he himself had done after coming out of the Observation Center for Minors. Léaud agreed to attend courses regularly at the Centre psychologique et scolaire, an institution specializing in difficult cases.

François Truffaut "brought up" Jean-Pierre Léaud; being only twelve years Léaud's senior, he was like an older brother as well as a father figure. He was also a Pygmalion, for he was very attached to the fictional character he had created; their relationship was complex but fulfilling. Truffaut drew from it the elements that would later constitute the material for some of his films—not just the "Doinel cycle" films, but also *The Wild Child, Two English Girls, Small Change,* and *Day for Night.* As for Léaud, he was literally kept afloat by his protector.

Though he enjoyed family life, in some ways Truffaut must have felt caught in a trap. Even during periods when the couple enjoyed harmony and deep affection, he wasn't faithful. Or rather, he had a very personal interpretation of fidelity: He lived with Madeleine, but pursued both old and new love affairs, and continued to visit prostitutes, as in his youth. He felt no guilt or shame; this kind of love life seemed almost natural to him, so much so that during those first years of marriage, he kept an intimate diary meticulously detailing his amorous encounters. In 1959, for example, he resumed his liaison with Evelyne D., which dated back to the mid-fifties, and saw her regularly in Paris. At the Cannes Festival the same year, even though he was with Madeleine for the official screening of *The 400 Blows,* he felt free enough to approach a beautiful green-eyed brunette several days later. Liliane David, a young actress, was staying in Saint-Tropez during the Festival. "I passed in front of a bistro, Le Festival, right next to the Palais, and a friend introduced me to two people at a table. One of them, the journalist Pierre Rey, was interviewing a guy whose first name was François. He looked at me with an intense gaze. It was our first meeting; I knew nothing about him, or about *The 400 Blows.*"[62] The following day, the two met again at the terrace of Sénéquier in Saint-Tropez: "We spent a long period of time together, talking; we were both shy. I felt I could trust him. He was delighted to hear that I'd been kicked out of the Centre dramatique de la rue Blanche." After a round trip between Saint-Tropez and the Colombe d'Or, Truffaut returned to pick up Liliane David and drove back to Paris with her. He dropped her off in front of her house in Paris, on rue du Colonel-Moll, a street which is perpendicular to the rue Saint-Ferdinand, where he and Madeleine were living at the time. Liliane was living in a maid's room above her parents' apartment. This was the beginning of an affair that would last four years, a tumultuous, intermittent passion, indulged in on weekends away from Paris, on visits to provincial film societies, and during festivals.

His life with Madeleine was constantly threatened by the possibility of embarrassing revelations. It soon became apparent to Truffaut that though he considered his marriage happy, it was unlikely to last. Furthermore, the articles in the press insinuating that he had married for career advancement created tension between the two. "François may have had the feeling of compromising," says Madeleine Morgenstern, "either in his ideas or with regard to his friends, by becoming someone important. This uneasiness is explicit in *Shoot the Piano Player,* and one had to be as blind as I was at the time not to have seen it, but I couldn't do anything about it."[63] During this time, Truffaut used Les Films du Carrosse as a shield, to give himself the appearance of a settled family man, a hard worker whose thoughts revolved only around cinema—the films he liked to see, and the films he planned to make. Methodical, obsessive, Truffaut did not want to waste time. This was also why he kept his relationships with friends separate from his professional relationships. He used Les Films du Carrosse to start another family, parallel to his real family, which allowed him to establish very strong and faithful ties, most often based on one-to-one relationships.

In May 1959, the Carrosse moved into the offices of SEDIF, which belonged to Ignace Morgenstern, on rue Quentin-Bauchart, very near to the Champs-Elysées. Marcel Berbert soon became the manager of the little production company, whose staff included a secretary, Lucette Deuss, and a receptionist, Christiane. Nine years Truffaut's senior but from a similar petit bourgeois background, Berbert was a discreet and serious man, with a face that was both stern and childish; he was sensible and prudent, not very talkative, and always direct. He had been there to advise Truffaut in 1957, when he was an inexperienced, very young director, and he would be there to the bitter end, in an office adjoining Truffaut's, whose door was never shut.

After the success of *The 400 Blows* and the move to the rue Quentin-Bauchart, Ignace Morgenstern went only rarely to the office. "He was ill and sad, yet he was a big strong guy, like a peasant,"[64] Marcel Berbert recalls. This ailing man had not been told the truth about his medical condition. He had been made to believe he was suffering from the aftereffects of a 1957 heart attack, when in fact he had had a ruptured aortic aneurysm, an extremely serious condition. Madeleine knew her father could die at any moment. The doctors had ordered complete rest.

Truffaut had great esteem for his father-in-law. First of all, he was grateful that Ignace had helped him by producing *The 400 Blows*, and more importantly, he valued his moral rigor and professionalism in managing his business. Truffaut was eager to manage his own Carrosse business wisely, under Marcel Berbert's guidance, so as not to disappoint his father-in-law, much less cause him financial difficulties. Morgenstern was far from enthusiastic about *The 400 Blows* (his tastes in motion pictures ran closer to *Chiens perdus sans collier*); nonetheless, despite this and the fact that he was from another age and of a different character, he instilled in his son-in-law a sense of responsibility in business.

In January 1962, when Ignace Morgenstern died at sixty of a second ruptured aneurysm, Marcel Berbert dedicated himself completely to Les Films du Carrosse. "The company kept forging ahead after *The 400 Blows*, with an uninterrupted series of films. François was solely in charge of the artistic end, and me, of managing production. I was executive producer, and line producer—in those days we did everything. I was also in charge of foreign sales."[65] The company operated in this kind of closed circuit, with the sole aim of ensuring Truffaut's independence. Conflicts between the two men were rare, primarily because they trusted each other, but also because Truffaut was reasonable and never made extravagant demands for his films. Life was quiet at the Carrosse, except in periods just prior to filmings. Then frenzy reigned in the cramped offices. Truffaut shut himself in his. He read the newspaper or a book, and wrote letters, trying to subdue the anxiety that gripped him.

## FOREIGN CORRESPONDENTS

Starting with *The 400 Blows*, Truffaut began building up an important network of foreign correspondents for the Carrosse. Many were film critics who already knew Truffaut by reputation from his days as a critic and who had translated his writings. There were also directors of festivals and film libraries, with whom he established long-lasting, dependable ties on his trips abroad. They kept Truffaut well informed about the distribution of his films and those of his New Wave friends in every country and actively promoted his films and his books on cinema. These informants also kept him up-to-date on the emergence of new talent in various places. They played a decisive role in the early sixties, in propagating the international renown of the New Wave.

On October 25, 1959, at the opening of *The 400 Blows* at the Curzon Theater in London, Truffaut met Richard Roud, of the British Film Institute, who subsequently played an important part in getting him and the New Wave recognized by magazines and the daily press—first in England and later in the United States, when he moved to New York to become director of the New York Film Festival, where Truffaut regularly presented his films. *The 400 Blows* also had success in Germany, where Truffaut found an efficient intermediary in the person of Enno Patalas, who was editor in chief of the magazine *FilmKritic* in Munich. In Genoa, Gianno Amico, a close friend of Rossellini, translated and published Truffaut's first writings. Franco's Spain, which would always be more resistant to his films, was approached through Antonio Vega de Seoanne at the Festival of San Sebastian, which Truffaut attended in July 1960, and in Barcelona by José Sagré, who translated and published a good many of Truffaut's pieces.

Truffaut regularly wrote to his many foreign correspondents, informing them of his activities, whether scripts in progress, films he was directing, or book projects that might be translated. He welcomed them when they came to Paris, aware of the stakes involved in his films being internationally recognized. Somewhat unexpectedly, it was in Japan that he found his most fervent and efficient supporters. For example, Shukichi Okada, who translated excerpts of Truffaut's first films for his magazine, *The Art of Cinema,* and wrote an essay on the New Wave. In addition to this devoted critic, to whom Truffaut constantly sent material, there was Hisamitsu Nogushi, painter, graphic artist, and jazz musician; he had designed the Japanese poster for *The 400 Blows,* showing Antoine Doinel with his face half hidden by a black turtleneck pulled up to his nose. Truffaut liked the poster enormously, so much so that he used it as part of the set of Doinel's bedroom in his short 1962 film, *Antoine and Colette* (an episode in the film *Love at Twenty*). It has also adorned one of the walls of Les Films du Carrosse since 1960.

## PARIS BELONGS TO US

Boosted by the success of *The 400 Blows,* and by the support of Marcel Berbert, François Truffaut wanted to help his New Wave colleagues. First, Jacques Rivette, who hadn't been able to finish his first film, *Paris nous appartient,* which he had begun to shoot in the summer of 1958. Truffaut rescued this film, provided partial financing, and then fought to ensure its Paris release at the Studio des Ursulines in December 1961. He did so because he felt indebted to Rivette, without whom the daring of the New Wave would not have been possible: "The release of *Paris nous appartient* (*Paris Belongs to Us*) is a score for every member of the [*Cahiers du cinéma*] team—or of our Mafia, if you prefer. . . . For Rivette is the source of many things. The example of *Le Coup du berger,* his short film of 1956, made me decide to shoot *Les Mistons,* and Claude Chabrol to be adventuresome enough to make a full-length film from *Le Beau Serge;* and at the same time it moved the most prestigious short-subject filmmakers, Alain Resnais and Georges Franju, to try their first full-length films. It had begun. And it had begun thanks to Jacques Rivette. Of all of us he was the most fiercely determined to move."[66] In exchange for his help, Truffaut borrowed from Rivette, for his future films, his two most important collaborators—Jean Gruault, the scenario and dialogue writer of *Paris nous appartient,* and Suzanne Schiffman, "the omniskilled assistant."

In 1959, Jean-Luc Godard was the only member of the "*Cahiers* Mafia" who had not directed a feature. When *The 400 Blows* was in the works, Truffaut, who greatly admired Godard, tried to convince some producers to gamble on him. Several projects were discussed—for example, an adaptation of Georges Bernanos's *Mouchette.* In the spring of 1959, Truffaut failed to convince Ignace Morgenstern to coproduce with Pierre Roustang Godard's project *Prénatal,* the first version of what was to become in two years *Une Femme est une femme* (*A Woman Is a Woman*). Several weeks later, still hoping to attract his friend's father-in-law, Godard came to Truffaut with the plan of adapting a Simenon novel, *Quartier nègre,* with Nicole Courcel, but once again Godard's project ran aground. It was only with the triumph of *The 400 Blows* in Cannes that his prospects improved. For producers started to pounce on young directors' projects, provided their films required very small budgets. Godard found in Georges de Beauregard a person who was convinced of his talent, but Beauregard would only commit himself if Godard had a story "that made sense." Having run out of ideas, Godard remembered the synopsis of *Breathless* that Truffaut had given him a few years earlier. He asked his friend to flesh out the story quickly, for he wanted to shoot the film very fast, by the end of the summer of 1959. "If you have the time to round out in three lines the idea for a film started at the Richelieu-Drouot métro station (those were the good old days), though I don't have access to Françoise Sagan, I could whip up the dialogues,"[67] he wrote Truffaut. Truffaut's four-page synopsis was enough to convince Beauregard. Out of friendship, and so as to not to add to the film's budget, Truffaut relinquished all royalties for a modest sum, 1 million old francs. He made a point of telling Georges de Beauregard that he didn't want to appear in the publicity for the film except as the author of the original screenplay, and he offered to give his opinion on the final script. "I'm very grateful to you for being so interested in my film," Beauregard replied on July 20. "I know it's out of friendship for Jean-Luc, but believe me, a producer doesn't often have the opportunity to encounter such disinterestedness. Therefore, thank you."[68] On the eve of his first day's shoot for *Breathless,* August 17, 1959, Godard wrote Truffaut to take stock of the situation:

> I'll have you read the continuity in a few days. After all, it's your screenplay. I think you'll be surprised once again. Yesterday, I discussed it with Melville. Thanks to him, and from having seen grand Momo's rushes, my spirits are in fourth gear. There will be a scene where Jean Seberg will interview Rossellini [in the end, the part would be played by Jean-Pierre Melville] for the *New York Herald.* I don't think you'll like this film, though it's dedicated to *Baby Doll,* but via *Rio Bravo.* I'd like to write you a lot longer still, but I'm so lazy that this effort will prevent me from working until tomorrow. And we're shooting on the 17th, come rain or shine. Roughly speaking, the subject will be the story of a boy who thinks of death and of a girl who doesn't. The adventures are those of a car thief (Melville will introduce me to specialists) in love with a girl who sells the *New York Herald* and who takes French civilization courses. What bothers me, is having had to introduce something of my own in a screenplay which

was by you. But we've become too difficult. We should get down to filming in large quantities and stop being wise guys. Kind regards from one of your sons.[69]

When it opened in Paris in December 1959, *Breathless* was almost as great a commercial success as *The 400 Blows*. The critics regarded it as the New Wave's aesthetic manifesto, a supplement to Truffaut's film, which had marked its public advent. The mission was accomplished: Youth had risen to power in French cinema. Now considered a full-fledged director, Godard no longer needed help from his friend Truffaut; he was already in preproduction for *Le Petit Soldat*, his second film (released in 1963). Completed at the height of the Algerian war, it would cause much ink to flow and incur Gaullist censorship.

## FRIENDS FIRST

Even established directors needed help from Les Films du Carrosse, and Truffaut gladly came to the rescue of some of his masters. One of Jean Cocteau's last dreams, at seventy, was to shoot *The Testament of Orpheus*, the third part of the triptych that included *Blood of a Poet* and *Orpheus*. Truffaut and Cocteau had known each other for about ten years and had been friends since the 1959 Cannes Festival. Their friendship can be gleaned from this surprising letter that the poet wrote to Truffaut when the latter was not yet thirty: "I saw in your eyes as you had in mine a heartfelt sincerity whose light the Cannes Festival ignores. By helping you I was helping myself: I was cleansing my soul of so much filth. My film is beginning to take shape. I've established refundable shares of five million based on the work's chances. If you're the delightful madman who wants to embark on my phantom yacht, just write to Gérard Worms, Edouard Dermit or Jean Thuillier. My film will belong to that logic which reason is spared and I'm happy you're intrigued by it. Write me often. Letters like yours are what allow me to live in this world."[70] In June 1959, Les Films du Carrosse promised to cofinance *The Testament of Orpheus*, despite the skepticism of Ignace Morgenstern and Marcel Berbert. Over the summer, Truffaut collaborated on the script with Cocteau, who began shooting in Les Baux-de-Provence in September. Jean-Pierre Léaud had a cameo role, "like a good-luck charm reminding me what I owe you,"[71] the elderly director wrote to his "producer."

Truffaut wanted to help another one of his masters, Roberto Rossellini, who had returned from his long trip with a magnificent film, *India*, which went unrecognized. At that point, Rossellini was on a fresh course, engaged in making didactic and historical films and planning one on Socrates, but obtaining financial backing proved tricky. Finally, the deal was concluded, with Greek, Italian, and Swedish financiers, in association with Les Films du Carrosse. Truffaut seemed happy to help one of his masters extricate himself from a period of dejection and stagnation. "The more I think about your Socrates, the more I believe this is the film you should make right now and that it will be magnificent,"[72] he wrote the Italian director on July 5, 1962.

In September 1960, Truffaut decided to produce an episode film based on Edgar Allan Poe's *Tales of the Grotesque and Arabesque;* it would be a way for New Wave directors to sponsor young directors of short films. Truffaut explained it in a memo to Marcel Berbert: "It seems to me that this collective film deserves to be attempted, for individual short films are fine but difficult to sell. One possibility would be for each episode to be filmed by a new director—Lachenay, Marcel Ophuls, Varesano, de Givray, Gégauff, Demy—but supervised by an established filmmaker—Godard, Malle, Astruc, Resnais, Franju, Chabrol, me. . . . This would give the enterprise a fraternal and even slightly polemical, anti–old wave, quality that would appeal to me. In short, we must fight and take advantage of the door being left ajar to get our friends in before it's too late."[73] Of this collective project, only *The Gold Bug,* a short film by Robert Lachenay, would see the light of day in 1960.[74]

In his dream of making Les Films du Carrosse into a ministudio and spearhead for the New Wave, Truffaut placed great hope in Marcel Ophuls, the son of the director of *Lola Montès,* and in Claude de Givray, formerly the youngest member of the *Cahiers du cinéma* group. In March 1960, the Carrosse signed a contract with Marcel Ophuls for the screen adaptation of Arthur Schnitzler's *The Return of Casanova.* Though the project never came to fruition, a friendship was born. While he was directing *Peau de banane (Banana Peel)* in 1963, starring Jeanne Moreau and Jean-Paul Belmondo, Marcel Ophuls acknowledged his debt to Truffaut: "For three years, it's been you, François, and Jeanne, who have made my film possible. Your loyal friendship has been the most creative I've ever known. I'll never forget it."[75]

Truffaut regarded Claude de Givray as a promising young director and was enthusiastic about producing his first feature, *Tire-au-flanc (The Army Game).* As soon as the Mouëzy-Eon play had been adapted for the screen, the shooting began, in February and March of 1961, in the area of Nice, with a Carrosse team that included Raoul Coutard, Suzanne Schiffman, Robert Lachenay; in the principal roles were Ricet-Barrier, Christian de Tilière, Jacques Balutin, Serge Davri, Bernadette Lafont, Cabu, Jean-François Adam, and Truffaut, who played a rank-and-file soldier. *Tire-au-flanc* was a commercial flop when it opened in December, but this did not prevent Truffaut from entrusting de Givray with the writing and direction of a second picture several months later, *Une grosse tête* with Eddie Constantine, Georges Poujouly, and Alexandra Stewart. Cowritten in August 1961 by Truffaut and de Givray and shot in the autumn, this film flopped as well. From then on, Truffaut gave up trying to be a producer except for his own films, but he had shown unflinching determination throughout the endeavor.

## THE STORY OF A SHY PERSON

François Truffaut was eager to begin work on a second feature. Wishing to remain faithful to his agreement with Pierre Braunberger, his first thought was to reconsider adapting *Temps chaud,* with Bernadette Lafont. He worked on the screenplay with Godard, whom Braunberger hired for 130,000 francs in early April 1959. The shooting was scheduled for July 15 to August 30, in Mougins. But the success of *The 400 Blows* changed matters. Truffaut realized he should dispel the image some film professionals and journalists had of him—of a simple little Parisian who had achieved success through nerve and ambition. Childhood and casual love stories had become fashionable subjects, and he felt he should stay away from these, even if this meant revealing other facets of his personality—those of an often anxious, rather pessimistic, pathologically shy seducer. So his second picture would not be the story of success, but of failure, of inner withdrawal, reflecting a more intimate aspect of himself, which Madeleine Morgenstern describes as follows: "Sometimes, when faced with certain situations, François could no longer speak, especially when more than one person was involved or when he felt he was in foreign territory. He had this slightly childish and disconcerting attitude of remaining silent with people who didn't speak the same way he did."[76]

Truffaut found an ideal surrogate in the person of Charles Aznavour. He was captivated by Aznavour's performance in Georges Franju's *La Tête contre les murs* (*The Keepers*). He liked his "fragility, his vulnerability, his humble and graceful figure, which made him resemble Saint Francis of Assisi."[77] The two men even looked alike: Short, with the same bearing and the same expressive face, they were both vivacious, excitable, and anxious, but with an elegance in gesture and deportment, and an iron will. They first met in Cannes, on the morning of May 11, 1959, at the bar of the Carlton Hotel. They felt an immediate bond, so much so that they saw each other often in Paris, and wanted to make a film together. Truffaut put aside *Temps chaud* and decided to adapt a David Goodis novel, *Down There,* which had been published in Gallimard's *Série Noire* under the title *Tirez sur le pianiste*

(*Shoot the Piano Player*). Goodis was one of Truffaut's favorite American writers. What he liked about the novel was its fairy-tale aspect treated in a *noir* manner, the plot twists combining unbridled fantasy with the most sordid tragedy—gangsters conversing about everyday life, crooks discussing love, and lovers turned killers. Truffaut gave Aznavour the novel to read; he was enchanted. Then Pierre Braunberger had to be convinced. He accepted Truffaut's conditions: 6 million old francs for himself and 2 million for Marcel Moussy, who would write the screen adaptation and the dialogue. He also acquired the rights to the novel (2 million) and guaranteed Aznavour's salary (5 million). *Shoot the Piano Player* would cost 75 million francs, almost double the budget of *The 400 Blows*, but a sum that was still moderate compared to the budgets for many French films of the period.

In June 1959, Truffaut asked Marcel Moussy again to write the screenplay. They spent two weeks in Saint-Tropez, at the Ferme d'Augustin, and a week at the Colombe d'Or in Saint-Paul-de-Vence. In Saint-Tropez, Truffaut was accompanied by Liliane David and Jean-Pierre Léaud. The young woman was there incognito in another hotel; she was supposed to be watching the adolescent Léaud while Truffaut worked with Moussy. The situation led to an imbroglio, for Truffaut was very worried about protecting his privacy. "I had to keep an eye on Jean-Pierre, who got into a lot of mischief," David recounts. While Truffaut and Moussy were working on the screenplay, Jean-Pierre Léaud, still basking in the glory of *The 400 Blows,* was the darling of the press. A young photographer in Saint-Tropez wanted to do a shoot for *Elle* of Léaud posing with the Saint-Tropez personalities Françoise Sagan, Jean-Pierre Aumont, and so on. "Jean-Pierre succeeded in borrowing the photographer's car," Liliane David says, "and getting into an accident with it. François was furious, since he had to pay the repair costs."[78]

In July, Madeleine and François Truffaut returned to Saint-Paul-de-Vence with little Laura, who was six months old. Then the couple spent time in Saint-Tropez at the Ferme d'Augustin, where Marcel Moussy's wife also joined them. Work progressed rapidly, and on July 17, the screenplay for *Shoot the Piano Player* was ready. Pierre Braunberger was pleased with it. Charlie Kohler is a short, somber, and mysterious man. A dance-hall pianist at Mammy's Bar, pampered by a prostitute, Clarisse, and secretly loved by Léna, the waitress at the bar, he lives alone with his younger brother, Fido. His past first catches up with him when his other brother Chico turns up at Mammy's Bar, with two gangsters hot on his trail. Charlie is reluctantly swept into this shady story by the two gangsters, Momo and Ernest, even though they turn out to be more eccentric than expected. His past catches up with him a second time when Léna declares her love, seduces him, and lures him home. The young woman knows that Charlie Kohler is the pseudonym of Edouard Saroyan, a young piano virtuoso. Charlie/Edouard then tells her the whole story: his young wife, Thérésa, had sacrificed herself for his career by becoming the mistress of an impresario, Lars Schmeel. When she confessed to the misdeed to which he owed his success, Saroyan could not bear the truth and walked out on Thérésa, who committed suicide by throwing herself from the window. Success and glory having shattered his conjugal happiness, Edouard became Charlie Kohler. After a night of love, Léna and Charlie must track down Fido, who has been kidnapped by the two gangsters. They go to the Saroyan family house, deep in the mountains, where they find Chico and Richard, the two other brothers who are hiding out there. A chase begins between the Saroyans and the gangsters. As the story draws to an end, it is Léna, the innocent one, who is struck by a stray bullet, slides to the snowy, bloodstained ground, and dies in Charlie's arms.

"One day," Claude de Givray recalls, "François said to me, 'That's it, this film with Aznavour will be the story of a shy person.' It's true François was shy, but on the other hand, when he spoke about cinema, even when he was very young, he already spoke like a film director. It was his terrain, he could be as daring as he pleased. He, who sometimes had difficulty speaking, became a bulldozer when speaking about things he had knowledge of. François learned to use his shyness. In *Shoot the Piano Player*, this can be seen in Aznavour's part, when he doesn't dare ring a doorbell. François films the gesture in four shots; he was very pleased with this because he had found a filmic device for transmitting this feeling. François used to bite his nails (he used to say that it was very good to bite one's nails, because there was always a woman who wanted to prevent you from doing it!), but as soon as he spoke about things that concerned him—that is, cinema—he would turn into a true professional."[79]

Truffaut was increasingly excited by this story of a shy man who began to bear a likeness to himself. It was not so much the plot as certain significant details that betrayed his most private obsessions. In their poetic dialogue, the gangsters referred to the "magical" power of women, while the Charlie/Edouard character, a famous pianist who had compromised himself to obtain success and had embraced anonymity out of despair, a man pathologically shy yet just as pathologically a womanizer, was of course Truffaut's double.

## GOODIS QUENEAU-STYLE

In this film, Truffaut experimented with a new style, based on constant changes in tempo. *Shoot the Piano Player* continually played on these breaks in rhythm, which recall both Queneau and Trenet. For Truffaut, it was "practically a musical film,"[80] composed like a score, mixing several styles. On Pierre Braunberger's advice, he contacted Georges Delerue, a former student of Darius Milhaud at the Paris Conservatoire who would later be the conductor of the Orchestre de la Radiodiffusion française. Truffaut and Delerue understood each other perfectly, as Truffaut himself recalled: "We were at the painful rough-cut stage. Delerue looked and grasped my intentions immediately. 'Okay! This is a *noir* thriller treated in the style of Raymond Queneau, I see what to do.' "[81] This first job would mark the beginning of a long and intense collaboration.

Boby Lapointe is the other musical revelation in the film. Guided by Audiberti, Truffaut picked him out at the Cheval d'Or, a club of cabaret artists: "the house went into a frenzy of joy when he struck up 'Léon,' then 'Marcelle,' and finally 'Avanie et Framboise.' "[82] With their constant puns and rapid syncopated rhythms, these pieces immediately filled Truffaut with enthusiasm, for they illustrated what he wanted to accomplish in *Shoot the Piano Player*. The director hired Boby Lapointe to play himself and sing "Avanie et framboise" in front of the camera in its entirety and in real time on the stage of Mammy's Bar, where Charlie Kohler plays the piano. Pierre Braunberger, who felt it was impossible to understand the meaning of the words, requested that Truffaut cut the song, or add subtitles to the scene. Truffaut refused to make cuts, but he liked the idea of the "subtitled"[83] singer. Later, Aznavour got Boby Lapointe hired for the first half of his recital at the Alhambra, which led to the singer's making his first record.

Simultaneously detective thriller and intimate journal, *Shoot the Piano Player* is surely François Truffaut's true New Wave film. Indeed, he had hired Raoul Coutard, the movement's preeminent cameraman since *Breathless*. "What attracted me to him," Truffaut wrote, "is the originality of his camerawork but also his extraordinarily crude language. . . . Coutard's rudeness makes visitors run away and particularly female visitors. He has no servility in him, and will address a producer, a technician or the female star in exactly the same way."[84] As for Coutard, who was accustomed to working quickly, the shooting conditions of this modest-budget film appealed to him: "I arrived with the bad manners of a press photographer," Coutard explained. "I like quick, candid work. I find the pretty and the 'polished' sickening. I started by eliminating from my films all the so-called artistic effects, all those things cameramen thrive on, and instead of asking for an army of projectors, I used daylight. . . . The result: we shot fifteen times more quickly for ten times less money, and our casual, lively films had more ambiance."[85]

Suzanne Schiffman was also a new recruit for Truffaut. She was an old-time acquaintance from the days of the Cinémathèque and the Ciné-Club du Quartier Latin, a friend of Rivette, Godard, and Gruault. In 1956, after getting a literature degree at the Sorbonne, she went to Chicago for a year on a fellowship given for her work with Edgar Morin, and then lived in Mexico for a year. On returning to Paris, she collaborated on the shoot of *Paris Belongs to Us* in the summer of 1958; then she was hired as script supervisor on *Shoot the Piano Player.* "Braunberger wasn't displeased," she recalls, "because he could pay me far less than the union wage. I found it so wonderful to be paid that I had no desire to argue."[86] Though she lacked professional experience, Schiffman was interested in all aspects of the shoot and had no preconceived ideas. Very soon, her job resembled that of an assistant director. She eventually became Truffaut's indispensable partner, his closest collaborator.

To work with Charles Aznavour, Truffaut hired several actors whom he had initially planned to use in *Temps chaud.* Hence, Nicole Berger plays Thérésa, Edouard Saroyan's wife, who commits suicide; Serge Davri has the part of Plyne, the limited, strapping bar owner with facial injuries, whose loutish appearance conceals great sensitivity and naïve love attachments; Catherine Lutz plays the role of his wife, Mammy, the melancholic owner of the bar. As for Albert Rémy, Antoine's stepfather in *The 400 Blows*, he becomes Chico, Charlie Kohler's crazy, blundering brother. Truffaut also freely punctuated his film with friends, such as the director Alex Joffé; the writer Daniel Boulanger, in the role of a gangster; and the filmmaker Claude Heymann, playing the impresario Lars Schmeel. Still to be cast were the two other main female parts, Léna, the waitress, and Clarisse, the prostitute. On October 14, 1959, Truffaut put a small announcement in *Paris-Flirt* before proceeding to auditions. He had promised the part of Clarisse to Liliane David, who had just appeared in *Breathless* (the friend Jean-Paul Belmondo comes to pinch money from in the wardrobe of the hotel where she is living). Afraid of mixing his love life with his work, Truffaut decided to give the part to Michèle Mercier, the future "Angélique" and star of the sixties. At a second audition, Truffaut fell head over heels for Claudine Huzé, a twenty-two-year-old actress with a round face, blond curls, and charming eyes and mouth, whom he had noticed in a television drama. After a highly comical screen test in which he asked the rather shy young actress to insult him with swearwords, Truffaut offered her the part of Léna. He thus launched Claudine Huzé's career and gave her her stage name, Marie Dubois, in homage to Audiberti's novel: "Marie Dubois is neither a 'chick' nor a 'doll,' she's neither 'titillating' nor 'impish,' but she's a pure and dignified young girl whom one could conceivably fall in love with and be loved by in return. One might not turn around to look at her in the street, but she's fresh and gracious, a bit boyish and very childlike. She's vehement and passionate, modest and tender,"[87] Truffaut wrote in presenting his discovery.

The filming of *Shoot the Piano Player* began in the last days of November 1959, mostly at Levallois-Perret, then in a brasserie at the Porte Champerret, and ended in mid-January, in a chalet in Le Sappey, located in the Massif de la Grande-Chartreuse, not far from Grenoble. This is where the last scenes of the film take place, in the snow, when Léna is killed by a stray bullet during the shoot-out between the Saroyans and the gangsters. Two nights before the end of the shoot, Marie Dubois's twenty-third birthday was celebrated with cakes and champagne. Good humor and conviviality dominated the filming. Truffaut was satisfied, but he realized the editing and postsynchronization processes would be essential, for the construction of the film was peculiar: There was a long flashback in the middle and constant rhythm changes and mixing of genres. It was also a "musical film," so the sound track was particularly important.

## THE AMERICAN FRIEND

On January 6, 1960, while he was completing his shoot in Le Sappey, François Truffaut received a telegram from Les Films du Carrosse: *The 400 Blows* had just been given the prize for best foreign film by the New York critics. The good news came with an invitation from Daniel Frankel, head of Zenith International Film Corporation, the film's New York distributor. Truffaut agreed to make his first trip to the United States. *The 400 Blows*, which had opened on November 16, 1959, at the Fine Arts theater, had received glowing reviews. For instance, the day after it opened, Bosley Crowther, the influential *New York Times* critic, had written, "Words cannot state simply how fine is Jean-Pierre Léaud in the role of the boy. . . . He will live as a delightful, provoking and heartbreaking monument to a boy." As for the film itself, it is "a small masterpiece" that "encourages an exciting refreshment of faith in films,"[88] Crowther said. The other important critics all agreed, such as Paul Beckley in the *New York Herald Tribune:* "A film everyone with a serious concern for fine films will not want to miss,"[89] or Archer Winsten in the *New York Post:* "*The 400 Blows* brings us one of those great timeless French pictures that wring your heart with their beauty, truth and despair."[90]

The United States was pivotal for Truffaut's reputation and commercial success. It was also the country of the directors he most admired, American directors and European exiles—Hitchcock, Hawks, Lang, Aldrich, and Nicholas Ray. And Truffaut realized that his own critical and popular success would compel recognition for the New Wave in the United States. But in his ambition to win over America, he had a serious handicap: He didn't speak English. From then on, learning English would become a lifelong obsession.

On January 20, 1960, Truffaut left Paris for New York. The New York Film Critics award ceremony was scheduled for the evening of January twenty-third. He planned to spend two weeks in the United States—one week in New York, a short stay in Chicago, and then a visit to Los Angeles to meet people and visit the mythical studios in the company of Jeanne Moreau. During the award ceremony, Truffaut was deathly pale, unable to utter a single word in English. By his side was one of the actors he most admired, James Stewart, receiving an award for his performance in Otto Preminger's *Anatomy of a Murder.* Audrey Hepburn and Elizabeth Taylor also received prizes, as did William Wyler's *Ben-Hur,* which was chosen as the best picture that year. They all posed for a group photograph. Truffaut smiled shyly, gazing with slight awe at Jimmy Stewart. Earlier, Daniel Frankel had introduced him to the critics in the *New York Times* reception rooms: "M. Truffaut has made his first trip to this country from Paris to be here tonight. This is his very first picture. He is only 27. He is a former movie critic, and the only one we ever heard of who got busy and made a good picture. For showing the rest of the world, New York Film Critics included, how to make a good picture and a masterpiece, may we give him the warm welcome he deserves."[91]

As soon as he arrived in New York, Truffaut made an acquaintance that would be crucial for his American career. Helen Scott was in charge of public relations at the French Film Office, whose director was Joseph Maternati. In this capacity, she welcomed Truffaut at the airport upon his arrival in New York and served as his guide and interpreter. Cultivated, fluent in French, a great film enthusiast blessed with a good New York Jewish sense of humor, Scott had been active in the American Left, and later would be in the feminist movement. During the McCarthy period, she had been blacklisted for so-called anti-American activities along with many other writers, screenwriters, left-wing film directors, and members of the American Communist party. With her thorough knowledge of the New York cultural scene and the press, Scott was an indispensable ally for Truffaut in the United States. She admired *The 400 Blows* and the other first films of the New Wave and devoted all her energy to promoting them, introducing Truffaut, Godard, and Resnais to the American critics as the foremost representatives of the new French cinema. Truffaut was her favorite. During the trip to Chicago, François Truffaut and Helen Scott became friends; they talked for hours on end about movies, their youth, and politics, with "him proclaiming he was of the 'politically uncommitted' generation and me, on the contrary, an old-time activist, trying to explain to him the conditions of my youth in America and of the war in Africa, which had led me to my left-wing convictions."[92]

A snowstorm in Chicago forced Truffaut to cancel the California leg of his journey. Eager to screen a first rough cut of *Shoot the Piano Player*, he decided to return to Paris, happy, thanks to Helen Scott, that he had met David Goodis, whose novel he had just adapted, as well as Henry Miller,[93] for whom he had the utmost admiration. On January 26, Helen Scott also organized a dinner to introduce him to Elie Wiesel, who suggested that Truffaut make a film on World War II and the concentration camps.

When he returned to Paris, Truffaut stayed in contact with Helen Scott, maintaining a faithful, extremely rich correspondence, in which they kept each other informed about the Paris and New York film scenes. Usually very discreet about his relationships with lovers and friends, Truffaut wrote openly to Helen about his moods and feelings at work and of his difficulties in his private life. Of course, he was secure in the knowledge that the distance between New York and Paris guaranteed him a certain discretion; but his willingness to confide in Helen Scott was also due to her abilities at persuasion, for she very much wanted their relationship to transcend the professional. In a letter dated March 3, 1960, several weeks after their parting in Chicago, she complained to Truffaut: "Without expecting you to be as effusive as me, I had nevertheless hoped to receive some personal news from you—your concerns about the new film, your return to Paris, whatever—in short, a sentence, any kind of sentence through which I could recognize my friend Truffaut. But your letter, all bizness [*sic*], could have been written by Tati or any other producer. The handwritten message? You know my mania against formulas; for me only substance counts. In any case, I began to wonder if the tone of my correspondence wasn't inappropriate. . . ."[94] Cut to the quick, Truffaut immediately apologized: "You were right to scold me, for I let myself take the easy way out, dictating several letters every morning to 'expedite current business' and that way I feel like I'm a *big business man*, a *self-made man*, a *first class quality* man [italicized words indicate English in the original], and what not. In short, thanks to you, I'll improve my behavior, I'll resume my habit of typing a few letters myself at home, and my provincial and foreign friends will wonder why I've become so affectionate without suspecting they owe it to Helen Scott, my dear Helen."[95] Beyond the countless puns ("Truffe," also called "Truffaldin: the valet in Italian comedy, hypocritical, cunning and untruthful"), an obvious tenderness ("Scottie" or "Mascotte"), and all sorts of secrets, this correspondence that Truffaut diligently kept up throughout the sixties offers a veritable intimate journal of the New Wave. "Everything you write me is so important to me. I like you almost as much as I like myself, which, God knows, is not saying little,"[96] he wrote her after his second trip to New York in April 1962.

## THE ALGERIAN TRAGEDY

On his return from the United States, François Truffaut started to move toward the Left ideologically, no doubt under Helen Scott's influence. On February 12, 1960, he confided to a screenwriter friend his desire "to shoot a political film in the next two years."[97] The idea was derived from his long conversations with Helen Scott and Elie Wiesel. While he liked Scott's outspokenness, caustic humor, political experience, and practical sense, he rather mistrusted Wiesel's "bruised good conscience": "This guy is more moving than likable; I mean that he must be dreadful to live with, moaning and crying over himself, but I admire him greatly."[98] Nevertheless, the subjects discussed during the New York dinner—the war, the Resistance, deportation, the death camps—fascinated the director. Elie Wiesel had given him the proofs of his novel *Le Jour* (*The Accident*) in the hope that he might adapt it for the screen, but Truffaut did not pursue the project. The two men then considered a film entitled *Le Dernier Déporté*, the story of the last convoy of Jews to leave France for the death camps on July 31, 1944, and the return of one survivor. In December 1960, Wiesel wrote to Truffaut: "Now, if you want, or still want, we could start working on your film subject. *Le Dernier Déporté*: the scores to be settled with the men of the past and the future, the anxieties that overwhelm him, the doubts (did it really happen?), the silences—a subject overflowing with rich possibilities."[99] Truffaut spent two months doing research, reading many works on the "final solution" and "on Hitler, Nuremberg, and particularly the wonderful American book by [William] Shirer on the Third Reich."[100] He met a survivor from the last convoy, Alexandre Chambon, French consul in Rio de Janeiro, who had written his recollections of the Buchenwald concentration camp, a grim eyewitness account, in a book entitled *81.490*, his number as a prisoner. For a while, Truffaut considered adapting the book, but then decided against it, rejecting the idea of "staging the false reality of horror": "I couldn't resolve to have characters weighing 30 kilos played by 60 kilo extras, for here, the physical, visual and bodily reality is too important to be sacrificed."[101] But even if Truffaut quickly shelved the project, his initial interest marks a clear ideological change from his attitude as a critic in the fifties, when he categorically rejected any "politically committed" work, met with the wartime collaborator Lucien Rebatet, and was ironical about all "left-wing films."

If his political convictions, and consequently his public image, had changed, this was in large part due to events connected with the Algerian war. Although no subject outside the movies had led him to take a public stance while writing for *Arts*, now the situation in Algeria sometimes caught his attention. Twice, Truffaut took a skeptical position with regard to the French military involvement there. First, on March 12, 1958, in his review of *Paths of Glory*, Stanley Kubrick's anti-militarist World War I film, banned in France for undermining army morale, Truffaut himself adopted a clearly antimilitarist stance, derived, no doubt, from his own bad memories of military prisons and hospitals. On October 8, 1958, in one of his last reviews, he reaffirmed the same bias in discussing the revival of Jean Renoir's *Grand Illusion*. In a long digression, Truffaut alluded to his conversation with the director Pierre Schoendoerffer, a former news reporter in Indochina, and, breaking a taboo of the French press, he drew a parallel between the anti-colonial struggle of the Vietminh and the NLF in Algeria, clearly enjoining the French army to withdraw. Feeling deep indignation at the torture practiced by French officers in Algeria, he had absolutely no faith in the army's ability to resolve the crisis, and he let this be known in the right-wing *Arts*, thereby creating a controversy.

The Algerian war would affect Truffaut directly on March 9, 1960, when Cécile Decugis, his editor for *Shoot the Piano Player*, was imprisoned for having rented an apartment in her name that was used as a headquarters by NLF activists. In a matter of days, Truffaut raised over 20,000 new francs for Decugis's appeal.[102] During the spring of 1960, he made regular trips to the Roquette prison to assure her of the loyalty and solidarity of the *Piano Player* cast and crew.

It was not so much the Algerian cause itself that moved Truffaut as it was the defense of basic liberties in time of war. He made financial contributions to a good number of independent periodicals—banned and clandestine—that sympathized with the NLF, such as the newspaper *Liberté-Vérité*, edited by Pierre Jean Oswald (he subscribed by sending a check for 4,000 new francs), or *L'Espoir d'Alger*, the "last free newspaper" published in Algeria, whose editor, Guy Teisseire, was a film enthusiast.[103] In June 1960, Truffaut also became passionately interested in the Maurice Audin affair, the case of a twenty-five-year-old scientist and member of the Algerian Communist party who had been arrested three years earlier by French paratroopers and had never been heard from since. The French army's official explanation was that the young academic had been inadvertently shot during an attempted escape. The "Audin committee," made up of Chatenet, dean of the Paris Law School, Pierre Vidal-Naquet, Jacques Panijel, Michel Crouzet, and Luc Montagnier, thought, on the contrary, that he had died under torture and that there had been an attempted cover-up. The Audin affair shed a very harsh light on the military practices that revolted Truffaut. He even considered making a film about Audin, but then reconsidered, writing in *Clarté*, the Communist student monthly:

> The affair is so clear in itself that it needs no comment. Perhaps it could be done by sticking to the facts. But a fiction film entails looking for other people's motives, not just their political motives but their personal motives. In the end, the film would merely consist in showing a victim, a man who had been subjected to an entirely unjust and appalling fate, and, on the other, the mechanism leading up to it. This would be inappropriate, for to show something is to ennoble it. A film of this kind would satisfy neither Madame Audin nor the Audin committee, because other people's motives would have to be investigated. Which would require being interested in the agonies of conscience of—this will make you bristle—General Massu, who allowed torture in Algeria and covered it up.[104]

Freedom of expression, the struggle against censorship and torture, antimilitarism—all these causes reinforced Truffaut's convictions, but he still hesitated to take a public position. He had always hated "the good conscience of the Left," he told Helen Scott, "those who suddenly discover one day that everyone on this earth ought to have enough to eat."[105] He would overcome his reluctance thanks to the damning testimony of his friends Claude de Givray and Claude Gauteur, who served in Algeria for two years and gave him an inside description of the army's despicable conduct. On August 28, 1960, Gauteur wrote Truffaut a distressing letter that thoroughly convinced him:

> I swear to you that when you see kids that are all skin and bones, pustules and rags, creep through the electrified barbed wire to lick an empty sardine can or pick up a few centimes that an irresponsible soldier has purposely thrown in that precise spot, I swear to you that when you realize the extent to which these "full-fledged French people" have been exploited, you switch from feeling to reason, from dilettantism to vigilance, from noncommitment to receptiveness. . . . To this day I have seen only four *fellaghas* [independence fighters], beaten up, "fate unknown" (wonderful euphemism), and they disturb my sleep twice every night. What's in store for me in the next eight months of duty? The reconquest of Morocco under the orders of Comrade Soustelle? Everything's swaying, you feel you're changing; you watch yourself disintegrate, a rather repulsive sight. . . . Yesterday I murdered my first "fellouze." Disgusting. The guy had a bullet that

literally came out of his rear, he was shitting blood. He didn't die on the spot and we evacuated him by helicopter. Fortunately for him, he succumbed to his wound, because with the bundle of coded documents he was carrying, he wasn't about to lead the good life! Lady torture was getting ready for a feast! Dear old boy, I can't tell you how fed up I am; I feel I've aged ten years. It's getting rougher and rougher. I'm no more distressed by the "friendly" losses than by the "enemy" losses, for everything here is pettiness in trying to keep oneself alive, a vegetative, absurd life.[106]

## THE MANIFESTO OF THE 121

On September 13, 1960, Truffaut received the "Declaration on the right to insubordination in the Algerian war," which Dionys Mascolo sent to him: "If it meets with your approval, as we all hope, could you please send it back, with your signature, as well as the typewritten text included with it, to D. Mascolo or Marguerite Duras, 5, rue St-Benoît, Paris 6e. It's urgent, of course. Kindest regards."[107] The famous "Manifesto of the 121"—so named because of the 121 artists, writers, and academics who first signed it—had been circulating illegally since early July. It had been initiated by Dionys Mascolo, Marguerite Duras, and Maurice Blanchot, soon joined by Jean-Paul Sartre and Simone de Beauvoir. It appealed for the support of all the French soldiers who had deserted in Algeria or before being sent to fight, and also of all the French who were in some way helping the NLF. As far as the government, the army, and much of public opinion was concerned, this declaration was treasonous; it was denounced as defeatist, anarchist, and left-wing, and legally prosecuted as such. For Truffaut, the manifesto expressed his own indignation—it denounced torture, rejected the army's actions, demanded freedom of expression, and supported deserters. Some of his friends were among the original 121: Florence Malraux and Alain Resnais, Maurice Pons and Claude Sautet. Truffaut signed on September 13, and though the manifesto and the names of the signers were banned from the French press, his gesture did not go unnoticed; his former allies and friends at *Arts* and *La Parisienne* responded en masse to the 121 with their own "Manifesto of French Intellectuals," published in the October 12, 1960, issue of *Carrefour*. They denounced the "professors of treason" and proclaimed their loyalty to the French army, which was "fighting for France in Algeria" and had "been accomplishing a civilizing, social and humane mission for years." This was signed by about three hundred academics, clearly right-wing, as well as by the "hussars" Roger Nimier, Jacques Laurent, Thierry Maulnier, Michel Déon, and Antoine Blondin.

The Algerian problem had become a source of painful conflict among French intellectuals,[108] reshuffling the alliances of the postwar period. Truffaut's own public and spectacular shift from the Right to the Left pleased his friends—particularly Helen Scott and David Goodis, who sent him warm congratulations from New York. Even some erstwhile opponents gave him credit: Robert Benayoun, for example, himself a signer of the Manifesto of the 121, an "anti-Truffaut" critic of the fifties and scourge of the New Wave, wrote him in the beginning of October 1960: "I heard they were making trouble for you and I want to assure you of my complete sympathy. I knew that your outstanding qualities were honesty and sincerity. I now know to add courage."[109] Aside from Truffaut, Jacques Doniol-Valcroze and Pierre Kast were the only ones from the *Cahiers* group to sign the manifesto.

On September 28, 1960, the Council of Ministers retaliated against the signers of the manifesto. Questions were raised in the opposition newspapers: "A WITCH-HUNT WOULD BE DEADLY FOR FRENCH CINEMA" was Georges Sadoul's headline in *Les Lettres françaises* on October 6, while in the Communist weekly *France nouvelle*, Jack Ralite compared the "Gaullist repression" to a "French McCarthyism."[110] In Italy, England, and Germany, journalists raised the possibility of shattered careers for Alain Resnais, Truffaut, Françoise Sagan, Roger Blin, Alain Cuny, Simone Signoret, Laurent Terzieff, and Danièle Delorme, all of whom had signed the manifesto. Truffaut, somewhat panic-stricken, wrote to Helen Scott on October 1, 1960, dramatizing matters:

Events have worsened significantly in the last few days, politically. If you read the French newspapers, you know that the "artists" who have signed the manifesto supporting insubordination are now on an official blacklist: banned from TV and radio appearances, or from performing in subsidized theaters. For movies, it is very complicated (fortunately), for there is talk of depriving us of the automatic subsidy granted to all French films, and the different types of existing quality bonuses and advances on box-office receipts. Malraux is in charge of working out the details of this sanction. In short, it's a terrible mess! All of this has plagued me of course and prevented me from concentrating on my work. If I spoke English, I would seriously consider trying my luck in America, but I have a terrible complex about languages; there would also be possibilities in Italy, where I have lots of friends. I'm simultaneously discouraged—because every day there are new charges and threats and my shady military past as a deserter will no doubt be exploited by the right-wing papers—and stimulated, for it is enough for me to be prevented from making films and all my doubts on the subject are removed. The 121 signatures have grown to 144

over the summer, and to over 400 since, and now the police are carrying out searches to prevent the number from growing; many teachers
who have signed might be dismissed. Strange climate. It will be very
tricky for me to supervise *Tire-au-flanc* officially and I'm afraid they
will eliminate the quality bonuses on the shorts I produced. Will I
have to leave France to shoot my next film?[111]

After "hiding out" at the Colombe d'Or, Truffaut was summoned to
police headquarters, on quai des Orfèvres, to testify as soon as he returned
to Paris, on October 7, 1960. But he chose not to appear and stayed cloistered at home. Several days later, thanks to campaigns in the French and
international press, the sanctions against the signers of the manifesto were
lifted. The blacklist was abolished; de Gaulle would not be another
McCarthy. Truffaut's commitment against the Algerian war was a meaningful step in his life; it gave him legitimacy as a left-winger and reinforced his
reputation as an honest, sincere, and courageous artist. He would always
bear a deep grudge against General de Gaulle and the France of the early
sixties: "A country that can say 'yes' to de Gaulle is a country that doesn't
give a damn whether culture disappears or not, hence that doesn't give a
damn about my films,"[112] he wrote to Helen Scott on the eve of the referen-
dum to elect de Gaulle president through universal suffrage.

## THEY SHOOT AT THE PIANO PLAYER

*Shoot the Piano Player* had been a pleasant film for Truffaut to shoot, but
turned out to be a difficult and tedious one to edit. He admitted to a feeling
of "blind panic about any screenplay structured around flashbacks."[113] The
editing of *Piano Player* had been conceived around one long flashback concerning the tragic love affair between the pianist Edouard Saroyan
(Aznavour) and his wife, Thérésa (Nicole Berger). The sound track was
equally complex, with a proliferation of false leads, changing atmosphere
and songs. Claudine Bouché, the editor of films by Michel Boisrond and
Alexandre Astruc, stood in for Cécile Decugis at the last minute. Truffaut
offered to show her the rushes at the Boulogne studios. "Since François had
used playback on the set, all the rushes were postsynchronized, with no
clear preference on his part. It was a nightmarish screening, endlessly long.
François didn't utter a word. I didn't know what to say to him; I was afraid to
commit a blunder. I hadn't read the screenplay, and the whole thing seemed
strange to me, because I wasn't used to films that were so minimally structured. The sound wasn't always audible. At around one in the morning,
Truffaut asked me if this could make a film. This made me furious: How

could a director like him ask me such a question? By chance, I told him it reminded me of Queneau. I later found out that I hadn't been mistaken."[114]

When the film was shown to the actors and some friends in June 1960, and to a few journalists later on, reactions were mixed, which depressed Truffaut and undermined his confidence. Pierre Braunberger found the film puzzling. It was true that Truffaut had wanted it to stand in stark contrast to *The 400 Blows.* Rather than present another story about children or adolescents and simple emotions, he gave his audience gangsters, prostitutes, and a pianist undermined by melancholy—a pure fantasy picture, constantly alternating between tragedy and comedy, part thriller, part musical. His radical change of genre took the public by surprise.

In addition, there were problems with the censors. Truffaut had cut a sequence that might have proved offensive—of a little cat run over by the gangsters. But another scene, where Michèle Mercier gets into bed with Aznavour and exposes her breasts, was considered too risqué. Truffaut shortened the scene but refused to cut it. The censorship board remained inflexible: *Shoot the Piano Player* was banned to those under eighteen.

Truffaut eventually lost interest in his film, which was badly received when it opened over the summer in several resort towns like Vichy, Deauville, and Biarritz. He turned his thoughts to other projects, including the *Tire-au-flanc* script he was to write with his friend de Givray. Braunberger tried to motivate him: "You're the greatest director, the most intelligent man in movies, a wonderful friend, and I'm very fond of you," he wrote him from Saint-Jean-de-Luz on August 20, 1960. "I'm prepared to start all over again on the same film under the same conditions. . . ."[115] But a week or two later, when it began to look as if *Piano Player* might be a commercial flop, Braunberger's tone changed; he harassed Truffaut with telegrams, enjoining him to promote his film: "Paris is where your career will be decided for the next five years and specifically how your film will fare in the world. This is why I'm in no hurry to release it and am looking for the best way of presenting it. It's not easy: should it be called 'a comic *film noir,*' 'an eccentric *film noir,*' a 'drama of love and humor,' a 'burlesque tragedy,' a 'film where the good guys are sometimes bad and the bad guys are sometimes likable'? You're much more qualified than me for this kind of game. So pull yourself together and help me. I'm really counting on you. . . ."[116]

When all was said and done, *Shoot the Piano Player,* which opened in three Paris theaters on November 25, 1960, did not do particularly well—71,901 ticket sales after a six-week run. Its run ended on January 3, 1961, and Truffaut considered it a dreadful failure, even though this hardly jeopardized Les Films du Carrosse. Earlier that fall, Jean Cocteau had tried to cheer him up. "I can't abide your fears, my darling François," he wrote him.

"Of course it's difficult, but you couldn't do anything badly even if you went out of your way to try."[117] At least Truffaut found out who his true friends were, for far fewer people came to congratulate him than at the release of *The 400 Blows*.


## THE GREATEST SWEETHEART

In his disappointment over *Shoot the Piano Player*, François Truffaut found comfort with Jeanne Moreau, an actress he had long admired. In 1957, he had written, "[She is] the greatest sweetheart in French cinema. While gangsters and gangs kill each other, she dances in a tutu in a circus, is tortured by a sadist and makes her way through bursts of submachine-gun fire, with thoughts only of love. With trembling lips, wild hair, she ignores what others call 'morals' and lives by and for love. Messieurs, producers and directors, give her a real part and we will have a great film."[118]

Jeanne Moreau had since become a star and had appeared in several noted films, including Louis Malle's *Ascenseur pour l'échafaud* (*Elevator to the Gallows*) and *Les Amants* (*The Lovers*) and Roger Vadim's *Les Liaisons dangereuses* (*Dangerous Liaisons*). Truffaut had met her for the first time in Cannes in 1957, at the screening of *Elevator to the Gallows*. "François gave me *Jules and Jim* to read and we met regularly to discuss it," Moreau explains. "François wasn't a very talkative person, but this did not prevent a deep bond from developing between us very quickly. Usually, when people first get to know each other, they exchange a lot of memories. For us it was silences—we exchanged a lot of silences. Fortunately, there was the correspondence; we soon talked a lot by letter."[119]

In *Arts*, François Truffaut defended *The Lovers*, which caused a scandal when it was shown at the Venice Film Festival in September 1958: "Louis Malle, with Louise de Vilmorin's admirable support, has pulled off a film which is perfectly familiar and almost banal, absolutely tasteful and morally unassailable."[120] Later the same year, Jeanne Moreau made a cameo appearance in *The 400 Blows*, on Jean-Claude Brialy's arm. She became an important person in Truffaut's life, embodying professional success, the glory and myth of the star, and the free woman in love with life. For the former critic, who had long been smitten with actresses on screen, the meeting with Jeanne Moreau was like a revelation. Florence Malraux recalls, "He was enthralled by her for several years, partly because she was a star, probably the only one he knew. Sometimes François called me at midnight to ask me if I knew where Jeanne was. I was a witness to this fascination, which he didn't hide from me. But I wasn't intimate enough with him to ask questions."[121]

"I was accustomed to fame," confides Moreau, "and my life consisted of enjoying only its pleasant aspects. Moreover, my Anglo-Saxon origin constituted an additional opening to the world, to different lifestyles and cultures. I made François discover Henry James and drink champagne."[122] Generous and convivial, Jeanne Moreau had a lifestyle that was indeed very different from Truffaut's; he always went to the same restaurants and had no interest in sharing the pleasures of good food. His friendship with her would unlock his ambitious strivings. For Truffaut could think of nothing else but making a great film with the woman who had become his friend. And this great film would be *Jules and Jim.*

But the adaptation of Roché's novel wasn't quite ready. In the meantime, Truffaut considered making another film with Jeanne Moreau, *Le Bleu d'outre-tombe,* based on a novel by René-Jean Clot; it is the story of a schoolteacher who is persecuted by an entire town when the parents of her students learn that she had once been put away in a psychiatric hospital. Les Films du Carrosse had already optioned the novel, published by Gallimard, and Clot had been hired to adapt it and write the dialogue.[123] But then tragedy struck. In February 1960, Jeanne Moreau was in Blaye, near Bordeaux, for the shooting of *Moderato Cantabile* (the Peter Brook film based on the novel by Marguerite Duras, in which Moreau plays opposite Jean-Paul Belmondo) when her son Jérôme, aged ten, was seriously injured in a car accident. The child remained in a deep coma, hovering between life and death, for two weeks. To comfort her, Truffaut went to join her for several weekends. *Le Bleu d'outre-tombe* was postponed for a year and then abandoned. After *Moderato Cantabile,* Jeanne Moreau immediately started work on Antonioni's *La Notte,* while Truffaut finished the screenplay of *Jules and Jim* as quickly as possible.

## WAVERING WAVE

The failure of *Piano Player,* and the uncertainties threatening this third film, occurred in a climate that had become inimical to the New Wave. In 1960–61, the films of young directors suffered serious commercial setbacks; ticket sales for Godard's *A Woman Is a Woman* were 65,000; for Chabrol's *Les Godelureaux,* 53,000; for Demy's *Lola,* 35,000. Furthermore, Godard's second film, *Le Petit Soldat,* fought a losing battle against censorship—in September 1960, with the Algerian war raging, it was banned in France and French territories overseas. Truffaut painted a very pessimistic picture for his friend Helen Scott: "I'm not a persecuted victim, and I don't want to talk about a plot, but it's clear right now that films by young people, as soon as they stray from the norm, come up against a barrier on the part of exhibitors and the press. Such is the case for Mocky and Queneau's *Un couple,* De Broca's *Farceur (The Joker),* and also *Piano Player.* It's true that this year there are a great number of old-fashioned big French films that will stay in the theaters for a long time. It smacks of the revenge of the Old Wave— Clouzot's *La Vérité (The Truth), La Française et l'Amour* (a despicable film), Cayatte's *Le Passage du Rhin (The Crossing of the Rhine),* and even Vadim's *Et mourir de plaisir (Blood and Roses)."*[124]

Many journalists and professionals held the New Wave films responsible for the desertion of the movie theaters during the early sixties. The movement became a scapegoat, its pictures considered too intellectual or boring, and so keeping the crowds away. "The turning point," Truffaut wrote to Scott, "the switch from praise to systematic denigration, occurred with La Patellière and Michel Audiard's film, *Rue des Prairies,* which was presented as an anti–New Wave film in its publicity: 'Jean Gabin settles his accounts with the New Wave.' "[125] In *Arts,* the screenwriter Michel Audiard accused the new directors of being responsible for the public's disgust with movies and hence playing into the hands of television:

> Ah! rebellion, how novel! Truffaut went through it. A charming boy. One eye on the little anarchist's manual, the other on the Catholic ratings; one hand clenched at the future and the other hiding his bow tie. Monsieur Truffaut would like to persuade the Fouquet customers that he's a menace, a dangerous individual. This makes the connoisseurs laugh, but it impresses poor Eric Rohmer. Because, while in the old days people who had nothing to say used to get together around a teapot, today they get together in front of a screen. Truffaut applauds Rohmer, who, the previous week, applauded Pollet, who next week will applaud Godard or Chabrol. These men operate like one big family. Such has been the game of French cinema for over a year. The practical result—1960 ends with hits by Delannoy, Grangier, Patellière, Verneuil, those baldies, those hideous professionals. Yuck! This is what they've achieved, or rather what they had achieved. For it wouldn't make sense to still talk about them in the present tense. The *Nouvelle Vague* is dead. And now we know it was really more vague than new.[126]

Jacques Lanzmann wondered in *Arts:* "Does the young French cinema have its future behind it?" In 1960, the magazine *Positif* published an entire issue against the New Wave. And in February 1960, Jean Cau, Sartre's former secretary at *Les Temps modernes,* went to see "some new French films" for *L'Express.* His opinion was harsh: "I'd say that for ten years these 'young people' kept yelling at us something like, 'Oh, if only we were given a camera!' . . . We ended up taking them up on it. We gave them one. What do they have to say? Oh how amazing, nothing! What do they have in their heads? Oh how surprising, a pea! And in their hearts? Oh, how pitiful, water! I admit I'm absolutely speechless with astonishment and sadness. . . . We now know the young directors have virtually nothing to say."[127]

These accusations came at a time when Godard and Truffaut, the leaders of the new cinema, were feeling particularly vulnerable and demoralized. "Me too, I'm feeling completely lost, *caro* Francesco," Godard wrote his friend. "I'm shooting in a strange zone. I feel there's something very beautiful hovering around me. But each time I tell Coutard to pan and capture it, it's gone."[128] The ban on *Le Petit Soldat* increased his distress.

Privately, Truffaut had no hesitation about expressing some harsh criticisms about films that were labeled "New Wave" but that "badly harmed" young French cinema, "stories that group together in a few minutes everything that young directors have been justifiably reproached with for some time—amateurism, snobbishness, and eccentric and incomprehensible characters."[129] But in reply to attacks, some by journalists who had been fervent supporters of the movement two years before, he decided to counterattack. "Before, in interviews, Godard, Resnais, Malle, Chabrol, I and others, we all used to say, 'The New Wave doesn't exist, the term is meaningless.' Then I proclaimed my membership in the movement. One had to be proud of being New Wave just as one had to be proud of having been Jewish during the Occupation,"[130] he said. In spite of *Piano Player*'s lack of success, Truffaut wanted to remind people that there was a "New Wave spirit." He wrote his friend Helen Scott, "Good films are shot in rooms, with one's ass in a chair."[131]

In October 1961, Truffaut granted Louis Marcorelles a long interview in *France-Observateur*. Truffaut spoke as a director, producer, former critic, and, above all, as the leader of the New Wave:

> I recognize that there's a malaise, a bad moment to get through and a need for solutions. I attribute this malaise to the following paradox: the "new cinema's" main concern was to emancipate itself vis-à-vis the motion picture industry. Because of various pressures, films had become impersonal. We believed that everything had to be simplified so we could work freely and make *humble* films on *simple* subjects, hence the quantity of New Wave pictures whose only common feature is a sum of rejections—the rejection of extras, of theatrical intrigue, costly sets, explanatory scenes; these films often have three or four characters and very little action. Unfortunately, the linearity of these films ties in with a literary genre that very much annoys the critics and the first-run public right now, a genre that we might call "Saganism"

[i.e., from the novels by Françoise Sagan]: sports cars, bottles of scotch, short-lived love affairs, etc. The deliberate lightness of these films passes for frivolity—sometimes wrongly, sometimes rightly. The confusion lies in that the qualities of this new cinema—gracefulness, lightness, a sense of propriety, elegance, a quick pace—parallel its faults—frivolity, lack of thought, naïveté. The result? All these films, whether good or bad, work against each other! The paradox is that this praiseworthy effort at lightness has borne fruit three years too late, at a time when audiences are being lured with an offering of the most solemn, most spectacular pictures ever made. In the old days, there used to be one superproduction a year, biblical or otherwise. Today, in the wake of *Ben Hur,* there's one a month. These are antitelevision films; our touching or humorous little films, shot casually and quickly, don't stand a chance against them.[132]

For several months, Truffaut remained on the offensive. He even took up the pen again, to support some "films by friends." In *Arts,* on December 20, 1961, he published a long, favorable article about Rivette's film *Paris nous appartient* (*Paris Belongs to Us*), entitled "The New Wave Is Not at Death's Door." Later, he praised Jacques Rozier's first film, *Adieu Philippine,* and called it an "uninterrupted poem," stating it was "the clearest success of this new cinema, a film where spontaneity is all the more powerful when it is the result of long and careful work. . . . If for no other reason, the new wave had to come in order to portray characters fifteen and twenty years old—a gap of only ten years between them and the directors, just right for the directors to have gained some perspective without losing along the way the accuracy of tone that is an end in itself, as in certain Raymond Queneau novels."[133] Then it was Godard's *Vivre sa vie* (*My Life to Live*) that received Truffaut's enthusiastic support; he even admitted to Helen Scott that he had cried on seeing it, even on seeing it a second time, "and my God I don't often cry at the movies."[134]

In the defense of the New Wave, Truffaut put pressure on *Cahiers du cinéma* to adopt a more committed attitude toward the films that best represented its spirit. Under the editorship of Eric Rohmer, the yellow-covered magazine—which Truffaut was still very attached to—was rather circumspect about new French films and preferred to champion Hollywood films of the early sixties, such as those directed by Vincente Minnelli, Otto Preminger, Alfred Hitchcock, Howard Hawks, Samuel Fuller, and Franck Tashlin, thus resisting any systematic, militant defense of the New Wave. First surprised, Truffaut became indignant. With the support of Doniol-Valcroze and Godard, he saw to it (not without a bad conscience, and later even remorse) that Rivette replaced Rohmer as the editor in chief of

*Cahiers.* From then on, the magazine would openly defend the films of the New Wave.[135]

Truffaut also strongly supported Janine Bazin's and André S. Labarthe's project for a series of made-for-television portraits called *Cinéastes de notre temps* (*Directors of Our Day*). In January 1962, Janine Bazin contacted the research services of the RTF [Radio Télévision Française] headed by Pierre Schaeffer, with the idea of giving young New Wave directors the opportunity to tape long interviews with the directors whom they regard as their masters. Janine Bazin included *Cahiers du cinéma* critic André S. Labarthe in her project, as well as François Truffaut. A trial film was shot in February 1962 in Rome, in which Truffaut interviewed Roberto Rossellini at length on his films and his conception of cinema; the trial was enough to convince Pierre Schaeffer to gamble on *Cinéastes de notre temps*. The first portrait was of Luis Buñuel and was shot in Spain over the summer of 1963 by Labarthe and a television crew directed by Robert Valey. The series was launched; fifty-odd portraits followed one after the other throughout the sixties. Truffaut himself would be honored in 1965; his portrait, *François Truffaut: L'esprit critique* (*François Truffaut: A Critical Mind*) was directed by Jean Chartier and consisted of interviews intercut with excerpts from his first films.

## THE WHIRLWIND OF LIFE

Truffaut couldn't afford another flop after *Piano Player.* Les Films du Carrosse's financial situation was not very solid. And since Ignace Morgenstern's death, Truffaut, with the help of Marcel Berbert, was solely responsible for his little production company. "I have the additional responsibility of not squandering his widow's money and that matters," he wrote to Helen Scott. "I'm dreadfully tense right now. This is certainly partly out of pride, vanity, careerism and God knows what other dishonorable but irresistible drives: I desperately want *Jules and Jim* to be an absolute success, not like *Piano Player.*"[136]

In September 1960, Truffaut spent two weeks alone at the Colombe d'Or, in Saint-Paul-de-Vence, reworking the adaptation of *Jules and Jim,* for he was dissatisfied with the version he had presented to Henri-Pierre Roché three years earlier. Taking inspiration from the *Carnets* (*Notebooks*) which Roché had kept for nearly sixty years, starting in 1901, and the triangular affair of Helen Hessel, Franz Hessel, and Roché, Truffaut refocused the screenplay on Catherine's simultaneous love for two men, two very dissimilar friends—Jim, the cultured, elegant Frenchman and womanizing dandy (Roché's self-portrait), and Jules, the more naïve, generous, gentle German,

whom Catherine would marry and who would become the father of her little girl, Sabine.

For one weekend, Jeanne Moreau joined Truffaut in Saint-Paul-de-
Vence. The film would clearly reflect their relationship, as Truffaut admitted to Helen Scott: *"Jules and Jim* will be a hymn to life and death, a
demonstration through joy and sadness of the impossibility of any love combination apart from the couple."[137] But the screenplay, too faithful to the
novel, was still wobbly. So Truffaut decided to hire Jean Gruault, whose
recent theatrical adaptation of Diderot's *La Religieuse* (*The Nun*) had very
much impressed him. Gruault was instantly attracted to Roché's novel and
accepted Truffaut's offer. In January 1961, the two men set to work structur-
ing a story focused on this pure *"amour à trois,"* a term that they planned to
use as the film's subtitle.[138]

Truffaut chose Henri Serre to portray Jim; he was a young, as-yet-
unknown actor who was performing a comedy duo at the Cheval d'Or
Cabaret. Truffaut was struck by his physical resemblance to the youthful
Roché: Tall and thin, he had a deep, gentle voice, and terse, rapid gestures.
Choosing someone to portray Jules was trickier. Truffaut wanted a foreign
actor, for he was convinced that an accent and hesitant speech would help
make the character moving. At one point, he considered Marcello Mastroianni, which would have facilitated an Italian coproduction. But out of
faithfulness to the book, Truffaut finally opted for a German-speaking actor,
Oskar Werner. A famous stage actor in Germany and Austria, he was the
director of the Vienna Burgtheater and had received much acclaim for his
role as Hamlet in the early fifties. Though he had not had any big screen
parts, Truffaut had been very struck by his appearance in Max Ophuls's *Lola
Montès*. Contacted through Marcel Ophuls, Werner accepted Truffaut's
offer, after an interview in the presence of Jeanne Moreau. She was the real
star of the film, and Truffaut was convinced that he was offering her a part
commensurate with her talent. Jean Moreau was at the height of her fame,
but she had been slightly frustrated by her last two films, particularly *La
Notte,* which she hadn't much liked. Truffaut picked up on this when he
stated his desire for *Jules and Jim* to contrast with *La Notte.* "Antonioni had
exploited the 'Bette Davis' side of Jeanne Moreau—the sullen face; she
never laughed. I wanted to lift her features up; she has a surprising laugh. In
fact there's a scene in the film when she says, 'But I also know how to smile.'
And then you see she can have another face."[139]

For Jeanne Moreau, this first real collaboration with Truffaut partook, as
she puts it, of those "ineluctable harmonies that some call chance." "After
the fulfillment I had experienced with Louis Malle, I was a bit of an orphan
as far as movies were concerned. And sharing such a wonderful debut with
François was something that reconciled me with myself."[140] In the part of

Catherine, Moreau would portray Truffaut's vision of the supreme woman, fragile and *fatale*, intelligent and lively, funny and tragic, free and haughty, a woman who followed the impulses of desire to the bitter end. The fusion between the fictional character and the actress seemed obvious, and Truffaut wanted to be a witness to it.

Before the preproduction and shooting of *Jules and Jim*, Truffaut went to stay with Jeanne Moreau on several occasions, in the house she owned at La Garde-Freinet. "It was a refuge for François, not only because of my presence, but also because of the people I had working for me, including one woman called Anna, who was wonderful and looked after him. This place suited him. Usually, I sensed it was linked to personal and emotional crises, though he didn't spell it out. He could read or write; he felt protected by our friendship."[141] There, Truffaut saw Jean-Louis Richard again, the actress's former husband, whom he had met a few months before at a private screening of *The 400 Blows*. He was very struck by Jean-Louis Richard's qualities—his devastating humor, his rejection of fashion, and especially his playful personality. The two men became friends, and immediately discussed the possibility of several common projects. Above all, they had a lot of fun together. Jeanne Moreau's relationship with her former husband was one of friendship and great tenderness; she admired him and cared about his opinion on everything that concerned her professional life. Richard was friends with Danièle and Serge Rezvani, who also had a house at La Garde-Freinet. Naturally, he introduced them to Truffaut, who then had the idea of including a song by Rezvani in *Jules and Jim* (or rather a song by Cyrus Bassiak, the name he used as a composer, though in the film he acted under the name Boris Bassiak), "Le Tourbillon de la vie (The Whirlwind of Life)," sung by Jeanne Moreau.

At La Garde-Freinet, the group of friends banded together and enjoyed great merriment. With Jeanne Moreau, Truffaut experienced moments of euphoria, the most harmonious, youthful moments of his life, and the most amorous as well. "After dinner, Jeanne would sit under the linden trees and start singing," recalls Florence Malraux, who was an assistant on the film, her only Truffaut film, after which she began her long collaboration with Alain Resnais. "There was already something of *Jules and Jim*."[142] Truffaut was caught up in this ambiance, so that sometimes he joined in the singing. "François and I used to perfect our song numbers together," says Jean-Louis Richard. "We used to sing Trenet's 'Le Soleil a rendez-vous avec la lune,' something he could never have done in public. Sometimes we also disguised ourselves."[143] *Jules and Jim*, one of Truffaut's most solemn films, took shape in these lighthearted and happy surroundings. "It was a time when everything was possible and nothing was solemn," says Jeanne Moreau, "as though François were discovering joie de vivre: Serge's songs, car trips, going to the market. . . . Time was devoted to reading, to making discoveries, rather than foreseeing the future or making ambitious plans. This was due to the house, but it was also a true liberation of the body."[144]

## THIS PURE TRIANGULAR LOVE

Once the screenplay was completed, François Truffaut was struck with a case of nerves as the shoot date approached. "We didn't have a distributor yet," Marcel Berbert recalls. "The only financing we had came from SEDIF. Truffaut asked me, 'What should we do? Should we drop it or continue?' I answered, 'Let's continue!' " Berbert was aware of the financial risks, having noticed how hesitant distributors became upon reading about the project. Most of them had no faith in the film. " 'What kind of subject is this? A man stands idly by while his wife is making love to another man?' Some of the reactions we got were incredible; they really annoyed François and me,"[145] Berbert says.

As a result *Jules and Jim* would be made very inexpensively, before the budget had been fully accounted for. Truffaut completed the casting with Marie Dubois and the little Sabine Haudepin. Locations were hastily found and a large number of scenes would be shot in places loaned by friends. Hence on April 10, 1961, the first day of the shoot, they all convened at the Moulin d'Andé in Saint-Pierre-du-Vauvray, in Normandy, where Truffaut had filmed the last scenes of *The 400 Blows*. Truffaut used a minimal crew, about fifteen people, which was what he liked. To set his mind at rest, he first shot a few secondary scenes. He covered himself with multiple takes— seven on average for each scene at the beginning of the filming, as opposed to three during the last weeks. Finally, to create an atmosphere that he felt would be propitious to this story of amorous excitement, Truffaut requested that all the actors be present at all times, even if they weren't in the scenes being filmed. But the early stages of the shoot were difficult because of the many location and set changes (Normandy, followed by Ermenonville, Paris, and Beaumont-sur-Oise for several World War I scenes in the trenches). The days were clouded by a host of problems—Marie Dubois twisted her ankle; Jeanne Moreau had the beginnings of a sore throat; Henri Serre wounded his left heel in a trench, so that he was tense and not very credible in the boxing sequence, which was shot two days later at the Lamotte gymnasium on rue Louis-le-Grand.

Thanks to Jeanne Moreau, Truffaut gradually regained confidence. "There was harmony in our work, the idea of a tandem—riding on the same bike and at the same rhythm." Truffaut himself acknowledged this: "Jeanne Moreau gave me courage each time I had doubts. Her qualities as an actress and as a woman made Catherine real before our very eyes, made her plausible, crazy, possessive, passionate, but above all adorable, i.e. worthy of adoration."[146] Motivated, focused, and happy during the shoot, "full of generosity, ardor, a feeling of collusion, and an understanding for human frailty,"[147] Jeanne Moreau strongly believed in the film and in Catherine, the character she was portraying. Liliane David, who stopped by the set, recalls a very unusual, quasi-passionate ambience: "It was complicated because everyone was in love with Jeanne Moreau—the producer Raoul Lévy, who came by unexpectedly, Henri Serre, François himself. He was literally fascinated by her. The ambiance was euphoric at times and at times painful, almost tragic."[148] Jeanne Moreau realized that shoots are always intense, collaborative moments, and even more intense when the picture depicts amorous passion. The relationship between a director and his actress is almost always altered. "It's an extraordinarily intimate exchange, which can lead to a romantic relationship, and sometimes to a much more complex, subtle relationship which is difficult to imagine and which is akin to artistic creation,"[149] Moreau confides.

Oskar Werner and François Truffaut maintained an excellent relationship during the filming; the Austrian actor turned out to be cheerful, perceptive, focused, and very friendly. The cast and crew had dinner together every evening. "François usually sat at the end of the table, and some evenings he didn't open his mouth," Florence Malraux recalls. "He sort of relied on me, asked me to handle Oskar Werner, to whom I was teaching some French, which he spoke poorly. Werner sang some Mozart in the car. He was wonderful."[150]

In May, the cast and crew moved near Saint-Tropez, and afterward near Saint-Paul-de-Vence, to shoot a few happy *ménage à trois* sequences. Marcel Berbert took this opportunity to go to Cannes, while the festival was in full swing, in the hope of finding a distributor. "In extremis, I was able to sell *Jules and Jim* to Cinédis for 20 million old francs, which wasn't much money for a film that cost seven times that amount."[151] But this money was vitally needed to finance the last weeks of filming. The most important scenes were shot from mid-May to early June in Jules and Catherine's large German-Style chalet in Molkenrein, which is located in the Vosges. Some of the sequences were tricky. A camera crane and a helicopter were required for the train scenes taken at the Landenbach-Vieil Armand station, while Jim and Catherine's lengthy mutual confessions had to be shot in "day for night," with a special filter that would re-create a nocturnal atmosphere.

In mid-June, after the cremation scene of Catherine and Jim had been shot at the crematorium in the Strasbourg cemetery, the entire cast and crew returned to Paris for a few additional sequences. Then everyone separated sadly; Oskar Werner returned to Vienna for an opera; Henri Serre went back to his cabaret comedy duo with Jean-Pierre Suc; Jeanne Moreau got ready to shoot *Eva,* directed by Joseph Losey. The relationship between her and Truffaut gradually changed over the filming, from a tumultuous passion to a tender and affectionate friendship—enduring, strong, and vital. An impossible love had finally found an aesthetic form—this film they had made together, which the director summarized to Helen Scott as follows: "In spite of some scenes that didn't come off that I'll cut or maybe fix up, I think the characters are more alive than in my other films. It's a risqué melodrama yet very moral."[152]

As soon as the filming was over, Truffaut was worried once again, for the first rough cut of *Jules and Jim* was two and a half hours long. The film therefore had to be tightened up in the editing. In contrast to *Shoot the Piano Player,* with its free tone and unbridled rhythm, *Jules and Jim* played on a certain formal classicism, as if to emphasize its daring subject. "What seems acceptable today, a woman in love with two men and the lover of both, was not so unobjectionable thirty years ago," says Claudine Bouché, who edited Truffaut's film. "We recorded part of the narration to measure its duration. Then we recorded it in its entirety, with the voice of the actor Michel Subor, and we edited it with the picture. We got Georges Delerue's music, which was very beautiful. When we listened to the mix of music and voice-over, things got complicated. Sometimes the fortes were too loud and covered the narration. And François wouldn't consider giving up these musical moments, which were so beautiful and lyrical. For the scene where Catherine picks Jim up at the station after the war and takes him back to the chalet, there was very beautiful music. To work in Michel Subor's voice, the narration had to be rerecorded in relation to the music."[153] She also confirms the free and easy style of the filming: "When Jeanne Moreau sings 'Le Tourbillon de la vie,' there's a moment when she makes a gesture because she's made a mistake and switched two verses. This is the take François and I chose. Being very professional, Jeanne didn't ask for the take to be interrupted; she simply made this gesture to indicate she had made a mistake. I knew François would accept this take, because Jeanne's gesture gives her even more charm."[154]

In need of an independent opinion, Truffaut called in Jean Aurel, the former *Arts* journalist turned filmmaker, whom he trusted completely when it came to editing or narrative structure. "I had just made a film, *14-18,* with a narration that Truffaut admired," says Jean Aurel. "He wanted to make sure the voice-over matched the picture, that it corresponded to the image, so the film would be effective. The narration cast the film in a sort of fictional past. This meant a lot to François. The film didn't exist without the narration. We watched it several times, and I made a few suggestions for moving the voice in relation to the picture. It was an interesting experiment, which made it possible to space out a sentence in relation to the picture."[155] "Showing a film to Aurel is like calling in a plumber who would not just repair a leak, but also locate it. He comes in, watches the film, takes notes in the dark, and then we talk"[156]—this is how Truffaut would describe the person whom he would thereafter always turn to at the final-edit stage of his films. As for Aurel, he defines himself as an "adviser" specializing in the "moving around of sequences,"[157] valuable work, requiring both critical judgment and the ability to imagine new solutions. Thanks to Aurel, *Jules and Jim* acquired its definitive shape, particularly the voice-over narration, which takes up nearly fifteen minutes of the sound track.

During the whole four months required for the editing and postsynchronization of *Jules and Jim,* Truffaut was haunted by a relentless, irrational fear of death. Though he was not even thirty, he identified, somehow, with Henri-Pierre Roché: "I tried to make the film as though I were a very old person, and at the end of my life. It was probably the first time I really experienced a fear of death,"[158] he said. In *Jules and Jim* as in *Shoot the Piano Player,* melancholy ultimately takes possession of all the characters. "This is the third time it's happened to me—starting a film with the thought that it's going to be amusing and realizing along the way that it will be saved only by its sadness,"[159] he wrote to Father Jean Mambrino on the eve of *Jules and Jim's* first sound-mixing session. Exhausted, he realized he had made his most difficult and daring film. But he felt confident, convinced he had given a wonderful part to a great actress—Jeanne Moreau—whose friendship he had won in the process.

## THE WOMEN CRY

Truffaut was much encouraged by the first private screenings of *Jules and Jim* before its release. His close friends found the film moving and his writer friends—including Queneau, Audiberti, and Jules Roy—were enthusiastic. "The women cry, many of the men are slightly bored. It's my first deliberately boring film (1 hour and 50 minutes). Frankly, thanks to the three actors, it holds up better than my previous films,"[160] he wrote to Helen Scott.

The response that meant the most to him was that of Jean Renoir, who was very moved by the film. Truffaut kept the letter Renoir had sent him from Hollywood in February 1962 tucked in the inside pocket of his suit jacket for a long time:

> I wanted to tell you that *Jules and Jim* seems to me the most accurate expression of contemporary French society that I've seen on-screen. By situating your film in 1914 you gave your depiction an even more exact tone, for the birth of today's way of thinking and behavior dates back to cars trimmed with gleaming brass. The hint of immorality which apparently crossed the mind of some confreres seems inexplicable to me. The observation of a consequence can't be immoral. Rain wets; fire burns. The resulting wetness and burn have nothing to do with morality. In a few years we've gone from one civilization to another. The leap is more formidable than the one made by our forefathers between the Middle Ages and the Renaissance. For the Knights of the Round Table, sentimental adventures were the subject of great fun, for the Romantics, the pretext for a flood of tears. For the characters in *Jules and Jim* it is something else again, and your film contributes in making us understand what this "something else" might be. It is very important for us men to know where we stand with women, and equally important for women to know where they stand with men. You help dissipate the fog that envelops the essence of this question. For this, and for many other reasons, I thank you with all my heart.[161]

Cocteau saw in *Jules and Jim* the revelation and recognition of a great literary figure hitherto unknown to the public: "He was the most delicate and noble soul,"[162] he wrote concerning Henri-Pierre Roché, who had been one of his friends. Denise Roché's reaction was of course very important to Truffaut: "I wish I could have seen your *Jules and Jim* with a fresh eye," she wrote him. "But in spite of wanting to create a vacuum I watched your film as though I myself were Pierre—and I know he would have felt great joy and a passionate interest. I am quite moved. In any case, I spent an extremely interesting two hours, steeped in freshness, poetry, innocence, impetuous ardor and anxiety. Yes, Pierre would have been very happy."[163] But the most moving and most unexpected response reached Truffaut at the end of January 1962. "I am, at 75, what is left of Kathe, the awesome heroine of Pierre Roché's novel, *Jules and Jim*. You can imagine the curiosity with which I waited to see your film on the screen. On January 24, I ran to the movie theater. Sitting in that dark auditorium, in the dread of veiled resemblances and more or less irritating parallels, I was soon swept along, gripped by the magical power—yours and Jeanne Moreau's—with which you revived what had been lived through blindly. The fact that Pierre Roché was able to tell the story of the three of us and kept it very close to the actual events, has nothing miraculous about it. But what disposition in you, what affinity, could enlighten you to the point of making the essence of our intimate emotions perceptible? As far as this goes, I'm your only authentic judge, since the other two witnesses, Pierre and Franz, are no longer here to express their 'yes' to you. Affectionately yours, dear Monsieur Truffaut."[164] This magnificent letter was signed by Helen Hessel, Roché's real-life heroine.

Nearly all the critics sung the praises of the film. A CELEBRATION OF TENDERNESS AND INTELLIGENCE was the headline of Jean-Louis Bory's review in *Arts*. "The first engaging film of the New Wave," admitted René Cortade in *L'Express,* while Georges Sadoul gave his column in *Lettres françaises* the title "Making Others Feel Good." The large-circulation papers—*Le Monde, Combat,* and *Le Figaro*—all concurred. The only negative article was Bernard Dort's in *France-Observateur;* he panned the films and the personality of François Truffaut: "Instead of an elderly man's account of a dreamily remembered youth, Truffaut's *Jules and Jim* is the film of a young man gambling on old age. A film of a New Wave which, with the help of a star, winks allusively at 'old fogeys.' "[165]

Though the critical response was excellent, Truffaut feared censorship, for he was aware that this *amour à trois* could be considered shocking to those of conventional morals. Unfortunately, his fears were well founded. After screening the film on November 24, 1961, the monitoring committee, whose president was Henri de Segogne, authorized its distribution but restricted it to audiences over eighteen, a severe handicap for the film's commercial prospects. Truffaut immediately appealed to have the restriction lifted. But despite prestigious testimonials by Renoir, Cocteau, Armand Salacrou, Pierre Lazareff, and Alain Resnais, who all vouched for the film's "nonimmoral character," the decision was upheld. *Jules and Jim* started its exclusive Paris engagement on January 24, 1964; it had a run of almost three months and an audience of 210,000 people, meaning it was a relative success. Truffaut then threw his energies into the promotion of the film, traveling all around the provinces to show it to full and attentive houses. The regional press no longer welcomed him as an *enfant terrible* or ambitious youngster, but as a serious, human, timid, polite filmmaker.

Alain Vannier, who had met Marcel Berbert in the days when he worked at Cocinor, was in charge of selling the foreign rights to *Jules and Jim.* "I was instantly enthusiastic, although the screenings were really going rather badly,"[166] he says. Vannier immediately called the boss of the English company Gala Film Distribution, which he represented in Paris. "Buy the picture!" replied Kenneth Rive, who caught a plane from London to sign a contract with Les Films du Carrosse. Later, during his first trip to the United States, Alain Vannier spoke highly of *Jules and Jim* to two Harvard students, Cyrus Harvey and Brian Halliday, who ran a film society and had created a small independent distribution company, Janus Films, in Cambridge, Massachusetts. So on February 20, 1962, SEDIF, acting on behalf of its coproduction with Carrosse, signed a contract with Janus Films for the U.S. distribution of *Jules and Jim,* "excluding Puerto Rico" but including "ships flying U.S. colors," with a guaranteed minimum sum of forty thousand dollars on American box-office receipts. From that time on, Alain Vannier was put in charge of the foreign sales of Truffaut's films, except for his American coproductions (primarily with United Artists). Very close to Gérard Lebovici, the head of Artmédia, Vannier would become an important associate in the production and financing system that Truffaut set up, with Marcel Berbert's help, in the course of his career.

*Jules and Jim* was banned outright in Italy on June 22, 1962. Truffaut went to Rome to support the public protest orchestrated by Dino de Laurentiis, the distributor of the film; the protest was also supported by such illustrious intellectuals as Alberto Moravia and Roberto Rossellini. On July 2, the ban was lifted, and *Jules and Jim* opened to critical acclaim in Rome, Turin, and Milan on September 3.

Truffaut traveled to many major European cities with his film—Brussels, London, Munich, Berlin, and Stockholm—and later to the Mar del Plata festival in Argentina, to Rio and Puerto Rico, and finally to New York. These efforts bore fruit: The film was a success in Germany, as well as in England, Belgium, and Sweden. But for Truffaut, the New York release was of vital importance. He arrived in New York with Madeleine on April 11, 1962, after attending the Mar del Piata festival. They were welcomed by Helen Scott, who had organized everything according to her friend's wishes; he had expressed a desire to meet such American film directors as Joshua Logan, Sidney Lumet, John Cassavetes, and Arthur Penn. The day after his arrival, the French Film Office in New York threw a reception in his honor. Truffaut mentioned a project that was dear to his heart—establishing a French Cinema Week in New York, with unreleased New Wave films such as *Lola, A Woman Is a Woman, My Life to Live,* and *Shoot the Piano Player.* The idea was realized several years later by the critic Richard Roud when he made this a part of the New York Film Festival. On April 17, Truffaut was due in Cannes as a member of the festival jury, but *Jules and Jim* opened in New York on April 25, where it enjoyed an exclusive four-week engagement and received glowing reviews. Jo Morgenstern (no relation to Madeleine) hailed the "Return of Movie 'Boy Wonder' " on the front page of the *Herald Tribune,* while Bosley Crowther in the *New York Times,* Andrew Sarris in the *Village Voice,* Archer Winsten in the *New York Post,* and Paul Beckley in the *New York Herald Tribune* all heralded *Jules and Jim* as one of the most original and engaging works in French cinema.

## A MUSICAL INFATUATION

In June 1961, François Truffaut accepted a commission to direct a short subject produced by Pierre Roustang, which he promised to deliver at the beginning of the following year. This was the first and last time he would bow to the requirements of a commission. His main motivation was to follow up on the adventures of Antoine Doinel. Roustang wanted five young directors from different countries each to make a short film on the theme of adolescent love as part of an episode film to be entitled *Love at Twenty*. Truffaut recommended Marcel Ophuls and Renzo Rossellini (Roberto's nephew) to Roustang, who had already recruited the Polish film director Andrzej Wajda and the Japanese director Shintaro Ishihara.

Truffaut drew on his youthful memories for the screenplay of *Antoine and Colette,* essentially taking his inspiration from his thwarted love for Liliane Litvin in the very early fifties, but he changed a few details. For instance, Antoine and Colette, his two protagonists, meet at a youth concert, not at the Cinémathèque; and Antoine works in record manufacturing, not as a factory worker. Though he had accepted the commission with enthusiasm, Truffaut was exhausted by the shooting and promotion of *Jules and Jim.* "I'm very bored at the thought of making this short film," he admitted to Helen Scott. "I would have liked to leave *Jules and Jim* with renewed virginity. I haven't prepared anything, I have no script, no notes, no ideas, I'm exhausted, dried up, sterilized."[167]

He placed an announcement in *Cinémonde* to cast the part of Colette: "François Truffaut seeks fiancée for Jean-Pierre Léaud and for *Love at Twenty.* Jean-Pierre's partner must be a real girl, not a Lolita, not a leather-jacket type, not a little young woman. She must be simple and cheerful, and have a good average culture. If too 'sexy' please abstain." He immediately received a note from Mario Brun, a journalist at *Nice-Matin,* who sent along a picture of a young girl from Nice, Marie-France Pisier, whom he had noticed in an amateur theatrical troupe. Truffaut had planned to schedule his auditions in the beginning of January 1962, just before the start of the shoot. In the meantime, he had wanted to stay at the Colombe d'Or for a few days around mid-December in order to rest and finish writing the screenplay. He had lunch in Saint-Paul-de-Vence with Mario Brun, who introduced him to Marie-France Pisier. He made her read for the part that very afternoon. Already under her spell, he asked to see her again the following day.

On returning to Paris, Truffaut continued casting. The two adolescents from *The 400 Blows* had matured. Jean-Pierre Léaud, whom Truffaut had lodged and educated over the last three years, was more disciplined, and also more melancholic. Patrick Auffay was cast as René again, Antoine's friend. In *Antoine and Colette,* they meet, talk, reminisce about an incident in *The 400 Blows,* and evaluate their respective chances as suitors, Antoine with Colette, René with his cousin. After choosing Rosy Varte and François Darbon to play Colette's parents, Truffaut scheduled auditions for the part of the young girl. Two candidates stood out—Marina Bazanov, the granddaughter of Helen Hessel, the real-life Kathe of Roché's novel, and Marie-France Pisier. More joyful, more charming, and also more casual, Pisier fit the character better. During the screen tests, she recalls, "he didn't really look at me, he was only interested in my voice. François always attached great importance to voices and their rhythm. For this he kept urging me, 'Faster, faster, Jeanne used to say it faster.' He liked the fact that I could speak quickly, and I later realized the importance this had for the character in the film: the girl had to be more comfortable with words than Léaud."[168]

The filming of *Antoine and Colette* began on January 15 with a small crew of Carrosse regulars grouped around Raoul Coutard and Suzanne Schiffman. It lasted only a week and took place near Place Clichy and Batignolles, with a few sequences shot in the Pleyel concert hall. "I recall a very important scene, the scene of 'musical infatuation,'" Marie-France Pisier remembers, "one of the first we shot. We had to make a series of incredibly specific gestures, which François insisted on, probably because they had a very intimate resonance for him. He said to Jean-Pierre, 'Turn your head to the side, no not too much,' and to me, 'Grasp the chain you're wearing around your neck, lift it up to your mouth, not twice, just once, do it again, cross your legs, not twice, just once, more decisively. . . .' It was really like a musical score."[169]

In the end, the shoot went well. It was well paced, lively, and sometimes improvisational, which suited Léaud's and Pisier's acting. Truffaut ended up liking this picture, which had initially bored him, and even regretted that he hadn't made it into a feature. But the film into which this episode was inserted was not particularly good. Truffaut supervised it, working with Claudine Bouché, whose editing table was at Les Films du Carrosse. "The episodes were all too long," she says, "We had to make cuts and find an order for them."[170] Marcel Ophuls's sketch was the only one that Truffaut liked. Jean Aurel was in charge of finding elements that would link the five episodes. He decided on a song with the recurrent theme of "love at twenty" (sung by Xavier Depraz), and photos by Cartier-Bresson. The film was greeted with indifference and closed after two weeks. Truffaut was quite disappointed, for he had grown to like his surrogate's timid, fruitless loves. The tone for the "Antoine Doinel adventures" had now been set, a lighter, more whimsical and melancholic one than could be anticipated from *The 400 Blows.*

Truffaut had already become enamored of Marie-France Pisier during preproduction on the film—so much so that he wanted to leave Madeleine and the children. He confided in Helen Scott, in an unusually intimate letter: "I'm very tired, very much on edge and sad, because I'm terribly in love with a young girl who is seventeen and a half; just for her, to make myself available for her, I'm going to bring tragedy around me and it's distressing. Not counting the fact that I might be ruining the next two or three years for her too. Dear Helen, I'm up to my neck in tragedy and havoc. You'd like the girl; she's modern, very feminist, left-wing, Sartre-Beauvoir, very hardworking (political economics in order to become a legal adviser) and an actress since I met her when I was looking for a girl to play opposite Jean-Pierre. This girl is very frank, direct, very strong and at the same time very childlike. She'll be very tough with me, that I know . . . ; we'll fight, I'm sure; I admire her enormously and I'm very distraught."[171]

Indeed, on December 25, 1961, Truffaut left the apartment on rue du Conseiller Collignon and moved into a hotel. He would return a month later. But for Madeleine, his unexpected departure was a trauma. At first, he didn't mention Marie-France Pisier, of whose existence Madeleine was completely unaware; instead, he talked about their disagreements, his need for solitude, and "the hypocrisy involved in staying together."[172] *Jules and Jim* (the filming itself as well as the subject of the film) made him come to the painful realization that he found living as a couple at once indispensable and unbearable.

At the beginning of 1962, Truffaut believed his breakup with Madeleine was virtually inevitable. This saddened him immensely, as did the prospect of being separated from his daughters, Laura and Eva. And once he had moved out, he grew fearful of committing himself to Marie-France Pisier, bewildered by this girl of seventeen who was now giving him a hard time. To make matters worse, Jeanne Moreau had fallen in love with someone else and was neglecting him, as he angrily reported in a letter to Helen Scott.[173] As always in his periods of romantic depression, Truffaut immersed himself in his work; the shooting and editing of *Antoine and Colette* occupied him full-time.

After a month-long "truancy," a shamefaced Truffaut decided to return home. His reconciliation with Madeleine was sealed with a journey: She accompanied him on a business trip to the United States in April. The girls were left in the care of their governess, Sylvia, while the couple traveled with Marcel Berbert to the Mar del Plata festival (where *Jules and Jim* was awarded the prize for best direction), and then to Rio and New York. Truffaut was visibly bolstered and relaxed, thinking he had resolved his romantic crisis. Several months later, after spending a quiet summer with Madeleine at the Colombe d'Or, he seemed to have rediscovered the virtues of marriage, even if professional anxieties assailed him once again: "Right now I'm going through a period where my morale is low," he wrote to Helen Scott on October 18, 1962, "for no reason, really, since things are going very well with Madeleine and the two girls are wonderful; like a bureaucrat, I come home every evening at around six and play with them for two hours. I no longer go to the office in the morning for the same reason."[174] The "pure triangular love" had temporarily been dispelled by conjugal happiness regained.

## THE TRIAL OF THE NEW WAVE

In early 1962, French cinema was in a new crisis. Not only had attendance at movie houses plummeted since the end of the fifties, but so had the New Wave euphoria. It was once again very difficult for a beginner to set up his own business, and the movement, which had been heterogeneous from the start, had now been fragmented by rivalries. A mentality of "everyone for himself" sometimes developed into outright confrontation; war was declared, a prelude to what the large-circulation papers had been calling the "death of the New Wave" since the beginning of 1962. "I'm therefore depressed for no good reason," Truffaut wrote to Helen Scott later that year. "Business is not going too badly, in spite of the crisis we're facing; I'm among the five or six directors whose forthcoming film people have faith in and *Jules and Jim* is still doing very well in France, Belgium and Italy. You're right, dear Helen, when you say I want it all, but for the time being, I myself don't even know what I'm missing."[175]

This crisis revolved around a specific conflict in which Truffaut was one of the main protagonists. The trouble had started back in 1960, with *La Bride sur le cou*, which was to have been Jean Aurel's first film, starring Brigitte Bardot. On December 4, 1960, only three days after shooting started, the producers brought in Roger Vadim, Bardot's ex-husband, to supervise the filming. On December 12, Aurel understood that this was not mere supervision but outright replacement. He left the set, denouncing the behavior of his star and Vadim. They defended themselves, citing Aurel's inability to direct Bardot.

Truffaut, siding with his friend Aurel, exposed the situation in a vitriolic article in the December 22, 1960, issue of *France-Observateur*. He upheld the "moral code of the film auteur" and denounced Vadim's "unfraternal" attitude. The article was perceived, of course, as an internal family quarrel. Truffaut's conclusion amounted to a strict warning: "The fact is, as far as I'm concerned, Roger Vadim now belongs to that group of film people who are capable of anything and of whom one should be wary." In addition, twenty-seven directors signed a declaration in support of Aurel, upholding the rights of "the film auteur" and the freedom of each person "to improvise at will on the set"—two fundamental principles for the New Wave. Vadim counterattacked by taking Truffaut to court for libel.

The affair led to a sensational trial that opened on January 29, 1962, before the Seventeenth Magistrate's Court in Paris. In the Vadim camp were Louis Malle, Michel Subor, and Brigitte Bardot, who was there in person to certify her good faith and discredit Aurel's "cinematic improvisations." In the Truffaut camp were Resnais, Melville, Godard, Chabrol, Kast, Sautet, and de Broca. After a farcical session, with Bardot pouting in the witness box and Godard banished from the courtroom for "insulting a witness," the judge ruled in favor of Vadim and sentenced Truffaut to pay him one franc in damages.

The sensational atmosphere surrounding the trial, as created by the large-circulation dailies, was revealing of the crisis of confidence at the time—the crisis in French cinema generally and in the New Wave specifically. It marked the end of an era, the (ephemeral) reign of the young directors. For the press, the producers, the public, the new French cinema was dead and buried.

Truffaut escaped the general negative climate; thanks to *Jules and Jim*, he was one of the five or six directors with a future. Paradoxically, this exceptional status was probably the main cause of his depression. The death of the New Wave gave rise to strong feelings of guilt: "I'm in the process of becoming a bastard. But I'm not yet hardened enough and it's very difficult, very painful,"[176] he confessed to Helen Scott. His feelings were exacerbated by the fact that he had to relinquish all coproduction projects and concentrate solely on his own films. It was during this period, for example, that he gave up the idea of producing Rossellini's *Socrates;* his reasons were irrefutable, but he realized he was disappointing a close friend, and he was disappointed in himself. "The truth is," he wrote Rossellini with a heavy heart, "we don't have the same ideas on how to make movies. I find everything you do good, right and logical as long as you're doing it. If I were to meddle, we would be heading for catastrophe."[177]

Family crisis and professional difficulties and rifts combined to make Truffaut feel isolated. He was successful, but the others had failed; the contrast caused quite a number of misunderstandings and accusations. Some protégés, who had been discovered and financed by the director of *The 400 Blows,* reacted with great violence when he withdrew into himself. "You have gone over to the powerful, we remain poor,"[178] wrote Michel Varesano, a director of shorts who had hoped to find a producer in Truffaut. Even Robert

Lachenay, his childhood friend and long-standing confidant, felt forsaken, and he expressed his bitterness in a moving appeal in the spring of 1962:

> I'm sorry to feel a kind of coldness and embarrassment coming between us. You're in large part responsible. I have so much respect and admiration for you that I can no longer behave as your equal and friend, though I would very much like to. My financial dependency makes matters even worse. But though I can't at present reach up to you, nothing prevents you from reaching down to me and treating me the way you treat Jean-Pierre [Léaud], for example. Material help means nothing if you can't give me help from the heart. We must become the complicitous friends and companions of former days again, the complicitous friends and companions of *The Story of a Cheat* and *Pépé le Moko*.[179]

Jean-Luc Godard wrote him a short, melancholic note at this time: "We never see each other anymore, it's silly. Yesterday I went to Claude's [Chabrol] set, it's terrible, we have nothing in common anymore. Like in the song—come the pale morning, there isn't even friendship left. We've each gone off on our own planet, and we can't see each other in close-up anymore, only in full shot. The girls we sleep with separate us each day even more, instead of bringing us closer. It's not normal."[180]

# 5.
# THE SLOW YEARS:
# 1962–1968

I n spite of the favorable reception of *Jules and Jim*, François Truffaut was plagued with what he called the "melancholy of the third film." "I think I've noticed," he admitted in an interview, "that generally speaking, every director has three films to make in his lifetime, the first three that spring from his most secret self. After that, he engages in a career, which is different."[1] For Truffaut, the only way to shatter this inevitability was to undertake an extremely ambitious and personal film.

*Fahrenheit 451* would provide such a challenge. He first heard about Ray Bradbury's novel on a Sunday in August 1960, during an evening at Jean-Pierre Melville's. Liliane David, who was with him, remembers this dinner, where the producer Raoul Lévy was also a guest: "Raoul Lévy, who was a wonderful storyteller, started to tell the story of *Fahrenheit*. François was hanging on his every word; then he asked who the author of the novel was."[2] Lévy promised to get Truffaut a copy.

## SCIENCE FICTION

Though he was no great lover of science fiction, the story of *Fahrenheit 451*, in which books are of primary importance, was bound to make an impression on François Truffaut. For here was a man who collected all kinds of books, old and recent, from thrillers to art books, and spent hours in bookstores—a passion both intellectual and physical. Bradbury's novel was part science fiction, part philosophical tale, blending political analysis with a defense of literature—all themes that fascinated Truffaut. Montag, *Fahrenheit*'s hero, is a fireman who is regularly sent on book-burning missions to destroy the books discovered in the homes of private individuals—books having been banned by a sanitized society where the audiovisual is king. But books, considered responsible for all evils, take revenge when Montag falls under the influence of a young woman and neighbor and—in defiance of his captain, his wife, and common sense—starts to look at them, preserve them, and read them. Informed on by his wife, pursued by the state police for his immoral attitude, he ends up taking refuge on the other side of the river, in the forest of the "book-men," a dissident minority who have decided to preserve the written heritage of the world by each adopting the identity of a book and even taking its title as a last name, thus incarnating the book as a way of rescuing it from the flames.

Truffaut was aware that a screen adaptation of *Fahrenheit 451* would be a costly project, because of the costumes, the many extras, and the futuristic set and atmosphere. At first, he considered a coproduction with Raoul Lévy, out of loyalty to the person who had inspired the project, but then changed his mind because the producer of *And God Created Woman* had a reputation for indecisiveness.[3] He then had the idea of a French-American coproduction between Carrosse and Astor Films—the New York distributor of *Shoot the Piano Player*—starring Paul Newman. This was the first time Truffaut contemplated making a film in the United States. In April 1962, he met Paul Newman at the Mar del Plata festival. That February, he had written to Ray Bradbury, who lived in Los Angeles, and the two met several weeks later in New York, in the offices of Don Congdon, the writer's agent. Helen Scott acted as interpreter in a conversation involving the rights to *Fahrenheit 451*. But Bradbury expressed his preference for a screen adaptation of one of the short stories included in his *Martian Chronicles*. Congdon confirmed that Bradbury was not very excited at the prospect of a screen adaptation of *Fahrenheit 451*, which had already been given a theatrical adaptation several years earlier.[4] A possible plan was that Truffaut and Bradbury first collaborate on an adaptation of *Chronicles*. With this in mind, Bradbury and his family would spend two months in France, at the expense of Les Films du Carrosse, so that the two men could work on a screenplay in French. *Fahrenheit* would be put on the back burner. "If everything goes well with their work on the short stories, we would then be very happy to make arrangements for Monsieur Truffaut to buy and produce the novel *Fahrenheit 451*,"[5] Don Congdon wrote in a memo to Helen Scott on the day following their meeting.

Truffaut left New York having misunderstood the arrangement; he thought he was in a position to acquire the rights to *Fahrenheit,* while Bradbury was actually only offering to first collaborate with him on an adaptation of *Martian Chronicles.* As soon as he returned to Paris, he wrote Bradbury a long letter explaining his motivations:

> To do a good job on a film taken from several of your short stories, a big effort would have to be made, in preproduction, scouting futuristic locations, ultramodern costumes and props, so that later I might be less inspired for *Fahrenheit.* Also, I only shoot one feature film every eighteen months. If I were to first shoot a film based on your *Chronicles,* this would put *Fahrenheit* off till 1964, and I think it would be too late by then, even for the producers of the film—since Gagarin [Soviet cosmonaut, first manned space mission, 1961], the same films can't be made. It's very important for *Fahrenheit* to be the first European science-fiction film. Hence I think we should negotiate the rights to *Fahrenheit* with Mr. Don Congdon immediately and work together this summer, at dates convenient to you, in conceiving a film which we could begin to shoot at the end of the year.[6]

But Bradbury turned down Truffaut's proposal: "I have spent so much time, over the years, on various aspects of FAHRENHEIT 451, both as a novel, and as a stageplay, never produced, that I feel I would be the wrong person to try to adapt it for the screen. I am very tired, very exhausted, on this novel, and would do you a disservice if I accepted the commission to write it for you in screenplay form. Therefore I suggest you arrange to buy the rights from my agent Don Congdon and hire another writer to do the screenplay."[7] Having developed a certain wariness from his first experiences collaborating with writers,[8] Truffaut actually felt relieved. Bradbury and he had become friends and would correspond regularly, with Truffaut keeping the writer informed of his progress.

On July 19, 1962, Les Films du Carrosse bought the rights to *Fahrenheit* for $40,000, a significant sum for a small production company. Truffaut had to seek outside financing to make the film. Since it was clear to him that it would be in French, he gave up the idea of casting Paul Newman in the part of Montag and thought of Jean-Paul Belmondo instead. Truffaut and Belmondo discussed *Fahrenheit* when they met at the Berlin Film Festival at the end of June 1962. But the actor was not free until the spring of 1963 because he was scheduled to act in Jean-Pierre Melville's *Le Doulos,* and his financial requirements were such that collaboration was impossible. The project got mired again.

*Fahrenheit* got passed around to several screenwriters over a period of several months. Still enthusiastic because of his work on *Jules and Jim,* Gruault took up the project first. Then Marcel Moussy labored on a second version of the screenplay. Dissatisfied, Truffaut started work on a third version, this time with Jean-Louis Richard, Jeanne Moreau's ex-husband, whom he had first met in the days of *The 400 Blows.* Richard, an actor by training, was not a professional screenwriter, but the two men got along extremely well. Richard's sense of humor offset Truffaut's anxieties, and his independent spirit and personality—which, as Madeleine puts it, was "as countertrendy as can be"—appealed to Truffaut. "Our friendship and our conversations were transmuted into work,"[9] says Richard.

In February and March of 1963, Truffaut moved into the apartment of the Résidence Saint-Michel—bought by Madeleine's parents and located in the hills above Cannes—with his wife and two daughters. At the same time, he rented a room for Jean-Louis Richard at the Hotel Martinez. Every day he joined his friend at the hotel and the two men worked in a euphoric spirit. As Truffaut recounted it, "One of us would climb on top of a piece of furniture, the other would lie down on the floor, and we would continue talking and miming a scene. One day, a bellhop walked in. He saw Jean-Louis Richard on an armoire and me lying on the fireplace at the other end of the room. We looked at him casually. He let out a funny scream."[10]

In March 1963, the *Fahrenheit* screenplay was completed. Truffaut thought he had found in Henry Deutschmeister a reliable producer who would provide financing for two-thirds of the budget, estimated at nearly 3 million new francs. With Belmondo out of the running, Truffaut considered Charles Aznavour for the part of Montag. Aznavour read the novel and accepted. "The other firemen will be short and thin like him. They'll be small men,"[11] Truffaut wrote to Bradbury, explaining his casting decision. Then he scouted numerous locations, searching for the ideal set for the film. Since Deutschmeister usually coproduced his films with Dino de Laurentiis, he tried to convince Truffaut to shoot in Italy, but the idea was quickly rejected. The south of France was considered, and then the Paris suburbs. "I'm going to visit the housing blocks in Sarcelles, Meudon, Antony, etc. I think of you a lot while writing the screenplay, the Montag character will be rather strong, I think, and better than in the novel,"[12] Truffaut wrote to Aznavour. Meanwhile, he also mobilized the Carrosse team—Delerue for the music, Coutard for the camera (for the first time, Truffaut planned to make a color film), and Suzanne Schiffman. But just when everything seemed settled, it all fell apart again. Truffaut no longer found Aznavour right for the part of Montag. Then Deutschmeister failed to find financing, in France or abroad; the project didn't seem to convince any of the major distributors. " 'People won't believe in it, it's science fiction, leave that to the Americans,' this is what I hear all day every day whenever the labor strikes give me the opportunity,"[13] the director wrote to Helen Scott.

In the meantime, Truffaut reworked the screenplay. He considered hiring an unknown to help him—Maurice Pialat, whose short film, *Janine,* he had admired. Truffaut proposed a collaboration and Pialet accepted, but in the end, Truffaut preferred to turn to Claude de Givray, his longtime collaborator. The following autumn, a fourth screenplay of *Fahrenheit 451* was ready. Through these successive versions, Truffaut was really seeking to reassure himself and forget the setbacks and delays in the production. From one postponement to another, over two years would go by without his making a film, even as his "writing studio" was working at full capacity. "This left him with very bad memories," Marcel Berbert recalls. "He said he would never again lose two years getting a film into shape."[14] Les Films du Carrosse was in a difficult situation, and the moderate success of *Jules and Jim* was a mere memory: "Most of our liquidity has been absorbed in the relatively expensive rights of *Fahrenheit,* the four successive treatments, and a variety of production costs,"[15] Truffaut himself admitted to his Canadian distributor, André Pépin.

## HITCHCOCK

While waiting to direct *Fahrenheit 451*, François Truffaut pursued another project: interviewing Alfred Hitchcock, one of his "filmmaking masters," on his career and work. The idea had occurred to him during a trip to New York in April 1962, in the course of a luncheon with Bosley Crowther, the *New York Times* critic, and Herman Weinberg, the head of the film department at the Museum of Modern Art. Truffaut was astounded by the American critics' deep disregard of Hitchcock's work; for them, he was merely a good technician, a cynical and clever "master of suspense," a "moneymaker." Truffaut and Helen Scott conceived the interview project together and decided to divide up the work. Helen was put in charge of finding a New York publisher, while Truffaut would submit his proposal to Robert Laffont as soon as he returned to Paris. "The goal of this book is to change the idea Americans have of Hitchcock,"[16] he wrote to Don Congdon at the end of April 1962.

Truffaut had already encountered this lack of comprehension of Hitchcock's work in France in the fifties. As far as he and his friends at *Cahiers* were concerned—Rohmer, Chabrol, Rivette, and Godard—the "master of suspense" concealed his genius and intelligence behind a good-natured, humorous veneer, in order to better attract a large audience.[17] Truffaut suggested the following explanation for this dissimulation: Hitchcock was the "biggest liar in the world," for he himself was a Hitchcockian character, haunted by a secret that had to be kept and that he feared having to reveal. "The man who excels at filming fear is himself a very fearful person, and I suspect that this trait of his personality has a direct bearing on his success. Throughout his entire career he has felt the need to protect himself from the actors, producers, and technicians who, insofar as their slightest lapse or whim may jeopardize the integrity of his work, all represent as many hazards to a director. How better to defend oneself than to become the director no actor will question, to become one's own producer, and to know more about technique than the technicians?"[18]

On June 2, 1962, Truffaut wrote Hitchcock a long letter. He reminded him of their first meeting: "A few years ago," Truffaut wrote, "in late 1954, when I was a film journalist, I came with my friend Claude Chabrol to interview you at the Saint-Maurice studio where you were directing the post-synchronization of *To Catch a Thief*. You asked us to go and wait for you in the studio bar, and it was then that, in the excitement of having watched fifteen times in succession a 'loop' showing Brigitte Auber and Cary Grant in a speedboat, Chabrol and I fell into the frozen tank in the studio courtyard. You very kindly agreed to postpone the interview which was conducted that same evening at your hotel. Subsequently, each time you visited Paris, I had the pleasure of meeting you with Odette Ferry, and the following year you even said to me 'Whenever I see ice cubes in a glass of whisky I think of you.' One year after that, you invited me to come to New York for a few days and watch the shooting of *The Wrong Man*, but I had to decline the invitation since, a few months after Claude Chabrol, I turned to film-making myself. I have made three films, the first of which, *The Four Hundred Blows*, had, I believe, a certain success in Hollywood."[19] Then Truffaut got down to the main point, the project of a long tape-recorded interview that would cover Hitchcock's entire career, in view of a book that would be published simultaneously in New York and Paris. He mentioned Helen Scott, who would translate this long conversation. While waiting for Hitchcock to agree, Truffaut planned to research and prepare several hundred questions on each film, covering both the English and American periods of the director. And he ended his letter with the kind of praise that couldn't fail to move the recipient: "The body of the work would be preceded by a text which I would write myself and which might be summarized as follows: if, overnight, the cinema had to do without its soundtrack and become once again a silent art, then many directors would be forced into unemployment, but, among the survivors, there would be Alfred Hitchcock and everyone would realize at last that he is the greatest film director in the world."[20] Flattered, moved, delighted, Hitchcock wasted no time in answering with a long telegram, in French, sent from Los Angeles: "Dear Monsieur Truffaut, your letter brought tears to my eyes and how grateful I am to receive such a tribute from you. Stop. I am still shooting *The Birds* and this will continue until July 15. Stop. Then I will have to begin the editing which will take several weeks. Stop. I think I will wait until the shooting of *The Birds* is finished and then contact you with the idea of getting together around the end of August. Stop. Thank you again for your charming letter sincere regards cordially yours Alfred Hitchcock."[21]

In seclusion at the Colombe d'Or, Truffaut set to work preparing the interviews. He gathered substantial research material, not just books and articles on Hitchcock but also the novels and short stories that the director had adapted for the screen, including those of Boileau and Narcejac and of Daphne du Maurier, the filming of whose novel *The Birds* Hitchcock was just then wrapping up in California. Meanwhile, in New York, Helen Scott was collecting American research material, including the then-unpublished interviews conducted by Peter Bogdanovich, the young American critic and future director who would contribute most to the recognition in the United States of Hitchcock's importance. In mid-July 1962, Truffaut went to Brussels, where Jacques Ledoux, the director of the Royal Cinémathèque of Belgium, organized three days of screenings for him of Hitchcock's British films, with which Truffaut was ill acquainted (and liked only moderately), including all his silent films. Truffaut also took advantage of all the summer revivals in Paris—*North by Northwest, I Confess, Rear Window,* and *Rope.* He then had to attend to the practical details of his first trip to Hollywood. He estimated its cost at $3,500, a sum that was lent to him by Les Films du Carrosse. "Choosing the right tape recorder is important," he wrote to Helen Scott on June 20, 1962, "because it shouldn't be an ordeal for me to carry it, and yet we have to be able to record for a long time without changing tapes. Please find out."[22] Inevitably, the plan was that Hitchcock and Truffaut would each speak in his own language, and Helen Scott would be their interpreter. Truffaut prepared a long questionnaire on each of the films, covering the genesis of each project, the drafting of the screenplay, the direction, and Hitchcock's feelings about the final result. Everything was minutely worked out. The goal was "accurately describing one of the finest and most complete directing careers." Truffaut wanted the book to be "very specific in terms of the intellectual, cerebral, but also manual and material 'crafting' of films," a book that would finally divulge the "secrets" that Truffaut had been trying to unveil for a long time: "This book on Hitchcock is merely a pretext for self-instruction. I would like all the people who make films to learn something from it as well as all those who want to make films."[23]

Helen Scott's role in this project was crucial, and Truffaut willingly acknowledged as much: "Don't let me down, or I'm cooked. If I didn't have you, I never would have considered, or dared to undertake, half of my American activities and especially the Hitchcock book."[24] He used all his influence to stand up for her with publishers who tended to overlook her contribution because they preferred to list only the two film directors as the authors: "If Helen had not been such a brilliant intermediary, the idea for this book would not even have occurred to me,"[25] he wrote to Simon and Schuster, his American publisher. Helen Scott received a first installment of six hundred dollars plus 10 percent of the royalties. Last but not least, Truffaut was convinced that Helen Scott would get along marvelously with Hitchcock: "He'll fall madly in love with you, and having always remained slightly anti-American, he'll be seduced by your European (Continental) liveliness and especially your sense of humor."[26]

Then they had to wait for Hitchcock to reply and set the date for their meetings. On August 9, Truffaut finally received a telegram from Hollywood: "Could you and Miss Helen Scott come to Beverly Hills to start work Monday August 13? If possible can you come by plane to be here Sunday or Monday morning? Reservations will be made for you Beverly Hills Hotel. In that case could work all week."[27] After a brief stop in New York, Helen Scott and the one she called her "hitchcoquin" (*coquin* meaning "little rascal") arrived in Los Angeles on August 13, Hitchcock's sixty-third birthday.

The two friends first dropped off their luggage at the Beverly Hills Hotel; then they went to dinner at the Hitchcocks' house on Bellagio Road in Bel Air. An appointment was made for the following day, in one of the offices of Bungalow 142, at Universal Studios. Hitchcock's chauffeur would come to pick them up in their hotel on Sunset Boulevard. At the appointed time, the master of the house turned on his charm—anecdotes, witticisms, jokes that made Helen laugh heartily, but not Truffaut, who didn't always grasp their full meaning and was eager to get down to serious matters. "Puritanical or not," said Helen Scott, "Hitchcock would occasionally interrupt the taping to give a salacious variant of the Cinderella story or make a nasty remark about an ex-co-worker. To put us at ease, the Master immediately told us to call him 'Hitch,' which I did. But throughout our entire stay, François continued to call him respectfully 'Monsieur Hitchcock,' while the latter answered with 'François, my boy.' "[28]

The interviews between Hitchcock and Truffaut lasted six days. During this time, their lively conversation included anecdotes, bawdy jokes, and discussion of shooting techniques and plot construction. Everything happened as Truffaut and Scott had hoped; Hitchcock was specific, voluble, spirited, and delved willingly into the technical or interpretative details suggested by his interlocutors. He even discussed aspects of his childhood and adolescence, and his ambivalent relationships with actresses—subjects about which he was usually not forthcoming.

After this long series of interviews, Truffaut returned to Paris, where he immediately felt nostalgic about the "week when I fulfilled an old dream—talking with Hitchcock to my heart's content about cinema."[29] This California sojourn greatly contributed in drawing Helen Scott and François Truffaut closer together—not only because they had proved a good team but also because something of a misunderstanding arose, causing a greater complicitous bond between them. For Helen Scott, of course, was in love with Truffaut, while he saw her as a caring "Jewish mother," with a marvelous sense of humor, but not at all as a mistress. The relationship inspired many sexual jokes. "I feel terribly like a bachelor since our painful separation at the Los Angeles airport,"[30] Truffaut wrote her as soon as he arrived in Paris. From that time on, Helen Scott would have but one desire—to work by Truffaut's side. She wanted not only to help him and become his "political mentor" but to feel like and be recognized as a full-fledged collaborator. But for the time being, Truffaut primarily needed Helen posted in New York to watch over the American publication of the Hitchcock interview book.

In September, Truffaut arranged for the interviews to be transcribed, more than forty hours on tape. On Helen Scott's advice, he hired a young American student, Linda, gave her board in Paris, and paid her to type up the English part of the interview. Meanwhile, two secretaries from Les Films du Carrosse, Lucette Desmouceaux—who had recently become Claude de Givray's wife—and Yvonne Goldstein, set to work transcribing the French version. But soon, "due to Helen's strange diction,"[31] the French version started to lag behind. So they adopted another approach; Yvonne and Lucette used Linda's transcribed English text as the starting point, and with the help of Truffaut's old friend Aimée Alexandre, they did their best to translate Hitchcock's words into French. Then, in his free time between the different screen adaptations of *Fahrenheit*, Truffaut made a great many changes and corrections, which had to be made in the English version, as well: a real headache.

In March 1963, Truffaut was already worried about the considerable delay his book had incurred. But in April, when he found the time to reread the first version of the manuscript, he was pleasantly surprised. He shut himself up in his office for ten days and dictated the quasi-definitive French version to Lucette de Givray. Each time he introduced a change in the interviews translated from the English, Truffaut was careful to make note of the fact for Helen Scott. "On the whole," he wrote her, "I try to maintain a conversational tone and avoid academic turns of phrase. I would like you to do your translation work with the same casualness, even if it means keeping some familiarities and possibly even some bad language. The only scruples to have concern the purely technical passages (which in the end are rather few), where you will have to get help from someone in movies, like Arthur Penn, or, better yet, someone bilingual like Sidney Lumet, who would be happy to help us out."[32] By late summer 1963, the double transcription work was completed, which both relieved Truffaut and left him with a big void. "My dream would be for this book never to be published," he wrote to Helen Scott, "and that you and I spend a month bringing it up to date every year, adding new questions and new 'interviews' with the maestro, in short, a yearly Hollywood vacation of a few weeks."[33] The illustrations still needed to be taken care of, for the book required an iconography that would give full meaning to the visual examples described by Hitchcock. Truffaut contacted all the distributors systematically—in France, Italy, and England—to obtain sets of publicity stills, he visited press agencies and Cinémathèque archives in search of precious documents, and borrowed films from the Paris offices of Universal, Paramount, MGM, and Warner Brothers and had individual frames printed at the expense of Les Films du Carrosse. In early March 1964, he spent three days in the British Film Institute's photographic lab, scanning through fourteen old dupes of English films for frames to develop and print. This is how Truffaut came to know by heart each sequence Hitchcock had shot in the course of his long career.

Two long years after recording the interviews, Truffaut set himself the goal of "finishing the book by the end of 1964."[34] The complexity of the task had been underestimated by all concerned; however, it allowed Truffaut to acquire an even more intimate knowledge of Hitchcock's films and gave him the opportunity to fulfill a long-standing desire—of following, from A to Z, religiously and in detail, the making of a book. At a time when Truffaut was involved telling the story of "all books, from Gutenberg to our day"[35] in *Fahrenheit 451*, he was also personally living his daily life with a "book in his head."

## TRIP TO TOKYO

In late 1962, with *Fahrenheit 451* and the Hitchcock interview book progressing too slowly, Truffaut sometimes wanted to "close down Carrosse and put the key under the mat."[36] He decided to travel. His aim was to promote his films, but for Truffaut, who felt himself at the time to be in a state of "romantic availability,"[37] each trip was also the occasion for encounters with women. His first destination was Stockholm, in January 1963, where *Jules and Jim* was being highly praised in the press. In the beginning of March, Truffaut was welcomed in Israel by his Tel Aviv distributor, Lucas Steiner.[38]

*Jules and Jim* also met with success in Israel. In the spring of 1963, he went to Japan for the first time. In the beginning of April, he was received for about ten days in Tokyo by Marcel Giuglaris, the director of Unifrance Japan, and by Kashiko Kawakita, whose company was distributing *Jules and Jim*. Truffaut made the acquaintance of Koichi Yamada, a young French-speaking Tokyo film enthusiast, who would become his official Japanese correspondent and, over the years, one of his closest friends. Truffaut would play host to him regularly at the Carrosse office during his long stays in Paris in 1965 and 1966; he showered him with books and journals, and recommended films to him, introducing him to Langlois's Cinémathèque. He even coproduced Yamada's short film, *La Marchande de poèmes* (The Vendor of Poems), shot in Japan in the summer of 1964. Truffaut made this 1963 trip to Tokyo under the auspices of Unifrance, as part of a delegation that included Alain Delon and Marie Laforêt—in connection with René Clément's film *Plein Soleil* (*Purple Noon*)—France Roche, Françoise Brion and Alexandra Stewart, the beautiful Canadian-born actress. "François took me under his wing, and it was in Tokyo that I saw *Jules and Jim* for the first time. I shed many a tear. . . . We spent the night talking,"[39] says Stewart. Tokyo became the birthplace of the amorous friendship between Truffaut and Alexandra Stewart, the woman whom he soon called in intimacy "Sandra, my vague star," a tender allusion to Visconti's 1965 film with Claudia Cardinale, *Sandra* (*Vaghe Stelle dell'Orsa*). It was a carefree relationship, "nothing serious or passionate, I made him laugh; he could let himself be light and childish,"[40] comments Stewart, reminiscing about a thirty-year friendship. As proof of his attachment, Truffaut would recommend her to Arthur Penn in 1964, when the American director was looking for an actress to play opposite Warren Beatty in *Mickey One*.

Truffaut met two women in Japan who would later appear in his fictional universe, fused in the guise of Kyoko, Doinel-Léaud's pretty mistress in *Bed and Board*. The first was called Kyoko K., a young model and friend of Koichi Yamada. Later she would write him ardent little notes, rather like the messages given to Antoine Doinel by his Japanese mistress: "Come back to Japan, please, please, please . . . François. And promise to give me a day with you. I'd like to spend the day talking, laughing and strolling with you; Kyoko and François only . . . Kyoko loves François. . . ."[41] The second was a charming and very distinguished woman, discreet and passionate, whose name was Shinobu. This first trip to Japan was an intense, lighthearted period in Truffaut's life, which made him forget his Paris worries. "I was melancholic on returning to Paris, for of all the many foreign trips I've made for Unifrance over the last three years, this one, to Tokyo, was the most instructive, most exciting and most pleasant,"[42] he wrote his Japanese distributor immediately upon his return.

## *THE SOFT SKIN*

Since conditions were not yet ideal for filming *Fahrenheit 451*, and the transcription of the Hitchcock interviews left him with time on his hands, Truffaut decided to undertake a new film. "The film will be indecent, completely shameless, rather sad, but very simple. Quick in the writing, quick in the filming, quick to be released and, I hope, quick to pay for itself,"[43] Truffaut announced to Helen Scott. On July 20, 1963, Jean-Louis Richard and he met again at the Hotel Martinez in Cannes. They wrote the script for *La Peau douce* (*The Soft Skin*) in less than a month, holed up, as though the fact of exploring this adulterous story required complete isolation.

The starting point was a double erotic fantasy, as Jean-Louis Richard tells it: "Originally two images had struck François's imagination. A woman and a man kissing in a taxi and the sound of their teeth clinking. And female legs in silk stockings, crossing and uncrossing, and the sound of stockings rubbing against one another. The kiss in the taxi of course is an adulterous kiss. I don't think there are many husbands who kiss their wives making their teeth clink."[44] The screenplay was completed on August 20, 1963. As Truffaut had predicted, *The Soft Skin* is the autopsy of a couple, "an incredibly depressing film, hopeless, with no solution."[45] Pierre Lachenay is a well-known intellectual, a Balzac specialist, and editor of a literary journal, *Ratures*. He is often invited to give lectures in France and abroad. He leads a bourgeois life with his wife, Franca, and their little girl, Sabine. During a trip to Lisbon, for a Balzac conference, he is seduced by a young airline stewardess, Nicole, who is staying in the same hotel. Lies begin to undermine Pierre's hitherto-stable marriage. Lachenay sees Nicole again in Paris, takes her along for a weekend conference in Reims, and wants to live with her. Franca, who has learned of his affair, throws him out after a bitter quarrel. Pierre moves out of the couple's apartment, but Nicole, who values her freedom, refuses to move in with him. Lost, Lachenay decides to go back to his wife. But Franca bursts into the restaurant where he is lunching alone at his usual table and shoots him dead.

When Truffaut sent Helen Scott the script of *The Soft Skin* in September 1963, he explained that he drew his inspiration from true stories. "These ideas about adultery have been running around in my head for such a long time that one might not sense the haste with which I worked,"[46] he pointed out, asking Helen to be as discreet as possible about the project. Truffaut always filed away press clippings on news items he found interesting, with the thought that he might one day use them to write a screenplay. *The Soft Skin* drew inspiration from the famous "Jaccoud affair" in Geneva in the mid-fifties, and from the "Nicole Gérard affair," named after the forty-one-year-old woman who walked into le Petit Chevreau, a restaurant on rue de la Huchette in Paris, on June 26, 1963, and killed her unfaithful husband with two shots from a hunting rifle.

But though the tragic outcome is identical, the characters, situations, feelings, and dialogues in the film are radically different. To better situate *The Soft Skin* in Truffaut's filmography, these news item should be treated as decoys for deflecting the curiosity of journalists and critics. Other details hint at an autobiographical inspiration. At first sight, the character of Pierre Lachenay seems remote from the director. He is older and an academic, probably modeled on the writer Raymond Jean, with whom Truffaut presented *Jules and Jim* to the students at the University of Aix-en-Provence in June 1962, and on Henri Guillemin, a prominent Balzac specialist and one of the best-known literary critics in the sixties. He is also meant as a tribute to his childhood friend Robert Lachenay, with whom Truffaut discovered Balzac. But there is no doubt that the character of Pierre resembles Truffaut himself, with his obsession for detail, his timidity and awkwardness, his need for social recognition and material comfort, and, somewhat paradoxically, his lack of adjustment to bourgeois routine and married life. The fact that Truffaut, for budgetary and practical reasons, used his own apartment on rue du Conseiller Collignon as the Lachenay apartment in the film furthers the autobiographical hypothesis. Was this an immodest desire, or an obsession with realism? The scenes of the Lachenay couple certainly bear a relation to those of the Truffaut couple. *The Soft Skin* is a film on adultery as told by Truffaut; it is studded with intimate details related to his love life, with his expressions and fantasies—for example, the sable-colored Scandale stockings and delicate garters worn by Nicole. *The Soft Skin* condenses Truffaut's romantic adventures into one story, centering on his marital crisis with Madeleine a year before. Nicole, the airline stewardess, brings to mind Truffaut's long affair with Liliane David, who remembers a trip to Le Mans where Truffaut presented *The 400 Blows*. "All I saw was the hotel room and a street giving out on a little square where the film was showing. I couldn't even go see the film because it was sold out."[47] The scene in the hotel, the compulsion to hide Nicole from the conference organizers, the scene in which Lachenay runs out to buy his mistress stockings—*The Soft Skin* literally recaptures several incidents from this affair, which actually came to an end at the time of the filming, when Liliane David married Michel Dreyfus, on October 19, 1963.

But even more than his relationship with David or that with Marie-France Pisier, with whom Truffaut had made a plan, finally aborted, to run away, above all *The Soft Skin* reflects his relationship with Françoise Dorléac. The film was born of their meeting during a trip to Tel Aviv organized by Unifrance Film in March 1963. Twenty-one, a former Christian Dior model, Dorléac was the eldest of the four daughters born to the actors Maurice Dorléac and Renée Simonet. Like her sister Catherine Deneuve, she was beautiful, refined, and graceful. During this trip in Israel, Truffaut and Françoise Dorléac overcame a certain mutual reticence. "I had an inexplicable prejudice against him and he later admitted to me that he had one against me as well," Françoise Dorléac confided at the time. "He thought I was unbearable. And then we got to know each other. I read books voraciously and he lent me some of his. We discussed them and this was the beginning of a mutual discovery."[48] They saw each other again in Paris, just before the actress flew to Brazil to shoot the film that would make her famous, Philippe de Broca's *That Man From Rio,* with Jean-Paul Belmondo.

When she returned from Brazil, Truffaut offered her the part of Nicole in *The Soft Skin.* On reading the script, she didn't like the part, finding the character too harsh. Truffaut would have to exert all his persuasive powers and charm to convince her. "Nicole ended up resembling me, François made her talk like me, tell stories that happened to me with slight changes. This explains why today I'm not so sure about not liking her anymore,"[49] the actress explained when the film opened. Indeed, "Framboise," as Truffaut nicknamed her, alluding to Boby Lapointe's song in *Shoot the Piano Player*—"Avanie et Framboise"—lent her voice, gestures, and rhythm to the woman she played in *The Soft Skin,* making her elegant, lively, reserved, and sensitive, at times violent, and always mysterious.

Truffaut sought an experienced stage actor for the part of Pierre Lachenay, finally selecting Jean Desailly, a member of the Comédie-Française, whose performance had impressed him in December 1961 in a production of René-Jean Clot's *Arc en Enfer,* where he played opposite Silvia Monfort. Truffaut cast Nelly Benedetti, a stage actress whom he had noticed in Claude Autant-Lara's film *Les Régates de San Francisco,* in the part of Franca. She confers upon her character an unquestionable seductiveness, which bears no resemblance to the cliché of the abandoned wife. Truffaut chose Daniel Ceccaldi for the part of Clément, Lachenay's provincial, clinging friend. And he reenlisted Sabine Haudepin, two years after *Jules and Jim,* to play the couple's little girl.

For his fourth film, Truffaut trusted his usual team—Raoul Coutard for the cinematography, Georges Delerue for the music, Claudine Bouché for the editing, and Suzanne Schiffman as script supervisor. He also hired Jean-Pierre Léaud, as well as his friend Jean-André Fieschi from *Cahiers du cinéma,* as apprentice assistant directors. Truffaut's cast and crew worked as an extended family on all his films, but this did not prevent him from being tense and nervous at the beginning of each shoot. Doubtless under the influence of his conversations with Hitchcock, he wanted his film to be intricately edited, with multiple shots and framings. "Up to now, on the first day of a shoot, I've always felt as though I were sending a boat out to sea and that my work thereafter consisted in standing at the helm day after day and avoiding the shipwreck to which I might inevitably be led by my mistakes in calculation at the preproduction stage. Keeping a ship on course in the storm is very tiring, but it's also very thrilling. If you're going to bring a wreck back to port, you might at least hope for a beautiful wreck. Now, I'm weary of this maritime imagery and I'd like my fourth film not to be a ship in distress, but a train crossing through the countryside. I'd like it to be a fine journey, smooth and harmonious, devoid of chaos or switching errors. Instead of hurriedly covering up weaknesses through improvisation, I'd like improvisation to be limited to the oiling of wheels, or the adding of a car without veering off course or slowing down."[50]

On Monday, October 21, 1963, the filming of *The Soft Skin* began at the Auberge des Saisons, in Vironvay, near Louviers in Normandy. For three days, Truffaut shot the most intimate scenes of the film in La Collinière, the ones in which Pierre Lachenay and Nicole spend a weekend together in a bungalow. For several erotic, not to say fetishistic, shots (Pierre removing the sleeping Nicole's stockings and caressing her thighs), Truffaut used a small six-man crew. Unexpectedly, on the second day of filming, the whole crew found itself rushing around in pursuit of a small cat who obstinately refused to lap up the milk from the bowl on the breakfast tray left by the lovers in front of their door. Irritated and amused, Truffaut would reuse this incident ten years later in *Day for Night*.

To minimize expenses, Truffaut had decided to concentrate shooting in the Paris area. There were many scenes that were filmed in the Orly airport over a three-day period, with Nicole as an airline stewardess.[51] The scenes of the Lisbon hotel where Pierre first meets Nicole, and Lachenay's lecture, were actually filmed at the Hotel Lutetia in Paris. The famous elevator sequences, cut and edited in a Hitchcockian rhythm, were taken at the renowned Roux and Combalusier elevator factory in Paris. The shots of the Lisbon street scenes would take only a few hours. A minimal crew accompanied Truffaut, Desailly, and Dorléac; they took the plane on November eighteenth from Orly and returned the following day. The director even managed to ground the plane with several Portuguese extras on an isolated runway of the Lisbon airport and film some additional footage, from 7:00 to 10 a.m., of airline stewardesses at work on board. Back in Paris, the domestic scenes were filmed, first at Nicole's, in Florence Malraux's studio on rue du Télégraphe in the twentieth arrondissement; then, December 2–9, 1963, in Truffaut's own apartment on rue du Conseiller Collignon. "Since no error of taste makes me recoil, the domestic rows will take place in my apartment, if you see what I mean . . ."[52] he had earlier written to Helen Scott. The last three days of filming, just before Christmas, were done at night in the restaurant Le Val d'Isère on rue de Berri, very close to the Champs-Elysées. This is where Franca bursts in and kills Pierre with a hunting rifle.

By the time he had finished this shoot, Truffaut was exhausted, weary, demoralized, and thinner, for his relationship with the actors had not always been ideal. Though Françoise Dorléac had been "charming, excellent, and as well-behaved as Jeanne on the set of *Jules and Jim*," Jean Desailly didn't "like the film, the character, the subject or me,"[53] Truffaut admitted. Truffaut's relations with him—an actor who was used to the quiet tempo and customs of the best Paris theaters—remained "hostile and deceitful"[54] throughout the filming. "Desailly was not happy on the set," says Jean-Louis Richard, who makes a brief appearance in the film.[55] "He was a terrific actor but also François's antithesis on the set. They didn't understand each other at all."[56] Claudine Bouché, who edited *The Soft Skin,* also recalls the tense relationship between Desailly and Truffaut. "François hated Desailly for a silly reason—he disliked physical clumsiness. In one scene, Desailly couldn't close his attaché case at the first try. François's fussiness and tyranny was such that he couldn't bear it when an actor needed a second try for a gesture. Also François didn't like to direct actors who were taller than he. Later he told me he should have chosen Jacques Dutronc for *The Soft Skin,* because he was his height. It was a quip of course, for François had a taste for paradox."[57]

The editing lasted three months. Bouché shortened the film by over forty minutes, cutting entire sequences and speeding up the rhythm. Truffaut was rather pleased: "The Nicole character improved greatly along the way, thanks to Dorléac and my interviews with three air stewardesses prior to the filming. . . . This picture will be more powerful during the marital sequences when 'things are going badly' than when things are 'going well.' Finally, I admit that while I despise Desailly the man, Desailly the actor did a good job playing the part of the bourgeois trapped by events. I've shown him as hyper-nervous, almost on the edge of madness, to avoid (a) blandness (b) a bourgeois tragedy. I like the film. I have only one reason to be worried: the 'mass audience' might dislike the leading character. Aside from that, I don't think it's possible to feel bored and as a whole it won't be too sordid."[58]

## THE THICK SKIN

Truffaut had to get the mix of *The Soft Skin* done by the beginning of April so he could have a print by May, since the film had been selected to compete in the Cannes Film Festival. Five years after *The 400 Blows,* the director once again experienced the ordeal and excitement of an official screening on the Croisette. Claudine Bouché and Jean-Louis Richard supervised the finishing touches, as Truffaut was in New York during most of April working with Helen Scott on the manuscript of the Hitchcock interview book. Prospects seemed excellent since, for the first time in his career, no cuts or restriction had been imposed by the censorship board. Yet Françoise Dorléac's thighs had been closely scrutinized by the censors, since about thirty photos from the La Collinière sequence can still be found today in the board's archives.

Everything went well until the screening in Cannes on May 9. "Everyone wanted to see the film,"[59] recalls Marcel Berbert, who was so harassed that he had to buy tickets, since he didn't have enough invitations to go around. The morning press screening went badly, and so did the subsequent press conferences. Truffaut was tense and on the defensive. The evening screening was, the director admitted, a "complete fiasco."[60] Claudine Bouché, who was by his side, still remembers "the way people shifted in their seats."[61] *The Soft Skin* was very badly received, almost booed. The financial consequences were immediate; the Italian and Spanish distributors withdrew their initial offers. "The day after the screening, no one at the festival knew me anymore; I had become anathema,"[62] Berbert recalls. The contrast with the triumph of *The 400 Blows* in the very same place was striking, and noted by many journalists in their articles the following day. Once the trial was over, however, Truffaut found his good spirits again, as can be seen by the telegram he sent Helen Scott on May 10: "Fortunately I have a thick skin. Stop. In spite of the flop we're having a lot of fun and all is well."[63]

But this slightly ironic, whimsical distance with regard to his own disappointments concealed a very deep malaise. This extremely personal film in which he put so much of himself was being rejected. His clinical view of the couple had been unconvincing, both to those who saw him as the filmmaker of rebellion (*The 400 Blows*) and to those who had become accustomed to his being more feverish in his depiction of feelings (*Jules and Jim*). There was quite a bit of misunderstanding on the part of the critics; (the Communist) *L'Humanité* as well as (the right-wing) *Le Figaro* referred to the director's "*embourgeoisement*," even though this was certainly Truffaut's most "experimental" film, for even if the subject was bourgeois, it was treated in a very daring way. "Soft-skinned François comes after hard-nosed François," confirmed *Le Parisien libéré*, while for the weekly *Candide*, "The New Wave lions have been tamed." *L'Express* and *Carrefour* hammered the point home, finding the film "boring" and denouncing a "distressing Truffaut." There were only a few articles to comfort the director, who was wounded by all those negative reviews: Michel Mardore's in *Lui* ("a beautiful film, reactionary and moral") and André Téchiné's, in his first essay for *Cahiers du cinéma*. But Godard's comments made him happiest. "I saw your film again on the big screen of the Olympe. It was even bigger than the screen. Warm kisses to Françoise Dorléac. If she hears people say it is acted like [a play by Henri] Bernstein, she can just answer: Why, don't you like Jews?"[64]

*The Soft Skin* opened in Paris on May 20, 1964. Burned by the Cannes reception, the distributors chose to show it in only three movie houses. The film would nevertheless run for twenty-three weeks, though attracting an audience of only 120,000, which just about covered Carrosse's investment. The company was soon heartened by the film's unexpected success in the Scandinavian countries, and in Germany, England, Canada, and Japan. In December 1964, Truffaut would make a triumphant Scandinavian tour. Three hundred and fifty articles appeared in the Swedish, Norwegian, Danish, and Finnish press, three hours on television, the University of Aarhus's Honored Artist prize—his success was impressive. In 1965, *The Soft Skin* was the number-one box-office hit in Copenhagen and number four in all of Finland.

## THE SEPARATION

Truffaut was deeply hurt. "My spirits are low, I'm eager to leave Paris and rest, I'm tired."[65] He received the following note from his friend Claude Jutra, the Québécois director: "I found your characters very sad. As a friend, this vague bitterness that the film exudes frightened me a bit, since I know your films resemble you, point per point, at the time when you make them. I therefore hope the next one will be cheerful."[66] After *The Soft Skin*, the breakup with Madeleine was imminent and, this time around, definitive. "We are separating, Madeleine felt very alone during this filming,"[67] Truffaut wrote Helen Scott, aware that marital hypocrisy was no longer appropriate. It was Madeleine who had taken the initiative to separate. "François was relieved; that was just what he was waiting for," she says today. "I felt it had to be done; he wasn't very pleasant at home, probably because he was very much in love with Françoise Dorléac."[68]

Truffaut left the family home for a three-room apartment he rented on February 18, 1964, at 35 avenue Paul Doumer, a minute away from Madeleine's. The hardest thing, Truffaut admitted, was "not seeing the children every day, but I'm entirely to blame for it all."[69] Laura and Eva, ages five and two and a half, respectively, came regularly to see him. The couple maintained an excellent relationship, affectionate and friendly, so much so that Madeleine seriously contemplated François's return. Yet Truffaut himself, who promised to return to rue du Conseiller Collignon, did not want to rush matters. For nearly a year, their relationship teetered between hope and disappointment, but by the end of 1964, they had to admit to a dead-lock: "Our mutual efforts were no more successful than a disarmament con-ference," he wrote to Helen Scott on November 27, 1964. "I do nothing with my freedom and yet I feel I can't do without it. We will soon have been separated for a year and we have become accustomed to it, each in a differ-ent way, and our quirks and habits have only increased."

In early 1965, Madeleine took the initiative in asking for a divorce. The proceedings started on February 8 and the divorce was granted on December 6, with Truffaut promising to pay a monthly alimony of 1,000 francs for each child. "The divorce posed no problems," says Madeleine, "first of all there was no financial problem, no inordinate demand, on either side. Furthermore, the intellectual esteem we had for each other remained unchanged, and his love for his daughters was visible."[70] In the meantime, Truffaut moved once again, on May 15, 1965, into a five-room apartment on rue de Passy, not far from his family. He could have his daughters over and have a live-in governess "to take care of the housework, the cooking and the sewing."[71] From then on, he devoted part of his free time to Laura and Eva, who grew up seeing a father on weekends "who systematically preferred to resort to jokes rather than fatherly authority, but was clearly a father, not a friend, capable of getting mad and punishing us on occasion, when jokes were no longer enough!"[72] Laura now recalls.

Truffaut's romantic adventures were still numerous, but none was really fulfilling to him; he admitted as much to Helen. He did not seem comfort-able, and was often "depressed," "feeling awful," and "incapable of lov-ing. . . . I still have nothing serious in my life and my critical attitude, which now reaches beyond obsessiveness to pure madness, prevents me from falling in love. I know that in talking to you about the sex lives of these ladies I'm only talking to you about my own, but too bad."[73]

At the same time, there were mounting problems at Les Films du Car-rosse. Aside from *The Soft Skin* and *Mata-Hari*, the film directed by Jean-Louis Richard and starring Jeanne Moreau, the production house really had no immediate projects lined up, and *Fahrenheit* was too costly: "We couldn't find money in France. The film was difficult to make because of the special effects, the fires,"[74] recalls Marcel Berbert. The situation was so precarious that in September 1965, Berbert expressed his desire to work on other pro-ductions so as to relieve Carrosse's cash flow. "François thought I wanted to leave Carrosse, which wasn't the case."[75] Though hurt, Truffaut nonetheless convinced him to stay with the company full-time, promising that, after *Fahrenheit*, he would resolve to produce a greater number of movies, more quickly and on limited budgets.

Truffaut's relationship with his mother-in-law, which had never been wonderful, was more and more tense. Now that her daughter was divorced,

1. François Truffaut and Jeanne Moreau during the filming of *Jules and Jim*, 1961. *A story focused on this pure triangular love . . .*

2 and 3. RIGHT & BOTTOM: Françoise Dorléac and François
Truffaut during the filming of *The Soft Skin*, 1963. *The film
will be indecent, completely shameless . . .*
4. BELOW: Jeanne Moreau and François Truffaut during the
filming of *The Bride Wore Black*, 1967. *It is an extremely
intimate exchange that can lead to an amorous
relationship . . .* (Jeanne Moreau)
5. OPPOSITE, TOP: Jean-Pierre Léaud, Claude Jade, and
François Truffaut during the filming of *Stolen Kisses*, 1968.
*The new adventures of Antoine Doinel . . .*
6. OPPOSITE, CENTER: Claude Lelouch, Jean-Luc Godard,
François Truffaut, Louis Malle, Roman Polanski at the
Cannes Festival in May 1968. *The country was paralyzed
and it was logical to stop the festivities . . .*

8. Jean-Paul Belmondo, Catherine Deneuve, François Truffaut during the filming of *Mississippi Mermaid,* 1969.
—*Does love hurt?*
—*Yes, it hurts. It hurts when I look at you.*
—*Yesterday you said it was a joy.*
—*Yes. It's a joy and a misery.*
9. François Truffaut, Jean-Paul Belmondo, Suzanne Schiffman during the filming of *Mississippi Mermaid,* 1969.

10. The end of the shoot of *The Wild Child*, 1969. *First row, left to right:* Jean-François Stévenin, Suzanne Schiffman and Pierre Zucca. *Second row:* François Truffaut, Catherine Deneuve, Jean-Pierre Cargol (fourth from left). *Third row:* Nestor Almendros (seventh from left). *Last row:* Marcel Berbert (far left).

11. François Truffaut and Nestor Almendros during the filming of *Two English Girls*, 1971.
12. François Truffaut, Kika Markham, Jean-Pierre Léaud and Stacey Tendeter during the filming of *Two English Girls*, 1971.

13. Marie-France Pisier and
François Truffaut during the
filming of *Stolen Kisses*, 1968.
14. Jacqueline Bisset and
François Truffaut during the
filming of *Day For Night*, 1972.

Jean-luc. Pour ne pas t'obliger à lire
cette lettre désagréable, jusqu'au bout, je
commence par l'essentiel : je n'enterrai pas
en co-production dans ton film.
Deuxièmement, je te retourne ta lettre
à jean-Pierre Léaud : je l'ai lue et je
la trouve dégueulasse. C'est à cause d'
elle que je sens le moment venu de te
dire, longuement, que selon moi tu te
conduis comme une merde.
En ce qui concerne jean-Pierre, si malmené
depuis l'histoire de la grande Marie et plus
récemment dans son travail, je trouve
dégueulasse de hurler avec les loups, dégueulasse
d'essayer d'extorquer, par intimidation, du fric
à quelqu'un qui a quinze ans de moins
que toi et que tu payais moins d'un million
lorsqu'il était le centre de tes films qui
t'en rapportaient trente fois plus.
Certes, jean-Pierre a changé depuis les
400 coups mais je peux te dire que c'est

15. Jean-Luc Godard and
François Truffaut, 1967. *From
solidarity . . .*
16. *. . . to breakup.* First page
of Truffaut's letter to Godard
breaking relations with him,
1973.

17. Yul Brynner giving François Truffaut the Oscar for best foreign film for *Day For Night*, 1974. *I'm very happy because* Day For Night *is about film people like you; it's your trophy* . . .

18. Steven Spielberg, François Truffaut during the filming of *Close Encounters of the Third Kind*, 1976. *I needed a man who would have the soul of a child* . . . (Steven Spielberg).

19. Éva, François, and Laura Truffaut.
20. Truffaut directing little Gregory during the filming of *Small Change*, 1975.
*My films are a critique of the French way of bringing up children . . .*

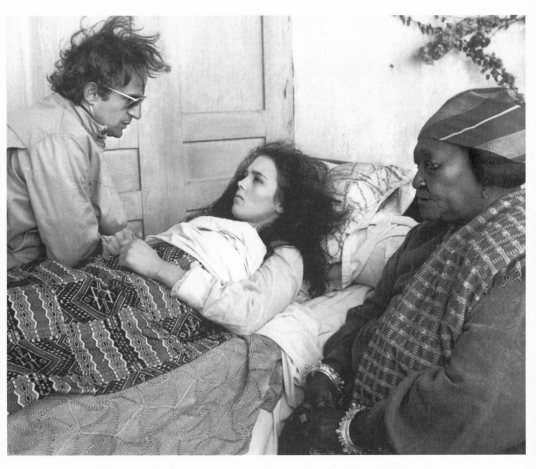

21. *I watch her act, I help her as I can, uttering thirty words when she would like a hundred . . .* François Truffaut, Isabelle Adjani, Madame Baa during the filming of *The Story of Adèle H.*, 1975.

*8/ Cette scène n'est pas satisfaisante car confuse.*
*Il faut qu'on comprenne qu'elle a demandé des renseigne-*
*-ments sur Pinson mais en demandant à Lenoir de ne 11 pas*
*parler d'elle ... c'est ce qui doit ressortir du dialogue ...*

8 . <u>CABINET DE MAITRE LENOIR . INT. JOUR</u>

*il faut*
*revoir cette*
*scène*
*scrupu-*
*-leusement.* }

L'avocat dit à Miss Lewly, quelques jours plus tard,

qu'il a bien réussi à retrouver le Lieutenant Pinson,

mais que celui-ci ne peut la voir actuellement, étant          *Vaseux*

gravement malade. *Il mentionne l'adresse du*
*casernement mais ;l'a obtenu celle d'une*
*maison privée où Pinson se rend souvent, chez une*
Il ne peut ajouter aucune précision et laisse sans          *jeune veuve ...*

réponse les questions inquiètes de sa cliente.

                    *quelles questions*

9: CAMPAGNE      Celle-ci lui règle ses honoraires et sort.

*Ici devrait se placer la scène où elle marche*
*dans la campagne parallèlement au régiment de*
*Pinson - Longtemps il ne la voit pas puis il sera la*
*reconnaître et ils*
*prennent le galop*
*( Page 84 )*

10. <u>RUES D'HALIFAX . EXT. JOUR</u>

~~Miss Lewly ~~erre dans les rues~~, désemparée.~~
*Filature*

~~Soudain elle est dépassée par~~ *une* voiture découverte *où*
*se trouvent Pinson et la femme aux chiens*
~~qui~~ s'arrête ~~un peu en avant d'elle,~~ devant une librai-

rie militaire "la maison "Gossip". ~~Une ordonnance se~~

~~précipite pour ouvrir la portière à un officier très "dan-~~

*( Oui, on peut conserver l'adresse )*

*\*) Faut-il à cheval ou*
*à pieds ? Hésitation*

22. Excerpt from the script of *The Story of Adèle H.,* annotated by François Truffaut.

23. Catherine Deneuve, François Truffaut, and Suzanne Schiffman during the filming of *The Last Métro,* 1980.

24. Fanny Ardant and François Truffaut during the filming of *The Woman Next Door,* 1981. *Neither with you nor without you . . .*

25. François Truffaut, Fanny Ardant, and Jean-Louis Trintignant during the filming of *Confidentially Yours*, 1983.

26. Gérard Depardieu and François Truffaut during the filming of *The Woman Next Door*, 1981.

27. Jean-Pierre Léaud and
François Truffaut, at the time
of *Love On the Run*, 1979.
*The end of the Doinel
cycle . . .*
28. Charles Denner and
François Truffaut during the
filming of *The Man Who
Loved Women*, 1976. *The
story of a skirt-chaser . . .*

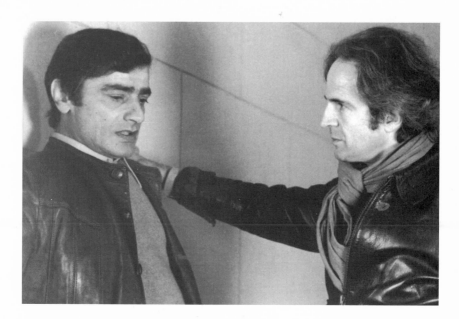

29. François Truffaut in *The Green Room*, 1978. *I'm faithful to the dead, I live with them . . .*

Elizabeth Morgenstern saw no reason to do her ex-son-in-law any favors. Up until then, Les Films du Carrosse had been renting space at a preferential rate in the offices of SEDIF, the company she and Madeleine had inherited. When a much higher rent was demanded in renewing his lease, Truffaut decided to move out. By chance, Alain Vannier, who handled the foreign sales of Truffaut's films, knew of an available space. Les Films du Carrosse moved into new offices on June 20, 1965, at 5 rue Robert Estienne, a dead-end street off rue Marbeuf. Originally a third-floor apartment, it had been renovated with wood paneling and Japanese wallpaper. In this dream office, surrounded by books and magazines, Truffaut welcomed his friends and collaborators in comfortable leather armchairs.

During this same period, an unpleasant plagiarism case upset life at Carrosse. In the spring of 1963, François Truffaut and Jean-Louis Richard had written a screenplay for Jeanne Moreau based on the life of Mata Hari, the famous German spy who had been active in Paris during World War I. Directed by Jean-Louis Richard and entirely produced by Les Films du Carrosse, *Mata-Hari* opened with some success on January 29, 1965, attracting an audience of 180,000 in two months. The following June, a plagiarism suit was filed against the film. Michel Binder, director of the Société Financière de Production Cinématographique, accused Richard and Truffaut of having lifted ten specific details from a preexisting screenplay by Paul and Cathy de Sainte-Colombe, authors who were under contract to him for a projected film on the same subject, to be directed by the American Edgar G. Ulmer. The Paris Court of Appeals ruled in favor of the plaintiff, and on June 16, the judges ordered the confiscation of all prints of the film and the deduction of 250,000 francs from box-office receipts, the equivalent of the sum Binder had paid his scriptwriters.[76] This put a severe dent in Carrosse's finances. The lawyer defending the company in this affair was Georges Kiejman, and this occasion marked the beginning of a long collaboration and deep friendship between him and Truffaut.

In the autumn of 1965, to rescue his company, Truffaut began assigning projects to his team of scriptwriters. In a letter dated November 27, he enumerated these to Helen Scott: "(1) *The Wild Child* (the story of the wolf-child I told you about); (2) *La Petite Voleuse* (like Bergman's *Monika*, the birth of femininity and flirtatiousness in a delinquent girl, a female *400 Blows*); (3) a story in the style of *Piano Player* or Godard's *Bande à part* (*Band of Outsiders*) for Jean-Pierre Léaud, perhaps an early Goodis novel; (4) a comedy drama about a young couple who separate and make up, possibly for Romy Schneider and Belmondo; (5) and finally, the film I've been talking about for a long time, in which all the action would take place in a school. That makes five projects, of which at least two will be under way next month. All of this is confidential. I'm telling you because I tell you everything, but keep it to yourself."[77] Truffaut inaugurated a regimen he would follow all through the succeeding years with his screenwriters—Jean Gruault, Jean-Louis Richard, Claude de Givray, and Bernard Revon. He would see them separately, for weekly "feverish and fast"[78] work sessions. This spate of projects, initiated simultaneously, would keep him busy for a time, and result in a series of films shot at a rapid pace.

## BONNIE AND CLYDE

Offers to work on other projects came to him from abroad. He gave two of them very serious consideration. One involved directing an episode of *Les Trois Faces,* produced by Dino de Laurentiis, with Princess Soraya in the lead. Truffaut was interested in the offer of a 300,000-franc salary, "enough money to buy an apartment,"[79] he admitted to Helen Scott. Intrigued, as well, at the thought of giving Soraya her film debut, he went to Rome in mid-July 1964 and met Franco Brusati, the Italian screenwriter. But soon thereafter, Truffaut changed his mind about directing a commissioned work and apologized to Soraya: "Yesterday, I gulped down a huge glass of tomato juice that was probably too chilled and it made me ill all evening and all night and I realized that Roman life was not for me. I was discouraged, tired and above all in need of a vacation. So I left for France and gave up the idea of shooting the episode. . . ."[80]

The other project was far more exciting. In mid-December 1963, Truffaut received a telegram from Lewis Allen, an independent producer he had met in New York, informing him that he owned the rights to a script being written by two young screenwriters, Robert Benton and David Newman. Friends of Helen Scott, Benton and Newman had selected Truffaut as their first choice for director, for they had admired *Jules and Jim* and *Shoot the Piano Player.* The story they were working on was being serialized at the time as a comic strip in *France-Soir*—which was how Truffaut first learned of Bonnie and Clyde's mad and murderous rampage through prewar Texas. On January 2, 1964, Elinor and Norton Wright, the producers who had taken over the project in New York, sent Truffaut a first version of the *Bonnie and Clyde* screenplay. Claudine Bouché immediately gave him a reading of it in French. It was then passed around the Carrosse office and aroused much enthusiasm. Convinced of the story's cinematic qualities, Truffaut contemplated directing his first American film.

On March 26, 1964, he flew to New York for a monthlong visit. He stayed at the Algonquin Hotel, on Jeanne Moreau's recommendation. Fortunately, in New York, he had Helen Scott, with whom he worked very hard reconciling the two versions of the Hitchcock interview book and solving some final translation problems. This was the first time he was staying for such a long time; "New York seems very provincial to me, and that's a surprise. But the other times, with films to present, journalists to meet and so on, American life seemed less calm to me. On this occasion, I take my time."[81]

During his stay in New York, Truffaut met several times with Robert Benton and David Newman to discuss *Bonnie and Clyde*. "I think the script could really be terrific," he wrote to Berbert; "we could substitute this project for *Fahrenheit*."[82] But Truffaut still felt a certain apprehension about making a film in the United States—because of his poor knowledge of English, for one, but also because he knew shooting conditions would be significantly different from those he was used to and which he owed to his extremely loyal technical crew and the financial independence of Les Films du Carrosse. The producers at the time had already started scouting locations in Texas, with the aim of shooting the film the following summer in the Dallas area, where small towns had barely changed since the thirties. With an estimated budget of $500,000, the film would be less costly than the average American film, which reassured Truffaut, who was frightened by big-budget Hollywood productions.

At the end of April, Truffaut was hesitating between *Fahrenheit 451*, whose production problems were still unsolved, and *Bonnie and Clyde*, the B film to be directed in haste over the summer of 1965. The American offer appealed to Truffaut; he considered Jane Fonda for the part of Bonnie, particularly since she had said she would be delighted to work with him. The producer Jacques Bar arranged a meeting between Truffaut and Fonda, but nothing came of it. Leslie Caron—a close friend of Warren Beatty, who traveled to Paris in the sole hope of being cast as Montag in *Fahrenheit*—arranged a lunch date with Truffaut at the Berkeley on avenue Matignon. This would also be an opportunity for her to make Truffaut's acquaintance. "Like a military officer on a campaign, Warren wanted everything to be fully planned out. He said to me, 'Listen, I don't speak French; it would be too long for me to spend the whole meal with Truffaut, so I'll join you for coffee.' "[83] At the end of the luncheon, Truffaut brought the conversation around to *Bonnie and Clyde* and praised the script, describing the story of the two youthful gangsters in the America of the thirties. On the following day, Beatty flew to New York and met with Robert Benton. "He phoned me immediately," Leslie Caron recounts, "and told me the screenplay was terrific, though he was a bit worried because Westerns were not doing well at the box office. He sent me the script, and I immediately told him it was wonderful, and not really a Western."[84]

After much thought, Truffaut decided against accepting the offer: "You should know that of all the screenplays I've turned down in the last five years, *Bonnie and Clyde* is by far the best,"[85] he wrote to Elinor Jones. And he added in his letter, "I took the liberty of giving *Bonnie and Clyde* to read to my friend Jean-Luc Godard and he too liked the script a lot." Godard sent Truffaut a telegram from the Venice Film Festival, where he was presenting *Une Femme mariée* (*A Married Woman*): "Am in love with Bonnie and also with Clyde. Stop. Would be happy to speak with authors in New York."[86] The first contacts between Godard and the screenwriters were fruitful, but the deal eventually fell through because of scheduling problems.

Truffaut's decision not to do *Bonnie and Clyde* was founded on new hopes of making *Fahrenheit 451*. It seemed, briefly, like the shoot could take place over the summer of 1965, but then coproduction problems cropped up once again. Hearing that Truffaut was free, Elinor Jones approached him again for *Bonnie and Clyde*. Truffaut, who was very tempted by this new offer, demanded a salary of $80,000, and set two conditions—that Helen Scott be hired as his personal assistant, and that he be allowed to cast Alexandra Stewart in the part of Bonnie Parker. Jones agreed to these conditions. Now all that remained was to find a star for the part of Clyde Barrow in order for shooting to begin in early July. The New York producers sent a telegram suggesting Paul Newman. Truffaut turned the suggestion down, arguing "The film would become too important and disproportionate. Stop. Scooter Teague and Robert Walker seem to me adequate for the two male parts. Stop. I don't see stars in this film, but cable me your suggestions as you go along."[87] The producers gave up the idea of Paul Newman, but they insisted on a star for financial reasons, and suggested Warren Beatty. This time, Truffaut's opposition was forceful and unequivocal. "Actually," he wrote to Elinor Jones, "I have no admiration for Warren Beatty and, moreover, he seems to me an extremely unpleasant person. As far as I'm concerned, he and Marlon Brando, and several others, are on a little list that I've classified in my head as 'Better not to make films at all than to make films with these people.' "[88] In the meantime, though, Warren Beatty, who liked the project, had bought the rights to the screenplay and had decided to hire Arthur Penn as director; he had just worked with Penn on *Mickey One*. Truffaut was thus definitely out of the running. *Bonnie and Clyde* would be filmed over the summer of 1966, starring Beatty and Faye Dunaway, and would become one of the biggest commercial hits of the decade.

## DEGREES FAHRENHEIT

Under the impetus of two young independent American producers, Eugene Archer and Lewis Allen, *Fahrenheit 451* was once again moving forward. "The time is ideal for a gifted young French director to make a low-budget film in America," Eugene Archer wrote Truffaut. "More than anything, the industry needs the example of a really brilliant film made in a wholly personal and artistic way for a moderate cost. It could be a decisive factor in starting a new trend, away from the super-spectacles with costs of millions of dollars, toward the kind of personal cinema that you and Jean-Luc and André Bazin—and I, in my own way—have always tried to encourage."[89]

Attracted by this offer, which testified to the New Wave's recognition abroad, Truffaut had the *Fahrenheit* script translated into English and gave it the title *Phoenix,* which seemed more international. Lewis Allen, who took personal charge of the project, proved to be efficient. In 1963, he bought the rights to the Bradbury novel from Les Films du Carrosse ($34,000) as well as the adaptation made by Truffaut and his successive screenwriters ($30,000). "Lewis Allen's involvement was unhoped for," Truffaut wrote enthusiastically to Helen Scott. "Les Films du Carrosse is presently staying afloat thanks to the advance he paid us for the *Fahrenheit* script. Our arrangement stipulates that the film can't be made with any other director but me, which reassures me. I can't lose the script."[90] Truffaut began to believe seriously in an American version of the film. Under Allen's aegis, a number of American movie stars were contacted for the part of Montag. Allen submitted the names of Marlon Brando and Paul Newman, the latter having already been contacted by Truffaut the previous year: "He is very handsome, particularly when he is filmed in color, and I prefer him to all the Hollywood actors who have box-office appeal—Hudson, Peck, Heston, Brando, Lancaster."[91] But Truffaut expressed skepticism, terrified at the prospect of his film being engulfed by the star system. "A costly film, a costly Newman . . . What would become of my independence then?"[92] Truffaut suggested other names: Montgomery Clift, Sterling Hayden—the hero of *Johnny Guitar* (one of Truffaut's cult pictures), but who hadn't appeared on screen for nearly five years—or Terence Stamp, "a sort of English-speaking Oskar Werner,"[93] who had impressed him in Peter Ustinov's *Billy Budd.* Contacted by Lewis Allen, Paul Newman was prepared to commit himself to the venture, either immediately, or in a year, in the summer of 1964. Truffaut and his producer opted for more time: The filming of *Fahrenheit,* starring Paul Newman, was scheduled for July 1964.

In September and October 1963, while Truffaut was shooting *The Soft Skin,* preproduction proceeded on *Fahrenheit.* The American producers scouted locations for futuristic scenery—Toronto, Seattle, for its elevated subway, Philadelphia. Allen favored Toronto, whose "advantages are now more and more considerable,"[94] but also expected to shoot several sequences in the Seattle elevated train. The next task was to complete the casting for Linda, Montag's wife; Clarisse, his young girlfriend; and the captain of the fire brigade. Truffaut and Allen agreed on Jean Seberg for the first and Jane Fonda for the second, and they sent the script to Albert

Finney, Max von Sydow, Peter O'Toole, and Sterling Hayden for the part of the captain. Then a few technical points had to be settled, particularly the question of color. Shooting in color was a commercial imperative, of course, but Truffaut had no experience with color. Allen suggested hiring the photographer Richard Avedon as an adviser, but Truffaut categorically refused: "I don't like the idea of cinema being a plastic art; I prefer to think of it as a dynamic art. And color is dynamic, thus naturally filmable."[95] To facilitate his relations with the American producers, Truffaut needed an intermediary, someone he completely trusted who was familiar with his work methods. He succeeded in getting Helen Scott hired, who dreamed of assisting him on a set.

Bad news: Paul Newman had decided not to accept the part of Montag. Lewis Allen explained. "Mainly, Paul visualizes the picture as something quite different from the way you and I see it. He thinks it is a sociological document and he is very interested that these political and sociological aspects be emphasized."[96] Allen then suggested Kirk Douglas, but Truffaut preferred Terence Stamp, of whom he had said a month before: "I'm convinced this actor will someday become very important in American cinema."[97] Allen, though wary, sent the screenplay to Stamp.

Truffaut had by then completed the shoot of *The Soft Skin*. Though he was still skeptical about the financial backing of *Fahrenheit 451*, his real concern was linguistic. How would he manage to communicate with non-French-speaking actors and technicians? With Helen, he twisted the problem around: "As for English, don't worry, I won't learn a word until the first day of filming. Don't tell me I should know English to make this film, since I'm making the film so I can learn English!"[98] But the problem still remained. He made a great effort and in January and February of 1965 took an intensive six-week course of daily private lessons. By the end of the six weeks, he could read letters, articles, and even novels, but his conversational skills remained limited, and his ability to express himself in public even more so.

In the spring of 1964, good news arrived: Terence Stamp liked the script and accepted the part of Montag. His financial requirements were reasonable, but he was unavailable for the next year because of a previous commitment to make *The Collector,* directed by William Wyler. Truffaut had finally found the ideal lead actor for the film, and Lewis Allen still had a year to complete the budget requirements, which were estimated at around $900,000. The American producer was in negotiation with MCA, a European subsidiary of Universal Studios, headed in London by the director Tony Richardson and Oscar Lewenstein. This meant filming in a studio in suburban London.

In the meantime, Truffaut contacted Oskar Werner and offered him the part of the captain of the fire brigade. The Austrian actor replied two days later: "Enthusiastic to work on *Fahrenheit* with you. Stop. Love."[99] As far as the two female parts were concerned, Clarisse (the young woman who intrigues Montag, seduces him, and incites him to clandestine reading) and Linda (his lawful wife, who ends up denouncing him to the chief of the fire brigade), Truffaut and Allen had contacted Jane Fonda and Julie Christie, the latter replacing Jean Seberg, who had dropped out. Fonda and Christie both accepted. Finally, Welles's and Hitchcock's composer, Bernard Herrmann, whom Truffaut admired and whose every record he owned, agreed to compose the musical score for the film. The two men met in London and enjoyed hours of conversation about *Citizen Kane* and *The Birds*. In that late autumn of 1964, everyone fully expected to meet again in Toronto or London in the spring, when the camera would begin to roll on the set of *Fahrenheit 451*, now the title preferred over *The Phoenix*.

Then Sam Spiegel entered the picture. Considered one of Hollywood's most important independent producers, he had just had an enormous commercial hit with David Lean's *Lawrence of Arabia*. In his negotiations with Lewis Allen, he threw everything into question. The names of Robert Redford, Richard Burton, and Elizabeth Taylor were bandied about, so that the projected budget now reached the $3 million range. Truffaut, who was kept out of the negotiations, became very worried. Fortunately, in mid-June 1965, Spiegel abandoned the project because of casting disagreements. Lewis Allen then signed with MCA, and granted Universal worldwide distribution rights. *Fahrenheit* was to be the first of MCA's independent coproductions in London; the second was *The Countess from Hong Kong*, which Charlie Chaplin was to shoot almost simultaneously, with Sophia Loren and Marlon Brando. The negotiations with Spiegel had again delayed matters; Truffaut's filming, now to be held at Pinewood Studios in suburban London, was postponed to January 1966.

In June and July 1965, Truffaut went regularly to London to meet with Terence Stamp and get ready for the shoot. The two men got on instantly, particularly since Stamp was of French descent on his mother's side and absolutely bilingual. Stamp, who was sometimes difficult and temperamental, was clearly enthusiastic about working with Truffaut and, at twenty-five, had just earned the award for best actor at Cannes for his performance in *The Collector*. In the beginning of August, Lewis Allen came up with an idea that appealed to Truffaut, namely to cast Julie Christie in both female roles—as the cold and elegant Linda and, wearing a wig of very short hair, as the playful, mischievous, slightly boyish Clarisse. Putting his producer in charge of explaining this sudden casting change to Jane Fonda, Truffaut wanted to tell Julie Christie the news in person. In early September, he flew to Madrid, where the actress had been shooting *Doctor Zhivago* for over six months. She was delighted at the prospect of playing both female parts. She and Truffaut were immediately drawn to each other; it was love at first sight. The young Englishwoman, who spoke French well, was impressed by Truffaut's imagination and enthusiasm, while he was seduced by her liveliness and wit. "Julie's was the first miniskirt I laid eyes on. It wasn't common at the time: I thought she was a bit crazy. . . . In fact, she was merely ahead of the times. There was also her voice, which somewhat contradicted her looks. As though she had drunk 1,800 whiskies, which wasn't true. She doesn't smoke, she doesn't drink, but she bites her nails badly. Like me. We hit it off immediately."[100] This close, amorous liaison would last for the entire period of the *Fahrenheit* filming.

Things did not go so smoothly when Truffaut told Terence Stamp that he had decided to give Julie Christie two parts. Convinced that Truffaut and she were stealing his show and shrinking his part, Stamp threatened to resign. Truffaut pleaded with him: "My dear Terry, you possess extraordinary talent and doubtless a marvelous career awaits you. You're a very great actor, the sort of poetical actor who is so needed in today's cinema, now that Hollywood is incapable of recruiting anything but playboys or G-men. . . . Using Julie Christie to play both Linda and Clarisse finally allows me to solve the eternal problem of the thankless part versus the glamorous part, show two aspects of the same woman, and also prove visually that for most men, wife and mistress are the same."[101] Truffaut used countless arguments, reminding him that *Fahrenheit* was "first and foremost the story of Montag the fireman," and how they had remained loyal to him when Sam Spiegel, in the course of negotiations, had demanded another actor for the part of Montag. But Truffaut's efforts were to no avail. Stamp was jealous and hurt; he felt betrayed. His decision was final.

Truffaut and Allen came up with a hasty compromise solution. They offered the part of Montag to Oskar Werner, who accepted, though the change made him ill at ease. He began the filming in a tense state, and suddenly required more money. For the part of the captain, Allen and Truffaut considered Sterling Hayden again, but he hesitated, having just completed a strenuous shoot, Stanley Kubrick's *Dr. Strangelove*. Then British Actor's Equity demanded a British actor, since Terence Stamp had dropped out. Faced with union pressure, Truffaut preferred to wait until the beginning of the filming rather than hire the first British actor to walk in the door: "In any case they all have a crooked face and a theatrical accent."[102]

*Fahrenheit* had exhausted Truffaut even before he had gotten around to making the film. He had been nurturing the project for four years, through four different versions of the script with four different screenwriters. At least a half dozen producers had shown interest in it, and about twenty actors had been considered. Now that he would finally be making the film, he seemed indifferent, nearly passive, as though inwardly drained, and crushed by the excessive weight of the production. Truffaut liked to say, and liked to have his screen characters say, that love stories have a beginning, a middle, and an end. In many ways, the same could be said of films: *Fahrenheit 451* seemed to have outlived its life span before being made.

## THE FOREST OF BOOK-MEN

In late 1965, François Truffaut made frequent trips from Paris to London to work with the actors and the crew of his film. He stayed in a suite at the Hilton from January 1966 until mid-June. Typically, Truffaut was not distracted by the swinging London of the sixties, with its effervescent musical scene and its innovative fashions, the most dynamic metropolis of the day. He didn't even see his friends, such as Roman Polanski and Françoise Dorléac. All he knew were the streets along a few taxi routes—the road to Pinewood Studios, and to the screening rooms of the British Film Institute or the National Film Theatre.

On the eve of his first day of filming, Godard came to see him; Truffaut took him around the sets and showed him the footage of his color tests. Then the two men buried themselves in a screening room at the British Film Institute to watch von Sternberg's *The Scarlet Empress,* with Marlene Dietrich, a film Truffaut called "the best, the craziest, the best performed."[103] Obsessed by his work, he saw himself as a director in exile, a state that suited him. He was accompanied throughout his London stay by his two personal assistants—Helen Scott and Suzanne Schiffman. "During the *Fahrenheit* shoot," the latter remembers, "there was an English script supervisor, of course, and I discovered the joy of not having to do production reports or log sheets every night. I spoke English, which François refused to do, and I was completely available: we worked together continuously."[104] Nicknamed "Suzanna the perverse," an allusion to Luis Buñuel's *Suzana la Perverse,* Suzanne Schiffman was completely integrated into Truffaut's creative process—there wasn't a single idea, a single new line of dialogue, a single detail, that wasn't discussed with her before he tried it out on film.

On January 11, 1966, two days before the shoot was to begin, Truffaut had to find, in extremis, an actor for the part of the captain of the fire brigade. On seeing Martin Ritt's *The Spy Who Came In from the Cold,* in which Oskar Werner had a role, he noticed an actor of Irish descent with an inimitable accent, Cyril Cusack, who he felt would be good for the part. Now that the cast was complete, the shooting could begin on Thursday, January 13, at Pinewood, stage 106.[105] These large studios, forty-five minutes away from the center of London, constituted a regulated world, Truffaut discovered, with very strict standards and numerous highly competent technicians. Indeed, Nicholas Roeg, *Fahrenheit*'s director of photography, had a team of nearly fifty people working for him. For the first time, Truffaut had two makeup girls and four wardrobe girls. Often these constraints irritated him: "Union rules are very strict, since, for example, if we're using two cameras, Nick Roeg doesn't have the right to be the cameraman on one of the two."[106] But there are also advantages: "Pinewood is a real studio, comfortable and wonderfully well equipped. At an hour's notice, I can ask for one or two additional cameras, and they come with camera operators and focus pullers recruited on the spot, who are available at all times."[107] His overall feelings were mixed. "For or against my will—more likely against—*Fahrenheit* will be slightly too English for my taste," Truffaut confided to Marcel Berbert. "I'm snowed under with work by this insufficiently prepared film. Every weekend I must write memos for the sets, the costumes, the props, etc., to avoid bad surprises. The quality of the work is improving a bit, but it's so slow!"[108] For this shoot, Truffaut adapted and changed his style, shooting a maximum of three takes and developing only one. Only the action scenes were filmed with three cameras.

Philippe Labro, who was then a star reporter for *France-Soir,* spent several days in London on the set of *Fahrenheit 451.* "I was taken over by a woman, a sort of domineering whale, likable in a syrupy way, but also metallically protective: She was Helen Scott."[109] She was both François Truffaut's interpreter and personal assistant; she could tell him if the actors' performances were convincing or not, since Truffaut, with his inadequate knowledge of English, was sometimes unable to judge. "It was the first time I saw Truffaut on a set," Labro explains, "he looked puzzled, wondering if he was right to make this film. He seemed like a stranger on the set, as though the film were at the mercy of some other, completely undefined entity, which was the foreign language."

Truffaut recalled only a few good days in a shoot that lasted three and a half months. One such was that of the firemen's book-burning scenes. Truffaut had personally chosen the books in a flea market and in a couple of London bookstores. A whole intimate library went up in flames—Proust, Klossowski's *Roberte de soir,* Audiberti's *Marie Dubois,* Genet's *The Thief's Journal,* Miller's *Sexus,* Paul Gégauff's *Rébus,* Queneau's *Zazie,* and a pleiad of Anglo-Saxon writers he admired, such as Twain, Dickens, Melville, Salinger, Defoe, Lewis Carroll, and Thackeray. There were also books on cinema, such as Chaplin's *My Autobiography,* and issues of *Cahiers du cinéma,* one with a still from *Breathless* on the cover, the other with a picture of Anna Karina as a nun—Truffaut's way of showing his solidarity with

Rivette at a time when *The Nun* had been banned in France by the Gaullist censors.[110]

There was another happy period as the filming drew to a close in April 1966, when the cast and crew met at Black Park, a forest near Pinewood, for exterior shots. This was the spot Truffaut had selected for the kingdom of the "book-men"—those victims of the authoritarian regime who had learned certain works by heart, such as Plato's *Republic, Wuthering Heights, Ulysses, Waiting for Godot, Henri Brulard,* Saint-Simon's *Memoirs, Martian Chronicles,* and *David Copperfield,* as a way of rescuing the literary heritage of past centuries from the flames. The weather was dreadful—cold, rainy, and windy. The first takes were catastrophic, and Truffaut had to reshoot all the sequences. Yet, with the passing days, the director gradually found his hallmark style. The last scenes of the film, in the snow, were the only improvised moments in sixty-seven days of shooting.

On the advice of Jean-Louis Comolli, editor in chief of *Cahiers du cinéma,* Truffaut kept a diary describing in minute detail the various stages of the "saddest and most difficult"[111] moviemaking experience he had had to date. *Cahiers* published the diary from March to June 1966. In it, Truffaut tells of his tense relationship with Oskar Werner. Their reunion, four years after *Jules and Jim,* was initially warm and friendly. But by the end of the first week, their relations began to deteriorate. Increasingly haughty, Werner demanded star billing and constantly challenged the director's decisions, insisting on explanations that Truffaut refused to give him. On February 1, the director recounted their first conflict in his journal: "Because of a flamethrower dangerously handled near his back by Cyril Cusack, Oskar Werner becomes nervous, and the two of us break out into a violent quarrel for five minutes."[112] Truffaut resented Werner's starlike capriciousness, his timorousness in the face of difficulties, his heavy-handed acting, and, above all, his lack of humor and imagination. The two men had very different conceptions of the Montag part. Werner wanted to portray a hero, while Truffaut detested heroism. "I soon rediscover my antiheroic bias. I'll never be able to film courage, probably because it doesn't interest me. Courage seems to me an overrated virtue, compared to tact, for example. I'm sure that General Oufkir, the 'bad guy' in the Ben Barka affair, is a courageous man, but in terms of tact, he's got a long way to go."[113]

The constant power struggle between the director and his lead actor dominated the filming of *Fahrenheit.* On February 18, Werner refused to act a scene with his flamethrower, and Truffaut had to use his stand-in. On the 22nd, Werner took the liberty of giving Julie Christie and Cyril Cusack acting instructions. "We must put up with each other until the end of April," the director told his actor. "It isn't the film you envisioned and it isn't the film I envisioned, it's somewhere in between, and that's the way things are.

Now, if you don't like the scene the way I'm filming it, you can just stay in your dressing room and I'll shoot without you or use your stand-in."[114] Werner finally yielded, but he sabotaged the last line in the sequence, which Truffaut sacrificed in the editing. The actor refused to give in completely, and he showed up on the set after Easter weekend with his hair cut very short at the nape of the neck and the back of the head, claiming he had fallen asleep at the hairdresser's. Furious, Truffaut could only shoot him facing the camera or wearing a cap, and he had to use his stand-in for scenes where Montag would be seen from the back. After a thirteen-week shoot, completed on April 15, 1966, Truffaut could finally write: "This is the end of my collaboration with Oskar Werner, whom I won't see again before his departure for Hollywood tomorrow, nor, I hope, in the near future."[115]

In early May, the director worked at Pinewood Studios with his English editor, Thom Noble, on a first rough cut of almost two hours. Truffaut wasn't pleased with it. In the beginning of June, he summoned Jean Aurel to London for advice. Aurel felt the film was slow in taking off, and that the female characters should be introduced in reverse order. Truffaut also relied on Bernard Herrmann, who composed almost an hour of music to match the mood of Nicholas Roeg's cinematography, essentially the aggressive red inspired from Hitchcock. Thanks to Herrmann's sharp, strident score, *Fahrenheit* sometimes takes on the tense rhythm of a suspense film.

*Fahrenheit 451* was finally completed on July 20, 1966. Though Truffaut was pleased with some of the scenes because of their color or music, or because of Julie Christie's gesture, expression, or the intonation in her voice, he didn't like the film as a whole. Was his poor English at fault? "Unfortunately," he wrote Thom Noble, "we won't have the opportunity to work together on my next films, for, after seeing *Fahrenheit* over and over again, I realize I should give up the idea of making films in English until I really know the language."[116] On June 10, Luigi Chiarini, the director of the Venice Film Festival, came to London to screen the film and decided to present it as an official selection. For Truffaut, this was a first, and also an encouragement. In August, there was another piece of good news from California. Ray Bradbury had seen *Fahrenheit 451* at a Universal screening and liked it: "How rare it is for a writer to walk into a motion picture theater and see his own novel faithfully and excitingly told on the screen. Stop. Truffaut has given me back a gift of my own book done in a new medium by preserving the soul of the original. I am deeply grateful."[117] Even if Truffaut didn't share the writer's enthusiastic reaction, he was touched by it.

In Paris the critical response was cool, polite at best. Michel Cournot, in *Le Nouvel Observateur,* was frankly hostile and rebuked Truffaut for having tried to imitate American movies. *Cahiers du cinéma's* attitude was emblematic of the press's embarrassment about *Fahrenheit 451. Cahiers* was proud of printing Truffaut's journal of the shoot, but Jean-Louis Comolli's positive review of *Fahrenheit* read like a personal favor. In *Cahiers'* list of best films of 1966, *Fahrenheit* would be ranked as number fourteen.

*Fahrenheit* was well received in Venice, at the September 7 screening, though it was not among the prizewinners three days later. On September 15, on the eve of its commercial release, a gala was held at the Marigny theater in Paris. Among those attending was a radiant Julie Christie, who was wearing a dressy miniskirt. Truffaut had arranged for everyone in the audience to receive a copy of the Bradbury novel, and among the guests, there were about fifteen members of the Académie française who had been invited to "celebrate books." This tie-in with established writers made Truffaut's cinema seem slightly stilted and outmoded, poles apart from the new cinema emerging at that time everywhere in Europe, under the influence of the French New Wave, whose standard-bearer he had been just a few years earlier.

*Fahrenheit 451* could not be considered a box-office success, selling only 186,000 tickets during its eighteen-week run. This was not a good return, given the cost of the film. It fared no better in New York, where it opened on November 2, 1966. When all was said and done, Truffaut felt only relief at being rid of a project that had occupied him for six years. "I can tell you quite frankly that I can breathe more easily now that our long, common adventure of *Fahrenheit 451* has come to an end," he wrote to Ray Bradbury. "Even if it was an exciting adventure, I must admit I often felt crushed by the scope of the project. Perhaps I was too ambitious, and I constantly feared my efforts wouldn't be equal to your work."[118]

## THE HITCHBOOK

In the summer of 1965, at the same time as he was starting the preproduction work for *Fahrenheit 451*, François Truffaut was finishing his book of Hitchcock interviews, exasperated at being behind schedule. He had to write the preface, which was "terribly difficult to do,"[119] he wrote Helen Scott, for it had to be addressed to critics and film enthusiasts as well as to a wider American and French readership. Truffaut completed the first version in mid-May, twenty-odd pages, which he sent to Scott for translation.

In mid-August 1965, Hitchcock received a copy of the interviews in English, just when he was immersed in the preproduction of *Torn Curtain*. Truffaut felt impatient and worried; with no news from Hitchcock, he no longer had control of the project. Then, in October, he received a long letter, in which Hitchcock poured out all his feelings about his new film, its structure and the choice of actors, and concluded with just two quick sentences on the interviews: "You have done a wonderful job. Two or three small changes will have to be made so as not to offend anyone. All is well."[120] Included with this letter was a carefully annotated copy of the interviews. Truffaut and Helen Scott were relieved. It was only later, when the book was in galleys, that Truffaut learned that Hitchcock was not quite satisfied with the English text, which he felt wasn't "sufficiently colloquial,"[121] and that this was delaying American publication. On July 27, 28, and 29, 1966, the three collaborators met at Claridges in London for a final interview devoted to *Marnie* and *Torn Curtain,* bringing the entire undertaking to a close. In August 1966, Truffaut had the huge manuscript of *Le Cinéma selon Alfred Hitchcock* delivered to his publisher, Robert Laffont—over 750 pages and 300 photos. "If I were to produce the book according to your specifications," the publisher wrote Truffaut, "it would be 416 pages long in a large 15.5 × 24 cm. format and carry a minimum price tag of 57 francs. I feel this price would be prohibitive for a certain kind of customer."[122] He raised the possibility of a paperback edition, which would require substantial cuts in the manuscript. Truffaut refused and managed to persuade Laffont that the book had chances of attracting a wide readership—not just film enthusiasts.

The following summer Laffont produced a large, almost square edition of 260 pages, including nearly 350 photos. It looked splendid—and Truffaut was very proud of it. It came out in October 1966. The American edition, *Hitchcock* by François Truffaut, was published by Simon and Schuster in November 1967 and looked even more elegant than the French book. Though sales in France stagnated at around 5,000 copies, in the United States the book was a commercial success—it sold 15,000 copies in hardcover and 21,000 in paperback. Between 1967 and 1973, Truffaut earned $23,000 in royalties. He set the money aside for Helen Scott, without whom he could never have successfully completed the book. Loyal in friendship, discreet in his way of helping friends, Truffaut would make several deposits in her bank account to "feed the brat,"[123] as he put it.

Critics in France hailed this new type of book: "a revolution in film criticism,"[124] wrote *Les Nouvelles littéraires.* Just as Truffaut got news of the first foreign publications, in Germany, Italy, Spain, Denmark, and England, he also received the compliment that moved him most, from Hitchcock: "I think the book has turned out wonderfully well, and I must congratulate you. I think the illustrations make a big difference to it. *Bravo et milliers de mercis.*"[125] The two men had become friends and would write to each other regularly—short, affectionate notes, long letters, and mutual words of advice on scripts in progress. Up until Hitchcock's death in 1980, Truffaut would never fail to visit the "master of suspense" whenever he was in California; he wrote articles and prefaces about him, and took part in tributes to this man who, largely thanks to Truffaut himself, was finally recognized in the United States as a full-fledged auteur and true creative genius.

## DEATHLY PALE THRILLER

To live up to his promise to Marcel Berbert, who was worried about Les Films du Carrosse's financial situation, François Truffaut planned to get back to work very quickly and direct what he called a "B picture." He had in mind a small film with a budget of $400,000 for the spring of 1967. *La Mariée était en noir* (*The Bride Wore Black*) was a project that actually dated back to the summer of 1964; it had been conceived as a tribute to Jeanne Moreau, a woman he loved and one who had become an intimate friend.

At that time, Jeanne Moreau had just broken up with Pierre Cardin. She had left the Paris designer's apartment and moved in with Micheline Rozan, her agent, before going to stay in her own house in the Var. Feeling extremely despondent, she had called Truffaut, who, having just broken up with Madeleine six months before, was also undergoing a crisis in his personal life. They picked up the thread of a love affair that had started during the pre-production of *Jules and Jim*. "In the Midi, we were perfectly happy together. As always, I am confronted with the same problem—whether to fight it or not fight it, whether to wait for things to happen or make things happen, pessimism or optimism, whether to live for the future or the present, whether to want or not want, etc."[126] Their liaison lasted all summer and into the filming of *Mata-Hari* in the fall. "We're not too easy on each other, but we treat each other with great gentleness and tenderness, we're a bit fearful of each other but not too much. . . ."[127] Truffaut wrote to Helen Scott. The desire for a second shared project was born from this brief new love affair.

Truffaut started looking for a really good part for Moreau. In August 1964, he asked Helen Scott to help him acquire the rights to a detective novel by William Irish, *The Bride Wore Black*, which he had read as an adolescent. Irish, whose real name was Cornell Woolrich, was a literary celebrity in the early thirties. Later, he lived as a recluse with his mother in a New York hotel room. A diabetic and an alcoholic, he had found it difficult to recover from his mother's death in 1957, but he had lived on for eleven years in desperate solitude. Affected with gangrene, he had had to have a leg amputated. At his death, he left Columbia University a trust fund of a million dollars. He was the bard of *noir*, of black gloom and darkness, words that recur obsessively in almost all his titles: *The Bride Wore Black, The Black Angel, The Black Path of Fear, Rendez-vous in Black, Waltz into Darkness*. Truffaut was fascinated by his work and would end up adapting two of his novels—*The Bride Wore Black* and *Mississippi Mermaid* (*La*

*Sirène du Mississippi* was the French title of *Waltz into Darkness*). He also wrote two very appreciative articles about him. "I see Irish . . . as the artist of fear, terror and sleepless nights. There are very few gangsters in his books. When there are, they are in the background. The plot usually centers around an ordinary man or woman with whom the reader can easily identify. But Irish's heroes never do things by halves and no unforeseen event can stop their march toward love and death. His world frequently also includes amnesia and mental problems, and his hypervulnerable, hypersensitive fictional characters are at the opposite extreme from the usual American hero. Just as there is a touch of Queneau in David Goodis, there is a touch of Cocteau in Irish, and it is this combination of American violence and poetic French prose that I find moving."[128]

Through Helen Scott, Truffaut learned that William Irish lived at the Sheraton-Russell Hotel on Park Avenue. He assigned Don Congdon, who had become his American agent, the task of negotiating with the writer for the movie rights to *The Bride Wore Black*. "I suggested to William Irish that we meet for lunch or a drink," Don Congdon recalls, "and he answered that this wouldn't be possible because he wrote in the afternoon. So we agreed to meet at breakfast. When I saw him approaching, I was taken aback; he looked like he had risen from the grave: He was pale, with grayish skin. He was a very secretive, solitary person."[129] Truffaut made a point of telling Don Congdon that he wanted to sign "a simpler, more advantageous contract than the one for *Fahrenheit 451*.[130] On September 17, 1964, Congdon informed Truffaut that Irish's asking price was fifty thousand dollars. Finding the amount excessive, Truffaut limited himself to an option, while Les Films du Carrosse tried to find cofinancing for the film. Oscar Lewenstein, coproducer at MCA of *Fahrenheit 451*, was the first to come to his rescue. Negotiations lasted until the autumn of 1965, with Lewenstein eventually buying the rights to *The Bride Wore Black* for forty thousand dollars. Given this partnership with Lewenstein, Truffaut briefly considered making another film in English at Pinewood Studios in the spring of 1967, but the lukewarm response to *Fahrenheit 451* led him to reconsider. His next film would be made in France and, if possible, co-produced by Carrosse and United Artists, the company with which Lewenstein had reached an agreement.

United Artists delayed in answering, so Truffaut began to consider other projects for Jeanne Moreau. In early 1967, Ray Bradbury suggested that Truffaut direct a short feature adapted from one of his short stories, *The Picasso Summer*. It had a wonderful plot: On a beach in Biarritz, a rich American tourist, George Smith, suddenly sees a small, lean, suntanned man emerge from the water. Using his finger, the man begins to draw on the moist sand with such skill that George Smith is enthralled. Then the little man goes back into the water as suddenly as he had appeared. This man was none other than Picasso. The tide rises and soon his drawings are washed away by the sea. Picasso himself had been contacted by Bradbury and had agreed to take part in the film; Truffaut wrote back to Bradbury immediately to accept his offer. But when he read the screenplay Bradbury sent him, Truffaut was far less tempted: "To be completely frank, since we've always been frank with each other, I must tell you that for me this detailed treatment fails to capture the inventive originality of your short story."[131] In the end, *The Picasso Summer* would be directed by Serge Bourguignon, "but the film was so bad," Bradbury confessed, "it never had a theatrical release."[132]

French offers abounded, as well, but none would retain Truffaut's attention. Certainly not the one made by Nicole Stéphane, the actress who had played in *Le Silence de la mer* and *Les Enfants terribles* (*The Strange Ones*) and who was now a producer. "On rereading *Swann's Way*," Truffaut wrote her, "it became patently obvious to me that I shouldn't touch it and that it just shouldn't be touched. . . . There was no doubt in my mind that you'd have to be a butcher to accept to film the Verdurin Salon and I learned that, far from being at all worried by my silence, you recently contacted just such a butcher, René Clément, who once again demonstrated his shameless vulgarity and instantly jumped on the opportunity."[133]

In December 1966, Oscar Lewenstein finally persuaded United Artists to let Truffaut shoot *The Bride Wore Black* in France and in French. A coproduction arrangement was reached between Les Films du Carrosse and UA that would last about ten years and allow Truffaut to make his films with greater financial peace of mind. Also, in early 1967, Helen Scott decided to move to Paris to be closer to Truffaut, with whom she hoped to work regularly. "François had tried to warn Helen about moving to Paris, feeling she might be under illusions,"[134] says Madeleine Morgenstern. Indeed, Truffaut kept a certain distance from Helen, as was sometimes his way with his best friends, out of self-protection and to avoid causing disappointment. This often gave rise to misunderstandings and a coolness in his friendships, for Truffaut was guided by a strict work ethic that was not to be weakened by personal ties. In Paris, Helen Scott first worked as an agent for Universal Studios, then as a translator, writing the English subtitles for French films. She rented an apartment on rue de la Pompe, very close to rue de Passy, where Truffaut lived. He looked after her, of course, and introduced her to his best friends, eager to increase Helen's chances of finding work. "When Helen came to France, we became good friends," Claudine Bouché recounts. "She used to tell me about her life with François on a daily basis, their quarrels. She wasn't past making nasty cracks. She had a complex about her physical appearance and in her professional capacities had a constant need for some kind of recognition. François advised her to write and do translations in her free time."[135]

In February 1967, Truffaut published an article in *Le Nouvel Observateur* praising Claude Berri's first feature, *Le Veil Homme et l'Enfant* (*The Two of Us*), an autobiographical story of a Jewish child who is taken in during the German Occupation by a retired worker (marvelously played by Michel Simon) "who is fiercely and adamantly anti-Semitic."[136] "He believed in me; he helped me a lot; he encouraged me enormously,"[137] says Claude Berri. A true friendship would develop between the two directors; Truffaut would even be Claude Berri's witness at his marriage to Anne-Marie Rassam in October 1967. A bachelor again, since his divorce from Madeleine, Truffaut found a real family in the Berris—a warm, enthusiastic, rather eccentric family, in whose midst Helen Scott was also welcomed. Claude Berri's brother-in-law, Jean-Pierre Rassam, the most imaginative young French producer of the late sixties and early seventies, became one of Helen's best friends, the person who rivaled Truffaut in her heart.

Several months earlier, during the 1966 Christmas vacation, François Truffaut had moved into the Hotel Martinez in Cannes with Jean-Louis Richard to adapt *The Bride Wore Black* for the screen. The writing of the script progressed rapidly. The plot centered around serial killings, the murderess being Julie Kohler, a young widow in pursuit of her victims. The task facing Richard and Truffaut was to make these murderous acts of revenge seem credible without blackening the part played by Jeanne Moreau. The heroine couldn't be either crazy or hysterical, but obsessive, determined to execute her plan methodically.

In February, Truffaut had a 237-page script; it was rather faithful to Irish's novel, though the names of the characters had been Frenchified. *The Bride Wore Black* is a film with a logical construction and studied effects, carefully calculated to create tension and suspense. Truffaut was particularly mindful not to reveal the plot before the film's release. For this, he pledged the entire cast and crew to secrecy and even distributed a misleading synopsis to the press describing the story as "a woman investigating her husband's disappearance. . . ."[138]

The early days of spring 1967 were devoted to casting, location scouting, and resolving technical details. Six male actors were needed to play opposite Jeanne Moreau, and Truffaut was happy for the opportunity to direct actors whom he had long admired. Among them, his friend Jean-Claude Brialy, "the only dawn to dusk actor," whom he cast in the part of Corey, the only man to escape Julie Kohler's murderous revenge because he had no part in her husband's murder. As Julie Kohler's five victims, Truffaut cast Claude

Rich, Michel Bouquet, Michael Lonsdale, Charles Denner, and Daniel Boulanger.

## THE COLORS OF THE BRIDE

On May 16, 1967, Carrosse's usual crew, gathered around Raoul Coutard and Suzanne Schiffman, met in Cannes to begin shooting in a rented apartment at the Résidence Saint-Michel. The fourteen outfits worn by Jeanne Moreau in the film, all in black and white, were designed for her by Pierre Cardin. But *The Bride Wore Black* was a color film and this soon became a subject of dissension between Truffaut and Coutard, his cinematographer. From the very first day of the shoot, Truffaut found the scenes underlit. He quarreled with Coutard for the first time, and interrupted the filming for two days. *The Bride* would turn out to be their last collaboration. "Coutard had always had a bad temper," says Claudine Bouché, the editor of the film, "and François didn't like Coutard's intransigence, particularly since he loved to fiddle with an image and reframe it when he so desired. Coutard called this 'mistreating the film stock.' "[139] As a result of this discord, the filming was tense, with Truffaut expending a great deal of energy on trying to convince Coutard, so that part of the job of directing the actors fell to Jeanne Moreau and Jean-Louis Richard. "It was a difficult shoot," Jeanne Moreau recalls. "There were tensions between François and Coutard because the light was supposed to change radically every week to suggest different locations, while in fact our shooting locations were geographically close. François was very mysterious, very secretive. He never spoke on the set. In *Jules and Jim,* there had been a lot of improvisation, in *The Bride,* none at all. The mood was very different."[140] Aside from the disagreement between Truffaut and Coutard, another difficulty was that the male actors had small parts, which gave them very little time to get into the atmosphere of the film. Truffaut, absorbed in sticking to the logic of his shooting script and more secretive than usual, put Jeanne Moreau in charge of explaining to each actor his part. "François would say to me: 'Listen, you take care of it. . . .' So each time, I had to take over and reassure my next murder victim."[141] The only moment when the cast and crew felt comfortable was when they shot the scenes between Charles Denner and Jeanne Moreau in the painter Fergus's studio. Truffaut had rented Victor Herbert's Paris studio, on rue du Val-de-Grâce, and commissioned Charles Matton to make some paintings, including several portraits of Jeanne Moreau. Truffaut got along well with Denner and put into his mouth many of his own personal expressions and fantasies. Fergus's entire speech on women, which foreshadows *The Man Who Loved Women,* could be likened to the "intimate journal of a womanizer," which Truffaut could have kept on a daily basis. Truffaut spent August through October 1967 editing his film with Claudine Bouché, assisted by Yann Dedet. He commissioned Bernard Herrmann for the music, but this time he was a bit disappointed with the result.

Truffaut had hoped this film would help Jeanne Moreau during a difficult period in her life. But the opposite occurred: Throughout the entire filming, it was Jeanne Moreau who came to his aid. Truffaut extolled her good humor and sense of solidarity to Hitchcock:

> On the set, she is ready to perform quickly or slowly, be funny or sad, serious or nutty, do anything that the director asks. And when misfortune strikes, she sticks by the captain of the ship: with no fuss or to-do, without singing "Nearer, my God, to Thee . . . ,' she will just go down by his side. The danger for her in *The Bride* is that her part is simply too extraordinary; the heroine, a woman who dominates men and then kills them, is too "prestigious." To counterbalance this, I asked Jeanne to play the part with simplicity, in a manner that is familiar and would make her actions unexpected, plausible and human. As I see it, Julie is a virgin, since her husband was killed at the church on the day of their wedding. But this revelation doesn't come out in the film and will have to remain a secret between Jeanne Moreau, you and me.[142]

Truffaut blamed himself and felt guilty for not rendering Jeanne Moreau's beauty on the screen. She looked tired, her face reflecting the trials she had been through in the mid-sixties. Furthermore, Truffaut disliked Cardin's costumes. Of all his films, *The Bride Wore Black* would be the one he liked least, except for the Charles Denner episode and the sequence with Michael Lonsdale.

Released on April 17, 1968, *The Bride Wore Black* sold 300,000 tickets during its fourteen-week exclusive run in Paris and the Paris area; it was therefore an unquestionable success. Furthermore, contrary to Truffaut's expectations, the reviews were not bad. But only one comment on the film really touched Truffaut, and that was Hitchcock's: "I especially liked the scene of Moreau watching the man who had taken poison Arak dying slowly. I think my particular sense of humour might have taken them a little further so that Moreau could have picked up a cushion and put it under his head so that he could die with more comfort."[143] Truffaut wrote two long letters in reply, with lengthy comments on the scripts of *Frenzy* and *Topaz,* which Hitchcock had sent him. However, the French director's "Hitchcockian" period—which started with *The Soft Skin,* included *Fahrenheit 451,* and ended with *The Bride Wore Black*—had not been a resounding success, as Truffaut himself was the first to realize.

## FRAMBOISE

"Françoise, Framboise, death in the summer. I knew it was painful. What is solitude? It is the intolerable,"[144] Truffaut wrote ten days after his friend's death. On June 27, 1967, Françoise Dorléac was killed on the road to the Nice airport, burned alive in a car accident. Truffaut was shattered by this tragedy; it left him distressed during the filming of *The Bride*, which took place not far from the scene of the actress's death. Françoise Dorléac and François Truffaut had shared the same literary and cinematic tastes, and they had seen each other very often after their brief romance in the days of *The Soft Skin*. They had remained very close, sharing a tender and solid friendship, almost like Truffaut's friendship with Jeanne Moreau. A month prior to the accident, he had written to her London agent, stressing his intention of working with the twenty-five-year-old actress far into the future: "The problem, for many young actresses, is to make a successful transition from young girl to woman, to switch from juvenile parts to adult ones. Françoise Dorléac, who will always be Framboise Dorléac for me, won't have these difficulties, for she is a precocious, premature woman, with a constructed face and body, constructed firmly, to last. She is the only young actress who might very conceivably have greater and greater appeal. She has nothing to fear from added years, for time works in her favor. I'm delighted to think that I'll be collaborating with her again in 1970, 1976, 1982, 1988, etc., etc. See you soon, Framboise!"[145]

This life cut short intensified François Truffaut's deep melancholy, in a decade of collective vigor and enthusiasm. For him, those years were punctuated by separations, professional and emotional disappointments, hesitations, and bereavements. This was not immediately apparent in the two films he had just directed, *Fahrenheit 451* and *The Bride;* they seem well mastered and clear, indeed almost academic, as many critics pointed out at the time. However, there is a detectable vulnerability in them, a shadow, as suggested by Jean-Louis Comolli in the profile he wrote of Truffaut in *Cahiers du cinéma* in May 1967: "Behind these more or less obvious virtues—an air of such mastery, calm and seriousness that it is sometimes irritating—there is one virtue that is so concealed and secret that it is generally overlooked; it could be antagonistic to all the others except that it is precisely the mainspring of them all—anxiety."[146]

Truffaut remained whimsical and imaginative, but these setbacks and difficulties affected him deeply. Jean-Pierre Melville, in whom Truffaut had confided far into the night of March 20, 1963, when plans for the French production of *Fahrenheit* had fallen through, saw these successive trials as a painful but vital way for him to assert himself: "The failure of *The Soft Skin* and especially of *Fahrenheit*," Melville said at the time to Raoul Lévy, "will allow him to become an adult who will finally know life, thanks to the truly negative experiences of moviemaking, those that enrich even more than they impoverish. This will allow him to change the direction of his work and set it on the right course—not with peace of mind but with true freedom in relation to himself—toward expressing what *one has to say* and no longer what *one would like to say.*"[147]

# 6.
# PARALLEL LIVES:
# 1968–1971

## DETECTIVE DOINEL

In 1968, Truffaut thought of a new project involving Antoine Doinel, his creation and alter ego. At first, he had wanted Doinel to be a journalist, in a film with the tentative title *Un jeune homme à Paris* (A Young Man in Paris). But finally he gave up the idea of journalism, as conventional and too literary and instead decided to make Doinel a private detective. The idea came to him from reading the back of a telephone directory: "Dubly Agency: Research, surveillance, investigations." He gave Claude de Givray and Bernard Revon the task of conducting a preliminary investigation into a detective agency, stressing that they be discreet and not mention his name. "Say it's a series for television!"[1] he told them. De Givray and Revon spent the entire spring of 1967 on preproduction work at Dubly Détective, a private agency on rue Saint-Lazare, run by a passionate cinema lover, Albert Duchenne. Claude de Givray recalls these work sessions with Duchenne, who ended up being a genuine collaborator on the script. "Albert Duchenne told us how to draw up a fake adultery report. A detective need only catch a wife in a hotel room with her lover; he requests that the husband be present, but the husband's testimony is insufficient, since he is both judge and litigant. The detective advises the husband to break everything in the room, until the night watchman calls the police. That way, the night watchman is a witness to disturbance of the peace. And it will be on record that the person who caused the disturbance is a jealous husband who had caught his wife in bed with her lover."[2] In the screenplay Doinel, who has just left the army, first gets a job as a night watchman in a Paris hotel and then as a private eye. To complete their research, de Givray and Revon questioned the personnel at the Terrass Hotel overlooking Montmartre cemetery—the very hotel where Truffaut had met Jean Genet sixteen years earlier.

In June, they gave Truffaut a first screenplay while he was completing *The Bride Wore Black*. It was entitled *Baisers volés (Stolen Kisses)*, a title chosen as a tribute to the singer Charles Trenet.[3] Ilya Lopert, head of the French branch of United Artists, was not entirely convinced by the screenplay, but he wanted to continue collaborating with Truffaut. United Artists reached an agreement with Carrosse, whereby they would invest up to $250,000 in the film and the profits would be split between the two companies. This was a smaller financial contribution on the part of United Artists than had been expected, which obliged Truffaut to keep his costs down in making the film.

In December 1967, helped by Revon and de Givray, Truffaut wrote a second version of the script of *Stolen Kisses*, for he wanted it to be a flexible chronicle "so improvisation can have the last word."[4] After the highly structured screenplays of *Fahrenheit 451* and *The Bride Wore Black*, Truffaut returned to moviemaking that renders the small events of life, leaves room for the imagination and the mood of the moment, and draws its inspiration from Renoir and Lubitsch rather than Hitchcock. A few months before the radical student uprisings of May 1968, Truffaut created a hero who seemed anachronistic, from another era, a romantic incapable of adapting to life or finding a stable job. The director's inspiration was entirely culled from the past, from his own youthful memories—the army, the visits to brothels, his desire to be accepted into a family.

Nine years after *The 400 Blows* and six years after *Antoine and Colette*, Truffaut was about to engage in a new collaboration with Jean-Pierre Léaud for the third Antoine Doinel adventure. Now twenty-three, the actor had become one of Godard's emblematic figures; between 1965 and 1967, he had appeared in *Pierrot le fou, Masculin-Féminin, Made in USA, La Chinoise, Weekend,* and the director's episode in *Le Plus Vieux Métier du monde.* He had acquired sufficient presence and strength of character so that Antoine Doinel began to resemble him more and more. In fact, beginning with *Stolen Kisses,* Doinel is part Truffaut, part Léaud. Increasingly, the character's gestures, attitudes, anecdotes, and even memories belong to Léaud himself. Truffaut was fully aware of this and encouraged it, never curbing Léaud's inspiration and improvisations. Léaud still lived in the bosom of the Carrosse family. He was lodged, most of the time, two flights above the company's offices, on rue Robert-Estienne, in an apartment rented by Truffaut on the fifth floor of the building. Except for periods when they were filming separately, Truffaut and Léaud would see each other regularly. There wasn't a single screenplay, a single film, television, or theater project offered to Léaud that wasn't first examined by Truffaut, whose opinion the actor always sought.

In January 1968, with advice from Gérard Lebovici and Serge Rousseau, his friends at the Artmédia agency, Truffaut began casting *Stolen Kisses*. The two women over whom Antoine Doinel is torn, Christine Darbon and Fabienne Tabard, must endow the film with romantic credibility. In the part of Fabienne—a "beautiful woman with a very vague, very gentle air"[5]—Truffaut had always visualized Delphine Seyrig, an actress he had admired in her two Alain Resnais films, *Last Year at Marienbad* and *Muriel*. On December 10, 1964, Truffaut saw Seyrig perform in Harold Pinter's *The Lover* at the Hébertot theater and was very impressed. She invited him to dinner that evening at her house on Place des Vosges. She reminded him of Louise de Vilmorin, the author of *Madame de . . .* , who had captivated him in 1950 when he was a young man; he found a similarity in her delicate traits and, to use Doinel's words, her "very pure oval" face, her pale complexion, "luminous, as though lit from the inside," and her very distinctive phrasing, "an admirable, deep tone." The actress was touched that she was selected for the part: "For me, I told you, the film will be like you and that is what counts. As for Fabienne 'de Mortsauf' I *adore* her. Though I have questions I'd like to ask you about her, and about Félix Antoine Léaud de Vandemesse. In any case, I'm having a lot of fun thinking about them."[6] Truffaut based the plot and atmosphere of the Antoine Doinel–Fabienne Tabard encounter on Balzac's *The Lily in the Valley*, which Jean-Pierre Léaud is reading at the beginning of the film. The analogy suited Delphine Seyrig perfectly; she was the ideal reincarnation of Madame de Mortsauf, the heroine of the Balzac novel.

Though the filming of *Stolen Kisses* was only several weeks away, the part of Christine Darbon, the pretty girl whom Antoine Doinel marries at the end of the picture, was still not cast. In late November 1967, Truffaut had attended the dress rehearsal of Pirandello's *Enrico IV*, directed by the well-known actor-director Sacha Pitoëff at the Théâtre Moderne, and saw a young nineteen-year-old actress, Claude Jade, perform onstage. He returned several times to see her perform, and a month later, he offered her the part of Christine Darbon. Thus did Claude Jade enter the life of Antoine Doinel—and of François Truffaut. From a good Protestant family of university teachers, she had a baccalaureate degree in philosophy and had came to Paris from Dijon, where she had studied dramatic art at the conservatory. Truffaut "was completely taken by her beauty, her manners, her kindness and her joie de vivre."[7] Claude Jade says, "I must have fit the image of the pure young girl. I was the right age and he felt Jean-Pierre Léaud, alias Antoine Doinel, and I could make a plausible couple. The first time I met him, François told me I looked like I belonged in a salon; he had been very amused because I used to answer politely, 'Yes, Monsieur, fine, Monsieur.' He stole little details from everyone—from me, my good upbringing, in my character's nickname, 'Peggy Proper'—Peggy because of her slight British air and because François knew I was the daughter of an English professor, and it amused him."[8]

Daniel Ceccaldi and Claire Duhamel were cast as the likable and friendly Darbon parents: "François said he liked girls who had nice parents,"[9] Claude Jade adds. Michael Lonsdale plays the unforgettable Monsieur Tabard, owner of the shoe shop, nicknamed "the Dinosaur" by his employees. Others in the cast include Jacques Robiolles, who was a friend of Truffaut; André Falcon as the owner of the detective agency; and Harry Max and Jacques Rispal. Truffaut felt very strongly about these supporting roles, for they were to instill life into the milieu in which the film was set. Marie-France Pisier replays Colette in a brief appearance, while Serge Rousseau plays the strange man in the trench coat who trails Christine Darbon and declares his "definitive" love at the end of the film.

In early February 1968, Truffaut was ready to film *Stolen Kisses*, with a crew that was almost entirely new. Clearly, this was a minor revolution. Suzanne Schiffman, acting as script supervisor and assistant, was one of the few people he kept from his previous team. He hired Denys Clerval as director of photography, Agnès Guillemot as editor, Antoine Duhamel to compose a tune "à la Charles Trenet," Jean-José Richer, formerly at *Cahiers,* as first assistant, and Roland Thénot, who had already worked on *The Bride,* as unit manager. All the preproduction work for the film had been accomplished in a mere two months; the success of a project is "10 percent inspiration and 90 percent perspiration,"[10] as the owner of the Blady detective agency observes in *Stolen Kisses.*

On February 5, 1968, on the eve of his thirty-sixth birthday, Truffaut was back in his childhood neighborhood—Villiers and Montmartre, Notre-Dame-de-Lorette and Place Clichy. The filming of his seventh feature took place at a swift, lively pace over the course of seven weeks. The actors remained true to their ways—Léaud read his lines only at the very last minute, while Claude Jade memorized them as soon as she could. But the ensemble worked harmoniously. The only sequence to present problems was the one in which Fabienne Tabard offers herself to Antoine Doinel in his furnished room; it was filmed on March 1 and 2 at the Avenir Hotel on boulevard de Rochechouart. Delphine Seyrig felt nervous, dissatisfied with her acting. "I very quickly realized how little I contributed to *Stolen*

*Kisses,*"[11] she later wrote to Truffaut, though he was sincerely captivated by her elegance and presence. "I'm in despair that I'm so lacking in inventiveness; Jean-Pierre Léaud impressed me—and everyone, I think—with his charm and freedom of movement and speech in front of the camera. You see, he has exactly the qualities I wanted to have. His freedom with words, his ease in improvising, this is what I would most like to acquire. And he has this naturally. I wish I had been more equal to the task."[12] Truffaut, however, felt that all his actors had performed at their best. He thought of *Stolen Kisses*—a light project, hastily written and shot—as one of those movies "saved in the filming,"[13] the kind he generally liked, dear to him because of the good memories they evoked.

## SCANDAL AT THE CINÉMATHÈQUE

The filming of *Stolen Kisses* would always remain associated in Truffaut's mind with one of the most exciting periods in his life—the mobilization to save Henri Langlois's Cinémathèque. One of Truffaut's last shots was filmed on March 29, 1968, in front of the locked gates of the Cinémathèque at the Palais de Chaillot. "This film is dedicated to Henri Langlois's Cinémathèque française," it says at the beginning of *Stolen Kisses*. And then we see a sign (in French) that reads CLOSED. THE DATE OF REOPENING WILL BE ANNOUNCED IN THE PRESS.

On February 7, 1968, two days into the filming, Jean-Louis Comolli, editor in chief of *Cahiers du cinéma,* tried to reach François Truffaut on the set. Rumors were circulating about the Cinémathèque's board of directors meeting in two days. It seemed Henri Langlois, the founder and director, was being seriously threatened with removal.[14] A visionary with insatiable energy, though he thrived in constant chaos, Langlois was a veritable symbol, for Truffaut as well as for scores of film lovers. Dismissing him would be a crime of "lèse-cinema." Truffaut, a member of the Cinémathèque's board of directors since the beginning of 1968, had not always agreed with Langlois's conception of his duties as film collector and programmer,[15] but he would be on the front line of the struggle to keep him in his position. Absorbed by his shoot, Truffaut had not planned to attend the board of directors meeting and had sent his proxy vote to Langlois. But Comolli's phone call had made him change his filming schedule for the day; he was at the Cinémathèque headquarters on rue de Courcelles on Friday morning, February 9.

Logically, the board of directors should have extended Langlois's mandate as director of the institution which he had created in 1936. But after paying him a glowing tribute, Pierre Moinot, an official from the Ministry of

Cultural Affairs and also the new president of the Cinémathèque, suggested, oddly enough, that Langlois be replaced by Pierre Barbin, director of the Tours and Annecy festivals. Several members of the board requested a week to make up their minds, but their request was denied. A vote was taken. The minority of independents, among whom were Jean Riboud, Ambroise Roux, Yvonne Dornès, François Truffaut, and several others, walked out of the meeting without voting. Barbin was elected to succeed Langlois. Quite obviously, everything had been arranged beforehand. One month before, rumors had already been circulating in the corridors of the Centre national de la cinématographie (CNC), an organization directed by André Holleaux. Langlois's friends had been wrong not to take these rumors seriously, so untouchable did Langlois seem to them. Two weeks before, during the Tours festival, a secret meeting had taken place among Barbin, Holleaux, Moinot, and Chevasson, an attaché in the cabinet of Minister of Culture André Malraux, to iron out the final details of a scheme that had originated at the highest levels. The maneuver seemed like an attempt to put the CNC, a supervisory government body, in control of the Cinémathèque, an independent nonprofit association with almost 780 members. Only the government subsidies the Cinémathèque received placed it in a dependent position vis-à-vis the Ministry of Cultural Affairs. There lay the great argument of the anti-Langlois faction: He was not a good administrator and put a serious strain on the institution with his odd habits and expenses.

The former *Cahiers* collaborators—Truffaut, Godard, Rivette, Chabrol, as well as Doniol-Valcroze, Kast, Astruc, and Renoir—defended Langlois. And now the protagonists of the fifties rebellion against "official" cinema were famous and had the support of the new generation—Marcel Ophuls, Claude Berri, Luc Moullet, Jean Eustache, Philippe Garrel, and the entire *Cahiers* editorial staff. A Defense Committee was led with ardor by Truffaut; its headquarters were at the offices of *Cahiers du cinéma.*

Undoubtedly thinking the matter was settled, André Holleaux left for a two-week vacation. On February 9 Pierre Barbin, accompanied by a small group of faithful supporters, moved into Langlois's office, making sure to change the locks. Several days later, Langlois's colleagues were fired—Marie Epstein, Lotte Eisner, and Mary Meerson.

On the morning of February 10, Langlois's friends began working shifts to gather the signatures of French and foreign directors. A hundred telegrams were sent from the post office on rue Clément Marot, near the *Cahiers* offices. The magazine's staff and the Carrosse secretaries were glued to the phone. They went through lists of personalities, letting their New Wave elders—excited by this renewed rebellious spirit—do the talking when appropriate. By early afternoon, a motion invited "all friends of cinema to show solidarity with any action that might reverse the arbitrary decision made against Henri Langlois."[16] On February 11, Renoir, Pagnol, and Tati responded, banning the screening of their films at the Cinémathèque if Langlois was not reinstated. Others followed suit—Gance, Resnais, Franju, Godard, Marker, Astruc, Chabrol, Bresson, Mocky, Robert Florey, Richard Lester, Lindsay Anderson, Henri Cartier-Bresson, Michel Simon, Busby Berkeley. They received signed petitions—from members of the association of Danish directors, headed by Carl Dreyer, and from the association of American critics, led by Andrew Sarris—and a manifesto of Japanese film-makers, drafted by Kurosawa, Oshima, Naruse, Yoshida, and sixteen others. There were also impressive telegrams from such well-known personalities as Josef von Sternberg, Jerry Lewis, Gloria Swanson, Chaplin, Rossellini, and Fritz Lang, all of whom banned further screenings of their films at the Cinémathèque pending Langlois's reinstatement.

On February 10, the press joined in. Henry Chapier in *Combat* and Jean de Baroncelli in *Le Monde* both carried the headline SCANDAL AT THE CINÉMATHÈQUE. "France is in no way short of good accountants or good administrators. But there was only one Henri Langlois. Will we accept his being snatched away from us?" wrote Baroncelli. On the 12th, Truffaut, Chabrol, Philippe Tesson, and Henry Chapier (with the famous headline THE MALRAUX MYTH HAS LASTED LONG ENOUGH) all published articles in *Combat*. Truffaut attacked Malraux violently: "Since taking office, all of André Malraux's decisions concerning cinema have been disastrous. A small frenetic figure, isolated in his dream factory which the striking filmmakers have evacuated, André Malraux should be aware that we don't have a short-term antimemory and that we won't forget he 'dropped' Henri Langlois just as he previously 'dropped' Jacques Flaud, Pierre Boulez, Jean Genet, Gaë-tan Picon, Rivette and his friend Diderot."[17]

On February 12, at 10:00 p.m., in response to an appeal launched by Michel Simon and Claude Berri, two to three hundred directors, critics, film enthusiasts, and actors, including many from the cast and crew of *Stolen Kisses* led by Truffaut, Léaud, and Claude Jade, blocked the entrance to the Cinémathèque screening room on rue d'Ulm. The CNC timidly counterattacked—an unsigned article in *France-Soir* criticized "the confusion into which French cinema and the Cinémathèque have been sinking for years."[18] Claude Autant-Lara was the only one to agree; he attacked Langlois and the New Wave rally around the Cinémathèque on the France Inter radio station. At the same time, the closing of the two Cinémathèque screening rooms for "inventory and reorganization" seemed like the first sign of weakness on the part of the new administration. The mobilization culminated on February 14, a day that marked a milestone—never before had policemen been seen charging into a demonstration of directors and actors. In response to an appeal from the "Children of the Cinémathèque," three thousand people reassembled on the esplanade of the Trocadéro. At 3:00 p.m., about thirty vanloads of police and security forces surrounded the neighborhood, barring access to the Cinémathèque. Television cameras were present; the government-owned French stations avoided reporting the events, but they were reported, briefly, on the foreign stations. A tract was distributed and read publicly by the actor Jean-Pierre Kalfon. Then the crowd headed toward the Palais de Chaillot, chanting, "Holleaux resign!" and "No to the Barbinthèque!" The first police cordon and the first clashes occurred in the gardens of the Trocadéro. Godard succeeded in crossing the barriers but found himself alone, surrounded by police, who let him retreat. The demonstrators bypassed the police cordons, headed back up the esplanade, and marched down the avenue du Président Wilson, blocking traffic. At the corner of the avenue Albert de Mun, where most of the security forces were parked, there was a new, more aggressive police barricade. Several ranks of police charged into the demonstrators. Some people were wounded and required help; Truffaut, severely shaken, was cared for in the entranceway to a building. Godard, stunned, looked for his lost sunglasses; Tavernier had blood dripping down his face; Yves Boisset's wife had been thrown to the ground. The crowd surged back to the Trocadéro and Godard, who was now directing operations, shouted orders to disperse. The troops had been driven back by the police assault, but their fighting spirit lived on. Above all, thanks to this demonstration, public opinion took up the cause of Langlois's defenders. It seems unlikely that the police prefect was congratulated by Malraux, or President Charles de Gaulle, that evening.

Taking advantage of this moral victory, on February 16 Langlois's supporters held a press conference at the Studio Action attended by three hundred journalists and five foreign television stations. By then, a new communiqué had come down from the ministry, retreating from the CNC's initial positions and suggesting that Langlois should be appointed to "new artistic duties." The text also announced the shelving of the plan dear to Pierre Barbin, of copyrighting films at the Cinémathèque, along the lines of the Bibliothèque Nationale. That plan would have placed Langlois's museum (shaped by his own personal view of the history of cinema) under permanent government control. Langlois's supporters could therefore adopt a confident, victorious tone at the press conference. Godard and Truffaut were still the main speakers, but Rivette, Chabrol, Kast, Doniol-Valcroze, Astruc, Resnais, and Rouch also had their say, advised by the lawyer Georges Kiejman. The journalists left the conference convinced that it was only a matter of days before Langlois would be reinstated, but no one let up the pressure. On February 20, at about 6:00 p.m., following an appeal by Françoise Rosay, Jean Marais, and René Allio, four hundred demonstrators surrounded the Cinémathèque offices on rue de Courcelles. On the

26th, a "committee for the defense of the Cinémathèque française," made up of about twenty film personalities, was created on Truffaut's initiative, with him as treasurer. This committee was in charge of coordinating the actions that were multiplying in France and around the world in support of Langlois. Renoir was the committee's honorary president and Resnais its acting president. On this occasion, Renoir offered a vibrant tribute to Langlois in the press, calling him "the creator of our very own Louvre" and "the only man who can bring together all filmmakers of goodwill."[19]

## VIVE LANGLOIS!

André Malraux understood that he had to back down. On March 5, at a meeting of the Cinémathèque's board of directors, Jean Riboud—head of the Schlumberger oil drilling company and a friend of Langlois and his long-time companion, Mary Meerson—suggested an "advisory committee" be set up with the task of finding a compromise. An independent figure, Georges Vedel, former dean of the Faculté de droit et de sciences économiques de Paris, was appointed director. As another proof of goodwill, Rivette was included among the five "wise men" on the committee. The members decided to schedule an extraordinary general meeting of the Cinémathèque membership on April 22, 1968, the only authority that could officially reverse the February 9 decision.

In the meantime, there were ongoing power struggles. Pierre Moinot, the president of the Cinémathèque, tried to eclipse Pierre Barbin, who clung to his prestigious position of artistic director. Lotte Eisner and Mary Meerson were still undesirables at rue de Courcelles. The defense committee began to worry about management's tergiversations and thought the latter might try to take advantage of a deteriorating situation to set up the new Cinémathèque. Truffaut decided to come out once again in the press and denounce the ministry's compromise solutions. He wrote in *Combat* on March 11, 1968:

> If the Moinot-Barbin duo were just dolts eager to have their blunder forgotten, the fight would indeed be almost won and we could believe that the administration was preparing Barbin's departure and Langlois's return within a proper lapse of time so as not to lose face. In my opinion the opposite is true. For we are facing ill-intentioned people who on some days are afraid, but on others are carried away by the disproportionate promotions they gained through political connections. . . . Formerly, the government used to get rid of blunderers, tactless fools and boors by sending them to Algeria or New Caledonia. In the France of

1968, the Moinots and Barbins cling to Paris, they want to eat at Lipp's, bring festivals to a close, hand out little medals to visiting foreigners and bouquets of flowers to female stars; they dig in their heels, take root, irritate, and they aggravate their cases.

The Langlois affair took a political turn. On March 21, Grenoble rallied to the cause, at the initiative of the two city's film clubs and the local section of the PSU (Socialist party). Le Rex movie theater was too small to accommodate the audience that came to listen to the eminent speaker defending Langlois—Pierre Mendès-France, elected several months earlier as deputy of the city. Truffaut organized this meeting personally, with the help of Jean-Louis Comolli and Georges Kiejman, who was close to Mendès-France. "Grenoble is the biggest punch we could throw at present," Truffaut wrote Comolli on March 8. "Also, I think we should let it be known. . . . Let's try to see each other tonight after the shoot, possibly at my screening of dailies (8:00 p.m., Ponthieu theater), to look into the situation."[20] Several days earlier, during questions addressed to the government at the National Assembly, François Mitterrand had tried to destabilize Malraux on the Langlois issue. The conflict had thus turned overtly political, a development that the committee for the defense of the Cinémathèque wanted to take advantage of. Indeed, on March 26, Truffaut sent Mitterrand a letter and a packet of information on the subject, for use on April 8, when the opposition leader was to appear on the television program *Face à Face*: "We hope that on April 8 you will take advantage of the opportunity to break the silence that the ORTF [French government radio and television] has maintained on this affair since the beginning,"[21] Truffaut wrote to Mitterrand.

On Monday, April 22, 1968, several hundred members of the Cinémathèque française assembled at the auditorium of Arts et Métiers on avenue d'Iéna for the special general meeting on Langlois's fate. Dean Georges Vedel read out the advisory committee's conclusions: "The Cinémathèque, a nonprofit association, will be organized and managed like a private group without state interference into its internal affairs. . . ."[22] Langlois was unanimously reelected to his duties as artistic and technical director. Pierre Moinot and Pierre Barbin were removed, as was the board of directors. On May 2, the theater on rue d'Ulm reopened its doors. Moved and beaming, Langlois encouraged lengthy applause for Truffaut and ended his welcoming speech with a resounding "Make way for the movies!"

For the public present that day, the event was essentially political. Directors and film enthusiasts had had their first taste of territorial struggles waged against the administration and the Gaullist government—street demonstrations, militancy, and defense committees. Every Langlois supporter had lived through his own May '68 two months early. Pierre Kast showed foresight in pointing this out in April, in the two-hundredth issue of *Cahiers du cinéma,* which was dedicated to Langlois: "I realize that though it's impossible to shout 'Long live Castro' without shouting 'Long live Langlois,' it's perfectly possible to shout 'Long live Langlois' without thinking 'Long live Castro.' But still, these scuffles, these tracts, these committee rooms, these discussions reach way beyond the Cinémathèque affair. . . . Cinema has become much more than a commodity retailed in specialized places. And defending the existence of the Cinémathèque française is a political act, oddly enough."

In April 1968, though he willingly shouted "Long live Langlois!" Truffaut had no desire to shout "Long live Castro!" Yet his political commitment against the Gaullist government definitely left a deep mark. From the Manifesto of the 121 in the fall of 1960 to the committee for the defense of the Cinémathèque in the spring of 1968, he showed consistency in thought and action. He always rallied to the cause of freedom of expression against a government that he saw as clumsy, interventionist, censorial, and tactless. However, though Truffaut had rubbed shoulders with people on the Left, and considered them more upright and more attentive to creative freedom, he was not ready to commit himself politically, for he deeply distrusted political discourse and people in politics. "There's the blockheadedness of an impossible régime," he wrote to Louis Marcorelles to explain Langlois's eviction, "but also the fact that, from De Gaulle to Mitterrand and Deferre, except for the modest Mendès-France, too many so-called 'elites' don't understand a thing about cinema and never will."[23]

## CURTAINS IN CANNES

After his difficult *Fahrenheit* years, François Truffaut's support of Langlois was a marvelous, "rejuvenating experience." The spring of 1968 infused him with unexpected, renewed enthusiasm. He lived through the period in a feverish, intoxicated state, on very few hours' sleep, his energies divided between a lively, quick shoot and the time-consuming demands of activism. "I can still see him on the avenue Albert de Mun," his friend Georges Kiejman says, "running like a rabbit and jumping over a row of cars to reach the front ranks and join those who were about to get beat up by the police. When I saw him bolting in front of me, he seemed the adolescent from *The 400 Blows* and I remember thinking at the time that no matter what age he would live to, he would remain an eternal adolescent."[24]

Undoubtedly, Truffaut was also happy in the spring of 1968, because he was in love with Claude Jade. The feelings were mutual; and for Claude Jade, who had just turned twenty, Truffaut was her first love. Sacha Pitoëff's wife had even gone and told Claude Jade's parents about their daughter's June marriage plans. Before leaving for England to spend time with her sister, Claude had chosen a wedding dress. The decision to get married had apparently been made on an impulse; Truffaut hadn't warned anyone, outside of his family. He had asked Berbert in passing, "Are you free on such and such a day? . . . Fine! You'll be my witness."[25]

In early May, France was shaken by the great student uprisings in the section of the city near the Sorbonne and the erection of barricades on rue Gay-Lussac. On the 13th, a million demonstrators marched down the streets of Paris, from the République to Denfert-Rochereau, and the whole country was paralyzed by the first day of general strikes involving the electrical company (EDF), public transportation (RAPT), railroads (SNCF), post office, and telephones (all government-owned)—strikes that immediately spread to the private sector. Meanwhile, in Cannes, at the start of the twenty-first film festival, all activity was suspended for twenty-four hours, at the request of the majority of film critics present; the screenings of Carlos Saura's *Peppermint frappé* and Frank Perry's *Trilogy,* based on stories by Truman Capote, which had been scheduled for that day, were postponed to May 18. Truffaut happened to be in Cannes between the 11th and 13th, preparing for two events he felt very strongly about. On Saturday, May 18, he was to join Claude Berri, Roger Vadim, Jacques Robert, and Claude Lelouch, for a press conference, presided over by Alain Resnais, explaining the initiative of the committee for the defense of the Cinémathèque; in the afternoon, he and Henri Langlois were to preside over a tribute to Georges Sadoul, the Communist critic who had died the previous fall. On May 13, given the scope of the general strikes and the first factory sit-ins, Truffaut advised the festival director, Robert Favre Le Bret, simply to interrupt the festival proceedings. He refused. That evening, Truffaut was back in Paris, supervising the editing of *Stolen Kisses* with Agnès Guillemot. The student movement was gaining momentum, and so were the factory strikes; Truffaut followed the events closely on the radio. But not even for a minute did he consider joining the street demonstrations; he remained an attentive witness.

On May 17, in the late morning, he drove back down to Cannes, making good time on deserted roads. At noon on the same day in Paris, a meeting of the technicians' union had been joined by a delegation of striking directors, and it was decided to call for a meeting of all industry professionals, that very night, at the Ecole de Photographie et de Cinéma on rue de Vaugirard, which was occupied by its students. At 9:00 p.m., the entire profession was gathered shoulder-to-shoulder on rue de Vaugirard. The meetings and demonstrations surrounding the Langlois affair had mushroomed into the "Etats généraux du cinéma français" (Estates General of French Cinema), an open call for greater freedom in film and television. Over twelve hundred professionals and students held regular meetings for over two weeks; they took part in endless debates, worked on committees, and presented plans for changing and renewing the film industry. This was tantamount to a small revolution in French cinema, which up to then had customarily been compartmentalized, torn with dissension, and under the supervision of the CNC. Two decisions were made in the course of this first meeting of the Etats généraux: first, a vote in favor of a film workers' strike, effective the next day—thereby interrupting the filming of Gérard Oury's *The Brain* at the Saint-Maurice Studio and the editing of *Stolen Kisses;* second, a motion requesting the shutdown of the Cannes festival, as a show of solidarity for the striking workers and students.

That night, Jacques Rivette, who was present at the first meeting of the Etats généraux, contacted Truffaut at the Hotel Martinez and informed him of these developments. Truffaut in turn notified the other directors attending the festival (Godard, Malle, Lelouch, the Czech filmmakers Jan Němec and Miloš Forman, Resnais, Richard Lester, Roman Polanski, Carlos Saura), suggesting they take action as quickly as possible. Those whose films were in competition—Forman (*The Firemen's Ball*), Resnais (*Je t'aime, je t'aime*), Lelouch (*Grenoble*), Němec (*A Report on the Party and the Guests*), Lester (*Petulia*), and Saura (*Peppermint frappé*)—were advised to withdraw their films, while Malle and Polanski promised to resign from the jury. On the morning of May 18, Truffaut, speaking on behalf of the Etats généraux, called on the many critics and directors attending the press conference on the Langlois affair to shut down the festival. One hour later, Godard suggested occupying the large auditorium of the Palais where the films were to be shown. As the hall filled up with spectators for Saura's film, a delegation made up of Truffaut, Malle, Godard, Gabriel Albicocco, Berri, and Lelouch walked onstage and announced the festival shutdown. The "conspirators" were joined by other directors and friends, such as Jean-Louis Richard and Jean-Pierre Léaud. In an unbelievable brouhaha, everyone awaited the decision of the jury as it deliberated on whether to resign, and that of the competing filmmakers while they discussed whether to withdraw their films. Stormy discussions took place during this waiting period; the majority "reformists" suggested a festival overhaul (more unofficial selections, possible retrospectives and discussions, repeal of the prize giving) while the "radicals" demanded an immediate shutdown. The news they received reinforced the latter's stance: Four members of the jury had resigned (Roman Polanski, Monica Vitti, Terence Young, and Louis Malle), and an ever-growing number of directors were withdrawing their films. Robert Favre Le Bret then proclaimed the festival noncompetitive but still on. Most of the public attending the festival was satisfied and loudly requested the showing of Saura's *Peppermint frappé*, starring Geraldine

Chaplin. Onstage, the "radicals" stuck to their position and tried to prevent the screening. Shoulder-to-shoulder, they faced a turbulent, enraged audience. Cheers rose from the public as the lights came down and the screening began. But the curtain was held firmly closed by the rebels, including Saura and Geraldine Chaplin, who were soon roughed up by police forces. Godard was slapped in the face and once again lost his glasses; Truffaut was tackled at the waist and thrown to the floor by an angry audience member. Several minutes later, the lights went on and Favre Le Bret made a second statement, announcing the cancellation of the afternoon and evening screenings. Interminable discussions continued far into the night in the large auditorium of the Palais. The "radicals" succeeded in their bid for power: At noon the following day, Favre Le Bret, feeling unable to pursue his mission, brought the festival to a close.

The "saboteurs," the "luxury fanatics" were violently attacked by the Gaullist press and the Cannes audience, for having "torpedoed" the festival "for good."[26] Truffaut justified himself in an interview: "No one seemed to want to understand that the country was paralyzed and that it was logical to stop the festivities. We had to get the festival to shut down and we did. This could have been done more elegantly, but in such circumstances you leave elegance in the cloakroom and even mislay the key. I know that a lot of people will reproach us for our attitude in Cannes for a long time to come, but I also know that two days later, when there were no more planes, no more trains, no cigarettes, no telephone service and no fuel, the festival would have been held up to incredible ridicule if it had continued to function."[27]

Meanwhile, in Paris, the Etats généraux tried to organize a mobilization. On May 19, the technicians union joined the directors from the government-owned radio and television stations (ORTF), the students from the Institut des Hautes Etudes Cinématographiques (IDHEC) and the Etats généraux in proclaiming an unlimited strike with sit-ins in the workplaces: "We film professionals (directors, technicians, workers, students and critics) are on strike for an unlimited period of time to denounce and destroy the reactionary structures of a cinema which has become a commercial commodity. We will give up our fight only when we have become the administrators and managers of our own profession."[28] The determination to do away with the existing state-controlled structures was affirmed on May 21. On that day, the Etats généraux voted on a motion declaring the abolition of the "CNC's privileges": "The Etats généraux of French cinema consider the CNC's reactionary structures abolished. It follows that its existence, representativeness and rules are no longer recognized by the profession. The new structures of our profession will have to grow out of the Etats généraux."[29] The motion of May 21 would be a milestone in cinema's utopian May landscape, even if nothing came of it. Three other general assemblies met on May 26 and 28 at the Centre culturel de l'Ouest parisien, in Suresnes, and presented nineteen plans for restructuring French cinema; June 5 was devoted to a tricky synthesizing project, which would quickly fall into oblivion—particularly since the legislative elections (June 23 and 30) gave General de Gaulle an overwhelming majority at the National Assembly. Abolishing the CNC was now out of the question.

When he returned from Cannes on May 19, Truffaut refused to become involved in the Etats généraux. On the 21st, he became disenchanted when attending a session where he found the idealism, lack of realism, and lack of preparation profoundly irritating: "There were workers there who wanted to shoot 140 films a year instead of 80," he said, "which is impossible; there were creative people who wanted greater freedom, hence fewer union constraints with all the same acquired benefits; and budding directors whose chances of entering the profession were so slight that they hoped for a revolution so that everything could start again from scratch. These meetings were bound to fail, and I should add bound to fail even if a left-wing government had come to power, because cinema will always be at the bottom of any government's list of concerns."[30] Similarly, Truffaut refused to join the Société des réalisateurs de films (Society of Filmmakers), which was being created then at the initiative of some of his friends, among whom were Kast and Doniol-Valcroze. In justification, he explained, "I feel solidarity for Rivette, Godard and Rohmer because I like them and admire their work, but I don't want to have anything to do with Jacqueline Audry, Serge Bourguignon, Jean Delannoy or Jacques Poitrenaud. The fact of having the same profession is meaningless to me if admiration and friendship don't come into play."[31]

On the other hand, Truffaut felt close to the student movement, especially at the end of May and the beginning of June, when it began to flag under political pressure and police repression. "I admire the students and I approve of their fight," he wrote in *Les Nouvelles littéraires*. "I didn't have the luck to be a student, only a schoolboy who had to earn a living at fourteen. Some people pursue their studies, me, I've been pursued by studies. Because of that, my knowledge is full of holes and I'm slower than others at understanding what has to be understood."[32] As a show of support for the student cause, on May 8, at the request of Marguerite Duras, he had signed a manifesto on their behalf. On the 15th, he had donated one thousand francs to the Committee on Direct Action and Creativity. Though he refused to visit the occupied Sorbonne—"I didn't want to act like a tourist, a member of the Paris 'smart set' "[33]—he often dropped by the Théâtre de l'Odéon, which was occupied and the scene of permanent discussions until it was "cleaned out" by the police on June 14: "I went there often, almost every evening at one point. One felt the need for a place where anyone could say anything they liked, as you can in the streets of London."[34]

Moreover, in a spirit of solidarity and for the first time in his life, Truffaut took part in the last big student demonstration in the Latin Quarter on June 1, 1968; he had refused to do so on May 24, when the Etats généraux du cinéma had marched for the day of social action organized by the CGT (union). "I've always been an individualist. I've always considered the people in the political contest as opponents. This may be for personal reasons: the cops beat me up when I was a kid, and I've always felt that political parties never concerned themselves with the one thing that touched me in life, antisocial people. . . . So what moved me about the students was that they were returning the blows they'd received from the police. I followed their entire movement; I even marched, though I had never marched before. I feel an enormous admiration for young people who are capable of chanting 'We're all German Jews!' I never thought we'd ever see intelligence, humor, strength and justice in the street at the same time. This is what stirred me."[35]

## THE FAMILY SAGA

After these weeks of political unrest and excitement, Truffaut backed down, in a somewhat cowardly fashion, from marrying Claude Jade, pleading he didn't feel ready for the commitment. The May events—the disorderly spectacle, which he had witnessed with delight—probably played a part. Truffaut became aware of the generation gap between the young actress and himself, but also of their different views of life. Helen Scott, in whom he had confided, had had no compunctions about dissuading him: "You'll just gobble her up!"[36] she had said about Claude Jade. His close friends, such as Helen and Claude de Givray, saw him as a bit of a Bluebeard. And suddenly, at thirty-six, the ghosts of his childhood revisited him.

Several months earlier, when he was finishing *Stolen Kisses*, Truffaut, like the clients in the film, met with Albert Duchenne, the owner of the Dubly detective agency. His purpose was to request a confidential search for his biological father—the man who had seduced his mother, Janine de Monferrand, made her pregnant in the spring of 1931, and then mysteriously disappeared.

Albert Duchenne took personal charge of the case and after several weeks of investigation handed Truffaut a confidential report.[37] According to his findings, Truffaut's father was Roland Lévy, born in Bayonne in 1910, son of Gaston Lévy and Berthe Kahn. After attending secondary school on the Basque coast and obtaining his baccalaureate degree, he moved to Paris in the late twenties and attended dentistry school in the Lorettes neighborhood. This was where he met Janine de Monferrand. He saw her in the early thirties but then left her before François's birth. After his studies, Roland Lévy settled in the Opéra neighborhood and began practicing dental surgery in 1938. Being Jewish, the man presumed to be François Truffaut's father had had to leave German-occupied Paris and take refuge in the provinces. The detectives tracked him down in Belfort, where he had settled in 1946. There he became engaged to a fellow dental surgeon, Andrée Blum, almost ten years younger than he, whom he married in July 1949. They lived in a building on boulevard Carnot, in the center of town, and had their dental practice on the third floor. The couple had two children, but they separated in 1959 after ten years of marriage.

François Truffaut was simultaneously distressed and relieved by this revelation. So he didn't completely belong to *her* family. He was deeply troubled to discover that the person who was probably his father was Jewish —the discovery gave the May students' chant "We're all German Jews" a truly stirring overtone. In a long, unpublished conversation with Claude de Givray at the end of his life, Truffaut confided that "he had always felt Jewish."[38] He connected this feeling with his penchant for outlaws, martyrs, social outcasts, marginal people, and his affirmation of the "other," which he claimed he himself had been all through his youth. He had already discovered his Jewishness in September 1945 at the Cinéac-Italiens when he saw the films of the liberation of the concentration camps. As he sat in the dark theater all alone, the young François—ignored by his mother, beaten by police, and sent away to a reformatory—felt like the "Jew" of the Truffaut-Monferrand family. Later, cinema contributed to his feelings of identification: There in the movies, which he saw over and over again, was a free space, separate from the world, a smuggled "other world" where the "Jew" could finally live a full life, with no constraints. Subsequently, in a certain sense, he created a double for himself,[39] which was the inverted portrait of the "Jew"—the young "hussar," the brilliant journalist fascinated by Rebatet, the ambitious director, the bourgeois, the politically uncommitted artist. At every opportunity, however, the "Jew" would resurface and peer through the overly smooth portrait presented to the press, and then his true personality would be revealed—that of the adult still affected by his battered childhood, the man who had constant feelings of guilt (in both his romantic disappointments and his professional setbacks), the loner fleeing society. This wild side always prevailed over his civilized alter ego, and it drove him to live like an outlaw in the midst of his success, and on the fringe of society in spite of the recognition he had gained. This conflicting impulse had nothing to do with the lifestyle of an "accursed artist"; it had a deeper origin, in a fate he had accepted since childhood—being the "Jew" of others, especially of an intolerant family.

In the spring of 1968, Truffaut kept his Jewish origins secret. He told only Madeleine and Helen Scott, and two film producers, Pierre Braunberger and Ilya Lopert. But it was reflected in some of his actions. For example, at a time when many of his friends leaned toward an anti-Zionist leftism, a year after the Six-Day War, he became, at Ilya Lopert's request, a member of the Fonds de solidarité avec Israël, and thereafter regularly contributed several thousand francs in annual dues.

On August 22, 1968, Janine de Monferrand died of cirrhosis of the liver. His mother's death abruptly thrust François Truffaut back to the wounds of his childhood. "Helen Scott had to push him to get him to go to the funeral,"[40] Madeleine Morgenstern recalls. For Truffaut was far from reconciled with his mother, for whom he felt a deep-seated resentment. The funeral ceremony on August 28 at the Church of Saint-Vincent-de-Paul, near the rue La Fayette, was particularly painful for him, since the Monferrand family was hostile to him. It was only after his mother's death that Truffaut's anger would gradually be dispelled. He even felt touched when he emptied her apartment on rue de Navarin and found documents that she had lovingly kept—"press clippings about him, with deletions and markings, which proved that she had been interested in him and not indifferent,"[41] says Madeleine.

All these events occurring in rapid succession in a period of months—Françoise Dorléac's death, the discovery of his real father, his mother's death, his hasty retreat from marriage—led François Truffaut to reexamine his life in detail. At the end of the summer of 1968, he immersed himself in the papers he found in the family apartment, his school and personal notebooks, his letters as an adolescent, the traces of his early life—his arrest and detention, his passion for films, and his military detention in 1951. He also worked on the various intimate journals he had kept in his youth, made rewrites, and gave them shape and focus. Moreover, he set down on paper various parts of his life: "My Childhood," "My Military Life," "My Articles," "My Films," "My Women," "My Friends." He contemplated using these meticulously kept documents—in which dates and facts were amassed in a precise, almost compulsive way—to write his autobiography, a project he abandoned in order to put together a collection of his main articles on cinema, *Les Films de ma vie*. During this same period, he came up with the idea for several more intimate and autobiographical films, including *L'Homme qui aimait les femmes* (*The Man Who Loved Women*), *La Chambre verte* (*The Green Room*), and *L'Amour en fuite* (*Love on the Run*). In sum, Truffaut tried to "explain his life" and come to terms with his own history; looking backward, he reworked the different strands of his life, from film to film, woman to woman, death to death,[42] recording everything in writing and putting it away in his most secret files.[43]

Yet one vital part of his life remained unknown: Why had his real father left Janine de Monferrand? Why wasn't his name François Lévy? Had the young dentist rejected a woman he considered too different from him, given his ambitions and his religion? Or had the Monferrand family interfered in the romance and wrecked it forever? Truffaut wrote to his family requesting information concerning his birth and his real father. The only person to reply to his letter was Suzanne de Saint-Martin, his maternal grandmother's sister-in-law: "I want to assure you on the subject of your birth (not that I know the exact name of your father), but I was in Paris at that time for my final teaching exams. I used to spend Sundays at your grandmother Viève's house. Your grandfather, Jean, very much the snob and very devout, was furious about Janine's follies with the workers in the neighborhood, people of common birth; but he never mentioned Jews, and he certainly would have with even greater wrath. . . . No, you're a real Frenchman from the Languedoc, from Brugnac, where your grandmother was born. . . ."[44] This letter, by its very denial, strengthened Truffaut's conviction that Roland Lévy had been banished from Janine de Monferrand's life because of anti-Semitism.[45] As practicing Catholics, titled nobles, and former anti-Dreyfusards, the men in the Monferrand family couldn't accept a Jew among them.

Though Truffaut tried to reconstruct the family saga, the story of his origins, certain doubts remained. One day in September 1968, he went to Belfort. He kept in his archives a map of the city with the route from the station to the boulevard Carnot neatly mapped out in pen.[46] Starting at seven in the evening, he posted himself at the foot of a six-story building dating from the early postwar period. According to the detective's report, Roland Lévy went out every night after dinner for a short walk in the neighborhood. He lived alone and followed a strict daily routine. At 8:30, a man in his sixties, stout and of medium height, muffled up in a gray coat, a scarf tied around his neck, opened the door to the building. But just then Truffaut turned away; he felt he couldn't disrupt a man's habits with the sudden revelation that he was his son. That night, he took a room in town and isolated himself in a movie house where they were showing Chaplin's *Gold Rush*.

## WHAT IS LEFT OF OUR LOVES?

This succession of events in spring and summer 1968 sheds light on François Truffaut's many separate, compartmentalized lives—interconnected by secret pathways. A hardworking, active movie director; a militant film devotee when championing Langlois; a "saboteur" at the Cannes festival, determined that cinema be in sync with a country on strike; a "student" in May; a "Jew" who discovered himself as such at the death of his mother; a womanizer—Truffaut succeeded in being all these personalities simultaneously; he showed no loss of composure with close friends and family, though, within himself, these many interconnections troubled him deeply.

Unexpectedly, thanks to *Stolen Kisses*, Les Films du Carrosse was financially sound once again. This film, which Truffaut had shot in a carefree spirit, with the Langlois affair absorbing his energies almost every evening, had been, as he himself put it, "sacrificed."[47] Simultaneously whimsical and rather nostalgic, it also seemed completely out-of-date in the atmosphere of May '68. Paradoxically, what might have seemed a handicap turned into an asset. The carefree spirit of the shoot gave the film rhythm, freedom, and melancholy, and its slightly outmoded ambiance proved perfectly attuned to audience expectations; after a spring of feverish political activism, the autumn mood was light and frivolous. The revolution had failed and, with it, the documentary and the political film. The audience returned to fiction, dreams, nostalgia, and smiles. This turn of events doesn't detract at all from Truffaut's personal merit, but it explains the unusual commercial fate of this small film.

*Stolen Kisses* was shown in preview on the closing night of the Avignon Festival, August 14, 1968. In 1968, the festival itself was an event, rocked by the "spirit of May." There were violent protests against Jean Vilar, the director of the festival; the Living Theatre imposed its conception of happenings; and the CRS (National Guard) was deployed in the streets. *Stolen Kisses* seemed completely out of step with this atmosphere. But the thirty thousand viewers present made the film into a triumphant success. The paradox was immediately apparent: The film captivated audiences but was perceived as anachronistic, almost reactionary. Released on September 4, 1968, in three Paris movie theaters, *Stolen Kisses* was favorably received by the press, which kept alluding to the "timeless" theme of the film. *Freshness, spontaneity, intensity, humor, freedom, emotion, tenderness, modesty*, and *comedy* were words used constantly with reference to it. In *Paris-Soir*, Michel Aubriant painted a revealing portrait of a mellowed Truffaut, "all sugar and spice": "It is incredible how much he has changed in ten years, the insolent young man who used to fight tooth and nail against a certain kind of old fogy cinema. Only imbeciles don't change. And grand principles are meant to be transgressed. Yes, Truffaut has evolved. One can't forever be breaking windows and throwing cobblestones."[48] Truffaut's reputation was now based on this rejection of trendiness and modernity: For the popular press, he incarnated the cinema of bygone days. These critics were all unaware of the fact that, deep down, this "acceptable" and "mellowed" Truffaut concealed secrets and facets of his personality that were far more somber and morbid. This gloomier side is revealed in his film in the disquieting character played by Serge Rousseau (one of Truffaut's best friends and Marie Dubois's husband), the man in the trench coat, who suddenly materializes at the end of *Stolen Kisses* to declare his "definitive love" to Claude Jade, a love stronger than death.

After a four-month run in Paris, the success of the picture was clear: 335,000 tickets had been sold. Awarded the Louis-Delluc Prize, on January 9, 1969, it attracted almost fifty thousand new viewers. *Stolen Kisses*, which had been made for a modest sum, brought in three times its investment. It was very well received in New York, by the press and by the public. "Everything Truffaut touches seems to be spontaneously invested with the lyricism that marks his greatest films. It is one of Truffaut's best,"[49] wrote Vincent Canby in the *New York Times*. It did very well at the Fine Arts Theater, where it opened on March 3, 1969. Not since *The 400 Blows* had any Truffaut film "brought as much money into the till."[50] Les Films du Carrosse thereby recovered from its troubled period of the late sixties and got a new start. *Stolen Kisses*, a "sacrificed," modest, outmoded film, set Truffaut back on the path to success.

## BELLE DE NUIT

The unexpected popularity of *Stolen Kisses* allowed Truffaut to finally take on a more ambitious film, *La Sirène du Mississippi* (*Mississippi Mermaid*), which he had nurtured for a long time. He had read William Irish's novel *Waltz into Darkness* about ten years earlier, when Madeleine Morgenstern had given it to him while visiting him in Nîmes on the set of *The Mischief Makers* in August 1957. But the idea of adapting it to the screen dated to the summer of 1966. He was completing *Fahrenheit 451* when the brothers Robert and Raymond Hakim offered to finance his next film, provided he cast Catherine Deneuve in it. The actress was working with Luis Buñuel at the time, on *Belle de jour*, a Hakim production. Truffaut was invited to view some rushes and have lunch with her. He was completely won over. A very short time later, he went to the Hakim brothers with the idea of adapting *Waltz into Darkness* with her in the lead female role and Jean-Paul Belmondo playing opposite her. During the autumn of 1966, negotiations took place between the Hakim brothers and Gérard Lebovici, the owner of Artmédia and the agent of the two stars, but they broke off abruptly when the "Brothers Zaquime," as Truffaut nicknamed them, demanded the right to approve the final cut.[51]

The *Mississippi Mermaid* project then made the rounds. A German producer offered to buy back the rights from the Hakims and cast Brigitte Bardot and Jean-Paul Belmondo as the couple. Truffaut refused; he would have no one but Catherine Deneuve for the film and she would have no other director. Then in autumn 1967, Truffaut was notified by Don Congdon, his New York literary agent, that the Hakims didn't actually own the rights to the Irish novel and that he had been "completely hoodwinked."[52] The rights belonged to Twentieth Century–Fox, which was asking fifty thousand dollars for them. Though Les Films du Carrosse couldn't afford to pay this amount of money, Truffaut could fortunately count on the help of three friends, Jeanne Moreau, Claude Lelouch, and Claude Berri, who put up the required amount. At that point, Truffaut and Marcel Berbert started working out the financing of the film with United Artists. It was budgeted at 8 million francs, which made it the director's costliest production. The shoot, which was to take place in Corsica and last twelve weeks, starting in December 1968, was the only "folly" Truffaut ever allowed himself: Each scene would be filmed in the exact order of the screenplay, "in order to respect the dramatic progression needed for the acting couple's performance."[53]

Truffaut worked alone on adapting the Irish novel, for none of his usual screenwriters were available. He wished to remain faithful to the novel but decided to transpose the action from the New Orleans of 1830 to present-day Corsica. Louis Mahé, the rich owner of a wine-producing estate, marries Julie Roussel, a young woman from the Continent, whom he meets through the personal ads. When the *Mississippi* arrives in the port of Calvi, Louis is surprised by Julie's youth and beauty and falls madly in love with her. They marry, but shortly thereafter the young woman robs him of all the money in their joint bank account and disappears. She had actually been manipulated by her gangster boyfriend, Richard, into impersonating the real Julie Roussel, who had been thrown overboard. Depressed and bitter, Mahé moves to the Riviera, runs into Julie Roussel by accident, and wants to kill her. She then explains her behavior in a long confession: Her real name is Marion Bergamo; she had been a ward of public welfare, shuttling from orphan homes to reformatories, before prostituting herself in the bars of Antibes and Nice. This is where she had met Richard, her lover and procurer, recently arrested. Marion begs Louis's forgiveness, saying she wants to reform her ways. Louis is still in love with her. The couple get back together and live happily in a large house near Aix-en-Provence—until Detective Comolli comes on the scene, the detective hired by Mahé and Julie Roussel's sister to track down Marion. To protect her, Louis kills Comolli. The couple then has to go on the run, fleeing first to Lyon, then to the Alps, in the hope of crossing the frontier. There, in a snowbound chalet,

Louis realizes that Marion is killing him with rat poison so she can get rid of him and escape. Out of love, he accepts his fate. When Marion becomes aware of this sacrifice, "love opens her eyes" and the two lovers wander off together in the snow.

Truffaut's screenplay is not so much a detective story as a *noir* love story, about a passion that can lead only to death. *Mississippi Mermaid* was to be an intimate account of a tragic romance. Everything hinged on the couple and the verisimilitude of their amorous relationship. This was why Truffaut was so eager to work with Jean-Paul Belmondo and Catherine Deneuve, France's two biggest stars and also, in his opinion, her two best actors. On the surface, Louis Mahé, the character Belmondo was to play, is a well-connected, rich, attractive, and amusing man. But he is also shy, awkward, betrayed, swindled, constantly made a fool of by Marion, and pathologically in love. Truffaut's secret twist consisted in reversing the roles: "Catherine Deneuve is the tough guy, the hood who has been through hard times; Jean-Paul Belmondo is the frightened young girl who expects everything from marriage. He finds a wife through the personal ads. I was tempted to have him say, during the credits, 'Young male, twenty-nine, virgin, seeks marriage, etc., etc.' Though he doesn't say it, for me Belmondo is actually a virgin!"[54] At the height of stardom, Belmondo had to accept this ambiguity and risk disappointing his public by going against his virile image as an actor. He would have to convey both strength and fragility. Hesitant, Belmondo finally let himself be convinced by Gérard Lebovici and accepted the part. But deep down, he had certain misgivings about the character; he realized he might "look like an ass,"[55] he admitted to Suzanne Schiffman.

Catherine Deneuve also accepted a part that did not match her image and was fraught with paradoxes. "What I like about her," Truffaut wrote, "is her mysterious quality. She is wonderfully suited to parts involving a secret, or a double life. Catherine Deneuve adds ambiguity to any situation and any screenplay, for she seems to be concealing a great many secret thoughts, we sense there are things lurking behind the surface. . . ."[56] Catherine Deneuve formally accepted the part at the beginning of February 1968, then left to spend most of the summer and fall in Hollywood for the filming of an American film, Stuart Rosenberg's *The April Fools*, costarring Jack Lemmon. Every so often, she wrote Truffaut long letters, expressing her expectations and doubts and requesting information about the screenplay. On September 2, Truffaut clarified his intentions and explained his belief in the intrinsic value of what he called "films with couples": "American films were never better than when James Stewart played opposite Katharine Hepburn, Cary Grant opposite Grace Kelly, Bogart opposite Bacall. With *Mermaid*, I very much want to show a new glamorous and striking pair: Jean-Paul, alive and fragile like a Stendhal hero, and you the blond siren whose chant would have inspired Giraudoux."[57] The success of the film therefore depended on this harmony, provided the sensitivities of each could be overcome. Truffaut asked Catherine Deneuve to be the "stronger half of the couple" in the film and during the shoot, "including being slightly bitchy," which would be bound to hurt or perturb her male alter ego. He described to her a "film of mad love," which assumes a great "familiarity" between the two characters in the drama: "Concentration and perfect harmony among the three of us will restore intimacy to this love life. I won't ask you play any sexually explicit scene, but an underlying sexuality must be felt at all times."[58] In *Mississippi Mermaid,* Catherine Deneuve's costumes are by Yves Saint-Laurent, her favorite designer, whom she introduced to Truffaut. "They met once, they didn't need to talk much, there was such an understanding," she later told Laurence Benaïm, Saint-Laurent's biographer. "Truffaut's ideas about clothes were very close to those of Saint-Laurent, even though he didn't like pants. He always spoke about women's legs. He only liked skirts with movement, he never liked anything straight, tight, stiff. . . ."[59]

During the fall of 1968, Truffaut asked Michel Bouquet to play detective Comolli, a secondary role but important in conveying the threat of the police hanging over this passionate love story. The part of Jardine, Louis Mahé's trusted right-hand man, quite naturally went to Marcel Berbert, since this was very much the part he played in daily life at Les Films du Carrosse: "It was to save money,"[60] Marcel Berbert admits. They had decided to cancel the shoot in Corsica, though Truffaut had stayed there for a week in the spring of 1968, scouting for locations. It lacked mystery. Above all, it was impossible to imagine, for the coherence of the plot, that Louis Mahé could live in Corsica and be so completely out of step with Continental France. Marcel Berbert recalls that on a Sunday morning, he received a call from Truffaut: "I've thought about it; we'll shoot in New Caledonia. Could you tell me how much more it will cost?" Berbert says, "I had a planisphere on my desk. I looked: New Caledonia, twenty thousand kilometers away. Then I saw Réunion Island, ten thousand . . . A cost-saver in the same amount!"[61] A mere four weeks before the start of the shoot, everything had to be rearranged, but the idea of shooting on Réunion Island appealed to Truffaut. A French overseas department, Réunion Island had a deeply colonial economy and society. It is a little island with a hilly, tortuous landscape, situated east of Africa's southernmost tip; here, Louis Mahé would become a believable character; a descendant of one of the oldest families of French settlers, living in a beautiful, large, inherited house, it was just possible that he might have kept his virginity and innocence while managing one of the island's biggest tobacco plantations.

## THE *MISSISSIPPI* CREW

On November 15, 1968, barely two weeks before the beginning of the filming, François Truffaut flew to Réunion Island. No plans had been made there yet. Jean-José Richer, Roland Thénot, Marcel Berbert, and Truffaut had two weeks to scout for locations, reserve hotels, find a house and a cigarette factory for Louis Mahé, a steamship for Julie Roussel's arrival, and a small church in the bush for their marriage. In a letter, Truffaut described his first impressions of the island: "On arrival, dismay, distress and disappointment. Then, after a few days, its charm begins to take effect. . . . The landscapes were often beautiful (not always) and the human types gorgeous, especially as far as the women and children are concerned. For the film, that's a definite advantage over Corsica. . . ."[62]

Indeed, the location scouting was fruitful—the Sainte-Anne chapel for the marriage, about thirty miles from Saint-Denis, in the heart of a magnificent volcanic landscape; for Louis Mahé, the Bel-Air villa, a stately white mansion owned by a big family of settlers in Tampon, a property above Saint-Denis; and the Law Son cigarette factory, right in the center of town. As for Truffaut, he stayed at the Relais Aériens Français, a residence overlooking Saint-Denis, with a magnificent view on the Indian Ocean. The rest of the crew and the two stars arrived at the end of November. Jean-Paul Belmondo took up residence at the Hotel Saint-Gilles, in the heart of Saint-Denis, while Catherine Deneuve moved into the Relais Aériens. "I strut around self-confidently, but as you might suspect, I'm petrified three days before the shooting, and plagued with the usual escapist fantasies: 'What if Catherine Deneuve were to break a leg . . . or Jean-Paul were to come down with tonsillitis . . .' In other words, once again they'll have to literally drag me to work, la Schife [Suzanne Schiffman] will have to kick me in the ass to get me going,"[63] Truffaut wrote to Helen Scott, forecasting a difficult shoot because of the distance from Paris, as well as the demands and whims of his actors.

"The filming is ideal and everything is going for the best,"[64] Truffaut wrote to Lucette Desmouceaux, his secretary at Les Films du Carrosse. The director was happy, reassured by his harmonious relationship with Catherine Deneuve. During the first few days, communication on the set had been rather tense, and strong gusts of wind had prevented them from filming a series of helicopter shots. But very soon, everything went smoothly. Catherine Deneuve dispelled all her director's apprehensions. "I had a certain preconception of Catherine Deneuve before filming *Mississippi Mermaid*. I thought she had an exaggerated sense of her interests as an actress and that this would go before the interests of the film. I suspected she was a perfectionist, hence always disappointed. I didn't think she was wholeheartedly behind the film, so I was slightly wary of her; I thought she would be too concerned with details and would often request explanations and justifications. In sum, in spite of my desire to work with her, I started the film with certain prejudices that she immediately guessed. While she was in America working on *April Fools,* I wrote to her in Hollywood and sent her some sly little warnings, like: 'When working on my films everyone is in a good mood,' or 'We must not think we'll make a masterpiece. We'll try to make a lively film.' Because of this, during the first days of the shoot, we were on our guard, then I discovered very fast that we thought the same way and agreed on everything."[65]

Truffaut's portrait of Catherine Deneuve in his long text, soberly entitled "Working with Catherine Deneuve," is not just an encomium of the actress he had just directed. No doubt Truffaut wrote the essay in part to promote his film and to justify the choice of Catherine Deneuve as its star alongside Jean-Paul Belmondo. However, it is also possible to read between the lines and see it as a discreet and modest declaration of love to the woman herself—her ambiguity, her personality, her beauty. "Indeed, Catherine Deneuve is so beautiful that any film she stars in could almost dispense with telling a story. I am convinced that the spectator will find happiness in just looking at Catherine and that this contemplation is worth the price of admission!" When he praises Catherine Deneuve, Truffaut describes the actress's physical appearance—her gentle face enhancing the occasional severity of her gaze—as well as her character, her way of moving, talking, dressing, wearing makeup; he is under the spell of her voice and mysterious quality.

During the filming of *Mississippi Mermaid,* Truffaut was not unlike the above-mentioned spectator watching his favorite screen heroine. Not only did the shoot take place under ideal conditions, but it was over those eighteen days on Réunion Island that their love story began. "Usually François was incredibly naive and thought no one noticed his affairs during filmings. In this instance, there was no attempt at secrecy. For her and for him, it was serious, not just a filming fling,"[66] recalls Marcel Berbert.

Though he remained tactful and in good spirits, Jean-Paul Belmondo felt slightly jealous of the favored treatment his partner received from the director. Witnesses remember that he and his girlfriend, Ursula Andress, who had joined him on Réunion Island, preferred not to take meals with the others on the set and isolated themselves in their villa. On December 23, before leaving the island, the producers threw a cocktail party for the actors and crew and also invited the island officials who had facilitated the making of the film. "Belmondo dropped by for only fifteen minutes; he smiled the whole time but didn't linger,"[67] Marcel Berbert recalls.

The shoot resumed on December 30 in Nice, following the screenplay in sequence. First came the scenes in the clinic where Louis Mahé, in a state of severe depression, is undergoing a sleeping cure to recover from Julie Roussel's departure and betrayal. This required three days of filming in the gardens of the Musée Masséna and in an adjoining clinic on the Promenade des Anglais. Then came the principal scenes between Louis Mahé and Marion, a "very spoken and very spontaneous dialogue which I draft from day to day a few hours before shooting the scenes."[68] This intimate ceremonial begins with Marion's long confession to Louis Mahé. For this monologue, Truffaut reworked, word for word, excerpts of a tape he had made in October 1965 of Mireille G., the first woman with whom he had ever lived, back in 1949, and whom he saw again in the south of France[69]—her reminiscences included receiving public welfare, acquiring her first pair of high heels at fourteen, stealing money from wallets, having kleptomania, and going to reform school.[70]

As an homage to his friend Jacques Audiberti, who had died in 1965, Truffaut had the idea of filming this sequence in a hotel that was situated on a square named after the writer in his native city of Antibes. He also rebaptized the hotel "Monorail," which is the title of an Audiberti novel. A night scene had to be filmed in which Belmondo, as usual refusing a stuntman, was to climb up the facade of the hotel and make his way into Marion's room. During the climb, he slipped, smashing a neon light, and was left suspended in space. Two hours later, the scene was reshot, after the crew had repaired the set.

The filming proceeded near Aix-en-Provence, where Louis Mahé and Marion renew their romance: declarations, love games, caresses; the transition from the formal *vous* to the informal *tu;* the double confession in front of the fireplace; the scene of Catherine Deneuve undressing by the side of the road;[71] the purely fetishistic sequences where the woman wears the "clothes of sexual fantasies" (sable-colored stockings, a pink silk slip, a scant little dress with eight buttons that the man unfastens one by one); the embraces that follow the dramatic events (the murder of detective Comolli and Louis returning with the money). It is a very intimate world that is depicted in *Mississippi Mermaid,* as Catherine Deneuve very insightfully points out: "François made love stories in which sexuality was always present. Usually the sexuality is ethereal, with modesty prevailing. But if his films are looked at attentively from that specific angle, for example *Mermaid,* you can see just how sexually violent and explicit they are."[72]

Late January and mid-February 1969 found the cast and crew in Lyon, then in Le Sappey, north of Grenoble, in the Chartreuse mountain range, where Truffaut had filmed the last scenes of *Shoot the Piano Player*. In fact, he used the same chalet for the last scenes of *Mississippi Mermaid,* when Deneuve poisons Belmondo with rat poison. This is where the last lines of the picture are exchanged: "Does love hurt?" asks Marion. "Yes, it hurts," Louis replies. "It hurts to look at you, you're so beautiful." And Marion says, "Yesterday you said it was a joy." In conclusion, Louis responds, "Yes. It's a joy and a misery." On the evening of February 15, the entire cast and crew partied together and belatedly celebrated Truffaut's thirty-seventh birthday: "The *Mississippi* crew requests the pleasure of your company at the Mermaid Party in honor of François Truffaut beginning at 10:00 p.m. at the Hotel des Skieurs (evening dress not required . . .)."[73]

Between March and May 1969, François Truffaut edited his film with Agnès Guillemot, assisted by Yann Dedet. For the opening credits, he used a montage of personal ads read in a voice-over and an excerpt from Jean Renoir's *La Marseillaise,* of which he had just seen a restored print.[74] "It's a great source of happiness for me to be associated with this picture,"[75] Renoir wrote, touched by this gesture. In the beginning of June, as was his habit, Truffaut scheduled a screening of *Mermaid* for his friend Jean Aurel, who suggested a few editing changes. "The film isn't fantastic, but it isn't a failure; the two lovers are very good,"[76] Truffaut confided to Helen Scott.

When the film opened on June 18, 1969, the critics all expressed disappointment. Jean-Louis Bory set the tone in *Le Nouvel Observateur:* "The 'Truffaut' touch makes for a gorgeous film which leaves me cold. Because of all the sauce? Is the bride too beautiful? Too haute couture? It's the metamorphosis of *Shoot the Piano Player* into an ultraposh boutique product. Ideal colors and international stars. I miss the old film, the poor one, in black and white. For these stars, in point of fact, are an encumbrance. . . ."[77] The intimate, passionate love story went unnoticed, overshadowed by the reputation of the stars and the "mass audience" look of the film. *Mississippi Mermaid* was then and still is misunderstood. In spite of its two big stars, audiences didn't flock to see it; it barely sold 100,000 tickets by the end of July 1969, when it was pulled from the theaters. It was a severe letdown. Les Films du Carrosse pulled through relatively well, but United Artists was very disappointed.

Paradoxically, Truffaut was little concerned by this flop. Spring 1969 was the happiest period of his life. Overlooking his usual extreme discretion, he couldn't resist confiding in two or three friends. To François Weyergans: "I'm the happiest man on earth. . . ."[78] To Helen Scott: "My personal life is very good. . . ."[79] And he wrote to Aimée Alexandre, his old friend of Russian descent, then aged seventy-seven years old, "My personal life is once again organized around the happiness of an amorous relationship."[80] This happy "amorous relationship" bore the delicate, regular features of

"Kathe de Neuve," as Truffaut sometimes called her with tenderness and irony.

The filming of *Mermaid* brought them together. The very theme of the movie, the story of a passionate love in which there is no other woman or man, probably had something to do with it. "It's the first time I've really dealt with a couple," said Truffaut to a reporter from *Télérama.* "In *Jules and Jim* or *The Soft Skin,* the scenes with couples always refer to a third person—the one who isn't there. Here the man and woman are happy together, or when they hurt each other, it comes only from themselves."[81] While he was shooting *Mermaid* in sequence—which allowed him to "construct" his couple on screen in precise fashion from one location to the next, charting a progression that was both physical and emotional—Truffaut was having a romance with the star of his movie. The bond that united them brought a perceptible, sensual joy to the filming, such as Truffaut had not felt on a set since *Jules and Jim;* it also gave the film the appearance of a real declaration of love. During the entire shoot, no one knew of their liaison outside of the cast and crew, even though there was a hint in the fact that Catherine Deneuve gave the first dance to François Truffaut at a soirée at the Hotel des Skieurs in Sappey. Several days later, *Paris-Match* published a photograph of the couple, "Catherine and Truffaut beneath the same umbrella,"[82] arm in arm in the snow.

"We agree on everything," said Truffaut gladly, alluding ambiguously to his professional relationship with the actress. "Catherine is not much of an actress in life," he added. "In fact, she is uncalculating and prefers to take things as they come, very comfortable in some situations and very unhappy in others. But she doesn't show it and has a propriety that I greatly appreciate. She has none of the vanity of her talent. For her, happiness is the only important thing. The rest is derisory. Catherine is like that."[83]

For Truffaut, this relationship was at once a consecration and the source of a deep upheaval in his life. Generally quite reticent, he confided movingly to his friend Claude de Givray: "My life is like a Hollywood comedy!"[84] To Helen Scott he wrote: "My private life is much more exclusive than before."[85] And to Aimée Alexandre: "We hardly ever go out to dinners, because of all the plays to see, the movies, and the evenings we spend watching television."[86] The couple indulged in no offbeat behavior, and led a very discreet life shared with only a few select friends. Very infrequently, photos of them at movie premieres appeared in the press, but they were both careful to protect their private life from the social gossip columns and the rumor mill.

In October and November 1969, Truffaut spent several weeks in Toledo, Spain, where Catherine Deneuve was filming one of her best roles, *Tristana,* directed by Luis Buñuel. Truffaut stayed at the El Marron Hotel, taking advantage of his vacation to work on the script for *Bed and Board.* His co-scenarist, Claude de Givray, who came for a short stay to discuss the screenplay, remembers that Truffaut had absolutely no interest in tourism. "He never set foot in the old quarter of town. He had a theory that cities were not meant for sight-seeing, like Cocteau's old saying: 'He dies, struck by the picturesque.' For him, it was really obscene to visit a city where people lived."[87]

## THE WILD CHILD

By the end of June 1969, it was clear to Truffaut that *Mississippi Mermaid* was his biggest box-office failure. Fortunately, by then he was already completely immersed in the preproduction of *L'Enfant sauvage* (*The Wild Child*), which he was to begin shooting on July 2. Ever since *The 400 Blows*, Truffaut had been interested in educational experiments with difficult—autistic or delinquent—children. During the spring of 1964, his curiosity had been aroused by the review in *Le Monde* of a book by Lucien Malson, *Les Enfants sauvages: Mythe et réalité* (*Wild Children: Myth and Reality*). The author, better known as a jazz specialist, was a professor of social psychology at the Centre national de pédagogie, where he studied "children who had been deprived of all human contact and had grown up, for one reason or other, in complete isolation."[88] The most instructive of the fifty-two cases analyzed by Malson was that of Victor of Aveyron, a child who in 1798 had been discovered in the forest by hunters.

Truffaut immediately bought about ten copies of Malson's book, as he customarily did when he was interested in a book for his work. Jean Itard, a brilliant physician who specialized in the study of auditory processes, had conducted an experiment that fascinated Truffaut. In December 1800, at twenty-nine, Itard was appointed director of the Institut national des sourds-muets (National Institute for Deaf-Mutes) in Paris, where he had been working for some time—specifically on the ten-year-old wild child found in Aveyron, who had become an object of public curiosity. Two opposing theories prevailed in medical circles at the time. For some, the child was a mental defective or idiot whose parents had tried to kill him—he had a deep scar on his throat—and who had been left for dead in the forest. Given this hypothesis, he was at best a fun-fair curiosity, who really should have been locked up in Bicêtre hospital with madmen and other incurables. For others, including Jean Itard, the child had indeed escaped his parents' knife but was not retarded. Isolation, absence of human communication, and want of affection had made him "wild." Itard obtained permission to place the child under his care, on condition he demonstrate the results of his instruction. He undertook the task of educating the child, whom he baptized Victor. Little by little, the child learned to use his senses and intelligence, to walk erect, behave properly at the table, and dress on his own; after a time, he could understand simple speech and pronounce some words. Eventually, Victor went on to live to age forty, under the care of a governess, Madame Guérin, in a little house on rue des Feuillantines, near the Institut; he worked at small tasks and lived very frugally.

François Truffaut first considered making a film based on this story in the autumn of 1964 and assigned it to Jean Gruault. By mid-January 1965, the latter suggested a possible theme for the story but his idea didn't completely satisfy Truffaut, so the scriptwriter did further research. He consulted educational treatises on deaf-mutes, read Condillac's *Treatise on the Sensations* (1754), and delved into articles in medicine and psychology that dealt with autistic children. By mid-November 1965, Truffaut had annotated Gruault's 243-page typewritten manuscript and returned it to him for a rewrite. A year later, after more "Ping-Pong work"[89] as Gruault called it, the script had grown to almost four hundred pages, meaning over three hours of film time by Truffaut's calculations. It had to be shortened by half. Finally, with some advice from Jacques Rivette, Truffaut and Gruault pared it down to 151 pages in the summer of 1968. The screenplay was dense, tense; Truffaut used the words *rigorous, logical, scientific,* and *poetic,* to describe it.[90]

To make this film, Truffaut met with an ear, nose, and throat specialist who was experimenting with the use of tuning forks on deaf-mute children. He involved Roger Monnin, the father of one of his friends, a deaf-mute who was in charge of several associations for the handicapped. Lastly, he again consulted Fernand Deligny (as he had for *The 400 Blows*), who now ran an experimental clinic for autistic children in Monoblet, a small hamlet in a remote section of the Cévennes.[91] In the autumn of 1968 Truffaut asked Suzanne Schiffman to go to Monoblet to observe a young boy whose behavior, according to Deligny, was surprisingly similar to Victor's. "Your description of his behavior is so similar to what Itard described in his writings and to what we want to achieve in the film that I find it extremely disconcerting," Truffaut wrote to Deligny. "In any case, I think your boy should serve as our model in selecting the boy who will actually play the part and should inspire us for his style of bodily comportment."[92]

With *The Wild Child,* Truffaut wanted to take a strong position regarding a cause for which he had fought with consistent determination and energy—the welfare of unhappy children. Along with freedom of the press and military insubordination, it was the only cause Truffaut was ready to take up at any time. Children, he felt, lack any protection and are helplessly trapped when those around them become violent and abusive. Truffaut took a radical position and accused politicians of indifference to this serious social problem:

> There can be no doubt that the number of abused and merely unhappy children will increase considerably in the years to come. Naturally the same is true for juvenile delinquents. Anyone can point to the reasons for this: too many unwanted children, housing crises, overcrowded schools, teacher shortages, derisory social assistance. The only solutions to such social problems are concrete—hence financial—hence political—and we know that elected officials only think about children when they reach voting age. Greater severity toward physically abusive parents is also a solution to be considered. Unfortunately, this solution will not be adopted by the administration because it is unpopular. Which is why we have every reason to be pessimistic, completely and unequivocally pessimistic.[93]

Given his deep concern, Truffaut collected press clippings on cases that appalled him—child suicides, health-care establishments found guilty of mistreating retarded children, physical cruelties inflicted by parents. In March 1964, he had become a member of the sponsorship committee of the Secours populaire français and in the spring of 1967, he had been made president of the benefactors' committee for SOS Villages d'enfants, an association that had centers for taking in battered children. Finally, in April 1968, he accepted the radio station France-Culture's offer to devote a day-long program to him, provided the broadcast focus exclusively on the cause of abused children. The program was aired on April 2, from 2:00 p.m. to midnight, and the station's switchboard was flooded with calls and testimonies. The broadcast was covered extensively in the press and Truffaut received almost two hundred letters from listeners. Some of these were from former abused children, or from watchdog committees, attesting to the accuracy of Truffaut's views. Truffaut had stood up against the rule of silence and the misuse of parental authority with the aim of initiating a real public debate. Likewise, the film about Victor of Aveyron, the abused and abandoned wild child, was an attempt to use cinema for educational purposes. Truffaut's pedagogical vocation was never better expressed than in *The Wild Child*, a film that is both optimistic and despairing—optimistic, because of its great confidence in the acquisition of culture; despairing, because this education brings with it the realization that society is a den of torturers and cowards.

Truffaut went to United Artists for financing, but Ilya Lopert was reluctant to commit himself; he found the screenplay "too documentarylike," as he told Jean-Louis Livi. Furthermore, Truffaut specifically wanted the film to be in black and white. Things looked bleak, so much so that, in September 1968, for the first and only time in his career, he applied for an advance on box-office receipts from the CNC. Gérard Lebovici then played a decisive role in convincing Lopert to rescind his decision and invest 2 million francs in *The Wild Child*. Jean-Louis Livi, Lebovici's right-hand man but also Ilya Lopert's son-in-law, remembers these negotiations between Truffaut and Lopert, the European production head of United Artists. "Imagine offering a big American company a black-and-white film with no stars when Truffaut was getting ready to make a film with Deneuve and Belmondo!" Still skeptical, Lopert agreed, on one condition—combining the box-office receipts of *The Wild Child* and *Mississippi Mermaid*, a film he was certain would bring in profits. "The Americans were counting on the success of *Mermaid* to absorb the losses of *The Wild Child;* the exact opposite occurred,"[94] recalls Marcel Berbert. "Ilya was smart to accept both films, for he didn't want to risk losing Truffaut,"[95] Jean-Louis Livi concludes.

On the advice of his location manager, Roland Thénot, Truffaut decided to shoot *The Wild Child* in Aubiat, in Auvergne, where the Thénot family owned a nineteenth-century manor house that could be made into Dr. Itard's house. For the black-and-white cinematography, Truffaut hired Nestor Almendros, Eric Rohmer's director of photography on *My Night at Maud's*, whose very refined, original, and simple lighting he had very much admired. This was the start of a long collaboration, a close artistic and professional bond, and an enduring friendship: Almendros and Truffaut would make nine films together, including Truffaut's last, *Vivement Dimanche!* (*Confidentially Yours!*)

During the preproduction of *The Wild Child*, Truffaut and Almendros viewed several films: Arthur Penn's *The Miracle Worker*, about the childhood education of Helen Keller, Bresson's *Diary of a Country Priest*, Bergman's *Monika*, and several silent films by Griffith and Dreyer. With its grainy black-and-white quality, the opening and shutting of an iris, used here by Truffaut as a recurrent punctuating device, *The Wild Child* is also an homage to the classical age of cinema. "Truffaut wanted me to create a certain archaic tone," Almendros later explained, "he likes the transitions and fades of the silent cinema. I had to study the problem: how to produce fades outside the laboratory (the dupe negative lowers the quality of the shots). I came up with the iris that was used in silent filmmaking. . . . J. C. Rivière, my assistant, set out to find an old iris, one of those used in the early days of the cinema. He found one. . . . The outline of the iris was . . . precise, and we got a perfect effect of a dark ring slowly closing until it isolated the essence of the image and then ended in total darkness."[96] At the same time, Suzanne Schiffman made the rounds of the schools around Nîmes,

Arles, Marseilles, and Montpellier, looking for a boy who could be cast as Victor. Schiffman interviewed and photographed nearly 2,500 children, five of whom were selected as finalists and summoned to Paris for screen tests. On June 6, Truffaut wrote to Helen Scott that he "had found the little boy."[97] He was Jean-Pierre Cargol, a twelve-year-old gypsy with a dark complexion, a "very animallike" profile, a lively and nimble body. The boy was the nephew of the guitarist Manitas de Plata. "He's a very handsome child, but I think he really looks like he came out of the woods," Truffaut wrote to Helen Scott.[98]

Truffaut cast stage actors in the other parts: Françoise Seigner of the Comédie-Française as Madame Guérin, and as Pinel, Jean Dasté, director of the Saint-Etienne theater and an actor in films by Jean Vigo (*Zéro de conduite* and *L'Atalante*) and Renoir (*Boudu Saved from Drowning, The Crime of Monsieur Lange, Grand Illusion*). Finally, he cast his collaborators in the small parts—Claude Miller, his wife, Annie, and their baby, Nathan, play the Lémeri family, whom Jean Itard occasionally goes to see with Victor, while Jean Gruault appears as a visitor in the sequences shot at the Institut national des sourds-muets.

Truffaut would vacillate for a long time over the part of Dr. Itard. He first considered television actors, then the journalist Philippe Labro to emphasize the educational tie between Itard and the wild child. Then he looked for someone unknown, who would make the character more believable. In fact, though he didn't dare admit it, Truffaut saw himself in the part. Suzanne Schiffman was the only person he let in on the secret, days before the beginning of the shoot. Even Berbert didn't know. "It's true, he didn't have the nerve to tell me. As in many instances, he told Suzanne and she went by my desk one day and said, 'You know who's going to be Dr. Itard? François!' I said, 'Oh, really? No kidding!' "[99] Truffaut thought he would feel more comfortable "inside the frame," directing a child who never talks. "Casting someone else in the part of Dr. Itard would have put an intermediary between Jean-Pierre Cargol and me, and I'd have had a lot of trouble directing him."[100] Gruault fully agreed: "Itard is seen almost exclusively in his professional capacity, which is very close to that of director."[101]

The filming of *The Wild Child* began on July 2, 1969, deep in the forest, with takes of the child hurriedly climbing up a tree to escape the dogs pursuing him, then finding shelter in a burrow. Thanks to small, specially made invisible sandals, Jean-Pierre Cargol could run around in the undergrowth without difficulty. The ambiance on set was studious; Truffaut stuck to his screenplay, which he found "well constructed," and harmony reigned. "Here in this manor, lost in the gentle rolling hills of la Limagne—to quote the guidebooks—far from the telephone, the traffic jams, the news, and even vacationers, work is going very well."[102] Catherine Deneuve joined him on location for much of the summer, which made Truffaut happy.

The Wild Child presented Truffaut with a new challenge—directing a child while being both in front of and behind the camera. To instruct Jean-Pierre Cargol, he used comparisons: "For the expression in his eyes, I would say, 'like a dog'; for his head movements, 'like a horse.' I mimed Harpo Marx when wide-eyed wonder had to be conveyed. But nervous laughter and rage were difficult for him, because Jean-Pierre is a very gentle, happy, well-balanced child who could only do quiet things."[103] While Truffaut was acting his part, Suzanne Schiffman took on the duties of assistant director; she was in charge of shouting "Roll" and "Cut" and stood in for Truffaut during rehearsals. Truffaut found this first experience as an actor extremely enriching: "On a movie set, the look in an actor's eye is very surprising; it reflects both pleasure and frustration. Pleasure because the feminine side in every man (and to a greater extent in every actor) feels fulfilled in being an object. Frustration, because there is also always some greater or lesser degree of virility that wants to rebel against this same condition."[104] With The Wild Child, he would learn in concrete, physical terms all that the directing of actors implies.

At the end of August, the cast and crew were back in Paris, for a last week of filming at the Institut national des sourds-muets. Then, after a shoot that had lasted fifty days, everyone separated. As a parting gift, Jean-Pierre Cargol was given a small 8-mm camera and he vowed to become "the first gypsy film director."[105]

## THE CARROSSE KEEPS ROLLING

Before The Wild Child was even released, François Truffaut was in the streets of Paris filming Domicile conjugal (Bed and Board), the third install-ment in the adventures of Antoine Doinel. This would be his fourth movie in two years. Cinema came first in his life. But Truffaut also worked con-stantly because of an obsessive need for a busy schedule; he never allowed room for the unexpected. He planned things compulsively, months, even years, ahead of time, and compartmentalized his various projects so his screenwriters would remain separate. This sometimes frightened his friends, such as Jean-Louis Richard, who recalls how Truffaut sometimes scheduled work sessions twelve to eighteen months into the future.

Leaving nothing to chance and putting filmmaking before his personal life were two of Truffaut's basic character traits. There was a madness in this dizzying immersion in work as the only salvation and escape from the melancholy of life. Shooting film after film kept him in a state of elation, and it was also the best way of retaining a group of trusted collaborators, including scriptwriters and technical crew. Constant work also allowed him to suppress his deep anxieties as the head of a company. ("The Carrosse keeps rolling [*carrosse* means "horse-drawn coach"],"[106] he wrote.) "I am a director-producer in charge of my own filmmaking projects. . . . Since I have been working with American companies for several years, I have lost contact with French producers. For these same years, I must say I've been lucky to work in complete freedom and I have carte blanche to the extent that my films require only medium-sized budgets."[107]

His full acceptance of the status of boss-cum-artist was rather unusual in the post-1968 context, a time when many intellectuals and artists chose ideological commitment on the extreme Left or a life on the margins of society. Some regarded his choice as the ultimate in bad taste. Jean-Luc Godard, for one, in his complete commitment to militant cinema, denigrated Truffaut as "a businessman in the morning and a poet in the afternoon."[108] To those who classified him as a bourgeois director, Truffaut quite frankly didn't know how to respond. "Almost everyone feels insulted when they're called bourgeois, but I don't feel insulted. In fact, I don't feel concerned, probably because, in general, I scarcely take part in life. . . . The designation 'bourgeois' attacks a way of life. I don't have a way of life (I don't live, outside cinema), I don't feel it applies to me and if it's a misunderstanding, I'm in no rush to clear it up."[109]

This insistence on remaining outside society was, of course, the primary characteristic of his protagonist Antoine Doinel, to whom he returned in the seventies with *Bed and Board,* on the advice given him by Henri Langlois after the screening of *Stolen Kisses:* "I want to see this little [Doinel-Darbon] couple again, in the first few months of their married life."[110] In April 1969, in a few work sessions with Claude de Givray and Bernard Revon, the main outline of a new screenplay was worked out. The idea was to give Antoine Doinel work, then a son, then a mistress, and in the end plunge him deep into marital conflict. Of course, Truffaut's personal recollections form the framework of the narrative, mixed together with the real life of Jean-Pierre Léaud. However, as with *Stolen Kisses,* de Givray and Revon added elements from their investigations in the field. Antoine Doinel has a most unusual job—dyeing bouquets of flowers for a florist. This was one of Truffaut's childhood memories: "At 10 rue de Douai, in my neighborhood, there was a florist who dyed flowers in the yard." Even if no one did so anymore, the idea appealed to him, and he decided to keep it as part of the film's antiquated charm. Similarly, Christine's profession—violin teacher—is a clear reference to Monique de Monferrand, Truffaut's young aunt, who became a violin teacher after graduating from the Conservatoire. Using specific recollections as starting points, Truffaut practiced what he called "verification through life,"[111] which involved concealing the autobiographical elements with real details and anecdotes collected by his screenwriters. He thereby made the autobiographical more concrete, but also more universal. For his guiding principle was always the same—avoid trends and clichés, and don't try to be up-to-date.

He was perfectly aware of the disparity between his Doinel of the early seventies and French youth so heavily influenced by the deep upheaval in intellectual fashions and mores effected by the events of May '68. But he fully accepted this, just as he accepted not being a revolutionary director. When he described Doinel, Truffaut was clearly describing himself: "Doinel is certainly asocial, but he isn't revolutionary the way people are today. Given this statement, I can see my films being condemned politically. Doinel isn't out to change society; he's leery of it and protects himself from it, but he's full of good will and wants to be 'accepted.' "[112] In this sense, Truffaut's films were poles apart from Godard's, which were always attuned to the language and forms of the present. Both directors used Jean-Pierre Léaud as an actor, but in opposite ways. Truffaut was often appalled or wounded by Léaud's personal choices and his commitment to left-wing militancy. The actor for his part surely felt closer to Godard, even though, on a human level, he remained extremely attached to Doinel's creator. But Léaud often considered the Doinel persona a burden, and his involvement and work with Godard was a necessary emancipation, even if it meant hurting Truffaut's feelings.

In *Bed and Board,* the Doinel couple's life is depicted in a light comic mode, with a touch of the burlesque. While Christine gives violin lessons, Antoine dyes flowers in the courtyard of their building; there, people come and go—clients from the nearby bistro, a waitress who is in love with him, the occupants of the building, including an old recluse who misses Pétain, and a mysterious stranger nicknamed "the strangler." Failing to achieve "absolute red" for his carnations, Antoine changes jobs; he is hired by the Paris branch of an American hydraulics company to operate ship models. The Doinel couple is expecting a child—Alphonse. But Antoine meets a young and beautiful Japanese woman, Kyoko, who becomes his mistress. Christine finds out about his affair when she comes upon the love notes Kyoko has sent Antoine in a bouquet of flowers; this provokes a crisis in their marriage. She banishes Antoine from their home. He then decides to write a novel about his life. But they miss each other, and Antoine interrupts a tête-à-tête dinner with Kyoko to declare his love to Christine over the telephone. In an epilogue, one year later, we see the young couple back together again, in a reconciliation that is probably illusory.

## SCENES FROM A MARRIAGE

An overtly amusing film, *Bed and Board* was also, Truffaut said, a "settling of scores."[113] For the director wanted to put Antoine Doinel to rest. He decided to do so in order to "liberate" Léaud from Doinel, "because it would get in the way of his career,"[114] and also because Truffaut felt he had fully exhausted the character's possibilities. He had made him into a married man, a father and head-of-family, and had given him a job, even though Doinel still oscillated between adolescence and adulthood. "Doinel isn't antisocial, but simply out of step with society. He doesn't reject society; it is society that takes issue with his spirit and style of life. Antoine Doinel, who is bound up with youthfulness, cannot be integrated into a normal society. In adulthood he becomes an impossible character."[115] Yet before parting with his double, Truffaut gave him two gifts—a film, *Bed and Board,* and a book, *The Adventures of Antoine Doinel.*[116] The latter is a kind of novel that traces Doinel's development, from runaway adolescent in *The 400 Blows,* to *Antoine and Colette* and *Stolen Kisses,* to the married man of *Bed and Board.* This narrative, consisting of four screenplays, recounts the birth, life, and personal fulfillment of one of the most famous screen characters in the world.

By mid-November 1969, he had a completed screenplay for *Bed and Board.* Marcel Berbert's estimated budget was modest—3.5 million francs. Truffaut had been annoyed by United Artists' procrastination over *The Wild Child* script and now he wanted to show his resentment by boycotting the American company. Furthermore, Ilya Lopert, with whom he had enjoyed a marvelous working relationship, died of a stroke in January 1970. So Truffaut turned to Hercule Mucchielli, an independent producer (Valoria Films), who contributed 40 percent of the budget and brought in a small Rome-based production company, Fida Cinematografica, which contributed an additional 10 percent. Les Films du Carrosse invested the other 50 percent, and the foreign sales were again entrusted to Alain Vannier. An agreement was signed with Columbia Pictures for American distribution.

Besides Jean-Pierre Léaud and Claude Jade, Truffaut used largely the same cast as in *Stolen Kisses,* most notably Daniel Ceccaldi and Claire Duhamel as Christine's parents. Two weeks before the shoot was to begin, Claude Jade came down with jaundice and had to be looked after by her parents in Dijon. This was just the first contretemps in a film that would soon try Truffaut's patience and goodwill. In the secondary roles, Truffaut cast stage and television actors. Jacques Robiolles and Daniel Boulanger made repeat appearances, and there was one newcomer, Philippe Léotard, aged thirty, a member of Ariane Mnouchkine's Théâtre du Soleil. Last but not least were two parts he felt very strongly about: Kyoko, and "the strangler." Truffaut asked Hiroko Berghauer, a former Cardin model and a "magical" woman, refined and elegant, to be Doinel's Japanese mistress. And in the role of "the strangler"—the strange, slightly effeminate, solitary man who sows terror until the day he is seen performing a skit on television—Truffaut cast his childhood friend Claude Thibaudat, alias Claude Vega. The son of the concierge on rue des Martyrs had become a stand-up comic—known, among other things, for his impersonation of actresses, such as Delphine Seyrig.

As of the first day's shoot of *Bed and Board,* on January 21, 1970, in a small courtyard near Sèvres-Babylone, Truffaut insisted that each scene be reperformed at a faster pace, as fast as possible, to emulate the rhythm of American screwball comedies by Howard Hawks, Leo McCarey (he had gone to see *The Awful Truth* again days before the shoot), and Frank Capra. "Very often," said Nestor Almendros, "he used Capra's technique: he would time the take and if it lasted 20 seconds, he would say, 'Now, let's do it in 10 seconds,' so the actors spoke like submachine guns and sometimes that was the take he'd keep."[117]

Shooting at a fast pace with frequent set changes involved some sacrifices. "*Bed and Board* is probably the least aesthetically pleasing of the films I have made for Truffaut," writes Almendros. "Its interest is concentrated in the situations and characters, and visual quality was of secondary importance."[118] Started in the middle of winter, *Bed and Board* was often filmed in subzero temperatures. Yet the screenplay clearly states that the characters' costumes are "in keeping with the spring season." Dressed in light clothes, Jean-Pierre Léaud, Claude Jade, and the other actors were numb with cold, while the members of the crew were bundled up in overcoats. "Filming a comedy in winter is particularly difficult," admitted Almendros.[119] The days were short, and so the crew was rushed, and Almendros was deeply distressed about shooting in congested streets filled with gawkers. Truffaut was made so nervous that he decided he would never again film in the streets of Paris.

Fortunately, the last part of the shoot, between February 23 and March 18, 1970, was inside. First, there were a few sequences at Christine Darbon's parents' house in Patin, the same house as in *Stolen Kisses.* Then the scenes in the Doinel couple's home, which, for budgetary reasons, Truffaut filmed in his fifth-floor rented apartment above the offices of Les Films du Carrosse on rue Robert-Estienne. Almendros and his crew very much disliked working in such a confined space. As for Truffaut, these last days on the set put him in a state of perpetual irritation.

The irritation would last beyond the forty-three days of filming. He wasn't pleased with the editing or the music of *Bed and Board,* finding neither spirited, light, or rapid enough. This would be his last collaboration with the editor Agnès Guillemot and the composer Antoine Duhamel. Usually very loyal to his technical crew and collaborators, Truffaut could be merciless in his judgments. He never replaced people during a shoot, but those who dissatisfied him were not hired again. Marcel Berbert or Suzanne Schiffman, his close guardian-protectors, did the dirty work of informing people of their dismissal. As time went on, Truffaut became increasingly demanding about craftsmanship. On this score, *Bed and Board,* though not as depressing as the shoots of *The Soft Skin, Fahrenheit 451,* or *The Bride Wore Black,* deeply dissatisfied him. His next films would be made under different circumstances, far from Paris and its problems, and with new collaborators.

## THE CAUSE OF CHILDREN

When *The Wild Child* opened on February 26, 1970, François Truffaut was still shooting *Bed and Board.* He considered *The Wild Child* austere and too rigorous to attract a large public. However, whether because of his reputation as a director, the appeal of the story, or the interest in childhood, within several weeks *The Wild Child* sold 200,000 tickets. The critics' unanimous praise certainly helped. Even before its foreign release, the film inspired no less than 150 articles—a quite impressive number.

On September 9, 1970, *Bed and Board* started a successful exclusive run in the same Paris movie houses that had shown *The Wild Child.* Ticket sales were good the first week, at 40,000, then tapered off slightly, but the film still attracted 220,000 people. With his last two features totaling ticket sales of over 400,000 in Paris, Truffaut began to be generally regarded as a popular director—this without even counting the success of *Stolen Kisses* and regardless of the box-office failure of *Mississippi Mermaid.* His fame can be gauged by the quantity of letters he received on *The Wild Child,* many from teachers or high school students. Truffaut conscientiously replied to each student, explaining his ideas, autographing a photo, sending a gift of a record or a book based on one of his films.

During this period of intense professional activity, Truffaut had more than his usual number of television and radio appearances and he used them to cultivate his image as an educational director. He also stressed his interest in childhood, at times polemically. "My films are a critique of the

French way of bringing up children. I only realized this gradually, through travel. It struck me that the happiness of children is completely unrelated to the wealth of their parents or their country. In Turkey, a poor country, the child is sacred. In Japan, it is inconceivable that a mother show indifference to her son. Here [in France] adult-child relationships are always ugly and petty."[120] Given these observations, Truffaut suggested adopting a personal moral code, behavior that is neither "politically committed" nor "model behavior," but deeply sincere and human. At a time when Leftism was triumphant in intellectual circles, he was content to reassert a few basic principles founded on self-determination, humanism, and cunning.

> I see life as very hard; I believe one should have a very simple, very crude and very strong moral system. One should say "yes, yes," and do exactly as one pleases. This is why there can't be any direct violence in my films. Already in *The 400 Blows,* Antoine is a child who never rebels openly. His moral system is more subtle than that. Like me, Antoine is against violence because it signifies confrontation. Violence is replaced by escape, not escape from what is essential, but escape in order to achieve the essential. I think I illustrated this in *Fahrenheit.* This is the most important aspect of the film, the apology for cunning. "Oh, really, books are banned, are they? Fine, we'll learn them by heart!" This is ultimate cunning.[121]

Eager to assert his convictions, Truffaut agreed to be the radio host on the midday news show on RTL from June 22 to 26, 1970. He conceived each broadcast as briskly covering a wide range of controversial topics, including the military, arms sales, and television censorship (the canceled broadcast of the film *The French Under the Occupation,* or the fact that Marcel Ophuls's *The Sorrow and the Pity* and Jean Aurel's *L'Affaire Dreyfus* were never broadcast). There were lighter moments as well—a daily tribute to Charles Trenet, music from films, and excerpts from Jeanne Moreau's latest record. Truffaut innovated by having the station commercials read by amateurs or children against the background noise of the city. And every day, Jean Servais read excerpts from *Madame Bovary.*

During this series of broadcasts, Truffaut also made public his "Open Letter to Annie Girardot,"[122] which was very polemical in tone. The actress had just agreed to play the lead in André Cayatte's film, *To Die of Love,* about Gabrielle Russier, a schoolteacher in Aix-en-Provence who had committed suicide when her love affair with a seventeen-year-old student had been disclosed. Truffaut first attacked Cayatte: "Some directors look for subjects, others find subjects, André Cayatte picks them up, he's even capable of digging into the pockets of warm corpses, like Thénardier salvaging the watches of dying soldiers at Waterloo." Then he appealed to Annie Girardot, in the hope that she would reconsider her decision to take part in Cayatte's film: "Gabrielle Russier killed herself because she couldn't bear it anymore, she regurgitated what was being done to her. Self-destruction was her way of shattering the mirror reflecting her hated image. The image is destroyed and it is sacrilegious to reconstruct it, even with talent, even with a sense of propriety. . . ."

The position he took on this event, which was rocking French society at the time, triggered a heated controversy. It was covered in the press and Truffaut received several hundred letters. When he chose to enter the fray, Truffaut made able use of his status as a public personality. His public stand on certain issues contributed to the portrait of a "man who makes no concessions, and is therefore solitary and sovereign," as he described himself to the critic Jean Collet after his RTL broadcasts. "I left the heads of the radio on rather cool terms after several last-minute conflicts: management's refusal to air certain reportages viewed as 'explosive.' "[123] Truffaut took advantage of heated debates to provoke embarrassment and to shed light on hidden facets of French society, politics, and culture. His image as the classic kindly, shy director then reversed itself and he was seen as a sensitive, sincere man, uncompromising in his convictions.

## THE NEW RENOIR

François Truffaut's image outside France was clearer: For some American critics, he was a "new Renoir." The success was paradoxical, following as it did the flop of *Fahrenheit 451*, his only film in English. As the United Artists New York press representative put it, in America his films were beginning to cross "the popcorn barrier"[124] separating the elitist culture of certain avant-garde artists from a wider, cultivated public that included students and academics.

Truffaut contributed to his success by traveling abroad with each of his films, whenever he was not tied up on set or in preproduction. As usual, he was methodical and rigorous: "He spoke to each interlocutor—whether a small-time correspondent for a provincial paper, a journalist for a big American weekly, or an important critic for a big Paris daily—with the same clear diction: He made you feel you were his best friend,"[125] says Philippe Labro. It is true that Truffaut also followed up with friendly thank-you notes to critics and journalists for their articles, picking up on a detail from a previous exchange. Claude Chabrol remembers attending one of the first screenings of *Jules and Jim:* "[With the critics] François began a fantastic campaign of seduction. Keeping a serious, skeptical air, he was very shrewd and had them eating out of his hand. He had a terrific trick with women critics of about forty, who liked him a lot. . . . He acted like a baby with his mother, and this worked very well with the ones who literally felt a maternal affection for him. From then on, he succeeded in tracing a rather cushy path for himself with the critics. . . . He had very few bad surprises."[126]

During these last ten years, he had devoted a great deal of energy to consolidating an astonishing network of foreign friends and correspondents. With each, he maintained a steady exchange of letters, as he did with Koichi Yamada in Japan. This was an asset no other French director possessed. For Alain Vannier, the difference between Truffaut and the others is obvious: "François knew how to take his time; he would spend a week in the United States, when any other director stayed only two days. He liked to schedule only three interviews a day with American journalists, giving time to each. As a result, they couldn't get over his kindness."[127]

In 1970, he made constant trips to present *The Wild Child* and *Bed and Board:* Barcelona, Stockholm, London, Lausanne, Geneva, and Zurich, Vienna and Milan, and even Tehran, where *The Wild Child* was awarded the special prize of the jury at the sixth international film festival. This suggests the breadth of the audience for Truffaut's films; his popularity also extended to Japan and Israel. But apart from Paris, the gauge of a reputation was New York, and here in the early 1970s Truffaut's was unquestionably on the rise. Eighty thousand dollars in box-office receipts for *Stolen Kisses* was hardly trivial for auteur cinema. Similarly, *Bed and Board* was a success in January 1971, bringing in $21,657 in box-office receipts during its first four days. Thanks to Vincent Canby in the *New York Times,* Pauline Kael in *The New Yorker,* and Andrew Sarris in the *Village Voice, Bed and Board* was above all a critical triumph. "*Bed and Board* will turn out to be one of the loveliest, most intelligent movies we'll see in all of 1971,"[128] Canby wrote. In September 1970, *The Wild Child* spread from the movie pages to the columns of magazines, becoming a controversial social and sociological subject in the major American papers. It was programmed on campuses with lecture series on education and child abuse. The film was shown at the eighth New York Film Festival. This was the first time Truffaut presented one of his films at the festival. Two years earlier, the festival's selection committee had rejected *Stolen Kisses,* deeming it too casual for New York critics and audiences. But now they were pleased to schedule Truffaut's film for the festival's opening night, September 10, 1970, in the presence of François Truffaut, Catherine Deneuve, and Jean-Pierre Léaud, to whom *The Wild Child* is dedicated. Honored by the mayor himself, Truffaut was unquestionably the star of the festival.

When the film opened on September 27 at the Fine Arts Theater on East 58th Street, the *New York Times* ran a two-page spread on Truffaut. The article delved into his acting performance in *The Wild Child* and painted a very laudatory portrait of him as a man—his life, his opinions, his relationships with American directors such as Arthur Penn, Mike Nichols, and Stanley Kubrick; even his relationship with Catherine Deneuve was mentioned, a taboo subject in Paris and an indication of Truffaut's relaxed, trusting mood during his stay at the Sherry-Netherland Hotel on Fifth Avenue. As for the film, its box-office performance was quite respectable; it brought in nearly $210,000 in the United States and garnered numerous prizes from associations of critics, writers, and clergymen. Three books by Truffaut were published in the United States during that period, which also contributed to his fame. In May 1969, Grove Press issued the translation of *The 400 Blows;* in 1971, Simon and Schuster published *The Adventures of Antoine Doinel;* then in 1973 Washington Square Press brought out the screenplay of *The Wild Child.*

The many letters sent to Les Films du Carrosse attest to Truffaut's celebrity in the United States. Like Bergman and Fellini, he had become a favorite European director on campus and among American intellectuals. Filmmakers like Stanley Kubrick, screenwriters like Robert Benton and David Newman, actors like Gene Wilder, producers like Daniel Selznick, and editors like Michael Korda all heaped praise and kind regards on him. The director of *Vertigo* sent Truffaut a wonderful tribute, written in awkward French: "I screened your wild child which I find wonderful. Please send me an autograph of the actor who plays the doctor. He is terrific. I desire this autograph for Alma Hitchcock. This film flooded her eyes with tears."[129]

## SARTRE'S CAUSE

As a public personality, François Truffaut was often asked to take a position regarding important issues in the political life of his country. But though he was passionately interested in politics and read the papers assiduously, he never ceased being wary of political commitment. In 1967, he turned down membership in the Legion of Honor from Minister of Cultural Affairs André Malraux. "I gladly accept rewards for any of my films, but it is not the same where the duty of the citizen is concerned, which I've never known how to fulfill, since I don't even have a voting card. I think you will understand, therefore, that since I have no civic sense, it would be dishonest of me to solicit any national honor."[130] What most bothered him about any political commitment was the simplification of reality, the Manichaeism implied in any militant discourse, for, as he put it, "life is neither Nazi, Communist, nor Gaullist, it is anarchistic."[131]

Given the political and ideological effervescence of France in the beginning of the seventies, inevitably some of Truffaut's friends urged him to commit himself to the Left—Helen Scott, for example, who was now living in Paris and still passionately interested in politics. Or Marie-France Pisier, who had made her acting debut with him in *Antoine and Colette* in the early sixties and had become a militant left-wing feminist. Truffaut maintained a friendly but stormy relationship with her. "François often feigned not to be interested in politics, to the point where sometimes he would tell me that things were going in the right direction in France after May '68 and that it was pointless to always take issue. In fact, François loathed watching people cast themselves self-importantly in political roles, or as moral spokesmen,"[132] says Pisier. As he himself said, he felt no "affection" for society, but he didn't wish to build another one which he would have no great faith in, either. "I would like to be wrong, but when I hear people say, 'We'll build a different society,' I don't believe it. When they say, 'In the future society the factories will belong to the workers,' I don't believe it. The factories might belong to the state, they'll be managed by government employees, but they'll never belong to the workers. I feel there's a huge amount of hoodwinking going on here."[133] As Truffaut swam against the fashionable tide of left-wing ideas and utopianism, there was no trace of cynicism in his remarks, just a spontaneous mistrust, dating back to his adolescence, of grand, generalizing, and (seemingly) generous concepts. For him, the artist—a term he rarely used and never with reference to himself—must defend his own cause before any other, the cause of artistic freedom, a position he discussed at length in a 1967 interview in *Cahiers du cinéma:*

I'm well aware that in troubled periods, the artist feels himself wavering and is tempted to abandon his art and place himself at the service of a specific, immediate ideal. It's the discrepancy between the frivolousness of his task and the seriousness of history's events that haunts the artist; he wishes he were a philosopher. When these kinds of thoughts come to my mind, I think of Matisse. He lived through three wars and served in none; he was too young in 1870, too old in 1914, a patriarch in 1940. He died in 1954, between the war in Indochina and the Algerian war, and had completed his life's work: fish, women, flowers, landscapes, with sections of windows. The wars were the frivolous events in his life, the thousands of paintings he left were the serious events. Art for art's sake? No. Art for beauty's sake, art for the sake of others. Matisse began by comforting himself, then he comforted others.[134]

Truffaut remained impervious to the revolutionary enthusiasm that was sweeping over a great many of his friends in those days. His reaction to a statement supporting Régis Debray, presented to him by his friend Francesca Solleville, is highly revealing. In November 1969, Régis Debray, a young French supporter of Che Guevara, was facing possible execution after two years' military detention in Bolivia. Many Paris intellectuals rallied to demand that he be pardoned by the Bolivian president. Truffaut refused to add his name to a list that already included Jacques Monod, François Jacob, Laurent Schwartz, and Jean-Paul Sartre. This refusal, for which he gave no reason, seemed natural to him, for he lacked the romantic streak that might have led him to join the international revolutionary movement. He was just as skeptical concerning something much more clear-cut, the war in Vietnam, and refused to come out against the American imperialist intervention. This drove Helen Scott to despair, particularly when he told her he could understand the reasons for the American presence in Vietnam: "For me, Johnson, who is trying to withdraw without losing face, is no more responsible for this war than Ho Chi Minh, who declares, 'We will fight until the last man!' Who knows whether the Vietnamese won't become tyrants in turn?"[135]

Truffaut was just as distrustful of the ideological discussions raging in the movie profession. "As you know, I'm completely unfamiliar with 'protest' cinema and my contribution to such a discussion would really be too slight,"[136] he replied, for example, to the director of the Venice Film Festival, who had invited him to take part in a conference entitled "Cinema and Politics" in September 1968. Truffaut also distrusted the Société des réalisateurs de films (Society of Filmmakers), which was born out of the events of May '68, even though its board of directors included several of his friends, such as Jacques Doniol-Valcroze, Pierre Kast, Claude Lelouch, Louis Malle, Edouard Molinaro, and Claude Sautet. Though he replied to its survey on censorship, he stayed away from its press conferences and refused to give the SRF clips from his censored films (*Shoot the Piano Player* and *Jules and Jim*) to use in a montage aimed at popularizing its struggle against censorship. "I cannot agree to join my filmmaker friends in signing a statement against censorship," he wrote in a private letter to Doniol-Valcroze, "because I feel there are countless ways of outwitting censorship and triumphing over it. I won't fight for principles, but for practical solutions."[137] Truffaut rejected grand abstract concepts and mobilizations on general themes. He suggested to Doniol-Valcroze another strategy: "My idea would be to create an anticensorship committee that would include filmmakers, journalists and public figures. These committee members would give maximum publicity to all the outrageous decisions of the censorship board. They would arrange to publish the dialogue or stills of censored scenes in weekly or monthly magazines, and circulate the material to foreign newspapers, radio and television stations. If this were done diligently, the members of the censorship board would eventually be made to feel that, as the saying goes, 'the game isn't worth the candle.' "[138]

Amid all the post-1968 effervescence of ideas, Truffaut preferred to remain a spectator. He favored gradual reform while admitting that "true reforms have been obtained or rather extracted for the last two years thanks to 'revolutionary actions.' Pompidou promises us Sweden with 'more sunshine.' For the moment, he gives us Sweden with more child abuse, more prison suicides, more unemployed, more needy elderly, more censorship, etc."[139] He hadn't liked Pompidou's predecessor, General de Gaulle, either. The only politician Truffaut admired was Pierre Mendès-France, the former president of the Council under the Fourth Republic and General de Gaulle's political opponent, a man of the Left who was upright, rigorous, and competent. Truffaut's reformism was based on confidence in honest, skilled politicians. The ground he trod was rather unusual in the French political landscape of the time; it was a path with no future, but original, wary of leftism and of the more reliable route that led to the founding and eventual success of François Mitterrand's Socialist party.

On occasion, however, issues that were dear to his heart—such as childhood, opposition to the army, freedom of expression, or women's struggle for legalized abortion—brought Truffaut temporarily closer to the Left. On May 22, 1969, for example, he signed a petition supporting Eric Losfeld, the editor of a small anarchist publishing house, Terrain Vague, who was ordered to submit his books to the Ministry of Justice prior to publication. Similarly, in January 1970, he publicly supported the three young conscripts who were sentenced to military detention for being in possession of left-wing antimilitary news publications.

On June 20, 1970, Truffaut joined Jean-Paul Sartre, Simone de Beauvoir, and many other personalities, including Marie-France Pisier, Alexandre Astruc, and Patrice Chéreau, in selling the leftist newspaper *La Cause du peuple* at the open-air market on rue Daguerre and on the avenue du Général Leclerc, in the fourteenth arrondissement. *La Cause du peuple* was the organ of the Proletarian Left, the foremost Maoist movement to emerge out of the events of May '68; the group had been disbanded by the Interior Ministry in spring 1970, and its paper banned; selling it meant arrest, followed by referral to the Cour de sûreté de l'Etat (high court). Sartre had agreed to become the paper's managing director and, in a show of militancy and solidarity, decided to sell it personally in the streets of Paris. Would the police be so bold as to arrest a Nobel Prizewinner? Asked by Liliane Siegel, an intimate friend of Sartre's, to join the protest, Truffaut enthusiastically agreed. "Sartre had drawn up a list of well-known people to contact to sell *La Cause du peuple*," Liliane Siegel recalls.[140]

Marie-France Pisier remembers Truffaut walking in the street, timidly selling *La Cause du peuple:* "He didn't give a darn about the content of the paper, but the idea that a paper could be banned seemed to him utterly objectionable. As soon as it was a matter of fighting for greater freedom, he was there, capable of proving as much by demonstrating."[141] The demonstration went well, even if one policeman, who had recognized Truffaut but not Sartre, briefly tried to arrest the philosopher and haul him into a police van!

On September 8, 1970, during the trial of the militants of *La Cause du peuple,* Truffaut justified his actions before the president of the high court: "I have never engaged in political activity and am no more a Maoist than a Pompidou supporter, as I am incapable of having feelings for any head of state. But I happen to love books and newspapers, and I cherish freedom of the press and the independence of the judicial system. I also happen to have made a film entitled *Fahrenheit 451,* which depicted and denounced an imaginary society in which the government systematically burned every book; I therefore wanted my ideas as a director to be consistent with my ideas as a French citizen."[142]

The year before, Truffaut had taken part in rescuing *Cahiers du cinéma,* which had become, after May '68, a spearhead of militant extreme-Left ideology. The press magnate Daniel Filipacchi, its majority owner since 1964, felt uncomfortable with the theoretical and political commitment of *Cahiers,* whose monthly pages, he felt, neglected cinema news in favor of analyses influenced by structuralism, psychoanalysis, and Marxism. In October 1969, Filipacchi decided to disassociate himself from these views, and on the 21st of that month the two editors in chief, Jean-Louis Comolli and Jean Narboni, were locked out of their offices on rue Marbeuf. Filipacchi and his associates extended the lockout. The publication of *Cahiers* was therefore interrupted, the majority shareholders formulating "specific demands concerning the liberalization of the magazine, which, according to them, had become obscure and dense and was completely devoid of objectivity in the hands of an uncompromisingly totalitarian editorial staff."[143] In ordering the magazine's suspension, Filipacchi demanded that the journal "be solely devoted to defending and illustrating the seventh art."

A meeting was scheduled for October 23 to try to find a compromise. In the presence of Georges Kiejman, the lawyer for *Cahiers,* and the minority partners, Truffaut and Doniol-Valcroze, Filipacchi demanded the replacement of the current editorial staff by a heterogeneous group of known critics, a spectrum that would include Samuel Lachize from *L'Humanité* and Louis Chauvet from *Le Figaro.* When this proposal was rejected, he gave the staff the opportunity to buy its independence—at a high price: 280,000 francs. Truffaut and Doniol-Valcroze each put up 30,000 francs. They then solicited help from all their friends—Nicole Stéphane, Jean Riboud, Pierre

Cardin, Gérard Lebovici, Michel Piccoli, Claude Berri, Pierre Braunberger, Constantin Costa-Gavras. Three members of the editorial staff, Jean Narboni, Jean-Louis Comolli, and Sylvie Pierre, brought the fund-raising to a close. A first agreement was signed on December 30, 1969, between Filipacchi and Doniol and Truffaut, and the purchase was concluded.

Truffaut thus helped to rescue *Cahiers* even though he no longer recognized himself at all in the magazine's tone, as he confided to Sylvie Pierre on November 20, 1970: "I fear things will go from bad to worse with regard to advertisement, cover choices, punctuality of subscriptions, dates of publication, etc., etc. All of this saddens me, even if it no longer concerns me. So much the better if I'm exaggerating and if reality is less bleak."[144] Since he disagreed with the staff and couldn't attend editorial meetings, Truffaut soon requested that his name be removed from the editorial committee. And so it was, in October 1970. The break between Truffaut and *Cahiers* was then complete; it would last six years, a bitter memory for the filmmaker.

## BREAKUPS ARE NECESSARY

After directing four films in two years, François Truffaut was exhausted and felt the need to take a break. He confided to Helen Scott that he had no film project scheduled until 1972: "I'll be able to get down to work on several books devoted to cinema and this will take all my time."[145] It was during this period that he collected his reviews in an anthology, *The Films of My Life,* and wrote the prefaces to the books by his "masters," Bazin, Guitry, and Audiberti.

Just as he was hoping to profit from his time off to pull together his book projects and live his new love life to the fullest, François Truffaut would go through one of the most acute emotional crises of his life. After a few months of living with Catherine Deneuve, a breakup seemed inevitable in the fall of 1970. For Truffaut, love of cinema, his desire to make films and his obsession with work were absolute priorities—to which his love life had to yield place. He probably secretly believed that harmonious love relationships were more likely to exist on screen than in real life. At the end of 1970, during the Christmas vacation, while his companion was off skiing, François Truffaut left the apartment and moved into a hotel. Perhaps it was all a complete misunderstanding. Truffaut confided to Madeleine, "I thought she wanted me to leave!"[146] In the belief that he was resolving a crisis, he brought on a break that threw him into a much deeper crisis. "The *Mermaid* is primarily the story of a degradation by love, the story of a passion. I think that most of my films are built around a chain of events in which the protagonist—who is always weaker than his partner—gets caught," he said about his film.[147] These words could not be more appropriate: *Mississippi Mermaid* allowed Truffaut to live a great love story, with a beginning, a middle, and an end. The end, unfortunately, was more like a tragedy than a Hollywood comedy.

This breakup left Truffaut devastated. To his old friend and confidante Aimée Alexandre, he mentioned "a distressing end of year, in morale and love life."[148] She tried to comfort her "dearly beloved little François" in a beautiful letter written on December 31, 1970: "I feel terribly sad about your sadness. Today, I can't prevent myself from telling you what my white hair knows and what you must be aware of from your perceptiveness: there are no accidental breakups. Breakups are always necessary. But we never realize it when they occur, and we suffer as though we had lost the essential, and we blame ourselves for not having known how to overcome circumstances. This suffering is useless, inadequate, yet it is bitter for it absorbs all actions and all thoughts. You've had all the opportunities, too many opportunities, you say. It is true. And you deserved them. But you will still have the one of encountering the essential."[149]

Truffaut had the feeling of a missed opportunity. Undoubtedly, at the time, he even had a deep sense of failure in part of his life, for once again a serious relationship, *la vie de couple*, had eluded him. As his depression worsened, he couldn't sleep, no matter how exhausted; sometimes he spent entire days without leaving the suite he had rented in mid-December in the Hotel George V. Later, he moved temporarily to the fifth-floor apartment in the building of Les Films du Carrosse, where he stayed alone with his dark thoughts. Jeanne Moreau advised him to consult Dr. René Held. This elderly man of seventy-eight, a psychoanalyst and specialist in psychosomatic medicine, completely charmed Truffaut, who found him "colorful and unbelievably full of vitality . . . very talkative and rabidly anti-American."[150] He recommended an anti-asthenia treatment, prescribed sedatives and sleeping pills, and advised Truffaut to take a ten-day sleeping cure. This was the same radical but effective treatment that had brought the Jean-Paul Belmondo character back to normal life in *Mississippi Mermaid*. On January 27, 1971, Marcel Berbert drove Truffaut to the Villa-des-Pages clinic in Le Vésinet, near Versailles, where he remained for a week. Using pep pills and sedatives, Truffaut tried to overcome his depression. As he wrote Aimée Alexandre, with a touch of irony, "the colors of my pills have become my only landscape." Yet, he added, he only felt he had returned to the world of humans when he opened "his window to throw them all out like multicolored confetti."[151]

# 7.
# CINEMA MAN:
# 1971–1979

" I hope you'll soon see me as I used to be, more cheerful,"[1] François
Truffaut wrote to the screenwriter Jean-Loup Dabadie in the beginning of 1971. After his sleeping cure he remained under medical
supervision for several months. Subject to sudden attacks of depression, his
mood was melancholic. "I am probably in less danger than I was a few weeks
ago," he confided to Liliane Siegel. "But the little nightly nightmare, eight
times out of ten about Catherine, of course, reminds me of the black hole.
In adversity—the word is too strong—one feels one can easily sink into bitterness, denigrating everything and everyone, and this I really don't want."[2]
Until spring, Truffaut, under sedatives, lived at a slower pace, conscious of
"returning from afar."[3] During this entire period, Marcel Berbert handled
the company's business, for which Truffaut was thankful to him: "At the
beginning of the year, the Carrosse really had one wheel over the edge; you
helped me, quietly but very energetically, to get things back on track. I hope
everything will go smoothly from now on."[4]

Madeleine Morgenstern remembers this depressive period as "very violent; it stemmed from his distress at being rejected by Catherine Deneuve.
François thought he was in control of the situation—he thought things
would evolve slowly, that Catherine would change her mind—but he was
brought up short when she did break up with him. He fell apart then; I had
never seen François like that."[5] Truffaut lived waiting for Catherine

Deneuve's phone calls, was thrown into a panic at the slightest delay, looked anxiously and incessantly at his watch, and chain-smoked. "I would have done anything to put an end to it," Madeleine added.

During this whole period, Truffaut avoided Paris. Whenever he was obliged to visit at least briefly, he took refuge in a hotel or in his office, and spent much of his time rereading the childhood papers and documents he had recovered in 1968, at the time of his mother's death. This aroused a feeling of guilt which only increased his melancholy. His mourning, two and a half years late, for a mother whom he had never understood, added to the depression caused by his love life and reinforced his feelings of solitude and abandonment. Thanks to the support of his loved ones, he tried to get back on his feet. Madeleine, though she had remarried (a marriage that would last only a few months), was by his side as often as possible. She accompanied him to Nice, where he stayed for a few weeks at the Négresco Hotel, until Jean-Louis Richard joined him to work on a new screenplay (*Day for Night*). Then he went to Jeanne Moreau's for a rest in her house at La Garde-Freinet.

## *TWO ENGLISH GIRLS*

During this dark period of his life, Truffaut found a veritable lifeline in Henri-Pierre Roché's novel *Les deux Anglaises et le Continent* (*The Two English Girls and the Continent*), which he had already read and thought of adapting several years earlier.[6] He read it over and over again, to the point where he knew every single line by heart. Giving up all thought of a sabbatical year, he decided, as a matter of urgency, to make this his next film. Jean-Claude Brialy, his confidant during his depression, fully understood the stakes involved in *Two English Girls* when he wrote to Truffaut: "My thoughts are very much with you right now as you start work on the film which you suddenly called forth to chase the bad clouds from your mind. I hope the work and joy of shooting prevent your being sad."[7] Filming to live, shooting to heal—rarely would cinema have such a vital function.

Ten years after *Jules and Jim*, Truffaut reimmersed himself in Roché's world—though, actually, he had never really cut himself off, since after the writer's death he had remained in touch with Denise, Roché's wife, and their son, Jean-Claude. He had arranged for his secretaries to type up Roché's numerous intimate notebooks, which would certainly have been lost or dispersed if not for Truffaut's stubborn determination to get them published. But his submissions to publishers—Robert Laffont, Flammarion, Hachette, and Gallimard—were rejected.[8] Truffaut would use some passages from these notebooks for the screenplays of *Two English Girls* and, several years later, *The Man Who Loved Women.*

Truffaut had started negotiating with Gallimard for the screen rights to *Two English Girls* in 1968. The publisher had requested 150,000 francs, a sum Truffaut found exorbitant. He had reminded Gallimard that his film *Jules and Jim* had greatly contributed to reviving the sales of Roché's novel. Fifteen thousand copies were sold during the sixties, and translations were published in Italy, England, Germany, and Holland. Truffaut also used as part of his argument Claude Gallimard's refusal to publish Roché's notebooks: "I know that I shouldn't necessarily see a connection between your financial demand for the rights to *Two English Girls* which seems excessive to me, and the minimal interest the Gallimard house shows for Roché's posthumous works, but nevertheless I feel your offer was made without your realizing everything I have done to champion one of your writers and make him known."[9] Gallimard responded by halving their asking price for the screen rights to *Two English Girls.*

Gruault started working on the adaptation, using Truffaut's annotated copy of the novel. He also read Roché's notebooks. It was an arduous task, for Truffaut wished to use extensive material (the novel and the notebooks) to draft a simple and linear screenplay. One year later, in March 1969, Gruault dropped off four large manuscript notebooks at Les Films du Carrosse; these amounted to the first version of the screenplay of *Two English Girls.* Typed, the script, divided into ninety-five sequences, came to 552 pages.

The story is set at the beginning of the century, over a long stretch of time punctuated by separations, trips, reunions, and deaths; it tells of several intertwining lives in a novelistic manner. Two young sisters from Wales, Muriel and Anne Brown, are in love with a Frenchman, Claude Roc, whom they call "the Continent." Claude, a young Parisian (in reality, Henri-Pierre Roché in his youth), plans to make a literary career for himself and gradually becomes an art lover. He was brought up by his widowed mother. In Paris, Claude first meets Anne, who secretly sees him as a good match for her sister, Muriel, whom she fervently admires. Claude then goes to spend the summer in Wales with the Brown family. At first, he hardly notices Muriel, but then he has a sudden revelation of his love for her, so much so that he wants to marry her. But Claude's mother is strongly opposed to their marriage and requests that the two young people separate for a year. When he returns to Paris, Claude has other affairs and sends Muriel a breakup letter that deeply hurts her. Anne, who has settled in Paris to study sculpture, becomes Claude's mistress. When Muriel comes to Paris and her sister tells her of their liaison, she feels completely shattered. She returns to England immediately. Claude sinks into depression, then recovers by telling the story in a novel, *Jérome and Julien.* Several years later, after Anne's death, he sees Muriel again in Calais and they make love for the first time, with Muriel demanding as a condition their immediate and definitive separation.

Discouraged by the scope of the project and the thick script, Truffaut had put it aside for two years. It wasn't until March 1971 that he began to work again on Jean Gruault's enormous opus. Armed with a pair of scissors and Scotch tape, he reduced it to two hundred pages, then asked Gruault to work on it again. While refocusing their attention on *Two English Girls,* they read all the biographies of Charlotte and Emily Brontë, "who were also English, puritanical, novelistic and impassioned,"[10] as well as Marcel Proust's recollections of his youth. "The hero of *Two English Girls* is a bit like a young Proust who might have fallen in love with Charlotte and Emily Brontë, and loved both of them for over ten years without being able to choose one or the other."[11] Anne's dying words—"My mouth is full of earth"—are taken from Emily Brontë. In the final screenplay, *Two English Girls* has shed much of its initial Belle Epoque setting and focuses solely on the feelings that bind Claude, Anne, and Muriel. "This isn't a film about physical love, but a physical film about love," Truffaut pointed out. "It is a romantic story that I wanted to make novelistic. I think that with this work, I wanted to squeeze love dry like a lemon."[12]

But it is a painful love story, and because the film shows this suffering, it can be read as the intimate journal of its convalescing director. Therein lies the true key to this work: the feverishness that binds human beings in passionate intimacy; the impulses that overpower the body and from which no one can free himself—such as Muriel's onanism, the ailing expression in Muriel's eyes when she loses her virginity, Claude's broken leg and his premature aging, Anne's thirst for life and her fatal tuberculosis. Physical and spiritual pain are the raw material of this film, the pain of human beings subjected to the ordeals of intense affections. These sufferings shed a harsh light on the distress of the director, who had himself loved two sisters, one of whom had deserted him in death, and the other in life.

Roché's writing burns like a smoldering inner flame in Truffaut's film. Rarely has the very substance of a book been filmed more forthrightly. Indeed, during the credits, one is shown the pages of Roché's book annotated by Truffaut, his deletions, his hesitations, and the words he circled in ink. The writing is also embodied in the voice-over, read by Truffaut himself with a haste and concentration that shows how deeply he identified with the characters' feelings.

After the success of *The Wild Child* and *Bed and Board,* Truffaut had no trouble finding financing for the film. Berbert and he maintained their collaboration with the independent producer-distributor Hercule Mucchielli.

The estimated budget was 3,850,000 francs, which was modest for a period film requiring several sets and a twelve-week shoot. Columbia Pictures contributed a $400,000 advance for the American distribution rights.

Preproduction, between March and April 1971, was rapid and intense. The Carrosse crew rallied around Suzanne Schiffman. Roland Thénot (location manager), Jean-Pierre Kohut-Svelko (assistant set designer), and Jean-François Stévenin found landscapes in the Norman Cotentin peninsula, which closely resembles Wales, where much of the film is supposed to take place. This choice suited Truffaut, since it made shooting conditions simpler. Stévenin also found a beautiful location in the Jura, near a beautiful lake, and an antiquated railroad surrounded by a forest in the Ardèche.

Truffaut didn't hesitate for a moment in casting Jean-Pierre Léaud as Claude Roc, the attractive, indecisive, fragile young dandy. Truffaut also hoped to dissociate the actor from the Antoine Doinel character. "It's as though you were playing the part of Jim," Truffaut wrote when sending him the screenplay. "This will be the most difficult part for you because you'll have to act as though you were born rich and powerful."[13] To cast the parts of the two English girls, Truffaut turned to Oscar Lewenstein, his friend in London who had produced *Fahrenheit 451* and *The Bride Wore Black*. Almost as soon as Truffaut came out of the clinic, he asked him to set up a casting call for about one hundred young actresses. "They should be between eighteen and twenty-four years old, not too tall to play opposite Jean-Pierre Léaud, and speak French as well as possible."[14] In mid-March, Suzanne Schiffman traveled to London for a first selection. Truffaut traveled himself for final auditions in early April and chose Kika Markham and Stacey Tendeter—the first for the part of Anne, the second for the part of Muriel. The brunette and redhead were unacquainted with each other, nor did they resemble each other, but they would get along perfectly during the filming. While in London, Truffaut also hired Sylvia Marriott, a known British stage actress, for the part of Mrs. Brown, the girls' mother.

Truffaut completed the casting with Philippe Léotard, Irène Tunc, and Marie Mansart, and as was his custom, assigned some of the secondary parts to his collaborators. Georges Delerue appears as Madame Roc's businessman, and Marcel Berbert as the owner of an art gallery. Laura and Eva, his daughters, are in the opening shot of the film, playing by the swing with Mathieu and Guillaume, Suzanne Schiffman's children.

On April 28, 1971, barely three months after leaving the clinic, Truffaut welcomed the cast and crew of the film at the Hague-Dick Hotel, a pension in Auderville in the Cotentin area. The shoot of the *Two English Girls* began nearby, on a beautiful estate rented from the Anquetil family, the ideal set for Mrs. Brown's "Welsh" house. Truffaut had some trees cut down in the garden to clear the view to the sea, but in every other respect the spot was perfect for his project, particularly the wild moor on the edge of the cliff where Claude, Anne, and Muriel pour out their feelings. When it rained, as it occasionally did there in the spring, the cast and crew remained cloistered inside the Anquetil house for the many interior scenes. When the rain stopped, they shot exterior scenes on the cliff. On May 8, Truffaut shot the big reunion scene between Claude and Muriel that occurs at the end of the story; it was shot in Cherbourg, though it is supposed to be set in Calais. Claude is on the quay waiting for Muriel, who disembarks from the boat; they meet again after a separation of several years and will have their sole night of lovemaking. "The sun was reflecting off the water in such a way," said Almendros, "that it was shedding waves of light on the hull of the ship. I said to François, 'Look how beautiful it would be if we could have them meet in front of this shimmering light.' He said, 'Let's go, quickly, we must do it.' We shot the scene and then in the editing he eliminated the dialogue. He put in Delerue's music and said to me, 'When you have an image with light like that, it is the equivalent of a line of dialogue.' It was as though the passion, the inner vibration, were projected in the image. When he saw a strong idea, he was eager to adopt it."[15]

In the beginning of June, one part of the cast and crew went to Lamastre, in the Vivarais, to shoot the station and antique railroad in Cheylard. Then they filmed in Paris and its environs, in various interiors and in the Musée Rodin for the last scene in the film, where, ten years later, Claude thinks he recognizes Muriel's daughter among the visiting English schoolgirls looking at the sculptor's works. The filming ended in July in the Jura, near the Lac de la Motte.

All in all, Truffaut was very satisfied with the shoot and felt he had made his masterpiece. Thanks to the steady support of his friends on the set, he had regained his self-confidence. "I was not alone in digging this first tunnel under the Channel, which, I hope, *Two English Girls* is."[16] Filmmaking turned out to be the most effective way for him to chase away his "dark thoughts" and finally sleep "without sleeping pills."[17] The idea of living alone in Paris became less frightening to him. Truffaut knew that work was his only remedy, the only thing that mobilized him completely and engaged his strongest emotions. "When I am working, I become attractive," he wrote to Liliane Dreyfus during the filming, "I feel it and at the same time this work, which is the best in the world, puts me in an emotional state that is propitious for the beginning of a *love story* [in English]. Before me, there is usually a young girl or woman, agitated, fearful and obedient, trusting and ready to surrender herself. What happens next is always the same. Sometimes the *love story* is synchronized with the filming and ends with it; at other times it continues afterward, by the will of one or both. . . ."[18] His affair with Kika

Markham, which started during the filming of *Two English Girls,* lasted for several months thereafter.

Truffaut gave himself a few weeks' vacation, from July 20, 1971 to the end of August, in a rented house in Antibes, the Villa Mirasol, on boulevard du Cap. It was only a part-time vacation, for he supervised Yann Dedet's editing of his film in the Victorine Studios in Nice. But he could also see Madeleine, Laura, and Eva, who were spending the summer at the Résidence Saint-Michel in Cannes, and entertain a succession of friends—Bernadette Lafont, Liliane Dreyfus, Suzanne Schiffman, Jean Aurel, Jean-Loup Dabadie, Jean-Louis Richard, and Jean Gruault. The last three were each working, separately, on Truffaut's next films—*Such a Gorgeous Kid Like Me, Day for Night,* and *The Story of Adèle H.* Truffaut recovered his good spirits by playing with his daughters, whose "cheerfulness and health" were of great help to him; they recounted the "funny, salacious stories told to them by older girls and which they only half-understand. We laugh a lot. They are thriving, and are far less jealous of one another. . . ."[19]

After a first screening of *Two English Girls* at the Victorine Studios, in the presence of Aurel (his "personal consultant,"[20] as Truffaut called him), Dabadie, and Jean-Louis Richard, the director was confident. "They think it's the most beautiful of my films, thanks to the photography,"[21] he wrote a short time later to Nestor Almendros. At the beginning of September, Truffaut was back in Paris for another screening, on rue de Ponthieu, attended by Léaud, Delerue, Gruault, Gérard Lebovici, Serge Rousseau, and the technical crew. "Everyone is very pleased,"[22] he wrote euphorically to Almendros on September 11. For those close to him, *Two English Girls* is unquestionably his most moving, most formally successful, and most novelistic film. The critic Louis Marcorelles wrote to him: "I felt very close to you in this film which seems to concern you so intimately, not because of any immodesty, but because your sensitivity, your passion show through constantly."[23] Before the film was released, Truffaut received about fifty letters, all laudatory, from friends who had had the privilege of seeing the film at a private screening. "Not only is this your most beautiful film, but the beginning of a new oeuvre, ripened by time and pain,"[24] the director Paul Vecchiali wrote to him, for example. "François, in spite of my enthusiasms at the time, I never believed that the New Wave meant anything else than the desire to take the place of others. Now, thanks to you, a work provides a deep justification for this change,"[25] wrote Jean Eustache. And Denise Roché: "This film is so important that the audience will have the patience and humility to understand it. I watched it—throughout—as though Pierre had been by my side."[26]

After a warm preview screening at the Cinémathèque française, the film came out in seven Paris movie theaters on November 24, 1971. The first two weeks were disastrous—barely thirty thousand tickets were sold. Curiously, the press was clearly divided into partisans and detractors. Many would criticize the film for being cold, gratuitous, even vulgar: "Truffaut dwells on things and even indulges in bad taste by drenching the sheets of a bridal bed with blood,"[27] wrote Robert Chazal about the sequence where Muriel loses her virginity. Truffaut, who had read, annotated, and underlined these remarks, was deeply affected by them. Faced with a double failure, commercial and critical, he reacted violently and decided to pull the film from the Paris theaters and cut it by fourteen minutes. With the running time of *Two English Girls* reduced to one hour and fifty-eight minutes, exhibitors could schedule one additional showing a day. In so doing, Truffaut tried to avert disaster and minimize the loss of money to Hercule Mucchielli, his financial partner, who had already complained about the "length of the film, the occasional unnecessary narration, and especially the bloodstain."[28] "I don't scorn money," Truffaut tried to justify what some saw as self-censorship, "I have no consuming love for it, but the idea of making someone else lose money is unbearable to me. I like my work enough to believe it is interesting, but not enough to believe it is indispensable or irreproachable."[29] Truffaut trimmed his voice-over narration but refused to cut the shot of Muriel's bloodstain, certainly the most intimate shot he ever filmed. He was very attached to Roché's sentence about this: "There was red on her gold." For Truffaut, this moment represented the imprint of unleashed passions. Furthermore, if he chose to shoot *Two English Girls* at a difficult period of his life, it was because he felt that the return to life entailed an excess of lovesickness. Truffaut had recovered perhaps, but *Two English Girls* still preserved the indelible trace of fevered anguish.

Abroad, the reception was better than in Paris. Truffaut traveled to various places with his film, primarily to escape depression. In places other than Paris, he felt more confident, far from the escalating failures that seemed once again to have taken hold of his life. This is clear from the interview he gave to Canadian television in December 1971, where he spoke openly and at length about his childhood and adolescence, his army desertion, the setbacks in his career—all subjects that he was reluctant to broach with French journalists. Truffaut sojourned in Montreal with Madeleine from December 13 to 17. It was then that he recorded the three-hour televised interview with Aline Desjardins, as part of the program *Femme d'aujourd'hui* (*Today's Woman*), directed by Gilles Derome: "What I said on that day, I'd never said elsewhere, and I'll never say again."[30] Then Truffaut spent the Christmas and New Year holidays in Athens, with his family—Madeleine, Laura (who was beginning to study Greek and would thereby be encouraged), and Eva. Family harmony, "a very happy moment in a time of distress,"[31] he wrote to Liliane Siegel on December 30, 1971.

## THE FEMALE HOODLUM

"When I've just shot a sad film, I have only one desire: to make a cheerful film."[32] To quickly forget the *Two English Girls* disaster, Truffaut started work on a new film three months later. If romantic passion was not understood, perhaps farce would help put him back on the road to success and deliver him from this difficult period. Deliberately funny and nutty, *Une belle fille comme moi* (*Such a Gorgeous Kid Like Me*) rests entirely on Bernadette Lafont's talent. Launched by Truffaut and Chabrol in the early years of the New Wave, the actress had married the sculptor Diourka Medveczki and had had three children. In the late sixties, she made her screen comeback and worked at a frenetic pace, appearing in films by Louis Malle, Philippe Garrel, Jean-Daniel Pollet, and Nadine Trintignant. But her career was truly relaunched in 1969 by *A Very Curious Girl*, directed by Nelly Kaplan. "Bernadette Lafont," as Jacques Audiberti put it, "performs as though her life depended on it." And Truffaut, it could be said, filmed "as though his life depended on it."[33] This shared energy brought the filmmaker and actress close at a time when both needed to immerse themselves in cinema in order to forget life's misfortunes.

In November 1969, Truffaut had read the novel *Such a Gorgeous Kid Like Me* by the American writer Henry Farrell; it had been published the year before in Gallimard's Série Noire under the French title *Le Chant de la sirène*. "One day I happened to start reading this novel on a Paris–Madrid flight," Truffaut explained, "a stewardess who heard me roar with laughter at every page went to warn the head pilot that a passenger had gone crazy and perhaps the control tower should be alerted."[34] The story is about a sociologist (Stanislas Prévine, in the French version) who is investigating female criminals. Through his work, he becomes particularly interested in the case of Camille Bliss, a petulant prisoner whose slang is irresistible and who is suspected of having killed her father and one of her many lovers. Truffaut was attracted to Camille because she was a "female hoodlum,"[35] like Deneuve's character in *Mississippi Mermaid*. A reserved man brimming with contradictions, Truffaut was always attracted by these kinds of women, who reminded him of certain women in his youth.

He learned from Gallimard that the screen rights to the novel were owned by Columbia Pictures. On March 15, 1971, he wrote to Columbia producers Stanley Schneider and Jack Wiener, offering to direct the film for the American company. Columbia temporized, for the project had already been offered to Blake Edwards. But in August, when Edwards turned it down, the way was open for Truffaut. It was then only a matter of specifying the terms of the coproduction deal between Les Films du Carrosse and the Hollywood studio; the latter agreed to finance a film with a budget of about 3 million francs.

While he was in Antibes in the summer of 1971, Truffaut invited Bernadette Lafont to come stay with him and discuss the film with him and Jean-Loup Dabadie. A young screenwriter, Dabadie had just made a name for himself with two Claude Sautet films, *Les Choses de la vie* and *Max et les Ferrailleurs*, and two Philippe de Broca comedies, *La Poudre d'escampette* and *Chère Louise.* "The screenplay of *Louise* is what made me want to work with you, because for the first time I felt I was reading a French script that could be shot as is,"[36] Truffaut wrote to Dabadie in January 1971. Paradoxically, Truffaut's dream was to have a script that was "ready to go," that he wouldn't have to constantly "fill in" and "patch up."[37] "This is what I want and what I need," he emphasized to Dabadie, momentarily preferring a degree of professional comfort in the writing of the screenplay to the "amateurism of his usual collaborators." Dabadie and he hit it off well, with Truffaut finding his "new acolyte funny, friendly and stimulating."[38] The two men worked together for three weeks in Antibes, sketching out the outline of the screenplay, which Dabadie would write the following autumn.

In *Such a Gorgeous Kid Like Me* the sociologist Stanislas Prévine finds out the details of Camille Bliss's past. After causing the death of her alcoholic father as a child, she had been sent to a center for juvenile delinquents. She ran away and married the first man she met, Clovis Bliss, whose mother was hiding a tidy sum. After searching for it in vain, Camille, who dreams of a nightclub singing career, deceives her husband with a singer, Sam Golden. Mad with rage, Clovis gets run over by a car and ends up paralyzed in a wheelchair. Camille then takes up with Arthur, a mystical rat exterminator who loses his virginity with her, but she ends up the victim of a shady lawyer, Murène, who makes her sign compromising papers. Cornered, Camille tries to kill off Clovis and Murène with Arthur's rat-exterminating machine. Arthur saves them but wants to draw Camille into a double suicide by jumping from church towers. Arthur jumps alone. Camille is charged with murder and finds herself in jail. Stanislas Prévine is secretly in love with the woman who is becoming his thesis subject. He succeeds in getting his hands on an amateur film shot at Arthur's death which proves Camille's innocence. Freed, she becomes a famous singer. But Clovis tracks her down and threatens her; she kills him and manages to pin the murder on Stanislas. The sociologist ends up in jail.

The first screenplay didn't satisfy Truffaut. He felt that the character of Stanislas, the investigating sociologist, had been sacrificed in favor of

Camille, the female criminal. Because of this imbalance, Camille Bliss's slang dwarfed Stanislas Prévine's scientific interpretations. "My dear Jean-Loup, I'm not the least bit worried about the way you make Bernadette talk. All will go well. We must rework the 'report' side of the narrative, which will allow us to shoot a film that won't be presented as a comedy, but will be 100 percent deadpan."[39] Dabadie reworked the screenplay, but when Truffaut started the shoot, he was still not satisfied.

He started casting the film in the middle of winter, 1971–1972, with Philippe Léotard in the part of Clovis, Camille Bliss's young alcoholic husband; Guy Marchand in the part of Sam Golden, the star of the Colt Saloon, a slightly vulgar singer with charm; and Claude Brasseur as the shady lawyer who goes by the gentle name of Murène. Arthur, the rat exterminator, is played by Charles Denner, who is different from the other characters, "in his more mystical, more pompous, more puritanical style."[40] Truffaut considered playing the part of Stanislas Prévine himself. He had enjoyed acting in *The Wild Child* and felt ready to renew the experience, for "I'm sure I would be impassive and that a contrast would be created between Bernadette and me,"[41] he wrote to Dabadie. Once the script was completed, however, Truffaut gave up the idea, since he didn't feel prepared to take on comedy. Instead, he chose André Dussollier for the part, a twenty-six-year-old first-prize graduate in comedy from the Conservatoire and a new member of the Comédie-Française. This would be Dussollier's first screen role, and his sober and elegant appearance conferred a suitable air of bourgeois respectability on the part.

Nestor Almendros, who was in great demand with other directors, was unavailable on Truffaut's shooting dates. So the director hired Pierre-William Glenn as director of photography for this comic film, in which speed of execution and pacing were more important than aesthetic qualities. Glenn was to be assisted by his cameraman Walter Bal, and Jean-Pierre Kohut-Svelko was hired as set designer. Aged twenty-six, a graduate of the Ecole des Beaux-Arts in Paris, Kohut-Svelko had already been assistant set designer for *Mississippi Mermaid* and *Two English Girls*. His collaboration with Truffaut was to be long-lasting.

In early February, Truffaut went to live in Béziers for the filming, in a large apartment he had rented in the center of town. He appeared relaxed, and the mild Languedoc winter seemed to agree with him; he took advantage of his housekeeper Marie's presence to invite his actors to dinner as they showed up on location for the shoot. "François loved jokes, and Denner and Brasseur certainly didn't abstain. Twice I saw François laugh so hard that he had to leave the table to go throw up,"[42] Bernadette Lafont recalls. The shooting, which started on February 14, unfolded in a very pleasant atmosphere. "Bernadette, really funny, is always laughing and easy to work with, Claude Brasseur is excellent, Charles Denner sublime,"[43] Truffaut wrote to Liliane Siegel. The film was mostly shot in Béziers, at the B.G.M. Brasserie, on Place d'Espagne, where a set had been created for the Bliss home. The courtyard of the prison where Camille is detained was erected in the former Béziers slaughterhouse; the visiting-room scenes were shot in the courthouse on Place de la Révolution. The cast and crew later moved to the outskirts of the city, then to Sète, and finally to Lunel, where Suzanne Schiffman had found a bar and dance hall with a western ambience, Le Rodéo, which was perfect for Sam Golden's singing act.

Bernadette Lafont's part fit her like a glove, and she was happy to work again with the person who had launched her acting career. "François was very attached to the character of Camille Bliss," she recalls. "He even said that if he had been a woman, he would have been like her, for this woman wasn't rehabilitated by society. She predated original sin."[44] Everything went smoothly until the day following the last day of the shoot. On that day, Truffaut, who was staying at the Hotel Imperator in Nîmes, "forgot" to stop by to pick up Bernadette Lafont, who was living in Lunel with the rest of the cast and crew. "He had said to me, 'Do you want me to give you a ride back to Paris? We're leaving very early tomorrow morning. Be in front of your hotel at nine o'clock.' I was there waiting with my suitcases. I waited until eleven o'clock, but he never showed up! In the evening, I phoned him, hurt, and François burst out laughing: 'My dear Bettine, listen, I forgot about you!' He didn't need me anymore!"[45] After a forty-six-day shoot, Truffaut was exhausted. He had just made two films right after recovering from a depression, and his mind was already on the problems of the next one. Very shortly after returning to Paris, he decided to give himself a few days' rest in Normandy, in the beautiful house Liliane Dreyfus and her husband had acquired in 1968. From then on, the Ranconnière manor near Deauville would become one of Truffaut's favorite spots. "He came often," says Liliane Dreyfus. "He did a lot of work there."[46]

In the meantime, Georges Delerue composed a rhythmical orchestral score and Guy Marchand set to music the two songs written by Jean-Loup Dabadie—Sam Golden's song and the song sung to great acclaim by Camille Bliss at the end of the film. Before it opened, on September 13, 1972, *Such a Gorgeous Kid Like Me* was shown in preview in Lyon, in the presence of François Truffaut and Bernadette Lafont, to inaugurate the renovated Bellecour movie theater. Bernadette Lafont also presented the film in Béziers on the eve of its Paris release, to an audience of local officials and most of the extras who lived in the city. The actress already felt she was shouldering this film on her own, a film in which she doesn't stop running, and which rests entirely on her energy. "When François saw the audience reactions, he said to me, 'This film belongs to you, this character is you, so you handle it!' He had sensed that the response was unexceptional for him, while things would go well for me."[47]

Indeed, the reviews of the film focused on Bernadette Lafont's performance. After a seven-week exclusive run, ticket sales for the film fell just short of 100,000. It did better in Italy, where it was shown in the spring of 1973 under the title *Mica Scema la Ragazza!* and was helped by catchy slogans such as "*Supercomico, Supersexy, Super-film.*" In the United States, *Such a Gorgeous Kid Like Me* was released simultaneously in eight large cities (an exceptional event for a Truffaut film), and it was a reasonable success in spite of a lukewarm, disappointed response from the press. But the director's mind was elsewhere; his thoughts were already on his next film.

## DAY FOR NIGHT

During the editing of *Two English Girls* at the Victorine Studios, François Truffaut had become intrigued by the remains of a huge exterior set that had been erected several years earlier for an American production of *The Madwoman of Chaillot*. Though it was slightly damaged, the set consisted of several building facades, a subway entrance, and a Paris sidewalk café. He started to explore the Victorine Studios thoroughly, with a mind to "shooting a film about cinema."[48]

It would be *La Nuit américaine* (*Day for Night*), which he wanted to write with Jean-Louis Richard, with whom he hadn't collaborated since *The Bride Wore Black*. The two men set to work in a rented house in Antibes; using a roll of blank white paper, they set down the main events of the script. "When we had an idea, our problem was to integrate it at a chosen moment in the film and we would inscribe it at a specific place on the big roll. That way we had an almost graphic overview of the film, a story line from which we could deviate, but which allowed us to maintain a pacing,"[49] Jean-Louis Richard explains. The fleshing out of the film progressed rapidly and by mid-August 1971, Truffaut already had the first draft of a screenplay telling the story of a film shoot.

*Day for Night* was then held in abeyance while Truffaut filmed *Such a Gorgeous Kid Like Me*. In January 1971, he met with Jean-Louis Richard again at Le Martinez, his hotel in Cannes. This was when they came up with the story for *Je vous présente Pamela* (*Meet Pamela*), the film within the film. A young man introduces his fiancée to his father, who falls in love and runs off with her. Suzanne Schiffman, with her thorough knowledge of the technical and human aspects of life on a film set, helped them with the final version of the screenplay. This would be the first time she would be listed as co-scenarist, as well as assistant director, in the credits of a Truffaut film.

*Day for Night* takes place during a film shoot and mixes the actors' private lives with the plot of the film in which they are acting, thereby showing the ties that bind all the members of a cast and crew. The shooting of *Je vous présente Pamela*, under the direction of Ferrand, is about to begin in the Victorine Studios. The extras are milling in front of a big set. The technicians bombard the director with questions, while the actors gradually arrive on set, each with his or her problems and private concerns. The film's female lead, Julie Baker, a psychologically fragile American star, is expected any minute with her husband, Dr. Nelson. Alphonse, the male lead playing opposite her, has arrived with his girlfriend, Liliane, whom he has succeeded in getting hired as an apprentice script girl. Alexandre, an elderly French actor and veteran of eighty-four films, plays Alphonse's father. In *Je vous présente Pamela,* he has to play opposite a long-lost former mistress, Séverine, an ex-Hollywood star who has been cast as his wife. All the members of the cast and crew are lodged in a hotel, where Ferrand prepares the following day's scenes and dialogues with his assistant, Joëlle. The filming progresses but seems at times to escape Ferrand's control because of the actors' and technicians' personal lives. Thus, when Liliane walks off the set with an English stuntman, Alphonse threatens to bring the entire movie to a halt. Ferrand tries to convince him to continue, while trying to protect Julie Baker, who has just spent the night with Alphonse. The following morning, Alphonse tells Dr. Nelson that he has slept with his wife. Julie is in despair. Her husband forgives her and reassures her. The shooting can now resume. However, the production manager then arrives on the set with dreadful news: Alexandre has just had a fatal car accident on the road to the airport.[50] Thanks to the efforts of the entire cast and crew, the shoot is completed in five days, with a stand-in and some script changes.

## LIKE A TRAIN GOING ALONG IN THE NIGHT

With this picture, Truffaut was fulfilling a longtime dream, that of showing the inside workings of a shoot. "I won't reveal the whole truth about filming, but just some real things that happened in my past movies or in other movies."[51] *Day for Night* was meant as a profession of faith in cinema—cinema, the thing he loved best in the world and which often came before his personal life, indeed before life in general. Through fiction, he was able to reveal the things that he was generally loath to bring up in interviews with journalists, or which he saw no point in describing in documentaries about his shoots. *Day for Night* mixes documentary and fiction: It would be a true and sincere film on an artificial world, the world of cinema, where "we do a lot of kissing because we must show our love,"[52] as one of the characters in the picture puts it. A facade of unanimity, a world of pretense, which the production manager's wife, alone in a corner of the set, is the sole person to demythologize: "What is this movie world?" she cries out. "What is this profession where everyone sleeps with everyone else? Everyone is chummy and everyone lies. What's it all about? Do you find it normal? Well I think it stinks. I despise it."[53] In the part of Ferrand, Truffaut—who rarely addressed his collaborators with the informal *"tu"*—did his utmost to give a neutral, professional image of the working film director, and he quite clearly avoided portraying him as an artist. But he was very eager to show the hidden side of moviemaking, the excitement of a shoot and a successful endeavor, with its bonds of friendship and its occasional love stories. Moments of depression, inspirational burnout, quarrels—nothing, not even death, will stop the film, which is like "a train going along in the night."[54]

Yet the film within the film that they are shooting at the Victorine Studios has nothing particularly exciting about it. It is obviously not an "auteur film," but a "bad film," as Jean-Louis Richard says. But the banality of the screenplay of *Je vous présente Pamela* doesn't in the least hamper the crescendo of the shoot, nor does it interfere with the fellowship felt by the cast and crew, or dampen the actors' enthusiasm. For Truffaut, *Day for Night* was a love story, a film devoted to the love of cinema *regardless of everything*. "Foremost in my mind was the Charles Trenet song 'Moi, j'aime le music-hall' where he enumerates with kindness and humor all the popular singers of the day, though they're his competitors. I shot *Day for Night* in the same spirit, my intent was to make the audience happy on seeing a film in the making, to infuse joy and lightheartedness from all the sprocket holes of the film. 'Moi, j'aime le cinéma.' "[55] Many would reproach Truffaut for his kindliness in describing the small world of the most banal kind of cinema—Jean-Luc Godard, for example, who felt Truffaut had sold out with this film.

Once the screenplay was completed, Marcel Berbert drew up a reasonable estimated budget of 3.5 million francs. Yet United Artists refused to finance *Day for Night* because they felt the script was too risky, "too intellectual," and they feared that an uninitiated audience might find the plot of a film within a film disconcerting. Berbert then approached Robert Solo, Warner's London representative, who was a Truffaut admirer. He agreed with alacrity after a first meeting in November 1971. The contract was signed in May 1972.

In the meantime, Truffaut began thinking about the casting with Jean-Louis Richard. Truffaut eventually cast Jean-Pierre Aumont as Alexandre and Valentina Cortese as Séverine.[56] Jean Champion was cast as the producer of *Je vous présente Pamela,* Marcel Berbert's double. Truffaut did not hesitate to cast himself in the part of Ferrand, giving the character his own childlike personality and love for his profession. Jean-Pierre Léaud was to play Alphonse—romantic, often capricious and unstable, to the point of interrupting the shoot. He resembles in every detail the Léaud of the early seventies, whom Truffaut had encouraged to pursue a "real acting career."[57] After *Two English Girls,* Léaud had worked with the directors Glauber Rocha (*The Lion Has Seven Heads*), Luc Moullet (*Une aventure de Billy le Kid*), Bernardo Bertolucci (*Last Tango in Paris*), and notably Jean Eustache, with whom he had just shot *La Maman et la Putain* (*The Mother and the Whore*).[58] Nonetheless, the actor had difficulty ridding himself of the Antoine Doinel persona and his image as "the son of Truffaut." His life consisted of a series of depressions, euphorias, about-faces, money problems, romantic setbacks, so that his fellow professionals found him unsettling. On the set of *A Sentimental Education,* which Marcel Cravenne made for television in 1972, the screenwriter François-Régis Bastide complained to Truffaut: "Everyone in the cast and crew hated him during those three months, and Cravenne didn't utter a single impatient word even though Jean-Pierre called everybody and anybody 'fascist.' . . ."[59] In *Day for Night,* Alphonse is as fragile as the real-life Jean-Pierre Léaud, and his relationship with Ferrand seems modeled on Léaud's relationship to Truffaut. In the scene where Ferrand lectures Alphonse in order to rekindle his self-confidence, Truffaut is clearly addressing Léaud: "Movies are more harmonious than life. There are no traffic jams in movies, no dead spots. Movies go along like trains, you understand, like trains in the night. People like you and me, as you know, should seek happiness in our work, in our movie work. I'm counting on you. . . ."[60]

Truffaut felt Jacqueline Bisset would be ideal for the part of Julie Baker. Of Scottish descent on her father's side and French on her mother's, she began her career as a model and made her first screen appearances in England (Richard Lester's *The Knack* and Roman Polanski's *Cul-de-Sac*), before moving to Hollywood in 1968. Her appearances in Peter Yates's *Bullitt* (with Steve McQueen), Gordon Douglas's *The Detective* (with Frank Sinatra), George Seaton's *Airport* (with Dean Martin and Burt Lancaster), and John Huston's *The Life and Times of Judge Roy Bean* (with Paul Newman) had catapulted her to Hollywood stardom. Her introduction to Truffaut, whom she had admired for a long time, occurred in an odd way. While she was staying for a few days in Paris, Bisset received a phone call at her hotel from Gérard Lebovici: "I'm François Truffaut's agent and I'd like to know what you thought of the script." At first, she thought it was a hoax, and told him she had no knowledge of any script. The misunderstanding was cleared up and Bisset requested that a copy of the script be dropped off at her hotel. "I thought the part wasn't very big, but I'd have taken it even if I'd had only one line to deliver." Later, she had a conversation over the phone with Truffaut: "He told me he didn't have much money to make the film, so he couldn't pay me very much, that it wasn't a particularly big part, that the film had several leading characters. He said all this with great courtesy and humility."[61] Usually, Jacqueline Bisset commanded a salary that was the equivalent of *Day for Night*'s entire budget. But the contract she signed with Carrosse in March 1972 stipulated that beyond her salary of 200,000 francs, she was to receive a 20 percent royalty on the profits. This was clear proof of her desire to work with Truffaut, one of the directors she most admired, along with Ingmar Bergman.

For the supporting roles, Truffaut met two young actresses with whom he would work again in the future: Dani, whom he cast in the part of Liliane, Alphonse's girlfriend, and Nathalie Baye, just out of the Conservatoire, whom he cast in the part of Joëlle, the script girl of *Je vous présente Pamela*, whose duties were those held in real life by Suzanne Schiffman from film to film. Baye recounts that one day, as she was coming out of a restaurant on rue Marbeuf with Serge Rousseau, her agent at Artmédia, they ran into Suzanne Schiffman across the street, who was probably on her way to the Carrosse offices. A short time later, Rousseau received a call from Suzanne: "Who was the young girl I saw you with on rue Marbeuf?" Several days later, Nathalie Baye was summoned to the Carrosse. "As soon as he saw me, Truffaut said, 'No, she's not right at all!' We continued our conversation and after a while he said to me, 'Come back tomorrow; we'll do a reading.' The next day we read a scene together from *Such a Gorgeous Kid Like Me*. I had stage fright; I was as red as a beet. At the end, he said to me, 'I'll take you, but you'll wear glasses!' "[62]

To complete his cast, Truffaut hired Bernard Menez, a comic actor, who would give piquancy to the role of Bernard, the propman on the set. Nike Arrighi would play Odile, the makeup girl, and David Markham, the father of Kika Markham, who had played in *Two English Girls*, was cast as Dr. Nelson, Julie Baker's husband. Truffaut gave his friend Alexandra Stewart the part of Stacey, the actress who gets hired in *Je vous présente Pamela* and conceals that she is pregnant. Finally, to give the film within a film greater verisimilitude, Truffaut asked his technicians to play themselves onscreen—Jean-François Stévenin as assistant, Pierre Zucca as unit photographer, Yann Dedet and Martine Barraqué in the cutting room, Georges Delerue as musician, and Walter Bal as cameraman.

On September 26, 1972, the actors and technicians assembled at the Victorine Studios in Nice for a shoot that would last only forty-two days. The lead actors lived in rented villas in the area, near Antibes. Jacqueline Bisset shared her house with Nathalie Baye. *Day for Night* was far from a quiet, restful shoot. Jacqueline Bisset didn't really feel at ease, at least for the first few days: "My French wasn't very good at the time, until François reassured me, 'Don't worry, you're not playing a Frenchwoman; you're an American actress performing in France.' This greatly relieved me,"[63] she says. Alexandra Stewart remembers a preoccupied, unavailable Truffaut: "François was anguished because he was doing everything—he had an acting part, Léaud was causing problems," she recalls. "Walter Bal, the cameraman, had a motorcycle accident; that's why he appears in the film with his arm in a sling. For reasons I couldn't fathom, François had a grudge against me; he blamed me for being late, which was just an excuse, for I've always been punctual. But it's true there were only two makeup girls for several actresses."[64] On Christmas Eve, right after the last days of the shoot, Alexandra Stewart, to her astonishment, even received a very harsh letter from Truffaut accusing her "of having messed up his film."[65] After a falling-out lasting several months, Truffaut apologized. Alexandra Stewart isn't the only close friend to have received this kind of letter from Truffaut, particularly during this period when his life was still unstable and when his character and feelings were subject to sudden swings, from euphoria to melancholy to anger.

Yann Dedet, assisted by Martine Barraqué, started editing *Day for Night* while the film was still being shot. In mid-November, Truffaut could already screen a first version, which he found too disjointed. Three months later, after Jean Aurel had given him some useful advice—for example, to rebalance the film around Ferrand by using a voice-over as much as possible—the film found its true, spirited tone, punctuated by lovely, stirring music. Truffaut was satisfied with the first screenings in March 1973. "I know that the film is touching—and deeply touching—to people in the profession,"[66] he said to Helen Scott. The actors in the film were enthusiastic: Jean-Pierre Aumont said he was "very moved" and "proud to have taken part"[67]; Nathalie Baye hoped to have been "worthy of what you gave me and hoping you'll always be pleased with your former script girl!"[68] Confident, Truffaut agreed to show his film outside competition at the Cannes Film Festival. The official screening took place on the evening of May fourteenth. There, joined by Jacqueline Bisset, Valentina Cortese, Nathalie Baye, Dani, Jean-Pierre Aumont, and Jean-Pierre Léaud, he presented himself to the public as an actor, which would have been unthinkable two years earlier, while he was in the depths of depression.

The following day, *Le Parisien* wrote of a "memorable night,"[69] and Louis Chauvet in *Le Figaro* maintained that the film would certainly have won the Palme d'or if it had been entered in the competition.[70] But Truffaut had wanted to be "outside the Cannes dealings," for "everything in Cannes is really unpredictable, everything is tactical, everything is strategic."[71] *Day for*

*Night* opened in eight Paris theaters on May 24. The reviews were full of praise. Jean-Louis Bory called it a "perfect film," from "François Truffaut's golden Carrosse," and "a little marvel of comedy, charm and emotion."[72] Jean de Baroncelli saw it as "one of his best films,"[73] and Chauvet hailed it as "the most accomplished work of its kind."[74] But Truffaut's primary concern was the audience's verdict; he hoped to erase his two recent commercial disappointments. Box-office results in Paris were good (nearly 300,000 tickets sold) but mediocre in the provinces. Truffaut thought he knew why: A large segment of the public was under the misapprehension that it was a documentary on cinema, an "overly intellectual" film. He decided that any mention of a "film within a film" in the publicity should be avoided. This is what he wrote to Simon Benzakein, his coproducer: "We should use another slant for the film: 'a movie of love and adventure.' The publicity department should refrain from explaining the title *Day for Night* as the trick effect 'day for night' but stress the double meaning—'a French-Hollywood night of love between Jean-Pierre Léaud and Jacqueline Bisset.' "[75] Truffaut had no qualms about misleading the public if this could benefit a film that was close to his heart.

## THE CONFRONTATION

Godard and Truffaut had lost sight of each other since 1968. For quite a while, they had each been engaged in a totally different kind of cinema. While Truffaut openly admired all of Godard's first films (up to *La Chinoise* in 1967), Godard, for his part, didn't conceal his indifference to Truffaut's films, except for *Shoot the Piano Player.* Even today, Godard admires Truffaut the critic, "who knew how to point out what was in a film, or compare two films."[76]

Up until the breakup of the New Wave in the mid-sixties, Truffaut and Godard stood by each other as true and loyal friends. Subsequently, however, while Truffaut carved out a niche for himself and protected his independence as best he could with the help of the American majors, Godard advocated a militant, revolutionary cinema directly connected with reality; he and two allies, Jean-Pierre Gorin and Jean-Henri Roger, were the driving forces behind the Dziga-Vertov Group. "He is engaged in another kind of cinema," Truffaut said of Godard. "He feels that since May '68 it's impossible to make the same kinds of movies and he resents people who still do. I've made a choice, my thoughts are perfectly clear, I want to make normal films, it's my life."[77] The two men kept up an intermittent correspondence. When Godard had a serious motorcycle accident in the fall of 1971 and was hospitalized for a long time, Truffaut contacted him. But they were no longer kindred spirits when it came to cinema or politics, or, consequently, when it came to feelings.

Godard initiated hostilities at the end of May 1973, right after the Cannes Film Festival. He came out of *Day for Night* exasperated and couldn't resist letting Truffaut know immediately. He wrote Truffaut a rather contemptuous letter, whose informal tone is consistent with their long-standing friendship as well as with the left-wing language of the period. "Probably no one else will call you a liar, but I will. It's no more of an insult than 'fascist,' it's a critique, and it's the absence of a critical view such films leave us with—those of Chabrol, Ferreri, Verneuil, Delannoy, Renoir, etc.—that I object to. You say: films are big trains that go along in the night, but who is taking the train, in what class, and who is the conductor with the management's 'stool pigeon' by his side? Such people make film-trains as well. And if you don't mean the Trans-Europ, then maybe it's the train to the suburbs, or the Dachau–Munich train, a station that you can be sure you won't see in Lelouch's film-train. Liar, because the shot of you and Jacqueline Bisset the other night at [the restaurant] Chez Francis isn't in your film, and one wonders why the director is the only one who isn't screwing around in *Day for Night*." Then Godard gets to the point. Using the tone of a formal request, he asks Truffaut to finance his next project, *Un simple film,* with an investment of 10 or 5 million francs. "After *Day for Night,* you ought to help me, so that audiences don't think that the only kind of movies being made are your kind." He writes in conclusion, "If you want to discuss it, fine,"[78] words that sound more like a challenge than an invitation to dialogue.

Truffaut could hardly have been pleased by Godard's tone or attitude. He felt that Godard had overstepped his bounds and didn't refrain from telling him so. His answer,[79] which runs to about twenty pages in the original, is unrestrained in its violence. He goes over everything point by point. First, their respective relationships with Jean-Pierre Léaud, whom they had both directed over the last several years. Truffaut resented Godard for insulting Léaud in a letter where he reproached him for acting in *Day for Night* and for working with other "*capitulard*" (sell-out) directors, and then demanded money from him. "I'm sending you back your letter to Jean-Pierre," Truffaut says in his answer, "I've read it and I find it disgusting. Because of that letter I feel it's finally time to tell you, at length, that in my opinion you've been behaving like a shit." Truffaut denounces Godard's lies, his superior tone, his "knack for passing himself off as a victim . . . whereas in fact you've always managed to do exactly what you wanted, when you wanted, as you wanted, and have always managed, above all, to maintain the pure, hard-line image you've cultivated, even at the expense of defenseless people. . . ." The image of the subversive artist, the poseur (a shit on a pedestal) annoys Truffaut, who has always had a preference for humble artisans: "The more you love the masses, the more I love Jean-Pierre Léaud, Janine Bazin,[80] Helen Scott, whom you snubbed when you ran into her in an airport. . . ." "The behavior of a shit," Truffaut reiterates in his letter, turning Godard's own political moral system against him, a system whose ostensible leftism fails to conceal a deep elitism. Truffaut also reminds him of his cowardice when they were selling *La Cause du peuple:* "I felt nothing but contempt for you when I saw the scene in *Vent d'est* on how to make a Molotov cocktail, and yet a year later you chickened out when we were first asked to distribute *La Cause du peuple* in the street with Sartre. The idea that all men are equal is theoretical with you, not sincerely felt." Finally, Truffaut calls Godard an impostor and a pathological egoist: "You need to play a role and the role has to be prestigious. I've always felt that true militants are like cleaning women, performing a thankless, daily, necessary task. But you, you're like Ursula Andress, you make a four-minute appearance, just enough time for the cameras to flash, for you to make two or three startling pronouncements, and then you disappear, shrouded in appealing mystery. In the opposite camp are the small men, ranging from Bazin to Edmond Maire and including Sartre, Buñuel, Queneau, Mendès-France, Rohmer, Audiberti, who ask others how they're doing, help them fill out their social security forms, and reply to letters. They have in common that they can forget their own egos and above all are more interested in what they do than in what they are or what they appear to be." He concludes like Godard: "If you want to discuss it, fine." They never would discuss it. The breakup between them was complete and irrevocable. The time of the "friends in the New Wave"[81] was gone forever.

Though he had unhesitatingly poured it all out and freed himself of the countless misunderstandings that had made his relationship with Godard increasingly awkward and insincere, Truffaut was nonetheless upset. It was a severe shock, a painful falling-out. Janine Bazin, in whom Truffaut had confided, wrote him a long, warm letter: "Your telephone call distressed me and I can't stop thinking about it. You had such a sad voice, just as hurt by Jean-Luc's letter as by the one you had to write him. And I don't know whether you were right to answer him because I don't know if Jean-Luc can quite understand it; I mean I don't know if he can understand that your insults are commensurate with your sadness and friendship for him. I don't mean that Jean-Luc is so lacking in feeling, but still I think his insults are insults that come from the head, whereas yours come from the heart, from your morality of the heart."[82]

In those days, Truffaut's obsession with ideological neutrality appeared to many as faint-hearted opportunism. Some did not hesitate to offer reproachful reminders of his youthful ideals. This attack from the Left disturbed Truffaut, particularly since the criticism came just as he was pulling out of his depression. "Truffaut the traitor" was the refrain, publicly and in several personal letters. Those who judged him with such severity were clearly fueled by a negative view of *Day for Night,* whose moral, they felt, was overly optimistic and conciliatory, vaunting the "magic" of classical cinema and compromise among the members of the profession's one big family. Godard had set the example. Jean-Louis Bory soon followed suit; after an initially favorable reaction to the film, several months later the critic denounced its "consensual and *capitularde*"[83] philosophy. He published an attention-grabbing article in *Le Nouvel Observateur,* "Should We Burn Down the Champs-Elysées?" Truffaut was particularly appalled by one sentence: "Truffaut, Chabrol, Demy, Rohmer have sold out to the system." Truffaut wrote Bory a long letter to justify himself. He went over his entire career, film by film, and explained how each one stemmed from a vital need and had a strictly personal character. "I haven't sold out to the system, I have my own way of working within the system."

My dear Jean-Louis Bory, we have something in common—we both enjoyed our biggest success right at the start. You had the good fortune of immediately being published and recognized, and I did too. Since then, you've published many books with different publishers, and none of your manuscripts was ever rejected, since you had demonstrated your abilities from the beginning. Suppose one day you were to read in the paper: "The manuscripts rejected by publishers, mimeographed booklets, and books published at authors' expense are what constitute the true literature of our time: Genet fell silent in 1968; as for Sartre, Bory, Cayrol, Rezvani, they have sold out to the system." Wouldn't you think, "Here's someone who's completely mixed up and mistakes the container for the thing contained"? You're not a "marginal" author, you're a professional writer; your books are published because they're good, because you have a following, and because the projected printing can be expected to earn back the initial investment. True or false? Though they may not be hot sellers in train stations like Simenon or Guy des Cars, your books can be bought in drugstores and that doesn't make them any worse. True or false? I may be wrong, but as a film director I feel I work in the same spirit as you do as a writer: we choose our subjects freely, we handle them as we see fit and we put them on the market. . . . Good or bad, my films are the films I wanted to make and none other. . . .[84]

Refusing to play the martyr (he left that to Godard), Truffaut pleaded his cause, that of an independent director whose career was punctuated with both success and failure. "I take complete responsibility for the films I make, their qualities and faults, and I never blame the system."[85] Paradoxically, Truffaut's truthfulness sounded false to many of his contemporaries. This exchange with Bory is emblematic of his estrangement from some of the figures from his past during that period.[86] He considered these breakups necessary, though each was painful.

## PRIVATE LIVES

The success of *Day for Night* allowed François Truffaut to slow down. Having just directed three films in rapid succession, he decided to take a two-year breather to do other things and travel. This intense activity had exhausted him, though it had helped him climb out of the "abyss" into which he had sunk at the beginning of 1971. Truffaut had spent most of his time away from Paris, making films; hence, he had practically never been alone.

At the time when he decided to give himself a rest, he had no less than four screenplays in progress—*The Story of Adele H.* and *L'Autel des morts* (*The Altar of the Dead*) with Gruault; *Small Change* with Suzanne Schiffman; *Le Cavaleur* (The Skirt-Chaser) with Michel Fermaud—as well as several book projects. Truffaut also spent time completing the "chronologies" of his life, noting down childhood memories and recollections about people he had met. He even promised the publisher Robert Laffont an autobiographical book, which could only be ready in "about ten years, primarily for family reasons."[87] For in describing his youth and his background, his first concern was not to hurt his father, Roland Truffaut.

Having recently turned forty, Truffaut felt the need to put his life in order. But he still had to protect himself, because he knew he was vulnerable. For a while, he continued to live in a suite at the Hotel George V: "He didn't want to leave the hotel," Liliane Siegel recalls, "except perhaps to go to the movies when the theater was already dark. When I came to dinner, he would have the meal sent up to his suite. Since he wanted to determine himself what kind of ties he would have with others, the fact of living in a hotel protected him. It was a way of preventing any woman from moving in with him."[88] Then for several months, he lived in the apartment above the offices of the Films du Carrosse. Finally, he decided to rent a large, sun-lit six-room apartment on avenue Pierre 1er de Serbie, which had two big advantages: It was close to his office and it had a view of the Eiffel Tower. The view from his living room was "his best source of inspiration."[89] Truffaut lived alone, with his housekeeper, Marie; her death in January 1973 would deeply affect him, for this energetic, discreet woman in her sixties had been completely devoted to him. She was succeeded by Emilienne briefly, and then by Carmen Sardà-Canovas, a perpetually sunny and cheerful woman, and a great admirer of the comic actor Fernandel (Truffaut recorded the actor's films for her when they were shown on television). Carmen wasn't a particularly good cook and "if she had been, this was not a quality that would have meant anything to my father,"[90] Laura points out. This is confirmed by Jean Gruault, who was used to seeing his friend Truffaut eat "his eternal overcooked steak smothered in mustard."[91]

Laura and Eva each had a room in the newly rented apartment and would usually spend the weekends with him. In the spring of 1973, Laura was fourteen and Eva twelve. When he was not busy with filmmaking, Truffaut would spend a great deal of time with them, sharing books and movies and deliberately nurturing their different personalities. Laura, the elder, was a daydreamer with a literary bent; Eva was more active and less romantic. "For me, we always chose the more fast-paced, dry, violent films," Eva recalls. "Lang, Sturges, Aldrich, Kubrick. This was the kind of film he couldn't see with Laura. With her, he revealed another side of his personality, other tastes and feelings, more romantic and colorful, like Cukor, Fellini, Hitchcock, musical comedies with Fred Astaire, W. C. Fields comedies, or films like *Pandora* and all the great Chaplin classics, which were rereleased during the seventies. We all three converged on some Mankiewicz films, *A Letter to Three Wives, All About Eve . . .* some Polanski films, and on Dalton Trumbo's *Johnny Got His Gun.*[92] Apart from a love of books and the pleasure of movies, Truffaut also shared with his daughters a love of song; Trenet was their favorite, and some singers from the new generation, like Julien Clerc and Alain Souchon. They also liked humorists, particularly Raymond Devos, for whom Truffaut had immense admiration and whose performances he often attended in Paris and the provinces. And they liked Pierre Dac and Francis Blanche, whose sketches all three found very funny.

When he didn't go to his office, Truffaut received friends and collaborators at home. In the evening, when he wasn't watching television—his favorite pastime—he would share his apartment only with women. "I wouldn't consider having dinner with a man," he wrote in *Paris-Match.* "I have this in common with Hitler and Sartre: I can't stand male companionship after seven in the evening. For me, the evening means private life, in a private place; it's the time for whispered words, shared secrets, sincere exchanges. The only moment which can rival the joy of filming."[93] These were special moments, which he safeguarded and wouldn't sacrifice for any social occasion. Those women closest to him were Madeleine Morgenstern and Helen Scott, and also Liliane Dreyfus, Leslie Caron, Alexandra Stewart, and Liliane Siegel. "Very soon we started talking about ourselves," says Liliane Siegel. "We saw each other often, just the two of us, and spent long evenings sharing a mutual trust and confiding in each other."[94] He often talked about Jean-Paul Sartre with her, for she knew him intimately and Truffaut was fascinated by him. "We spoke a great deal, very freely, it was good," Truffaut wrote her on April 20, 1971, the day after their first dinner. "We did a year's worth of confiding in one evening, which allows me to switch from 'fondly' to 'affectionately.'"[95] With his female friends and former mistresses, Truffaut felt good, providing they each respected what he considered certain essential rules. Discretion was vital and foremost. Whoever infringed the pact of secrecy exposed herself to a violent breakup, usually in writing. Truffaut partitioned his relationships to avoid any short circuits and "complications that bore me."[96] There again, he was capable of great anger when a woman—for example, Helen Scott, whom he sometimes reproached for her lack of discretion—proved unable to keep a secret. Truffaut's relationships with his female friends took various forms. He set the limits between intimacy and friendship. "I'm afraid of ties, I'm afraid of making promises and not keeping them," he wrote to Liliane Siegel. "You shouldn't scare me, when I'm with you I'm happy, very quickly and durably, but it's abnormal that on the following days I'm tortured with the thought that I should be phoning you, as though I were in the wrong, as though I owed you an explanation, as though I were going to be bawled out."[97] With some of his women friends, Truffaut shared the pleasure of going to a film or spending an evening at the theater, activities that he valued infinitely more than a good dinner.

This partitioned, complex life was actually based on simple principles. First among these was the exclusive pleasure of a relationship *à deux*, for Truffaut disliked society life, a waste of time as far as he was concerned. When he couldn't avoid a social event, he didn't seek to impress or be clever; he preferred to listen, laugh, and be a good audience, particularly when he had accepted a dinner invitation because he had been curious to meet someone he admired or whose books he had read. When trapped in a conversation that didn't interest him, he remained silent, allowing long pauses to set in, which eventually embarrassed those around him. "François acted as though he hadn't heard anything, an angel was passing. A person had to be very brave to try to say anything again," Madeleine Morgenstern says. Truffaut found it difficult to bring romantic relationships to a close, so he pursued several simultaneous affairs, which he sought to keep compartmentalized, as discreetly and hermetically as possible. "Once there had been an extended emotional tie, François could not imagine that a woman would no longer be part of his landscape," Madeleine confirms. The relationship between her and Truffaut had never ceased to exist; it was close and intimate, romantic and friendly, with occasional periods when they differed immensely. "The fact that I was a kind of ever-present family reference was not very pleasant for the other women in his life,"[98] Madeleine admits, quite perceptively. When he wanted to break off a liaison, he could be harsh, but usually his love affairs would turn into strong and durable friendships.

After his yearlong depression, François Truffaut resumed a restless love life. He saw Kika Markham again, one of the stars of *Two English Girls,* when the film was being promoted in France, and during several of her Paris trips. Then he had a number of affairs, sometimes with former lovers, sometimes with new ones. And he still had a distinct penchant for visiting prostitutes. On the other hand, since his last romantic breakup, he refused to live as a couple with anyone. "I can only love now through casual meetings,"[99] he wrote to a woman friend. "He had acquired a phobia for conjugal life which he had trouble reconciling with the tender affection he felt for his close relatives and friends," Gruault points out. "He once told me that as he walked up to his landing he always fleetingly felt the same pang of anguish from the recollection of several periods in his life where he knew he would be welcomed by a spouse or female companion whose conversation and possible recriminations he would have to endure, and who would criticize his eating habits, etc. And what a relief it was for him now to know that he would turn the doorknob and walk into an empty apartment where he would be alone with all his books and his television. Yet he wasn't spared the anguish of loneliness. One morning I found him very worried: he had slept very badly, he had had a discharge from his ear and traces of pus on his pillow, he feared a recurrence of the chronic ear infections that had plagued him in his childhood. He admitted to me that he had experienced that night a painful feeling of abandonment."[100]

During *Day for Night,* Jacqueline Bisset was the only woman who really succeeded in sharing his solitude. Their relationship, which started timidly during the filming in Nice, lasted for some time thereafter. Jacqueline Bisset remained in France after *Day for Night,* where she immediately started working on Philippe de Broca's *Le Magnifique* with Jean-Paul Belmondo. She and Truffaut met regularly over the spring of 1973, in Nice, Paris, and Cannes, where they presented *Day for Night* at the festival. Then Truffaut spent the entire summer in Los Angeles, which gave him the opportunity to visit Jean Renoir and to spend time with Jacqueline Bisset again, in her beautiful white house in Benedict Canyon. "Thanks to her, I regained my confidence,"[101] he admitted to Jean-Claude Brialy.

Truffaut was perpetually unfaithful, more out of a need to seduce and be loved than out of Don Juanism. These "other women" were strangers, collaborators, or foreign journalists. First and foremost, they were the actresses in his films. "Women, for him, were always part icon part woman. That's why he loved his actresses: It made his life easier—loving cinema more than anything else, his activity as a director, and the beautiful actresses he cast in his films. Above all, it was a way of perpetuating childhood: woman as mother, woman as doll, woman as fiancée,"[102] says Alexandra Stewart, providing a perfect description of Truffaut's dual obsessions and how they were secretly intertwined—love of cinema and love of women.

Truffaut was not free of remorse vis-à-vis Madeleine and his daughters. Hence the guilt feelings, which partially explain his periods of depression and the more serious crises that affected him in his adult life. When he was not out of town filming, Truffaut spent all his weekends at rue du Conseiller Collignon, to be with his daughters, but also to be with Madeleine, for maintaining a relationship with her surely soothed him. "Those strange moments resembled a true family life," Madeleine explains, "it provided him with a kind of peace. I accepted this situation, for myself and the children, because you can't expect to live for several years with someone as interesting as François and not want something to remain, somehow or other, later."[103]

In Truffaut's life, there was an odd need for stability, even for a certain routine, which coexisted with the need for amorous adventures. Whether alone or with a woman, he needed established markers and rituals to maintain an atmosphere conducive to work (hence his habit of rehiring the same crew from film to film).

## THE CALIFORNIA SUMMER

During this two-year respite, François Truffaut spent as much time as possible abroad. He lived in Los Angeles in the summer of 1973, from June to August. "I'm leading a very luxurious life, a bungalow with a patio, a big red car with an automatic shift! For the time being, great solitude,"[104] he wrote to Liliane Siegel. Very soon, some producers interpreted his presence in Hollywood as an indication that he wanted to make a film there. Simon Benzakein, for example, who was working for Warner Brothers, made him the offer of directing a remake of *Casablanca*. Truffaut refused of course:

> It's not my favorite Humphrey Bogart film, and I rate it much lower than *The Big Sleep* or *To Have and Have Not*. So, the thought of directing a new version should logically scare me less and I realize the film would take place in a French ambiance. However, I know American students adore this film, especially the dialogue, and they know every line by heart. I would be equally intimidated by the actors; I can't imagine Jean-Paul Belmondo and Catherine Deneuve succeeding Humphrey Bogart and Ingrid Bergman. I know that people see these things differently in America. The idea of directing a remake doesn't shock me, provided it's a very good, bold story which could be treated with greater candor today, and a title that doesn't carry too

much weight in the history of American cinema. If Warner Brothers really wants me to direct a film, I suggest you send me a list of titles I could select from.[105]

Though being solicited by Hollywood amused him, Truffaut nevertheless turned down all the offers, explaining his reasons at length, courteously and with great professionalism. He never closed the door on the possibility, for the idea of someday making a film in the United States was a rejuvenating prospect. As soon as his situation in France seemed too precarious, as soon as he felt any ideological or professional pressure, he found solace in the thought that Hollywood was prepared to welcome him. It was a way of asserting privilege or special status in the French film industry. It was also Truffaut's discreet way of divorcing himself from the auteur cinema, which he liked (the films of Jean Eustache, Jacques Rivette, or Philippe Garrel) but which he deemed hard to export. A show-business professional and a great admirer of Lubitsch and Hitchcock, Truffaut felt competent to make films in Hollywood, the movie mecca, "provided the story not be too specific in setting or Americanness."[106]

The discrepancy between Truffaut's position as an independent auteur-producer and the rest of the French movie industry was a constant source of misunderstandings—with journalists and critics, but also with his best friends. There is a definite resemblance between the Truffaut of the early seventies and Ferrand, the director in *Day for Night,* a conscientious, budget-conscious craftsman who creates an old-fashioned movie family with his actors and collaborators. During this entire period when French auteur cinema was perpetually confronted by its own fringe status, Truffaut reserved judgment. "I've had too much luck to attack those who have been less lucky than me, it's as simple as that," he said with great honesty to the journalist Guy Teisseire.[107]

Truffaut loved California, first of all for its lifestyle, and secondly because this was where all the directors he admired lived—Renoir, Hitchcock, Hawks, Capra. He felt at ease there, considerably freer in his movements than in Paris. When Leslie Caron asked him one day why he was so fond of California, Truffaut replied jokingly, "Because you can always find a parking space!"[108] To take full advantage of America, he made it a point of honor to lick "the great problem of his life," his difficulty in speaking English. Such was his motive for this long Californian sojourn—taking lessons "with a teacher who has obtained results with morons." So he settled at the Beverly Hills Hotel and took daily six-hour lessons with Professor Michel Thomas, who literally fascinated him. An exceptional teacher and founder of a language school, Thomas was a Frenchman and former Resistance fighter who had been living in the United States since 1947. He had been head of an underground network near Grenoble, and had been tortured by Klaus Barbie in Lyon; after the Liberation, he had become an American counterespionage agent. The student had every reason to be attentive, the more so since his teacher had successfully taught French to Grace Kelly and Otto Preminger in a matter of months, and had made Yves Montand proficient in the language of Shakespeare and Marilyn. Yet, in spite of painstaking efforts, Truffaut made very little progress, as he himself admitted to Helen Scott: "My teacher says that he finds it more difficult to get me out of the habit of my mistakes than to teach me the correct forms. He never blames me, he behaves a bit like a psychoanalyst, and he has the patience of an angel, but I can sense he is astonished by the extent of my mental block. The truth is that there is in me a refusal to learn that is as powerful as my desire to know."[109]

During that summer of 1973, he, like the rest of America, was completely enthralled by the Watergate affair. American investigative journalism impressed him enormously, compared with the "great amateurishness of French journalism, its fraudulence."[110] He mixed work with pleasure as he watched the live broadcasts every morning and followed the latest developments in the political scandal implicating a large part of the Nixon administration. The public spectacle of government confronted with its own lies and manipulations fascinated him, and he tried to take advantage of the daily reportage to improve his English. But despite all his efforts, his knowledge of English remained stagnant—though, in its issue of September 2, 1973, the *Los Angeles Herald Examiner* devoted a whole page to an enthusiastic article entitled "Three Hours of Watergate a Day Helped Truffaut Master English." However, Truffaut did acquire a good reading knowledge of English, which allowed him to immerse himself in film literature and historical studies. The first English-language book he bought for himself was Selznick's *Memo*,[111] which he read attentively by the pool of his luxurious California hotel in early July 1973.

In Hollywood as in Paris, François Truffaut's life followed a detailed, immutable ritual. But his outward appearance differed. While dressing austerely, in a dark suit and tie, on the Right Bank of the Seine, around Passy, and on the Champs-Elysées, Truffaut used to undergo a radical metamorphosis as soon as he arrived in California. "He looked fifteen years younger," says Claudine Bouché, the editor of his early days, who had moved to the United States in 1967; she remembers his "elegant, informal outfits."[112] Leslie Caron describes a relaxed, easygoing person, at the wheel of a beautiful American convertible. Indeed, Truffaut liked the style and rhythm of California life. Furthermore, since there was no equivalent in Paris, he would often spend hours browsing at Larry Edmunds', the famous cinema bookstore on Hollywood Boulevard. Truffaut adored American biographies of actors and directors, for they were a gold mine of fascinating behind-the-scenes details on the history of cinema, the making of films, and the romances of the stars.

Todd McCarthy, the *Variety* critic and journalist, one of the main people Truffaut associated with when he was in the States, remembers his friend "sitting in a deck chair, a bit isolated, at the edge of the pool at the Beverly Hills, the posh hotel where he stayed whenever he came to Los Angeles. When you know he'd been afraid of water all his life, his presence amidst tanned Californians, sun worshippers and athletic swimmers, seemed all the more incongruous. Even stranger was the fact that it was his favorite place in the world for reading American books on film, for which he had an insatiable appetite. . . . Beautiful women would stroll back and forth wondering who that man was—was it really François Truffaut?—and from time to time, one of them would muster up the courage to go up to him and try to start a conversation. Indifferent to their beauty, which he almost overlooked, François would usually assume a polite but resolutely closed air, with that pregnant silence that reigned around him when he wanted to keep someone at a distance. . . . Finally, slightly embarrassed and at a loss what to say, the gorgeous creatures would withdraw and François would go back to his book."[113]

Truffaut's main purpose in being there was to rest. The only exception was on Saturday nights, when he enjoyed "acting the Frenchman" at parties in beautiful Hollywood villas. Sometimes he became a scathing chronicler of the Hollywood smart set in his correspondence with friends. He wrote to Helen Scott:

> I went to two parties recently. The first was at a charming woman painter's, Barbara Poe, the ex-wife of the *script-writer* [in English] James Poe. When the conversation revolved around food pollution, a woman asked me: *"Et en France, est-ce que vous mettez des préservatifs autour des légumes?"* [And in France, do you put condoms (*préservatifs*) around your vegetables?] It was a *nice party* [in English], everyone was left-wing, great supporters of the town's new black mayor. . . . Last night, another party, much more typical of Hollywood, thrown by the young Peter Guber, head of production at Columbia, the spitting image of the character in *What Makes Sammy Run?* Billiards in a room where the ceiling is decorated with the Company's illuminated posters, barbecue on the lawn, followed by a screening of an unreleased comedy which I didn't watch because I was flirting with Buck Henry, who is really adorable.[114]

Truffaut's favorite ritual was to pay a visit to the Renoirs every Saturday afternoon. Jean and Dido Renoir lived in a redbrick building at the top of

Leona Drive. Renoir had drawn the plans of the house himself, in 1950, before going to India to shoot *The River.* Some twenty olive trees were planted around the house, like those at Colettes, the family house in Cagnes-sur-Mer. In July 1973, Truffaut found Renoir "very old and very tired"; he refused to walk, but regained "his liveliness every afternoon when he dictates his memoirs to his secretary."[115] To his Paris friends, Truffaut stressed Renoir's vitality regardless of his advanced age. "Every morning, Dido Renoir wakes up at seven and waits for the deliveryman to throw the *Los Angeles Times* in front of the house; when her husband wakes up, Dido reads him the most interesting news. At around nine, Greg arrives, a young actor who was a nurse in Vietnam; he comes to massage Jean Renoir's wounded leg, a 1916 war wound that never healed and which caused Octave's famous bearlike gait [referring to the character Renoir played in *The Rules of the Game*]. Renoir then answers his mail, declining all invitations to speak at universities, all offers to preside on juries, and all requests to authenticate his father's paintings—all with the utmost kindness. His politeness is legendary."[116]

The Renoirs considered Leslie Caron, who had been living in Hollywood since the early seventies and was married to an American producer, like their daughter. "I was 'little Leslie'; I never grew up in their eyes,"[117] remembers Caron. A faithful among faithfuls, she met Truffaut at Leona Drive on countless occasions. "Jean had complete confidence in François, who was like a second son. And François venerated him, tried to cheer him up by talking to him about France. Jean used to regain his liveliness when François was around."[118] There was a screen that could be unrolled in the Renoir living room. By removing a painting on the wall opposite, you could aim the beam of a 16-mm army projector, which was permanently installed inside a closet in the hall, at the screen. Jean, Dido, and their guests occasionally watched films, old or new, brought to them by Peter Bogdanovich, Todd McCarthy, or some other faithful friend. "He is sometimes tormented by the thought that he will probably never make another film," Truffaut said, "because he feels he could have done better and more, but we who see his films and love them so, know that he has done the most and done the best."[119]

Truffaut recorded his meetings and experiences in his letters to Madeleine, a tender and light little travel diary.

My little bunny,

Veronica Lake died, so did Betty Grable, and Robert Ryan, yesterday; this afternoon Nixon went into the hospital and I myself don't feel very well. . . . I've always been told that the great step forward would be to dream in English, actually I wake up at night screaming, "*I am going to buy some for you. . . . I want to buy any,* [in English] etc." In fact, I'm starting to read the newspapers rather well, but speaking is another matter and as far as understanding is concerned, it won't be this year. I should tell you, my bunny, that if my teacher doesn't leave Los Angeles, I'll stay here longer, until around August 18 or 20 because I don't want to return with the feeling of having failed; if I can do another forty or fifty hours, I must do them. . . . I almost forgot your birthday since I have no reason to look at dates here but, fortunately, one of my nightmares was about you (!) and the alarm went off in my head.° [°*"Gift postponned to sept (sic)."* (Footnote, in English, in the original letter)] . . .

Collective kisses to all 3, I think of you a lot, not just when I write or call (rarely, the telephone *is very expensive* [in English]), tenderly, François.[120]

After his summer in California, Truffaut spent time in New York. At the end of September, three years after the success of *The Wild Child,* he came to attend the screening of *Day for Night* at the New York Film Festival at Lincoln Center. The picture triumphed on the evening of October 1, 1973. Truffaut entered the large hall to enthusiastic applause; at his side was a radiant Jacqueline Bisset, wearing a white dress with a plunging neckline; New York mayor John Lindsay; Jean-Pierre Léaud, and Lillian Gish, to whom, with her sister, Dorothy, Truffaut had dedicated the film. Six days later, *Day for Night* opened to rave reviews at the Fine Arts Theater. All the most important movie critics—Vincent Canby in the *New York Times,* Pauline Kael in *The New Yorker,* Rex Reed in the *New York Daily News,* Judith Crist in *New York* magazine, and Archer Winsten in the *New York Post*—had nothing but praise, and Jacqueline Bisset made the cover of *Newsweek:* A BEAUTY NAMED BISSET. *Day for Night* received several prestigious prizes: It was named best picture by the National Society of Film Critics and was awarded Best Motion Picture and Best Direction by the New York Film Critics. After twenty-three weeks in the theaters, it earned over a million dollars in box-office receipts, as much as all the other Truffaut films distributed in the United States to that date.

Encouraged by this success, during October Truffaut traveled to all the major American cities with *Day for Night.* Four days in Boston, a detour to Montreal, then the San Francisco Festival, where the film was shown on October twenty-fourth prior to the Los Angeles preview scheduled for November third. In the reception room of the Directors Guild, Vincente Minnelli, flanked by William Wilder and George Cukor, extended Truffaut a warm welcome, ending his speech by saying, "And now this film should be listed among the five Oscar nominees for best foreign film." Prestigious supporters such as these were an undeniable asset for Truffaut, who certainly had a chance of winning the famous trophy. He had almost won an Oscar twice before. In 1959, *The 400 Blows* had been nominated for Best Original Screenplay, and in 1968, *Stolen Kisses* had lost the award for Best Foreign-Language Film to Sergei Bondarchuk's *War and Peace*. This time, not only was *Day for Night* nominated, but so was Valentina Cortese as Best Supporting Actress.

Several months later, on April 3, 1974, Truffaut attended the nationally broadcast Academy Awards ceremony at the Los Angeles Music Center. George Roy Hill's *The Sting* was the big winner of the evening, garnering seven awards. But French cinema was honored when an Oscar for Lifetime Achievement was given to Henri Langlois, the director of the Cinémathèque française. Later in the evening, the proceedings were disrupted by a naked man who climbed onstage and interrupted Jack Lemmon's acceptance of the Best Actor award for his role in *Save the Tiger*. It was Yul Brynner who unsealed the envelope to announce the winner in the Best Foreign-Language Film category. Truffaut, seated in the audience in a black tuxedo, betrayed a slight momentary tension when his name was read. Then, onstage, he thanked the audience in English: "I'm very happy because *Day for Night* is about film people like you; it's your trophy. But if you'll agree, I'll keep it for you."[121]

The Oscar added to Truffaut's fame in the United States; like Fellini, Bergman, and Kurosawa, he now belonged to the select group of foreign directors considered dependable box-office draws there. As a result, he received even more film offers from Hollywood, including one for a film on the lives of Ernest Hemingway and F. Scott Fitzgerald, *One Last Glimpse*, based on a novel by James Aldridge. But Truffaut still didn't feel ready for the challenge; he preferred to take advantage of his fame to negotiate better American distribution for his independently made films.

It was then that he decided to use Roger Corman as his distributor. Six years his senior, Corman had directed almost seventy films in England and Hollywood, including six screen adaptations of Edgar Allan Poe, between 1960 and 1964, starring Vincent Price. Since the mid-sixties, Corman had also become a producer and distributor, and the head of his own company, New World Pictures. In Hollywood, he also established a reputation as the most prolific discoverer of new talent: Francis Ford Coppola, Monte Hellman, Peter Bogdanovich, Martin Scorsese, and Joe Dante all made their debut films for him, some featuring the future star Jack Nicholson. As a distributor, Corman specialized in European films, with success, as in the cases of Bergman's *Cries and Whispers* and Fellini's *Amarcord*. This was what persuaded Truffaut to sign up with him for his next four films. "I think that with him I've finally found the ideal distributor. He's Hollywood-based. He feels close to the films he takes on, watches them attentively, has a network of well-established theaters and a very competent staff that includes Jim McBride and Todd McCarthy."[122]

For Truffaut, it was most important to be recognized by his peers—Alfred Hitchcock, Robert Aldrich, Nicholas Ray, Tay Garnett, Samuel Fuller, among the older generation; Miloš Forman, Robert Benton, Arthur Penn, Sydney Pollack, among the younger—these directors were his main champions on the other side of the Atlantic. He was without a doubt the only French director of his generation to have been so respected and honored in Hollywood. In this, he may even have surpassed the other greats of world cinema, Bergman, Fellini, Buñuel, and Kurosawa, who put less energy into following the fate of their films in the United States.

Truffaut also became one of the best-liked directors on American campuses and universities. In the seventies, there were numerous retrospectives and university courses and seminars devoted to his work—Paul Michaud's at Harvard; James Monaco's and Donald Spoto's at the New School for Social Research; Dudley Andrew's at the University of Iowa; Annette Insdorf's at Yale. Truffaut often met young American film enthusiasts in his travels—for example, Leo Moldaver of Cleveland, who organized a tribute to him and wrote him enthusiastic fan letters, or the young Alfred Dolder, who wrote him from Los Angeles on July 12, 1974: "It is thanks to you that I'm in movies, your films are my inspiration, and your love affair with cinema my dream. This letter is a homage to you, the greatest movie director of our time."[123]

## POLITICAL COLUMNS

During the whole summer of 1973, François Truffaut was fascinated by Watergate: "I don't understand it at all, but it's fascinating,"[124] he admitted to Liliane Siegel. Richard Nixon, who had "the lead part," interested him less than Nixon's secretary, who had to lie in order to cover up for her boss. Here was politics as suspense, with all the twists and turns and mysteries of an action film, politics that had nothing in common with the politics that grew out of ideological clashes. When politics put society on show like this, Truffaut felt concerned; he even felt stimulated to express his point of view—like a demanding viewer, or film critic.

Hence, when Georges Pompidou died at the beginning of April 1974, Truffaut agreed to write a weekly column in Le Monde on the presidential campaign until the election of a successor. He drafted five articles but finally decided against publishing them, doubtless afraid of exposing himself on a terrain that was not his own. Written during the election campaign, these pieces are those of an attentive but sarcastic spectator, voicing his opinion on the performance of the play he is watching. Indeed, the first column is entitled "At the Show":

> Being listened to, being looked at, appearing interesting, that's what matters. The way something is said is more important than substance, this must be acknowledged even though it's shocking. The presidential campaign is show business, and subject to its laws. Experience counts, but not much: there are some good supporting roles—Royer, Krivine, Le Pen, Laguiller, Dumont; there are those who have chosen the wrong vocation and shouldn't be appearing on-screen for lack of talent; there is the fallen star, Chaban-Delmas, foundering in his performance of an outdated play; there is the uninspired but reliable actor, François Mitterrand, who has become a star through hard work; and there is the great actor, the star, Giscard d'Estaing, the one whose quality performance makes one forget the work that went into it, who would triple the number of votes of the other candidates if he were to substitute for them. Giscard d'Estaing with his masterful act of sobriety. You find the term "act" shocking, excessive? Asserting that one will look "deep into the eyes of France," or that the best reforms are those that cost nothing, quoting Napoleon in Corsica and Marcel Pagnol in Marseilles—isn't this performing an act? The French like great men and they have one—Giscard d'Estaing. Thanks to his acting talent, which is immense, he suggests as efficiently as De Gaulle but more subtly, more indirectly, that he is one of those great men, a man who is more than just a president of the Republic, and that he would therefore be making us a gift in accepting to look after us.[125]

Truffaut felt that the opposition press in France was not doing its work, that it "shouldn't let lies and unkept promises go unnoticed." He was still very influenced and impressed by the role played by the *Washington Post* reporters in uncovering the Watergate scandal. "These people should be called liars when they deserve it, we should tirelessly stress the political world's inadmissible lies and preferential treatments. The serious, opposition press must resolve to inform and oppose; they should take a look at the *Washington Post, Newsweek, Time. . . .*" It was because of this need for vigilance, for a permanent countergovernment, that Truffaut—though politically so moderate—paradoxically praised the French left-wing movement, the only organized force that could make up for the failure of opposition journalism: "Leftism is useful, it has harassing value and can force yesterday's U.D.R. State, tomorrow's Giscardian or Socialist State, to keep their promises."

Given this show, how did Truffaut see the ideal politician? He was extremely wary of the "great man," the "providential savior," and sought to demystify political life. "There are no great men, there are only men, and as far as politics are concerned I tend to prefer those who behave like cleaning women: punctuality, modesty, liveliness, equilibrium, the fight against dust, for cleanliness is daily, carries no prestige, is indispensable and unremitting. I don't necessarily want a little man, but a man who has the disposition of Mendès-France, a man whose commitment is as daily and calm as Sartre's."

In his last column, written on the eve of the presidential election's first round of votes, Truffaut finally justified his own choice. Why did he support François Mitterrand, even though he disliked both the "political actor" and the "man"? Indeed, he had joined the Mitterrand support committee and made a contribution of five thousand francs on May 10, 1974. Even though his convictions were closer to those of Michel Rocard, whose candidacy he had wished for in these presidential elections. For Truffaut, Rocard was among those politicians who displayed a certain skepticism and great lucidity concerning political power, like Pierre Mendès-France, Pierre Cot, and Edmond Maire. Nevertheless, and still without having registered to vote, Truffaut officially backed Mitterrand. "Mitterrand should be supported, not to be 'with it,' to look like good guys, or seem youthful, but simply because it seems to me just."

Sartre occupied a major place for Truffaut in the realm of political and moral ideas and was his main point of reference. He was constantly reading and rereading the philosopher's works. Upon rereading *The Words,* he wrote to Liliane Siegel, "Of course, we have a greater or lesser need for a given book depending on the period of life we are going through, and right now, this book hits the bull's-eye in terms of my fears. I feel that other books by Sartre can give me courage at the present time."[126]

As always with Truffaut, the friendly relationship he maintained with Liliane Siegel was very ritualized. He would go to pick her up at her house, on boulevard Raspail, at around eight o'clock, then take her to dinner in Montparnasse, often at the Palette, one of Sartre's favorite restaurants, and their conversation often revolved around Sartre. Siegel even finds similarities between the two men, "the same way of living a life as regular as clockwork, with mental compartments. . . ."[127] A similar pleasure in the company of women and a similar desire to seduce them. "These kinds of men always wonder if they are loved for what they really are or for what they represent socially," Siegel adds.

During the fall of 1974 came an opportunity for a real rapprochement between Truffaut and Sartre. Marcel Jullian, who had been appointed head of Antenne 2, wanted to undertake a bold television project with Sartre: a series of ten broadcasts of one hour and a half that would present the history of France in the twentieth century. Sartre was very eager for Truffaut to be the director for the broadcasts. Truffaut was very touched and considered the project worthwhile, but he turned the offer down, since his own films claimed too much of his time. Furthermore, he couldn't see himself working for television, which he regarded as "unfair competition" for cinema. And he feared that his public and professional fame might get in the way of Sartre's team, or that, somehow, he might become a pawn for Antenne 2's managers. Though "he stood by cinema," Truffaut nevertheless devoted some time to Sartre's television project. He discussed it regularly with Liliane Siegel, at dinner or in his letters, and she relayed his opinions to Sartre. "So I'm in the background helping you, out of admiration, friendship and a feeling of kinship for Sartre,"[128] he wrote her. For example, he went to the trouble of drawing up a list of potential directors, which included Roger Louis, a journalist and television director whom he admired, and his friend Claude de Givray. But in the meantime, the Sartre project was beginning to fall apart because of internal dissension among the collaborators,[129] violent hostility on the part of the political and television authorities toward a project that they considered left-wing and subversive, Sartre's mistrust, his demand for freedom in his work, and, as a result, his rejection of Jullian's request for a pilot broadcast. In September 1975, the affair broke out publicly; state television, despite its new veneer of advanced liberalism, missed its opportunity with an intellectual of Sartre's stature and censored his project. People say that Jacques Chirac, the then prime minister, had something to do with it.

## ISABELLE'S FACE

Truffaut made no films in 1973 and 1974, which put Les Films du Carrosse in financial difficulty. He urgently needed to knock at the door of American financial backers with some new projects. In 1974, the one that was furthest along and which Truffaut was most enthusiastic about was Jean Gruault's, based on the *Journal of Adèle Hugo,* which had been published in the late sixties by Editions Minard and edited by an American university professor in Ohio, Frances Vernor Guille. Captivated by the book, Truffaut had lost no time in giving it to Gruault—not to adapt, but with the idea of fleshing out one episode in the life of Victor Hugo's second daughter, a linear story of mad, unrequited love, with no hope of a happy ending.

In 1863, Adèle Hugo goes to live in Halifax, Nova Scotia, under the borrowed name of Miss Lewly. She has come to join a British army lieutenant,

Pinson, with whom she is madly in love. She takes lodgings with a solitary elderly woman and keeps her real identity secret. But the lieutenant rejects her and asks her to leave. Adèle persists obstinately, redoubling her stratagems and declarations of love to Pinson. She tells her father, Victor Hugo, who is living in exile on the Channel Island of Guernsey, that she has married, and thereby obtains a living allowance from him. Madness gradually takes possession of her soul. Feverish and distracted, she writes diary entries every night, in which she talks about her love and her writing ambitions, and repudiates her father and his name. Then Lieutenant Pinson's regiment is sent to Barbados, in the West Indies. Adèle Hugo follows him. She is found in Bridgetown, distraught and in rags, a madwoman whom children cruelly pursue with their taunts. The last time she runs into Lieutenant Pinson in the street, she doesn't even recognize him. A West Indian woman, Madame Baa, finally takes her in and then accompanies her to France with financial help from Victor Hugo. Adèle is then locked up in an asylum in Paris, where she dies in 1915, still believing in her eternal love.

While Gruault was working on the screenplay—it took him two long years—relations with Frances Vernor Guille became complicated; she demanded a considerable sum for the screen rights (30,000 francs) and the status of coscenarist (with payment of 200,000 francs). Truffaut considered these demands unacceptable. While expressing his "deep disappointment" to her, he contemplated giving up the project "all the more sadly and bitterly as we have never encountered such a situation in our fifteen years of filmmaking."[130]

In fact, Truffaut was playing a tricky game, pretending to be discouraged and on the point of giving up the project, with the sole aim of getting Guille to back down. For he very much wanted to make the film. Indeed, he put all his energy into overcoming the reluctance of Jean Hugo, a writer and painter living in Lunel, who was Adèle's grand-nephew and Victor Hugo's great-grandson, and hence the direct heir and owner of the rights to this adaptation. Jean Hugo hesitated for a long time: "I wonder if this sad story, which was always a jealously guarded family secret, won't be shocking on the screen. Doesn't mental disease, whose signs were very soon apparent in Adèle Hugo, give a pathological overtone to this love story and take away all its human value?"[131] he wrote, somewhat fearfully, to Truffaut. It was only after reading Gruault's first treatment that Victor Hugo's descendant gave his consent, on the sole condition that the writer not appear as a protagonist on-screen. In the meantime, Truffaut had to settle his dispute with Frances Vernor Guille. A compromise was reached involving payment of fifty thousand francs for the "historical supervision" of the screenplay, a nonbinding honorary status.

Marcel Berbert's estimated budget for *L'Histoire d'Adèle H.* (*The Story of Adèle H.*), a period film shot outside, was slightly over 5 million francs. This was too expensive a film for Carrosse to produce on its own. Berbert quite naturally turned to Robert Solo, in the belief that after the success of *Day for Night* and the Oscar for Best Foreign-Language Film, he would encounter no difficulty in putting together a coproduction deal with Warner Brothers. But the company's representative in France turned down the *Adèle H.* screenplay on the grounds that it was too literary. Several weeks later, Truffaut and Berbert, who were used to such unexpected reversals, found a better reception with Jean Nachbaur, the French representative for United Artists, Carrosse's erstwhile partner for *The Wild Child.* But Nachbaur thought the budget too big, which necessitated a revision of the screenplay. Though he had set out to write a novelistic film "à la *Gone With the Wind,*"[132] Gruault condensed his scenes and pruned the story as much as possible. The screenplay he handed to Truffaut in November 1973 was shortened considerably, from 373 to 116 pages. With Suzanne Schiffman's help, Truffaut eliminated most of the costly historical scenes and decided to center the film around Adèle, her madness, her psychotic behavior, and her persecution mania. This was where the whole strength of the film would lie, focused on obsessive love, a theme that was dear to Truffaut.

Now Truffaut had to find the ideal actress. Several years earlier, he had promised the part to Catherine Deneuve.[133] A short time later, he made screen tests with Stacey Tendeter—the actress who had played Muriel in *Two English Girls* and whose physical appearance was right for the part. But he now wanted the heroine to be younger and he began to look for an ingenue. Very soon, he noticed Isabelle Adjani, first in the television broadcast of the Comédie-Française production of Molière's *School for Wives,* and then in Claude Pinoteau's film *La Gifle,* a big hit when it opened in September 1974. Though he didn't know her, he wrote her an impassioned letter to convince her to accept the part of Adèle Hugo, which meant she would have to break her contract with the Comédie-Française: "You're a fabulous actress and, with the exception of Jeanne Moreau, I've never felt such a pressing desire to capture a face on celluloid, immediately, and without further delay. I accept the idea that theater is a noble cause, but my particular area is cinema and I came out of *La Gifle* with the conviction that you should be filmed every day, even on Sunday."[134]

Isabelle Adjani demurred. She was attracted by the part (even though she admitted she thought she was too young for it) and by the director's prestige, but she felt that breaking with the Comédie-Française would be an "act of betrayal, of disloyal severance."[135] Truffaut pleaded even more energetically to persuade her. Not only did he predict a "magnificent career" for her but he confessed his infatuation: "Your face tells a screen story unto itself, the expression in your eyes creates dramatic situations, you could even act in a film with no story line, it would be a documentary on you and would be as good as any fiction."[136] Truffaut wrote to Pierre Dux, the head of the Comédie-Française, on October 23, 1974, asking him to grant Adjani a fourteen-week leave, starting in January 1975. Dux categorically refused. Unwilling to give up on Adjani, Truffaut continued to exercise pressure. When the Comédie-Française threatened the actress with a breach-of-contract suit, Truffaut gave the case to his lawyer, Pierre Hebey, asking him to negotiate a compromise. Isabelle Adjani passively let the adults decide things for her. But by giving up the two parts she was to perform onstage, she was deserting the theater. "After my last performance, some people came to see me to tell me that what I was doing was very bad, that I would always regret it, that things would not go well in the movies. . . . That night I was really stigmatized. . . ."[137]

Now that he had almost kidnapped the nineteen-year-old actress, François Truffaut could get down to the preproduction work on the film. Suzanne Schiffman scouted locations: the filming was to take place in Guernsey, except for the Barbados scenes, which were to be shot on the island of Gorée off the coast of Senegal. *The Story of Adéle H.* would be filmed entirely on islands, in isolated conditions that would be hard on the entire cast and crew. To complete his casting, Truffaut went to London on December ninth, to audition English actors whom he wanted for the supporting roles. He hired Bruce Robinson for the part of Lieutenant Pinson, Joseph Blatchley for the bookseller Whistler, and Sylvia Marriott, the mother of Anne and Muriel Brown in *Two English Girls*, for the part of Mrs. Saunders, Adèle's landlady. Lastly, he had the idea of casting Ivry Gitlis, the famous violinist, in the part of a magician and hypnotist.

On January 3, 1975, Truffaut arrived in Guernsey. He stayed at the Duke of Richmond Hotel, which faced Cambridge Park in the heart of Saint Peter Port. This is the main town on this small island, with its very puritanical atmosphere; its main claim to fame is the fact that it extended hospitality to the exiled Victor Hugo for over fifteen years. The cast and crew had to spend two months there. Truffaut was delighted to work with Nestor Almendros again, four years after their last collaboration. He persuaded him to take on Florent Bazin—Janine and André's son—as assistant cameraman. From then on, Florent Bazin would be assistant cameraman or cameraman on all of Truffaut's films.

Because of the isolation, Truffaut organized a film society in a room of the Duke of Richmond Hotel. Two evenings a week, Claude Miller, the production manager, was in charge of showing films in 16 mm: Welles's *The Magnificent Ambersons,* Chaplin's *The Gold Rush,* Hitchcock's *Psycho,*

Richard Fleischer's *The Vikings,* Murnau's *The Last Laugh,* and Keaton's *The Navigator.* It was a way of relieving tension—"we were stuck,"[138] Isabelle Adjani said. But this austere life also had its advantages: The cast and crew concentrated on their work and the shooting atmosphere was quasi-religious. "Everything is fraught with tension and passion, but internally and with no outward show," Truffaut confided to Liliane Siegel. "For that reason it is rather hard on the nerves, but the rushes are really good. I'm on good behavior and strictly professional, if you see what I mean, and usually I'm thinking of my daughters as I lead Isabelle A. in the direction of children's books for young girls."[139]

Besides the isolation, there were reasons why the *Adèle H.* shoot was very tense and difficult. The film had to be made in two versions, in French and in English, so multiple takes were necessary in order to shoot each scene in both languages. Then, most important, the relationship between the actress and the director was sensitive, not to say passionate. "For Truffaut, *Adèle* is primarily a story about isolation," Isabelle Adjani said. "He knew how to create a claustrophobic atmosphere."[140] As on each of his shoots, Truffaut was in love with his female lead. "I spent my time warding him off as a woman and as an actress,"[141] Adjani later admitted. Truffaut's passion took the form of enthrallment. He seemed hypnotized, more than he had ever been on any of his films. "I watch her act, I help her as I can, uttering thirty words when she would like a hundred, or fifty when only one, but the right one, is needed, for everything is a matter of vocabulary in our strange association. I don't know Isabelle Adjani. Yet, in the evening, my eyes and ears are tired from having looked at her too hard and listened to her all day."[142]

As for Isabelle Adjani, she gave herself entirely to her part; she seemed possessed by Adèle Hugo, a young woman rejected by an older man, Lieutenant Pinson, who was supposed to be the same age as Truffaut. "Adèle was not in love with the young man but in love with her love for him, with her imagined idea of love,"[143] says Adjani. *The Story of Adèle H.,* then, is a film about love as an obsession, with the script reproducing—but with genders reversed—the relationship between the director and his actress. Truffaut was motivated to film extreme close-ups of the face and body of the young actress. "He needed me to be there so he could focus on me, and record this idée fixe he had of me, this rigidity he demanded of my body,"[144] Adjani adds.

"It is not unusual to see the little makeup girls and hair stylists crying behind the set as they hear our young Adèle performing,"[145] Truffaut wrote to Helen Scott. It was Adjani's practice not to rehearse so she could give herself completely during the takes; in this way, she created a climate that often left the director and his team in an overwrought emotional state. So he wrote to Liliane Siegel from Guernsey, asking her to keep her lips sealed for "fear of misunderstandings": "You mention the pleasure I must have directing Isabelle A. It's the opposite of pleasure, it's daily suffering for me, and almost an agony for her. For her profession is her religion, and because of that our shoot is a trial for everyone. It would be too easy to say she is difficult, she is not. She is different from all the women in this profession and since she isn't even twenty, add to all this (to her genius, let's not be afraid of words), an unawareness of others and their vulnerability which creates an unbelievable tension."[146]

After a two-month shoot on the island, one of the longest in his entire career, Truffaut, on the point of exhaustion, left Guernsey with his cast and crew on March 8, 1975. There still remained another week of work in Senegal, involving only part of the cast and crew. They left Paris on March twelfth for Dakar, where Truffaut granted himself a week's rest before tackling the editing of his film. He still had to confront what he called "the trial of the Moritone":[147] seeing Isabelle Adjani's face over and over again on the editing flatbed and wondering whether he had succeeded in obtaining what he had hoped for from her. *The Story of Adèle H.*, Truffaut realized very soon, was a film that had been abducted by his actress's face. Would this, which seemed a strength to him, seem so to others? The initial response of some of his close friends was stern. Gilles Jacob wrote him that "he had felt unmoved";[148] Marcel Ophuls said he was disappointed by the coldness of a film that was "frozen from within by the pallor of Adèle's face."[149] Even Gruault was not convinced by the film, the principal problem being that "Adèle does not go mad because she is in love; on the contrary, she seems mad from the beginning, on the wharf, as soon as she steps off the boat."[150] For Truffaut, this blow struck home, but he would need some distance to comprehend it. In two years, "he would be able to see the film again as though it had been filmed by someone else."[151] For the time being, however, he sensed that there was "something strange and unbalanced"[152] about this film that had sometimes made him shed tears while he was making it.

*The Story of Adèle H.* opened in Paris on October eighth. Attendance was good during the first week, with 55,000 tickets sold, but soon dwindled because word of mouth was poor. The film fared better in Japan and Italy. It opened in New York on December 22 and was well received by the press. A tragic coincidence: One week after seeing the film, to which she responded enthusiastically and with great emotion, "in tears from beginning to end,"[153] Frances V. Guille, Adèle's biographer, died of a heart attack.

## SMALL CHANGE

Even before the release of *The Story of Adèle H.*, François Truffaut was planning a new film—the best remedy for forgetting the tensions and passions of Guernsey. After depicting a young woman's obsessive love and madness, he started work on a film about children. He scheduled the filming of *L'Argent de poche* (*Small Change*) for July 1975, during the summer vacation, a mere four months after his return from Senegal. The screenplay would be built around several little anecdotes he had recorded. Some dated back to the period when he was working on *The Mischief Makers* and *The 400 Blows*—for example, the one of the little girl who had been left home alone by her parents and who yelled from the window "I'm hungry," a true story told to him by Madeleine. Some of the other incidents were autobiographical, like the one of his first kiss, at summer camp in August 1945. Others were taken from news items, or simply invented.

At the end of 1972, the project was still only at the synopsis stage—he had written about ten pages with Suzanne Schiffman. At that point, Truffaut had contemplated an "episode film illustrating different aspects of childhood," with each part a variation on the theme of "children's great powers of resistance and survival."[154] He even considered giving his film the ironic title *The Tough Skin*. In early summer 1974, Truffaut decided to resume work on the project with Suzanne Schiffman. He didn't intend to write a real screenplay, for he wanted to be free to improvise with the children who would act in the film and write the dialogue as he went along, using preestablished situations and including some of his ideas about childhood.[155] It is Truffaut himself—his words, ideas, and intonations—who is echoed in the teacher's long monologue to his young pupils, delivered by Jean-François Stévenin:

> I wanted to tell you that it is because of my own bad memories of my youth and because I don't like the way children are treated that I chose to become a schoolteacher. Life's not easy, it's hard and it's important you learn to steel yourself against it. Note, I said steel yourself, not become hard-boiled. Things balance out in an odd way, so people who have had a difficult youth are often better equipped to confront adult life than people who have been overprotected, or very loved. It's a sort of law of compensation. In time you will have children and I hope you will love them and they will love you. To tell the truth, they will love you if you love them. Otherwise they will transfer their love, affection, or tenderness to other people or other things. Because life is such that it is impossible not to feel love and be loved.[156]

In April 1975, after scouting locations in the center of France, Truffaut decided to shoot his film in Thiers, in the Puy-de-Dôme. At the end of May, he started auditioning and giving screen tests to children every Saturday at Les Films du Carrosse. Among the three hundred who auditioned, fifteen would ultimately be cast in the main parts of *Small Change*. Some children of friends were among the chosen, such as Georges Desmouceaux, the son of Lucette and Claude de Givray, or Philippe Goldmann, the son of the philosopher Lucien Goldmann. Truffaut's daughters also made their real screen debut—Laura as the young wife by the name of Madeleine Doinel, the mother of a baby, Oscar, who refuses to talk and only expresses himself by whistling; Eva in the part of Patricia, the teenager whose little boyfriends take her to the movies in the hope of kissing her.

In June, Truffaut settled in Thiers and hired some local schoolchildren as extras. The wife of the schoolteacher (Jean-François Stévenin) is played by Virginie Thévenet. Marcel Berbert, Roland Thénot, Monique Dury (the costumer) and Thi Loan N'Guyen (the makeup girl) also make appearances in the film, and so does the mayor of Thiers, René Barnérias, in a small part. The shooting of *Small Change* began on July 17, 1975, and lasted two months. Truffaut had rehired Pierre-William Glenn, the director of photography of *Day for Night,* because he wanted the new picture to be filmed at a similarly rapid pace. Truffaut wrote his dialogue hurriedly, every once in a while noting down expressions used by his "actors."

Rather cheerful, but physically exhausting because of the constant attention required by the children, the shoot of *Small Change* left him once again in a state of great fatigue. His physician prescribed a month of complete rest, which he decided to spend in Cannes, then in Los Angeles, at the Beverly Hills Hotel. When he returned to Paris at the end of October 1975, an arduous editing task awaited him—a three-hour rough cut that had to be brought down to an acceptable running time of around one hour and forty minutes.

Six months after the failure of *The Story of Adèle H.,* Truffaut found success again. *Small Change* was a big hit when it opened in ten Paris movie houses on March 17, 1976. Once again, the audience flocked to one of Truffaut's "small" films after keeping away from a more ambitious work. *Small Change* reached ticket sales of 470,000 after a six-month run, equaling the success of *The 400 Blows.* The film also did extremely well abroad—including the United States (it earned almost $1.5 million in box-office receipts), Germany, Scandinavia, and Japan. In the United States, Truffaut had two consecutive successes in the same year—*Adèle H.* and *Small Change*—he could now join the club of "million-dollar directors" whose films cost only half that amount to make.

## A MAN WHO WOULD HAVE THE SOUL OF A CHILD

François Truffaut had no further film shoots scheduled until the autumn of 1976. He was giving himself six months to rest, write a few prefaces, and tinker with the screenplay of *The Man Who Loved Women*. On March 2, 1976, his plans were changed by a telephone call from Los Angeles. A twenty-nine-year-old American filmmaker was on the other end of the line, offering him a part in his next film. It was Steven Spielberg, who had attracted attention in 1971 with his first television feature, *Duel*. Though the latter became an American cult movie, Spielberg was better known to international audiences for his second feature film, *Jaws,* the greatest box-office hit in the history of cinema at that time. Spielberg had just completed the screenplay for *Close Encounters of the Third Kind* and offered Truffaut the part of the French scientist specializing in UFOs. "I needed a man who would have the soul of a child," Spielberg later said, "someone kindly, warm, who could completely accept the extraordinary, the irrational."[157] A teenage prodigy, born in Ohio in 1947 and who later studied film at California State College, Long Beach, Steven Spielberg had seen *The Wild Child* and *Day for Night,* two films that had made a deep impression on him. He thought he could count on Truffaut's acting talent for the part of the "child-man," to whom he gave a very French name, Claude Lacombe.

The day after Spielberg's phone call, his producer, Julia Phillips,[158] who worked for Columbia Pictures, arranged to have the screenplay delivered to Truffaut, with French translations scrupulously provided for all the scenes in which he was to appear. About ten days later, on March 15, Truffaut sent the following telegram to Spielberg: "I like the script and I like Lacombe. Stop. I would like to be able to play the part, but I need time to think because I'm supposed to shoot a new film in the beginning of September. Stop. Sincerely yours."[159] Truffaut was tempted by the offer. The thought of acting in an $11 million Hollywood production directed by a talented young man was not only a real novelty but also an exciting challenge. He told Julia Phillips he could only accept under one condition: He had to be free in August to work on the screenplay for *The Man Who Loved Women* in Los Angeles. He also requested information concerning the dates and locations of the shoot, as well as payment he would receive. "I wonder if you'll understand my very special English, I hope so!"[160] he wrote. Truffaut contacted his lawyer in Los Angeles, Louis Blau, and his agent, Rupert Allen, to negotiate his contract. Spielberg and Columbia Pictures did everything to facilitate Truffaut's involvement with *Close Encounters.* They assured him that the shoot, scheduled to begin in May 1976, wouldn't exceed fourteen weeks, that he would be free for two weeks in mid-August, and they offered him a payment that was far from insignificant—$85,000. Truffaut accepted the part of Claude Lacombe, UFO specialist. When he arrived in Los Angeles on May 5, 1976, preproduction on the film was already nearly complete and the shoot was to begin a few days later in Gillett, in the mountains of Wyoming, near the local attraction, the strange cylinder-shaped peak called Devil's Tower.

As soon as he arrived in Hollywood, Truffaut was charmed by Steven Spielberg; the two men shared the same love of cinema, in particular an admiration for Howard Hawks.[161] Truffaut found Spielberg unpretentious, even though he was already "the director of the most *successful* [in English] film in the history of cinema,"[162] and fearless about directing such a huge production. He admired Spielberg's serenity and good humor in fulfilling his "childhood dream." Nevertheless, the first two weeks of the shoot in Gillett were trying. Truffaut was uneasy with the language, lost among several dozen technicians, and homesick. "I like America, but Los Angeles more than Wyoming or Alabama and I miss you, as well as our lunches at the *boulangerie*,"[163] he wrote to his friend Serge Rousseau, whom he used to meet often, when he was in Paris, at the bakery-restaurant on the corner of rue Marbeuf and rue Robert-Estienne, a few yards away from his office. Truffaut, who was never enticed by tourism, even declined visiting the famed Mount Rushmore and seeing the heads of the American presidents carved in stone—the location used by Hitchcock for the final sequences of *North by Northwest.* He spent most of his time just waiting. "It's sometimes amusing, but very slow, very long, and I must admit that the acting profession has its wretched side (or rather sides),"[164] he wrote to Nestor Almendros. Though he sometimes took undeniable pleasure in "acting without stage fright" and often succeeded in making the American cast and crew laugh, Truffaut discovered the frustration of actors, forced to wait between takes in complete passivity and idleness. This was completely foreign to his usual experience on the set, where he could control situations and master his schedule. He felt stymied, "almost like in a (gilded) prisoners' camp,"[165] he admitted to Marcel Berbert, saying that he would never again agree to be directed by other filmmakers. On the set of *Close Encounters,* he discovered special effects and technical processes that were all the rage in American moviemaking (that same year, Spielberg's best friend, George Lucas, started work on *Star Wars*). The actors were filmed performing their scenes with a matte on the upper half of the frame for the subsequent compositing of studio-made video and computer-generated special effects. Here, on this part of the image—and of the screen—the famed flying objects that Professor Lacombe was supposed to tame would eventually be seen. Though a highly sophisticated technique, marking an important stage in the history of cinematic special effects, it slowed the pace of the filming considerably, leading Truffaut to say that Spielberg shoots only three or four shots a day.

After a ten-day interlude in Los Angeles, during which they shot at Columbia Studios (and Truffaut had the pleasure of seeing Jean Renoir and staying at the Beverly Hills Hotel), in June 1976, the cast and crew left for Mobile, Alabama, for two months. There, inside a huge warehouse, gigantic state-of-the-art sets had been built. Truffaut wrote to Madeleine on July 13:

I can't describe the shoot in this enormous warehouse representing a secret, electronically equipped underground passage where the spaceship will land, because we're only beginning to shoot there tomorrow, I think. It's a bigger, larger and taller place than any Hollywood studio, which is why it was chosen—except the production people didn't know there were leaks in the roof (a catastrophe for the set), etc. Later. I saw the warehouse, not bad. We aren't shooting today, a giant mess. There are 120 people besides the cast and crew—extras, a hundred people equally divided into little groups: chemists, engineers, physicians, meteorologists, telephone operators. I don't really understand much; in principle, I direct a pseudo-French group called "the society of light." In the end, the little girls will fly off, the spaceship will arrive, we'll all touch each other, etc. all of this before October, I hope. . . . P.S. . . . : I was just told over the phone that I would have my office tomorrow. It's a wonderful life. Les Films du Carrosse will have an outpost in Mobile![166]

Truffaut eventually became accustomed to this world of technology and excess that was so foreign to him: "I'm learning all sorts of things that will never be of any use to me,"[167] he said facetiously to Marcel Berbert, fully appreciating the talent of his right-hand man at managing his modest film budgets. In Mobile, Truffaut used the private office the producers gave him inside the warehouse studio as a place where he could rest, read, and entertain friends—the star of the film, Richard Dreyfuss, or Bob Balaban, who also played in *Close Encounters,* or the director of photography, the Hungarian Vilmos Zsigmond.

Josiane Couëdel, his secretary at Les Films du Carrosse, sent him his mail from Paris regularly, as well as the newspapers and magazines he liked to read—*L'Express, Le Point, Le Nouvel Observateur, Télérama, Le Film français,* the movie page of *Le Monde.* Between takes, he wrote scores of letters to friends and worked on the script of *The Man Who Loved Women:*

The first version . . . is finished, I'm only 50 percent satisfied with it, but I have the feeling of seeing, much more clearly than usual, what has to be done to improve it considerably and I must say I have time to fine-tune it. . . . For the moment, the question that worries me is this: can women be sent out into the streets of Montpellier in November in summer dresses or would it be more reasonable to wait until the spring of '77 . . . ? The script is getting rather amusing. Since I know ahead of time that Denner's puritanism will prevent many things, I try to find indirect solutions so that, in spite of this, things will be charged with tension and eroticism. I only come up with one really good idea a week, but I've been at it for quite awhile already. . . . Good, fine, I know that eventually I'll be bawled out by everyone and when I say everyone, it starts very close to home. . . .[168]

In mid-August, Truffaut was free for two weeks, as planned. He arranged to have Suzanne Schiffman come to Los Angeles. There, in a suite at the Beverly Hills Hotel, they put the finishing touches on the screenplay for *The Man Who Loved Women,* which Truffaut hoped to shoot in October of the same year. In the beginning of September, he returned to Mobile for the last two weeks of filming. Steven Spielberg shot the end of his film in the huge warehouse that served as a set—the arrival of the spaceship and the fraternizing of the humans and the extraterrestrials, under Professor Lacombe's sympathetic gaze. Now, only ten days of filming remained, which was scheduled for the beginning of 1977—in India, this time, not far from Bombay, where Truffaut would go after directing his own film.

All in all, after a difficult period of adjustment, Truffaut was not unhappy with his experience. He was forced to put himself into someone else's shoes and, moreover, the shoes of a foreigner twice over. Spielberg's conception of Professor Lacombe presupposed a linguistic and cultural estrangement. But even if the world of Hollywood megaproductions was poles apart from Truffaut's conception of cinema—modest, craftsmanlike, uniting a small family of actors and technicians—he doubtless recognized in the character of Lacombe Dr. Itard's double—someone who seeks out extraterrestrials like so many wild children who need to be understood. Spielberg and Truffaut were thus united in the themes they explored.

With his neutral acting style, his luminous and passionate gaze, Truffaut is out of place in this typically American film. This was the effect Spielberg had desired; and for him, Truffaut was the "perfect actor,"[169] the kind who never asked questions and was always available to shoot extra scenes or dialogue. Spielberg wrote expressing his gratitude to Truffaut in December 1977, once the film was completed: "*Close Encounters* is doing beautifully—as I've indicated time and time again, your performance was superb!"[170] He even asked Truffaut to write the introduction to the book about the making of the film.

Released in the United States on February 6, 1978 (Truffaut's forty-sixth birthday), Spielberg's film was greeted with enthusiasm by the critics and the public. One month later, the two filmmakers met in London for a special screening of *Close Encounters* in the presence of Queen Elizabeth. In the meantime, the film had opened in Paris, where it had been preceded by a televised program devoted to Truffaut and hosted by Michel Drucker. The character of Claude Lacombe revealed François Truffaut to countless viewers all over the world who hadn't necessarily seen his films. In some sense, he became more than a director; he became "a humanist,"[171] as Steven Spielberg said of him.

## A SOLITARY HUNTER

For a long time, the film that was to become *L'Homme qui aimait les femmes* (*The Man Who Loved Women*) was entitled *Le Cavaleur* (The Skirt-Chaser). François Truffaut had as an epigraph to the screenplay a sentence from a book by Bruno Bettelheim: "It seemed that Joey simply never got through to his mother,"[172] proof, once again, of the autobiographical nature of the story. Truffaut intended to draw the portrait of a womanizer, a man who values the love of women above everything else in his life, as a way of simultaneously repressing and exalting a disappointed first love for his mother. Truffaut was always fascinated by these kinds of men, "who loved women." Not skirt-chasers or Don Juans, for whom seduction is a game, but men for whom seduction is a passion, an idée fixe, a serious, perpetual occupation—as though with every prospective conquest their lives were at stake. Truffaut had known men like this—Henri-Pierre Roché or Jacques Audiberti, for instance—and he himself, though he was shy and had a great sense of propriety, was a ladies' man. Diffidence was part of his charm, and he used it as an asset in seducing women, or in letting women seduce him. Liliane Dreyfus says, for example, "François had a female sensibility; he knew how to read expressions in people's eyes."[173] He sometimes could seem timid with a woman, in the periods of his life when he lacked self-confidence or was reluctant to commit himself. But he could be bold and was capable of badgering women who resisted him or considered him a friend or a pleasant companion rather than a lover. He was "very loyal, but possessive,"[174] by several accounts. "There was always a beginning, rarely an end," Liliane Dreyfus says. "He protected me, like a father, husband, and brother all at once, at every point in my life. Which didn't prevent him from sometimes being cruel, even with the people he loved."[175] "Deeply unfaithful, more out of an appetite for seduction, or a need to be loved, than out of an all-consuming need,"[176] is how Madeleine Morgenstern describes it. Love then changed into friendship, or continued in a more lasting, explicitly sexual way. Jeanne Moreau referred to "inescapable harmonies." The men who knew Truffaut well also have something to say about his charm and his obsessive desire to seduce. Claude Chabrol unhesitatingly says that Truffaut's great theme, in his life and work, was "the search for harmonious relationships," this constant, sometimes desperate quest, for a just equilibrium and happiness. "François was an absolutely charming man, in the literal meaning of the word: He charmed. But I've often asked myself whether he had been happy in his life. . . ."[177] Philippe Labro also describes "this drive, this thirst, this voracious need to seduce. However, François was not a hollow Don Juan. Because what counted most was his work, the idea of imposing his own style and his own world, the desire to exhibit all his talent."[178]

The idea for *Le Cavaleur* owed a great deal to Michel Fermaud. An old acquaintance, Fermaud had met Truffaut in the late fifties in the *Cahiers du cinéma* entourage. The two were about the same age, and they addressed each other with the informal "*tu,*" a privilege Truffaut accorded sparingly. "I often saw Truffaut at the *Cahiers*—saw, I can't say we knew each other then," Fermaud recalls. At about the same time, in 1958, Fermaud wrote a play, *Les Portes claquent* (The Doors Slam), starring Jean-Claude Brialy and Michael Lonsdale, which was a huge hit. "François came to see it. We met; we had long conversations. He knew that I loved women,"[179] Fermaud adds. Out of this shared passion for women, there arose a certain complicity between the two men. Thereafter, however, they lost sight of each other for about fifteen years.

In December 1974, Truffaut got back in touch with Fermaud and invited him to lunch in a restaurant on the Champs-Elysées. He requested that Fermaud help him in shaping his screenplay. As he always did with scriptwriters, Truffaut asked Fermaud to record as many anecdotes about his female conquests as possible. His regular appointments with an usherette in a movie theater, a pickup in a fitting room, a scene in the washroom of a restaurant or department store—all these romantic and sexual stories offer a wonderful gallery of female characters, including the "easy woman" who resists the skirt-chaser, the woman who "seems like an impregnable citadel" yet "pounces on him,"[180] and the married woman who uses all manner of cunning to meet with her lover.

On February 18, 1975, Michel Fermaud gave Truffaut a first set of notes, with a commentary in the form of a self-portrait. "If I understand correctly, the hero is neither a sex maniac nor a skirt-chaser. He just goes to great lengths to conquer members of the opposite sex, satisfy them and get rid of them, as though his life depended on it. Is he motivated by a fear of solitude? You must have had the experience, as I have, of bringing someone home at night not because you desired her all that much, but because you felt a certain anguish. Is he driven by the need to please, affirm himself, or conquer? Is he trying to appease a raging sexual appetite? What social milieu does he belong to?"[181] Truffaut sent his friend's sheets back to him with notes and comments. "François would say to me, 'More like this, more like that.' I would sometimes go against my instincts because I didn't always feel things the same way he did." Indeed, Fermaud was a carefree seducer, a hedonist, but Truffaut wasn't: "He saw me as blessed by the gods, a kind of freak," Fermaud adds. "François was very discreet about his romantic relationships with actresses; I realized this when I worked with him on avenue Pierre 1er de Serbie. I overheard many phone conversations, his imbroglios with women were incredible. There was always an unspoken, hidden undertone."[182] Fermaud furnished Truffaut with a series of anecdotes, light but detailed short scenes, to help him write his screenplay. The hero of *Le Cavaleur*, Bertrand Morane, is a depressive surrounded by women, a conception derived as much from Fermaud as from Truffaut. The autobiographical dimension is particularly obvious in the flashbacks of the film, made up of the hero's childhood and adolescent memories about his mother. "My mother was in the habit of walking around half-naked in front of me," Bertrand Morane writes in his journal. "Not in order to arouse me of course but rather, I assume, to confirm to herself that I didn't exist. Everything about her behavior with me when I was little implied: 'I'd have been better off breaking a leg on the day I gave birth to this little moron.' "

In the spring of 1976, when he joined Spielberg for several months in California, Truffaut took Fermaud's notes with him. Meanwhile, Suzanne Schiffman began outlining a story line and a narrative structure. As planned, the two met in August in Los Angeles and worked on the screenplay together for two weeks. Oddly, the script begins in a cemetery: A man is being buried and the only people at the grave are women who loved him. In his early forties, Bertrand Morane lived in Montpellier and was an engineer at the Institute for the Study of Fluid Mechanics. His job was to test the effects of atmospheric turbulence on model planes, ships, and helicopters. But his only passion was women. None left him indifferent—whether dark or blond, "tall filly" or "little kitten," each had characteristics that fit into a detailed glossary of femininity. Morane loved redheads for their smell, platinum blondes for their artificiality; he loved young women who believed the world belonged to them, mature women who remained flirtatious; and he loved widows because they were available, married women because they were not. For Bertrand, women's legs "measure the world like a compass, giving it balance and harmony."

The hero, as Truffaut conceived him in his work sessions with Michel Fermaud, is a solitary and anxious hunter, who seeks to conquer women even in the face of the worst difficulties—whether an unknown woman whose legs he spots in a laundry, a baby-sitter whose phone number he copies off a bulletin board in a supermarket, a car-rental employee, or the invisible operator of a telephone wake-up service, a café waitress proficient in karate, a deaf-mute usherette in a movie theater, a woman who comes back into his life after a long separation, or one who can make love only in precarious situations. One evening, a not-so-young woman who owns a boutique of fancy lingerie rejects Bertrand Morane's advances; though she enjoys his company, she confesses that she likes only younger men. This rejection induces Morane to write an autobiographical novel which he entitles *Le Cavaleur.* By recounting his adventures, the hero brings the women he has known back to life. He writes in a feverish state and, as he progresses, gives installments of his manuscript to a secretary to be typed. But after the third chapter she refuses to continue, shocked by the book's salaciousness. From then on, Bertrand Morane has to type his manuscript himself, with two fingers. He sends it to several Paris publishing houses. The manuscript appeals to Geneviève, an editor. The editorial committee at Editions Bétany, where she works, agrees to publish the book but suggests another title: *Le Cavaleur* becomes *L'Homme qui aimait les femmes.* Geneviève follows the stages of the project and goes to the plant where the book will be printed, near Montpellier. On that occasion, she spends the afternoon with Bertrand in a hotel room and becomes one of his lovers. After her departure, unwilling to resign himself to spending Christmas Eve alone, Morane roams the streets of Montpellier hoping to meet a woman. He spots one across the street, tries to catch up to her, and is hit by a car. He is taken to the hospital in serious condition. When he comes to, the first thing he sees is a nurse's pretty legs. Unable to resist, he tries to get up, falls out of bed, and dies, like the miser Grandet trying to grasp the priest's gold crucifix.[183] *The Man Who Loved Women* is certainly one of François Truffaut's finest screenplays.

From the very beginning, he had given his skirt-chaser the face of Charles Denner. "I wanted to hear his voice throughout the film. His seriousness appealed to me. I didn't want my womanizer to be too attractive, I saw him as rather anxious, not at all the stereotype of the smug and irritating playboy."[184] Truffaut liked the odd blend of humor and seriousness that characterized this passionate, unpredictable, sincere actor, who, following in the footsteps of Aznavour and Léaud, became Truffaut's screen double. They shared a similar physical appearance, a similar anguish, and a similar lively and worried intelligence. While he was writing his screenplay, Truffaut had discreetly asked Serge Rousseau, Denner's agent, if the actor would be free in the fall of 1976. It was only at lunch in a restaurant on rue François 1er, in November 1975, that Truffaut told Denner the plot of his film and offered him the lead.

Marcel Berbert, in the meantime, negotiated the film's financing with Jean Nachbaur at United Artists. Gérard Lebovici, whom Truffaut had asked to be his agent and negotiate his personal contracts as author-director as well as those of Les Films du Carrosse, raised the bid: He asked United Artists for 6 million francs, which they refused. Berbert showed himself to be more reasonable and reached a compromise. "François sought security; he had Lebovici and me, which represented two different styles, no doubt complementary in his eyes,"[185] Marcel Berbert now explains. As head of Artmédia, Europe's foremost talent agency, representing France's biggest movie stars, as well as screenwriters and directors, Gérard Lebovici was very much concerned about the evolution of the film industry, which had been deeply affected by the growing power of television. Though television had cut into theatrical film exhibition, it was nevertheless contributing more and more to financing film production. Lebovici's entire strategy consisted in making the stars and filmmakers he represented full-fledged producers in their own right. As such, François Truffaut served as a model, since he had always been auteur, director, and producer. Lebovici was conscious of Truffaut's commercial and symbolic value in France and abroad. "Gérard Lebovici gave Truffaut a global view of the system," says Jean-Louis Livi, who was Lebovici's closest collaborator for many years before becoming a producer himself. "They had a great deal in common. First a love for women, and exceptional literary culture. It was easy for the two men to communicate. But there was a fundamental difference; François was fearful in business matters, while Lebovici was adventuresome. François was impressed by this adventuresome side, and Gérard liked François's humility and wanted to help him achieve great things."[186]

In September 1976, when he returned from the United States, Truffaut set about casting all the female parts in *The Man Who Loved Women*. Brigitte Fossey is Geneviève, Bertand Morane's editor and last lover. Leslie Caron makes an appearance as Véra, the woman who had been Morane's great love and whom he unexpectedly runs into one evening. Caron thought that this scene, which resembles a confession of love, was directly autobiographical: "I thought my part in the film was Madeleine's in François's life. I discussed it with Madeleine, who thinks that Véra is more like Catherine Deneuve."[187] Geneviève Fontanel is Hélène, the lingerie shopkeeper whom Morane is attracted to but who turns him down because she prefers younger men. Faithful to Nathalie Baye, with whom he had remained on good terms since *Day for Night*, Truffaut cast her in a small but sparkling role, and he also asked her to do the voice-over for the wake-up service's operator, with whom Morane has a suggestive daily telephone relationship. Truffaut also wanted to work again with Nelly Bourgeaud, who had had a thankless part in *Mississippi Mermaid;* he cast her as Delphine, a married woman with impulsive desires, who leads Bertrand Morane to the edge of madness. Truffaut decided to find actors for the other secondary roles in Montpellier, the city where he planned to shoot his film, for he remembered it fondly from the time he presented *Small Change* there. "I had been told, and it's true, that it's the French city that has the greatest number of pretty girls per square meter,"[188] he wrote, justifying his choice.

In the beginning of October, Truffaut rented a beautiful old house in the center of town, on rue du Carré-du-Roi. He auditioned a great many actors from the south of France for the smaller parts, and called upon two Langue-doc personalities, the film director Roger Leenhardt, member of an important Protestant family of the region, and the critic Henri Agel, to act in the scene in which the members of the editorial committee give their opinion of Bertrand Morane's manuscript and accept it for publication. The filming, which began on October 19, 1976, lasted over two months. During that period, the cast and crew shot in the city streets and in the offices of the *Midi libre* newspaper, particularly the office of Monsieur Bugeon, the managing director, who kindly made the space available for the scenes in the Bétany publishing house. During the Toussaint [All Saints' Day] school holiday, Laura Truffaut took time off from her intensive literary studies to spend a few days in Montpellier with her father, whom she hadn't seen in several months. The days spent on the set of *The Man Who Loved Women,* where she was an apprentice script girl, were "unforgettable" for her, but also put her in a "real quandary"[189] over whether to pursue filmmaking as a career or to continue her studies. The experience occurred at a decisive moment in her life. Laura would finally choose the latter, but not without regret.

François Truffaut, who thought he was making a comedy, realized in the cutting room, as he often did, that his footage was melancholic—to the point where he now considered changing the title to *The Man Who Was Afraid of Women.* In Montpellier, Laura had a feeling of discomfort, almost of pain, because of "those vague cross-references between the story and life; I was seventeen and I understood that even harmonious divorces were synonymous with a true emotional split."[190] The critics didn't respond to *The Man Who Loved Women* as comedy, but as a picture with "a grave, bitter, possibly despairing element."[191] This didn't prevent the reviews from being generally favorable—and unanimous in their praise of Charles Denner's performance.

When *The Man Who Loved Women* opened in April 1977, feminists attacked it as misogynistic and macho. Claire Clouot, for instance, compared it to "an inventory of spare parts exhibiting broads like veal scallops."[192] Though Truffaut found these attacks inappropriate, they did not come as a surprise. A month before the film's release, he had expressly warned Charles Denner about possible criticism and advised him on how to reply: "What are the ladies from the M.L.F. [Mouvement pour la libération des femmes] going to think? On this point, my reply would be that we didn't seek to play up to the M.L.F., but that the female roles, though numerous and episodic, are strong enough to hold their own against Bertrand Morane."[193] Truffaut here disassociated himself from what he called a "servilely feminist atmosphere."[194] It is true that his female characters fit a traditional concept of women, and that, in their diversity, they illustrate his personal fantasies and fetishes: flowing skirts, stockinged legs, preferably in black high-heeled shoes, silk underwear. But this is not so much a misogynistic objectification as a passé image of femininity and female eroticism, bearing the clear stamp of the fifties, the decade of Truffaut's youth. Wary as he was of fashion, including the fashion of feminism, Truffaut took full responsibility for an admittedly dated—but, to his mind, not negative— vision of woman. Remarking on this, Jean-Louis Bory ended his article in the *Nouvel Observateur* with the following statement: "When Bertrand's amorous body, his flesh, is buried in the ground, his love of women continues to live thanks to his book, but it is a passé love in a world where women now wear pants and wish to establish new relationships with men beyond those of a cat and bowl of cream."[195]

In spite of the controversy, *The Man Who Loved Women* was a success, attracting 325,000 viewers in Paris over a twelve-week period. Truffaut traveled with the film to the provinces and other countries, along with Charles Denner and Brigitte Fossey; the success of the film varied according to the local image of the "seducer." In Latin countries, where ostentatious womanizing is traditional, the film was by and large misunderstood, while in Germany and Scandinavian countries, this skirt-chaser's seriousness and melancholy were well received. In the United States, the response was mixed and box-office earnings mediocre. As for American critics, they seemed to have difficulty relating this film—in spite of its significance to its creator—to Truffaut's work as a whole. Six years later, Blake Edwards directed a remake of *The Man Who Loved Women,*[196] starring Burt Reynolds; his brawny self-assurance and flaunted rakishness have little in common with the kind of womanizer portrayed by Charles Denner.

Several months before the release of *The Man Who Loved Women,* on his forty-fifth birthday, François Truffaut met Marie Jaoul de Poncheville, who was soon to become his girlfriend. This beautiful thirty-year-old brunette was brought by Marie-France Pisier to the small dinner party Truffaut was throwing to mark the occasion at avenue Pierre 1er-de-Serbie. "She is my cousin from the provinces," said Marie-France Pisier as she walked in with her and Georges Kiejman. Truffaut was intrigued and instantly attracted to Marie de Poncheville, an editor at the small publishing house Tchou. She reminded him of the fictional woman played by Brigitte Fossey in his film, and he lost very little time in calling her. Marie de Poncheville lived on Place des Vosges and was raising her little daughter, Alice, on her own. Poncheville now says, "It was out of the question for me to have a romantic relationship with him."[197] Truffaut laid siege: "One evening, François rang my doorbell. I had to go out, and he said, 'It doesn't matter, I'll stay here, read the newspapers, and baby-sit for your daughter.' When I returned, he left and said to me, 'See you next Friday!' " This happened several times, and brings to mind the scene in *The Man Who Loved Women* where Bertrand Morane arranges to have a baby-sitter come to his house, with the aim of seducing her. Then one day, this game Truffaut had initiated changed into a ritualized romance. "We saw each other on specific days, but not on weekends: three days at my house, two days at his. Our relationship was rather chaotic. I was free and independent, raising my daughter. I had a certain vision of life: I was in favor of free love, as they used to say at the time."[198] Poncheville upset Truffaut's habits. Her way of life, her many friends, her outspokenness, and the fact that she didn't belong to the movie world—all these things set her apart from Truffaut's usual women friends. They addressed each other with the informal *"tu,"* enjoyed going out to the movies and theater, and made a few trips to the provinces and abroad. Truffaut, who was usually so unsociable, didn't mind attending her parties. "Life was merry. He went along; he accepted being with me in public," she explains. This relationship, which would last two years, seemed to amuse Truffaut and give him some emotional stability. But ultimately, he was a man who didn't believe couples could live harmoniously—though he also claimed to be seeking tranquillity with the "ideal" woman. "He planned out what he conceived to be happiness, with his book collections, his time for reading, his work. He hoped to be happy, but he lived in great solitude," says Marie de Poncheville. Anxious, unable to conceal his disquiet entirely, he suffered regular headaches that kept him awake at night. Something deeper was troubling him, against his will or not, and undermining any romantic relationship.

## LIVING WITH ONE'S DEAD

François Truffaut felt a strong tie with the important people in his life who were now dead. "I'm faithful to the dead, I live with them. I'm forty-five and already beginning to be surrounded by dead people."[199] Since André Bazin, who had died immediately before the first day's shoot of *The 400 Blows,* the list of his departed friends had grown—ranging from women he had loved, like Françoise Dorléac, to men he had admired, like Cocteau, whose voice Truffaut "listened to every morning for several days."[200] In January 1977, he was saddened by the death of Henri Langlois, followed by that of Roberto Rossellini six months later. These two men had been like fathers to him, initiating him into the love of films and giving him the desire and courage to make his own. When Rossellini died in Rome, one month after presiding over the Cannes Film Festival, Truffaut paid tribute, in *Le Matin de Paris,* to "the most intelligent man, with André Bazin,"[201] whom he had ever known.

Cruelly, death and cinema seemed to get on well together, Truffaut observed at the time, after seeing his second film, *Shoot the Piano Player,* again. He noted with sadness that "half the actors in it were gone": Boby Lapointe, Albert Rémy, Nicole Berger, Claude Mansart, Catherine Lutz. He missed these departed ones and refused to forget them. "Why not have the same range of feelings for the dead as for the living, the same aggressive or affectionate relationships?"[202] he asked in *L'Express.* For several years, he had wanted to use this idea, that we can and must live with the dead, as the subject of a film, and he wondered "what it would be like to show on screen a man who refuses to forget the dead."[203]

The project dated back to December 1970 and his breakup with Catherine Deneuve. At that time, Truffaut had immersed himself passionately in the novels of Henry James, a writer whom he worshipped—he had visited his homes when he was in Boston, and he collected French and English editions of his books. He asked his friend Aimée Alexandre to translate "The Altar of the Dead," a James short story written in London in 1894 which hadn't been published in France. He collected biographical data, particularly the notebooks for James's autobiographies, in which the author described his lifelong worship of his dead young fiancée. Aimée Alexandre, who was a specialist in Russian literature,[204] recommended he read some short stories by Chekhov and Tolstoy on the same theme. Also, as she had been a friend of Gaston Bachelard, she suggested he read "La Flamme d'une chandelle [The Flame of a Candle]," a marvelous short essay (published in 1961), which made quite an impression on Truffaut.

Time went by and Truffaut made his films according to plan: *Two English Girls, Such a Gorgeous Kid Like Me, Day for Night.* Then in the beginning of 1974, Henry James's story collection *The Altar of the Dead* was issued by Editions Stock, in Diane de Margerie's French translation. "In Henry James's world, the dead have a specific significance—one might almost say, usefulness. In general, they enhance the life of the living by firing the imagination through memory: the hero chooses reminiscence as opposed to future plans, ritual as opposed to action, the past as opposed to the present, defunct loves as opposed to possible loves,"[205] Diane de Margerie writes in her preface, which Truffaut annotated heavily. This was when he asked Gruault (who had just finished the *Adèle H.* script) to adapt the James short story.

Jean Gruault received his contract for "The Altar of the Dead" adaptation in July 1974. "It's not fabulous," Truffaut admitted, "but this is a trial project and if, as is my hope, the film gets made under normal conditions, we can always renegotiate our agreement."[206] Truffaut had already drawn up the main outlines for his project and envisioned an element of "suspense"[207] around the idea of a worshipped dead fiancée and a "mysterious and charismatic" hero. In passing, he recommended Gruault read two other James short stories, "The Beast in the Jungle" and "The Friends of the Friends." He intended to change the atmosphere by transposing the setting from Victorian England to a small provincial French town in the twenties; the story would be "directly linked to the memory of the First World War."[208]

Gruault spent much of 1974 rereading Henry James and immersing himself in his world. By October, he had drafted a first outline of "five acts and around twenty tableaux." In March 1975, he completed a first screenplay entitled *La Fiancée disparue* (The Vanished Fiancée), three thick notebooks crammed with details, places, and situations. Truffaut deemed it too long and complicated and asked his friend to make cuts. This was done within a month, but Truffaut was still dissatisfied. They became uneasy with each other, in part because at this time Gruault had also voiced his disappointment with *The Story of Adèle H.* On November 21, Truffaut wrote to Gruault to sort things out: "I don't always hate misunderstandings, but I don't feel we should allow our friendship to be spoiled by silences for which I'm originally responsible. First, there was my disappointment on reading your *Altar of the Dead;* secondly, there was your disappointment on seeing *Adèle* on the screen. As far as *The Altar of the Dead* is concerned, I gave you too rigid a framework for you to invent anything and you did your best. In fact I liked your work better on a second reading, I had it typed and I'm getting ready to revise it with Suzanne before submitting the fourth version to you."[209]

During this whole period, Jean Gruault was not entirely free, for he was writing the screenplay of *Mon Oncle d'Amérique* with Alain Resnais. As a result, the project of *La Fiancée disparue* was almost shelved. Truffaut looked elsewhere, reread all the volumes of Proust's *Remembrance of Things Past,*[210] and threw himself into Japanese literature, primarily Tanizaki. He asked Koichi Yamada, his Japanese correspondent, to help him find references to the cult of the dead in Japanese literature. He also consulted Eric Rohmer, and sent him "The Altar of the Dead." But it failed to inspire the director of *Claire's Knee.* Truffaut also requested help for the "religious" scenes from the two film enthusiast friends he had met through Bazin—the Jesuit Jean Mambrino and the Dominican Guy Léger. This research shows Truffaut's attachment to this theme but also his hesitation in using it for a film.

Gruault's script remained in a file at Les Films du Carrosse for almost two years. It was only when he was getting ready to shoot *The Man Who Loved Women* that Truffaut decided to work on it again. Deliberately, he set out to refocus the story around a hopeless romantic relationship between Julien Davenne—the man obsessed by the idea that one must live with the dead—and Cécilia, a young woman who is prepared to join him in his cult of the dead because of her love for him. Truffaut also introduced other characters and places that aren't in the James short stories, the young deaf-mute, who is both confidant and wild child, and the quaint magazine *Le Globe*, for which Davenne writes the obituaries.

In mid-October 1976, Truffaut related his ideas to Gruault, who accepted them and went back to work with enthusiasm. In the meantime, Truffaut filmed *The Man Who Loved Women*. In February 1977, a new version of the script was ready, with a number of possible titles: *The Departed Fiancée, The Unfinished Figure, The Mountain of Fire, Those We Haven't Forgotten, Those We Have Loved, The Last Flame, The Others, Them, The Fête of Memory*. Upon reading this new version, Truffaut sent Gruault a telegram from Bombay, where he was filming additional scenes for *Close Encounters of the Third Kind*. "The screenplay is magnificent and I'm very pleased."[211] After some work with Suzanne Schiffman, the final draft was completed in late May 1977. The title was yet to be found, since no one felt happy with any of those suggested.

Truffaut cast Nathalie Baye as Cécilia, the heroine of the film. After her first screen appearance in *Day for Night* and a small part in *The Man Who Loved Women*, Baye had acted opposite Philippe Léotard in Maurice Pialat's *La Gueule ouverte*. She looks back on *La Chambre verte* (*The Green Room*) as an important film for her. "If François asked me to perform with him, it was because he knew I wasn't the kind of actress who caused problems. He could rely on me, which was very reassuring to him,"[212] she says. She would indeed be playing opposite Truffaut in the film, for he had decided to play the part of Julien Davenne himself, after briefly considering Charles Denner, who was not available. But Truffaut was afraid of appearing too old for the part. This so obsessed him that he consulted his hairdresser, who recommended a wig, which he ultimately didn't use. He hoped that by playing the part himself he would give the film a more intimate, authentic quality. "This film is like a handwritten letter," he said. "If you write by hand, the letter won't be perfect, the handwriting might be a bit shaky, but it will be you, your handwriting."[213] Truffaut feared that Julien Davenne might seem ridiculous, even pathetic—a madman with morbid passions. This was another reason why he decided to play the part himself. "He didn't want anyone to stand between him and Julien Davenne, for this undertaking was too intimate," Nathalie Baye confirms. The actress remembers that Truffaut sometimes had severe doubts: "He would say to me, 'It's madness; it will never work!' And he came close to wanting to stop everything."[214]

In addition to Truffaut and Nathalie Baye, the cast includes Jean Dasté (in the part of the *Globe* editor), Antoine Vitez (as a stern clergyman in a short but intense scene), Jean-Pierre Moulin (a widower whom Davenne comforts at the beginning of the film), and Patrick Maléon (a young deaf-mute actor in the part of Julien Davenne's protégé). Some Carrosse technicians and collaborators also make an appearance: Josiane Couëdel, his secretary, who plays a nurse; Martine Barraqué, his editor, who also plays a nurse; and Annie Miller, who plays a dead woman. Lastly, Marie de Poncheville appears in a scene of the film, as the woman whom Davenne's widower friend, Mazet, takes as his second wife.

The shoot, which was in preproduction during the summer of 1977, was to take place in Honfleur. Truffaut asked Nestor Almendros to exploit the contrast between electric light and a flood of candlelight to give the film a ghostly quality. On October 11, 1977, Truffaut began shooting in the Maison Troublet, a beautiful four-story old residence on rue Eugène Boudin. Since the shoot was to last only thirty-eight days and the film had only a 3-million-franc budget, financed by United Artists, he made the most of the large Honfleur house and used it for several sets. He repeated what he had done for *Adèle H.*, and, with the help of François Porcile and Patrice Mestral, prerecorded music taken from the *Flemish Concert* by Maurice Jaubert, a composer who had died at the front in 1940. Truffaut played the music on the set during the takes to help the actors and technicians get into the ritualized, quasi-religious atmosphere of the film. "It's not surprising to find, in the sudden explosive tension and somber conviction of his acting, a direct echo of Jaubert's style, with its gathering momentum and sudden restraint, its reticence and violence,"[215] wrote François Porcile. Several scenes were shot in exteriors; four days were spent in the Caen cemetery, three in the Honfleur auction room, and five inside the Carbec chapel, a small marvel of religious architecture discovered in Saint-Pierre-du-Val, near Pont-Audemer. Inside the chapel, in a set designed by Jean-Pierre Kohut-Svelko and among scores of candles set up by Nestor Almendros, Truffaut placed his personal photos, the faces of departed friends whose memory he was thereby perpetuating. Hence, the figures in Julien Davenne's life are the people in Truffaut's: Audiberti, Cocteau, Queneau, Jeanne Moreau and her sister, Louise de Vilmorin, Aimée Alexandre, Oskar Werner, and Oscar Lewenstein (the producer of *The Bride Wore Black*); there are also portraits of admired writers and musicians, such as Proust, Oscar Wilde, Henry James, Guillaume Apollinaire, Prokofiev, and Maurice Jaubert and his orchestra.

The making of *The Green Room* was in no way gloomy. In fact, it was festive, one of Truffaut's most joyful shoots. "We laughed a lot; we often had irrepressible laughing fits before takes," recalls Nathalie Baye, "so much so that Suzanne Schiffman sometimes had to reprimand us."[216] Marie de Poncheville, who used to join Truffaut in Honfleur on weekends, confirms that "Nathalie had a contagious laugh, like bells ringing!"[217] Truffaut played his part in an expressionless, nearly mechanical way, which inevitably put constraints on Nathalie Baye, who had to adjust her own acting and intonations accordingly. Simultaneously in front of and behind the camera, Truffaut was of no great help to her. Though she has a very happy memory of the shoot, she admits that she sometimes felt alone and missed the presence of a "real" director, more alert to her needs.

By March 1978, Truffaut was ready to show *The Green Room* to his friends. Not since *Two English Girls* was he so showered with praise. "Of all your films it is the one that most moved me and spoke to me, along with *Two English Girls*," Isabelle Adjani wrote. "I felt good crying in your presence."[218] "*The Green Room*, along with Clément, Visconti and very few others, is part of my secret garden,"[219] Alain Delon wrote him with sincerity. "I found your film deeply moving. I found you deeply moving in your film,"[220] said Eric Rohmer. "I haven't yet told you the emotion I felt on seeing *The Green Room*," Antoine Vitez wrote him. "What I see in it, deep down, is kindness, and that's what touches me most. Thank you for having included me in it."[221]

Except for François Chalais in *Le Figaro*, the critics were all in agreement. "In its simple and pure line, it resembles a cinematic testament. There will be other Truffaut films, but none that will ever be more intimate, more personal, more wrenching that this *Green Room*, altar of the dead,"[222] wrote Jean-Louis Bory in *Le Nouvel Observateur*. This reception marked a period of accomplishment and fulfillment.

## THE EMPTY ROOM

The release of *The Green Room*, on April 5, 1978, brought this state of grace to an abrupt end. It was a dismal failure commercially and Truffaut felt deeply hurt and disappointed. Though he was under no illusions about the odds of a hit, he had hoped the film would at least draw an audience of film lovers. "I don't want admiration, that doesn't interest me. But I want the audience to be really drawn in by the film for an hour and a half. Because I think this kind of theme can touch a deep chord in many people. Everyone has their dead,"[223] he wrote several weeks before the film's release. Truffaut was mistaken. Anticipating the difficulties, he put all his energies—even more than usual—into promoting the film. He wrote the press kit himself, saw to the poster and trailer, planned interviews with journalists and trips around the country. He even attended many of the press screenings prior to the film's release to try to convince reticent critics. He hired the best press agent, Simon Misrahi, a die-hard movie lover who had the reputation of being able to win over the most stubborn journalists. With the help of Misrahi and his collaborator, Martine Marignac, Truffaut attempted the impossible—to convince the public to go see a film on the cult of the dead.

Sensing failure, he decided to change strategies several days before the premiere and deliberately conceal the subject matter of the film, stressing instead his own reputation, the presence of Nathalie Baye, and the film's novel-like atmosphere. Hence he asked Michel Drucker, who was preparing a television broadcast in which *The Green Room* would be promoted, to include only two clips from the film, "which had the advantage of not mentioning death or the dead and presenting four of the film's protagonists."[224] Nonetheless, the public stayed away, refusing to associate François Truffaut's image with what they considered a morbid work. With slightly over thirty thousand tickets sold, the film was a commercial flop comparable to *Two English Girls*. It was more like *"The Empty Room!"*[225] Truffaut wrote to his musical adviser, François Porcile.

Deeply distressed, Truffaut accepted full responsibility for this failure, and even regretted that he had played the part of Julien Davenne: "Charles Denner would have been better than I,"[226] he said in *Paris-Match*, announcing his intention of never acting again for other directors, and of not playing in his own films for the next ten years. On May 10, 1978, he confessed to Annette Insdorf, a young American scholar who was writing a study of his work, that his morale was extremely low. As always, when everything was going badly, he found his only solace in the United States, where he felt he was best understood and best appreciated. In France, the reviews were good, he said to Annette, but "they mentioned DEATH so often that they've made the film as troublesome as *Johnny Got His Gun*. Keep all this to yourself, of course, since the film still has chances in N.Y. (after the next festival), in Scandinavia and Japan."[227]

Truffaut had great expectations for *The Green Room* in Japan, believing a country so attached to funeral rites was bound to respond to the film. He also relied on the New York Film Festival in September, where he would present the film to the American public. He arrived at the festival with Marie de Poncheville, Nathalie Baye, and Helen Scott. The New York premiere was morose, but the mood picked up considerably later in the evening, at a party thrown in Truffaut's honor in a New York apartment. Miloš Forman, the Czech director who had come to live in the United States, had an apartment in the same building. Truffaut and his women friends went to join him to finish off the evening. It was a cheerful evening and, having had a joint, "François didn't have a clue what was going on,"[228] recalls Nathalie Baye.

Truffaut made no secret of a certain weariness when he confided to his New York friend Annette Insdorf that he had "made too many films in the last five years, too many, too quickly. Les Films du Carrosse gives me undeniable freedom, but at great personal cost and above all it prevents me from stopping and thinking. Every month, I turn down offers from Hollywood . . . but one day I'll let myself be tempted before becoming a *has been* [in English]."[229] Was Truffaut already a has-been at forty-six? He imparted his anxiety to a *France-Soir* journalist: "I must hurry. I'm forty-six, I'm enjoying my last years of good health. I want to make as many films as possible so I won't have any regrets later on."[230] Marie de Poncheville confirms his unease: "François was not happy with the life he was leading. He was aware that life was in perpetual flux, which drove him crazy. He hoped to be happy, but he often said he was living like a dog, inflicting things he hated on himself."[231] During that same period, on hearing that Jean-Louis Bory was suffering from severe depression, Truffaut wrote him a letter to try to comfort and help him: "Pains of anguish that are like death, the feeling of a black hole, of no longer existing, the unreality of faces in the street—I have experienced all of that, as well as the conviction that it is impossible to make others understand what one is going through, the material world slipping away, this numb emptiness. I have experienced all of that and it took me a year and a half to get over it, before finding the inner strength to bounce back; and it was three more years before I could live normally and love without mistrust."[232] And he encouraged Bory to fight the uphill struggle, to show "valor, gaiety and vitality": "I know, when the time comes, you will find the strength to fight your way back to the surface again, among us." Nine months later, on June 12, 1979, the sixty-year-old novelist and film critic would commit suicide.

During this period, Truffaut first received warnings about his health, which hardly improved his morale. Except for a recurrent ear infection and an operation on his nasal septum in 1960, he had never really worried about his health. In the last days of 1977 and the first months of 1978, Truffaut consulted Dr. Lévy at the Saint-Antoine Hospital, where he underwent colon X rays. He also suffered from sciatica and was treated by Dr. Bénichou at the Saint-Cloud Hospital. On January 20, 1978, Dr. Alexanian prescribed ten days' rest after the filming of *The Green Room*. Several months later, he consulted a cardiologist, Dr. Pauly-Laubry at the Saint-Joseph Hospital; after a complete and satisfactory checkup, the physician put him on a diet and recommended that he exercise, walk, lose a few pounds, and follow a special regimen to reduce flatulence. Truffaut suddenly felt he was aging.

His dark mood and health problems were directly linked to the failure of *The Green Room*. His relationship with Jean Nachbaur deteriorated as well; Truffaut blamed United Artists for not having faith in the film and for not promoting it enough. The studio already had its eye on Truffaut's next film, preferring to forget the commercial failure of *The Green Room*. The director was making the same calculation: *L'Amour en fuite* (*Love on the Run*), a new Doinel film, a surefire success, would compensate for *The Green Room*'s financial loss. But on the advice of Gérard Lebovici, Berbert and he decided to do without United Artists and produce *Love on the Run*—which required a very small budget—on their own. Les Films du Carrosse would thereby get all profits. Jean Nachbaur was rather bitter and found the "maneuver rather questionable,"[233] and his reaction would only widen the rift between the two men.

The United Artists coproduction arrangement dated back to 1967 and *The Bride Wore Black.* It had allowed Truffaut to make eleven films, all financed by French or European subsidiaries of the Hollywood majors, United Artists, Columbia, or Warner, and benefit from virtually complete artistic freedom. From then on, Carrosse had to find other ways of financing Truffaut's films, relying primarily on French television and, to a certain extent, on advance foreign sales. The visionary Gérard Lebovici played a decisive role in working out this new strategy; he convinced Truffaut and Berbert to do without the American studios. Lebovici was on the point of becoming a producer and distributor himself; he had left Artmédia (whose management he had entrusted to Jean-Louis Livi) and created his own company, A.A.A. (standing for *"Auteurs Artistes Associés"*). Lebovici and the many companies he controlled (in production, distribution, sale of video rights, and foreign film export through Roissy Films, the company managed by Alain Vannier) were consolidating a strong empire covering the entire spectrum of the French film industry. A loyal friend of Lebovici, Truffaut was at the heart of this new structure, even if it was out of the question for him to give up his independence.[234]

## LOVE ON THE RUN

The commercial failure of *The Green Room* forced Truffaut to put off temporarily projects that were dear to his heart. He decided to postpone the filming of *L'Agence Magic,* though the screenplay, written by Claude de Givray and Bernard Revon, was at a very advanced stage. After *Day for Night,* his film about cinema, he wanted to make one about the milieu of variety theater, as part two of a triptych that would later include a film about theater. *L'Agence Magic* is about a small troupe of variety artists who go on an adventurous tour to Senegal in order to solve their financial difficulties. "François's idea was that the troupe had to be endangered,"[235] Claude de Givray says in summary. The film would follow several characters, young and not so young; show their family ties and romantic relationships, their petty jealousies within the troupe and their personal secrets; a love story between Leslie, a young girl, and an older man, Charles-Henri, nicknamed "the Dauphin"; the troupe's difficulty in finding a theater and their life in a shabby Dakar hotel. Leslie shoots and kills Charles-Henri because he no longer loves her. To avoid cliché, Truffaut had asked his screenwriters to draw inspiration from a news item describing how a man who had just been stabbed got up in normal fashion, walked to the refrigerator, opened it, drank some milk out of the bottle, walked back, and collapsed on his bed. At the end of the story, Leslie's mother, Viviane, turns herself in to the police as the murderess: "Since she was older, she would be entitled to greater leniency and less of a punishment. In any case, she was to blame for Leslie committing this act, for she should have brought her up differently,"[236] is the comment at the end of the seventy-page script. "We had taken inspiration from Michael Curtiz's *Mildred Pierce,* in which a mother, played by Joan Crawford, takes the blame for the murder committed by her daughter, played by Ann Blyth,"[237] Givray adds. But in the end, Truffaut didn't feel like going to Africa, which would have entailed an exhausting shoot. He preferred to put off the project, requesting that his two screenwriters rework the script, since the same story could take place during the Occupation in the unoccupied south of France.

In desperation, and eager to shoot a film quickly, Truffaut decided to go back to his mascot, Antoine Doinel. In his mind, *Love on the Run* was merely an "occasional" film, the opportunity to erase the failure of *The Green Room* and pull himself out of his depression. The film is deliberately structured as the last episode in the adventures of Antoine Doinel; all the stages in a man's life (youth, marriage, first adulterous affair, and divorce) are recapitulated, using many clips from the first four Doinel films. The idea of a film as "a kind of mosaic, the story of a life,"[238] seemed amusing and exciting to Truffaut, who didn't realize at first that it would turn out to be more complex—and even, at times, more agonizing—than anticipated.

At first, to justify the flashback structure, Truffaut considered using psychoanalysis as a narrative mainspring. Stretched out on the couch, Antoine Doinel would recount his life to a psychoanalyst, while scenes from *The 400 Blows, Love at Twenty, Stolen Kisses,* and *Bed and Board* would file by, like someone's memories. Marie-France Pisier would be cast as the psychoanalyst and Léaud as her depressed patient. But finally Truffaut rejected psychoanalysis as a conceit. Even though he had read Bruno Bettelheim for *The Wild Child* and had paid occasional visits to René Held during a difficult period of his life, the discipline was mysterious to him, and he didn't feel competent to use it as subject matter. He was afraid using a psychoanalyst might seem artificial, a concession to one of the fashions of the day. Marie-France Pisier, who collaborated on the screenplay with Suzanne Schiffman, then suggested making Colette a lawyer, with the story revolving around Colette and Antoine's amorous reunion, fifteen years after their flirtation at the youth concert. Antoine recounts his life to Colette during a train trip; she is on her way to another city to defend a client when he runs into her. They fall into each other's arms and the Doinel cycle has a happy ending: Antoine's first great love finally finds fulfillment fifteen years later. Suzanne Schiffman even suggested going one step further and revealing Doinel as a screen character. "This scene is the last scene in the film," she wrote at the end of the synopsis intended for Truffaut. "Antoine pursues Colette down the hallways, runs down the stairs after her and catches up with her, of course. At first, he has trouble calming her down, but since he loves her and she loves him, it will all end well with a final kiss. This is when F.T. enters the shot: he isn't convinced by this end, he shot it because Jean-Pierre and Marie-France wanted it, but he would like to think about it until the next day and try an alternate ending. The assistant comes up to François, who confirms that they will be shooting again the next day. While he goes around convening the crew for the next day, Jean-Pierre and François walk away gesticulating in heated conversation, their silhouettes etched against the light of the hallway leading to the street. THE END."[239] For Truffaut, this conceit was too similar to the one used at the end of *Day for Night*. Marie-France Pisier and Suzanne Schiffman set to work again, helped by Jean Aurel, the "structure specialist." The fact was, Truffaut didn't know how to part with Antoine Doinel. "The more I know him, the less I can make him do anything surprising,"[240] he said. He was willing to keep the reunion with Colette, but not her love story with Antoine. He thus invented a new female character, Sabine, a twenty-year-old woman attracted by Doinel's romanticism. This would be the romantic focus of the film, to avoid having *Love on the Run* find all its energy in the past. Truffaut thought of a new, modern female figure, "a young woman of her time,"[241] and in the part he cast Dorothée, the hostess of a Wednesday-afternoon children's television program, *Récré A2*. In fact, he found Dorothée by watching television. He contacted her on May 8, 1978, scarcely three weeks before the beginning of the filming. The young woman accepted his offer enthusiastically. The gamble of *Love on the Run* rested, in part, on this surprising choice.

A proofreader in a printing house, Antoine Doinel has an affair with Sabine, a saleswoman in a record store. He divorces Christine "by mutual consent"; their son, Alphonse, has grown since *Bed and Board*. In taking Alphonse to the station, Antoine runs into Colette, who has become a lawyer and is on her way to Aix-en-Provence, where she is to defend a case in court. Unexpectedly, at the last moment, Antoine boards the train to be with Colette, who just happens to be reading *Les Salades de l'amour* (*Love and Other Troubles*), the autobiographical novel Doinel was writing at the end of *Bed and Board*. She has bought it from Xavier, the bookseller with whom she is in love. Antoine recounts his life to Colette and tries to seduce her once again. Of course, Colette refuses.

Truffaut found the entire story rather implausible; he considered his script "flimsy, and very hard to improve upon,"[242] though he was about to shoot it. "François hated this project very early on," confirms Marie-France Pisier. "This film was certainly not a happy experience for him. He knew it would be the last Doinel film; but at the same time, he very much wanted Jean-Pierre to work again. He also felt that, with age, Antoine Doinel was becoming less credible because of his unidentifiable social status, and yet to give him a status would be a betrayal of the character's spirit."[243] Truffaut was perfectly aware of the fact that he was giving Jean-Pierre Léaud a poisoned gift, and this made him feel guilty and distressed. For it was risky for the actor to be playing a thirty-five-year-old whom the public was bound to see as antisocial—a person who doesn't drive, doesn't keep fit, and has no real profession. Doinel is "always on the run, always late, a young man in a rush. . . . Antoine should stop . . . running away . . . he should take advantage of the present . . . should stop settling a score with his mother through every girl he meets. . . ."[244] Truffaut wrote to Alain Souchon, requesting that the singer compose a song for the film.

When Truffaut did some final work on the dialogue with Suzanne Schiffman in April 1978, he was in a sullen mood. His relations with Suzanne were tense; and she remembers "ghastly arguments."[245] Feeling trapped, Truffaut wanted to give up or postpone the shoot, which was impossible because of the commitments of the actors and technicians. Marie-France Pisier was free only in June, since she was to start work on André Téchiné's *The Brontë Sisters* immediately afterward. Aside from the family of characters from the Doinel films—Jean-Pierre Léaud, Claude Jade, Dani, Marie-France Pisier, and Rosy Varte—to which he had added Dorothée and Daniel Mesguich (the bookseller Colette is in love with), Truffaut developed a character that had only been glimpsed at in one of the scenes of *The 400 Blows*—Monsieur Lucien, the lover of Antoine Doinel's mother, whom he surprises on Place Clichy. In Truffaut's first film, Jean Douchet, a *Cahiers du cinéma* critic, made a furtive appearance in the part. This time, the character has greater substance, thanks to the actor Julien Bertheau, who has an unforgettable scene, sitting opposite Antoine at a table in a café, not far from the cemetery where Madame Doinel has been laid to rest. Monsieur Lucien admits to Antoine that his mother "was a little bird," a passionate woman and an anarchist. Doinel becomes reconciled with his mother, at least with his memory of her, thereby giving a more poetic, or at least positive, image to the unworthy mother of *The 400 Blows*. This reconciliation, of course, owes a great deal to Truffaut's discovery, right after his mother's death, of the many documents among her belongings that proved her genuine attachment to him.

Beginning on May 29, 1978, the filming of *Love on the Run* lasted only twenty-eight days, for the most part in Paris. The editing, on the other hand, required time, given the complexity of the story, which is interwoven with flashback clips. Alain Souchon and Laurent Voulzy composed the lyrics and music of the film's title song, "L'amour en fuite." "I'm very, very pleased with your song," Truffaut wrote Souchon. "The film is a letter, your song is the envelope for the letter; it frames it. Doinel was always seeking a family, he is happy to play sponger at Souchon's."[246] The answer print was ready just after Christmas, after five months of editing and mixing. The commercial release was scheduled for January 24, 1979. Truffaut remained unconvinced by his film, certain he was "heading straight into a wall."[247] Fortunately, he was relieved by the first reviews. François Chalais, in *Le Figaro,* described a "romantic patchwork" and commented gently, "How time flies. . . ."[248] Jacques Siclier hailed "the collected Antoine Doinel" in an article in *Le Monde* that greatly moved the director.[249] "If I didn't know you, I wouldn't be writing this letter," Truffaut replied. "I'd be happy to just be happy! But we first met, when? About twenty, twenty-five years ago and I associate you with Teisseire, Gauteur, Claude de Givray, all of Doinel's cousins. And why not tell you the truth? After having had so many doubts during five months of editing, it's a real pleasure to feel I've been understood, yes, simply understood."[250]

He also felt reassured by the commercial fate of the film, since *Love on the Run* attracted 250,000 viewers during a three-month Paris run. For the Carrosse, this meant an excellent return on their investment. But Truffaut still felt that *Love on the Run* was a mistake. It would be one of the films that he would always hate to see again, along with *The Bride Wore Black* and *Fahrenheit 451*. His permanent emancipation from Antoine Doinel, a screen persona he had created and lived with for twenty years and who had been seen the world over, made Truffaut feel lonelier, almost like an orphan. For the first time in his life, he said he was a bit weary of making films. On February 12, 1979, when he was invited to be the editor of "Journal inattendu" on radio station RTL, Truffaut declared, unperturbed, "I have no project for the time being. And I'm not looking for one. I've decided to take a bit of a rest, after much strain and worry."[251]

# 8.
# THE UNFINISHED FIGURE:
# 1979–1984

After *The Green Room,* a box-office flop, and *Love on the Run,* which Truffaut wasn't pleased with, Carrosse needed a project that would be large and ambitious enough to reenergize it. Truffaut wasn't ready to shoot *L'Agence Magic,* for he felt the screenplay needed further development, and his friend Claude de Givray was still working on the script for *La Petite Voleuse* (The Little Thief). This was a long-standing project, since Truffaut had already referred to it in a letter to Helen Scott in November 1964: "*La Petite Voleuse,* a bit like Ingmar Bergman's *Monika,* the onset of femininity and flirtatiousness in a delinquent girl, a female version of *400 Blows,*"[1] loosely inspired by the story told him by one of his first mistresses, whom he had seen again in October 1965. "She has become a bit ugly, like me," he wrote a year later to Helen Scott, and she's done time in prison, has three kids . . . and a bit of everything."[2] The story of *La Petite Voleuse* takes place in postwar Paris, around 1950. The heroine, Janine, a delinquent, could be a younger sister to Antoine Doinel. First she steals cigarettes from American soldiers; then she filches a music box, spends time in a reformatory, and has a love affair.[3]

Jean Gruault was also put to work to find a subject. First they considered adapting *Julien et Marguerite,* a story of incest during the reign of Henry IV. Then the two friends contemplated working on another project, *Petit Roi,* which had been turned down by Jean-Loup Dabadie and Milan Kundera.

But neither of these two ideas led anywhere. Truffaut then suggested to Pierre Kast—whose last film, *Le Soleil en face,* he had liked—that he write a "story for four hands."[4] Kast suggested using two episodes drawn, respectively, from Stendhal's life and Joseph Conrad's life. The first was Stendhal's love affair with Clémentine Curial. He teaches her freedom, love, passion," Kast wrote. "She lets herself be seduced, then turns against him or carries on without him, using everything he gave her and taught her. In sum, he himself will have induced her to free herself of him."[5] The second project was taken from a Conrad novel, *The Arrow of Gold,* "an incredibly beautiful subject and novel,"[6] said Kast. But Truffaut admitted that he had trouble "visualizing"[7] either of these stories and conceded that he was unfamiliar with Conrad's world. During the same period, he also considered collaborating with Francis Veber, the writer of successful comedies directed by Georges Lautner (*The Girl in the Trunk*), Yves Robert (*The Tall Blond Man* series), Philippe de Broca (*Le Magnifique*), and Edouard Molinaro (*A Pain in the A——*). In 1976, Veber directed his own first feature, *The Toy,* with Pierre Richard. Contacted by Truffaut in March 1979, Francis Veber suggested an original screenplay, *Le Garde du corps* (*The Bodyguard*), but once again, this project never got off the ground.[8]

## THEATER DURING THE NAZI OCCUPATION

On April 29, 1979, François Truffaut burst into Suzanne Schiffman's office. "Here, I've got a file on theater and a file on the Occupation. We'll do a film with both."[9] He had had the idea of working on something set during this period for around ten years. "For me, who was an adolescent at the time, the image of France cut in two, divided into Germans and Resistance fighters, is false. I see a much calmer France. One day I'll make a film about it."[10] The idea was still vague, and it involved showing the everyday life of Parisians during the Occupation. By ruling out any ideological consideration and heroic vision, Truffaut wanted to show that the French "were never so free as under the German Occupation," as Sartre had put it. Truffaut had been impressed in 1969 by a film directed by his friend Marcel Ophuls, *The Sorrow and the Pity,* and had played a part in getting it released in a Paris movie theater.[11] Truffaut considered *The Sorrow and the Pity* the first film to show this period in French history as a "nonlegendary story." In an unpublished interview, he said, "It's a film that makes one very critical of films that claim to restore the climate of the Occupation. After Ophuls's work, you can't have clowns play Vichy people or militiamen anymore. Well, maybe I'll return to this someday."[12]

In 1975, when he was writing the preface for an anthology of articles by

André Bazin, *Le Cinéma de l'Occupation et de la Résistance,* Truffaut again felt "a pressing desire to make a film on that period."[13] This is when he first conceived of combining the subjects of theater and the Occupation as the third part of a trilogy on show business: After *Day for Night,* on the cinema, there would be *L'Agence Magic,* on the music hall, and a film on the theater, which he was determined to make someday. He delved into source material, and in October 1976, he asked Jean-Loup Dabadie to read a novel that had a character he found interesting: "In a city, possibly Paris, during the Occupation, a beautiful actress continues to practice her profession, regardless of the possible presence of German officers in the audience. Her husband, a Jew who is supposed to have died or escaped, is actually hidden in the basement of the theater. Such is the basis of the story that we can see oscillating between *The Diary of Anne Frank* and *To Be or Not to Be.*"[14] He also derived inspiration from a Renoir play, *Carola,* filmed for American television by Norman Lloyd. Leslie Caron, who had a part in the film, says, "François arranged to have the play published in *L'Avant-Scène.* And then he made *The Last Métro,* whose subject is very similar to the Renoir play. They have so many points in common that Ginette Doynel and I were very surprised; we thought he could at least have given credit to Jean Renoir. When he came to see me the first time after *The Last Métro,* I told him very frankly that I thought there were resemblances with *Carola.* He was very indignant, and took my comment as a reproach. And we didn't see each other again for a year and a half."[15]

During the Christmas season of 1978, Truffaut and Suzanne Schiffman started working on the "Theater Under the Occupation" file. They gave themselves two weeks to study the press and documents from the period, the books that had been published in those years, old posters, and the memoirs of actors and directors who had worked under the Occupation.[16] Truffaut had always enjoyed reading the recollections of actors and theater people because they were teeming with details about the profession and backstage life—for example, the recollections of Alice Cocéa who was a theater director, or those of Jean Marais, *Histoires de ma vie,* which contained the episode Truffaut would use in the film where the actor chastised Alain Laubreaux,[17] the anti-Semitic critic of *Je suis partout,* who had insulted Jean Cocteau in 1941. Truffaut also had his own specific recollections of the period. He had a daily acquaintance with fear and the need for resourcefulness; he had seen many films made during the Occupation and remembered his parents' conversations about the most talked-about shows and plays. He also went to specialized bookstores—L'Envers du Miroir on rue de Seine, and Les Arcades on rue de Castiglione—and saw certain relevant films again—Lubitsch's *To Be or Not to Be* and Mankiewicz's *All About Eve.* Finally, he gathered personal recollections from his women friends—Nelly

Benedetti, for example, an actress in *The Soft Skin,* who had started her career at the Conservatoire and at the Théâtre de l'Atelier during the war. Simone Berriau, at the end of her life, confided in him, as well; a powerful personality, she had been director of the Théâtre Antoine since 1943, and Truffaut greatly admired her.

Between May and August 1979, Truffaut and Schiffman worked on the script relentlessly. A synopsis was ready by the end of May, and three weeks later, a first detailed treatment of 150 pages. In the summer, Truffaut left Paris for Villedieu, near Vaison-la-Romaine, to take up residence with Marie de Poncheville in a beautiful rental, not far from Suzanne Schiffman's vacation home. They continued working, the result being a second treatment, with dialogue, entitled *Le Dernier Métro (The Last Métro).*

The story takes place in Paris in 1942. Bernard Granger, a young actor from the Grand Guignol, comes to the Théâtre Montmartre, where a new play is being produced, *La Disparue (The Disappearance),* directed by Jean-Louis Cottins. He is hired by Marion Steiner, who is now managing the theater, as her husband, the Jewish director Lucas Steiner, has presumably fled to South America. In fact, unbeknownst to anyone, Marion is hiding Lucas in the basement of the theater. The rehearsals begin. We see Bernard's repeated rejection by Arlette, the costumer; Marion's secret attraction to Bernard, who pursues all women, except the one he dares not approach; the entrance, in the midst of rehearsal, of Daxiat—the critic from the virulently anti-Semitic paper *Je suis partout,* on whom the consent of the censors and the fate of the play depend; the ham brought by a woman dealing in the black market and which Raymond, the stage manager, hides inside a cello case. After the premiere, which is a success, events gather momentum. Daxiat attacks the show mercilessly in *Je suis partout;* Bernard insists that he present his apologies to Marion Steiner and chastises the critic publicly—which angers Marion, whose primary concern is protecting her theater. Bernard, who has witnessed the arrest of one of his friends inside a church, announces to Marion his intention of leaving the theater and joining the Resistance. On the day of his departure, they make love in Marion's office. At the Liberation, Lucas Steiner finally comes out of hiding. Marion goes to visit Bernard, who is wounded, in the hospital. Then the curtain comes down, revealing that this was the last scene in a new play directed by Steiner.

Truffaut knew he was getting ready to shoot his costliest film. Indeed, Marcel Berbert estimated the budget at around 11 million francs. Without the usual backing of an American studio, Carrosse had difficulty financing the project. Over the summer of 1979, Marcel Berbert began by demanding all the money due from creditors for the exhibition of Truffaut's previous films. This was supplemented by a sum from the Fonds d'aide (Assistance

Funds), made available to Les Films du Carrosse by the C.N.C. At the same time, Gérard Lebovici entered into negotiations with the television network TF1, for both *The Last Métro* and Alain Resnais's next film, *Mon Oncle d'Amérique*. The network decided to invest in the Truffaut film, partly for production and partly as payment for the first television screening rights. This was still insufficient financing; a big distributor had to be convinced. Marcel Berbert offered the film to the A.M.L.F. distribution company, which turned it down. Lebovici approached Gaumont, which accepted the distribution of the film in extremis and convinced the Société Française de Production, a television company, to come into the deal, as well. Even though, as Marcel Berbert put it, he felt "he had expended a lot of energy" in these negotiations, Truffaut was relieved to know he could start filming at the beginning of 1980.

In the meantime, he and Marie de Poncheville had broken up after their summer vacation in Villedieu. Very soon after returning to Paris at the end of August, Marie de Poncheville, without warning Truffaut, left for Los Angeles to join an American, whom she would later marry. "That vacation was our last attempt at establishing a close relationship," she says. "It was becoming impossible for me to live according to François's preestablished plan, in which my position was more and more limited."[18]

## ANOTHER DOUBLE

Truffaut started casting of *The Last Métro* in September 1979. He had written the part of Marion Steiner with Catherine Deneuve in mind, for he considered her ideally suited to play this vital, energetic, but distant woman on whom the whole film rested. The actress had already agreed to this cinematic reunion with Truffaut at the beginning of the summer. Ten years had gone by since *Mississippi Mermaid*. Once again, Deneuve was to play a woman named Marion. And in the last scene of *La Disparue*—the play being performed on the stage of the Théâtre Montmartre—the lines Catherine Deneuve delivers to Gérard Depardieu are almost word for word the same lines she delivers to Jean-Paul Belmondo at the end of *Mississippi Mermaid*:

> *I come to love and it hurts. Does love hurt?*
> *Yes, love hurts. It hovers over us like big birds of prey, stops and threatens us. But this threat can also be a promise of happiness. You are lovely, Eléna, so lovely that it's painful to look at you.*
> *Yesterday, you said it was a joy!*
> *It's a joy and a misery.*

At the beginning of 1979, Truffaut greeted Jean-Louis Richard at Les Films du Carrosse with the following words: "You've been my scriptwriter, I've been your producer, now I want you to be my actor."[19] He then offered him the part of Daxiat. Richard accepted, on condition that he be allowed to "give the part as much prestige as possible."[20] He would endow Daxiat with a perverse, unsettling personality, a soft voice, a physical appearance that is both childish and imposing, with flashes of near madness in his eyes.

Truffaut contacted the little Sabine of *Jules and Jim* and *The Soft Skin,* who had now become—fifteen years later—a very gifted young actress. He cast Sabine Haudepin in the part of Nadine Marsac, an ambitious young actress determined to succeed, who acts onstage at night and on film sets in the afternoon. At the end of October, Gérard Depardieu was approached to play Bernard Granger, the male lead. Depardieu was in the Vercors at the time, on the set of Bertrand Blier's *Buffet froid.* Truffaut and he got in touch through their agents, Gérard Lebovici and Jean-Louis Livi, who were very favorably disposed to this first meeting, since they were both aware that Truffaut had written the script with Depardieu in mind. Initially, Depardieu was not very enthusiastic; for him, Truffaut had a somewhat passé image. "When Gérard Lebovici and Jean-Louis Livi told me that Truffaut had me in mind, I wasn't at all thrilled. I had loved *The 400 Blows* and *The Wild Child,* but his other films less, including the Doinel films, for I thought they lacked something, perhaps a mean edge."[21] During their first meeting, the actor made no secret of his qualms to Truffaut, who rather liked his frankness. Very rapidly, the two men hit it off; they discovered true affinities. "It was even love at first sight,"[22] says Jean-Louis Livi. More than sympathy, it was the feeling of coming from the same milieu that brought them close. "I was so afraid that he wouldn't be a little hood,"[23] Depardieu said of Truffaut. Won over by the man, he accepted with alacrity the part of Bernard Granger in *The Last Métro.*

For the part of Jean-Louis Cottins, the director who replaces Lucas Steiner and rehearses the actors in *La Disparue,* Truffaut first thought of Jean-Claude Brialy, but the actor had a previous commitment to Francis Girod's film *La Banquière.* He then contacted Jean Poiret, whom he had long admired.[24] The discreet, dandyish, and fashionable homosexual was a complex part to interpret, so different from the comic roles the actor usually excelled at. Truffaut was counting on a surprise effect, bolstered by the fact that Poiret had done very little film work over the previous ten years, appearing almost exclusively on the stage. Choosing an actor for the part of Lucas Steiner was difficult for Truffaut; he felt uneasy about this type of passive, reserved person and he agonized over what was meant by "looking Jewish." He thought of Heinz Bennent, a German actor whose French was excellent, and whom he had liked in two Volker Schlöndorff films, *The Lost Honor of Katharina Blum* and *The Tin Drum,* and in Ingmar Bergman's *The*

*Serpent's Egg.* But he continued to hesitate until Suzanne Schiffman finally convinced him to cast this non-Jewish actor in the part of a Jew.

He then completed casting the parts of all the individuals who contribute to the life of a theater, the technicians and administrators working in the wings. Paulette Dubost, Lisette in *The Rules of the Game,* was to play Germaine, the dresser. Maurice Risch was cast as the stage manager. Laszlo Szabo, the mascot actor of the New Wave, who had become a director, was to play the part of Lieutenant Bergen, a German officer who is a passionate admirer of Marion Steiner. Andréa Ferréol, who made her début in Marco Ferreri's *La Grande Bouffe,* was cast as Arlette Guillaume, the costume designer, who is wooed by Bernard Granger. Marcel Berbert would make a brief screen appearance as the manager of the Théâtre Montmartre, a part resembling his role in real life. ("He handles the finances,"[25] says one of the characters in *The Last Métro.*) Finally, Richard Bohringer, who was not yet a star, was cast as a Gestapo agent.

## THE BEST NOVEL OF THE YEAR

Before starting the shoot, François Truffaut was even more nervous than usual. *The Last Métro* was an ambitious and costly film, and after a bad flop (*The Green Room*) and a moderate hit (*Love on the Run*), he very much needed a career boost. In addition, he had no other script in the works, which was unusual for him. But he was also perfectly aware that the odds were on his side—he had a star duo for the first time since *Mississippi Mermaid.* The preproduction was trying nonetheless. Suzanne Schiffman had trouble finding a theater where Truffaut could shoot the rehearsal scenes. The producers finally resolved to use the Théâtre Saint-Georges a mere two weeks before the cameras were to begin rolling. Just before Christmas, Catherine Deneuve's father, Maurice Dorléac, died, which deeply affected her. And then Truffaut felt dissatisfied with all the scenes in the screenplay involving Marion and Lucas Steiner in the basement of the Théâtre Montmartre; he found the dialogue too literary or too programmatically about "Jews under the Occupation." For a while, he considered sacrificing the character of Lucas Steiner by never showing him on screen. However, two weeks before the beginning of the shoot, he saw a play by Jean-Claude Grumberg, *L'Atelier,* at the Théâtre du Gymnase. He was impressed by the authenticity of the characters, particularly of Léon, the small-time Jewish boss of the ready-to-wear garment workshop where the play is set. Four days later, with the encouragement of Serge Rousseau, he wrote to the author: "Your Léon is sublime, he has everything that my Lucas lacks. Would you accept to kollaborate [the *k* is supposed to look German]? Lucas Steiner will be played by Heinz Bennent, a very good

German actor (*The Tin Drum*) who speaks French well, without a thick accent. The problem is, I have not known how to make him speak, or come alive. There is no doubt in my mind: the solution will flow from the tip of your pen, which is a hell of a lot better than mine."[26] Jean-Claude Grumberg accepted and, several days later, gave Truffaut rewrites of the scenes between Catherine Deneuve and Heinz Bennent, and the scenes with Daxiat. Truffaut was relieved. "I might only keep 30 or 50 percent of your dialogue," he wrote to Grumberg, "either because I prefer my own wording or because I consider it more appropriate to the two actors, but there is no doubt, for me, that the character of Lucas will be enhanced thanks to you."[27]

But other worries claimed his attention. Some rumors in the press concerning *The Last Métro*—Pierre Montaigne in *Le Figaro* alluding to a "remake of *To Be or Not to Be*"—enraged Truffaut and led him to ban journalists from his set. To prevent any leaks, he sent an internal memo to all his coworkers: "We are going to work with the aim of telling an interesting and intriguing story. I suggest that we keep this story secret and avoid talking about it to journalists. Let us even avoid describing the characters. What happens in the Théâtre Montmartre, from the basement to the attic, concerns only us . . . and the public with whom we have an appointment, but not for another nine months (inevitably). . . ."[28]

*The Last Métro* shoot, which began on January 28, 1980, was therefore shrouded in secrecy. Nestor Almendros's crew spent ten days filming the rehearsals and staging of *La Disparue*. Though available and precise in his instructions to the actors, Truffaut was tense, enduring neither quarrels nor outbursts on the set. There was a muffled atmosphere, with everyone speaking in a low voice and using the polite *"vous"* form. In his letter to Janine Bazin, Truffaut mentioned a series "of catastrophes,"[29] that had upset his work schedule and led to a serious delay. "I hope that the seven remaining weeks of filming will be calmer." Indeed, Catherine Deneuve suffered a sprain from a fall, and Suzanne Schiffman was hospitalized for several days with a serious intestinal obstruction.

Thereafter most of the filming was in a large abandoned factory, the Moreuil chocolate factory, on rue du Landy in Clichy. The space was transformed into a real studio, the cast and crew moved within four different sets designed by Jean-Pierre Kohut-Svelko—Lucas Steiner's basement, Marion Steiner's dressing room and office, the courtyard and street in front of the Théâtre Montmartre, and the exterior and interior of a Paris restaurant during the Occupation. Truffaut took full advantage of this unique site, and the filming finally picked up speed. Nestor Almendros was particularly attentive to the lighting and the colors, using a chromatic palette restricted to browns, ochers, and reds, inspired by the German films of the war period, such as

Josef von Baky's *Münchausen* and Veit Harlan's *Die goldene Stadt* (a poster for the latter can be seen in the film). This precision work on color gives the film an artificial and gentle atmosphere—making all of French life under the Occupation seem like a theatrical stage. Truffaut's progress toward studio pictures, which had started with *Adèle H.* and *The Green Room,* was now complete.

In mid-March, the cast and crew shot a few exterior scenes, first the escape of the collaborator Daxiat, in front of a house in ruins on rue Massenet in Paris, then scenes where the critic goes to the offices of his newspaper, *Je suis partout,* filmed on the premises of *Rivarol,* a right-wing satirical newspaper located in the Passage des Marais in the tenth arrondissement. Then came the sequences in Marion Steiner's hotel room, shot at the Hotel Crillon on Place de la Concorde, followed by the long scene of the actors' dinner after the successful opening night of *La Disparue,* shot in a club near Place Pigalle. Finally, the church scene where Bernard sees the arrest of a Resistance fighter by the Gestapo was shot inside Notre-Dame-des-Victoires. From March 27 until mid-April, the crew moved back into the Moreuil chocolate factory for the basement scenes. The filming of *The Last Métro,* which had lasted fifty-nine days, ended on April 21, 1980. Two days later, Truffaut flew to Beverly Hills, leaving this memo for his helpmate Jean Aurel: "I'm going to sleep in Los Angeles, I'll be back in Paris around May 12. It would be wonderful for me if you were in Paris then, free for lunch, to talk and to look at *The Last Métro,* so ramshackle in its present state."[30]

Almost as soon as he arrived in Los Angeles, Truffaut received the news of Alfred Hitchcock's death, on April 29, 1980. Immediately, "his telephone wouldn't stop ringing,"[31] says Laura, who had been living and studying in Berkeley for several months and had come to spend a few days with her father. On May second, Truffaut and Laura went to the little church on Santa Monica Boulevard, in Beverly Hills, where a Mass was held in honor of Hitchcock. This was the same church where one year earlier, "a farewell to Jean Renoir had taken place," Truffaut wrote, comparing the two ceremonies. "Jean Renoir's coffin had been placed in front of the altar. Family, friends, neighbors, film lovers and people off the street attended the ceremony. For Hitchcock it was different. There was no coffin—it had been removed to an unknown destination. The guests, who had been invited by telegram, were checked in at the door by Universal's security men. The police dispersed the crowd outside. It was the burial of a timid man who had become intimidating and who, for the first time, was avoiding publicity, since it wouldn't help his work—a man who, since his adolescence, had trained himself to be in control of the situation."[32] With the deaths of the two directors he probably most admired in the world coming so close together, Truffaut knew he would no longer have the same pleasure visiting Hollywood, as he had been doing once or twice a year for some time.

The editing of *The Last Métro* lasted four months, and throughout the entire period Truffaut was worried and doubtful about the film's success. Jean Aurel came up with the idea of changing the beginning: "In its previous version, the film started differently. Depardieu went to the theater but didn't meet the woman played by Andréa Ferréol. After discussing the matter, we placed this meeting at the very beginning of the film, which changes an unimaginable number of things. Always following the efficiency principle. The beginning became better, thanks to that scene where Depardieu makes a play for Ferréol, unaware that she's not interested in men. It's a principle of indirect narration inspired by Lubitsch."[33]

Truffaut derived great pleasure from his musical collaboration with Georges Delerue. The two men used several songs from the period, tunes that the young Truffaut had known by heart during the Occupation, one of the great periods for French street songs, such as "Mon Amant de Saint-Jean" or "La Prière à Zumba." Reactions to the first screenings in early September, for friends and later the press, were good. "I'm almost completely reassured concerning the reception the film will get in France,"[34] he wrote to Richard Roud, the director of the New York Film Festival. Indeed, rarely had he received so many positive opinions from such very different quarters—Jean-Paul Belmondo, Federico Fellini, Samuel Fuller, Jean Marais, among others. Nicolas Seydoux, the head of Gaumont, was extremely pleased as well, and he insisted on organizing a glamorous preview screening. Attended by the director and his entire cast, the screening was held in one of the most beautiful picture palaces on the Champs-Elysées, the Paris, a large theater owned by Marcel Dassault. Truffaut used the opportunity to bring together two generations of actors—those who had lived through the Occupation, such as Jean Poiret, Paulette Dubost, Yves Montand, Jeanne Moreau, Jean-Marc Thibault, Julien Bertheau, Simone Berriau, Nelly Benedetti, or Marcel Dalio, who had fled France, and the younger generation, friends of Gérard Depardieu, such as Julien Clerc, Alain Souchon, Miou-Miou, and Nathalie Baye. In the midst of it all was a radiant Catherine Deneuve in an elegant red suit. The atmosphere was warm and confident, yet Truffaut remained tense throughout the entire screening, until the lights went back on. "I went up to François, he was green: 'We're done for,' he said to me, 'they didn't like the film,' " recalled Suzanne Schiffman. "He was never pleased with a film and managed to draw you into his anxieties."[35] But the audience stood and applauded; it was a triumph. The irony was that the following day, Marcel Dassault called Truffaut to tell him that now that he had seen the film, he had changed his mind. He considered the film interesting, but he didn't feel the subject matter, Jews during the Occupation and collaboration, was appropriate for *his* theater and *his* public. He therefore wanted to cancel the run at the Paris, the principal first-run theater for the film on the Champs-Elysées. Truffaut would have to use all his diplomatic skills to dissuade him.

Almost all the reviews were favorable. But Bernard Pivot's article in *Lire* was the piece that most pleased Truffaut. Under the title "The Best Novel of the Year," the host of the television program *Apostrophes* wrote: "Soon to come out, we are told, is a novel by Tournier, a new Sagan, and the latest Rinaldi. Well no, I won't wait to have read them to let you benefit from my discovery, to tell you, indeed to shout from the rooftops, the first and last name of the magnificent novelist whose work has deeply moved, enchanted and enthralled me—to the point where I'm about to commit a crime against this magazine entirely devoted to reading, a crime against its nature and spirit. For this novelist is a movie director—François Truffaut, and his novel is a film, *The Last Métro*."[36] On the very day of the film's opening, Truffaut wrote to Laura to tell her that everything was going well, but that "what counts above all is the paying public." A decisive moment that he called, humorously, "the opening of the mine."[37]

*The Last Métro* was a smash hit. The Gaumont officials were betting on 10,000 ticket sales a day and 120,000 in the first week. "The Carrosse is keeping the calculators clicking,"[38] Truffaut wrote to Laura. The forecasts turned out to be correct: *The Last Métro* pulled in 126,000 viewers in a week, a record number for a Truffaut film. The following week brought confirmation of the audience's infatuation—so much so that the media was forced to ponder the phenomenon. An overtly classical film, dealing with a period that had not had a good reputation up until then, drew a large public, ordinary people and youth, far exceeding the audience for Truffaut's previous films. By 1980, the French were beginning to show a lively interest in the Occupation and seeking a more accurate view of their own history.[39]

## TEN CÉSARS

On January 31, 1981, *The Last Métro* triumphed at the sixth César ceremony that was held at the Palais des Congrès. Nominated in twelve categories, Truffaut's film won ten César awards, France's equivalent of the Oscar, including the most important ones—best film, best director, best actress (Catherine Deneuve), best actor (Gérard Depardieu). But it also received the prize for best screenplay (Suzanne Schiffman), best cinematography (Nestor Almendros), best sound (Michel Laurent), best editing

(Martine Barraqué), best set (Jean-Pierre Kohut-Svelko). An unqualified success in the face of no small competition—Alain Resnais with *Mon Oncle d'Amérique,* Claude Sautet with *Un mauvais fils,* Maurice Pialat with *Loulou,* and Jean-Luc Godard's return to the screen with *Sauve qui peut (la vie).* *The Last Métro,* even more than *Day for Night,* attracted the honors of the guild that recognized itself in this film, and thereby, in a way, paid homage to itself. At the end of the ceremony, Truffaut, embarrassed by so many awards, expressed his gratitude by repeating almost word for word what he had said in English seven years earlier upon receiving the Oscar for *Day for Night:* "*The Last Métro* was inspired by the life of theater people, I attribute my success to them. I will keep this César for best director at home . . . but for them."

A few days later, Catherine Deneuve and Gérard Depardieu made the cover of *Paris-Match,* "a new film couple who succeeded in touching the public's heart." With its ten Césars, *The Last Métro* was given another boost and attracted an additional 200,000 filmgoers in Paris in the five weeks following the ceremony. Truffaut certainly had no complaint, and he even thanked Georges Cravenne for creating these Oscar-inspired prizes in 1975. "Between now and the end of the month, *The Last Métro* will clear a million in tickets sales in Paris and this is due to the Césars of course. In Montreal, New York, Los Angeles and Boston, we have beaten previous records in each movie house, and the publicity, every time, was based on the ten Césars. In sum, I'm surely not the first to tell you, you were darned inspired on the day you came up with the idea of creating the Césars—and then when you had the courage to carry out your idea. I wanted to express not just my enthusiasm, but also my gratitude, and tell you that you can count on me,"[40] he wrote Cravenne.

The success of *The Last Métro* was a momentous event for Les Films du Carrosse—particularly since no one, least of all Truffaut, had suspected it would do so well. "Today people think *The Last Métro* was bound to be a 'hit' even before it was made: not true, if that had been the case, it would not have been rejected by UGC and AMLF or German coproducers . . .,"[41] he would say later, recalling the many financing difficulties he had had. The euphoria was such that "no one noticed the swastika on the poster was reversed!"[42] Marcel Berbert remembered with irony.

Eager to protect his independence as best he could, Truffaut was tough in his negotiations with TF1, in an effort to postpone the network's first broadcast of the film to as late a date as possible.[43] He even got Gaumont to agree to a second nationwide release sixteen months after the first exclusive run. On March 9, 1983, *The Last Métro* was rereleased with an extra six-minute sequence and attracted close to another 100,000 viewers.

*The Last Métro* was a smash hit abroad as well. In the United States, box-office receipts were good, with earnings of over $1 million in a nineteen-week run. The film was also nominated for both a Golden Globe and an Oscar for best foreign film. Truffaut's oeuvre was being honored worldwide, with retrospectives in Chicago, London, and Lausanne, and subsequently in San Sebastian and Tokyo. In Florence, Truffaut received the Visconti prize for lifetime achievement, given to him during the David of Donatello ceremony—the Italian equivalent of the Oscars and Césars.

*The Last Métro*'s triumph in France did provoke a backlash in the press and in the profession. Two days after the César ceremony, Dominique Jamet wrote a scathing editorial on the first page of *Le Quotidien de Paris*. "On seeing Truffaut and his friends stagger under the weight of the ugly little objects with which we honor great success in the seventh art and wander off under the slightly bitter gazes of Jean-Luc, Claude, Alain, and the others, we couldn't help feeling uneasy. This was giving Truffaut the sole monopoly on talent, elevating him to the status of Commander of French cinema, Boss of the industry, indeed Godfather of the guild. If this were the case, we would have grounds for deploring the extreme poverty of French cinema. Just as one swallow doesn't make a summer, one man doesn't populate a desert."[44] Several months later, Alain Rémond in *Les Nouvelles littéraires* accused Truffaut of having joined the ranks of the "quality cinema" which he himself used to denounce. "It rolls along smoothly, it works, it takes not the slightest risk. This change in Truffaut does not date from today. The auteur has been left behind. It's a bit sad."[45]

Truffaut was not impervious to these attacks. Of course, he was a man who liked success, a necessary condition to his independence as a director and producer. He also made it a rule to accept only prizes related to his profession. Hence, based on this principle, he had turned down the Légion d'honneur and other awards. Truffaut had accepted the ten Césars because they had been awarded by his peers, but he had been embarrassed by the landslide, especially vis-à-vis directors he admired like Resnais, Sautet, and Pialat. And he was most embarrassed at being made into the "boss of French cinema." Though he refused to be on the fringes like Godard, his greatest wish was to remain an independent craftsman.

More than a director, Truffaut had primarily become a symbol, linking French cinema's different, indeed conflicting, families, tendencies, and clans. The number of screenplays he received at Les Films du Carrosse after the success of *The Last Métro* attests to this fact. In 1980 and 1981, over two hundred projects were dropped off at rue Robert-Etienne, a large number of them originating on the other side of the Atlantic. Many were written by eager young people seeking a godfather and a mentor.

## SAUVE QUI PEUT (L'AMITIÉ) . . .
## OR SALVAGING A FRIENDSHIP

It was also around this time that Jean-Luc Godard tried to reestablish a relationship with François Truffaut. After their falling out in 1973, the former friends saw each other only once, when they accidentally met in the same hotel in New York. "François refused to shake my hand," Godard recalls. "We ended up waiting for a taxi on the same sidewalk and he pretended not to see me."[46] At the end of the seventies, they kept up a dialogue only via the press. "I don't think François knows how to make films at all. He made one film that truly expressed him, *The 400 Blows,* and that was it: afterward, he merely told stories," Godard inveighed in a *Télérama* interview in July 1978. "Truffaut is a usurper. . . . If he could get into the Académie française, I'm sure he would. . . ."[47] Truffaut didn't react at the time. Then on August 19, 1980, Godard sent a letter to his old companions Truffaut, Jacques Rivette, and Claude Chabrol, suggesting that the three New Wave veterans get together with him in Rolle, Switzerland, where he was residing. He had just completed *Sauve qui peut (la vie)*, with Isabelle Huppert, Nathalie Baye, and Jacques Dutronc, his return to film after several years of political activism and experimentation with video. Chabrol was then finishing *Le Cheval d'orgueil,* based on the book by Pierre-Jakez Hélias, and Rivette, *Le Pont du nord,* starring Pascale Ogier. The only thing these films had in common was their release at around the same time as *The Last Métro.* "Couldn't we stage a 'conversation'?" Godard wrote to his old cohorts. "Whatever our differences, I would be interested in finding out viva voce what's become of our cinema. We could surely find a 'moderator' whom we would all approve of. We could make it into a book for Gallimard or some other house. Personally, I'm all set to invite you to Geneva for a day or two. If feasible, I'd love to show you my 'location.' While a reunion of just two of us might be felt as too explosive; with four of us there should be a way of underplaying the differences in potential so some connections could get through. Best regards anyhow."[48]

This time, Truffaut decided to break his silence:

Your invitation to Switzerland is extraordinarily flattering knowing how precious your time is. So now that you've put the Czechs, Vietnamese, Cubans, Palestinians and Mozambicans back on the right track, you will turn solicitously to reeducating the last outpost of the New Wave. I hope this plan of unloading a hasty book on Gallimard isn't a sign you now don't give two hoots about the Third World. Your letter is terrific and your pastiche of political style very convincing.

The finale of your letter is sure to remain one of your best touches, "Best regards anyhow." So you don't hold against us the fact that you called us crooks, dregs and scum. . . . As far as I'm concerned, I agree to come see your location—what a pretty expression . . . when I think of all the hypocrites who would just say my house—but it's a privilege I'd like to share with others, let's say four or five people who could receive your word and then spread it around everywhere. I therefore request that you invite Jean-Paul Belmondo at the same time as me. You said he was afraid of you and it may be time to reassure him. I'd also very much like Vera Chytilova to be present, whom you denounced as "revisionist" in her own country just at the time of the Soviet occupation. Her presence at our colloquium seems to me necessary, for I'm certain you would help her to obtain an exit visa. Why neglect Loleh Bellon, whom you called a real bitch in *Télérama*. Finally, don't forget Boumboum, our old friend Braunberger, who wrote me the day after your phone call: " 'Dirty Jew' is the only insult I can't tolerate." I'm not excessively impatient as I wait for your reply, for if you're becoming a Coppola groupie, you might be short on time and you should by no means hastily throw together the preproduction work on your next autobiographical film, whose title I think I know: *Once a Shit Always a Shit.*[49]

Truffaut also took advantage of a long interview in *Cahiers du cinéma* to set the record straight. It was an opportunity for him to seal his reunion with *Cahiers* after a long period of estrangement.[50] He assessed his career, discussed his relations with the public, with other directors, with people from the past, with actors, and with the United States. He also stated what he now found difficult to endure: solitude, nonconformism, and . . . Godard, who "belongs to a group of convulsively envious people." This time, the attack was not only private but also public, and it was radical. "Even at the time of the New Wave, friendship was a one-way thing for him. Since he was very talented and already clever at attracting pity, we used to forgive his pettiness, but, everyone will tell you, he already had his slippery side, which he now can't conceal. He had to be helped all the time, you had to do him favors and could expect an underhanded blow in return."

Aside from settling the score with Godard, Truffaut defined his ethics as a director, discussed his love and angst in making films, his abiding by rules of conduct he had set for himself since the beginning of his career—his not wanting other people to lose money, his refusal to pose as an artist, or to criticize those who had had less luck than he in their work. He situated himself at the center of French cinema, or rather "at the extreme center,"[51] independent though working within the system: This was the place Truffaut jealously wished to keep; he constantly dreaded appearing the head of a clique, or, worse still, the cornerstone of the French film industry.[52] He refused, for example, to preside over the Société des réalisateurs de films (Society of Filmmakers), when asked by Marcel Ophuls and Luc Moullet, who were then secretaries general of that organization. He reasserted his independence in a letter to Claude Autant-Lara, who accused him of having "all the powers in French film," stressed his voluntary isolation, and justified himself in these terms: "Anyone could give you confirmation of this—I'm not power-hungry. I have refused to accept the directorship of the *Avance sur recettes* [government subsidy—advance on box-office receipts], the presidencies of the Cinémathèque française and the Société des réalisateurs de films, or to sit on any jury since 1962, or to make the fate of a project depend on my personal taste, or to let my freedom be compromised. I have never made the slightest attempt to seize power in any institution whatsoever, for, as Serge de Gainsbourg would put it, '*J'en ai rien à cirer* [I couldn't give a flying fart].' "[53]

"My only tactic is alternating, shooting a very low-budget film after each costly film, so that I won't be drawn into an escalation that leads to serious concessions, megalomania and unemployment,"[54] said Truffaut to his *Cahiers* interviewers when they quizzed him about his projects after *The Last Métro*. His next film would therefore be in stark contrast to his latest hit. After a period film, he would direct a contemporary film; after one of his longest and costliest shoots, the next one would be among his quickest, and its budget among the most modest. He would abandon historical fresco and classical narrative and return to the intimate journal style to tell a story bordering on madness.

## NEITHER WITH YOU NOR WITHOUT YOU

In December of 1979, Truffaut, like a million of his countrymen, had been captivated by a series of five televised episodes on Antenne 2, *Les Dames de la côte* (The Ladies of the Coast), produced by Mag Bodard and directed by Nina Companeez. This historical saga covered a good part of the twentieth century through the fortunes and misfortunes of a French family. It had an illustrious cast—Edwige Feuillère, Françoise Fabian, Martine Chevalier, Evelyne Buyle, and Francis Huster. The female lead was played by Fanny Ardant, a thirty-year-old stage actress who had had very few prior screen appearances. Laura Truffaut, who was vacationing in Paris at the time, recalls being with her father at Avenue Pierre 1er-de-Serbie when they saw the first episode of *Les Dames de la côte*. "I saw my father charmed the first time he saw Fanny Ardant on television; he was really bowled over."[55] Confessing to "television love at first sight,"[56] Truffaut wrote to Ardant at the end of December, suggesting they meet at Les Films du Carrosse.

Their first meeting took place when Truffaut was getting ready to shoot *The Last Métro.* "The next film will be for you," he promised Ardant. They saw each other regularly thereafter, eating lunch together at the *boulangerie* on the corner of rue Marbeuf and rue Robert-Etienne, one of the director's favorite spots. They discussed his next film, which was already being written, and got to know each other. The daughter of a colonel in the cavalry, born in Saumur, Fanny Ardant first followed her father in his various missions around Europe, in Sweden, for instance, where Colonel Ardant was military attaché, then, in the sixties, in Monaco, where he was one of the advisers to Prince Rainier's personal guard. His daughter's education was in the pure aristocratic tradition, "à la Don Quixote," as Ardant would put it. Even though the family was not very wealthy, she lived in high style—private schools, good French lycées abroad, formal balls, and horse races. At twenty, she followed a three-year course of study in political science in Aix-en-Provence, where she wrote a paper on surrealism and anarchy. She then went to live in Paris after a short stay in London. But in the mid-seventies, she was lured away from the university by the theater. After taking an acting course at the Ecole Perimoni, she started to get her first parts. She played Pauline in Corneille's *Polyeucte,* produced as part of the 1974 Festival du Marais in Paris; then she was cast in Montherlant's *Le Maître de Santiago,* Racine's *Esther,* Giraudoux's *Electra,* Paul Claudel's *Tête d'or.* Finally, in 1978, she was noticed in a television drama based on Balzac, *Les Mémoires de deux jeunes mariées* (The Memoirs of Two Young Newlyweds). The following year, Mag Bodard and Nina Companeez gave her the lead role in *Les Dames de la côte.*[57]

On the evening of the César awards, January 31, 1981, Truffaut's first impression of the actress was reinforced. During the traditional supper at Fouquet's following the ceremony, Truffaut was surrounded by all the actors from *The Last Métro:* "Fanny Ardant came to join us, Gérard Depardieu and me, at our table. When I saw them together, it became plain to me that they were to be my lovers."[58] He was referring to the lovers in the script that he had started working on "clandestinely."[59] The desire to cast them together impelled him to speed up the preproduction work on this new film; he started drafting the dialogues daily and on weekends. Later, in talking about Fanny Ardant, Truffaut would admit that he had been seduced "by her large mouth, her deep voice and its unusual intonations, her big black eyes and her triangular face."[60] He liked the vitality of her acting, her enthusiasm and humor, her "penchant for secrecy, her distant, slightly unsociable side, and, above all, her vibrancy."[61]

The theme of *La Femme d'à côté* (*The Woman Next Door*) dated far back in Truffaut's work program, as was true for most of his films. "I could give royalties to Catherine Deneuve," he said in jest to Claude de Givray during their taped interviews in June 1984. For the screenplay of *The Woman Next Door* was inspired, in large part, by his amorous relationship with the actress. Truffaut had even written five pages at the end of 1972, a first synopsis entitled "*Sur les rails* (On the Rails)," the story of two former lovers who accidentally meet after an eight-year separation. The synopsis described this passionate but impossible reunion, the man's depression (changed to the woman's in *The Woman Next Door*), the "little multicolored pills" which more or less cure lovesickness, the emblematic song ("Without Love One Is Nothing"), and a less pessimistic ending than the later version. In 1972, Truffaut thought of bringing together Jeanne Moreau and Charles Denner as the couple whose passion can be summarized in this simple phrase, "neither with you nor without you."

Truffaut started working on this project again with Jean Aurel in the autumn of 1980. "We established an oral continuity, scene by scene, as we went along," Aurel recalls. "We had to have the meeting in the supermarket, the nervous breakdown for the dramatization, with the idea of intentional illness which came from my reading of Groddeck. The dramatic ending was planned. It could only end in death. . . . And then the idea, François's idea, which he told me bashfully, that they would die while making love."[62] Subsequently, Truffaut split his working time between Jean Aurel and Suzanne Schiffman. The first focused on the construction of the whole, finding ideas to fill out the twenty sequences in the synopsis; the latter shaped the continuity and deepened the psychology of the characters. Suzanne Schiffman developed the character of Madame Jouve, the manager of the tennis club the two couples belong to, a generous woman, haunted and traumatized by a former passion, who becomes the confidante of each of the lovers. By the end of February 1981, the last draft of the script for *The Woman Next Door* was finished—just over three months had gone by, from the first synopsis to the final version.

"Lovesickness is a disease. The doctor cannot cure it": Around this epigraph, taken from an old French song, the screenplay offers one of François Truffaut's most limpid and tragic stories. Bernard Coudray and Mathilde Bauchard had loved each other passionately and had gone through a painful separation. They meet again seven years later when Mathilde, recently married to Philippe, comes to live in the house next door to Bernard's, where he lives with his wife, Arlette, and their son, Thomas. Bernard has found happiness with Arlette, and they lead a calm and peaceful life in a small village about twelve miles from Grenoble. As for Mathilde, her marriage to Philippe, who is older than she, has given her a certain equilibrium.

Inevitably, the two couples establish neighborly relations; both Bernard and Mathilde are silent about their old relationship and try to stifle their feelings. In spite of their efforts, their passion is reignited. The lovers meet in a hotel room. But, during a party at Mathilde's, Bernard has a violent fit of rage on learning that Mathilde wants to break up. Mathilde undergoes a severe depression and is treated in a clinic. Her husband puts the house up for sale. One night, Bernard sees a light inside the house. It is Mathilde. The two lovers embrace. While they are making love, Mathilde shoots Bernard and then shoots herself.

Truffaut wanted to film *The Woman Next Door* quickly. His reasons were compelling: He wished to preserve the emotional power of its subject matter and dispel the new image of himself as an establishment director. Furthermore, Gérard Depardieu was in great demand and free for only six weeks, between March and April 1981. "Gérard Depardieu had been hired to act in Francis Veber's *The Goat*," recalls Jean-Louis Livi, who was then the actor's agent as well as Truffaut's agent. "François told me he wanted to shoot immediately. I asked him if he was ready and he answered, 'No, but after a success like *The Last Métro*, I can't wait.' I worked things out with Gaumont, which was producing *The Goat*, to put off the shoot so that Gérard would be free for *The Woman Next Door*."[63]

Truffaut was therefore obliged to work swiftly, which didn't displease him. He had no difficulty choosing actors for the remainder of the small cast. Henri Garcin was cast in the part of Philippe, Mathilde's husband, and Michèle Baumgartner,[64] in that of Arlette, Bernard's wife. Véronique Silver was to play Madame Jouve, and Philippe Morier-Genoud, an actor from the Centre dramatique national des Alpes, the part of the psychiatrist who tries to cure Mathilde.

At the end of March 1981, Truffaut moved to Grenoble, where the shoot was to take place from April 1 to May 15. He found the two neighboring houses that serve as the basic set for the film in a village about ten miles from Grenoble. The only significant change in his technical team was the camera crew, now headed by William Lubtchansky, assisted by Caroline Champetier and Barcha Bauer. *The Woman Next Door* was a coproduction deal between Carrosse, Gaumont (which would also be its distributor), and TF1. The financial arrangements were the same as for *The Last Métro,* but the budget was one-third the size and the shoot only half as long. The film fits in the category of Truffaut's happy shoots, like *Jules and Jim* and *Mississippi Mermaid,* made when the director was in love with the actress he was filming. As was his habit, Truffaut was secretive about this new affair. "François was extremely discreet," says Gérard Depardieu. "One night, coming home to the Hôtel du Commerce at around midnight, I was talking to the porter, as usual, when the elevator door opened and I saw François, who lived in town. He shut the door and I looked away as though I hadn't seen him, because I sensed his discomfort. What was he doing there? At first, I told myself that he had probably come to 'coach' Fanny. It was only later that I understood their relationship."[65] This love and harmony was apparent in Truffaut's praise of his actress: "As soon as a scene is shot, her face lights up, she remains silent and breaks into a smile that seems to say: 'I am satiated, I am fulfilled, I am gratified.' "[66]

A first rough cut was ready in mid-June 1981, a mere two and a half months after the beginning of the shoot. But Truffaut wasn't fully satisfied with its structure. Suzanne Schiffman then suggested that they make Madame Jouve into the narrator. At the beginning of the film, she would recount a news event to the viewer: "It was still night when the police car left Grenoble. . . . My name is Odile Jouve. . . . The business started six months ago. . . ." Then she would narrate the story of the lovers throughout the entire film, summarizing their tragedy with the line "Neither with you nor without you." Truffaut liked the idea and shot an additional sequence with Véronique Silver, on June 13, in front of the Corenc Tennis Club, about six miles from Grenoble.

The first reactions, prior to the release of the film on September 30, 1981, were unanimously positive and several commentators hailed the emergence of a great actress. "Fanny Ardant's entire being blazes with a strange, romantic flame. She is a sort of disquieting Fate whose dark gaze and obsession recall both the Maria Casarès of *Orphée* and the Adjani of *Adèle H.*,"[67] Michel Pascal declared over the radio, on Europe 1, while *Le Film français* prophesied: "*A Star is born*, unquestionably, and François Truffaut is the supervisor of this flamboyant metamorphosis."[68] But the most acute analysis of the film was offered by Serge Daney in *Libération*:

> If *The Woman Next Door* is such an effective movie and so moving in the end, it is because Truffaut, the enemy of exhibitionism in passions and ideas, the man of the golden mean and compromise, has tried this time to film compromise itself, to make it the substance and form of his film. . . . Truffaut's gamble with *The Woman Next Door*, is to escape from *The Green Room*, to combine the Hyde scenario (morbid, private passion) and the Jekyll scenario (other people, public life). To combine them without letting one prevail over the other, without making the viewer choose between them. . . . For, through a paradox that is unique to him, his art of compromise plunges him into a riskier cinema, without any safety net. In *The Woman Next Door*, his art of directing has become broad and free enough to accommodate Hyde and Jekyll in the same breath.[69]

## A SINGULAR COUPLE

François Truffaut's last great love reinstilled passion and intensity in his romantic life. After the editing of *The Woman Next Door,* he rented a large house not far from Paris, where, from the end of June to the end of August 1981, he hoped to spend what he called in a handwritten note "the FT/Fanny vacation in Fontainebleau."[70] But Fanny Ardant wasn't free, for she was working for most of the summer in the Bordeaux region, on a made-for-television movie, *Le Chef de famille* (The Head of the Family), directed by Nina Companeez. Feeling despondent and lonely, Truffaut preferred his Paris apartment to his summer rental, and he entertained Laura and her boyfriend, Steve Wong, who were vacationing in France. Though he had just undergone a serious dental operation from which he had not fully recovered, he submitted at the end of June and the beginning of July to lengthy interviews conducted by Jérôme Prieur and Jean Collet, for a film directed by José Maria Berzosa. In this *leçon de cinéma,* consisting of two one-hour interviews intercut with excerpts from his films, he discussed each film, often with a critical eye, as he sat in a screening room at I.N.A. (the Institut National de l'Audiovisuel), in Bry-sur-Marne, looking somewhat uncomfortable. In a letter to Jean Collet, he described himself at the time as "in very bad shape physically and mentally."[71]

Fortunately, in mid-September, he was reunited with Fanny and they took several trips together over the next two months, promoting *The Woman Next Door* in the provinces and abroad. At the beginning of October, Fanny Ardant and François Truffaut, joined by Helen Scott, presented *The Woman Next Door* at the New York Film Festival and stayed for a week at the Carlyle Hotel. They no sooner returned to Paris than they set off again for the United States, on November 4, 1981, for a longer stay—first in Chicago, where they attended a tribute to Truffaut, then in San Francisco and Los Angeles, where the couple stayed at the Beverly Hills Hotel. Truffaut introduced Fanny to his Californian friends, among them Dido Renoir, who was charmed by the young French actress.

François Truffaut and Fanny Ardant formed a singular couple. By mutual agreement, they had decided not to live together and to keep their independence, even though they were practically neighbors in the sixteenth arrondissement. "I adore large families," said Fanny in *Figaro Madame,* "but for me love must remain illicit, with no ring on the finger. I also love large houses, but not couples. The priest's benediction is like signing a contract to get trapped! One shouldn't live together. It's so wonderful to have assignations and be like a guest in each other's house."[72] At thirty, Fanny Ardant had arranged to live on the fringes. "Unconventional people like me often come from very strict, repressive families . . . because such families give you a fanatical taste for freedom."[73] She lived alone with Lumir, her daughter born in 1975, named after the Claudel heroine in *Crusts*. She and Truffaut shared this "fanatical taste for freedom" and had the same sense of humor, a certain lightness, a pleasure in telling stories, a desire to work together, and a mutual admiration. They had in common a passionate love of reading. At Fanny's, there were books everywhere, a piano, and some prints adorning the white walls. They both loved Balzac, Proust, Miller, and James; and Fanny also liked Julien Gracq, Jane Austen, Elsa Morante, and F. Scott Fitzgerald. They saw each other several times a week, in a restaurant, at the movies, at each other's house. Their quasi-illicit love began to mean everything to them.

## ON THE SIDELINES

In May 1981, France elected a socialist president, François Mitterrand. Passionately interested in politics but wary of political commitment, Truffaut had nonetheless supported the campaign publicly, and he joined the committee to elect Mitterrand in March, even allowing his picture to appear on one of the committee's posters, along with eighteen other personalities, among them Jean-Claude Casadesus, Vladimir Jankélévitch, Françoise Sagan, Alexandre Minkowski, Haroun Tazieff, Anna Prucnal, Catherine Lara, Gérard Depardieu, and Anny Duperey. Truffaut was disappointed by the picture they chose, which was taken from *The Green Room;* in it, he wore turn-of-the-century eyeglasses and looked pale and sweaty. At the committee's request, he delivered a speech at a UNESCO forum on March 19, at a meeting of about a thousand intellectuals from various countries. He also joined fifty film professionals—including René Allio, Gérard Blain, Claude Chabrol, Constantin Costa-Gavras, Gérard Depardieu, Jacques Demy, Michel Piccoli, Marie Dubois, and Brigitte Fossey—in signing an appeal to vote for Mitterrand "against fear, manipulation and the lies of the people in power." Finally, on April 26, on the eve of the first round in the presidential election, he joined a last-minute appeal to "defeat Giscard by casting a useful ballot in the first round."

Truffaut's real motive was to see a change in the political workforce, and other players active in public life. During his entire adult life, Truffaut had known only conservative governments. But he didn't commit himself to the point of personally going out to vote. In fact, Laura openly criticized him, for she was more than delighted to have acquired, thanks to Valérie Giscard d'Estaing, the right to vote at eighteen. "I told him this was not right—if you urge people to vote, you should vote yourself. He said the opposite, that he exerted a far greater influence by urging others to vote."[74] But Truffaut was as ever full of contradictions when it came to politics.

Truffaut supported Mitterrand but was only moderately fond of him, for he saw him as too political, a skillful strategist more than a moral authority. Yet the two men had made a determined effort to try to get to know each other and had lunched several times together at the Brasserie Lipp in the seventies.[75] As in 1974, Truffaut initially favored Michel Rocard, when the latter and Mitterrand were still the rival Left candidates in the presidential elections. On the day after a much-talked-about Rocard television appearance, Marcel Ophuls wrote to Truffaut to convince him to lend his support to the former head of the Socialist party: "Should it turn out to be necessary, I would try to convince you. I know that I have a certain prestige in your eyes as a 'political mind.' I would like to take advantage of it now because I think it's very important. . . ."[76] In mid-April 1980, Truffaut and Ophuls met Rocard, ready to lend their support to his candidacy. Several weeks later, when it became clear that a large majority in the Socialist party sided with Mitterrand, Rocard withdrew. Eleven months later, Truffaut joined the committee to elect Mitterrand, at the request of Jack Lang and Roger Hanin.

Undeniably, François Truffaut rejoiced at Mitterrand's victory on May 10, 1981. On May 21, the day of the inauguration, he was in the third row of the procession marching behind the new president to the ceremony at the Panthéon, and several days later, he was among the many personalities Mitterrand invited to the Intercontinental Hotel, where he thanked his supporters. The president had a long private conversation with him and thanked him warmly. Truffaut was delighted by two of the first measures taken by the new government—the television broadcast of *The Sorrow and the Pity* in May 1981 and the abolition of the death penalty, which was voted into law by the National Assembly on September 17. This latter measure had been proposed by Robert Badinter, the former lawyer of, among others, Roberto Rossellini, and now Minister of Justice in Prime Minister Pierre Mauroy's government.

But Truffaut's political commitment had no effect on the principles that guided his behavior. Hence, when Jack Lang, the new Minister of Culture, informed him that he was to receive the Légion d'honneur during the traditional presentation on Bastille Day, the national holiday, Truffaut declined to accept. He would still accept only "distinctions pertaining to his profession, the cinema."[77] Wary of any ruling power, whether on the Right or Left, Truffaut justified himself in an interview with Luce Vigo, published in the Communist weekly *Révolution*. "My first reaction was: 'Oh, that's good, the Left has won.' But we must not have a relationship with them because we must not 'suck up to them.' By definition, we must be against, or perhaps not necessarily against the government, but at any rate separate from it."[78]

In October of the same year, Jack Lang asked Truffaut to present himself for the presidency of the Cinémathèque française.[79] But the director wanted to "stay on the sidelines," as he bluntly told Jean Riboud, the head of Schlumberger, who had been a great friend of Langlois, Renoir, and Rossellini and who, as a board member of the Cinémathèque, wanted to give new prestige to the old institution. "Madame Jack Lang called me," Truffaut wrote to Riboud. "Having turned down medals, positions, receptions and official trips since the month of May, I didn't think I could get out of lunch at rue de Valois on Wednesday, November 3. I'll stay completely evasive concerning the Cinémathèque, since we decided to discuss it together later. It is my conviction that Jacques Rivette would be perfectly suited in this area, the ideal programming director in any case."[80] During this luncheon at the Ministry of Culture, Truffaut did indeed remain very evasive concerning the Cinémathèque française. It was also the occasion of a rather outspoken conversation between him and Jack Lang, the minister finding it difficult to understand Truffaut's attitude regarding the Socialist government. They discussed the "Yorktown affair," an episode where Truffaut had failed to obey protocol. Two weeks before this luncheon, François Mitterrand had made an official trip to Yorktown, the historic American city, for a meeting with Ronald Reagan. The French president had wanted to have a retinue of cultural personalities and, on the morning of October 12, Truffaut had been invited to join the delegation. But on that very day, he was in New York with Fanny Ardant, presenting *The Woman Next Door.* Jack Lang's office had been very insistent about his extending his stay in the United States and his going to Yorktown. A record of a series of rather curt exchanges can be found—recorded by Josiane Couëdel—on the register of telephone calls at Les Films du Carrosse: "I said you were returning tomorrow, because you had many appointments and that you had to leave for Germany on the 18th for the opening of *The Last Métro* there. Monsieur Lang answered that this was not about just anybody, but the president, Monsieur Mitterrand, and that consequently you would do well to change your attitude."

Six months later, another episode illustrates the reserve Truffaut intended to maintain with regard to the leftist government. In April 1982, he was in Tokyo for a week, for a retrospective devoted to his work. Mitterrand and a delegation of several ministers, including Jack Lang, were on an official visit to Tokyo at the same time. Earlier, in planning this trip with Koichi Yamada, Truffaut had informed him of his desire to avoid any political-diplomatic reception, preferring to "see two good recent Japanese films rather than play penguin with the ambassador."[81] Fearing he had made a faux pas, Truffaut eventually changed his schedule for April 16. "On Friday, we must absolutely change the schedule so that I can attend President Mitterrand's reception at the embassy," he wrote to Yamada, "for it would really be impolite not to attend. The conflict on the following day between the showing of *The Woman Next Door* and the Lang reception is less serious, but we might have to divide the book-signing session in two so I can spend fifteen minutes at the Jack Lang gathering."[82]

Truffaut was truly ill at ease with the Socialist protocol and eager to preserve his freedom of movement and opinion. Concrete action was what had always counted for him on issues that he felt personally concerned about. Hence, when he was contacted at the end of 1981 by the C.F.D.T. (French Democratic Confederation of Labor) because it intended to produce a film on troubled childhood, Truffaut immediately agreed to participate in a study group to define the guidelines of the project. In January and February 1982, he worked on the documents that the study group had assembled (the screenplay concerns a strike by women in a textile factory, with children joining the strikers in occupying the factory), but he eventually abandoned the project. He justified this to Edmond Maire, the secretary-general of the affiliated unions, as follows: "The esteem I have for you and your action at the C.F.D.T. made me want to try this experiment, but since I'm a director from before the advent of television, it intimidates me, and I prefer to continue working within the film industry for several more years."[83] Whatever happened, Truffaut, while curious and available, maintained a staunchly independent position in his relations with political power as with television.

## CONFIDENTIALLY YOURS!

While screening the rushes of the last scene of *The Woman Next Door*—where Mathilde, wearing a beige trench coat, shoots Bernard, her lover and neighbor, and then shoots herself—it suddenly struck Truffaut that Fanny Ardant looked like a *film noir* heroine. This immediately made him want to find a crime thriller to adapt, so he could cast his lover in the lead. A short time later, Suzanne Schiffman suggested a Charles Williams novel, *The Long Saturday Night* (*Vivement dimanche!*), whose rights Truffaut had wanted to acquire in the sixties as a possible vehicle for Jeanne Moreau.[84] What Truffaut most liked about it was the possibility of making the woman conduct the police investigation, "not a killer or a woman detective, but an ordinary woman, a valiant secretary, determined to prove her boss's innocence."[85] This was an ideal part for Fanny Ardant, a part where she could "gallop headlong into a trotting universe."[86]

During the entire autumn of 1981, Truffaut was busy with the release of *The Woman Next Door,* traveling incessantly, in France and abroad. At the beginning of the following year, he could finally start adapting *Vivement dimanche! (Confidentially Yours!)* with help from Suzanne Schiffman and Jean Aurel. The trickiest part consisted in overhauling the structure of the novel to make the screen heroine portrayed by Fanny Ardant more active and decisive. "In the Charles Williams novel, not his best," says Suzanne Schiffman, "it was the man, after all, who conducted the investigation and the woman who stayed in the agency.... She wasn't active enough! But what if the man were confined to the agency and she were to take over the entire investigation? François approved."[87]

In fact, François Truffaut wasn't really pleased with his script, finding it lacked credibility. So much so that he even considered giving up the film shortly before the shoot was to start. But he gave the script to Fanny Ardant to read and she found it amusing. "I laughed a lot on reading it," she now recalls, "but it was Gérard Lebovici's opinion that clinched matters. 'You'd be crazy not to make it! And this is not my opinion as a businessman, but as a connoisseur friend.' "[88] Oddly enough, Truffaut resented Suzanne Schiffman for having pointed him in the direction of that particular novel. The tension between them cast a shadow over their collaboration that never let up in the course of the shoot. Yet the other coscenarist, Jean Aurel, defends the project to this day: "It's a crazy screenplay, there's no logic of space or time, it's conceived as an entertainment. The subject of the film isn't exactly the action that unfolds, it serves as support for the rest."[89] At the end of May 1982, Truffaut and his screenwriters isolated themselves in a rented house in Villedieu, in Provence, and set to work again. The trio returned three weeks later with scripted dialogue that was practically a final screenplay. Truffaut finally completed the script after another work session at the Hôtel de Rochegude, near Avignon, this time in the company of Fanny Ardant and Suzanne Schiffman, spinning out an improbable plot of nearly two hundred pages.

Julien Vercel, the owner of a real estate agency in a small town, is accused of a double murder—that of his wife, Marie-Christine, and her lover, Jacques Massoulier, both brutally shot in the head one morning while hunting. With the circumstantial evidence against him, Julien Vercel decides to conduct his own investigation. But very soon, he becomes the suspect in a third murder and is forced to hide from the police and let his secretary, Barbara Becker, pursue the investigation. An ironical brunette, a graduate of the Cours Pigier (a secretarial school), and a clever amateur detective, Barbara throws herself into situations that are alternately alarming and unexpected in her attempt to discover the identity of the true guilty party, who is none other than Vercel's own lawyer, Maître Clément. As a romantic backdrop to this comic thriller, the relationship between Julien and Barbara changes from one of irritation to complicity, culminating in their marriage at the end of the film.

## FANNY IN BLACK AND WHITE

For Truffaut, it was obvious that *Confidentially Yours!* had to be made in black and white. His aesthetic gamble consisted in "restoring the mysterious and glossy nocturnal ambiance of the American detective comedies that used to delight us."[90] In fact, since he had doubts about his script, Truffaut knew that the best way to rescue his film was to find a rapid, spirited pace in the shooting. To conform to the *film noir* logic, black and white was essential, an idea that very much appealed to Nestor Almendros. He would try to re-create the stylized lighting of detective films by using a range of different black-and-white emulsions. During preproduction, Almendros even came upon some old Fresnel lamps from the fifties in a studio in the Paris suburbs; they produced a harsher lighting, illuminating clearly defined areas and projecting very distinct shadows. Truffaut and Almendros hired Hilton McConnico, an American production designer, who built entire sets painted in black and white. Similarly, Michèle Cerf's and Franckie Diago's costumes and props were conceived in the black, gray, and white spectrums.

But Carrosse's financial partners disapproved of this esthetic decision and considered it uncommercial. Television was particularly hostile, refusing to finance a film that wouldn't really fit into peak-hour programming. TF1's film subsidiary refused to coproduce *Confidentially Yours!* and Antenne 2 was interested but hesitant. Even Gérard Lebovici admitted he was reluctant. Truffaut did everything he could to convince him: "The Venice Film Festival just awarded the Golden Lion to *The State of Things,* which was made by Wim Wenders in black and white," he wrote him on September 9, 1982, in a rather vehement letter where he enumerated recent well-known black-and-white films—*The Last Picture Show, Manhattan, Raging Bull, Veronika Voss, The Elephant Man.* And his conclusion was marvelous: "Films are not cans of food. Like human beings, they must be thought about, scrutinized, and considered one by one."[91] In his plea, Truffaut stuck up for his film, of course, but also requested respect for his freedom as an auteur and independent producer. He felt slighted by the attitude of the television networks—slighted on principle, because their rejection of black and white stemmed from a desire to standardize film, which he objected to, and slighted on a personal level, because with *The Last Métro* and *The Woman Next Door,* he felt TF1 had concluded two excellent business deals, both financially and as a way of enhancing its reputation with television viewers. Lebovici finally came around to Truffaut's point of view.

And Antenne 2 agreed to coproduce *Confidentially Yours!* By the end of September 1982, after two months of anxiety and struggle, Truffaut finally balanced his 7-million-franc budget.

The ideal partner still had to be found for Fanny Ardant—a well-known actor who would still let her be the star. The Julien Vercel character is indeed full of contradictions: irritating but attractive, passive but conducting the investigation by proxy, a notable but slightly shady man, someone who likes only blond women but ends up marrying a brunette. His role in the story is not unlike that of a director who organizes everything on the set without appearing on-screen. Truffaut decided to cast Jean-Louis Trintignant in the part, an actor he had never previously directed. Trintignant had taken the first step, in 1979, by writing to Truffaut; he had found a casual way of saying he was available.

> I would love to be in your films. I am sure you would have been pleased with me as an actor and I'm sure I would have been very good. Perhaps there is something about me, or my acting style, you don't like. This letter isn't at all aggressive. Quite the opposite. We actors are often a bit dumb. We take a foolish pride in waiting to be selected. It's our slightly feminine side—feminine in the sense of our mothers, not our wives. There, I'm only writing you all this now because I've stopped thinking of myself as an actor really, or a director, or even less a car racer. I think of myself as a man who has the time to do all the things he likes to do. This might be a sign of aging, and I'm on the lookout for those very signs these days."[92]

Trintignant's frankness appealed to Truffaut, who later acknowledged that Trintignant was the only actor who could have played the parts he himself had played in his films—Dr. Itard in *The Wild Child,* Julien Davenne in *The Green Room,* Ferrand in *Day for Night.* Indeed, Truffaut and Trintignant were only two years apart in age and had the same physical appearance. Their voices were similar—original, almost colorless, neutral in tone and devoid of dramatic effect. "If you choose this part as you would choose a pair of shoes, your feet won't hurt, for we'll tread softly, as if we were wearing moccasins,"[93] Truffaut wrote to Trintignant when offering him the role of Julien Vercel.

The supporting cast in *Confidentially Yours!* was crucial to making the crime-thriller atmosphere convincing. For the part of the lawyer, Truffaut sought a reliable actor, but one who hadn't been seen too often in films or on television. He certainly didn't want a "bad guy" whom the public would instantly identify as a negative or suspicious character. This was why he tried to convince his friend Serge Rousseau to take the part. For Truffaut, Rousseau was kindness itself, and competent enough for the part, since he had begun his career as an actor before being an agent at Artmédia. But Rousseau turned him down. Two weeks before the filming, Truffaut still tried to convince him: "Time is pressing, for I've run out of options. You know that in casting, I'm never the least bit concerned with fashion or box-office appeal, but with appropriateness and plausibility. I need you for this part. Don't let me down, for as Raymond Devos says, the person who is let down goes down."[94] Serge Rousseau didn't change his mind, but it is he who recommended Philippe Laudenbach. For the part of Jacques Massoulier, an enigmatic priest who is conducting his own investigation and hindering Barbara's, Truffaut first considered the writer and *Nouvel Observateur* journalist Jean-François Josselin, then, strongly encouraged by his daughter Eva, he took Jean-Pierre Kalfon, the Rivette actor (*Out One*). He also cast Caroline Sihol in the part of Marie-Christine Vercel, and Philippe Morier-Genoud as the police superintendent. Lastly, he once again convinced Jean-Louis Richard to accept the part of the "bad guy," Louison, the shady owner of a Riviera nightclub.

Having shot one scene of *The Woman Next Door* in Hyères, in the Var—on Jean-Louis Richard's property, in fact—Truffaut very much wanted to shoot this new film on location in that region. Suzanne Schiffman, who was sent scouting for locations between Toulon and the Giens peninsula, found a huge abandoned clinic, Les Kermes, about six miles from Hyères. Hilton McConnico and his technicians would divide the space into several sets, offering nearly the same shooting conditions as a studio. The filming of *Confidentially Yours!* began on November 4, 1982, and lasted eight weeks. "It's a strange experience, as though everyone had been struck with color blindness,"[95] wrote a reporter for the *Matin de Paris* who visited the set and was surprised to find a dreamlike atmosphere where everything—set and actors' costumes—was black, gray, and white.

At the end of the shoot, François Truffaut and Fanny Ardant rested in Provence for about ten days before returning to Paris. Then the editing had to be done immediately and very fast to meet the release date, which had already been set for "around August 10 in the big cities, while the critics are in the country,"[96] he wrote to Georges Delerue, who had been living in Los Angeles for some time, and from whom he requested a score "recalling the Warner Brothers style, like the Max Steiner–Franz Waxman films, whose masterpiece was *The Big Sleep.*"[97] The answer print of *Confidentially Yours!* was ready on May 20. Truffaut had succeeded in making his film in a mere six months, under the shooting conditions of a French B film, with the woman he loved as star.

## THE LAST VACATION

It was a rather bold decision on the part of A.A.A., the distribution company founded by Gérard Lebovici, to release *Confidentially Yours!* in the middle of the summer, on Wednesday, August tenth, in a deserted Paris, overrun by tourists. In the meantime, François Truffaut contemplated taking a vacation. At the end of May, he gave himself a few days off in Rome, where Fanny Ardant was finishing the shoot of *Benvenuta,* directed by the Belgian filmmaker André Delvaux. On June 29, at the town hall of the sixteenth arrondissement, François Truffaut and Madeleine Morgenstern attended the marriage of their elder daughter, Laura, to Steve Wong, who worked at the Pacific Film Archive in Berkeley, California. Only a handful of close friends were present at the ceremony—Camille de Casablanca, a great childhood friend of Laura, and Nestor Almendros, whom she very much liked. Many more friends attended the dinner that evening, at the restaurant of L'Hôtel, on rue des Beaux-Arts, for it was also Eva's birthday celebration—among them Helen Scott, Claudine Bouché, and her daughter Tessa. By then, after a long period of estrangement, François had grown closer to his father, so Roland Truffaut was also present at the ceremony. He met Eva, whom he had never seen before, for she had always refused to acknowledge him as her grandfather. As for Laura, this was only the second time she had met Roland, whom she had first seen four years earlier, when her father's paternal grandmother died.[98]

On the following day, Truffaut and Fanny Ardant left for a vacation on the Norman coast. He had asked Marcel Berbert, who owned an apartment in Trouville, to find him a quiet house to rent, where he could rest, work on his forthcoming films, and entertain friends and collaborators. The choice of Normandy, not far from Paris, was to allow Truffaut to make a few round-trips in his convertible, to respond to journalists' queries and supervise the promotion of *Confidentially Yours!* Thanks to an auctioneer with whom he had maintained contact since the shoot of *The Green Room,* Berbert heard that the house owned by France Gall and Michel Berger, near Honfleur, was available for rent for two months in the summer. In June, Truffaut made a quick trip to see it and give his approval. Le Clos Saint-Nicolas was a pretty manor house in the hamlet of Vasouy. It was there that Truffaut and Fanny Ardant settled in the beginning of July.

By then, it was no longer a secret to anyone close to the couple that Fanny was expecting a child, due in September 1983. Having recently turned fifty-one, Truffaut felt no great eagerness to become a father again, yet he didn't feel he had to justify himself vis-à-vis his daughters, Laura and Eva, who were initially somewhat upset on hearing the news.

Thanks to this heralded birth, he seemed to believe in a new start. His optimism even led him to forsake his usual secrecy and to tell his friends the news: "I won't be coming to New York this year," he wrote to Annette Insdorf in June 1983, "mainly because I'm expecting a baby; Fanny Ardant won't be coming either and for the same reason! I preferred to tell you in writing before the rumors start spreading."[99] Fanny Ardant wanted a second child, "a quasi-visceral desire," she confided to *Figaro Madame* in the spring of 1981. In this early summer of 1983, she felt happy, fulfilled: "The child that will turn my life upside down,"[100] she said.

In accord with this new life, François Truffaut was poised to embark on a new cycle in his cinematic oeuvre. He was planning to use his two-month vacation in Honfleur to develop future scripts. "He no longer had any projects lined up," confirms Claude de Givray, "he who liked to have three or four scripts in process—one with Gruault, one with Jean-Louis Richard, one with Bernard Revon and me, and also one with Suzanne Schiffman. He had to get the storytelling machine going again."[101] Claude de Givray was invited to come stay in Honfleur. The two men soon had several projects in the works. Two were at a reasonably advanced stage, so much so that Truffaut expected to shoot them back-to-back in the same year, 1985. The first was a remake of *Nez-de-Cuir*, a new adaptation of La Varende's novel that he wanted to film with Fanny Ardant and Gérard Depardieu; the second was *La Petite Voleuse* (*The Little Thief*). "In La Varende's novel, there are two female characters, a twenty-year-old girl and a forty-year-old woman," says Givray. "François wanted them condensed into one, a thirty-year-old woman. He also said to me, 'No hunting scenes!' He felt that nothing could be more boring to film. However, the novel is filled with hunting scenes. . . ."[102]

With Jean Gruault, Truffaut considered adapting *Le Petit Ami*, the autobiographical novel by Paul Léautaud, a writer who fascinated him. Carrosse had acquired the rights to the novel in the spring of 1981 from Mercure de France and had also negotiated permission to use part of the writer's nineteen-volume *Journal littéraire*. Truffaut was also very interested by *Lettre à ma mère*, another autobiographical text by Léautaud. Taken together, these works would allow him to give a complete account of the writer's childhood, in the early part of the century, in the Lorettes neighborhood, and depict his complex relationship with his mother, who had abandoned him when he was very young and whom he saw periodically in his adult years. Of course, though derived from Léautaud, this narrative had an odd resemblance to Truffaut's own childhood, his personal development, his ambiguous relationship with his mother. However, he gave the project up when he learned that Pascal Thomas also intended to make a film based on Léautaud.

Truffaut then turned his attention to another ambitious idea, assigning the writing to Gruault: "oo-14" was the code name of a script about Paris during the *Belle Epoque*—a saga spanning the period between the world's fair at the beginning of the century and the declaration of war in August 1914. The script was to follow four characters and the events of their time and make them meet historical, political, and literary figures. These four characters were the industrialist Louis Renault—a part that would go to Gérard Depardieu; a young anarchist worker who gradually changed camps—Truffaut thought of Jean-Pierre Léaud; Alice, Louis Renault's mistress, played by Fanny Ardant; and Laure, Renault's young wife. Truffaut saw oo-14 as midway between Milos Forman's *Ragtime* and Ingmar Bergman's *Fanny and Alexander*, two works he particularly admired. Truffaut and Gruault gathered abundant research material on the *Belle Epoque* and read a great many biographies, memoirs, and journals; they became fascinated by the assassination of Gaston Calmette, the head of *Le Figaro*, in March 1914, by Henriette Caillaux, the wife of Finance Minister Joseph Caillaux, whom Calmette had slandered in the press. Truffaut and Gruault also acknowledged this project was partially inspired by Proust and they envisioned it as suitable for both film and television.[103] Following in the steps of Bergman's *Fanny and Alexander*, Truffaut wanted this script to be the basis for a three-hour film as well as a multiepisode television series. Indeed, Antenne 2 had virtually approved the project and was on the verge of signing a contract. After *Confidentially Yours!*, with a script he had regarded as weak, Truffaut was determined to take control over his stories again, to write them with pleasure and rigor, thanks to the collaboration of his different screenwriters. His projects were varied, far-ranging, and ambitious, combining a taste for history with an authentic autobiographical thread. Truffaut realized he had found an ideal alter ego in Gérard Depardieu; he wanted to conceive certain projects with him in mind, or as a partner again with Fanny Ardant. According to Depardieu, "Truffaut was done with his past"[104] and ready for a new cycle. He intended to inaugurate it in the coming months, resuming the rhythm of one film a year.

Other projects were in their early stages, like the story of a lady-killer, a Landru figure, a perfume-maker living in Grasse who was both a seducer and a criminal. A variation on the theme of *The Man Who Loved Women,* in which he would cast Guy Marchand, an actor whom he had enjoyed directing in *Such a Gorgeous Kid Like Me* and had liked in Pialat's *Loulou* and Diane Kurys's *Entre Nous*. Truffaut wrote him a little note: "One of these days, I'll bring you a script, but it will be the leading role or nothing. The idea is fomenting in my mind, I'll let it grow and, when the time comes, bingo, on paper, and then in the mail for you to read."[105]

Truffaut had also vowed to take time in Honfleur to update his book of interviews with Alfred Hitchcock, for he wished to establish a definitive edition that would include the director's last films. Between the publication of the book in 1966 and Hitchcock's death in 1980, the director had made *Topaz, Frenzy,* and *Family Plot.* Though Truffaut didn't consider these to be among Hitchcock's best films, he nevertheless wanted to discuss them in a final chapter and write a new preface for the book. His editor, Robert Laffont, had refused to consider the new, expanded edition, so Truffaut succeeded in recovering his rights to the book in March 1981. After several unsuccessful attempts at interesting Gallimard, Flammarion, and Daniel Filipacchi in a new edition, Truffaut followed the advice of René Bonnell, who was then working at Gaumont, which had just bought the Editions Ramsay. He signed a contract with Ramsay on June 30, 1983, just before leaving on vacation.

Truffaut therefore took his research material to Normandy so he could work on this expanded edition: "I wrote a sixteenth chapter 'covering' Hitchcock's last three films and describing the last three years of his life. For me, this version constitutes the definitive edition and I hope that some foreign publishers will use it when they reprint the book,"[106] he wrote to Koichi Yamada, his faithful Japanese friend and correspondent, on August 4. Truffaut had found it painful to write the chapter devoted to the films Hitchcock had made when he was ill. The definitive edition of the Hitchbook came out in November 1983 and sold extremely well.

Truffaut spent several days in Paris, as planned, in the beginning of August 1983 for the opening of *Confidentially Yours!* He attended the preview screening at the Cinémathèque française, where the picture was greeted with enthusiasm.[107] This was a great relief to him, for he had had little faith in it. On the evening of August 10, Laura, whose vacation in France was drawing to an end, accompanied her father to the offices of Gérard Lebovici on rue Keppler. "The results were coming in from each separate movie theater; Everyone was a bit euphoric because the film was doing well and holding its own against *Superman II,* which had opened on the same day,"[108] Laura recalled. Everyone was cheerful. Truffaut was delighted and relieved; Lebovici opened a bottle of champagne. A few hours later, Laura and her father parted; she set off for Berkeley to resume her university studies; he went to join Fanny Ardant again in Honfleur and serenely enjoy the last stretch of their summer vacation.

The following day, Truffaut made his way back to the Clos Saint-Nicolas in Vasouy, at the wheel of his black convertible. On the morning of August

12, Gérard Depardieu was passing through Normandy with his daughter Julie, who was the same age as Fanny Ardant's daughter, Lumir. The two men discussed common projects, *Nez-de-Cuir,* 00-14. On the same day, Truffaut worked until late in the afternoon with Claude de Givray. But at dinner, he suddenly felt faint, "as though a firecracker had exploded in his head,"[109] de Givray recalls. During the night, he threw up some blood. The next day, the physician in Honfleur diagnosed a case of acute sinusitis; his friends attributed this to the fact that Truffaut had driven between Paris and Honfleur with his head exposed to the wind. Three days went by, during which Truffaut talked with his friends, read, and rested. But the headache persisted. Alain Resnais and Florence Malraux made a short trip to Honfleur, for Resnais wanted to see Fanny Ardant, whom he was going to cast in his next film, *Love Unto Death.* In the train going to Trouville, Florence Malraux remembers Resnais saying, "François is such a fulfilled, happy man." Fanny Ardant came to welcome them at the station, alone. "François has been having very bad migraines," she said, "but he is expecting you." The four friends lunched together, but Florence Malraux says that "François was in a bad state"[110] and that a strange cloud hung over the otherwise-harmonious mood of the day, the pretty house, and the soon-to-be-born baby.

On the morning of August 16, still suffering from painful migraines, Truffaut went to the Honfleur medical center. The physician reassured him by prescribing an aggressive treatment against "ophthalmological-type migraine cephalitis."[111] Eight days later, Truffaut consulted an ophthalmologist in Deauville, Dr. Camille Malo. Alarmed by his examination of the back of Truffaut's eye, Dr. Malo immediately sent him to Professor Rozenbaum, at the Caen regional hospital center, specifying that "additional examinations would be advisable in order to establish etiologic certainty."[112] The following day, Dr. Rozenbaum detected "bell-shaped spots"[113] on the right temporal region, the sign of a persistent hematoma. There was the danger of a cerebral hemorrhage, a ruptured aneurysm, or a brain tumor.

While Fanny Ardant closed the vacation house in Honfleur, François Truffaut was transferred at once by ambulance to Paris; at his own request, he was checked into the American Hospital in Neuilly and examined by Professor Bernard Pertuisé, an internationally known neurosurgeon. He underwent an arteriograph under anesthetic. He then remained in the hospital for a week, where he was visited by his family and close friends. After a second scan, on September 3, he was given permission to leave the hospital—"demobilization," as he noted in the daily logbook he kept at the time.[114] He spent the weekend at home, at avenue Pierre 1er-de-Serbie, with his family at his side. On Monday, he was back at the American Hospital, in Professor Planchon's department of nuclear medicine. There, he underwent a "dynamic study by scintigraph camera,"[115] which allowed the brain to be scrutinized with extreme precision. The examination, according to Dr. Planchon's report, allowed the "hypothesis of an underlying aneurysm to be rejected," but it confirmed the presence "of a late diffuse fixation in the right temporal region,"[116] in other words, a brain tumor. Professor Pertuisé decided on an emergency operation. The physicians at the American Hospital tried to reassure Truffaut about his condition. In his letters, Truffaut described "an aneurysm from birth which provoked a cerebral hemorrhage," "an aneurysm that will be lessened by opening my head."[117] The word *tumor* was never mentioned in his presence. But Professor Pertuisé did explain to Madeleine Morgenstern that Truffaut had a malignant tumor, a glioma, in the right frontal region of the brain, which had bled on the evening of August 12 and caused his malaise. The condition was incurable and terminal. François Truffaut had only a few months to live, a year at most.

Before his operation, Truffaut wanted to legally recognize his unborn child, but French law doesn't allow a child to be recognized prior to birth. Truffaut then considered marriage, but time was short. The surgery was scheduled for September 12, and Truffaut had to enter the clinic on the 10th. On the eve of the 10th, in his apartment, he wrote a few letters to friends abroad—Dido Renoir, Leslie Caron, Koichi Yamada in Japan, Robert Fischer in Germany, Richard Roud and Annette Insdorf in the United States. Though these letters were often amusing and full of irony, behind their merry aloofness there lurked a gnawing anxiety. To his "old pal Richard" Roud, Truffaut announced that he was "entering the American Hospital to have my skull opened," and wanted to express to the director of the New York Festival his "gratitude for the almost annual celebration of which I was the beneficiary and you the conductor."[118] To Annette Insdorf, he confided that "he must be operated on for a brain aneurysm," and he added, "film critics were twenty years ahead of official medicine, for, as soon as my second film, *Shoot the Piano Player,* opened, they declared the film couldn't possibly have been made by someone whose brain was functioning normally."[119] He announced to Robert Fischer that he was to undergo "an operation following a vascular accident."[120] Finally to his friend Yamada, he said he was in "good spirits, but should things go wrong, I want to express to you my thanks, my friendship and my desire that you always be my representative-translator-friend-alter-ego—in a word, my Japanese brother. If all goes well, I'll be able to write you again in October, and by then I'll be the father of a small child, the one Fanny Ardant is expecting; goodbye, dear Yamada, see you soon, yes, see you soon, I very much hope so, love François."[121] Truffaut ended each one of his letters with a "soon, I hope" which was not quite his usual style, habitually lighter and less pessimistic.

The operation on September 12 lasted three hours but went exactly as planned. A great many get-well messages awaited him in his room, including those from President François Mitterrand, Dido Renoir, Lillian Gish, and Robert Bresson. Later, Isabelle Adjani wrote him, "I think you think I never think of you and I don't think you ever think of me, so I don't dare send you my thoughts, except to tell you that I've thought about you a great deal these last few days. I very much hope you feel better."[122] One week after his surgery, on September 20, Truffaut was back in his apartment. On the 24th, in a paparazzo photo published "exclusively"[123] in the *France-Soir* weekly supplement, he could be seen coming out of the hospital, looking tired and weak, his head completely shaved, supported by Madeleine Morgenstern and his servant Ahmed. Less than a week later, on September 28, Fanny Ardant gave birth to a baby girl named Joséphine, François Truffaut's third daughter.

## OBSERVING SILENCE

After his operation, François Truffaut settled back into his apartment. He was very weak, but he had been told—in somewhat vague terms—that his convalescence would be brief, as is indicated in Dr. Pertuisé's first letter to him, on the very day of his release from the hospital: "Don't forget that in medicine prediction is uncertain. Make a great film for us very soon. . . ."[124] In fact, the true gravity of his condition was never alluded to in his presence.

In the eighties, in France, cancer was still poorly understood, the word itself was still taboo, and obituaries usually made use of a conventional phrase, "died after a long illness." Truffaut himself seemed not to want to know the truth. And most of his immediate entourage, even Fanny Ardant, were not aware of just how seriously ill he was. With this kind of tumor, radiation treatment can add a few months to a patient's life, but remission is impossible. Truffaut, who had made a good recovery from his operation, was in less pain than before. His tumor was in the frontal cortex; it affected neither his language function nor his memory; however, he tired easily and had difficulty concentrating. He seemed more relaxed, and he joked with his daughters and friends. His mood darkened only when he was alone.

In November, Madeleine decided to share her secret. The first person in whom she confided and told the physicians' diagnosis was Marcel Berbert. She also confided in Laura and Eva. Several weeks later, in January 1984, she was invited for dinner at the home of Lucette and Claude de Givray in Puteaux. De Givray had just been asked to direct a television film, with the actress Nicole Courcel; he hesitated to accept the offer, since he had previous scriptwriting commitments with Truffaut. Madeleine took him aside and told him the truth: "Claude, you shouldn't turn down any work. François has terminal cancer. . . ."[125]

The Carrosse family rallied around Truffaut during his illness, protected him from rumors, and had orders not to breathe a word outside their circle. Josiane Couëdel transmitted the same message to all the countless people who phoned the office to ask after the director's health: "François had a ruptured aneurysm, his operation went well; he is now convalescing. . . ." More than ever, the Carrosse family mobilized and maintained its protective role toward Truffaut, but not without pain. "François, my only remorse is that, for a year, I watched you slowly sink into suffering without having the courage to live up to my old threat from the days when you used to get too much on my nerves: to knock you over the head with your Oscar!"[126] Josiane Couëdel would say after Truffaut's death.

"Fanny didn't yet know the truth, nor Jean-Pierre Léaud, nor Helen Scott, since François himself didn't know!"[127] says Claude de Givray. His very close friends—Suzanne Schiffman, Jean Aurel, Jean Gruault, Jean-Louis Richard, and Janine Bazin—asked after him regularly. Some of them knew the truth; most did not.

In the meantime, Truffaut showed forethought and, on the advice of Georges Kiejman, consulted a lawyer, who urged him to prepare for any eventuality. Every morning, at around eleven, Marcel Berbert—who had retired in 1982—came by the apartment on avenue Pierre 1er-de-Serbie to take notes for the drafting of Truffaut's last will and testament, a task that kept the director busy until Christmas 1983. "The document is very specific in its instructions; everything had to be clear,"[128] Madeleine recalls. Truffaut requested that Les Films du Carrosse cease all production activities and put Madeleine Morgenstern in charge of the future distribution of his films.

In December, Truffaut was so weak that he was unable to work. "Given the state I'm in, I'd no sooner step off the night train than I'd melt in the snow and disappear before having time to utter the master's name: 'Alfredd . . .' "[129] he wrote the director of the Avoriaz festival, who had invited him to a Hitchcock tribute. The prognosis now stressed the long term: "Everyone tells me to expect a three-year convalescence, of which only the first year is really confining."[130] Truffaut had to cancel his plans, such as presenting *Confidentially Yours!* at the British Film Institute in London, and activities tied to the promotion of his Hitchcock interview book. Knowing it would be some time before he would get around to making a new film, he decided to restore the uncut version of *Two English Girls*, a project that had been on his mind since the spring of 1983. He assigned the task to Martine Barraqué, his editor, who spliced back the scenes that had been cut in 1971, at the time of the film's release. Now restored to its original 132 minutes, *Two English Girls* was ready for a new commercial release; it would be his film for 1984.

François Truffaut gradually started working again. Madeleine encouraged him, as did all his close friends—Claude de Givray, Gérard Depardieu, Jean-Louis Livi, and Serge Rousseau. The screenplay of *La Petite Voleuse* was unfinished, but Truffaut felt that the material, as it was, was completely satisfactory and ready to be filmed. He even asked Serge Rousseau to find a young actress for the lead. Truffaut wanted everything to be ready for a shoot sometime in 1985, as soon as he would be sufficiently recovered. In the meantime, he resumed work on the script of *Nez-de-Cuir* with Claude de Givray, though less intensively than the preceding summer in Honfleur. Gérard Depardieu, who had visited Truffaut repeatedly at the American Hospital in September 1983, did everything to encourage him: "I said to François, 'Nez-de-Cuir has a hole in his mug, you have a hole in your head, we're doing well!' "[131] Depardieu continued to think about *Nez-de-Cuir* even when he was far from Paris, on the set of Alain Courneau's *Fort Saganne* in the Mauritanian desert, acting in a part that Truffaut had strongly urged him to accept: "You should play the part of a military man, like Gabin in *Gueule d'amour!*"[132] The actor even devised an original way of conveying his feelings to Truffaut: He recorded his impressions of the shoot on a cassette, which he gave to Jean-Louis Livi, who had come to see him in Mauritania, to give to Truffaut. He wrote him concerning the film they planned to shoot together: "Thank you, François, for your support and for taking on this romantic gentleman who has me daydreaming. Seen from here, I'm deeply moved and I feel it will be so strong, simple, funny and dignified. . . . Excuse me, Fanny, you know I don't always have words at my command. I prefer to think about the two of you, the three of you now, and about us later. I love you, you make me feel good."[133]

In the weeks following his release from the hospital, it was easiest for Truffaut to return to his own apartment; he gave up the idea of moving into a large apartment near Passy with Fanny Ardant. Fanny came every day, so he could see his little girl. But that year, the actress had a great deal of work. Two months after Joséphine's birth, she replaced Isabelle Adjani on short notice in Strindberg's *Miss Julie,* opposite Niels Arestrup. In spite of fatigue from his radiation sessions, Truffaut attended a performance of the play, and he was happy and proud of Fanny's triumph. Immediately thereafter, in February 1984, she went to work in Uzès, in the Cévennes, on Alain Resnais's film *Love Unto Death,* followed by Nadine Trintignant's film, *L'Eté prochain.* Madeleine Morgenstern went to the apartment on avenue Pierre 1er-de-Serbie every day to see Truffaut and attended to all practical matters. Dusk was the most difficult hour for him, a time when he was gripped by intense angst. "I was there to help him get through the nightfall,"[134] says Madeleine, who got into the habit of staying until dinner. At around nine, after watching television, Truffaut would fall asleep, a refuge and escape from exhaustion and anguish. His daughters Laura and Eva were also by his side, Laura having returned from Berkeley to spend Christmas 1983 with her family. Her memory of first seeing her ailing father is still painful: "He wasn't the same man; he was smaller, gray; the physical change was enormous." Laura arranged to stay almost a month in Paris to be near her father for as long as possible. "I lived that period like an egoist, for he was there, available, because of the illness. We had long conversations; he was almost my hostage,"[135] she recalls.

## LIFE REGARDLESS

At the beginning of 1984, Truffaut seemed to regain some strength. At the end of January, he spent a few days at the Colombe d'Or in Saint-Paul-de-Vence with Fanny Ardant. He regained some weight, got back some color; he could even drive his car and go to the movies and the theater with Fanny. He liked Fellini's *And the Ship Sails On,* Gérard Mordillat's *Vive la sociale,* and Woody Allen's *Zelig.* Filled with hope, he ordered a Mercedes convertible for the fine weather ahead. It was as if he wanted to ward off the rumor spreading in Paris.

On the occasion of the rerelease of five Hitchcock films in Paris and the simultaneous publication of the new edition of his interview book, Truffaut was the guest on February 12, 1984, of the RTL radio show, "Journal inattendu," and was interviewed at length by Philippe Labro. "I was very insistent that he come," Labro admits, "and no doubt François wanted to prove he could come to the broadcast."[136] After discussing Hitchcock at length, Truffaut signed off by giving news of his health. There again, the "official" version was far from the medical truth—to wit, the following dialogue between Labro and Truffaut at the very end of the broadcast:

> *I know you were somewhat ill; this is the first time you've spoken publicly in a long time.*
> *I was actually very ill, since I underwent a brain operation. But in consolation I told myself that the film critics—you know, when you're in this business you often blame film critics—that the film critics were twenty years ahead of official medicine, since, when I released my second film,* Shoot the Piano Player, *twenty years ago, some critics wondered whether my brain worked properly. Now that my brain's been operated on, maybe I'll be able to make films that will be more to their liking.*
> *RTL listeners hold you very dear and it's been ages since they've*

*had any worries about the way your brain works. And I hope to see*
*you beating the path back to the studios.*

Truffaut spent time in his office at Les Films du Carrosse again. He wrote
to his friends and recovered his taste for cigars. "I narrowly missed the great
crossing: a brain hemorrhage," he wrote to Liliane Siegel in February 1984.
"I have questioned some people who have had the same experience. The first
year is difficult, very difficult, you think you'll never make it. The second
year, work resumes, you regain your strength. The third year, you're out of
danger (almost). So I'm waiting and I'm prudent, in bed at nine almost every
night, plenty of sleep and naps, not just half a work schedule but a quarter
schedule. That's my diminished life, the life I'm leading at present."[137]
François Truffaut continued to believe in his recovery, and in this he was
encouraged by the case of his Japanese friend, Koichi Yamada, who had
recovered from an operation on his cerebellum in 1969, following a ruptured
aneurysm. Indeed, this experience strengthened the bond between the two
men, regardless of the geographical distance that separated them. Truffaut
resolved that from now on, out of both friendship and superstition, he would
give his "Japanese alter ego" the gift of a plane ticket every year. Three
months after his visit to Paris in June 1983, having learned of Truffaut's brain
operation, Yamada wrote to the man he admired most in the world: "I imagine you must feel a world of emotions after your operation. Let my friendship
reassure you: we are brothers in this kind of trial, since, you might remember,
I underwent exactly the same operation fourteen years ago. And you'll agree
that no trace of it remains either physically or mentally!"[138] The two men saw
each other one last time in Paris, from June 20 to 27, 1984, when Truffaut
received Yamada at his home. "I was unbelievably moved to see you, if not in
perfect health, at least well on the way," his Japanese friend wrote him on his
return to Tokyo. "You looked rather tired, but, confident from my personal
experience, I can tell you that it will only be a passing state and that the only
important thing is to be as patient as possible."[139]

Truffaut wished to show such confidence in broad daylight. On March 4,
1984, he therefore decided to attend the César ceremony at the Théâtre de
l'Empire, after he had been talked into it by his friend Claude Berri, whose
film *Tchao Pantin* had a good chance of winning some prizes. Fanny Ardant
had received a best-actress nomination for her performance in *Confidentially Yours!* and Truffaut was by her side during the award ceremony. He
also handed Maurice Pialat the César for best film for *A Nos Amours*. The
two men, who had known each other for many years,[140] embraced, and it was
a truly moving moment. Truffaut seemed cheerful that evening and many
people believed he was on the road to recovery. He later dined at Fouquet's
with Fanny Ardant and Isabelle Adjani, who wrote him a warm note the fol-

lowing day: "I was moved to see you, you looked both tired and happy. Life is so wonderful when one has been really ill. You had such tender gazes yesterday evening. I love you and admire you always and forever."[141]

On the day after the Césars, the press felt entitled to announce the return of François Truffaut: HE IS ACTIVELY RESUMING WORK was the *France-Soir* headline. "Truffaut is directing again: a film recounting the adventures of a little girl right after the war," ventured the magazine *Première*. In March, Truffaut spent a few days again at the Colombe d'Or, this time with Madeleine and their friends Serge Rousseau and Marie Dubois. This was right after the murder of Gérard Lebovici, on March 3, 1984, in a Champs-Elysées parking area. Truffaut and Rousseau were very attached to Lebovici, each for his own reasons. Truffaut trusted the man completely, was impressed by his intelligence and culture, and was fascinated by his double life as a public man in film and a politically committed publisher of Guy Debord and the situationists. As for Rousseau, he had worked with Lebovici at Artmédia for about twenty years. March 13 was Serge Rousseau's birthday. At the Colombe d'Or, Marie Dubois asked Truffaut, "Should we do something for Serge's birthday?" And, she says, "François had this marvelous reply, 'But life goes on!' "

In mid-April, Truffaut inaugurated a movie theater bearing his name in Romilly-sur-Seine, in the Aube; Marcel Carné was also present, for another theater was dedicated in his name. Truffaut was surrounded by Marie Dubois, Brigitte Fossey, Macha Méril, Jean-Pierre Léaud, and André Dussollier. He participated in Bernard Pivot's literary talk show, *Apostrophes*, on a night when it was devoted to cinema, and talked about the new edition of his Hitchcock interview book. With him were Roman Polanski, who had just published his memoirs, Marcello Mastroianni, who talked about his friend Fellini, and the daughter of Suso Cecchi d'Amico, Visconti's screenwriter. Frequently called upon by Pivot, Truffaut told many anecdotes about Hitchcock, including the famous episode of their first meeting at the Joinville Studios, when Chabrol and he fell into a pool of freezing water. For all those who were seeing him for the first time in months, the man's intense effort to overcome his physical weakness and transmit the ardor and clarity of his ideas was deeply moving.

## THE DIMINISHED LIFE

Truffaut's follow-up brain scan at the end of April 1984 was hardly cause for optimism. Stronger doses of cortisone would have to be administered, which meant he would have to rest over the summer and avoid travel. But he still wanted to believe in recovery. Nor did he give up the idea of making *Nez-de-*

*Cuir.* With this in mind, he arranged for a screening of the Yves Allégret version with Jean Marais, at the Cinémathèque française on May 25, 1984. Truffaut had invited cinematographer Nestor Almendros, Gérard Depardieu, Marcel Berbert, and Jean-Louis Livi, who had been assigned the task of negotiating the rights to the book. What he liked about the La Varende novel was the opportunity to rework the theme of *The Man Who Loved Women*, but in an entirely different context. A soldier returns from the Napoléonic wars completely disfigured, his face mauled. He assumes his life as a seducer is over; but the exact opposite happens: His leather nose becomes a fetishistic element that helps him seduce women. At the end of the screening, as they climbed up the stairs of the Cinémathèque, Gérard Depardieu had no real illusions: "François was already very weak. I remember everyone had already left; I was there, about to put on my motorcycle helmet. François was at the bottom of the Cinémathèque steps. He looked at me and pulled down his hat, but too far down, to just above his eyes, without realizing it. It was a dreadful sight! That's when I really saw the disease; I understood that he didn't really feel things anymore. That's actually the last image I have of him, because I didn't want to go see him at home; I preferred to phone him."[142]

In June, Truffaut spent his days in his room, in peace and quiet. He made some summer plans, including spending a holiday in Brittany with Fanny Ardant and little Joséphine. Ardant had asked Claude de Givray to accompany her to the region around Roscoff to find a house to rent. But Truffaut could no longer travel. It was then that Fanny learned the truth. "Me, whose life has always been organized around a schedule," he said to Serge Toubiana, "this is the first time I'm living in uncertainty, I'm no longer in command of my time," Truffaut confided at the time. Many of his friends were struck by his melancholy, as Jean-Claude Brialy put it: "François said to me: 'I'm getting used to the idea of death,' and the look in his eyes had become sad."[143] This state of mind did not dampen his determination to face up to the ordeal; and in his case, facing up meant keeping his sense of humor to the end: "The last time I saw him," said Jean-Louis Richard, "I asked him if I could do something for him. He was suffering at that moment and he said to me, 'Lend me your gun, I'll return it tomorrow.' And he burst into giggles. He laughed just like the two of us used to in the old days."[144]

He did have one last project, however: to summon whatever strength he still had to recount the story of his life and write his autobiography. This was a desire he had already confessed to his friend Annette Insdorf a few years earlier: "I'll open my files when the doctors forbid me to make films and I'll start writing my memoirs."[145] That day had now arrived, and this was an added reason why he wanted to see his oldest friends again, to refresh his memories of youth. He got back together with Robert Lachenay, his oldest friend and playmate. "Did we meet in '43 or '44?" Truffaut wrote him. "I'm opting for

October '43, when I was eleven. . . . These days my thoughts often turn to the past. Our common experience belongs to that period in life one never forgets, adolescence and the formative years. Everything related to that period is part of chemical memory, I think that's what biologists call it. In other words, should we become more or less senile, the only memories forever fresh and lively that will always stream before our eyes, like a film edited in a 'loop,' will be those that stretch from Barbès to Clichy, Abesses to Notre-Dame-de-Lorette, the Delta Ciné-club to the Champollion theater. . . ."[146]

Truffaut decided to put his archives in order, those numerous files that he had methodically kept since his youth. He reimmersed himself in his childhood and reread dozens of documents, letters, and intimate journals. In view of this projected autobiography—which he deeply cared about and which would primarily deal with the "critical years" in his life—he contacted a publisher. "In the life I now lead as a convalescent, my thoughts often turn to my childhood and youth, the thirties, forties, fifties," Truffaut wrote on July 6, 1984, to Charles Ronsac at Robert Laffont. "I don't know what cinema—or my health—have in store for me in the future, but I'm considering dusting off my portable typewriter and attempting an autobiography, entitled *Le Scénario de ma vie* (or *The Script of My Life*). What do you think of this idea, you who were just about the first person to have suggested it to me six or seven years ago?"[147] Charles Ronsac assured him he was interested in this manuscript, which would never see the light of day.

Truffaut had been unable to concentrate well enough to write. He had tried another approach—a series of taped interviews with Claude de Givray. The latter encouraged him, pointing to the example of *Fellini by Fellini,* which had just hit the bookstores. The interview sessions lasted for two afternoons, with pauses, for Truffaut had to recover from the fatigue provoked by the rush of memories. At the end of the last recording, made in June 1984, there is this exchange with Claude de Givray:

> *The excuse, at school after you played hooky, "My mother died," which comes from Alphonse Daudet and which you put in* The 400 Blows, *you didn't actually use that excuse in real life?*
> *Yes I did, I did use it. It was in 1943.*

Then the tape was interrupted, leaving *The Script of My Life* unfinished.

## THE FAREWELL CEREMONY

On July 10, 1984, a new brain scan showed that the tumor had spread. The press even announced "François Truffaut's hospitalization," an erroneous news item picked up on the TF1 evening news on July 16 and on Europe 1 on the morning of the 17th. Get-well messages began to stream into Les Films du Carrosse from everywhere, from artists, actors, directors, and many ordinary filmgoers. Other letters, from family and close friends, were sent directly to Truffaut. "I'm thinking of you all the time," said Floriana Lebovici. "I'm writing you what Gérard would have said to you: don't give up the fight, struggle with all your might. There are many alternate treatments, don't neglect them. You must try everything, absolutely everything, to the end. But really, above all, don't be defeated. Life is so strong for you and you have so much to do."[148]

With the onset of summer, changes had to be made in organizing Truffaut's daily life. Ahmed, his majordomo, would be absent from Paris for five weeks, and Fanny Ardant was starting work on a film with Nadine Trintignant. Since he couldn't remain home alone, Truffaut moved in with Madeleine Morgenstern, at rue du Conseiller Collignon. There he had frequent, thoughtful visits from his doctor, Jacques Chassigneux, whose moral support and deep humanity were of great help. In the absence of Professor Pertuisé, he was referred, thanks to Catherine Deneuve, to Professor Aron for a consultation about his eyesight, which had considerably altered. Laura, who was in France at the time, kept her father company and spent many long hours by his side. "François slept a great deal," says Madeleine Morgenstern, "but when friends came to see him, he was very brilliant, he laughed, and was lively and funny; visits stimulated him."[149] Fanny Ardant came to see him whenever she could get away from her work on the set. During the entire summer, a procession of friends dropped by, day after day: Dido Renoir, Jean Aurel, Alain Vannier, Claude de Givray, Suzanne Schiffman, Serge Rousseau, as well as Claude Berri and Milos Forman, who was visiting Paris for the opening of *Amadeus*. The three men shared a long-standing friendship, and they discussed Forman's new film, of course. In his eagerness to please Truffaut, Berri was prepared to do anything to make it possible for him to attend a private screening of *Amadeus*. "François so wanted to see the film that I said to Madeleine, 'Let him come in pajamas; we'll drive the car into the courtyard and François will only have to walk a few steps!'"[150] But Truffaut had no strength left. On the following day, Jean-Pierre Léaud stopped by the apartment on rue du Conseiller Collignon. Liliane Siegel remembers meeting Léaud not far from her house, wandering distraught down the boulevard Raspail: "I said to him, 'You look upset!' and Jean-Pierre answered, 'François is dying! He is very sick and is dying. . . .'"[151] Roland Truffaut stopped by to see François; he was, as Madeleine Morgenstern put it, "unhappy and dismayed." The conversation between father and son was slightly awkward, even though, deep down, Truffaut never really had any resentment toward Roland. In the beginning of September, he had visits from Jeanne Moreau,

Catherine Deneuve, Claude Miller, Marcel Ophuls, and Leslie Caron, and, at a later date, from Jean-José Richer, as well as Pierre Hebey and Anne François, who were working on the release of *Two English Girls*.

But the afternoons were long in these final days of the Parisian summer. Truffaut had difficulty walking; his headaches sometimes made him gloomy and silent. He didn't complain, but his anguish was increasingly pronounced. "My present vegetable state is degrading," he wrote to Liliane Siegel. "There's an enormous fatigue that begins after breakfast and sends me back to bed or to the corner of a window. This is bearable only by setting small goals, important dates, the birthday of one of my daughters, the visit of a faraway friend, the publication of such and such a book. Autumn is the next goal. Such is the state of my slow brain, dear Liliane."[152] The creator of *The Green Room*, fascinated by this crossing, was preparing to die. Most of his interests, visions, and readings concerned death. He discussed Sartre's death at length with Liliane Siegel. Simone de Beauvoir's *La Cérémonie des adieux* (in English, the book is entitled *Adieux: A Farewell to Sartre*), which recounts Sartre's last years, became his bedside book. "It was by reading Sartre and Beauvoir that he tried to prepare for death, to find a meaning for the end of his life,"[153] said Claude de Givray. Truffaut also read Painter's biography of Proust. In the correspondence between Proust and Madame Strauss, which was being issued at that time, he noted the passage where the dead are referred to as "so much more numerous than the living." His few hours of concentration were divided among reading, visits from his closest friends, and the screening of films on videocassette—films by Chaplin, Lubitsch, Renoir, Bresson, and Becker.

During the summer, François Truffaut told Madeleine Morgenstern he wished to be buried in the Montmartre cemetery. He also asked to see Father Mambrino, the Jesuit priest and film enthusiast who had been André Bazin's friend. When Jean Mambrino went to see him at Madeleine's, he thought Truffaut wanted to make his final confession. In fact, Truffaut questioned him about the next life. Madeleine recalls hearing the two men laugh. After Mambrino's departure, François said to Madeleine, "He knows no more than anyone else!"[154]

Claude Berri and Robert Lachenay would be his last visitors, on September 19. "In his bed, François looked like Sacha Guitry, in the picture—one of the last—where you see him editing a film," says Lachenay. "We talked about literature, like in the good old days. . . . Even on his deathbed, François was the same, merry, still forever joking. . . . When it was time to leave, he got up to walk me to the door. On the landing, I realized I wouldn't see him again, that this was the last time. . . . And, for the first time in forty years of friendship, we embraced. . . ."[155]

On the afternoon of September 28, François Truffaut returned to the

American Hospital, for his condition had suddenly worsened. He remained in the hospital for the last three weeks of his life, and he suffered a painful death. Fanny and Madeleine were by his bedside, and they were soon joined by Laura and Eva. He died on October 21, 1984, at 2:30 p.m.

As he had requested, he was cremated at the Père-Lachaise crematorium on October 24 and his ashes buried in the Montmartre cemetery. Thousands of people—first and foremost, his family, the women he had loved, his friends, actors, and film lovers—attended his burial under a splendid autumn sun. As had been Truffaut's wish, Claude de Givray and Serge Rousseau spoke a few words by his graveside. De Givray had first thought of using Sartre's famous line, "Any man who feels he is indispensible is a bastard!"—a line often uttered by Truffaut, who was aware of his fame but feared being too self-important in the eyes of his friends. In the hearse, de Givray scribbled down some notes on a piece of paper, taking inspiration from the Frank Capra film that Truffaut very much liked, *It's a Wonderful Life*. James Stewart plays a generous man who is saved from suicide by a guardian angel named Clarence, who lets him briefly visit a world where he wouldn't have existed; he is shown what the lives of his dear ones would have been like if he had not been born. And so it was that the friend delivered a fittingly cinema-inspired oration to the crowd gathered around the director's grave: "If François had not been born, if he had not been a director . . ."

One month later, on November 21, 1984, a Mass was celebrated at the church of Saint-Roch by the priest of the Artists' parish and by Father Mambrino. This had been Truffaut's wish; the ceremony had doubtless been discussed during that last interview with the Jesuit father at rue du Conseiller Collignon. Though a nonbeliever, Truffaut wasn't opposed to the ritual of a church benediction. And the church of Saint-Roch was associated in his mind with the yearly anniversary Mass celebrated every October in memory of Jean Cocteau. As in the scene in *The Green Room* where Julien Davenne, played by François Truffaut, celebrates the cult of the dead, hundreds of candles burned in the nave of Saint-Roch, creating a veritable forest of light.

# NOTES

## 1.
### A CLANDESTINE CHILDHOOD:
### 1932–1946

1. Birth certificate, town hall of the seventeenth arrondissement, number BL/178.
2. *Livret de famille* (family record book of the Truffauts), archives of Les Films du Carrosse, file "Archives très privées [very private archives] 1."
3. Interview with the authors, 1995.
4. Letter from Suzanne de Saint-Martin to François Truffaut, July 11, 1968, archives of Les Films du Carrosse, file "Archives très privées 1."
5. Claude de Givray's interview of François Truffaut, June 1984, archives of Les Films du Carrosse, pp. 22–23. These were taped interviews made in June 1984, when Truffaut was already very ill. He never had the time or strength to reread these interviews, as opposed to all the other interviews he gave, which he always corrected and reworked with great care. Hence their extremely chatty tone.
6. Archives of Les Films du Carrosse, file "Ma Vie [My Life] 2."

7. Salary statements of the Truffauts, archives of Les Films du Carrosse, file "Archives très privées 1."
8. Letter from Denise Dehousse to François Truffaut, May 13 1959, archives of Les Films du Carrosse, file "Ma Vie 1."
9. Letter from Henry Moins to François Truffaut, undated, archives of Les Films du Carrosse, file "Ma Vie 1."
10. Archives of Les Films du Carrosse, file "Archives très privées 1."
11. Subsequently, after nearly drowning in a kayak, François Truffaut developed a permanent loathing for water.
12. Archives of Les Films du Carrosse, file "Ma Vie 1."
13. Archives of Les Films du Carrosse, file "Archives très privées 1."
14. Ibid.
15. Truffaut/de Givray interview, archives of Les Films du Carrosse, p. 23.
16. Ibid., p. 24.
17. Ibid., p. 16.
18. Note for the project "Le scénario de ma vie [The Script of My Life]," archives of Les Films du Carrosse, file "Ma Vie 1."

19. Truffaut/de Givray interview, archives of Les Films du Carrosse, pp. 18–19.

20. Robert Lachenay quoted in *Le Roman de François Truffaut,* special issue of *Cahiers du cinéma,* December 1984, p. 19.

21. Truffaut/de Givray interview, archives of Les Films du Carrosse, p. 17.

22. Ibid., p. 16.

23. Ibid.

24. Ibid., p. 13.

25. Roland Truffaud, *Du Kenya au Kilimanjaro:* Expédition française au Kenya, 1952 (Paris: Julliard, 1953), p. 243.

26. Truffaut/de Givray interview, archives of Les Films du Carrosse, pp. 37–38.

27. Letter from Janine Truffaut to her brother, Bernard, undated, archives of Les Films du Carrosse, file "Ma Vie 1."

28. Archives of Les Films du Carrosse, file "Archives très privées 1."

29. The reason he did not take the exam is given in a letter written by Truffaut, quoted on pages 300–301. Clearly, the young Truffaut maintained a tremendous grudge against his parents for this mistake, which he considered a major cause of his failure at school.

30. Truffaut/de Givray interview, archives of Les Films du Carrosse, pp. 8–9.

31. Ibid., p. 9.

32. Ibid., pp. 30–31.

33. Ibid., pp. 39, 65.

34. Ibid., pp. 9–10.

35. Robert Lachenay quoted in *Le Roman de François Truffaut,* p. 15.

36. Monsieur Lachenay paid dearly for this position and these material advantages at the time of the Liberation. He was found guilty of collaboration and black-marketeering and incarcerated. He died in a military prison in the immediate postwar period.

37. Letter included in *François Truffaut: Correspondance* (Paris: Hatier, 1988), p. 20; U.S. edition: François Truffaut, *Correspondence 1945–1984,* trans. Gilbert Adair (New York: Noonday Press, 1988).

38. Claude Vega quoted in *Le Roman de François Truffaut,* p. 21.

39. Truffaut/de Givray interview, archives of Les Films du Carrosse, pp. 10–11.

40. Ibid., p. 11.

41. Ibid., p. 56.

42. Ibid., p. 15.

43. Robert Lachenay quoted in *Le Roman de François Truffaut,* p. 15.

44. Truffaut, *Correspondance,* pp. 20–22.

45. Jean Gruault, *Ce que dit l'autre* (Paris: Julliard, 1992), pp. 276–277.

46. François Truffaut, *Les Films de ma vie* (Paris: Flammarion, 1975), p. 15; U.S. edition: *The Films in My Life,* trans. Leonard Mayhew (New York: Simon and Schuster, 1978). This expression is also used by Eric Rohmer to designate the "film enthusiast period" in his life; see *Le Roman de François Truffaut,* p. 17.

47. Truffaut/de Givray interview, archives of Les Films du Carrosse, p. 19.

48. Ibid., p. 20.

49. Ibid., p. 32.

50. Truffaut often used to refer to Jacques Siclier's book, *La France de Pétain et son cinéma* (Paris: Veyrier, 1981): "Thanks to Siclier's thick book, which is remarkable, it's very easy for me to know all the films I saw during the war. He's the only guy to have seen the 200 films of the period. Me, I didn't see 200, but I must have seen a third or half and they're all in the book." Truffaut/de Givray interview, archives of Les Films du Carrosse, p. 20.

51. Truffaut, *The Films in My Life,* pp. 3–4.

52. Truffaut/de Givray interview, archives of Les Films du Carrosse, p. 21.

53. Ibid., p. 43.

54. Ibid., p. 44.

55. Ibid., p. 45.

56. Ibid., p. 43.

57. Ibid., p. 53.

58. Ibid., pp. 53–54.

59. Ibid., pp. 54–55.

60. Ibid., p. 55.

61. Ibid., p. 7.

62. In *The Last Métro,* this is the scene where the character Bernard Granger witnesses the arrest of a Resistance fighter with whom he has an appointment.

63. Truffaut/de Givray interview, archives of Les Films du Carrosse, p. 23.

64. Ibid., p. 27.

65. Archives of Les Films du Carrosse, file "Archives très privées 1."

66. Archives of Les Films du Carrosse, file "Ma Vie 1."

## 2.
## FOUR HUNDRED BLOWS:
## 1946-1952

1. This is according to Robert Lachenay, in *Le Roman de François Truffaut,* special issue of *Cahiers du cinéma,* December 1984, p. 16.
2. François Truffaut, "Sacha Guitry cinéaste," in Sacha Guitry, *Le Cinéma et moi* (Paris: Ramsay, 1977), pp. 19–20.
3. François Truffaut's journal from August 21, 1951 to May 31, 1952, archives of Les Films du Carrosse, file "Ma Vie 2," p. 56.
4. Truffaut/de Givray interview, archives of Les Films du Carrosse, p. 30.
5. Archives of Les Films du Carrosse, file "Ma Vie 1."
6. Robert Lachenay quoted in *Le Roman de François Truffaut,* p. 16.
7. Archives of Les Films du Carrosse, file "Ma Vie 1."
8. *François Truffaut. Correspondance* (Paris: Hatier, 1988), p. 25.
9. "André Bazin, l'Occupation et moi," in André Bazin, *Le Cinéma de l'Occupation et de la Résistance* (Paris: U.G.E., 1975), pp. 20–21. U.S. edition: *French Cinema of the Occupation and Resistance: The Birth of a Critical Esthetic;* trans. Stanley Hochman (New York: Ungar, 1981). Preface by François Truffaut.
10. Archives of Les Films du Carrosse, file "Ma Vie 1."
11. Ibid.
12. Truffaut/de Givray interview, archives of Les Films du Carrosse, p. 40.
13. Jean-Charles Tacchella quoted in *Le Roman de François Truffaut,* pp. 22–23.
14. *Libération,* December 30, 1948.
15. Truffaut/de Givray interview, archives of Les Films du Carrosse, p. 41.
16. A selection of articles from the *Revue du cinéma* can be found in the 1992 book *Anthologie* (introduction by Antoine de Baecque), published by Gallimard in its series "Tel": *La Revue du cinéma. Anthologie.* A facsimile edition of the *Revue du cinéma* was issued in 1979 by éditions Pierre Lherminier, edited by Odette and Alain Virmaux.
17. Truffaut/de Givray interview, archives of Les Films du Carrosse, p. 41.
18. Ibid.
19. Ibid., p. 42.
20. The discovery of American cinema by enraptured Parisian movie buffs in the postwar period was well described by two witnesses: Jean-Charles Tacchella and Roger Thérond, *Les Années éblouissantes. Le cinéma qu'on aime: 1945–1952* (Paris: Filipacchi, 1988).
21. *Bulletin du Ciné-Club du Quartier Latin,* April 1950.
22. "Citizen Kane: The Fragile Giant," in François Truffaut, *The Films in My Life,* trans. Leonard Mayhew (New York: Simon and Schuster, 1978), pp. 279–280.
23. André Bazin, "Pour en finir avec le profondeur de champ," *Cahiers du cinéma* no. 1 (April 1951).
24. Archives of Les Films du Carrosse, file "Archives très privées 1."
25. In Rouen, Jacques Enfer founded a small magazine in 1950 entitled *Les Cahiers du cinéma.* Since Jacques Doniol-Valcroze had come up with the same title for the magazine he wanted to start with André Bazin and Lo Duca, he had to negotiate with Jacques Enfer to buy the title before publishing the first issue of *Cahiers du cinéma* in April 1951.
26. Dudley Andrew, *André Bazin* (Paris: Editions de l'Etoile, 1983); preface by François Truffaut. U.S. edition: (New York: Oxford University Press, 1978).
27. Archives of Les Films du Carrosse, file "Archives très privées 1."
28. Robert Lachenay quoted in *Le Roman de François Truffaut,* p. 16.
29. Archives of Les Films du Carrosse, file "Archives très privées 1."
30. Ibid.
31. Ibid.
32. Ibid.
33. Ibid.
34. Archives of Les Films du Carrosse, file "Ma Vie 1."
35. Archives of Les Films du Carrosse, file "Archives très privées 1."
36. Ibid.
37. Ibid.
38. Ibid.
39. Ibid.
40. Ibid.
41. Minutes from the clerk's office of the justice of the peace in the ninth

arrondissement of Paris, file "Paul Martin, juge de Paix."

42. Archives of Les Films du Carrosse, file "Ma Vie 1."

43. Archives of Les Films du Carrosse, file "Archives très privées 1."

44. Ibid.

45. Louis Daquin, "Remarques déplacées," *L'Ecran français*, March 8, 1949.

46. Archives of Les Films du Carrosse, file "Ma Vie 1"; published in Truffaut, *Correspondance*, p. 32.

47. Ibid.

48. Antoine de Baecque, *Les Cahiers du cinéma: Histoire d'une revue*, vol. 1, (Paris: Editions de l'Etoile, 1991), pp. 221–222.

49. Charles Bitsch quoted in *Le Roman de François Truffaut*, p. 48.

50. Claude Chabrol, *Et pourtant je tourne* (Paris: Robert Laffont, 1976), p. 109.

51. Jean Douchet, *Artpress*, special issue on Jean-Luc Godard, January–February 1985, p. 70.

52. On the Parisian love of movies in the postwar period, see the published proceedings (eds. Antoine de Baecque and Thierry Frémaux) of the colloquium L'Invention d'une culture: Une histoire de la cinéphilie (1895–1995), Actes Sud/Institut Lumière, 1997.

53. Claude Chabrol quoted in *Le Roman de François Truffaut*, p. 38.

54. Jean Gruault, *Ce que dit l'autre* (Paris: Julliard, 1992), pp. 143–144.

55. Truffaut mentioned that his first critical essays were written in 1948 for *Cités,* the magazine edited by Jacques Enfer, but no trace of these can be found. On the other hand, in the file "Ma Vie 1" in the archives of Les Films du Carrosse, there is a fiction project entitled *Références,* which might well be François Truffaut's first piece of writing.

56. Archives of Les Films du Carrosse, file "Ma Vie 1."

57. Gruault, *Ce que dit l'autre,* pp. 147–151.

58. Truffaut's journal, p. 14.

59. Ibid., p. 15.

60. Archives of Les Films du Carrosse, file "Archives très privées 1."

61. Archives of Les Films du Carrosse, file "Ma Vie 2."

62. Ibid.

63. Archives of Les Films du Carrosse, file "Ma Vie 1."

64. Ibid.

65. Ibid.

66. Ibid.

67. Truffaut, *Correspondance,* p. 41.

68. Archives of Les Films du Carrosse, file "Ma Vie 1."

69. Ibid., letter published in *Correspondance,* pp. 42–44.

70. Ibid.

71. Ibid.

72. Ibid.

73. Ibid.

74. Archives of Les Films du Carrosse, file "Ma Vie 2."

75. Ibid.

76. Archives of Les Films du Carrosse, file "Ma Vie 1."

77. Ibid.

78. Ibid.

79. Ibid.

80. Ibid.

81. Ibid.

82. Excerpt from *The Thief's Journal (Journal d'un voleur)* recopied by hand by Truffaut, archives of Les Films du Carrosse, file "Archives très privées 1." Translation used is from Edmund White, *Genet: A Biography* (New York: Alfred A. Knopf, 1993), p. 8; the mistake ("My mother [*sic*] remains unknown") has been corrected here.

83. On this period in the life of Jean Genet, see White, *Genet,* pp. 372 ff.

84. Archives of Les Films du Carrosse, file "Ma Vie 1."

85. Archives of Les Films du Carrosse, file "Archives très privées 1."

86. Jean-Paul Sartre, foreword to *The Thief's Journal,* trans. Bernard Frechtman (New York: Grove Press, 1964).

87. Archives of Les Films du Carrosse, file "Ma Vie 1."

88. Archives of Les Films du Carrosse, file "Archives très privées 1"; photocopies of this correspondence were also kept in a file entitled "Ecrivains [Writers]."

89. Archives of Les Films du Carrosse, file "Ma Vie 1."

90. François Truffaut immediately sent Genet a letter of explanation and apology: "I returned from Stockholm last night; today I worked all day and took no calls because I'm leaving for the Midi again tomorrow morning. As soon as I heard you

were looking for me I called the Lutetia. I told you, I'll come at 7, we'll talk till 8. After your call, my wife phoned because my younger daughter was sick and there was medication to pick up at the pharmacy. Foreseeing a delay, I called my office so they would warn you: 8 o'clock instead of 7. I had to pick up the medications and bring them home, then go to the Lutetia, you know the rest. I'm not too mad at being called *petit emmerdeur* [damn little pain] because when I was a kid I was called a *petit merdeux* [little squirt]; this shows some progress. If your friend, who has nothing to do with our respective *emmerdements* [damned troubles], phones me Tuesday morning, I'll see him that same day or the next day, at the latest. In some sense, I dare say I was pleased to miss you and I thought of those days when I used to walk down the boulevard de Clichy hoping and fearing to meet you; when I think about it now, I tell myself you were very patient with me; my turn to say, greetings." "Archives très privées 1," and file entitled "Ecrivains."

91. Archives of Les Films du Carrosse, file "Ma Vie 1."

92. Ibid.

93. Archives of Les Films du Carrosse, file "Archives très privées 1."

94. Truffaut's journal, p. 1.

95. Ibid., p. 7.

96. Ibid., pp. 18–19.

97. Ibid., pp. 22–23.

98. Letter of July 27, 1951, from Lieutenant Le Masne de Chermont, archives of Les Films du Carrosse, file "Archives très privées 1."

99. Archives of Les Films du Carrosse, file "Archives très privées 1."

100. Ibid.

101. Ibid.

102. Ibid.

103. Ibid.

104. Truffaut's journal, pp. 174–175.

105. Ibid., pp. 177–178.

# 3.
## LIFE WAS THE SCREEN:
## 1952–1958

1. Archives of Les Films du Carrosse, file "Archives très privées 1."

2. François Truffaut's journal, archives of Les Films du Carrosse, file "Ma Vie 2," pp. 233–234.

3. Archives of Les Films du Carrosse, file "Bazin."

4. Ibid.

5. Janine Bazin quoted in *Le Roman de François Truffaut*, special issue of *Cahiers du cinéma*, December 1984, pp. 24–25.

6. Archives of Les Films du Carrosse, file "Archives très privées 1."

7. *Cinémonde*, May 14, 1953.

8. Olivier Barrot, *L'Ecran français; 1943–1953* (Paris: Editeurs français réunis, 1979).

9. The manuscript of this first version of what would finally be titled "A Certain Tendency of the French Cinema" can be found in the archives of Les Films du Carrosse, file "Archives très privées 2."

10. Truffaut's journal, p. 172.

11. Ibid., pp. 100–101.

12. On the genesis, publication, and effects of this essay, see Antoine de Baecque, "Contre la Qualité français: Autour d'un article de François Truffaut," *Cinémathèque* 4 (Fall 1993): 44–66.

13. Wheeler Winston Dixon, *The Early Film Criticism of François Truffaut* (Bloomington: Indiana University Press, 1993).

14. In his answer to this letter, Pierre Bost shows himself to be magnanimous and a good loser: "Dear Sir, your article in *Cahiers du cinéma* contains some things that are intelligent, some that are unfair, and others that are inaccurate. But there is also something else—and this is the only matter I will bring up today. In my day one did not come to a person's house to borrow writings, make public use of them, and exploit them for acerbic criticism. Especially not confidential writings, since we are talking about a script that has not yet been filmed. I admit that your behavior surprised me, and that I will now feel a mistrust that is not in my nature—here's the proof. I do not hold any of your reproaches against you. I merely wish that none of the many details you give should come from me (after all, I may have spoken to you too and your piece sometimes takes on the tone of a police report). In any case, you have lacked elegance, I'm sorry to have to tell you so, but I'm entitled to say at least that." Letter in the archives

of Les Films du Carrosse, file "Archives très privées 2."

15. *Cahiers du cinéma* 33 (March 1954).

16. Archives of Les Films du Carrosse, file "Archives très privées 2."

17. *Cahiers du cinéma* 33 (March 1954).

18. *Cahiers du cinéma* 36 (June 1954).

19. On this episode in the history of *Cahiers du cinéma*, see Antoine de Baecque, *Les Cahiers du cinéma: Histoire d'une revue*, vol. 1, (Paris: Editions de l'Etoile, 1991), pp. 89–125.

20. Archives of Les Films du Carrosse, file "Archives très privées 1." This synopsis was published in *Cahiers du cinéma* in May 1994.

21. François Truffaut, *Correspondance*, (Paris: Hatier, 1988), pp. 107–108.

22. François Truffaut, "Un colossal enfant" (written in 1973), *Approches*, February 1974.

23. Archives of Les Films du Carrosse, file "Ecrivains." Audiberti's writings on cinema were published as *Le Mur du fond: Ecrits sur le cinéma*, ed. Michel Giroud, with an introduction by Jérôme Prieur (Paris: Editions des Cahiers du cinéma, 1996).

24. Truffaut, "Un colossal enfant."

25. *Ibid.* Truffaut also had the project of directing an Audiberti play for the stage. On August 19, 1960, he told him in a letter of his desire to direct *Pomme, Pomme, Pomme.* Audiberti answered, "In any case, I would be *delighted* that we operate in concert on a theater stage, you as director and me as the directed!" When they met, Audiberti suggested another play to Truffaut, on the myth of Joan of Arc, entitled *La Pucelle*—written and first produced in 1950, but which he was then rewriting. Several months later, Audiberti and Truffaut found producers for their theatrical venture: Robert Yag and Madeleine Declercq, two friends of the playwright. In July 1961, the news could be announced in the press: TRUFFAUT SWITCHES TO THE-ATER was the headline in *Paris-Presse.* Over the summer, with the premiere scheduled for November 1961, Truffaut's main work consisted in casting the play: Marie Dubois, Albert Rémy, Pierre Mondy, Marie-José Nat, Françoise Vatel, Serge Gainsbourg, and Yvette Etiévant, as well as Henri Virlojeux, Jean-Pierre Léaud, Claude Mansard, François Darbon, Rosy Varte, so many actors used by Truffaut in his films. The project took shape, as well as the main directing ideas. But Robert Yag, the producer, found the casting excessive, risky, and too burdensome financially. In August 1961, Truffaut therefore abandoned the project of directing *La Pucelle* for the stage.

26. See Antoine de Baecque, "Contre la Qualité française."

27. Letter from François Truffaut to Charles Bitsch, September 1956, archives of Les Films du Carrosse, file "CCH 1 (1953–1957)."

28. Truffaut *Correspondance*, p. 103.

29. Pierre Braunberger quoted in *Le Roman de François Truffaut*, p. 51.

30. François Truffaut, "Les Dessous du Niagara," *Cahiers du cinéma* 28 (November 1953).

31. François Truffaut, "Vous êtes tous témoins dans ce procès: le cinéma français crève sous de fausses légendes," *Arts*, May 15 1957.

32. *Arts*, February 14, 1955.

33. Archives of Les Films du Carrosse, file "CCH 1 (1953–1957)."

34. Ibid.

35. *Les Temps Modernes*, December 1952.

36. *L'Express*, November 14, 1954.

37. *Positif* 21.

38. Ibid.

39. François Truffaut, "Si Versailles m'était conté," *Cahiers du cinéma* 34 (April 1954).

40. Ibid.

41. Robert Belot, *Lucien Rebatet: Un itinéraire fasciste* (Paris: Editions du Seuil, 1994). Rebatet wrote about his meetings with Truffaut in the newspaper *Dimanche-Matin*, February 3, 1957. Also relevant is Eric Neuhoff, *Lettre ouverte à François Truffaut* (Paris: Albin Michel, 1987), pp. 70–73.

42. Letter from Lotte Eisner to François Truffaut, undated (1978), archives of Les Films du Carrosse, file "CCH 1978 (2)."

43. Archives of Les Films du Carrosse, file "CCH 1 (1953–1957)."

44. Ibid.

45. Ibid.

46. *Le Roman de François Truffaut*, p. 42.

47. *Cahiers du cinéma* 36 (June 1954).

48. Eric Rohmer quoted in *Le Roman de François Truffaut,* p. 28.

49. Letter from François Truffaut to Robert Lachenay, undated, archives of Les Films du Carrosse, file "Archives très privées 1."

50. Ibid.

51. Lydie Mahias quoted in *Le Roman de François Truffaut,* p. 47.

52. François Truffaut subsequently drew inspiration from Robert Mallet's radio interviews with Paul Léautaud for his book on Alfred Hitchcock.

53. *France-Observateur,* March 24, 1960.

54. Archives of Les Films du Carrosse, file "CCH 1 (1953–1957)."

55. Ibid.

56. Jean-Claude Brialy quoted in *Le Roman de François Truffaut,* pp. 49–50.

57. Letter from Julien Duvivier to François Truffaut, of August 13 1956, archives of Les Films du Carrosse, file "CCH 1 (1953–1957)."

58. Interview with Marcel Ophuls, filmed by Michel Pascal and Serge Toubiana, for the documentary *François Truffaut: Portraits volés (Stolen Portraits),* 1992.

59. Letter from Max Ophuls to François Truffaut, February 17, 1955, archives of Les Films du Carrosse, file "CCH 1 (1953–1957)."

60. François Truffaut, "La Bataille du Marignan," *Arts,* December 19, 1955.

61. Letter from Max Ophuls to François Truffaut, January 7, 1956, archives of Les Films du Carrosse, file "CCH 1 (1953–1957)."

62. Roberto Rossellini's writings and interviews in *Cahiers du cinéma* were collected in *Le Cinéma révélé,* (Paris: Editions de l'Etoile, 1984).

63. On *Viaggio in Italia,* see Jacques Rivette, "Lettre sur Rossellini," *Cahiers du cinéma* 46 (April 1955).

64. Interview with the authors, 1996.

65. François Truffaut, "Il préfère la vie," *L'Express,* September 10, 1959.

66. Ibid.

67. Ibid.

68. *La Peur de Paris,* thirty-seven-page synopsis, archives of Les Films du Carrosse, file "Archives très privées 2."

69. Letter from François Truffaut to Robert Lachenay, September 16, 1956, archives of Les Films du Carrosse, file "Archives très privées 2."

70. See de Baecque, *Les Cahiers du cinéma,* vol. 1, pp. 147–152.

71. *Cahiers du cinéma,* 34 (April 1954).

72. François Truffaut, "Voici les trente nouveaux noms du cinéma français," *Arts,* January 15, 1958.

73. *Cahiers du cinéma* 47 (May 1955).

74. Ibid.

75. André Bazin, "De la politique des auteurs," *Cahiers du cinéma* 70 (April 1957).

76. *Cahiers du cinéma* 86 (August 1958).

77. *Cahiers du cinéma* 44 (February 1955).

78. François Truffaut, "Hitchcock est le plus grand inventeur de forme," *Arts,* December 4, 1957.

79. François Truffaut, "Ladmirable certitude," *Cahiers du cinéma* 46 (April 1955).

80. François Truffaut, "Journal du festival de Cannes: une histoire de fous," *Arts,* May 9, 1956.

81. Letter from Jean Delannoy to François Truffaut, November 13, 1955, archives of Les Films du Carrosse, file "CCH 1 (1953–1957)."

82. François Truffaut, "Cannes, un incontestable succès? Non, Monsieur le Ministre," *Arts,* May 16, 1956.

83. Truffaut, *Correspondance,* p. 120.

84. Interview with the authors, 1995.

85. Ibid.

86. François Truffaut, "Henri-Pierre Roché revisité," 1980 essay, a portion of which was published as a preface to the German edition of *Jules and Jim;* also as in François Truffaut, *Le Plaisir des Yeux* (Paris: Editions de l'Etoile, 1987); subsequently published as a foreword to Henri-Pierre Roché, *Carnets* (Marseille, Editions André Dimanche, 1990).

87. François Truffaut, "*Le Bandit* d'Edgar Ulmer," *Arts,* March 14, 1956.

88. Letter from Henri-Pierre Roché to François Truffaut, April 11, 1956, archives of Les Films du Carrosse, file "CCH 1 (1953–1957)."

89. Letter from Henri-Pierre Roché to François Truffaut, April 3, 1959, archives of Les Films du Carrosse, file "CCH 1 (1953–1957)."

90. Archives of Les Films du Carrosse, file "Archives très privées 1."

91. Ibid.

92. Ibid.

93. Ibid.

94. Maurice Pons, *Souvenirs littéraires* (Paris: Quai Voltaire, 1993).

95. "Les Mistons," in Maurice Pons, *Virginales* (Paris: Julliard, 1955), pp. 97–110.

96. Interview with the authors, 1995.

97. Letter from Bernadette Lafont to François Truffaut, July 8, 1957, archives of Les Films du Carrosse, file "CCH 1 (1953–1957)."

98. Interview with the authors, 1995.

99. Marcel Berbet quoted in *Le Roman de François Truffaut*, p. 68.

100. François Truffaut, "Vous êtes tous témoins dans ce procès: le cinéma français crève sous de fausses légendes," *Arts,* May 15, 1957.

101. Ibid. Quoted from François Truffaut, *The Films in My Life,* op. cit. p. 19.

102. François Truffaut, "Autant-Lara, faux martyr, est un cinéaste bourgeois," *Arts,* June 19, 1957.

103. François Truffaut, "Mefiez-vous fillettes: gangsters, filles, cinéastes, censeurs, dans le même panier," *Arts,* July 3, 1957.

104. François Truffaut, "Le Droit de répondre," *Arts,* June 12, 1957.

105. François Truffaut, "Le règne du cochon de payant est terminé," *Arts,* November 6, 1957.

106. François Truffaut, "Clouzot au travail ou le règne de la terreur," *Cahiers du cinéma* 77 (December 1957).

107. François Truffaut, "Si votre techniramage . . . ," *Cahiers du cinéma* 84 (June 1958).

108. François Truffaut, "Sacha Guitry fut un grand cinéaste réaliste," *Arts,* July 31, 1957.

109. François Truffaut, "Les critiques de cinéma sont misogynes: B.B. est victime d'une cabale," *Arts,* December 12, 1956.

110. Ibid.

111. Letter from Brigitte Bardot to François Truffaut, December 13, 1956, archives of Les Films du Carrosse, file "CCH 1 (1953–1957)."

112. *Midi libre,* August 4, 1957.

113. Interview with the authors, 1995

114. Truffaut, *Correspondance,* p. 130.

115. Interview with the authors, 1995

116. Truffaut, *Correspondance,* p. 130.

117. Interview with the authors, 1995

118. Truffaut kept a radioscopic test dated October 7, 1957, archives of Les Films du Carrosse, file "Santé [Health]."

119. Truffaut, *Correspondance,* p. 141.

120. *France-Soir,* November 19, 1958.

121. *France-Soir,* February 14, 1959.

122. Madeleine Morgenstern's interview with the authors, 1995.

123. Ibid.

124. Ibid.

125. Ibid.

126. Archives of Les Films du Carrosse, file "Archives très privées 1."

127. Interview with the authors, 1995.

128. Ibid.

129. Ibid.

130. Archives of Les Films du Carrosse, file "Archives très privées 1."

131. *L'Express,* January 14, 1964.

132. Archives of Les Films du Carrosse, file "CCH 1 (1953–1957)."

133. Letter from André Parinaud to François Truffaut, September 19, 1957, archives of Les Films du Carrosse, file "CCH 1 (1953–1957)."

134. Letter from François Truffaut to André Parinauld, September 21, 1957, archives of Les Films du Carrosse, file "CCH 1 (1953–1957)."

135. Archives of Les Films du Carrosse, file "Archives très privées 1."

136. Archives of Les Films du Carrosse, file "CCH 1 (1953–1957)."

**4.**
## NEW WAVE:
## 1958–1962

1. François Truffaut, *Correspondance* (Paris: Hatier, 1988), p. 139.

2. Ibid., pp. 138–139.

3. Letter from Pierre Braunberger to François Truffaut, February 15, 1958, archives of Les Films du Carrosse, file "CCH 1958."

4. Namely, in Nantes, at the end of March 1958, in Reims in mid-April, and then in the Brussels world festival of short films, where it received the prize for best direction.

5. *Arts,* May 14, 1958.

6. François Truffaut, "Si des modifications n'interviennent pas, le prochain festival est condamné," *Arts,* May 21, 1958.

7. Marcel Berbert's interview with the authors, 1995.

8. Interview with the authors, 1995.

9. François Truffaut's 1958 date book, archives of Les Films du Carrosse, file "Archives très privées 1."

10. Letter from François Truffaut to Robert Lachenay, April 30, 1958, archives of Les Films du Carrosse, file "Archives très privées 1." Other titles were considered for this film, including *Les petits copains [The Little Pals]*: "Because of my mother: 'Your little pals—always your little pals,'" Truffaut wrote to Lachenay on April 28, 1958.

11. Interview with the authors, 1991.

12. Truffaut, *Correspondance*, p. 144.

13. Ibid., p. 145.

14. Letter from Fernand Deligny to François Truffaut, February 4, 1959, archives of Les Films du Carrosse, file "Fernand Deligny."

15. Letter from Fernand Deligny to François Truffaut, August 20, 1958, archives of Les Films du Carrosse, file "Fernand Deligny."

16. Archives of Les Films du Carrosse, file "Fernand Deligny."

17. *Paris-Journal,* May 21, 1959.

18. Letter of January 27, 1958, archives of Les Films du Carrosse, file "Jean-Pierre Léaud."

19. Unpublished interview with Maurice Terrail, December 1979, archives of Les Films du Carrosse, file "CCH 1979 (2)."

20. François Truffaut, "Il faisait bon vivre," *Cahiers du cinéma* 90 (December 1958).

21. Ibid.

22. François Truffaut kept all the call sheets from his shoots, filed away by film. Thanks to the archives of Les Films du Carrosse, one can therefore follow the daily life on his sets.

23. Interview with the authors, 1995.

24. Ibid.

25. Ibid.

26. *Elle,* May 8, 1959.

27. Jacques Audiberti, "Avec ses '400 coups' d'essai, Truffaut a réussi un coup de maître." *Arts,* May 13, 1959.

28. Jacques Doniol-Valcroze, "Cannes 59," *Cahiers du cinéma* 96 (June 1959).

29. *Cinéma* 58, February 1958.

30. Jacques Siclier, *Nouvelle vague?* (Paris: Editions du Cerf, 1960); André S. Labarthe, *Essai sur le jeune cinéma français* (Paris: Editions Eric Losfeld,

1960); Raymond Borde, Freddy Buache, and Jean Curtelin, *Nouvelle Vague* (Lyon: Editions Serdoc, 1962).

31. *Cahiers du cinéma* 101 (November 1959).

32. See specifically *Positif* 46 (June 1962) and its special report, entitled "Feux sur le cinéma français."

33. *Lui,* September 1964.

34. *Santé Publique,* May 15, 1959.

35. *France-Soir,* June 6, 1959.

36. *Elle,* May 8, 1959.

37. *Cahiers des Saisons,* Fall 1959.

38. Philippe Labro's interview with the authors, 1996.

39. Interview with the authors, 1995.

40. Letter from Roland Truffaut to François Truffaut, April 17, 1959, archives of Les Films du Carrosse, file "Archives très privées 2."

41. Archives of Les Films du Carrosse, file "Archives très privées 2."

42. Letter from Roland Truffaut to François Truffaut, May 20, 1959, archives of Les Films Carrosse, file "Archives très privées 2."

43. Archives of Les Films du Carrosse, file "Archives très privées 2."

44. Ibid.

45. Letter from Madeleine Truffaut to Roland and Janine Truffaut, January 7, 1962, archives of Les Films Carrosse, file "Archives très privées 2."

46. Letter from Roland and Janine Truffaut to Madeleine Truffaut, January 11, 1962, archives of Les Films Carrosse, file "Archives très privées 2."

47. Interview with the authors, 1995.

48. Letter from François Truffaut to Roland Truffaut, May 28, 1962, archives of Les Films du Carrosse, file "Archives très privées 2."

49. Psychoanalysis always fascinated François Truffaut, and he read many books on child psychology, among other things. He considered undergoing analysis several times, but always changed his mind, probably because he felt that analysis would interfere with his work as a filmmaker. This is the opinion of his friend Liliane Siegel (interview with the authors, 1995): "When François mentioned psychoanalysis to me, I told him, 'If you start therapy, you'll never be the same and you won't make the same kinds of films.' He answered, 'I think

you're right, so I've been told.' I think he went to see a psychoanalyst two or three times, then decided not to undergo analysis. But he probably hesitated."

50. Letter from François Truffaut to Janine Truffaut, October 19, 1963, archives of Les Films du Carrosse, file "Archives très privées 2."

51. Interview with the authors, 1995.

52. Letter from Simone Jollivet to François Truffaut, June 12, 1961, archives of Les Films du Carrosse, file "CCH 61."

53. Interview with the authors, 1995.

54. Letter from François Truffaut to Helen Scott, December 27, 1960, archives of Les Films du Carrosse, file "Helen Scott."

55. Letter from François Truffaut to Helen Scott, March 1960, archives of Les Films du Carrosse, file "Helen Scott."

56. Interview with the authors, 1996.

57. Letter from François Truffaut to Helen Scott, March 29, 1960, archives of Les Films du Carrosse, file "Helen Scott."

58. Words used by François Truffaut in his letters to Helen Scott between 1960 and 1962.

59. Letter from François Truffaut to Helen Scott, March 14, 1963, archives of Les Films du Carrosse, file "Helen Scott."

60. Interview with the authors, 1995.

61. Letter of April 14, 1960, archives of Les Films du Carrosse, file "Jean-Pierre Léaud."

62. Liliane David's interview with the authors, 1995.

63. Madeleine Morgenstern's interview with the authors, 1995.

64. Marcel Berbert's interview with the authors, 1995.

65. Marcel Berbert quoted in *Le Roman de François Truffaut*, special issue of *Cahiers du cinéma*, December 1984, p. 44.

66. Article published in *Arts*, December 15, 1961; reprinted in François Truffaut, *The Films in My Life*, p. 321.

67. Undated letter from Jean-Luc Godard to François Truffaut, archives of Les Films du Carrosse, file "Jean-Luc Godard."

68. Letter from Georges de Beauregard to François Truffaut, July 20, 1959, archives of Les Films du Carrosse, file "Jean-Luc Godard."

69. Undated letter from Jean-Luc Godard to François Truffaut, archives of Les Films du Carrosse, file "Jean-Luc Godard."

70. Letter from Jean Cocteau to François Truffaut, May 20, 1959, archives of Les Films du Carrosse, file "Ecrivains."

71. Undated letter (June 1959) from Jean Cocteau to François Truffaut, archives of Les Films du Carrosse, file "Ecrivains."

72. Letter from François Truffaut to Roberto Rossellini, July 5, 1962, archives of Les Films du Carrosse, file "Roberto Rossellini." Several months later, Truffaut would give up the idea of coproducing this Rossellini project. For more information on this project, see Gianni Rondolino, *Roberto Rossellini* (Turin: Utet, 1989).

73. Archives of Les Films du Carrosse, file "CCH 60."

74. Truffaut and Les Films du Carrosse produced other short films during this period—by Claude Jutra (*Anna la bonne*), Jean Aurel (*Les Aventures extraordinaires*), Michel Varesano (*La Fin du voyage*), Fernand Deligny (*Le Moindre Geste*), Max Zelenka, Alain Jeannel, and Jean-Claude Roché (*Vie d'insecte*).

75. Letter from Marcel Ophuls to François Truffaut, dated "second day of shoot," archives of Les Films du Carrosse, file "Marcel Ophuls."

76. Interview with the authors, 1995.

77. Press kit, *Shoot the Piano Player*, 1960.

78. Liliane David's interview with the authors, 1996.

79. Claude de Givray's interview with the authors, 1996.

80. Letter from François Truffaut to Maurice Le Roux, May 11, 1960, archives of Les Films du Carrosse, file "CCH 60."

81. *Journal musical français*, September-October 1966.

82. François Truffaut, "Le chanteur soustitré," in *Boby Lapointe* (Paris: Editions Encres, 1980); republished in François Truffaut, *Le Plaisir des yeux* (Paris: Editions de l'Etoile, 1987), pp. 184–185.

83. *Le Plaisir des yeux*, pp. 184–185.

84. *Le Film français*, May 23, 1964.

85. *Lui*, February 1964.

86. Suzanne Schiffman quoted in *Le Roman de François Truffaut*, p. 52.

87. Press kit for *Shoot the Piano Player*, 1960.

88. *New York Times*, November 17, 1959.

89. *New York Herald Tribune,* December 14, 1959.

90. *New York Post,* November 17, 1959.

91. Archives of Les Films du Carrosse, file "CCH 60."

92. Helen Scott quoted in *Le Roman de François Truffaut,* p. 113.

93. Henry Miller, then sixty-nine, was a cult figure for the young Truffaut, one of the writers he most admired, particularly his book *Sexus,* which Truffaut always listed among the books that truly "changed his life." And Miller held Truffaut in high regard. The two men met again in New York in April 1962 and Miller gave Truffaut his first play, *Just Wild About Harry,* written in 1942 (unpublished and untranslated in France), at a time when the young director was not averse to directing for the stage. Truffaut, who couldn't read English at the time, gave it to his wife, Madeleine, to read and to Marcel Moussy. Madeleine liked the play, finding it "amusing, sentimental, and unusual," while Moussy had his doubts: "An outmoded, risky play," he wrote Truffaut at the end of May 1962. Meanwhile, on the basis of Madeleine's positive opinion, François Truffaut, recontacted Henry Miller by telegram while the writer was vacationing in the Formentor Hotel in Majorca: "Dear Mr. Miller. Stop. Possibility of staging play this winter and would very much like to do business with you. Stop. Yours with admiration. Stop." Henry Miller was delighted and immediately answered Truffaut with a letter written in French: "I should tell you right away that this is my first play and it might very well be bad. I call it 'melo-melo,' which means a mixture of farce, burlesque, slapstick and sentimentality. I think it is amusing and that no one will fall asleep. There are about twenty characters and four leads. I think there is a lot of 'business,' as they say—perhaps too much. But the Germans and Norwegians accepted it and up to now didn't criticize me for it. But you'll see for yourself. I'm flattered that someone like you is interested; believe me, I was very touched by your gesture. So see you soon, for I'll be in Paris next week— for only a few days." The two men did indeed meet in Paris, at the end of May 1962, and then spent a weekend working together near Nîmes, at the home of Lawrence Durrell, a great friend of Henry Miller. Yet the project never saw the light of day because of lack of enthusiasm on the part of Jean-Louis Barrault, the director of the Théâtre de France, who disliked the play and refused to mobilize twenty-odd actors at the Odéon theater for a work he considered "a bit lowbrow" and "very risky." (Letter to François Truffaut from Jean-Louis Barrault, Archives of Les Films du Carrosse, file "Ecrivains.") Miller would always have regrets about this aborted project.

94. Letter from Helen Scott to François Truffaut, March 3, 1960, archives of Les Films du Carrosse, file "Helen Scott."

95. Letter from François Truffaut to Helen Scott, March 29, 1960, Archives of Les Films du Carrosse, file "Helen Scott."

96. Letter from François Truffaut to Helen Scott, April 14, 1962, archives of Les Films du Carrosse, file "Helen Scott."

97. Archives of Les Films du Carrosse, file "CCH 60."

98. Letter from François Truffaut to Helen Scott, February 27, 1960, archives of Les Films du Carrosse, file "Helen Scott."

99. Letter from Elie Wiesel to François Truffaut, December 10, 1960, archives of Les Films du Carrosse, file "CCH 60."

100. Letter from François Truffaut to Helen Scott, November 16, 1960, archives of Les Films du Carrosse, file "Helen Scott."

101. Letter from François Truffaut to Alexandre Chambon, June 15, 1962, archives of Les Films du Carrosse, file "CCH 62."

102. Those responding to this appeal were Raoul Lévy, Pierre Kast, Philippe de Broca, Chris Marker, Jacques Doniol-Valcroze, Claude Chabrol, Pierre Braunberger, Marcel Ophuls, Alain Resnais, François Reichenbach, Jean-Luc Godard, Daniel Boulanger, Jacques Demy, Françoise Giroud, Agnès Varda, Georges Franju, Simone Signoret, Jean-Pierre Melville, Alexandre Astruc, Marguerite Duras, Louis Malle, Jean Rouch, Roger Vadim, Edouard Molinaro, and Georges de Beauregard.

103. Guy Teisseire, who died in 1993, later

became a journalist and film critic, writing for *L'Aurore, Parisien libéré, Matin de Paris,* and so on. He was also a screenwriter (*Il faut tuer Birgit Haas*) and a novelist (*Un peu plus loin que l'Occident* and *La Main d'Abraham,* both published by Editions Jean-Claude Lattès).

104. *Clarté* 42 (March 1962).

105. Letter from François Truffaut to Helen Scott, October 24, 1961, archives of Les Films du Carrosse, file "Helen Scott."

106. Letter from Claude Gauteur to François Truffaut, August 28, 1960, archives of Les Films du Carrosse, file "CCH 60."

107. Letter from Dionys Mascolo to François Truffaut, September 13, 1960, archives of Les Films du Carrosse, file "CCH 60."

108. For more information on this subject, see Jean-Pierre Rioux and Jean-François Sirinelli, eds., *La guerre d'Algérie et les intellectuels français* (Paris: Institut d'Histoire du Temps Présent, 1988), and Jean-François Sirinelli, *Intellectuels et passions françaises: manifestes et pétitions au XXe siècle* (Paris: Fayard, 1990).

109. Undated letter (October 1960) from Robert Benayoun to François Truffaut, archives of Les Films du Carrosse, file "CCH 60."

110. *France nouvelle,* November 4, 1960.

111. Letter from François Truffaut to Helen Scott, October 1, 1960, archives of Les Films du Carrosse, file "Helen Scott."

112. Letter from François Truffaut to Helen Scott, October 18, 1962, archives of Les Films du Carrosse, file "Helen Scott."

113. Letter from François Truffaut to François Leterrier, July 4, 1963, archives of Les Films du Carrosse, file "CCH 63."

114. Interview with the authors, 1995.

115. Letter from Pierre Braunberger to François Truffaut, August 20, 1960, archives of Les Films du Carrosse, file "CCH 60."

116. Letter from Pierre Braunberger to François Truffaut, August 30, 1960, archives of Les Films du Carrosse, file "CCH 60."

117. Letter from Jean Cocteau to François Truffaut, September 9, 1960, archives of Les Films du Carrosse, file "Ecrivains."

118. François Truffaut, "Petit journal du cinéma," *Cahiers du cinéma* 69 (March 1957).

119. Jeanne Moreau quoted in *Le Roman de François Truffaut,* p. 94.

120. François Truffaut, "Louis Malle a filmé la première nuit d'amour du cinéma," *Arts,* September 10, 1958.

121. Florence Malraux's interview with the authors, 1995.

122. Jeanne Moreau's interview with the authors, 1995.

123. René-Jean Clot, in a memo to Truffaut written in February 1960, offers his own adaptation in a few sentences: "The subject concerns a schoolteacher's reintegration into a primary school after a mental breakdown, her arrival in a new job, the reactions among her students and colleagues, and finally her removal from the community. It opposes two people, Madame Langlois, the newly arrived schoolteacher, tolerated at first and then hated, and Monsieur Fraipoint, a schoolteacher who will reveal himself to be the school's 'ringleader.' This man is rigid, meticulous, dissatisfied, and jealous of other people's success. He considers this new teacher 'suspicious,' with her superior culture and intellect; since he is frightened, he becomes aggressive and petty toward her and his fear gradually changes to hatred. He influences his colleagues to share his fear and very soon Madame Langlois becomes a sort of 'secular witch' who is harmful to the students and must be sent back where she came from. In spite of the kindness and generosity of the school inspector, stupidity will triumph and Madame Langlois will be transferred, but not without having to conceal a deep, new wound."

124. Letter from François Truffaut to Helen Scott, September 26, 1960, archives of Les Films du Carrosse, file "Helen Scott."

125. Letter from François Truffaut to Helen Scott, December 27, 1960, archives of Les Films du Carrosse, file "Helen Scott."

126. *Arts,* November 14, 1959.

127. *L'Express,* February 25, 1960.

128. Undated letter (1960) from Jean-Luc Godard to François Truffaut, archives of Les Films du Carrosse, file "Jean-Luc Godard."

129. Undated letter from François Truffaut to Jean Domarchi, undated, archives of Les Films du Carrosse, file "CCH 60."

130. *Signes du temps,* December 1959.

131. Letter from François Truffaut to Helen Scott, December 27, 1960, archives of Les Films du Carrosse, file "Helen Scott."

132. *France-Observateur,* October 19 1961.

133. François Truffaut, written in 1963 (press kit for the film); republished in Truffaut, *The Films in My Life,* trans. Leonard Mayhew (New York: Simon and Schuster, 1978), pp. 324–325.

134. Letter from François Truffaut to Helen Scott, October 24, 1961, archives of Les Films du Carrosse, file "Helen Scott."

135. For example, with its special issue "Nouvelle Vague" in December 1962. See Antoine de Baecque, *Les Cahiers du cinéma: Histoire d'une revue,* vol. 2 (Paris: Editions de l'Etoile, 1991), pp. 18–26, 70–86.

136. Letter from François Truffaut to Helen Scott, March 11, 1961, archives of Les Films du Carrosse, file "Helen Scott." Another explanation for Truffaut's prudence was the fact *Jules and Jim* was to be coproduced by Carrosse and SEDIF, which was then headed by his mother-in-law.

137. Letter from François Truffaut to Helen Scott, September 26, 1960, archives of Les Films du Carrosse, file "Helen Scott."

138. Jean Gruault describes the writing of the *Jules and Jim* screenplay in *Ce que dit l'autre* (Paris: Julliard, 1992), pp. 193–195, 199–200, 207–208.

139. *L'Alsace,* March 17, 1961.

140. Jeanne Moreau's interview with the authors, 1995.

141. Ibid.

142. Florence Malraux's interview with the authors, 1995.

143. Jean-Louis Richard's interview with the authors, 1992.

144. Jeanne Moreau's interview with the authors, 1995.

145. Marcel Berbert's interview with the authors, 1995.

146. "Henri-Pierre Roché revisité," in *Le Plaisir des yeux,* pp. 146–155.

147. "Jeanne Moreau, rieuse et tendre," in *Le Plaisir des yeux,* p. 187.

148. Liliane David's interview with the authors, 1995.

149. Jeanne Moreau's interview with the authors, 1995.

150. Florence Malraux's interview with the authors, 1995.

151. Interview with the authors, 1995.

152. Letter from François Truffaut to Helen Scott, November 9, 1961, archives of Les Films du Carrosse, file "Helen Scott."

153. Claudine Bouché's interview with the authors, 1995.

154. Ibid.

155. Jean Aurel's interview with the authors, 1995.

156. *Journal de Fahrenheit* 451, published with the screenplay of *La Nuit américaine* (Paris: Seghers, 1974), p. 228.

157. Jean Aurel's interview with the authors, 1995.

158. "Henri-Pierre Roché revisité," pp. 146–155.

159. Truffaut, *Correspondance,* p. 188.

160. Letter from François Truffaut to Helen Scott, December 20, 1961, archives of Les Films du Carrosse, file "Helen Scott."

161. Letter from Jean Renoir to François Truffaut, February 8, 1962, archives of Les Films du Carrosse, file "Jean Renoir."

162. Letter from Jean Cocteau to François Truffaut, February 7, 1962, archives of Les Films du Carrosse, file "Ecrivains."

163. Letter from Denise Roché to François Truffaut, February 4, 1962, archives of Les Films du Carrosse, file "CCH 62."

164. Letter from Helen Hessel to François Truffaut, January 30, 1962, archives of Les Films du Carrosse, file "CCH 62." Truffaut answered several days later: "I was very happy to receive your letter and I read it with much emotion. I filmed *Jules and Jim* with profound respect, for I've never liked a book as much as this one and I'm very worried about how the spectators who knew Henri-Pierre Roché will react. This is why your letter increases my anxiety while it also gives me great joy. On learning of your letter, Mademoiselle Jeanne Moreau felt the same emotion as I

and joins me in sending you our most respectful thoughts."

165. *France-Observateur,* February 1, 1962.

166. Interview with the authors, 1996.

167. Letter from François Truffaut to Helen Scott, December 20, 1961, archives of Les Films du Carrosse, file "Helen Scott."

168. Marie-France Pisier quoted in *Le Roman de François Truffaut,* p. 96.

169. Ibid.

170. Interview with the authors, 1995.

171. Letter from François Truffaut to Helen Scott, December 24, 1961, archives of Les Films du Carrosse, file "Helen Scott."

172. Letter from François Truffaut to Helen Scott, January 4, 1962, archives of Les Films du Carrosse, file "Helen Scott."

173. Letter from François Truffaut to Helen Scott, January 18, 1962, archives of Les Films du Carrosse, file "Helen Scott."

174. Letter from François Truffaut to Helen Scott, October 18, 1962, archives of Les Films du Carrosse, file "Helen Scott."

175. Ibid.

176. Letter from François Truffaut to Helen Scott, January 14, 1963, archives of Les Films du Carrosse, file "Helen Scott."

177. Letter from François Truffaut to Roberto Rossellini, November 30, 1962, archives of Les Films du Carrosse, file "Roberto Rossellini."

178. Letter from Marcel Varesano to François Truffaut, November 13, 1961, archives of Les Films du Carrosse, file "CCH 61."

179. Undated letter (1962) from Robert Lachenay to François Truffaut, archives of Les Films du Carrosse, file "Archives très privées 1."

180. Undated letter (1961) from Jean-Luc Godard to François Truffaut, archives of Les Films du Carrosse, file "Jean-Luc Godard."

## 5.
### THE SLOW YEARS:
### 1962–1968

1. *La Libre Belgique,* May 14, 1963.

2. Interview with the authors, 1995.

3. Jean-Dominique Bauby, *Raoul Lévy: un aventurier du cinéma* (Paris: Jean-Claude Lattès, 1995).

4. Interview with the authors, 1995.

5. Memo from Don Congdon to Helen Scott, April 24, 1962, archives of Les Films du Carrosse, file "Ecrivains."

6. Letter from François Truffaut to Ray Bradbury, April 27, 1962, archives of Les Films du Carrosse, file "Ecrivains."

7. Letter from Ray Bradbury to François Truffaut, May 3, 1962, archives of Les Films du Carrosse, file "Ecrivains."

8. From his experiences with Maurice Pons, René-Jean Clot, Jacques Audiberti, and Henry Miller, François Truffaut realized that it was very tricky for a film director to work directly with a writer. After a while, he preferred to collaborate with his screenwriter, who was rarely a professional writer.

9. Interview with the authors, 1995.

10. *La Cinématographie française,* May 7, 1964.

11. Letter from François Truffaut to Ray Bradbury, September 24, 1962, archives of Les Films du Carrosse, file "Ecrivains."

12. Letter from François Truffaut to Charles Aznavour, January 18, 1963, archives of Les Films du Carrosse, file "CCH 63."

13. Letter from François Truffaut to Helen Scott, March 20, 1963, archives of Les Films du Carrosse, file "Helen Scott."

14. Marcel Berbert quoted in *Le Roman de François Truffaut,* special issue of *Cahiers du cinéma,* December 1984, p. 46.

15. Letter from François Truffaut to André Pépin, July 16, 1963, archives of Les Films du Carrosse, file "CCH 63."

16. Letter from François Truffaut to Don Congdon, November 16, 1962, archives of Les Films du Carrosse, file "Congdon."

17. This is a point Truffaut makes at the end of an article on *Rear Window* written for *Arts,* April 6, 1955: "No, this devil of a man hasn't yet revealed all his secrets, but each new film allows us to better understand a very rich oeuvre that is one of the subtlest in contemporary cinema."

18. Introduction to François Truffaut, *Le Cinéma selon Alfred Hitchcock* (Paris: Robert Laffont, 1966). U.S. edition: *Hitchcock* (New York: Simon and Schuster, 1967), p. 8.

19. Letter from François Truffaut to

Alfred Hitchcock, June 2, 1962, archives of Les Films du Carrosse, file "Alfred Hitchcock." Excerpts from this letter are from François Truffaut, *Correspondance 1945–1984*, trans. Gilbert Adair (New York: Noonday Press, 1988), p. 177.

20. Ibid (Gilbert Adair's translation, p. 179).

21. *Archives* of Les Films du Carrosse, file "Alfred Hitchcock."

22. Letter from François Truffaut to Helen Scott, June 20, 1962, archives of Les Films du Carrosse, file "Helen Scott."

23. Letter from François Truffaut to Don Congdon, November 16, 1962, archives of Les Films du Carrosse, file "Congdon."

24. Letter from François Truffaut to Helen Scott, August 24, 1962, archives of Les Films du Carrosse, file "Helen Scott."

25. Letter of April 14, 1963, archives of Les Films du Carrosse, file "Simon and Schuster."

26. Letter from François Truffaut to Helen Scott July 5, 1962, archives of Les Films du Carrosse, file "Helen Scott."

27. Archives of Les Films du Carrosse, file "Alfred Hitchcock."

28. Helen Scott quoted in *Le Roman de François Truffaut*, p. 114.

29. Letter from François Truffaut to Helen Scott, August 24, 1962, archives of Les Films du Carrosse, file "Helen Scott."

30. Ibid.

31. Interview with the authors, 1995.

32. Letter from François Truffaut to Helen Scott, July 18, 1963, archives of Les Films du Carrosse, file "Helen Scott."

33. Letter from François Truffaut to Helen Scott, September 9, 1963, archives of Les Films du Carrosse, file "Helen Scott."

34. Letter from François Truffaut to Helen Scott, January 14, 1964, archives of Les Films du Carrosse, file "Helen Scott."

35. Press kit for *Les Deux Anglaises et le Continent,* 1971.

36. Marcel Berbert's interview with the authors, 1995.

37. Letter from François Truffaut to Helen Scott, September 27, 1963, archives of Les Films du Carrosse, file "Helen Scott."

38. Lucas Steiner is the name Truffaut gave to the character played by Heinz Bennent in *The Last Métro*—the Jewish director hidden in the basement of the theater.

39. Interview with the authors, 1995.

40. Ibid.

41. Archives of Les Films du Carrosse, file "CCH 63."

42. Letter from François Truffaut to Kashiko Kawakita, April 22, 1963, archives of Les Films du Carrosse, file "CCH 63."

43. Letter from François Truffaut to Helen Scott, August 20, 1963, archives of Les Films du Carrosse, file "Helen Scott."

44. Interview conducted by Michel Pascal and Serge Toubiana for the documentary *François Truffaut: Portraits volés (Stolen Portraits),* 1992.

45. Letter from François Truffaut to Helen Scott, January 1, 1964, archives of Les Films du Carrosse, file "Helen Scott."

46. Letter from François Truffaut to Helen Scott, September 9, 1963, archives of Les Films du Carrosse, file "Helen Scott."

47. Interview with the authors, 1995.

48. *Val d'or. Quotidien québecquois,* November 17, 1965.

49. Ibid.

50. Press kit for *La Peau douce,* 1964.

51. Truffaut shot so many sequences that he was able to edit the outtakes into a short ten-minute film, *Les Voix d'Orly (Voices of Orly),* which he himself defined as "a cinema poem structured around visual and sound relationships, a poem playing on the contrast between the noise of the jets on the runway and the idyllic three-note bell summoning passengers to waiting areas."

52. Letter from François Truffaut to Helen Scott, November 14, 1963, archives of Les Films du Carrosse, file "Helen Scott."

53. Letter from François Truffaut to Helen Scott, December 18, 1963, archives of Les Films du Carrosse, file "Helen Scott."

54. Ibid.

55. In one scene in the film, Jean-Louis Richard goes up to Franca in the street and offers to show her "dirty pictures." She publicly insults him.

56. Jean-Louis Richard's interview with the authors, 1995.

57. Claudine Bonché's interview with the authors, 1995.

58. Letter from François Truffaut to Helen Scott, January 1, 1964, archives of Les Films du Carrosse, file "Helen Scott."

59. Interview with the authors, 1995.

60. Letter from François Truffaut to Helen Scott, May 10–12, 1964, archives of Les Films du Carrosse, file "Helen Scott."

61. Claudine Bonché's interview with the authors, 1995.

62. Marcel Berbert's interview with the authors, 1995.

63. Archives of Les Films du Carrosse, file "Helen Scott."

64. Undated letter from Jean-Luc Godard to François Truffaut, archives of Les Films du Carrosse, file "Jean-Luc Godard."

65. Letter from François Truffaut to Helen Scott, May 28, 1964, archives of Les Films du Carrosse, file "Helen Scott."

66. Letter from Claude Jutra to François Truffaut, August 1, 1964, archives of Les Films du Carrosse, file "CCH 64."

67. Letter from François Truffaut to Helen Scott, February 22, 1964, archives of Les Films du Carrosse, file "Helen Scott."

68. Interview with the authors, 1995.

69. Letter from François Truffaut to Helen Scott, February 22, 1964, archives of Les Films du Carrosse, file "Helen Scott."

70. Interview with the authors, 1995.

71. Excerpt from the want ad in *Le Figaro,* May 19, 1965.

72. Interview with the authors, 1994.

73. Letter from François Truffaut to Helen Scott, November 27, 1964, archives of Les Films du Carrosse, file "Helen Scott."

74. Interview with the authors, 1995.

75. Ibid.

76. It was a tricky case for the defense, since Truffaut and Richard had indeed seen and read the Sainte-Colombe screenplay.

77. Letter from François Truffaut to Helen Scott, November 27, 1964, archives of Les Films du Carrosse, file "Helen Scott."

78. Ibid.

79. Letter from François Truffaut to Helen Scott, May 28, 1964, archives of Les Films du Carrosse, file "Helen Scott."

80. Letter from François Truffaut to Princess Soraya, July 17, 1964, archives of Les Films du Carrosse, file "CCH 64."

81. Letter from François Truffaut to Marcel Berbert, April 2, 1964, archives of Les Films du Carrosse, file "CCH 64."

82. Ibid.

83. Interview with the authors, 1995.

84. Ibid.

85. Letter from François Truffaut to Elinor Jones, September 7, 1964, archives of Les Films du Carrosse, file "CCH 64."

86. Archives of Les Films du Carrosse, file "Jean-Luc Godard."

87. Archives of Les Films du Carrosse, file "CCH 65."

88. Letter from François Truffaut to Elinor Jones, July 2, 1965, archives of Les Films du Carrosse, file "CCH 65."

89. Letter from Eugene Archer to François Truffaut, September 3, 1962, archives of Les Films du Carrosse, file "CCH 62."

90. Letter from François Truffaut to Helen Scott, August 20, 1963, archives of Les Films du Carrosse, file "Helen Scott."

91. Letter from François Truffaut to Lewis Allen July 3, 1963, archives of Les Films du Carrosse, file "CCH 63."

92. Letter from François Truffaut to Lewis Allen, June 5, 1963, archives of Les Films du Carrosse, file "CCH 63."

93. Letter from François Truffaut to Lewis Allen, July 3, 1963, archives of Les Films du Carrosse, file "CCH 63."

94. Letter from Lewis Allen to François Truffaut, November 7, 1963, archives of Les Films du Carrosse, file "CCH 63."

95. Letter from François Truffaut to Lewis Allen, September 13, 1963, archives of Les Films du Carrosse, file "CCH 63."

96. Letter from Lewis Allen to François Truffaut, November 7, 1963, archives of Les Films du Carrosse, file "CCH 63."

97. Letter from François Truffaut to Lewis Allen, October 18, 1963, archives of Les Films du Carrosse, file "CCH 63."

98. Letter from François Truffaut to Helen Scott, December 16, 1964, archives of Les Films du Carrosse, file "Helen Scott."

99. Telegram of October 29, 1964, archives of Les Films du Carrosse, file "CCH 64."

100. Interview with François Truffaut, *Elle,* September 28, 1966.

101. Letter from François Truffaut to Terence Stamp, December 21, 1965, archives of Les Films du Carrosse, file "CCH 65."
102. *Journal de Fahrenheit 451*, published with the screenplay of *La Nuit Américaine* (Paris: Seghers, 1974), p. 168.
103. Letter from François Truffaut to Jacques Doniol-Valcroze, January 17, 1966, archives of Les Films du Carrosse, file "CCH 66."
104. Suzanne Schiffman quoted in *Le Roman de François Truffaut*, p. 52.
105. For further information on this shoot, see the marvelous *Journal de Fahrenheit 451*, about which Peter Bogdanovich wrote to Truffaut in the fall of 1966: "I don't know which I prefer, your film *Fahrenheit* or your journal on the shoot. The latter will serve as inspiration to *all* directors and be a kind of guide." (Archives of Les Films du Carrosse, file "CCH 66.")
106. *Journal de Fahrenheit 451*, p. 168.
107. Ibid., p. 169.
108. Letter from François to Marcel Berbert, January 22, 1966, archives of Les Films du Carrosse, file "CCH 66."
109. Interview with the authors, 1996.
110. The issue of *Cahiers du cinéma* with Anna Karina on the cover was number 177, which had a special report on the censorship of Jacques Rivette's *La Religieuse* (*The Nun*). For more details about this matter, see Antoine de Baecque, *Les Cahiers du cinéma: Histoire d'une revue*, vol. 2 (Paris: Editions de l'Etoile, 1991), pp. 173–176.
111. *Journal de Fahrenheit 451*, p. 219.
112. Ibid., p. 177.
113. Ibid., p. 175.
114. Ibid., p. 186.
115. Ibid., p. 219.
116. Letter from François Truffaut to Thom Noble, October 10, 1966, archives of Les Films du Carrosse, file "CCH 66."
117. Telegram of August 31, 1966, archives of Les Films du Carrosse, file "Ecrivains."
118. Letter from François Truffaut to Ray Bradbury, January 1, 1967, archives of Les Films du Carrosse, file "Ecrivains."
119. Letter from François Truffaut to Helen Scott, May 3, 1965, archives of Les Films du Carrosse, file "Helen Scott."
120. Letter from Alfred Hitchcock to

François Truffaut, October 22, 1965, archives of Les Films du Carrosse, file "Alfred Hitchcock."
121. Letter from Alfred Hitchcock to Odette Ferry, June 17, 1966, archives of Les Films du Carrosse, file "CCH 66."
122. Letter from Robert Laffont to François Truffaut, January 13, 1966, archives of Les Films du Carrosse, file "CCH 66."
123. Letter from François Truffaut to Helen Scott, November 27, 1964, archives of Les Films du Carrosse, file "Helen Scott."
124. *Les Nouvelles littéraires*, November 22, 1966.
125. Letter from Alfred Hitchcock to François Truffaut, December 9, 1966, archives of Les Films du Carrosse, file "Alfred Hitchcock."
126. Letter from François Truffaut to Helen Scott, August 13, 1964, archives of Les Films du Carrosse, file "Helen Scott."
127. Letter from François Truffaut to Helen Scott, August 19, 1964, archives of Les Films du Carrosse, file "Helen Scott."
128. Press kit for *The Bride Wore Black*, 1968.
129. Interview with the authors, 1995.
130. Letter from François Truffaut to Don Congdon, August 19, 1964, archives of Les Films du Carrosse, file "Congdon."
131. Letter from François Truffaut to Ray Bradbury, January 25, 1967, archives of Les Films du Carrosse, file "Ecrivains."
132. Letter from Ray Bradbury to François Truffaut, May 14, 1969, archives of Les Films du Carrosse, file "Ecrivains."
133. Letter from François Truffaut to Nicole Stéphane, August 31, 1964, archives of Les Films du Carrosse, file "CCH 64." Nicole Stéphane produced *Un amour de Swann* (*Swann in Love*) in 1983, directed by Volker Schlöndorff.
134. Madeleine Morgenstern's interview with the authors, 1995.
135. Claudine Bouché's interview with the authors, 1995.
136. *Le Nouvel Observateur*, March 8, 1967.
137. Interview conducted by Michel Pascal for the film *François Truffaut: Portraits volés*, 1992.
138. Memo to the collaborators, artists, and technicians of *The Bride Wore Black*,

undated, archives of Les Films du Carrosse, file *"La Mariée. Feuilles de service."*
139. Interview with the authors, 1995.
140. Jeanne Moreau quoted in *Le Roman de François Truffaut,* p. 94.
141. Ibid.
142. Letter from François Truffaut to Alfred Hitchcock, August 31, 1967, archives of Les Films du Carrosse, file "Alfred Hitchcock."
143. Letter from Alfred Hitchcock to François Truffaut, June 17, 1968, archives of Les Films du Carrosse, file "Alfred Hitchcock."
144. Handwritten note, undated, archives of Les Films du Carrosse, file "CCH 67."
145. Letter of May 11, 1967, archives of Les Films du Carrosse, file "CCH 67."
146. *Cahiers du cinéma* 190 (May 1967).
147. *L'Express,* October 28, 1966.

# 6.
## PARALLEL LIVES:
## 1968–1971

1. Claude de Givray's interview with the authors, 1995.
2. Ibid.
3. The refrain from the song "Que reste-t-il de nos amours?": *"Bonheur fané/ Cheveux au vent/Baisers volés/Rêves mouvants/Que reste-t-il de tout cela?"*
4. Press kit for *Stolen Kisses,* 1968.
5. François Truffaut, in *Le Plaisir des yeux* (Paris: Editions de l'Etoile, 1967), p. 174.
6. Undated letter (January 1968) from Delphine Seyrig to François Truffaut archives of Les Films du Carrosse, file "CCH 68."
7. Press kit for *Stolen Kisses,* 1968.
8. Interview with the authors, 1991.
9. Ibid.
10. The writing and rewriting of the screenplay of *Stolen Kisses* is revealing of the "Truffaut method." Thanks to the different stages of the project, it is possible to shed light on his writing process. See the book by Carole Le Berre, *François Truffaut,* Ed. de l'Etoile, Paris, 1993. Truffaut revised the screenplay of *Stolen Kisses* in December 1967. This was the first time a fully researched and investigated story came to him virtually "ready to use." Though Truffaut kept all of his scriptwriters' research work for the film, he was very

critical of their character portrayals, situations, and dialogue. His notes on the original screenplay are very revealing. Truffaut also rejected the name "Martine"—"People who call their daughter Martine or Caroline are morons who have been under the spell of Martine Carol between 1950 and 1955. Like Brigitte later and now Sylvie, etc. ... Hence no Martine"—only the heroine herself from the Revon and de Givray script. Indeed, in the screen version of *Stolen Kisses,* "Christine Darbon" is no longer a slightly bitchy, very snobbish girl from the upper bourgeoisie of the sixteenth arrondissement, but the "serious daughter" of a couple from the petite bourgeoisie living in a house in the Paris suburbs. Similarly, Truffaut rejected the name "Cyprienne" for the "forty-year-old woman": "It's straight out of boulevard theater." Instead, he came up with the name "Fabienne Tabard." This elegant woman is no longer the wife of a military man stationed far away, but of a shoe store owner. He also changed his scriptwriters' suggested locations: the Opéra Comique would not be kept for the film, nor the fashionable restaurant, nor the social evenings in beautiful apartments, and opposite the tennis match at the Pierre-de-Coubertin stadium he noted, "I hate stadiums." Finally, Truffaut particularly objected to the dialogue in this original screenplay: "Very bad, 1937 dialogue for Renée Saint-Cyr"; "Terrible lack of invention. This is all banal"; "False, false. Not serious, not realistic. A cheat and too quick"; "All of this is hardly serious, really. I told you: do it as you would for yourself, not Chabrol"; "What film are we in? This smacks of Georges Conchon, i.e., Paris high society and boulevard satire which is to *Edouard et Caroline* what *L'Eau à la bouche* is to *La Règle du jeu*."
11. Undated letter (April 1968) from Delphine Seyrig to François Truffaut, archives of Les Films du Carrosse, file "CCH 68."
12. Ibid.
13. Press kit for *Stolen Kisses,* 1968.
14. G. P. Langlois and G. Myrent, *Henri Langlois: Premier citoyen du cinéma* (Paris: Denoël, 1986); republished by Ramsay (on the affair of February 1968, see pp. 319–357). Richard Roud, *Henri Langlois: l'homme de la Cinémathèque*

(Paris: Belfond, 1985). U.S. edition: *A Passion for Films: Henri Langlois and the Cinémathèque Française* (New York: Viking, 1983). Also, on the Langlois affair, see Antoine de Baecque, *Les Cahiers du cinéma: Histoire d'une revue,* vol. 2 (Paris: Editions de l'Etoile, 1991), pp. 177–183.

15. As of January 1969, François Truffaut wanted to stop working for the Cinémathèque Defense Committee. Indeed, he couldn't bear Langlois's "fumblings, constant improvisations, doubtful decisions concerning fundamental choices . . . particularly when they are institutionalized" (letter of September 5, 1969). Truffaut therefore wrote Langlois a "rather sad" letter in January 1969 to tell him of his resignation: "If the Defense Committee served any purpose in the course of 1968, it's not because it functioned *with* you, but *by your side* and definitively *for* you. If, as you say, the Prix Delluc for *Stolen Kisses* comes with a check, I'll give it to the Defense Committee and it will be the last check signed and endorsed François Truffaut, Treasurer. Naturally I'll withdraw without making a fuss or doing anything that could harm you; I'll simply transmit the files to Doniol-Valcroze, since he is the assistant treasurer, and that's all. . . ." (Letter of January 13, 1969, archives of Les Films du Carrosse, file "Henri Langlois").

16. Archives of Les Films du Carrosse, file "Henri Langlois."

17. *Combat,* February 12, 1968.

18. *France-Soir,* February 13, 1968.

19. Archives of Les Films du Carrosse, file "Henri Langlois."

20. Letter from François Truffaut to Jean-Louis Comolli, March 8, 1968, archives of Les Films du Carrosse, file "Henri Langlois."

21. Letter from François Truffaut to François Mitterrand, March 26, 1969, archives of Les Films du Carrosse, file "Henri Langlois."

22. Archives of Les Films du Carrosse, file "Henri Langlois."

23. Letter from François Truffaut to Louis Marcorelles, May 12, 1968, archives of Les Films du Carrosse, file "Henri Langlois."

24. Georges Kiejman quoted in *Le Roman de François Truffaut,* special issue of *Cahiers du cinéma,* December 1984, p. 133.

25. Interview with the authors, 1995.

26. *L'Intransigeant,* May 20, 1968; *Paris-Jour,* May 20, 1968.

27. *L'Express,* July 15, 1968.

28. *Le Cinéma s'insurge* 1 (May 1968), the brochure of the Etats généraux du cinéma, Eric Losfeld editor.

29. Ibid.

30. *L'Express,* July 15, 1968.

31. Ibid.

32. *Les Nouvelles littéraires,* July 25, 1968.

33. *L'Express,* July 15, 1968.

34. Ibid.

35. Ibid.

36. Letter from François Truffaut to Helen Scott, October 14, 1967, archives of Les Films du Carrosse, file "Helen Scott."

37. Archives of Les Films du Carrosse, file "Ma Vie 1." This report by Albert Duchenne should be read with some wariness. The details of the investigation are not given and his conclusions are subject to caution.

38. Truffaut/De Givray interview, June 1984, archives of Les Films du Carrosse, p. 34.

39. In an article on *La Femme d'à côté* (*The Woman Next Door*), *Libération,* September 30, 1981, Serge Daney referred to a "Jekyll Truffaut" and a "Hyde Truffaut."

40. Interview with the authors, 1995.

41. Ibid.

42. In a letter to Tanya Lopert, who had just lost her father, Truffaut expressed his feelings concerning "his" dead. It can be seen as the germ of what would later become *The Green Room:* "There are far too many dead around me whom I have loved, and since Françoise Dorléac's death, I have decided not to go to any funerals, which, as you can imagine, does not prevent the presence of sadness, darkening everything for a while and never really being completely obliterated, even as the years go by, for we don't just live with the living, but also with all those who have counted in our lives." Undated letter (February 1970), archives of Les Films du Carrosse, file "CCH 70 (1)."

43. It was then that he established the principal files of his intimate life: "Ma Vie 1," "Ma Vie 2," "Archives très privées 1," and "Archives très privées 2," which are presently kept at Les Films du Carrosse.

44. Letter from Suzanne de Saint-Martin

to François Truffaut August 24, 1969, archives of Les Films du Carrosse, file "Ma Vie 1."

45. The Monferrand family disagreed with this interpretation of the facts. Monique de Monferrand, for example, felt the breakup between Roland Lévy and Janine de Monferrand was the former's decision and that he had left his girlfriend of the time without even knowing that he had made her pregnant.

46. Archives of Les Films du Carrosse, file "Ma Vie 1."

47. Press kit for *Stolen Kisses*, 1968.

48. *Paris-Soir*, September 14, 1968.

49. *New York Times*, March 5, 1969.

50. Marcel Berbert's interview with the authors, 1995.

51. Archives of Les Films du Carrosse, file "Gérard Lebovici."

52. Letter from François Truffaut to Don Congdon, October 14, 1967, archives of Les Films du Carrosse, file "Don Congdon."

53. Letter from François Truffaut to Ilya Lopert, November 13, 1968, archives of Les Films du Carrosse, file "CCH 68."

54. Interview with François Truffaut, *Playboy*, January 1975.

55. Suzanne Schiffman's interview with the authors, 1995.

56. François Truffaut, "En travaillant avec Catherine Deneuve," *Unifrance Film Magazine*, 1969. Reprinted in *Le Plaisir des yeux*, pp. 175–177.

57. Letter from François Truffaut to Catherine Deneuve, September 2, 1968, archives of Les Films du Carrosse, file "CCH 68."

58. Ibid.

59. Laurence Benaïm, *Yves Saint-Laurent* (Paris: Grasset, 1993).

60. Interview with the authors, 1995.

61. Ibid.

62. Letter from François Truffaut to Jean Narboni, January 14, 1969, archives of Les Films du Carrosse, file "CCH 69."

63. Letter from François Truffaut to Helen Scott, November 29, 1968, archives of Les Films du Carrosse, file "Helen Scott."

64. Telegram of December 10, 1968, archives of Les Films du Carrosse, file "CCH 68."

65. François Truffaut, "En travaillant avec Catherine Deneuve," *Unifrance Film Magazine*, 1969.

66. Interview with the authors, 1995.

67. Ibid.

68. Letter from François Truffaut to Jean Narboni, January 14, 1969, archives of Les Films du Carrosse, file "CCH 69."

69. "I'm quite moved because I just saw my first mistress again," he wrote to Helen Scott in May 1965, "the first woman I ever lived with." (Archives of Les Films du Carrosse, file "Helen Scott.")

70. Mirieille G. also inspired the screenplay of *La Petite Voleuse*, written by François Truffaut and Claude de Givray, which was directed by Claude Miller in 1988, four years after Truffaut's death.

71. This sequence had been written for Françoise Dorléac in the script of *The Soft Skin*, then cut in the editing by Truffaut, who reshot it identically five years later with Catherine Deneuve.

72. Catherine Deneuve quoted in *Le Roman de François Truffaut*, p. 98.

73. Call sheets for *Mississippi Mermaid*, archives of Les Films du Carrosse, file "F. S. Sirène."

74. The island was baptized Réunion Island in 1793 following the events of August 10, 1792, the day of the taking of the Tuileries castle, the abolition of the monarchy, and the establishment of the French Republic, all events illustrated by Renoir in *La Marseillaise*.

75. Letter from Jean Renoir to François Truffaut, August 27, 1969, archives of Les Films du Carrosse, file "Jean Renoir."

76. Letter from François Truffaut to Helen Scott, May 14, 1969, archives of Les Films du Carrosse, file "Helen Scott."

77. *Le Nouvel Observateur*, June 30, 1969.

78. Undated letter (October 1969) from François Truffaut to François Weyergans, archives of Les Films du Carrosse, file "CCH 69."

79. Letter from François Truffaut to Helen Scott, June 6, 1969, archives of Les Films du Carrosse, file "Helen Scott."

80. Letter from François Truffaut to Aimée Alexandre, June 14, 1969, archives of Les Films du Carrosse, file "Aimée Alexandre."

81. Interview with Claude-Marie Tremois, *Télérama*, June 15, 1969.

82. *Paris-Match,* March 8, 1969.

83. "En travaillant avec Catherine Deneuve."

84. Interview with the authors, 1995.

85. Letter from François Truffaut to Helen Scott, June 6, 1969, archives of Les Films du Carrosse, file "Helen Scott."

86. Letter from François Truffaut to Aimée Alexandre, June 14, 1969, archives of Les Films du Carrosse, file "Aimée Alexandre."

87. *Le Roman de François Truffaut,* p. 58.

88. Lucien Malson, *Les Enfants sauvages: Mythe et réalité* (Paris: Union Générale d'Edition, 1964).

89. Jean Gruault, *Ce que dit l'autre* (Paris: Julliard, 1992), p. 238.

90. Letter from François Truffaut to Jean Gruault, November 29, 1965, archives of Les Films du Carrosse, file "CCH 65."

91. François Truffaut helped Fernand Deligny and Jean-Pierre Daniel to produce their film on autistic children, *Le Moindre geste* (1965). Then, between 1972 and 1974, he financed *Ce gamin-là,* a film made by Renaud Victor in Monoblet with Deligny.

92. Letter from François Truffaut to Fernand Deligny, November 15, 1968, archives of Les Films du Carrosse, file "Fernand Deligny."

93. Interview with François Truffaut, *Heures Claires,* December 1965.

94. Marcel Berbert's interview with the authors, 1995.

95. Jean-Louis Livi's interview with the authors, 1996.

96. Nestor Almendros, *A Man with a Camera,* trans. Rachel Phillips Belash (New York: Farrar, Straus and Giroux, 1984), p. 84.

97. Letter from François Truffaut, June 6, 1969, archives of Les Films du Carrosse, file "Helen Scott."

98. Ibid.

99. Interview with the authors, 1995.

100. Interview with François Truffaut, *Télérama,* February 28, 1970.

101. Letter from Jean Grualt to François Truffaut, August 2, 1969, archives of Les Films du Carrosse, file "CCH 69."

102. Letter from François Truffaut to Gilles Jacob, July 13, 1969, archives of Les Films du Carrosse, file "CCH 69."

103. *Télérama,* February 28, 1970.

104. Ibid.

105. Letter from Jean-Pierre Cargol to François Truffaut, May 22, 1970, archives of Les Films du Carrosse, file "CCH 70 (1)."

106. Letter from François Truffaut to Patrice Hovald, March 14, 1969, archives of Les Films du Carrosse, file "CCH 69."

107. Letter from François Truffaut to Jacques-Louis Roustant, September 20, 1971, archives of Les Films du Carrosse, file "CCH 71."

108. Letter from François Truffaut to Patrice Hovald, March 14, 1969, archives of Les Films du Carrosse, file "CCH 69."

109. Interview with François Truffaut, *Image et Son,* December 1970.

110. Press kit for *Bed and Board,* 1970.

111. Interview with François Truffaut, *Le Progrès,* October 20, 1970.

112. Interview with François Truffaut, *Le Journal du dimanche,* September 6, 1970.

113. Ibid.

114. Interview with François Truffaut, *Dernière heure lyonnaise,* October 22, 1970.

115. Interview with François Truffaut, *Le Journal du dimanche,* September 6, 1970.

116. *Les Aventures d'Antoine Doinel* (Paris: Mercure de France, 1970). U.S. edition: *The Adventures of Antoine Doinel: Four Autobiographical Screenplays,* trans. Helen Scott (New York: Simon and Schuster, 1971).

117. Nestor Almendros quoted in *Le Roman de François Truffaut,* p. 70.

118. Almendros, *A Man with a Camera,* p. 94.

119. Ibid., p. 93.

120. *Le Nouvel Observateur,* March 2, 1970.

121. Ibid.

122. "Lettre ouverte de François Truffaut à Annie Girardot," June 23, 1970, archives of Les Films du Carrosse, file "RTL 70."

123. Letter from François Truffaut to Jean Collet, June 26, 1970, archives of Les Films du Carrosse, file "CCH 70 (1)."

124. Letter of September 14, 1970, archives of Les Films du Carrosse, file "CCH 70 (2)."

125. Philippe Labro's interview with the authors, 1996.

126. Claude Chabrol's interview with the authors, 1996.

127. Alain Vannier's interview with the authors, 1996.

128. *New York Times,* January 18, 1971.

129. Archives of Les Films du Carrosse, file "Alfred Hitchcock."

130. Letter from François Truffaut to André Malraux, June 14, 1967, archives of Les Films du Carrosse, file "CCH 67."

131. *Le Nouvel Observateur,* March 2, 1970.

132. Interview with the authors, 1995.

133. *Image et Son,* December 1970.

134. *Cahiers du cinéma* 172 (November 1965).

135. *Le Roman de François Truffaut,* pp. 114–115.

136. Letter of May 7, 1968, archives of Les Films du Carrosse, file "CCH 68."

137. Letter from François Truffaut to Jacques Doniol-Valcroze, January 22, 1970, archives of Les Films du Carrosse, file "CCH 70 (1)."

138. Ibid.

139. *L'Express,* February 14, 1970.

140. Interview with the authors, 1995.

141. Interview conducted by Michel Pascal for the film *François Truffaut: portraits volés, (Stolen Portraits),* 1992.

142. Open letter from François Truffaut to the court, September 8, 1970, archives of Les Films du Carrosse, file "CCH 70 (2)."

143. Letter of October 21 1969, archives of Les Films du Carrosse, file *"Cahiers du cinéma."*

144. Letter from François Truffaut to Sylvie Pierre, November 20, 1970, archives of Les Films du Carrosse, file *"Cahiers du cinéma."*

145. Letter from François Truffaut to Helen Scott, April 23, 1970, archives of Les Films du Carrosse, file "Helen Scott."

146. Interview with the authors, 1995.

147. Anne Gillain, ed., *Le Cinéma selon François Truffaut* (Paris: Flammarion, 1998), p. 247.

148. Letter from François Truffaut to Aimée Alexandre, December 23, 1970, archives of Les Films du Carrosse, file "Aimée Alexandre."

149. Letter from Aimée Alexandre to François Truffaut, December 31, 1970, archives of Les Films du Carrosse, file "Aimée Alexandre."

150. Letter from François Truffaut to Liliane Siegel, December 6, 1971; letter loaned to the authors.

151. Letter from François Truffaut to Aimée Alexandre, March 10, 1971, archives of Les Films du Carrosse, file "Aimée Alexandre."

## 7.
## CINEMA MAN:
## 1971–1979

1. Letter from François Truffaut to Jean-Loup Dabadie, February 14, 1971, archives of Les Films du Carrosse, file "CCH 71 (1)."

2. Letter from François Truffaut to Liliane Siegel, August 15, 1971, letter loaned to the authors.

3. Undated letter (July 1971) from François Truffaut to Marcel Berbert, archives of Les Films du Carrosse, file "CCH 71 (2)."

4. Ibid.

5. Interview with the authors, 1995.

6. Henri-Pierre Roché, *Les Deux Anglaises et le Continent* (Paris; Gallimard, 1955).

7. Undated letter (May 1971) from Jean-Claude Brialy to François Truffaut, archives of Les Films du Carrosse, file "CCH 71 (2)."

8. Henri-Pierre Roché, The *Carnets* (Marseille: Editions André Dimanche, 1990), with a preface by François Truffaut.

9. Letter from François Truffaut to Claude Gallimard, October 14, 1968, archives of Les Films du Carrosse, file "CCH 68."

10. Press kit for *Two English Girls,* 1971.

11. Interview with François Truffaut, *Le Nouveau Cinémonde,* July–August 1971.

12. *AFP,* November 24, 1971.

13. As told by Truffaut in *Télérama,* August 14, 1971.

14. Letter from François Truffaut to Oscar Lewenstein, February 12, 1971, archives of Les Films du Carrosse, file "CCH 71 (1)."

15. Nestor Almendros quoted in *Le Roman de François Truffaut,* special issue of *Cahiers du cinéma,* December 1984, *op cit.* p. 72.

16. Press kit for *Two English Girls,* 1971.

17. Letter from François Truffaut to Liliane Siegel, May 20, 1971, letter loaned to the authors.

18. Letter from François Truffaut to Liliane Dreyfus, May 16, 1971, letter loaned to the authors (when she married in 1963, Liliane David took the name Dreyfus).

19. Letter from François Truffaut to Liliane Siegel, August 15, 1971, letter loaned to the authors.

20. Interview with the authors, 1995.

21. Letter from François Truffaut to Nestor Almendros, September 9, 1971, archives of Les Films du Carrosse, file "CCH 71 (2)."

22. Letter from François Truffaut to Nestor Almendros, September 11, 1971, archives of Les Films du Carrosse, file "CCH 71 (2)."

23. Letter from Louis Marcorelles to François Truffaut, November 22, 1971, archives of Les Films du Carrosse, file "CCH 71 (2)."

24. Letter from Paul Vecchiali to François Truffaut, December 5, 1971, archives of Les Films du Carrosse, file "CCH 71 (2)."

25. Letter from Jean Eustache to François Truffaut, December 12, 1971, archives of Les Films du Carrosse, file "CCH 71 (2)."

26. Letter from Denise Roché to Franço is Truffaut, November 28, 1971, archives of Les Films du Carrosse, file "Ecrivains."

27. *France Soir*, December 4, 1971.

28. Letter from Hercule Mucchielli to François Truffaut, December 17, 1971, archives of Les Films du Carrosse, file "CCH 71 (2)."

29. *L'Avant-Scène*, issue on *Two English Girls*, December 14, 1971.

30. This interview was published in 1972 by Radio Canada and republished by Ramsay in 1987, with the title *Aline Desjardins s'entretient avec François Truffaut*.

31. Letter from François Truffaut to Liliane Stegel, December 30, 1971, letter loaned to the authors.

32. *Pour la Presse*, February 4, 1972; Reused in the press kit for *Such a Gorgeous Kid Like Me*, 1972.

33. *L'Humanité*, May 18, 1967.

34. *Pour la Presse*, February 4, 1972.

35. *Le Soir* (Marseille), March 29, 1972.

36. Letter from François Truffaut to Jean-Loup Dabadie, May 7, 1971, archives of Les Films du Carrosse, file "CCH 71 (1)."

37. Ibid.

38. Letter from François Truffaut to Liliane Siegel, August 21, 1971, letter loaned to the authors.

39. Truffaut's memorandum to Dabadie concerning the first draft of the screenplay of *Such a Gorgeous Kid Like Me*, undated (December 1971), archives of Les Films du Carrosse, file "Scénario/Une belle fille. . . ."

40. Ibid.

41. Undated letter (September 1971), from François Truffaut to Jean-Loup Dabadie, archives of Les Films du Carrosse, file "CCH 71 (1)."

42. Interview with the authors, 1995.

43. Letter from François Truffaut to Liliane Siegel, March 3, 1971, letter loaned to the authors.

44. Bernadette Lafont's interview with the authors, 1995.

45. Ibid.

46. Liliane Dreyfus's interview with the authors, 1995.

47. Bernadette Lafont's interview with the authors, 1995.

48. François Truffaut, "Le Cinéma en action," written as an introduction to the screenplay of *La Nuit américaine* (Paris: Seghers, 1974). U.S. edition: *Day for Night*, trans. San Florès (New York: Grove Press, 1975).

49. Jean-Louis Richard quoted in *Le Roman de François Truffaut*, p. 63.

50. For Truffaut, the death of an actor is the only tragedy that can interfere with the completion of a shoot. This plot twist in *Day for Night* inevitably calls to mind the tragic death of Françoise Dorléac; her fatal car accident took place on the same stretch of road as the one that casts a pall on the cast and crew working at the Victorine studios.

51. Truffaut, "Le cinéma en action."

52. *La Nuit américaine*, p. 46.

53. Ibid., p. 76.

54. Truffaut had already used the expression "a train in the night" to describe a film shoot in the press kit for *The Soft Skin*. He uses it again here, spoken by the director Ferrand.

55. Press kit for *Day for Night*, 1973.

56. François Truffaut had initially wanted to cast Louis Jourdan in the part of Alexandre, but he was not available. He had also hoped to convince Simone Simon, who had retired in 1956, to make a movie

comeback and play the part of Séverine. Then he approached Madeleine Renaud, who had to turn the offer down because of a theatrical tour.

57. *Le Monde,* May 18, 1973.

58. See two articles about Jean-Pierre Léaud published at that time: *Le Monde,* February 14, 1972; *Elle,* May 21, 1973.

59. Archives of Les Films du Carrosse, file "CCH 72 (1)."

60. *La Nuit américaine,* p. 83.

61. Jacqueline Bisset's interview with the authors, 1995.

62. Nathalie Baye's interview with the authors, 1995.

63. Jacqueline Bisset's interview with the authors, 1995.

64. Alexandra Stewart's interview with the authors, 1995.

65. Letter from François Truffaut to Alexandra Stewart, December 23, 1972, letter loaned to the authors.

66. Letter from François Truffaut to Helen Scott, March 14, 1973, archives of Les Films du Carrosse, file "Helen Scott."

67. Letter from Jean-Pierre Aumont to François Truffaut, May 6, 1973, archives of Les Films du Carrosse, file "CCH 73 (1)."

68. Letter from Nathalie Baye to François Truffaut, June 11, 1973, archives of Les Films du Carrosse, file "CCH 73 (1)."

69. *Le Parisien,* May 16, 1973.

70. *Le Figaro,* May 17, 1973. But the fact that Jean Delannoy, Truffaut's inveterate enemy, was on the Cannes jury would certainly not have helped the film had it been entered in the competition.

71. Letter from François Truffaut to Gilles Jacob, May 27, 1973, archives of Les Films du Carrosse, file "CCH 73 (1)."

72. *Le Nouvel Observateur,* May 28, 1973.

73. *Le Monde,* May 16, 1973.

74. *Le Figaro,* May 15, 1973.

75. Letter from François Truffaut to Simon Benzakein, June 13, 1973, archives of Les Films du Carrosse, file "CCH 73 (1)."

76. Interview with the authors, 1996. Things are actually more complicated, since Godard included *The 400 Blows, Shoot the Piano Player, Jules and Jim,* and *The Soft Skin* in his "10 best films of the year" lists published by *Cahiers du cinéma* in the early sixties.

77. *Le Nouvel Observateur,* March 2, 1970.

78. Letter included in *François Truffaut: Correspondance* (Paris: Hatier, 1988), pp. 423–424.

79. Ibid., pp. 425–431.

80. Janine Bazin's television program *Vive le cinéma* was censored by the government (in June 1972), and Godard offered her no support whatsoever. Truffaut showed his solidarity with Bazin and André Labarthe by refusing to participate in *Dossiers de l'écran* on July 5, 1972, which had as its theme "freedom of thought," following the screening of *Fahrenheit 451.* "I'm willing to bet," he wrote to Armand Jammot, the producer of the program, "that the word 'censorship' won't even be mentioned in the discussion and that the true issues will be skirted over. From now on I wish to have nothing more to do, therefore, with the black *Dossiers de l'écran.*"

81. This is a reference to an expression coined by Truffaut to refer to his friendship with, and feelings of solidarity for, the young New Wave filmmakers, an expression which he reused as a part title in his book *The Films in My Life.*

82. Undated letter (June 1973) from Janine Bazin to François Truffaut, archives of Les Films du Carrosse, file "Bazin."

83. *Le Nouvel Observateur,* December 2, 1974.

84. Letter from François Truffaut to Jean-Louis Bory, December 11, 1974, archives of Les Films du Carrosse, file "CCH 74 (2)."

85. Ibid.

86. For example, Truffaut had a falling-out with the actor Oskar Werner. After the negative experience of *Fahrenheit 451,* the two men ignored each other. But at the beginning of January 1971, Truffaut, who was then in the midst of a depression—"in this port of shadows where I am, haunted by ghosts, shades and nightmares"—he recontacted him, hoping the actor would give him moral support. He sent him a copy of *Jules and Jim* as a gift. Werner was very touched by this show of friendship and expressed his "eternal affection" to Truffaut. But the relationship once again began to deteriorate when Werner asked Truffaut to cofinance his first film as a director, *So Love Returns,* with a New York company, newly created by Steve McQueen, Paul Newman, Sidney Poitier,

and Barbra Streisand, the First Artists Production Company. Truffaut turned him down on May 8, 1973, admitting to Werner that he had doubts about his ability to direct a film. "I was shocked by your letter," the actor replied on December 30, 1973. "It was written by a journalist, a gossip, not an artist. You allow yourself to pass judgment on me from evidence that you cannot possibly have. You are wrong, François, for you don't know me at all. Contrary to what you may think, I have no contempt for the world. I only hate megalomaniacs. I don't think that, in the one hundred and ten parts I have played on stage and twenty-five film parts, I have shown, as you say, 'a kind of arrogance and contempt for others.' However, I do believe this arrogance you accuse me of is very widespread among film directors, who are emblems of narcissism today. We are separated by about ten years, and that's enormous. You were 5 years old when I earned my first paycheck at 15 for a film. You were 6 years old when I saw the first Jews persecuted in the streets of Vienna, when I saw the SA use torches to burn the books of Freud, Werfel, Zweig, Heine, Friedell, Mann, Hesse, Adler (and, believe me, it was rather different from the way you showed it in *Fahrenheit 451,* and Cusack is like a choirboy compared to the SA and SS who burned synagogues). I also heard the cries from the crowd, vociferation from the masses, and how they were put in trances by this joyous spectacle. You were 8 years old when I was put in a Nazi labor camp and tried to commit suicide when my mother was arrested by the Gestapo. You were 12 years old when I was hiding as a deserter, to escape Hitler's army, with my 7-month daughter and my Jewish wife in the woods around Vienna. And this 'dance of death' which lasted four and a half months had nothing to do with Johann Strauss's Viennese waltzes. I am not telling you these stories to provoke pity. But when one survives such events— living hell—the rest is purgatory: one listens and sees the world more clearly. One can more confidently distinguish truth from hypocrisy, genius from phoniness, nobility from vulgarity, the sublime from the mediocre. You can see why I believe that though you were sometimes touched

by truth, genius, nobility and the sublime, with *Jules and Jim* and *The Wild Child,* your recent attitude and films seem to me hypocritical, false, vulgar and mediocre."

87. Letter from François Truffaut to Robert Laffont, March 8, 1974, archives of Les Films du Carrosse, file "CCH 74 (1)."

88. Interview with the authors, 1995.

89. *Pomme d'Api,* July 15, 1972.

90. Interview with the authors, 1995.

91. Jean Gruault, *Ce que dit l'autre* (Paris: Julliard, 1992), p. 282.

92. Interview with Eva Truffaut, *Cahiers du cinéma,* May 1994.

93. *Paris-Match,* May 14, 1974.

94. Interview with the authors, 1995.

95. Letter from François Truffaut to Liliane Siegel, April 20, 1971, letter loaned to the authors.

96. Letter from François Truffaut to Liliane Siegel, September 15, 1972, letter loaned to the authors.

97. Letter from François Truffaut to Liliane Siegel, December 6, 1971, letter loaned to the authors.

98. Interview with the authors, 1995.

99. Letter from François Truffaut to Isabelle Adjani, April 14, 1976, archives of Les Films du Carrosse, file "CCH 76 (1)."

100. Gruault, *Ce que dit l'autre,* p. 283.

101. Letter from François Truffaut to Jean-Claude Brialy, January 24, 1978, archives of Les Films du Carrosse, file "CCH 78 (1)."

102. Alexandra Stewart's interview with the authors, 1996.

103. Madeleine Morgenstern's interview with the authors, 1995.

104. Letter from François Truffaut to Liliane Siegel, August 14, 1973, letter loaned to the authors.

105. Letter from François Truffaut to Simon Benzakein, March 10, 1974, archives of Les Films du Carrosse, file "CCH 74 (1)."

106. Letter from François Truffaut to David Susskind (New York agent), May 16, 1975, archives of Les Films du Carrosse, file "CCH 75 (1)."

107. Letter from François Truffaut to Guy Teisseire about an interview for *Ciné Revue,* July 1973, archives of Les Films du Carrosse, file "CCH 73 (2)."

108. Interview with the authors, 1995.

109. Letter from François Truffaut to

Helen Scott, July 9, 1973, archives of Les Films du Carrosse, file "Helen Scott."

110. Ibid.

111. *Memo from David O. Selznick,* ed. Rudy Behlmer (New York: Viking Press, 1972).

112. Interview with the authors, 1996.

113. Todd McCarthy quoted in *Le Roman de François Truffaut,* pp. 157–158.

114. Letter from François Truffaut to Helen Scott, July 9, 1973, archives of Les Films du Carrosse, file "Helen Scott." (Helen Scott had introduced Truffaut to the actor-writer Buck Henry, who played in Milos Forman's *Taking Off* and wrote the screenplays for Mike Nichols's *The Graduate* and *The Day of the Dolphin.*)

115. Ibid.

116. François Truffaut, "Jean Renoir, 1273 Leona Drive," December 1975; published under the title "Jean Renoir: Quatre-vingts ans d'étonnements," *Le Nouvel Observateur,* March 4, 1978; reprinted in *Le Plaisir des yeux* (Paris: Éditions de l'Etoile, 1987), pp. 140–146.

117. Interview with the authors, 1995.

118. Ibid.

119. Truffaut, "Jean Renoir, 1273 Leona Drive."

120. Letter from François Truffaut to Madeleine Morgenstern July 13, 1973, letter loaned to the authors by Madeleine Morgenstern.

121. *Le Figaro,* April 4, 1974.

122. Letter from François Truffaut to Marcel Berbert, July 21, 1975, archives of Les Films du Carrosse, file "CCH 75 (2)."

123. Archives of Les Films du Carrosse, file "CCH 74 (2)."

124. Letter from François Truffaut to Liliane Siegel, August 14, 1973, letter loaned to the authors.

125. This series of unpublished articles is kept in the archives of Les Films du Carrosse, file "Politique."

126. Letter from François Truffaut to Liliane Siegel, August 15, 1971, letter loaned to the authors.

127. Interview with the authors, 1995.

128. Letter from François Truffaut to Liliane Siegel, January 4, 1975, letter loaned to the authors.

129. The project involved almost eighty people—political militants, historians, researchers, and academics.

130. Letter from François Truffaut to Frances Vernor Guille, April 13, 1973, archives of Les Films du Carrosse, file "CCH 73 (1)."

131. Letter from Jean Hugo to François Truffaut, January 31, 1971, archives of Les Films du Carrosse, file "CCH 71 (1)."

132. Letter from Jean Gruault to François Truffaut, July 6, 1974, archives of Les Films du Carrosse, file "CCH 74 (2)." See also Gruault, *Ce que dit l'autre,* pp. 298–299.

133. Catherine Deneuve's interview with the authors, 1995.

134. Undated letter (October 1974), from François Truffaut to Isabelle Adjani, archives of Les Films du Carrosse, file "CCH 74 (2)."

135. Interview with Isabelle Adjani, *Cinématographe,* December 1984.

136. Undated letter (October 1974), from François Truffaut to Isabelle Adjani, archives of Les Films du Carrosse, file "CCH 74 (2)."

137. *Cinématographe,* December 1984.

138. *France Soir,* September 30, 1975.

139. Letter from François Truffaut to Liliane Siegel, January 27, 1975, letter loaned to the authors.

140. *France Soir,* September 30, 1975.

141. Interview with the authors, 1995.

142. *L'Express,* March 3, 1975.

143. Interview with the authors, 1995.

144. Ibid.

145. Letter from François Truffaut to Helen Scott, February 9, 1975, archives of Les Films du Carrosse, file "Helen Scott."

146. Letter from François Truffaut to Liliane Siegel, February 14, 1975, letter loaned to the authors.

147. Letter from François Truffaut to Jean-Loup Dabadie, April 30, 1975, archives of Les Films du Carrosse, file "CCH 75 (1)."

148. Letter from Gilles Jacob to François Truffaut, November 15, 1975, archives of Les Films du Carrosse, file "CCH 75 (2)."

149. Letter from Marcel Ophuls to François Truffaut, November 6, 1975, archives of Les Film du Carrosse, file "CCH 75 (2)."

150. Letter from Jean Gruault to François Truffaut, of November 26, 1975, archives

of Les Films du Carrosse, file "CCH 75 (2)."

151. Letter from François Truffaut to Gilles Jacob, November 21, 1975, archives of Les Films du Carrosse, file "CCH 75 (2)."

152. Ibid.

153. Letter from Jean Hugo to François Truffaut, October 30, 1975, archives of Les Films du Carrosse, file "CCH 75 (2)."

154. *Projet pour un film sur les enfants* (Project for a film about children), 1972, memo for Suzanne Schiffman, archives of Les Films du Carrosse, file "Scénario/ Argent de poche." One of the anecdotes is taken from a Sacha Guitry anthology, *Si j'ai bonne mémoire*. It's the story of a boy who is in love with the mother of a friend and gives her a bouquet of flowers. She responds by saying, "Please thank your father for me." Among other stories, which he didn't use, there is the autobiographical one: "A thirteen-year old boy is home alone and discovers his father's old date books while rummaging around. Curiosity leads him to look up what his father wrote on the day of his birth. He notices that there is no mention of his birth on that day or on any of the following days. This is how he discovers that his father is not his father. He finds definite confirmation of this fact by consulting the family record book."

155. Truffaut continued his militant activity for children throughout the seventies, supporting various associations, Perce Neige for example, created by Lino Ventura, and the Association for the Support of Deaf Children, as well as schools and experimental centers for "maladjusted" or mentally handicapped children. He gave generously to these various associations and was always ready to make public statements in the press in support of this cause.

156. This schoolteacher's speech was published in *Télérama*, March 8, 1976.

157. Steven Spielberg quoted in *Le Roman de François Truffaut*, p. 121.

158. Truffaut remembered Julia Phillips from the Academy Awards ceremony he had attended in April 1974, where she went onstage to collect her Oscar for *The Sting*. He decided that if he ever made a Hollywood film, it would be with her, and he told her so in a letter of March 19, 1976. Their relationship deteriorated considerably in the course of the shoot, as can be seen from the following excerpt from his letter to Madeleine Morgenstern on July 13, 1976: "Instead of a noisy, refrigerated trailer I asked to have an office in this warehouse, and again this was a big deal. I had to pretend to be angry and prepared to go on strike to get what I wanted; for example, I won't go drink champagne with the producer tonight so she'll understand that she's the one I resent. She was lucky enough to produce *The Sting* and *Taxi Driver*, but actually she's lazy; next year she herself will be directing a feminist erotic film, *Fear of Flying*, and she thinks that by being glued to the camera all day and staring at the actors, she'll learn something!. . . ." And on July 29, 1976, he wrote to Madeleine again: "The funny thing is, I'm now on bad terms with the producer, we don't greet each other, we pretend not to see each other, and what I gain in this is that she doesn't dare sit next to the camera, she remains slightly on the sidelines." Julia Phillips described her experience as a Hollywood producer in *You'll Never Eat Lunch in This Town Again* (New York: Signet, 1991).

159. Telegram of March 15, 1976, archives of Les Films du Carrosse, file "Close Encounters."

160. Letter from François Truffaut to Julia Phillips, March 19, 1976, archives of Les Films du Carrosse, file "Close Encounters."

161. Spielberg was quite clear about the fact that *Close Encounters* was a homage to Howard Hawks's 1951 film *The Thing*. It was initially going to be entitled *Watch the Sky*, the last line in *The Thing*.

162. Letter from François Truffaut to Jean-Loup Dabadie, August 18, 1976, archives of Les Films du Carrosse, file "CCH 76 (2)."

163. Letter from François Truffaut to Serge Rousseau, July 29, 1976, archives of Les Films du Carrosse, file "CCH 76 (2)."

164. Letter from François Truffaut to Nestor Almendros, archives of Les Films du Carrosse, file "CCH 76 (2)."

165. Letter from François Truffaut to Marcel Berbert, July 19, 1976, archives of

Les Films du Carrosse, file "Close Encounters."

166. Letter from François Truffaut to Madeleine Morgenstern, July 13, 1976, letter loaned to the authors by Madeleine Morgenstern.

167. Letter from François Truffaut to Marcel Berbert, July 19, 1976, archives of Les Films du Carrosse, file "Close Encounters."

168. Letter from François Truffaut to Madeleine Morgenstern, July 13, 1976, letter loaned to the authors by Madeleine Morgenstern.

169. Steven Spielberg quoted in *Le Roman de François Truffaut,* p. 121.

170. Letter from Steven Spielberg to François Truffaut, December 22, 1977, archives of Les Films du Carrosse, file "Close Encounters."

171. Steven Spielberg quoted in *Le Roman de François Truffaut,* p. 121.

172. Bruno Bettelheim, *The Empty Fortress: Infantile Autism and the Birth of Self* (New York: The Free Press, 1967), p. 241.

173. Liliane Dreyfus's interview with the authors, 1996.

174. Ibid.

175. Ibid.

176. Madeleine Morgenstern's interview with the authors, 1995.

177. Claude Chabrol's interview with the authors, 1996.

178. Phillippe Labro's interview with the authors, 1996.

179. Michel Fermaud's interviews with the authors, 1995 and 1996.

180. *France Soir,* April 22, 1977.

181. Letter from Michel Fermaud to François Truffaut, February 18, 1975, archives of Les Films du Carrosse, file "CCH 75 (1)."

182. Michel Fermaud's interview with the authors, 1995.

183. Comparison comes from an article in *Midi libre,* January 9, 1977.

184. *Elle,* May 2, 1977.

185. Marcel Berbert's interview with the authors, 1995.

186. Jean-Louis Livi's interview with the authors, 1996.

187. Leslie Caron's interview with the authors, 1995.

188. Press kit for *L'Homme qui aimait les femmes,* 1977.

189. Interview with the authors, 1995.

190. Ibid.

191. Henry Chapier in *Le Quotidien de Paris,* May 5, 1977.

192. *Pariscope,* June 22, 1977.

193. Letter from François Truffaut to Charles Denner, March 29, 1977, archives of Les Films du Carrosse, file "CCH 77 (1)."

194. Interview with François Truffaut, *Lumière du cinéma,* May 1977.

195. *Le Nouvel Observateur,* May 9, 1977.

196. This remake was a lucrative deal for Les Films du Carrosse, since they were paid $300,000 for the rights to the film.

197. Interview with the authors, 1996.

198. Ibid.

199. *L'Express,* March 13, 1978.

200. Ibid.

201. *Le Matin de Paris,* June 5, 1977.

202. *L'Express,* March 13, 1978.

203. *Humanité-Dimanche,* April 7, 1978.

204. Aimée Alexandre died in 1981, at the age of eighty-seven. She had become blind and was never able to see *The Green Room,* a film which owed so much to her.

205. Henry James, *L'Autel des morts,* trans. and with a preface by Diane de Margerie (Paris: Stock, 1974).

206. Letter from François Truffaut to Jean Gruault, of July 21, 1974, archives of Les Films du Carrosse, file "CCH 74 (2)."

207. Ibid.

208. Ibid.

209. Letter from François Truffaut to Jean Gruault of November 21, 1975, archives of Les Films du Carrosse file "CCH 75 (2)."

210. The name of Paul Massigny, Julien Davenne's worst enemy, even in death, comes from this rereading of Proust, as well as many details throughout the screenplay. Note that it is possible to recognize Serge Rousseau, one of Truffaut's best friends, in the supposed portrait of Massigny.

211. Telegram, February 23, 1977, archives of Les Films du Carrosse, file "CCH 77 (1)."

212. Interview with the authors, 1996.

213. *L'Aurore,* April 3, 1978.

214. Interview with the authors, 1996.

215. Press kit for *La Chambre verte,* 1978.

216. Nathalie Baye's interview with the authors, 1996.

217. Marie de Poncheville's interview with the authors, 1996.

218. Letter from Isabelle Adjani to François Truffaut, April 9, 1978, archives of Les Films du Carrosse, file "CCH 78 (1)."

219. Letter from Alain Delon to François Truffaut, October 2, 1979, archives of Les Films du Carrosse, file "CCH 79 (2)."

220. Letter from Eric Rohmer to François Truffaut, April 26, 1978, archives of Les Films du Carrosse, file "CCH 78 (1)."

221. Letter (dated Whitsunday 1978) from Antoine Vitez to François Truffaut, archives of Les Films du Carrosse, file "CCH 78 (1)."

222. *Le Nouvel Observateur*, April 3, 1978.

223. *L'Express*, March 13, 1978.

224. Letter from François Truffaut to Michel Drucker, April 3, 1978, archives of Les Films du Carrosse, file "CCH 78 (1)."

225. Letter from François Truffaut to François Porcile, May 8, 1978, archives of Les Films du Carrosse, file "CCH 78 (1)."

226. *Paris-Match*, May 4, 1978.

227. Letter from François Truffaut to Annette Insdorf, May 10, 1978, archives of Les Films du Carrosse, file "CCH 78 (1)."

228. Interview with the authors, 1996.

229. Letter from François Truffaut to Annette Insdorf, May 10, 1978, archives of Les Films du Carrosse, file "CCH 78 (1)."

230. *France Soir*, November 3, 1977.

231. Interview with the authors, 1996.

232. Letter from François Truffaut to Jean-Louis Bory, September 1, 1978, archives of Les Films du Carrosse, file "CCH 78 (2)."

233. Letter from François Truffaut to Jean Nachbaur, January 26, 1978, archives of Les Films du Carrosse, file "CCH 78 (1)."

234. For information concerning economic changes in the French film industry, see Jean-Michel Frodon, *L'Age moderne du cinéma français: De la Nouvelle Vague à nos jours* (Paris: Flammarion, 1995), pp. 533–537, chapter entitled "Artmédia en position dominante."

235. Interview with the authors, 1996.

236. Archives of Les Films du Carrosse, file "Agence Magic."

237. Interview with the authors, 1996.

238. Letter from François Truffaut to Henning and Else Carlsen, October 13, 1978, archives of Les Films du Carrosse, file "CCH 78 (2)." Truffaut added, "To a certain extent I owe *Love on the Run* to you, for it was because of the Dagmar Theater's [movie house run by the Carlsens in Copenhagen] initiative of showing all the Doinel films chronologically in one day that I had the idea of making a last Doinel, which would include flashbacks excerpted from the four preceding films."

239. Archives of Les Films du Carrosse, file "Scénario/L'Amour en fuite."

240. *France Soir*, January 27, 1979.

241. Ibid.

242. Letter from François Truffaut to Annette Insdorf, May 10, 1978, archives of Les Films du Carrosse, file "CCH 78 (1)."

243. Interview with the authors, 1992.

244. Letter from François Truffaut to Alain Souchon, July 10, 1978, archives of Les Films du Carrosse, file "CCH 78 (2)."

245. Suzanne Schiffman quoted in *Le Roman de François Truffaut*, p. 54.

246. Undated letter (beginning of January 1979), from François Truffaut to Alain Souchon, archives of Les Films du Carrosse, file "CCH 79 (1)."

247. Jean-Louis Richard quoted in *Le Roman de François Truffaut*, p. 65.

248. *Le Figaro*, January 20, 1979.

249. *Le Monde*, January 25, 1979.

250. Undated letter (end of January 1979), from François Truffaut to Jacques Siclier, archives of Les Films du Carrosse, file "CCH 79 (1)."

251. RTL, "Le journal inattendu," February 14, 1979.

**8.**

**THE UNFINISHED FIGURE:**

**1979–1984**

1. Letter from François Truffaut to Helen Scott, November 27, 1964, archives of Les Films du Carrosse, file "Helen Scott."

2. Letter from François Truffaut to Helen Scott October 14, 1965, archives of Les Films du Carrosse, file "Helen Scott."

3. Truffaut and Claude de Givray worked on the script of *La Petite Voleuse* again in 1983, in Honfleur. It was one of the films

Truffaut wanted to shoot after *Confidentially Yours!* After his death, Claude Berri wanted to direct the film and acquired the rights to the screenplay as well as to the screenplay of *L'Agence Magic.* In the end, the film was directed by Claude Miller in the summer of 1988; it starred Charlotte Gainsbourg. Claude Berri was the producer of the film.

4. Letter from François Truffaut to Pierre Kast, May 14, 1979, archives of Les Films du Carrosse, file "CCH 79 (1)."

5. Undated letter (May 79), from Pierre Kast to François Truffaut, archives of Les Films du Carrosse, file "CCH 79 (1)."

6. Letter from Pierre Kast to François Truffaut, July 9, 1979, archives of Les Films du Carrosse, file "CCH 79 (2)."

7. Letter from François Truffaut to Pierre Kast, May 30, 1979, archives of Les Films du Carrosse, file "CCH 79 (1)." In his letter, Truffaut wrote, "The story about Stendhal is terrific, but I can't seem to visualize it, or rather I can't see filming, for an hour and a half, an actor who has to be chosen for both his talent and his physical resemblance to the original. But if you feel that Philippe Noiret would make a possible Stendhal, why don't you give him *Henri et Clémentine* to read?"

8. Truffaut felt that the ideal actor for *Le Garde du corps* would be Patrick Dewaere. "But I don't think he wants to work with me," he wrote to Jacques Veber on May 28, 1979. "This wouldn't be the case with Jacques Dutronc, whom I very much admire, but I have the impression that, consciously or not, you wrote with Dewaere in mind."

9. Suzanne Schiffman quoted in *Le Roman de François Truffaut,* special issue of *Cahiers du cinéma,* December 1984, p. 54.

10. *France Soir,* March 4, 1970.

11. Truffaut was also active in getting *The Sorrow and the Pity,* which was censored by the ORTF, broadcast on television. The film wouldn't be shown on television until 1981.

12. Unpublished interview with Mireille Le Dantec, December 1977, archives of Les Films du Carrosse, file "Robert Bresson."

13. Letter from François Truffaut to Michael Korda, May 25, 1982, archives of Les Films du Carrosse, file "CCH 82 (1)."

14. Letter from François Truffaut to Jean-Loup Dabadie, October 8, 1976, archives of Les Films du Carrosse, file "CCH 76 (2)."

15. Interview with the authors, 1995.

16. He also used Hervé Le Boterf's *La Vie parisienne sous l'Occupation.* He was a journalist Truffaut had met in the fifties at *Cinémonde.*

17. The character of Daxiat in *The Last Métro* is all the more believable in that he is modeled on the collaborationist critic Alain Laubreaux, who had written a play, *Les Pirates de Paris,* under the pseudonym Daxiat. He was a gifted and brilliant polemicist and famous for his insults at the time. He called Jean Marais "The man with the Cocteau [play on the word *couteau,* meaning "knife"] between his teeth." At the Liberation, Laubreaux fled to Spain, where he died in 1960.

18. Interview with the authors, 1995.

19. Truffaut coscripted *Mata-Hari,* a film with Jeanne Moreau, directed by Jean-Louis Richard and produced by Les Films du Carrosse.

20. Jean-Louis Richard's interview with the authors, 1992.

21. Gérard Depardieu's interview with the authors, 1992.

22. Jean-Louis Livi's interview with the authors, 1996.

23. Gérard Depardieu quoted in *Le Roman de François Truffaut,* p. 100.

24. Truffaut had written a very complimentary article in *Arts* about Jean Poiret's performance in Sacha Guitry's *Assassins et Voleurs.*

25. *Le Roman de François Truffaut,* p. 47.

26. Letter from François Truffaut to Jean-Claude Grumberg, January 15, 1980, archives of Les Films du Carrosse, file "CCH 80 (1)."

27. Undated letter (February 1980), from François Truffaut to Jean-Claude Grumberg, archives of Les Films du Carrosse, file "CCH 80 (1)."

28. This letter (January 21, 1980) was inspired by Spielberg's behavior during the filming of *Close Encounters.*

29. Letter from François Truffaut to Janine Bazin, February 28, 1980, archives of Les Films du Carrosse, file "Bazin."

30. Letter from François Truffaut to Jean

Aurel, April 23, 1980, archives of Les Films du Carrosse, file "CCH 80 (1)."

31. Interview with the authors, 1995.

32. Preface to the revised edition of François Truffaut, *Hitchcock* (New York: Simon and Schuster, 1984), p. 12.

33. Interview with the authors, 1991.

34. Letter from François Truffaut to Richard Roud, September 3, 1980, archives of Les Films du Carrosse, file "CCH 80 (2)."

35. Suzanne Schiffman quoted in *Le Roman de François Truffaut*, p. 54.

36. *Lire* 62 (October 1980).

37. Letter from François Truffaut to Richard Roud, September 3, 1980, archives of Les Films du Carrosse, file "CCH 80 (2)."

38. Interview with the authors, 1995.

39. Henri Amouroux's chronicles were appearing every week at that time and were very popular, "Les Années 40," "La grande histoire des Français sous l'Occupation," and "Les beaux jours des Collabos."

40. Letter from François Truffaut to Georges Cravenne, March 3, 1981, archives of Les Films du Carrosse, file "CCH 81 (1)."

41. Interview with François Truffaut, *Première*, August 1983.

42. Interview with the authors, 1995.

43. TF1 wanted to broadcast *The Last Métro* during the 1982 Christmas holidays and was legally entitled to do so. Truffaut did everything he could to get the broadcast legally postponed for a year. He finally succeeded, which allowed him to extend exhibition of the film in movie houses.

44. *Le Quotidien de Paris*, February 2, 1981.

45. *Les Nouvelles littéraires*, October 1, 1981.

46. Interview with the authors, 1996.

47. *Télérama*, July 14, 1978.

48. Letter from Jean-Luc Godard to François Truffaut et al., August 19, 1980, archives of Les Films du Carrosse, file "Jean-Luc Godard."

49. Undated letter (August 1980) from François Truffaut's to Jean-Luc Godard, archives of Les Films du Carrosse, file "Jean-Luc Godard."

50. *Cahiers du cinéma* 315 and 316 (September and October 1980).

51. Truffaut used this expression in an interview in *Les nouvelles littéraires,* September 17, 1980.

52. The only responsibility that Truffaut accepted at that time, out of film lover's loyalty, was presiding over the Fédération Internationale des Ciné-Clubs. Asked by Jean Roy, who was then a delegate to the FICC, he was elected during a general assembly in Marly-le-Roi in June 1979. Truffaut was reelected to the presidency of the FICC, in October 1981, somewhat against his will, and remained president until 1983.

53. Letter from François Truffaut to Claude Autant-Lara, of April 12, 1983, archives of Les Films du Carrosse, file "CCH 83 (1)."

54. *Cahiers du cinéma* 316 (October 1980).

55. Interview with the authors, 1995.

56. François Truffaut, "Introducing Fanny Ardant," press kit of *The Woman Next Door,* (October 1981, republished in *Le Plaisir des yeux* (Paris: Editions de l'Etoile, 1987), pp. 166–167.

57. Before being discovered by Truffaut, Fanny Ardant was given her first screen appearances by Alain Jessua (*Les Chiens*) and Claude Lelouch (*Les Uns et les Autres*).

58. *Le Matin de Paris,* October 2, 1981.

59. Letter from François Truffaut to Jean Collet, January 9, 1981, archives of Les Films du Carrosse, file "CCH 81 (1)."

60. Truffaut, "Introducing Fanny Ardant."

61. Ibid.

62. Jean Aurel quoted in *Le Roman de François Truffaut*, p. 67.

63. Interview with the authors, 1996. In 1981, Gérard Lebovici became a producer and left the management of Artmédia to Jean-Louis Livi, who then became Truffaut's agent.

64. Michèle Baumgartner, a young theater actress, died suddenly several months after the filming of *The Woman Next Door.*

65. Interview with the authors, 1992.

66. Truffaut, "Introducing Fanny Ardant."

67. Europe 1, September 29, 1981.

68. *Le Film Français,* October 2, 1981.

69. Serge Daney, *Libération,* September 30, 1981.

70. Archives of Les Films du Carrosse, file "CCH 81 (2)."

71. Letter from François Truffaut to Jean Collet, August 5, 1981, archives of Les Films du Carrosse, file "CCH 81 (2)."

72. *Le Figaro Madame,* September 26, 1981.

73. *Le Figaro,* September 3, 1981.

74. Interview with the authors, 1995.

75. According to Truffaut's date book Mitterrand and Truffaut had lunch together four times between 1975 and 1980.

76. Letter from Marcel Ophuls to François Truffaut, February 26, 1980, archives of Les Films du Carrosse, file "CCH 80 (1)."

77. Note of June 17, 1981, archives of Les Films du Carrosse, file "CCH 81 (1)."

78. *Révolution,* October 2, 1981.

79. It was also at that time that Professor Blin at the Collège de France suggested Truffaut apply for a position at that prestigious institution. Truffaut refused, even though, as Professor Blin put it, "he had every chance of being elected."

80. Letter from François Truffaut to Jean Riboud, November 2, 1981, archives of Les Films du Carrosse, file "CCH 81 (2)."

81. Letter from François Truffaut to Koichi Yamada, March 27, 1982, archives of Les Films du Carrosse, file "Yamada."

82. Letter from François Truffaut to Koichi Yamada, April 3, 1982, archives of Les Films du Carrosse, file "Yamada."

83. Letter from François Truffaut to Edmond Maire, February 3, 1982, archives of Les Films du Carrosse, file "CCH 82 (1)."

84. *The Long Saturday Night* was published by Gallimard, in their Série noire, in 1962, under the title *Vivement dimanche!*

85. Press kit for *Vivement dimanche!,* 1983.

86. *Le Matin de Paris,* August 10, 1983.

87. Suzanne Schiffman quoted in *Le Roman de François Truffaut,* p. 55.

88. Interview with the authors, 1996.

89. Jean Aurel quoted in *Le Roman de François Truffaut,* p. 57.

90. Letter from François Truffaut to Gérard Lebovici, September 9, 1982, archives of Les Films du Carrosse, file "CCH 82 (2)."

91. Ibid.

92. Undated letter (October 1979) from Jean-Louis Trintignant to François Truffaut, archives of Les Films du Carrosse, file "CCH 79 (2)."

93. Letter from François Truffaut to Jean-Louis Trintignant, July 9, 1982, archives of Les Films du Carrosse, file "CCH 82 (2)."

94. Letter from François Truffaut to Serge Rousseau, October 20, 1982, archives of Les Films du Carrosse, file "CCH 82 (2)."

95. *Le Matin de Paris,* January 14, 1983.

96. Letter from François Truffaut to Georges Delerue, September 30, 1982, archives of Les Films du Carrosse, file "CCH 82 (2)."

97. Ibid.

98. François Truffaut's grandmother died in June 1979 at the age of ninety-eight. He helped her a great deal in her final years.

99. Letter from François Truffaut to Annette Insdorf, August 3, 1983, archives of Les Films du Carrosse, file "CCH 83 (2)."

100. *Le Figaro Madame,* March 14, 1981.

101. Interview with the authors, 1996.

102. Ibid.

103. *Belle Epoque* was made for television in 1995 by Gavin Millar. Jean Gruault discusses the screenplay in *Le Roman de François Truffaut,* pp. 61–62, and in *Cahiers du cinéma* 447 (September 1991). Gruault published this screenplay as a novel with Gallimard.

104. Interview with the authors, 1992.

105. Letter from François Truffaut to Guy Marchard, April 28, 1983, archives of Les Films du Carrosse, file "CCH 83 (1)."

106. Letter from François Truffaut to Koichi Yamada, August 4, 1983, archives of Les Films du Carrosse, file "Yamada."

107. *Confidentially Yours!* inaugurated a cycle programmed by Truffaut and entitled "Série noire en noir et blanc." It included twelve black-and-white films adapted from Gallimard's Série Noire such as Melville's *Doulos the Finger Man,* Dassin's *Rififi,* Sautet's *The Big Risk,* Godard's *Band of Outsiders,* and Preminger's *Where the Sidewalk Ends.*

108. Laura Truffaut's interview with the authors, 1995.

109. Claude de Givray's interview with the authors, 1996.

110. Florence Malraux's interview with the authors, 1995.

111. Archives of Les Films du Carrosse, file "Santé."

112. Ibid.

113. Ibid.

114. Ibid.

115. Ibid.

116. Ibid.

117. Letter from François Truffaut to Koichi Yamada, September 9, 1983, archives of Les Films du Carrosse, file "Yamada."

118. Letter from François Truffaut to Richard Roud, September 9, 1983, archives of Les Films du Carrosse, file "CCH 83 (2)."

119. Letter from François Truffaut to Annette Insdorf, September 9, 1983, archives of Les Films du Carrosse, file "CCH 83 (2)."

120. Letter from François Truffaut to Robert Fischer, September 9, 1983, archives of Les Films du Carrosse, file "CCH 83 (2)."

121. Letter from François Truffaut to Koichi Yamada, September 9, 1983, archives of Les Films du Carrosse, file "Yamada."

122. Letter from Isabelle Adjani to François Truffaut, October 4, 1983, archives of Les Films du Carrosse, file "CCH 83 (2)."

123. *France-Soir,* September 24, 1983. There was also an article on the same page of *France-Soir:* "Two weeks ago, the American Hospital in Neuilly was taken by surprise by the emergency arrival of François Truffaut. His physician decided he should be hospitalized because of his violent and persistent headaches. Auscultation and X rays led to the discovery of a hematoma in the brain and the danger of a fatal cerebral hemorrhage. Dr. Pertuisé decided to operate on Monday, September 12. Three hours later, the operation was a success, the hematoma reduced and the patient back in his room. On the following day, almost completely well, he declared: 'I'm no longer suffering, it's wonderful.' Since he was healing well, he was able to leave the hospital last Monday for a month of convalescence at a slow pace."

124. Letter from Dr. Bertrand Pertuisé to François Truffaut, September 20, 1983, archives of Les Films du Carrosse, file "Santé."

125. Madeleine Morgenstern's interview with the authors, 1995.

126. Josiane Couëdel quoted in *Le Roman de François Truffaut*, p. 49.

127. Claude de Givray's interview with the authors, 1996.

128. Madeleine Morgenstern's interview with the authors, 1995.

129. Letter from François Truffaut to Lionel Chouchan, December 16, 1983, archives of Les Films du Carrosse, file "CCH 83 (2)."

130. Letter from François Truffaut to Robert Cortes, director of the Festival of Prades, February 17, 1984, archives of Les Films du Carrosse, file "CCH 84 (1)."

131. Gérard Depardieu quoted in *Le Roman de François Truffaut*, p. 101.

132. Ibid.

133. Letter from Gérard Depardieu to François Truffaut, October 10, 1983, archives of Les Films du Carrosse, file "CCH 83 (2)."

134. Madeleine Morgenstern's interview with the authors, 1995.

135. Laura Truffaut's interview with the authors, 1995.

136. Philippe Labro's interview with the authors, 1995.

137. Letter from François Truffaut to Liliane Siegel, February 17, 1984, letter loaned to the authors.

138. Letter from Koichi Yamada to François Truffaut, September 18, 1983, archives of Les Films du Carrosse, file "Yamada."

139. Letter from Koichi Yamada to François Truffaut, July 1, 1984, archives of Les Films du Carrosse, file "Yamada."

140. In 1968, Truffaut had indeed coproduced Maurice Pialat's *L'Enfance nue,* with Mag Bodard, Claude Berri, and Véra Belmont.

141. Letter from Isabelle Adjani to François Truffaut, March 5, 1984, archives of Les Films du Carrosse, file "CCH 84 (1)."

142. Interview with the authors, 1992.

143. Jean-Claude Brialy quoted in *Le Roman de François Truffaut*, p. 34.

144. Jean-Louis Richard quoted in *Le Roman de François Truffaut*, p. 65.

145. Letter from François Truffaut to Annette Insdorf, July 24, 1980, archives of Les Films du Carrosse, file "CCH 80 (2)."

146. Letter from François Truffaut to Robert Lachenay, December 22, 1983, archives of Les Films du Carrosse, file "CCH 83 (2)."

147. Letter from François Truffaut to Charles Ronsac, July 6, 1984, archives of Les Films du Carrosse, file "CCH 84 (2)."

148. Letter from Floriana Lebovici to François Truffaut, July 13, 1984, archives of Les Films du Carrosse, file "CCH 84 (2)."

149. Madeleine Morgenstern's interview with the authors, 1995.

150. Claude Berri's interview with the authors, 1995.

151. Liliane Siegel's interview with the authors, 1995.

152. Undated letter (June 1984) from François Truffaut to Liliane Siegel, letter loaned to the authors.

153. Claude de Givray quoted in *Le Roman de François Truffaut*, p. 58.

154. Interview with the authors, 1995.

155. Interview conducted by Michel Pascal and Serge Toubiana in 1992 for the film *François Truffaut: Portraits volés (Stolen Portraits)*. Truffaut very much liked this photo of Sacha Guitry, made by Willy Rizzo. For him, it showed the courage and valor of a man who worked on his film to the very last.

# BIBLIOGRAPHY

## FRANÇOIS TRUFFAUT'S PRINCIPAL WORKS

Selected articles (listed chronologically)

"René Clair au Ciné-Club." *Bulletin du Ciné-Club du Quartier Latin,* 4 (February 1950).

"*La Règle du jeu* (Jean Renoir)." *Bulletin du Ciné-Club du Quartier Latin,* 5 (May 1950).

"Avenue de l'Opéra: Trois ladies de Paname." *Elle,* June 12, 1950.

"*Sudden Fear* (David Miller)." *Cahiers du cinéma* 21 (March 1953).

"*Les Neiges du Kilimandjaro* (Henry King)." *Cahiers du cinéma* 23 (May 1953).

"*Le Bistro du péché* (Bruce Humberstone)." *Cahiers du cinéma* 24 (June 1953).

"Le Cinémascope: en avoir plein la vue." *Cahiers du cinéma* 25 (July 1953).

"*Niagara* (Henry Hathaway)." *Cahiers du cinéma* 28 (November 1953).

"F comme Femme." *Cahiers du cinéma* 30 (Christmas 1953).

"Une certaine tendance du cinéma français." *Cahiers du cinéma* 31 (January 1954).

"*Règlement de comptes* (Fritz Lang)." *Cahiers du cinéma* 31 (January 1954).

"*La Red* (Emilio Fernandez)." *Cahiers du cinéma* 32 (February 1954).

"*Touchez pas au grisbi* (Jacques Becker)." *Cahiers du cinéma* 34 (April 1954).

"*Si Versailles m'était conté* (Sacha Guitry)." *Cahiers du cinéma* 34 (April 1954).

"*Une femme qui s'affiche* (George Cukor)." *Cahiers du cinéma* 35 (May 1954).

"Un homme seul, Roberto Rossellini." *Radio-Cinéma-Télévision,* July 4, 1954.

"*Rivière sans retour* (Otto Preminger)." *Cahiers du cinéma* 38 (August 1954).

"Howard Hawks, intellectuel." *Arts,* August 18, 1954.

"Sir Abel Gance." *Arts,* September 1, 1954.

"*Un jour de terreur* (Tay Garnett)." *Arts,* September 29, 1954.

"Un trousseau de fausses clés (sur Alfred Hitchcock)." *Cahiers du cinéma* 39 (October 1954).

"Georges Sadoul et la vérité historique." *La Parisienne*, October 1954.

"Silence! Jean Renoir tourne *French Cancan*." *Arts*, October 27, 1954.

"*Le Démon des eaux troubles* (Samuel Fuller)." *Arts*, December 15, 1954.

"*Rossellini 55*." *Arts*, January 19, 1955.

"*Ali Baba* (Jacques Becker) et la politique des auteurs." *Cahiers du cinéma* 44 (February 1955).

"Crise d'ambition du cinéma français." *Arts*, March 30, 1955.

"*Johnny Guitare* (Nicholas Ray)." *Cahiers du cinéma* 46 (April 1955).

"Ingrid Bergman: 'J'ai échappé à Hollywood et à Sacha Guitry'." *Arts*, April 6, 1955.

"*Fenêtre sur cour* (Alfred Hitchcock)." *Arts*, April 6, 1955.

"*Voyage en Italie* (Roberto Rossellini)." *Arts*, April 20, 1955.

"Cannes: palmarès anticipé selon les règles du jeu." *Arts*, April 27, 1955.

"*La Tour de Nesle* (Abel Gance)." *Cahiers du cinéma* 47 (May 1955).

"Antoine et l'orpheline." *La Parisienne*, May 1955.

"Hulot parmi nous." *Arts*, May 11, 1955.

"*Battle Cry* (Raoul Walsh)." *Arts*, June 15, 1955.

"*Futures Vedettes* (Marc Allégret)." *Arts*, June 22, 1955.

"*La Comtesse aux pieds nus* (Joseph Mankiewicz)." *Cahiers du cinéma* 49 (July 1955).

"Les sept péchés capitaux de la critique." *Arts*, July 6, 1955.

"*En quatrième vitesse* (Robert Aldrich)." *Arts*, September 21, 1955.

"*Il Bidone* (Federico Fellini)." *Cahiers du cinéma* 51 (October 1955).

"*Les Mauvaises Rencontres* (Alexandre Astruc)." *Arts*, October 19, 1955.

"Portrait d'Humphrey Bogart." *Cahiers du cinéma* 52 (November 1955).

"*Chiens perdus sans collier* (Jean Delannoy)." *Arts*, November 9, 1955.

"*L'Homme de la plaine* (Anthony Mann)." *Arts*, December 7, 1955.

"Hitchcock aime l'invraisemblance." *Arts*, December 28, 1955.

"*Lola Montès* (Max Ophuls)." *Cahiers du cinéma* 55 (January 1956).

"*La Pointe courte* (Agnès Varda)." *Arts*, January 11, 1956.

"*Nuit et Brouillard* (Alain Resnais)." *Cahiers du cinéma* 56 (February 1956).

"*Entrée des artistes*: Joëlle Robin." *Arts*, February 22, 1956.

"*Les salauds vont en enfer* (Robert Hossein)." *Arts*, February 29, 1956.

"*Sept Ans de réflexion* (Billy Wilder)." *Cahiers du cinéma* 57 (March 1956).

"Comment peut-on être jeune turc?" *Cahiers du cinéma* 57 (March 1956).

"*Le Bandit* (Edgar Ulmer)." *Arts*, March 14, 1956.

"*La Fureur de vivre* (Nicholas Ray)." *Arts*, April 4, 1956.

"James Dean est mort." *Arts*, April 11, 1956.

"*Le Temps des assassins* (Julien Duvivier)." *Arts*, April 18, 1956.

"Cannes: un palmarès ridicule." *Arts*, May 16, 1956.

"*La Nuit du chasseur* (Charles Laughton)." *Arts*, May 23, 1956.

"*Monsieur Arkadin* (Orson Welles)." *Arts*, June 13, 1956.

"Les assassins du dimanche." *Arts*, June 27, 1956.

"Il y a dix ans, *Citizen Kane*." *Cahiers du cinéma* 61 (July 1956).

"*La Prisonnière du désert* (John Ford)." *Arts*, August 15, 1956.

"Présence de Marilyn Monroe." *Arts*, August 19, 1956.

"Venise, festival courageux, exemple d'austérité." *Arts*, September 12, 1956.

"*La Traversée de Paris* (Claude Autant-Lara)." *Arts*, October 31, 1956.

"*Le Pays d'où je viens* (Marcel Carné), une consternante pochade." *Arts*, October 31, 1956.

"*Un condamné à mort s'est échappé* (Robert Bresson)." *Arts*, November 14, 1956.

"Boxeur, officier, acteur, peintre, écrivain, cinéaste, John Huston ne sera-t-il toujours qu'un amateur?" *Arts*, November 14, 1956.

"Renaissance du court métrage français." *Arts*, November 21, 1956.

"*Et Dieu créa la femme* (Roger Vadim)." *Arts*, December 5, 1956.

"Les critiques de cinéma sont misogynes: B.B. est victime d'une cabale." *Arts*, December 12, 1956.

"En 1956, cinq grands films, sept bons films. Un événement: Il est démontré que le cinéma peut se passer des scénaristes." *Arts,* December 19, 1956.

"*Bob le Flambeur* (Jean-Pierre Melville)." *Arts,* December 19, 1956.

"Qui est Elia Kazan?" *Arts,* January 2, 1957.

"Derrière le miroir (Nicholas Ray)." *Arts,* February 20, 1957.

"*Ecrit sur du vent* (Douglas Sirk)." *Arts,* February 20, 1957.

"*Courte Tête* (Norbert Carbonnaux)." *Arts,* March 6, 1957.

"*Assassins et Voleurs* (Sacha Guitry)." *Cahiers du cinéma* 70 (April 1957).

"Avec Max Ophuls, nous perdons un de nos meilleurs cinéastes." *Arts,* April 3, 1957.

"*Un vrai cinglé de cinéma* (Frank Tashlin)." *Arts,* April 24, 1957.

"Vous êtes tous témoins dans ce procès. Le cinéma français crève sous les fausses légendes." *Arts,* May 15, 1957.

"Cannes: Un échec dominé par les compromis, les combines et les faux pas." *Arts,* May 22, 1957.

"Asphyxie de la critique: Nous sommes tous des condamnés." *Arts,* May 29, 1957.

"Claude Autant-Lara, faux martyr, n'est qu'un cinéaste bourgeois." *Arts,* June 19, 1957.

"*Méfiez-vous fillettes* (Yves Allégret): Gangsters, filles, cinéastes, censeurs dans le même panier." *Arts,* July 10, 1957.

"Sacha Guitry fut un grand cinéaste réaliste." *Arts,* July 31, 1957.

"Avec *Oeil pour oeil,* Cayatte et Curd Jurgens font reculer les bornes du grotesque à l'écran." *Arts,* September 18, 1957.

"*Un roi à New York* (Charlie Chaplin) est un film génial." *Arts,* October 30, 1957.

"Clouzot au travail, ou le règne de la terreur." *Cahiers du cinéma* 77 (December 1957).

"Hitchcock est le plus grand inventeur de formes." *Arts,* December 4, 1957.

"*Positif,* copie o." *Cahiers du cinéma* 79 (January 1958).

"Seule la crise sauvera le cinéma français." *Arts,* January 8, 1958.

"Voici les trente nouveaux noms du cinéma français." *Arts,* January 8, 1958.

"Les plus grands cinéastes du monde ont plus de 50 ans." *Arts,* January 15, 1958.

"*Bonjour tristesse* (Otto Preminger)." *Arts,* March 12, 1958.

"Redécouvrons Max Ophuls." *Arts,* March 26, 1958.

"*Charlotte et Véronique* (Jean-Luc Godard)." *Cahiers du cinéma* 83 (May 1958).

"Si jeunes et des Japonais (*Passion juvénile* de Kô Nakahira)." *Cahiers du cinéma* 83 (May 1958).

"*Le Beau Serge* (Claude Chabrol)." *Arts,* May 21, 1958.

"Si des modifications radicales n'interviennent pas, le prochain Festival est condamné." *Arts,* May 21, 1958.

"*Barrage contre le Pacifique* (René Clément)." *Cahiers du cinéma* 84 (June 1958).

"*La Soif du mal* (Orson Welles)." *Arts,* June 4, 1958.

"Le nouveau grand du cinéma mondial, Ingmar Bergman, a dédié son oeuvre aux femmes." *Arts,* June 11, 1958.

"*Jet Pilot* (Josef von Sternberg)." *Arts,* July 9, 1958.

"*En cas de malheur* (Claude Autant-Lara)." *Arts,* September 10, 1958.

"Louis Malle a filmé la première nuit d'amour du cinéma." *Arts,* September 10, 1958.

"Il faisait bon vivre." *Cahiers du cinéma* 91 (January 1959).

"Je n'ai pas écrit ma biographie en 400 coups." *Arts,* June 3, 1959.

"Aznavour donne le *la.*" *Cinémonde,* May 5, 1960.

"L'affaire Vadim." *France-Observateur,* December 22, 1960.

"L'agonie de la Nouvelle Vague n'est pas pour demain (*Paris nous appartient,* de Jacques Rivette)." *Arts,* December 20, 1961.

"*Adieu Philippine* (Jacques Rozier)." *Lui,* November 1963.

"*Muriel* (Alain Resnais)." *Lui,* January 1964.

"*Le Vieil Homme et l'enfant* (Claude Berri)." *Le Nouvel Observateur,* March 8, 1967.

"La savate et la finance, ou deux ou trois choses que je sais de lui (sur Jean-Luc Godard)." *Les Lettres françaises,* March 16, 1967.

"*La Marseillaise* (Jean Renoir)." *L'Express,* October 30, 1967.

# BIBLIOGRAPHY

"Jean Renoir le patron." *Le Monde,* January 18, 1968.
"Lubitsch était un prince." *Cahiers du cinéma* 198 (February 1968).
"L'antimémoire courte." *Combat,* February 12, 1968.
"À propos d'Audiberti." *Théâtre du Cothurne* (Lyon), December 1973.
"Les 80 ans de Jean Renoir." *Le Film français,* July 3, 1974.

François Truffaut's principal interviews for *Cahiers du cinéma* were published as *La Politique des auteurs* (Paris: Champ Libre, 1971; reprinted by Editions de l'Etoile in 1983 and by Ramsay in 1988).

## BOOKS

*Le Cinéma selon Hitchcock* (avec la collaboration de Helen Scott). Paris: Robert Laffont, 1966. Republished under the title *Hitchcock-Truffaut.* Paris: Ramsay, 1984.
*Hitchcock* (with the collaboration of Helen G. Scott). New York: Simon and Schuster, 1967; revised, expanded edition, 1984.
*Les Aventures d'Antoine Doinel.* Paris: Mercure de France, 1970.
*Les Films de ma vie.* Paris: Flammarion, 1975.
*The Films in My Life.* Trans. Leonard Mayhew. New York: Simon and Schuster, 1978.
*Le Plaisir des yeux.* Paris: Editions de l'Etoile, 1987.
*François Truffaut: Correspondance.* Paris: Hatier, 1988.
*Correspondence 1945–1984.* Trans. Gilbert Adair. New York: The Noonday Press, Farrar, Straus and Giroux, 1989.

The scripts of *Les Mistons, Histoire d'eau, Tirez sur le pianiste, Jules et Jim, La Peau douce, L'Enfant sauvage, Les Deux Anglaises et le Continent, L'Histoire d'Adèle H., La Chambre verte, L'Amour en fuite, Le Dernier Métro, La Femme d'à côté,* and *Vivement dimanche!* were published by *L'Avant-Scène cinéma.*

## PREFACES

*Le Trou* (script, Jacques Becker film). *L'Avant-Scène cinéma* 13 (1962).
*Vivre sa vie* (script, Jean-Luc Godard film).
*L'Avant-Scène cinéma* 19 (1962).
*Casque d'or* (script, Jacques Becker film). *L'Avant-Scène cinéma* 43 (1964).
Gheur, Bernard. *Le Testament d'un cancre.* Paris: Albin Michel, 1971.
Bazin, André. *Jean Renoir.* Paris: Champ Libre, 1971.
Bazin, André. *What Is Cinema?* Berkeley: University of California Press, 1971.
Bazin, André, and Eric Rohmer. *Charlie Chaplin.* Paris: Cerf, 1973.
Guarner, José-Luis. *Roberto Rossellini.* Madrid: Editorial Fundamentos, 1973.
*La Grande Illusion* (script and album of the Jean Renoir film). Paris: Balland, 1974.
Bazin, André. *Le Cinéma de la cruauté.* Paris: Flammarion, 1975.
Bazin, André. *Le Cinéma de l'Occupation et de la Résistance.* Paris: UGE, 1975.
Kostariski, Richard. *Hollywood Directors* (1914–1940). New York: Oxford University Press, 1976.
Aumont, Jean-Pierre. *Le Soleil et les Ombres.* Paris: J'ai lu, 1977.
Guitry, Sacha. *Le Cinéma et moi.* Paris: Ramsay, 1977.
Andrew, Dudley. *André Bazin.* New York: Oxford University Press, 1977 (French translation, Paris: Editions de l'Etoile, 1983).
Bazin, André. *Orson Welles.* New York: Harper & Row, 1978.
*La Toile d'araignée* (Nouvelles de William Irish) Paris: Pierre Belfond, 1980.
Almendros, Nestor. *Un homme à la caméra.* Paris: Hatier, 1980. (U.S. edition, *A Man with a Camera.* Trans. Rachel Phillips Belash. New York: Farrar, Straus and Giroux, 1984).
*Oeuvres de cinéma* (édition intégrale des scénarios et des écrits de Jean Vigo) Paris: Lherminier/Cinémathèque française, 1985.
Roché, Henri-Pierre. *Carnets.* Marseille: Editions André Dimanche, 1990.

## INTERVIEWS WITH FRANÇOIS TRUFFAUT (LISTED CHRONOLOGICALLY)

*Le Monde*, April 21, 1959.
*L'Express*, April 23, 1959.
*Arts*, April 29, 1959.
*Les Lettres françaises*, May 28, 1959.
*Cinéma* 59, June 1959.
*Télé-Ciné*, June 1959.
*Signes du temps*, December 1959.
*France-Observateur*, December 3, 1959.
*Le Monde*, November 24, 1960.
*Cinéma* 61, January 1961.
*France-Film*, February 1961.
*Télé-Ciné*, March 1961.
*France-Observateur*, October 19, 1961.
*Cinémonde*, October 31, 1961.
*Cinéma* 62, January 1962.
*Le Monde*, January 24, 1962.
*Les Lettres françaises*, January 25, 1962.
*Clarté*, March 1962.
*Script*, April 1962.
*New York Film Bulletin*, Summer 1962.
*Les Nouvelles littéraires*, November 15, 1962.
*Cahiers du cinéma* 138 (December 1962).
*L'Express*, January 24, 1963.
*Télérama*, February 14, 1963.
*Télérama*, February 2, 1964.
*Réalités*, May 1964.
*Cinéma* 64, May 1964.
*L'Express*, May 14, 1964.
*Les Nouvelles littéraires*, May 21, 1964.
*Le Monde*, May 22, 1964.
*Cinéma* 64, June 1964.
*Lui*, September 1964.
*Art et Essai*, March 1966.
*Télé-Ciné*, May 1966.
*Télérama*, August 14, 1966.
*Arts-Loisirs*, September 14, 1966.
*Les Lettres françaises*, September 15, 1966.
*Le Monde*, September 18, 1966.
*Télé-Cinéma*, October 1966.
*Paris-Match*, October 1, 1966.
*Télérama*, October 2, 1966.
*Lectures pour tous*, December 1966.
*Midi-Minuit fantastique*, December 1966.
*Cinéma* 67, January 1967.
*Les Lettres françaises*, April 14, 1967.
*Cahiers du cinéma* 190 (May 1967).
*Cinéma* 67, December 1967.
*Le Nouvel Adam*, February 1968.
*Les Lettres françaises*, April 10, 1968.
*Le Monde*, April 18, 1968.

*Télérama*, April 28, 1968.
*May 68: ce n'est qu'un début* 2 (May 1968).
*Jeune Cinéma*, May 1968.
*L'Express*, May 20, 1968.
*Télé-Cinéma*, October 1968.
*Cahiers du cinéma* 200 (April 1969).
*Le Monde*, May 21, 1969.
*Télérama*, June 14, 1969.
*New York Times*, June 15, 1969.
*Journal du show-business*, June 27, 1969.
*Télé-Ciné*, March 1970.
*Le Nouvel Observateur*, March 2, 1970.
*Cinémonde*, September 1970.
*Les Lettres françaises*, September 9, 1970.
*Les Nouvelles littéraires*, September 10, 1970.
*The National Observer*, October 12, 1970.
*Cinéma* 70, November 1970.
*Image et Son*, December 1970.
*Télérama*, August 14, 1971.
*Le Monde*, November 25, 1971.
*Les Nouvelles littéraires*, December 3, 1971.
*Ecran* 72, January 1972.
*Le Technicien du film*, March 15, 1972.
*Le Soir* (Marseille), March 29, 1972.
*Télérama*, April 15, 1972.
*Vingt Ans*, January 3, 1973.
*Le Monde*, May 18, 1973.
*Ecran* 73, July 1973.
*Cinématographe*, Summer 1973.
*Time Out*, November 30, 1973.
*Cinéma/Québec*, December 1973.
*Real Paper*, January 2, 1974.
*Village Voice*, January 24, 1974.
*Jeune Cinéma*, March 1974.
*Playboy* (France), January 1975.
*Télérama*, April 27, 1975.
*Cinématographe*, October 1975.
*Ecran* 76, March 15, 1976.
*Les Nouvelles littéraires*, March 18, 1976.
*Jeune Cinéma*, May–June 1976.
*Le Quotidien de Paris*, April 26, 1977.
*Lumière du cinéma*, May 1977.
*Cinématographe*, May 1977.
*L'Express*, March 13, 1978.
*Le Matin de Paris*, March 29, 1978.
*L'Humanité-dimanche*, April 7, 1978.
*Télérama*, April 8, 1978.
*Christian Science Monitor*, November 27, 1978.

*Sight and Sound* 4 (Winter, 1979).

*Le Matin de Paris*, January 24, 1979.

*Washington Post*, February 22, 1979.

*Les Nouvelles littéraires*, February 22, 1979.

*The Chronicle Review*, March 19, 1979.

*Le Quotidien de Paris*, June 11, 1980.

*Cahiers du cinéma* 315 and 316 (September and October 1980).

*Les Nouvelles littéraires*, September 18, 1980.

*Film-Bruxelles*, October 1980.

*New York Times*, October 14, 1980.

*Wide Angle* 4, 4 (1981).

*Le Journal de Montréal*, February 17, 1981.

*Le Devoir* (Montréal), February 21, 1981.

*La Presse* (Montréal), February 21, 1981.

*Télérama*, September 30, 1981.

*Première*, October 1981.

*Les Nouvelles littéraires*, October 1, 1981.

*Révolution*, October 2, 1981.

*L'Hebdo-Belge*, November 1981.

*Lire*, April 1982.

*Première*, February 1983.

*Pilote*, August 1983.

*Le Nouvel Observateur*, August 5, 1983.

*Télé 7 jours*, August 6, 1983.

*Le Matin de Paris*, August 8, 1983.

*Révolution*, August 12, 1983.

*Les Lettres françaises*, October 24, 1983.

*Cinématographe*, December 1984.

## BOOKS AND ARTICLES ON TRUFFAUT

Auzel, Dominique. *Truffaut: Les Mille et Une Nuits américaines*. Paris: Henri Veyrier, 1990. (Album of film posters.)

de Baecque, Antoine. "François Truffaut, spectateur cinéphile." *Vertigo* 10 (1991).

———. "Contre la 'Qualité française.' François Truffaut écrit 'Une certaine tendance du cinéma français'." *Cinémathèque* 4 (Autumn 1993).

Bastide, Bernard. *François Truffaut, Les Mistons*, Nîmes; Ciné-Sud, 1987.

Bonnafons, Elisabeth. *François Truffaut*. Lausanne: L'Âge d'homme, 1981.

*Cahiers du cinéma. Le Roman de François Truffaut*. Special issue, December 1984.

Cahoreau, Gilles. *François Truffaut*. Paris: Albin Michel, 1986.

*Cinématographe*. 105 (December 1984). "François Truffaut."

Collet, Jean. "L'oeuvre de François Truffaut, une tragédie de la connaissance." *Etudes*, December 1966.

———. *Le Cinéma de François Truffaut*. Paris: Lherminier, 1977.

———. *François Truffaut*. Paris: Lherminier, 1985.

Comolli, Jean-Louis. "Au coeur des paradoxes." *Cahiers du cinéma*. 190 (May 1967).

Dalmais, Hervé. *Truffaut*. Paris: Rivages/Cinéma, 1987.

*Aline Desjardins s'entretient avec François Truffaut*. Ottawa: Editions Léméac/Radio Canada, 1973; revised edition, Paris: Poche Cinéma, Ramsay, 1988.

Dixon, Wheeler Winston. *The Early Film Criticism of François Truffaut*. Bloomington: Indiana University Press, 1993.

Fanne, Dominique. *L'Univers de François Truffaut*. Paris: Le Cerf, 1972.

Gillain, Anne. *Le Cinéma selon François Truffaut*. Paris: Flammarion, 1988.

———. *François Truffaut: Le Secret perdu*. Paris: Hatier, 1991.

Insdorf, Annette. *François Truffaut*. Boston: Twayne Publishers, 1978, revised edition, New York: Simon and Schuster, 1989. (French translation entitled *François Truffaut: Le Cinéma est-il magique?* Paris: Ramsay, 1989.)

Le Berre, Carole. *François Truffaut*. Paris: Editions de l'Etoile, 1993.

Moullet, Luc. "La balance et le Lien." *Cahiers du cinéma* 410 (July–August 1990).

Petrie, Graham. *The Cinema of François Truffaut*. New York: International Film Guide Series, A. S. Barnes, 1970.

Rabourdin, Dominique. *Truffaut par Truffaut*, Paris: éditions du Chêne, 1985. U.S. edition: trans. Robert Erich Wolf. New York: Harry N. Abrams, 1987.

Simondi, Mario, ed. *François Truffaut*. Florence: La Casa Usher, 1982.

Toubiana, Serge. "François Truffaut, domaine public." *Trafic* 5 (1992).

Waltz, Eugene P. *François Truffaut: A Guide to References and Resources*. Boston: G. K. Hall, 1982.

# ACKNOWLEDGMENTS

This book could never have been written without the help of François Truffaut's many friends, relatives, and collaborators, who shared their recollections with us, offered their opinions, and gave us access to their personal archives. May we express our deepest thanks to them all, and particularly to: Fanny Ardant, the late Jean Aurel, Nathalie Baye, Janine Bazin, Marcel Berbert, Claude Berri, Jacqueline Bisset, Charles Bitsch, René Bonnell, Claudine Bouché, Jean-Claude Brialy, Leslie Caron, Jacqueline Caspar, Claude Chabrol, Don Congdon, Josiane Couëdel, Claude Davy, Gérard Depardieu, Jean Douchet, Liliane Dreyfus, Marie Dubois, Michel Fermaud, the late Odette Ferry, Claude Gauteur, Claude de Givray, Jean-Luc Godard, Jean Gruault, Pierre Hebey, Annette Insdorf, Claude Jade, Georges Kiejman, André S. Labarthe, Bertrand de Labbey, Philippe Labro, Robert Lachenay, Bernadette Lafont, Jean-Louis Livi, Monique Lucas (de Monferrand), Lydie Mahias, Florence Malraux, Claude Miller, François-Xavier Mollin, Jeanne Moreau, Luc Moullet, Jean Narboni, Marcel Ophuls, Marie-France Pisier, Marie de Poncheville, Jérôme Prieur, Jean-Louis Richard, Jean-José Richer, Eric Rohmer, Serge Rousseau, François-Marie Samuelson, Suzanne Schiffman, Jacques Siclier, Liliane Siegel, Alexandra Stewart, Bertrand Tavernier, Nadine Trintignant, Alain Vannier, Claude Véga. The authors are, of course, solely responsible for the interpretation given to their statements.

Thanks are also due to Colline Faure-Poirée, Patricia Guédot, Pierre Guislain, Hélène Quinquin, all of whom followed this project from the beginning and generously gave us the benefit of their attentive reading and remarks, as did Isabelle Gallimard, Emmanuèle Bernheim, Carole Le Berre, Sylvie de Baecque, Marc Grinsztajn, Manuel Carcassonne, and Laurence Giavarini.

Thank you to Michel Pascal, with whom the making of the film *François Truffaut: Portraits volés* (*Stolen Portraits*), in 1992, shed much light on François Truffaut's life and work.

Finally, Madeleine Morgenstern, Laura Truffaut, and Eva Truffaut gave us unrestricted access to the archives of Les Films du Carrosse. They also helped us on countless occasions, with their opinions, advice, recollections, and friendship. We were very touched by their trust and are deeply grateful to them; without them, this book would not exist. Monique Holvëck at Les Films du Carrosse gave us invaluable help and always showed great kindness and patience.

# INDEX

# INDEX

# PHOTOGRAPH CREDITS

**INSERT 1**

1. Coll. F. Truffaut family
2. "
3. "
4. "
5. "
6. "
7. "
8. "
9. "
10. Coll. Robert Lachenay
11. Ph. © André Dino/Films du Carrosse
12. Archives F. Truffaut
13. Coll. F. Truffaut family
14. Films du Carrosse D.R.
15. "
16. "
17. "
18. Coll. *Cahiers du Cinéma*
19. Coll. *Cahiers du Cinéma*
20. Ph. © Raymond Cachetier
21. Ph. © André Greffen/*Cahiers du Cinéma*
22. Coll. *Cahiers du Cinéma* D.R.
23. Coll. F. Truffaut family. D.R.
24. "
25. "
26. "
27. Ph. © Botti/Stills
28. Films du Carrosse D.R.
29. Coll. *Cahiers du Cinéma* D.R.
30. Ph. © André Dino/Films du Carrosse
31. Ph. © C. Werle/Films du Carrosse
32. Archives F. Truffaut
33. Films du Carrosse D.R.
34. Ph. © Robert Lachenay/Films du Carrosse
35. Coll. F. Truffaut family D.R.
36. "
37. Ph. © Philip Halsman/Magnum
38. "
39. "

# PHOTOGRAPH CREDITS

## INSERT 2

1. Ph. © Raymond Cauchetier/Films du Carrosse
2. Films du Carrosse/D.R.
3. Ph. © Raymond Cauchetier/Films du Carrosse
4. Ph. © Marilu Parolini/Films du Carrosse
5. Films du Carrosse D.R.
6. Ph. © Tourte/Stills
7. Ph. © Marilu Parolini/Films du Carrosse
8. Ph. © Léonard de Raemy/Coll. *Cahiers du Cinéma*
9. "
10. Ph. © Pierre Zucca/Films du Carrosse
11. Ph. © Léonard de Raemy/Coll. *Cahiers du Cinéma*
12. Ph. © Raymond Depardon/Magnum
13. Ph. © Raymond Cauchetier/Films du Carrosse
14. Ph. © Pierre Zucca/Films du Carrosse
15. Ph. © Marilu Parolini/Films du Carrosse
16. Coll. F. Truffaut family/D.R.
17. Ph. © Sheedy and Long USA
18. Coll. F. Truffaut family
19. "
20. Ph. © Hélène Jeanbrau/Films du Carrosse
21. Ph. © Bernard Prim/Films du Carrosse
22. Archives F. Truffaut
23. Ph. © Jean-Pierre Fizet/Coll. *Cahiers du Cinéma*
24. Ph. © William Karel/Sygma
25. "
26. "
27. Ph. © Dominique Le Rigoleur
28. "
29. "

## A NOTE ON THE TYPE

*This book was set in Caledonia, a face designed by William Addison Dwiggins (1880–1956) for the Mergenthaler Linotype Company in 1939. It belongs to the family of types referred to by printers as "modern," a term used to mark the change in type styles that occurred around 1800. Caledonia was inspired by the Scotch types cast by the Glasgow typefounders Alexander Wilson & Sons circa 1833. However, there is a calligraphic quality about Caledonia that is completely lacking in the Wilson types.*

*Dwiggins referred to an even earlier typeface for this "liveliness of action"—one cut around 1790 by William Martin for the printer William Bulmer. Caledonia has more weight than the Martin letters, and the bottom finishing strokes of the letters are cut straight across, without brackets, to make sharp angles with the upright stems, thus giving a modern-face appearance.*

*W. A. Dwiggins began his association with the Mergenthaler Linotype Company in 1929, and over the next twenty-seven years he designed a number of book types, the most interesting of which are Metro, Electra, Caledonia, Eldorado, and Falcon.*

*Composed by North Market Street Graphics,*
*Lancaster, Pennsylvania*

*Printed and bound by Maple-Vail Book Mfg.*
*Binghamton, New York*

*Designed by Iris Weinstein*